Cloud Computing Networking

Theory, Practice, and Development

Cloud Computing Networking

Theory, Practice, and Development

Lee Chao

CRC Press
Taylor & Francis Group
Boca Raton London New York

CRC Press is an imprint of the
Taylor & Francis Group, an **informa** business

AN AUERBACH BOOK

CRC Press
Taylor & Francis Group
6000 Broken Sound Parkway NW, Suite 300
Boca Raton, FL 33487-2742

© 2016 by Taylor & Francis Group, LLC
CRC Press is an imprint of Taylor & Francis Group, an Informa business

No claim to original U.S. Government works

Printed on acid-free paper by CPI Group (UK) Ltd, Croydon, CR0 4YY
Version Date: 20150724

International Standard Book Number-13: 978-1-4822-5481-5 (Hardback)

Library of Congress Cataloging-in-Publication Data

Chao, Lee, 1951-
  Cloud computing networking : theory, practice, and development / Lee Chao.
    pages cm
  Includes bibliographical references and index.
  ISBN 978-1-4822-5481-5 (alk. paper)
  1. Cloud computing. 2. Computer networks. I. Title.

QA76.585C439 2015
004.67'82--dc23

2015014928

Visit the Taylor & Francis Web site at
http://www.taylorandfrancis.com

and the CRC Press Web site at
http://www.crcpress.com

Contents

Preface

As the IT industry advances, cloud computing represents the next big computing platform change. It is the most significant transformation since the introduction of the Internet in the early 1990s. Cloud computing along with virtualization technology will literally revolutionize the way we run a business. The cloud provides a flexible, secure, scalable, and affordable IT infrastructure. E-commerce and educational institutions can particularly benefit from cloud-based IT infrastructures.

Through the Internet, cloud-based IT infrastructures allow companies and educational institutions to subscribe to software, an IT infrastructure, or an application development platform from a cloud provider. This way, it is not necessary for subscribers to build their own IT infrastructure for supporting their computation needs. As a result, subscribers can significantly reduce the cost of IT development and management. Companies and educational institutions can also develop their own private clouds to take advantage of the flexibility, security, availability, and affordability of a cloud computing environment.

To catch up on the cutting-edge technology such as cloud computing and network virtualization, this book is designed to provide enough networking theory and concepts for readers to understand cloud computing. In addition, the book provides hands-on practice in a cloud-based computing environment.

Motivation

More and more companies and educational institutions are planning to adopt a cloud-based IT infrastructure. Therefore, today's job market requires IT professionals to understand cloud computing and have hands-on skills for developing cloud-based IT infrastructures. Although professional development books in the cloud computing field are available, they are usually for more experienced IT professionals. For many university students and entry-level IT professionals, there are a handful of challenges to master cloud technology. It is difficult for them to understand cloud computing without adequate knowledge of networking and system administration.

Understanding the needs of entry-level IP professionals and university students has motivated the author to write this book, which includes systematic coverage of networking and system administration for better understanding cloud computing.

Objectives of the Book

With this motivation, this book is designed with the following objectives. First, it provides IT professionals with the necessary networking and system administration knowledge to better understand cloud computing. Second, it helps IT professionals to get a quick start in deploying cloud services. The book provides detailed instructions on establishing a cloud-based computing environment where IT professionals can carry out all the hands-on activities in this book. The cloud-based computing environment allows readers to develop cloud services collaboratively or individually. Third, it enhances readers' hands-on skills by providing lab activities. Through these lab activities, readers can develop a fully functioning cloud-based IT infrastructure with Microsoft Azure. Last, this book demonstrates how networking plays a key role in a cloud-based IT infrastructure. It helps readers understand how to set up networks for a cloud-based IT infrastructure. It also demonstrates how networks are used to construct cloud services.

Features of the Book

This book integrates networking and cloud computing. Networking and system administration theory and concepts are used to explain cloud computing technology. Hands-on practice is conducted in the cloud computing environment. To help IT professionals catch up with the trend in cloud computing, the public cloud provider, Microsoft Azure, is used to establish a cloud computing environment. This book also illustrates the development of a private cloud with Hyper-V. After systematic coverage of networking theory and concepts such as virtual network, private network, and certification, this book leads the reader to the development of a hybrid cloud that integrates the public cloud and the private cloud.

The following are the features that make the book valuable for readers who are interested in learning about cloud-based IT infrastructures.

- *Cloud computing*: This book focuses on networking used to construct a cloud computing environment. Microsoft Azure is used to build and manage virtual networks.

- *Real-world approach*: Many hands-on activities are added to help readers develop a cloud-based IT infrastructure that can be used for a real-world business.
- *Combination of theory and hands-on practice*: This book provides adequate networking theory, enough for readers to understand cloud computing. Comprehensive lab activities are used to help readers make the connection between theory and practice.
- *Online development*: This book provides detailed instructions and resources for creating and managing online computer labs by using the Microsoft Azure academic account.
- *Instructional materials*: To help with teaching and learning, this book includes instructional materials such as an instructor's manual, PowerPoint presentations, and solutions.

The book focuses on its goal to make sure that readers learn how to develop a cloud-based network system for a real-world business. The content of the book is suitable for undergraduate and beginning graduate courses related to networking as well as for IT professionals who do self-study on cloud computing.

For the convenience of entry-level IP professionals and university students, the book is designed in the following manner:

- *Self-contained content*: For readers' convenience, the book is self-contained. It includes some necessary basic networking concepts, hands-on activities, and information about cloud-based network services.
- *Suitable for self-study*: This book provides detailed instructions that are suitable for self-study. It not only presents the theory and concepts but also explains them through examples, illustrations, and hands-on activities.
- *Designed for Microsoft Azure*: The book is specially designed for Microsoft Azure. All the hands-on activities can be conducted with the Windows Server operating system.
- *Step-by-step instructions*: For hands-on activities, the book provides step-by-step instructions and illustrations to help beginners. It also provides instructions on setting up a cloud environment for hands-on practice.

With these features, readers will be able to implement a cloud-based IT infrastructure and other cloud-based services in a short time.

Organization of the Book

This book includes 11 chapters. Each chapter contains an introduction of its content, the main body of the chapter, a "Summary" section to summarize the discussion in the chapter, and a "Review Questions" section to help readers review the knowledge learned from the chapter. Each chapter also includes hands-on activities to help readers practice the skills learned in the chapter.

Chapter 1 introduces networking and network operating systems. It outlines the use of network operating systems in cloud computing. This chapter gives an overview of the commonly available public cloud providers and packages used for developing private clouds. The lab activity in this chapter prepares a cloud computing environment for the lab activities in later chapters.

Chapter 2 deals with the necessary network protocols to be used in cloud computing. Three hands-on activities are used to explore the network management tools provided by the Windows Server operating system.

Chapter 3 covers the topics related to network design and IP addressing. It describes how the Internet works. It also describes other types of networks used in implementing cloud computing. The hands-on practice of this chapter creates a virtual network on Microsoft Azure. The virtual network is used to illustrate the concepts of local area networking and subnetting.

Chapter 4 introduces directory services, which are the key components of cloud computing. The chapter describes how directory services are used in enterprise-level IT infrastructure management. It provides technical details on the development and implementation of directory services. In the hands-on practice of this chapter, the Active Directory service is implemented on virtual machines hosted by Microsoft Azure.

Chapter 5 introduces network services such as the dynamic host service and name service, which are often used in cloud computing. The theory and concepts of the dynamic host service and name service are described in detail. The hands-on activity in this chapter illustrates the implementation of the dynamic host service and name service in Microsoft Azure.

Chapter 6 demonstrates how to use Windows PowerShell for network and cloud management. This chapter introduces programming units such as cmdlets, PowerShell functions, and PowerShell Scripts. During hands-on activities, readers can experiment with such units in the Microsoft Azure cloud environment. This chapter also presents the use of Microsoft Azure PowerShell for cloud service management.

Chapter 7 discusses Internet data transaction protection. In the cloud computing environment, it is necessary to protect the data transaction between a cloud provider and a cloud service subscriber. The chapter introduces network security tools such as Secure Sockets Layer (SSL) and Certificate Services. The hands-on activity in this chapter implements Certificate Services in the Microsoft Azure cloud environment.

Chapter 8 covers IP Security (IPSec), which is used in later chapters to link the virtual networks created in Microsoft Azure to the on-premises network of an enterprise. IPSec is a security protocol to secure the network protocols above the Internet layer. The hands-on activities implement IPSec in the Microsoft Azure cloud environment.

Chapter 9 explains the theory and concepts of network routing. Routers are used to connect networks. In this book, the virtual networks in the cloud and the on-premises networks of an enterprise are connected with routers. This chapter also discusses Network Address Translation (NAT), which allows the virtual machines on a private network to share a single Internet connection. There are two activities for this chapter's hands-on practice. The first one creates a routing service with Windows Server and second one implements a NAT service.

Chapter 10 discusses the virtual private network (VPN) architecture. VPN allows an enterprise to integrate its own network with a virtual network in a cloud. This chapter gives the pros and cons of different types of VPN technologies. It focuses on the IPSec-based VPN and SSL-based VPN, which are used by Microsoft Azure to remotely access the on-premises network of a company from a virtual network in a cloud or vice versa. Two hands-on activities are included in this chapter. The first one is used to create a point-to-site connection between a local computer and Microsoft Azure. The second one creates a site-to-site connection between Microsoft Azure and an on-premises network.

Chapter 11 covers the hybrid cloud, which integrates public clouds with private clouds. It introduces hybrid cloud technology and its application in a cloud-based enterprise network. With the System Center Virtual Machine Manager (SCVMM) package, the hands-on activity of this chapter creates a hybrid cloud that integrates Microsoft Azure with a private cloud created on a local network.

One or more hands-on activities are included in each of the chapters. It is recommended that readers complete the activities in the previous chapters before starting the hands-on activity in the next chapter because some of the hands-on activities may depend on the ones in the previous chapters.

Acknowledgments

I thank my family for their continuous and loving support, patience, and understanding of my work.

My special gratitude goes to my students and Dr. Jenny Huang for their participation in the book proofreading process. They carefully reviewed the content of the manuscript. Their constructive suggestions and corrections greatly improve the quality of the book.

I also thank the outstanding editorial staff members and other personnel at Auerbach Publications of Taylor & Francis Group for their support of this project. I truly appreciate the encouragement and collaboration of John Wyzalek, senior acquisitions editor, and all the other people who have been involved in the book's production. The book would not have been possible without their inspiration and great effort.

Author

Lee Chao, PhD, is currently a professor in the Science, Technology, Engineering, and Mathematics Division at the University of Houston, Victoria, Texas. He earned his PhD from the University of Wyoming, Laramie, Wyoming. He has been teaching IT courses for over 20 years. His current research interests are database system development and cloud computing. Dr. Chao is also the author of more than a dozen research articles and books in various areas of IT.

1

Overview on Cloud and Networking

Objectives

- Draw an overview of network servers.
- Understand the role of network servers in networking.
- Learn about the process of implementing networks.
- Set up a cloud-based lab for hands-on practice.

1.1 Introduction

In an enterprise, IT infrastructure is needed to provide employees with the necessary hardware and software to do their job. The key component of the IT infrastructure is the network that connects servers, desktop computers, and mobile devices. The IT infrastructure in an enterprise is a high-cost and high-maintenance unit. It requires expensive hardware and software and skilled IT service staff members to keep it running.

Cloud computing is a technology that can be used to support online IT infrastructure. Cloud computing has become the new trend in delivering business applications and services. The cloud is a cost-effective, flexible, reliable IT infrastructure to support e-commerce and e-learning. With the cloud, employees across the world are able to access the hardware and software provided by an enterprise. In addition, an enterprise can allow its contractors to create their own virtual IT infrastructures on the cloud. Cloud computing can also provide a collaboration platform for developers to participate in an application development project anywhere and anytime. When an enterprise develops a cloud for its own use, this type of cloud is called a private cloud. When a cloud provides cloud services for the public to subscribe, this type of cloud is called a public cloud. When a cloud integrates both the public and private clouds, it is called a hybrid cloud. A large enterprise usually has its IT infrastructure created on a hybrid cloud.

Since a cloud can be considered an online IT infrastructure, the network is also a key component of the cloud. Networking theories and practice have been widely used in cloud computing. To understand the usage of the cloud in an enterprise, one has to have a thorough understanding of networking theories and practice. At the end of this book, a hybrid cloud will be developed. To get there, the reader needs to be familiar with the cloud-related networking theories and practice.

As networks play a key role in today's IT industry, networking has become a required subject in the computer science and information systems curricula. Networking theories and practice are taught at different levels in high schools and higher education institutions. Students majoring in IT-related fields are required to have networking knowledge and skills.

This chapter will first introduce the types of networks. Then, it will introduce the operating systems that are able to provide network services and manage network devices. It will analyze the functionalities of these operating systems and present their functionalities through network architecture. This chapter will explain how cloud computing is supported by the operating systems. It will discuss the networking process and illustrate how to implement a network system. At the end of the chapter, instructions will be provided on how to develop a cloud-based lab environment for conducting hands-on activities in later chapters.

1.2 Networks

To transmit data from one computer to another computer, the two computers need to be connected via network hardware and software. Computers, printers, copiers, or storage devices linked by a network are called hosts. Each host has a network interface card (NIC) to which a network cable or another connection medium is connected. The network cable or connection medium carries binary electronic signals back and forth between two hosts. When there are multiple hosts on a network, these hosts are connected to a network device called a switch through which electronic signals are distributed to other hosts. The network device, router, is used to connect two different networks. In the IT industry, it is known that a switch is used to construct a network and a router is used to connect networks.

There are different types of networks such as the local area network (LAN), wide area network (WAN), Internet, and cloud-based network. A LAN is a type of network that exists within a room or a building as shown in Figure 1.1. A WAN is a type of network that is highly scalable and may cover a large geographic area (Figure 1.2). The Internet is a worldwide network system formed by interconnecting LANs and

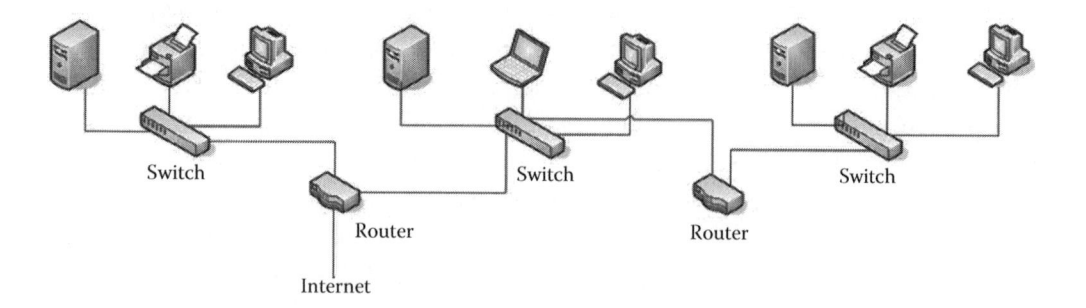

Figure 1.1 Local area network.

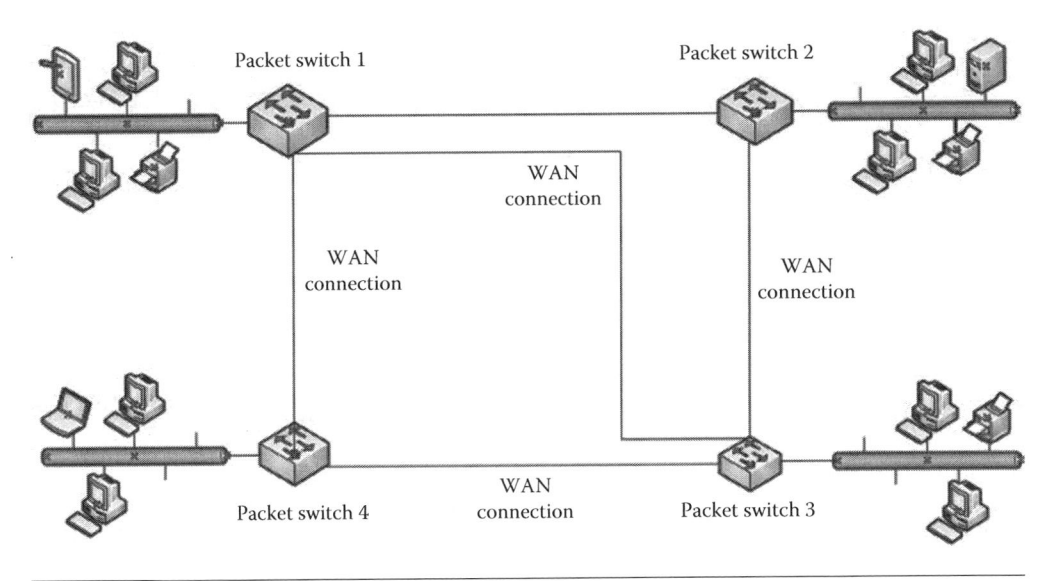

Figure 1.2   Wide area network.

WANs as shown in Figure 1.3. The LAN is connected to the Internet through one of the Internet Service Providers (ISPs). The ISP communicates with the regional network through an access point called a point of presence (POP). It can be a telecommunication facility rented by an ISP for accessing the global network, or it can be any facility used to access the Internet such as a dial-up server, router, or ATM switch. ISPs are connected through a network access point (NAP), which is a major Internet interconnection point.

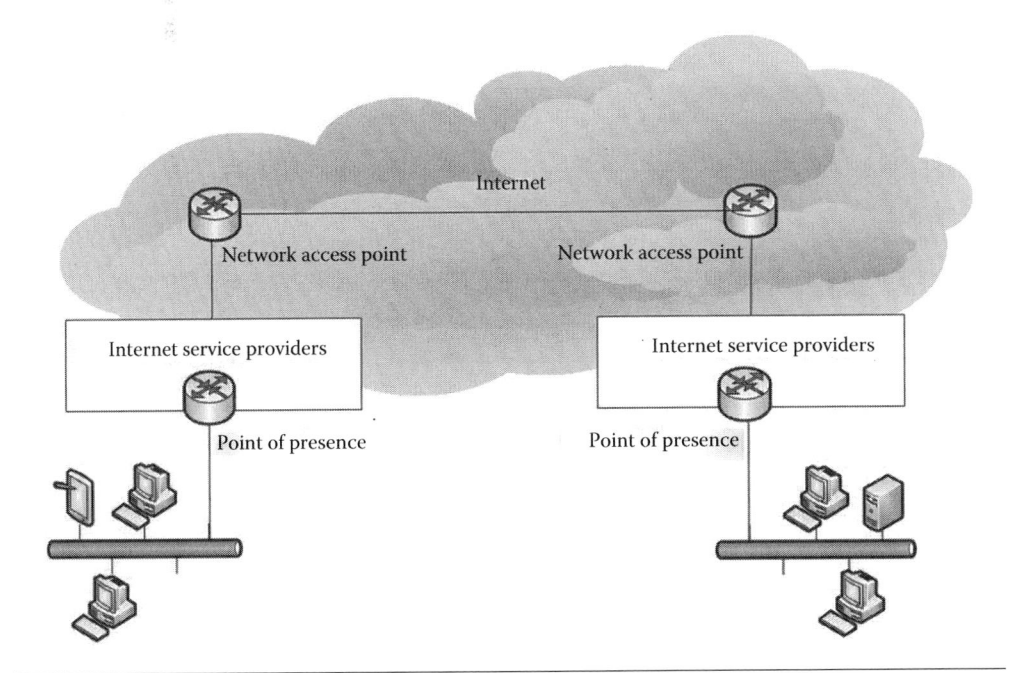

Figure 1.3   Internet.

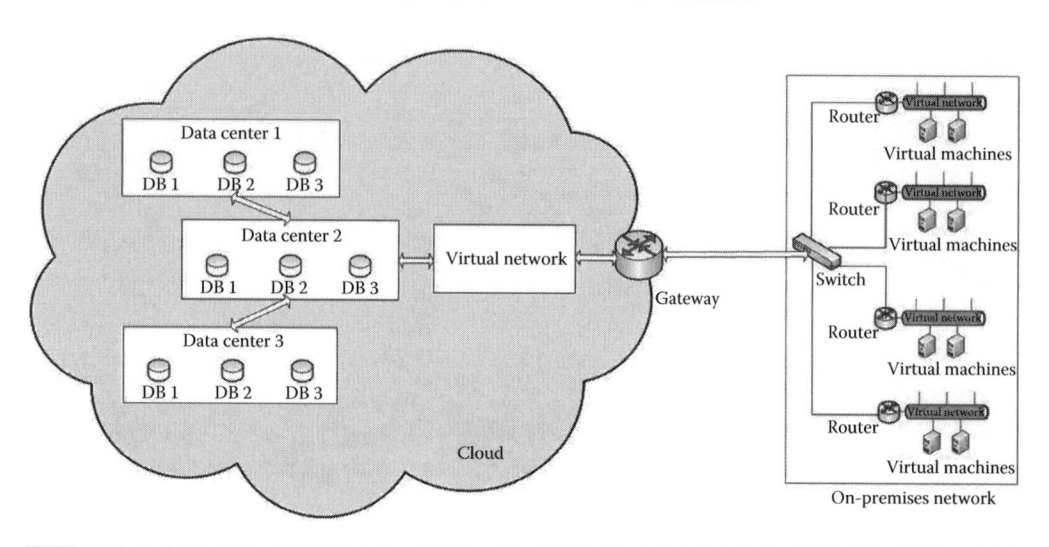

Figure 1.4   Cloud-based network.

A cloud-based network is an enterprise network that can be extended to the cloud shown in Figure 1.4. The cloud-based network allows an enterprise to distribute its network around the world. The cloud significantly simplifies the development of an enterprise network system. In the cloud, the underlying network is constructed by a cloud provider. All an enterprise needs to do is to connect its on-premises network to the network built in the cloud to form a global enterprise-class network system. There is no initial capital investment in this type of global network system.

Unlike the Internet, the cloud-based network provides centralized control over network visibility. Through the cloud-based network, the enterprise is able to provide a multitenant application, which is a software application that serves multiple tenants. Each tenant subscribes an instance of the application. Each tenant's data are isolated and remain invisible to other tenants. On the other hand, the maintenance and update of the application can be greatly simplified. The cloud-based network enables the enterprise to deploy IT infrastructures to remote locations in minutes (Figure 1.4).

The cloud-based network targets organizations with a large number of sites around the world. There could be a couple of hundred to ten thousand employees working in multiple sites such as branch offices, schools in a school district, clinics, manufacturing facilities, or retail stores. Through the management tools deployed in the cloud, network administrators are able to manage the enterprise-distributed networks anywhere and anytime. The management tools can be used to manage cloud-hosted virtual machines and mobile services. They are used to accomplish tasks such as centralized management, remote monitoring, remote software and app installation, remote wiping, and security auditing.

1.3 Network Operating Systems

Operating systems can be categorized as a server edition, desktop edition, and mobile edition based on the tasks performed by them. The server edition can be used to manage networks and is capable of providing network services. Here, our focus is on server edition operating systems. In the following, we will discuss several commonly available server edition operating systems that are capable of networking.

Most of the low-cost network server operating systems are developed to run on the ×86 platform, which is powered with the microprocessors from Intel and AMD. The ×86 platform was originally created for personal computers. Today's ×86 platform is built on multicore ×86 microprocessors, which can handle large-scale networking tasks. Popular operating systems such as Linux, Windows, and some versions of the UNIX operating system are all supported by the ×86 platform.

1.3.1 Windows Server 2012

For networking, Windows Server 2012 provides tools to accomplish the following tasks:

- *Network management*: The tasks may include network performance management, network device management, system backup and restoration, troubleshooting, and so on.
- *Network services*: The tasks may include developing and managing network services such as IP address management service, dynamic IP address assignment, name service, Web service, email service, VOIP service, and so on.
- *Network security*: The tasks may include user authentication, certification service, data encryption, network monitoring, setting up firewalls, virus protection, and so on.
- *Remote access and routing*: The tasks may include sharing network resources through VPN and DirectAccess. Windows Server 2012 can also accomplish tasks such as routing network traffic from one network to another network.
- *Cloud communication management*: The tasks may include extending a private cloud to a public cloud by securely connecting the private cloud to the public cloud. The public cloud can also be used to extend the data center located on the private cloud.
- *Virtualization*: Windows Server 2012 includes the virtualization tool, Hyper-V. With Hyper-V, we are able to accomplish the tasks of creating virtual machines, virtual networks, and virtual network devices such as virtual switches.

Compared with the older version of Windows Server, Windows Server 2012 was designed with the cloud concept in mind. New networking features have been added mainly to support cloud computing. The new features such as failover clustering, virtualization, and file services have all been added for this purpose. The virtualization tool Hyper-V has been modified so that it can help set up environments in the cloud.

Hyper-V is broadly used to create and manage virtual machines and virtual network devices such as virtual switches. With Hyper-V, one can create virtual networks that are independent of the underlying physical network. For network security management, the virtual networks created with Hyper-V can be isolated from each other. For example, the virtual network for hands-on practice in a networking class can be made to isolate itself from that of the Admissions office. Also, deploying the workload to multiple virtual networks can improve the performance of a large project such as a datacenter.

Hyper-V has a feature called live migration; that is, virtual machines hosted by virtual networks can live migrate anywhere without service disruption. These virtual networks can be migrated to a cloud while preserving their existing IP addresses. With the IP addresses preserved, the virtual networks on the cloud can emerge into the on-premises network. All the services provided by these migrated virtual networks can continue to function without knowing where the underlying physical network is. With Hyper-V, a true hybrid cloud can be established by seamlessly integrating a public cloud and a private cloud running on an on-premises network.

In Windows Server 2012, most of the management tasks can be done through the Server Manager interface shown in Figure 1.5. Networking tasks such as active directory administration, dynamic IP addressing, name service, virtualization, and remote access can all be handled in Server Manager.

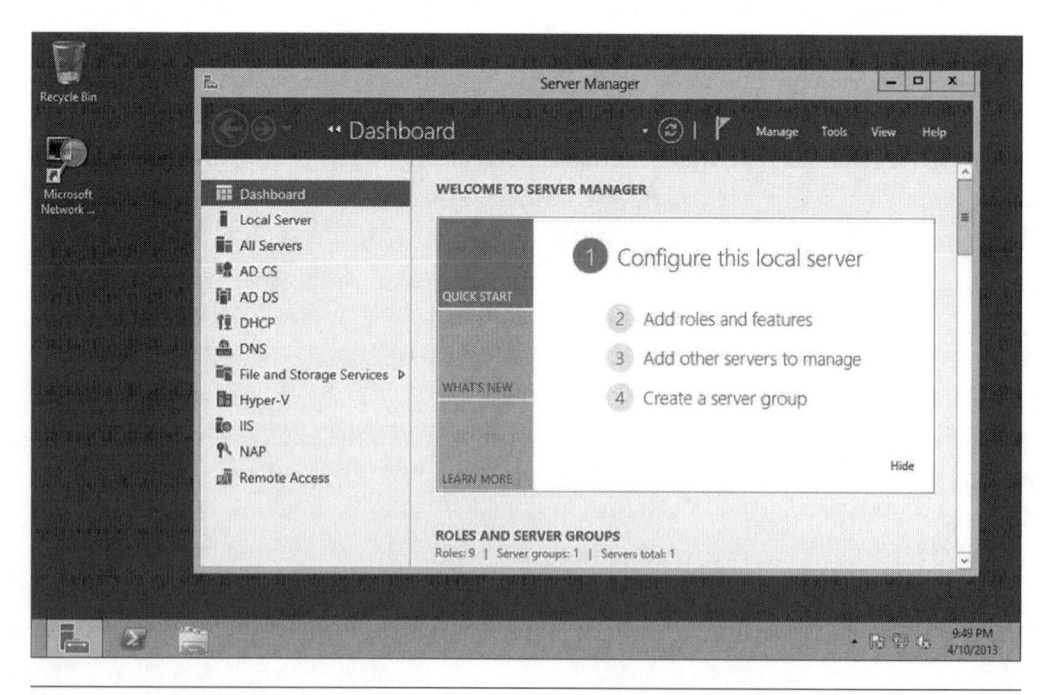

Figure 1.5 Server Manager.

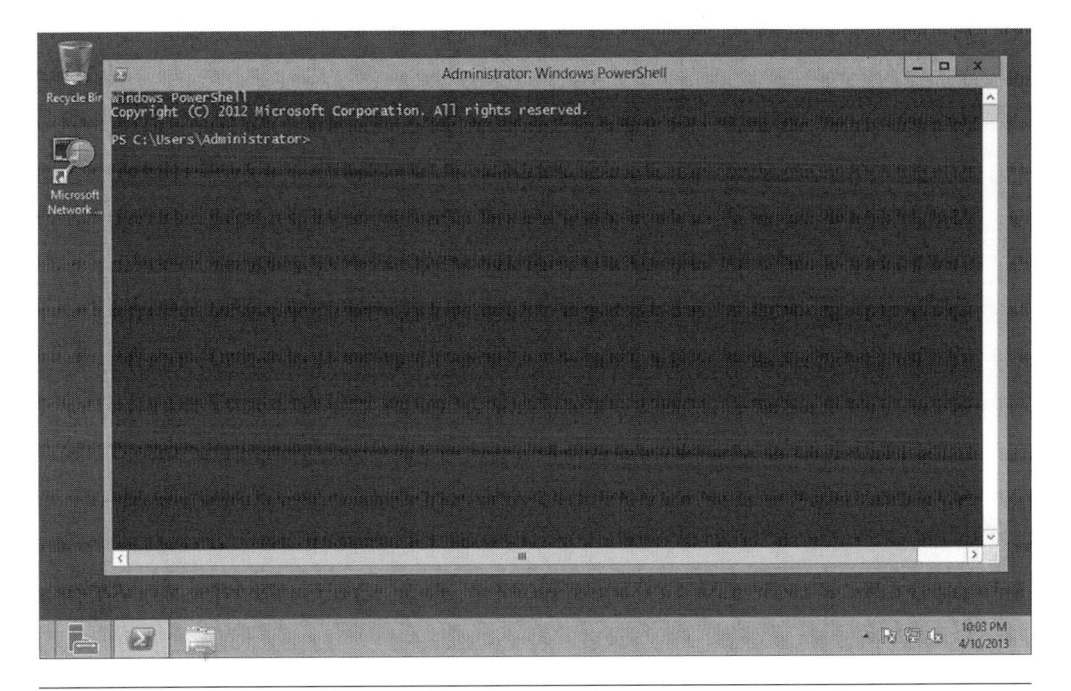

Figure 1.6 Windows PowerShell.

The management tasks can also be done through the command interface, Windows PowerShell (Figure 1.6). Windows PowerShell is a powerful management tool which includes 2430 cmdlets. A network administrator can write a script to automate a large task that needs to execute multiple cmdlets.

Windows Server 2012 uses a new Metro GUI design for touch-centric devices. In Metro GUI, the Start menu is a matrix of icons as shown in Figure 1.7.

1.3.2 Microsoft Azure

Microsoft Azure is a cloud computing platform built on a global network of Microsoft-managed datacenters. Microsoft Azure uses a customized version of Hyper-V known as Windows Azure Hypervisor to handle virtualization tasks. The operating system running on Microsoft Azure is used to manage computing and storage resources. It also provides security protection and remote access mechanisms. The Microsoft Azure development environment is highly scalable. Additional computation capacities can be added as desired until the subscription limit is reached. Microsoft Azure provides a highly available computing environment. With Microsoft Azure, IT professionals can work on their projects from anywhere and at any time. With Microsoft Azure, there is no initial cost on IT infrastructure development and management. However, users need to pay monthly for the storage and computing usage. Figure 1.8 shows the Microsoft Azure Management Portal.

Microsoft Azure provides three types of cloud services, Infrastructure as a Service (IaaS), Platform as a Service (PaaS), and Software as a Service (SaaS). For data storage,

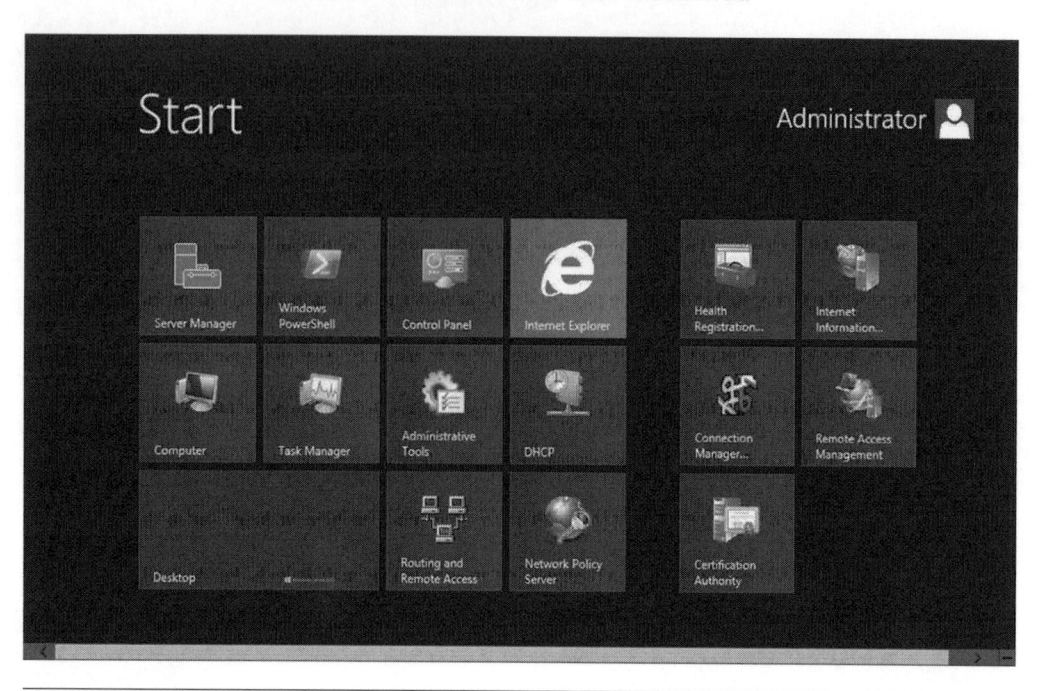

Figure 1.7   Metro GUI.

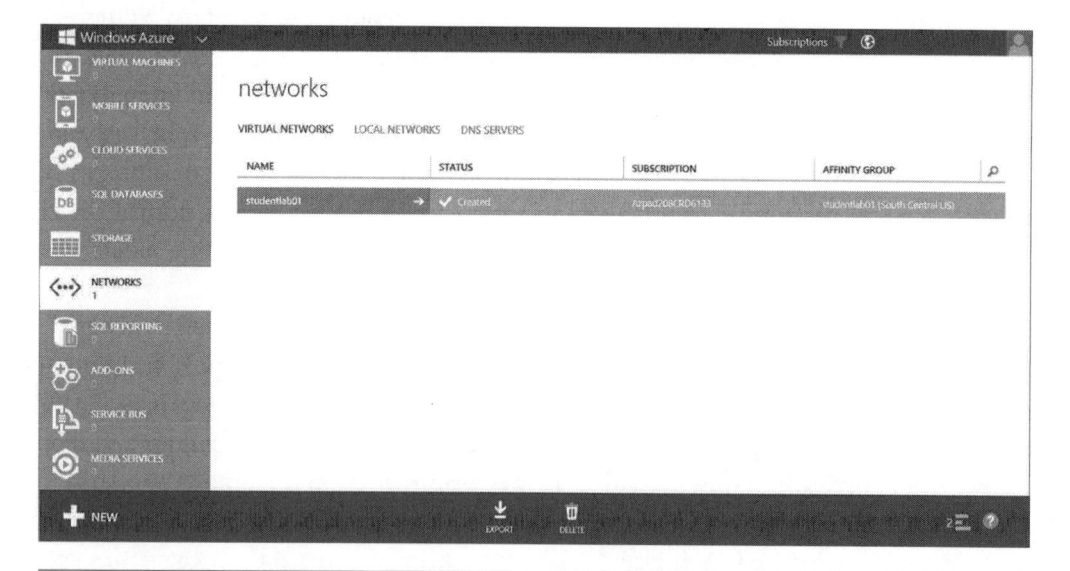

Figure 1.8   Windows Azure management portal.

Microsoft Azure offers Windows Azure SQL Database for storing and managing relational data and data storage services for storing and managing nonrelational data. Microsoft Azure provides software such as server operating systems like Windows Server 2012 and SUSE Linux Enterprise Server (SLES). It also provides database management system (DBMS) software such as Windows Azure SQL Database, which is the cloud version of Microsoft SQL Server. The Windows Azure emulation

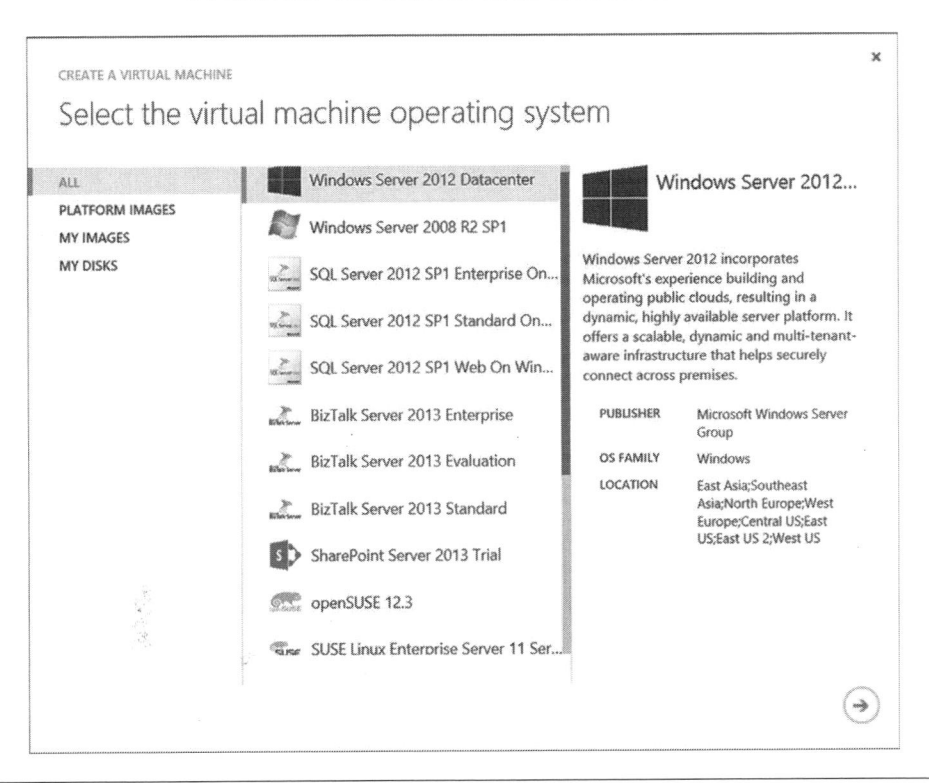

Figure 1.9 Operating systems provided by Windows Azure.

software and Windows Azure Software Development Kit (SDK) can be downloaded to students' home computers to emulate the Microsoft Azure cloud environment on a local computer. Figure 1.9 shows the operating system software provided by Microsoft Azure.

To help cloud subscribers to extend their existing networks into the public cloud, Microsoft Azure offers a range of networking capabilities such as Virtual Network, Windows Azure Connect, and Traffic Manager. Figure 1.10 shows the Virtual Network tools.

Windows Azure Virtual Network provisions and manages the VPN connection between the on-premises IT infrastructure and Microsoft Azure. Virtual Network is used to set up a hybrid cloud, which consists of the private cloud run on the on-premises network and the public Microsoft Azure cloud. With Virtual Network, an administrator can accomplish tasks such as setting up IP security service to provide a secure connection between the corporate VPN gateway and Microsoft Azure. Virtual Network can also be used to configure DNS service and IP address for virtual machines.

Windows Azure Connect is a tool used to connect the services provided by two machines; one is located on the on-premises network and the other one is on Microsoft Azure. This tool can be used to help application developers to build cloud applications hosted in a hybrid environment. It allows services such as Web service on

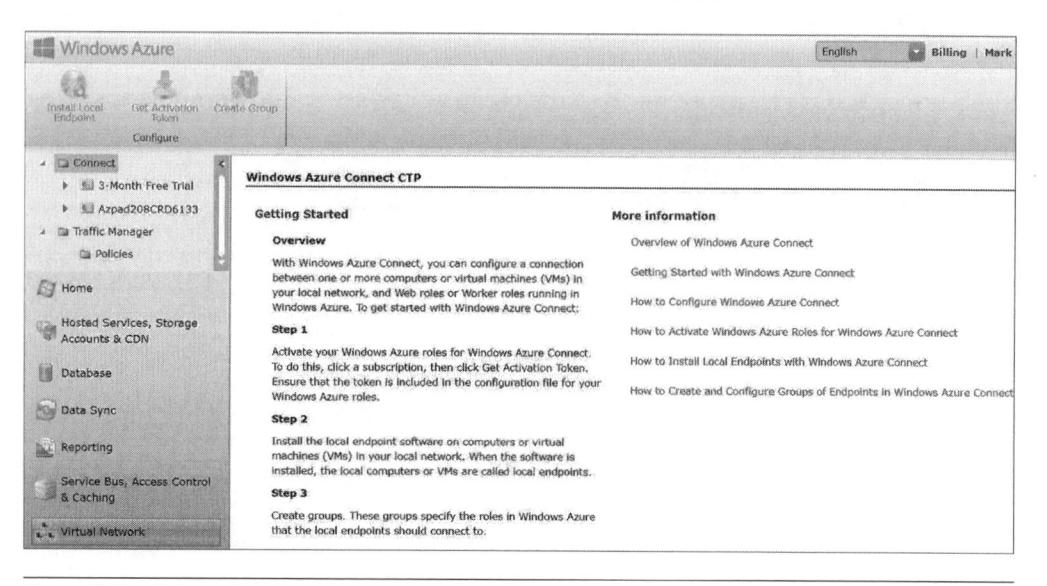

Figure 1.10   Virtual network tools.

Microsoft Azure to securely access an on-premise SQL Server database server. It can also authenticate users on Microsoft Azure against an on-premise Active Directory service. With this tool, application developers can use the debugging tools provided by the on-premises applications to do troubleshooting for the applications hosted on the Microsoft Azure cloud.

Traffic Manager is a tool used to balance the network traffic across multiple Microsoft Azure hosted services. This tool can help improve an application's performance, availability, and elasticity. To improve availability, Traffic Manager provides automatic failover capabilities when a service goes down. It also monitors Microsoft Azure hosted services. To improve performance, it allows the services to run at the datacenter closest to the end-user to reduce latency.

1.3.3 VMware vCloud Suite

The VMware vCloud Suite® is an integrated package used to provide a full cloud solution at the enterprise level. It includes the operating system, management software, and front-end user interface. The following are the main products included in the suite.

VMware vSphere: vSphere is a cloud computing virtualization operating system provided by VMware. vSphere provides a virtualization platform for enterprises to make use of both the public and private cloud services. One of VMware's goals is to be able to connect a private cloud to any public cloud provider. When there is a burst of workload, vSphere can seamlessly migrate some of the workload to a public cloud. To achieve this goal, VMware has developed the open-source standard, Open Virtualization Format (OVF), used for packaging and distributing virtual machines. Through OVF, VMware enables the sharing of virtual machines between

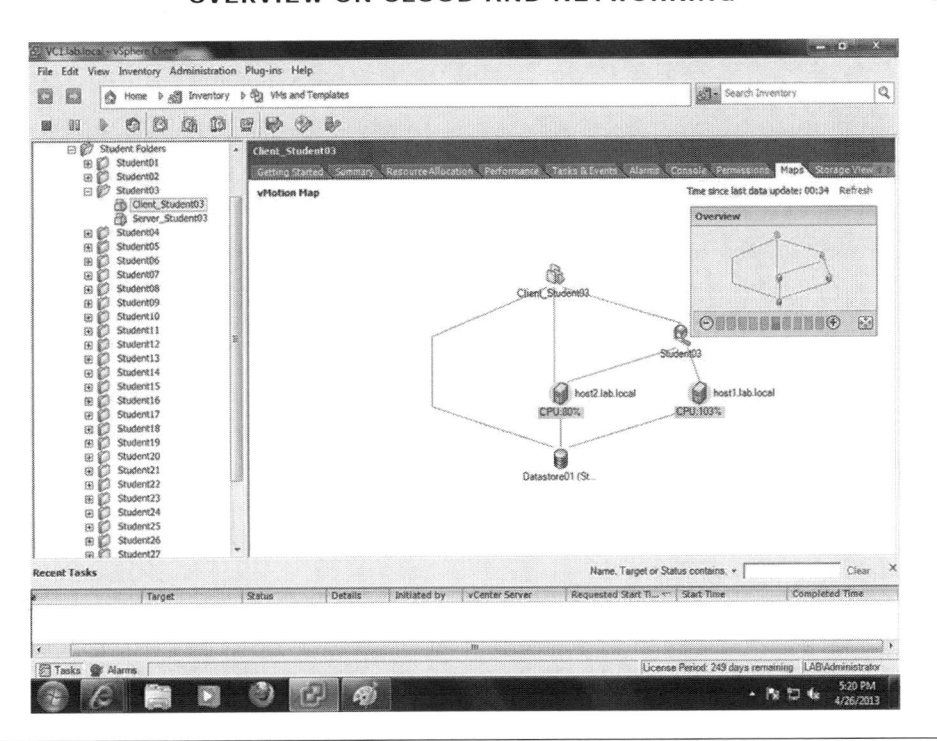

Figure 1.11   vMotion map.

two different virtual machine platforms and the sharing of virtual machines over the Internet. vSphere is able to migrate running virtual machines and attach storage devices to host servers. Figure 1.11 illustrates a map of host servers, virtual machines, and the centralized data store.

To enhance network security and manageability, VMware has been working on the new operating system NSX as the network and security virtualization platform. With NSX, to help with virtualization security, VMware provides tools to help users to store virtualized applications and data in a separated zone where no unauthorized user can access. NSX allows users to create virtual networks to accomplish tasks such as switching, routing, firewall setting, load-balancing, and so on. NSX also allows its partners to securely integrate their physical and virtual networks into the NSX platform. For security, NSX does not require disruptive hardware to be upgraded. To support virtual machines made by other server hypervisors, VMware is designed to support server hypervisors such as KVM and Xen. It can also work with any cloud management systems, for example, VMware vCloud, OpenStack, and CloudStack.

As a network operating system, vSphere can be used for datacenter-wide network integration by centralizing the network provision and network management. It provides management tools such as vSphere Distributed Resource Scheduler (DRS) for dynamically balancing computing resources and power consumption, vSphere High Availability for fault tolerance, data protection and replication, vShield Zones for securing vSphere with application-aware firewall and antivirus functions, and vSphere Auto Deploy for rapid deployment.

Applications developed by application developers such as those from Microsoft and Google all have their architectures, not to mention that many companies have their own applications. The architecture of an application may not match the architecture of a cloud provider. The difference in application architecture makes it hard to migrate these applications to the public cloud. Assisting the migration of applications to the cloud environment is another goal of VMware. VMware includes the plugins from application developers so that their applications can run on vSphere. VMware is also working on the technology that can help a company run their apps in a self-service provisioning enabled cloud. Self-service provisioning allows the end user to deploy and manage applications in the cloud computing environment.

For networking, vSphere provides four types of services for network system development:

- The first type of service is used to connect virtual network devices and virtual machines hosted by a vSphere server.
- The second type of service connects virtual network devices and virtual machines to the underlying physical network.
- The third type of service connects the services on the virtual network to the underlying physical network.
- The fourth type of service is used for managing the host server where the vSphere is installed.

VMware vSphere can virtualize network devices such as NICs and switches for connecting virtual machines. Figure 1.12 shows the virtual machines hosted by a vSphere server.

With VMware vSphere, various virtual IT infrastructures can be delivered as services. That is, the IT infrastructures designed for different types of businesses can be delivered without resetting the underlying physical network. VMware vSphere provides network performance analysis tools for network monitoring and management. Figure 1.13 shows a virtual machine performance chart and Figure 1.14 illustrates vSphere computing resources.

vCloud Director: This product is used to provide virtual datacenter services. It creates a secure multitenant environment to fully utilize the hardware capability and other computing resources. It allows the rapid cloning of the previously built virtualized IT infrastructure called vApps. It can also be used to deploy a virtualized multitier client–server IT infrastructure.

vCloud Networking and Security: This product offers a broad range of services including virtual firewalls, VPN, load balancing, and VXLAN extended networks. VXLAN is designed to allow an application to be scaled across clusters without any reconfiguration of a physical network. To protect data security, vCloud Networking and Security scans sensitive data and reports violations. The report can be used to assess the state of compliance with regulations.

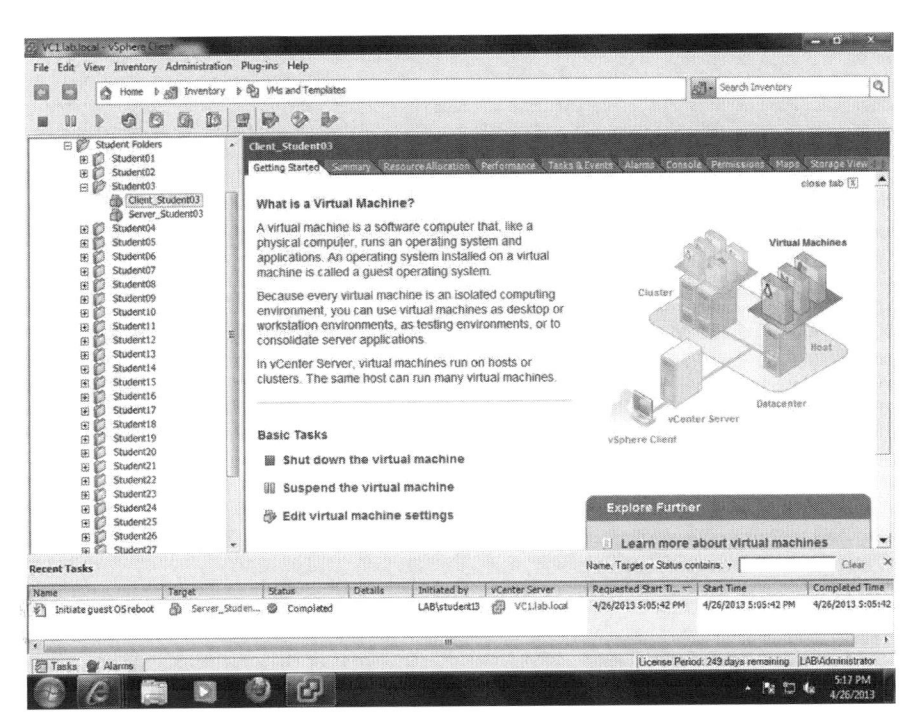

Figure 1.12 Virtual machines hosted by vSphere server.

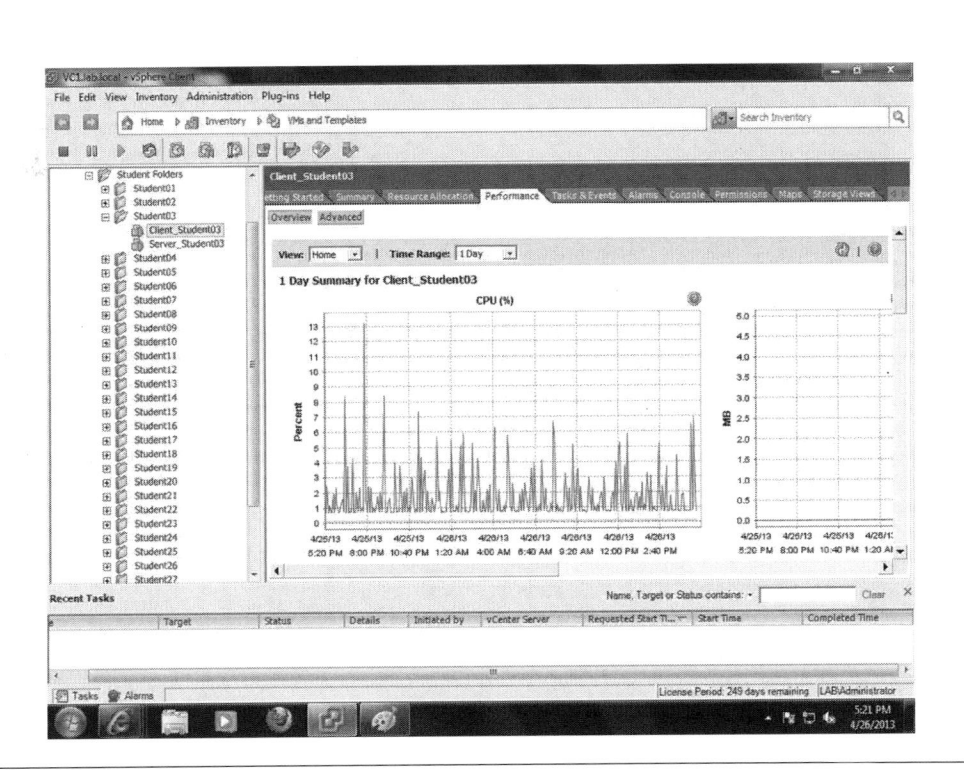

Figure 1.13 Performance monitoring.

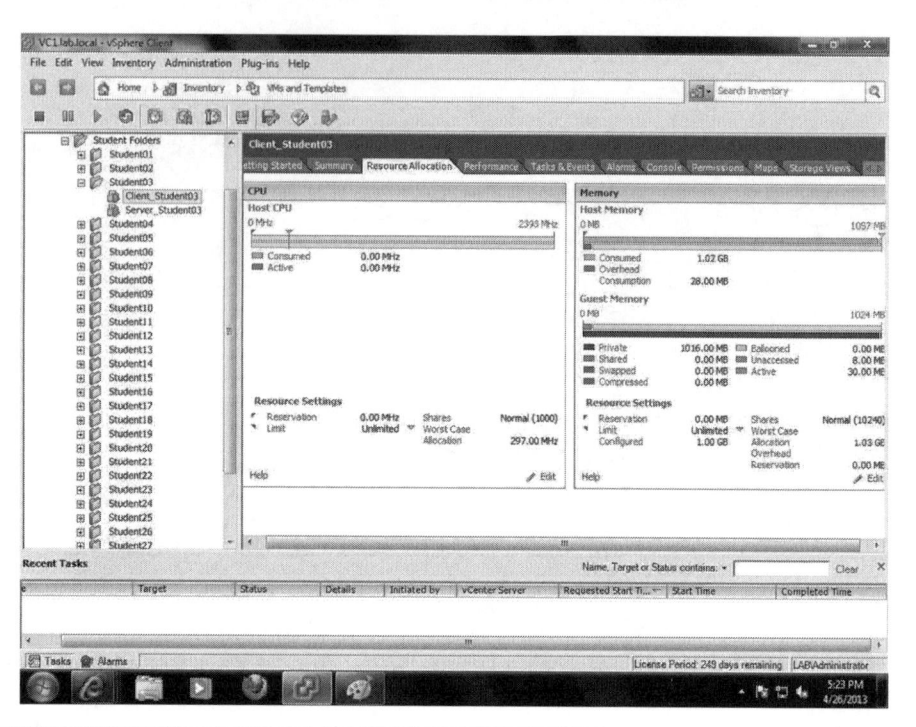

Figure 1.14   Computing resources.

vCenter Operations Management Suite: As a management tool, the product provides automated operations management through an integrated approach to performance, capacity, and configuration management. The vCenter Operations Management Suite enables IT organizations to get better visibility and actionable intelligence to proactively ensure service levels, optimum resource usage, and configuration compliance in dynamic virtual and cloud environments.

vFabric Application Director for Provisioning: It is a cloud-enabled application provisioning and maintenance solution. This tool simplifies the process of creating and standardizing application deployment across cloud services. With the tool, multitier applications can be deployed to any cloud.

vCloud Automation Center: With this tool, users can rapidly deploy and provide cloud services across private and public clouds, physical infrastructures, hypervisors, and public cloud providers. It provides user authentication service and helps to enforce business policies throughout the service lifecycle.

vSphere Client: vSphere Client is a GUI tool for managing vSphere. vSphere has two versions of vSphere Client, the regular vSphere Desktop Client, and the vSphere Web Client. Some of the new features of vSphere can only be managed with the vSphere Web Client. With the vSphere Desktop Client, a network administrator can accomplish tasks such as connecting to a vSphere host, VXLAN Networking, changing the guest OS on an existing virtual machine, editing virtual network attributes, viewing vCenter Server maps, and so on. Figure 1.15 demonstrates the guest operating system running on a vSphere host server.

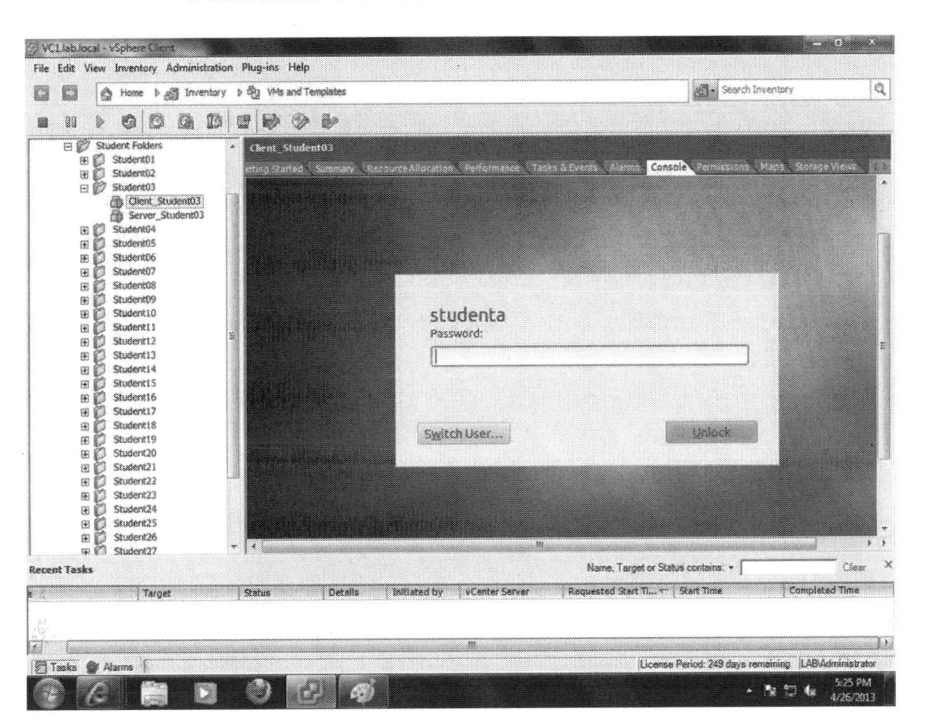

Figure 1.15   Guest operating system on host server.

By using the vSphere Web Client, the network administrator can perform tasks such as user authentication management, inventory management, vSphere replication, workflow management, virtual machine migration management, logging, virtual distributed switch management, and vSphere data protection.

1.3.4 Linux

Linux is an open source operating system, which is licensed under the GNU General Public License. The operating system source code can be freely modified, used, and redistributed by anyone. Since the World Wide Web and Internet-related protocols such as IP are open source technologies, it is convenient to include these protocols in the operating system. With these open source protocols, Linux is widely used as a network server to accomplish various networking tasks. Linux can be made to serve as an enterprise-level server operating system. It is built to multitask and allow multiple users to work on the same server computer at the same time. Therefore, a Linux operating system is often used in a grid system for distributed computing. As Linux is able to communicate with other network technologies such as Windows and Novell, Linux can also host the directory service. As an open source product, the total cost of using Linux is low. However, it requires technicians to have adequate knowledge to handle daily operations. The main cost of using Linux is the support and services offered by Linux distributions. In general, Linux requires less computing resources and is able to work with older network devices. The Linux operating system is able to run on a broad range of computing architectures such as ×86, POWER, SAPRC, and Itanium 2. This feature is especially suitable for organizations that have a limited budget and are not able to upgrade their equipment frequently.

Next, we will look at some of the Linux operating systems that are capable of supporting cloud computing. Among these Linux operating systems, you can find virtual machines preinstalled with SUSE Linux Enterprise or Ubuntu Linux on Microsoft Azure. Also, you can download a readymade virtual machine with Red Hat Linux installed for VMware.

Red Hat Linux: Red Hat, Inc. was founded in 1993. Red Hat has two editions of operating systems, Fedora and Red Hat Enterprise Linux. Fedora is the open source version of the Linux operating system, which is managed by the Linux user community and Red Hat employees. Even though Fedora is free, it is a fully functioning operating system. Red Hat uses Fedora as a testing platform for many new services and innovation tools. During the testing period, programmers from the user community and Red Hat work together to fix problems found in the new products. As Linux is updated frequently, Fedora is updated every 4–6 months. Since Fedora is a free operating system, Red Hat does not provide training and support for Fedora.

Red Hat Enterprise Linux is known as the Linux operating system for supporting enterprise-level computation. It charges fees for support and services. The support and services are necessary for developing and managing an enterprise-level IT infrastructure. Red Hat Enterprise Linux provides 24 × 7 integrated service. Customers can often get response within 1 h. In addition to the support and services, Red Hat also provides various training and certification service on Red Hat Enterprise Linux. Red Hat Enterprise Linux is a more stable operating system. It only includes those new services and innovation tools that are proven to work. Red Hat Enterprise Linux will be upgraded to a new version after three new upgrades of Fedora. Red Hat Enterprise Linux is going to be fully supported by Red Hat for 7 years after it is upgraded. It is widely supported by computer hardware companies such as Dell, HP, and IBM. It is also supported by over a thousand application software companies such as Oracle, CA, IBM, and so forth. The software from these companies is tested on the Red Hat operating system. Although the Red Hat operating system often runs on the ×86 platform, it is also able to run on other platforms.

For cloud computing, Red Hat provides an open hybrid cloud solution. Red Hat allows its customers to create a hybrid cloud in their own way and there is no vendor lock-in. That is, the customer has the freedom to access data in various structures, to build any application or service regardless of technology and platform. The open cloud allows customers to add a variety of features, cloud providers, and technologies from different vendors. With Red Hat, customers can fully utilize the existing IT infrastructure and build a cloud solution piece by piece. They are able to connect their private clouds to a wide range of public clouds such as Amazon and IBM.

Red Hat can make applications and data portable across different clouds. It also allows the management of applications across heterogeneous infrastructures.

Red Hat provides a number of products for developing cloud services. Among these products, CloudForms can be used to develop IaaS service and OpenShift can be used to develop PaaS service. With CloudForms, one can construct a virtualized system with a mixture of hypervisors and virtualization management software, and the technologies from various public clouds. CloudForms allows users to create a pool of virtual machine images consisting of an operating system, applications, and associated supporting software. It also allows users to manage, deploy, and monitor virtualized systems. OpenShift has two versions, OpenShift Online and OpenShift Enterprise. OpenShift Online is a public cloud providing PaaS service. OpenShift Enterprise is a comprehensive enterprise development platform. With OpenShift Enterprise, a team of developers can develop, deploy, and execute enterprise applications in either a private or public cloud environment.

SUSE Linux: SUSE Linux is another major Linux distribution owned by Novell. Like Red Hat Linux, there are two editions of SUSE Linux, openSUSE and SUSE Linux Enterprise. openSUSE is available in a free-download open source package. It is also available in a retail package, which contains a printed manual, a DVD, and bundled software. openSUSE also includes some proprietary components such as Adobe Flash. After Novell acquired SUSE Linux from a SUSE UNIX consulting company in Germany, Novell added the GUI-based system management software YaST2 to SUSE Linux. Novell also provides two proprietary editions of the Linux operating system, SUSE Linux Enterprise Server (SLES) and SUSE Linux Enterprise Desktop (SLED). These two editions of SUSE Linux are designed for developing and managing enterprise-level IT infrastructure. As a server operating system, SLES can run on servers with platforms such as ×86, PowerPC, Itanium 2, and so on. SLES includes over 2000 proprietary application software packages from Microsoft, Oracle, SAP, and WebSphere. In addition, it includes over 1000 open source applications. SLES is a relatively stable operating system. It is usually upgraded to a new version every 2 years. The new version will be supported by SUSE for 7 years. Figure 1.16 displays the SUSE Linux Enterprise login interface.

As a desktop operating system, SLED is designed for enterprise use. Like SLES, it is relatively stable when compared with openSUSE. It also includes proprietary software such as the antivirus software McAfee. Both SLED and SLES include technical support from Novell and certification by hardware and software vendors. SUSE Linux Enterprise is often installed on servers sold by hardware vendors such as IBM, HP, Sun Microsystems, Dell, and SGI. These hardware vendors install, configure, and test SUSE Linux Enterprise before their computer systems are shipped to customers.

As for cloud computing, the SUSE Cloud package is an open source, enterprise cloud computing platform. The platform includes an administration server used for setting up the cloud. The administration server is also used for configuring and

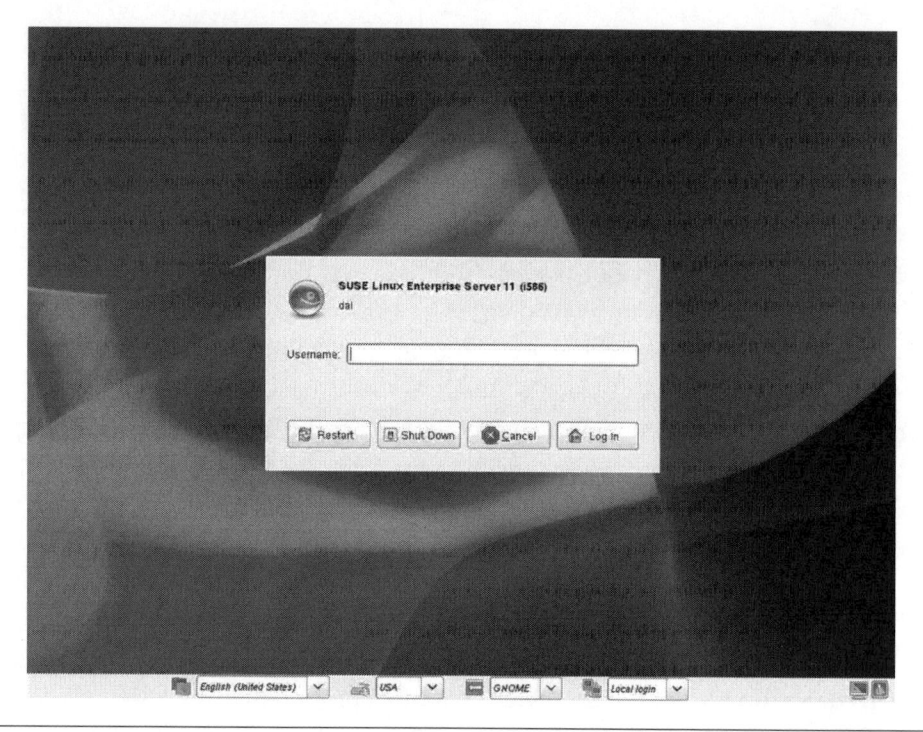

Figure 1.16   SUSE Linux enterprise server.

provisioning cloud control nodes and cloud compute or storage nodes. A control node automatically tracks the resource state of the cloud compute or storage nodes, identifies the available capacity within the cloud, and deploys workloads. The compute or storage nodes are physical servers that are either used to host virtual machines or to host storage devices.

SUSE Cloud is an OpenStack-based platform that supports multiple hypervisors such as Xen, KVM, QEMU, LXC, and Hyper-V. The support of Hyper-V enables enterprises to deploy their open source private clouds on the public cloud Microsoft Azure, or to be hosted by on-premises Windows Server machines. The collaboration with Hyper-V also facilitates the installation of compute nodes based on Hyper-V on the SUSE Cloud platform.

SUSE collaborates with the hardware vendor Dell to develop the enterprise-class private cloud infrastructure solution, which combines Dell's hardware and services with SUSE software. The Dell SUSE Cloud Solution gets support from both Dell and SUSE worldwide support organizations. It simplifies the IT infrastructure development process, enables an enterprise to set up clouds on an existing data center quickly, and reduces tasks needed to add capacity as the need continues to grow.

Ubuntu Linux: Ubuntu is also a major Linux distribution sponsored by Canonical Ltd., a private company from South Africa. The Ubuntu Linux operating system is free and consists of all open source products. It is updated every 6 months. It also provides a long-term support version of the operating system, which upgrades every 3 years.

The Ubuntu Linux operating system has three editions, the server edition, the desktop edition, and the mobile edition. The server edition of Ubuntu Linux includes the LAMP (Linux, Apache, MySQL, and PHP) package. The installation of Ubuntu is quick and simple. The LAMP package is installed automatically. The Ubuntu desktop edition is specially designed to be easy-to-use. It includes many utilities for handling multimedia content such as photo editing and media editing tools. Like the Windows operating system, it includes a large number of GUI tools for searching, calendaring, Web form spell checking, phishing detection, and system administration. It also includes e-mail and the latest Web browsing technology, the office suite OpenOffice.org, the instant messenger Pidgin, and the image editor GIMP. The mobile edition is designed to run multimedia content on mobile devices. The mobile edition operating system can run with small memory and storage space. It also delivers fast boot and resume time. Figure 1.17 illustrates the GUI interface of Ubuntu Server.

Ubuntu Cloud is designed to allow companies to provide fast and efficient cloud services. With Ubuntu Cloud, a pool of scalable compute and storage IT resources can be made available for on-demand access. Ubuntu is the reference operating system for OpenStack. That is, Ubuntu is the base operating system used by the developers of OpenStack. OpenStack is a free and open-source software platform on which cloud services can be built, tested, and deployed. As the reference operating system

Figure 1.17 Ubuntu Server.

for OpenStack, Ubuntu cuts down the complexity in developing an OpenStack cloud, which stops the lock-in to a specific cloud vendor.

Ubuntu is broadly supported by public clouds such as Amazon Web Services, Rackspace Cloud, HP Public Cloud, and Microsoft Azure, and so on. It can be used either as an underlying infrastructure or as a guest operating system on virtual machines hosted in a cloud. Ubuntu works with the leading public cloud infrastructures to enhance performance, handle updates, and achieve compliance and reliability on the public clouds. Ubuntu has been creating tools such as cloud-init to ease the process of bringing up new instances on a public cloud.

Ubuntu can also be used to create cloud services that are deployed on private IT infrastructures. With Ubuntu Cloud Infrastructure, a company can deliver all its compute, network, and storage resources as cloud service. Ubuntu provides necessary tools for developing a private Infrastructure as a Service (IaaS) cloud service on an existing private IT infrastructure. With these tools, one can quickly set up scalable storage and integrate the features into a cloud service. The private cloud created with Ubuntu is compliant with some of the public cloud standards including Amazon EC2 and Rackspace APIs. Therefore, it has the freedom to migrate the cloud services between the public cloud and the private cloud.

With Ubuntu Cloud Infrastructure, a private cloud can be extended into the public cloud to form a hybrid cloud. When Ubuntu is on both the private cloud and the public cloud, Ubuntu Cloud Infrastructure enables users to burst workloads from their private clouds to the major public clouds, or vice versa. Ubuntu provides a service orchestration tool called Juju to accomplish tasks such as automated arrangement, coordination, and management of virtual machines, middleware, and services. With Juju, one can define the Software as a Service (SaaS) and deploy it to a cloud, either a private cloud or a public cloud or both. Juju is so designed that it is cloud provider independent; therefore, it can deploy services to different cloud providers.

Earlier, we have discussed several operating systems that are capable of cloud computing and network virtualization. There are many other operating systems that may also be capable of cloud development and network virtualization. The selection of an operating system for networking depends on the tasks to be accomplished, the flexibility, the scalability, ease-of-use, and the cost. For most networking-related tasks, the operating system mentioned in this section should be able to do the job. Next, we will focus on network architecture which is the logic model used by the networking capable operating systems.

1.4 Network Architecture

This section will discuss network architecture and the tasks to be accomplished during a networking process. It will introduce the major components in a network system. We will take a look at how network functionalities are designed and implemented in an operating system. Network management tools will also be introduced in this section.

A network can be as small as two computers connected by a copper wire or as large as the Internet that links millions of computers and network devices. For computers to be able to communicate with each other through physical media, as an example, the Linux operating system provides four major components: application, service, protocol, and adapter.

A network system can be represented by a network model, also called network architecture, which is often presented as a layer system. The network architecture provides an overview of a network system by including the major components for a network and the interfaces between components. To be able to handle data transmission tasks on various networks, the network components in an operating system are built according to the network architecture. An operating system controls data transmission from the application software to the physical wire, which connects the computers. Figure 1.18 illustrates the network components in an operating system.

As a service interface between users and the operating system kernel, the application software manages data communication between the users and the operating system. It takes the users' requests for file transfer, database query, and message exchange, and then submits the requests to the operating system. Once the requests are submitted to the operating system, the network management component will collect the data and identify the network protocols to be used for data communication.

A network protocol serves as a service interface between the application software and the network driver. There are hundreds of protocols supported by an operating system.

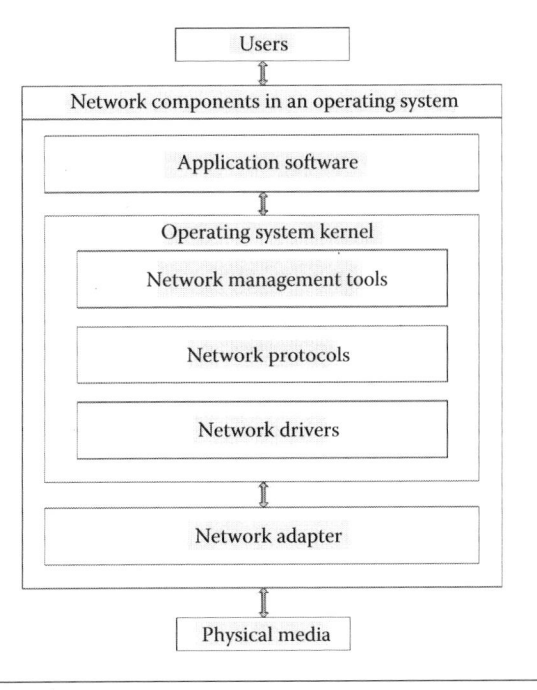

Figure 1.18 Network components.

The network protocols perform tasks such as establishing the communication ports, detecting data transmission errors, data formatting, controlling the data transmission process, resolving network addresses, maintaining network traffic, locating the destination computer and setting up the route to the destination, defining how the data are sent and received, and so on. For security, some of the protocols are used for data encryption and authentication.

A network driver serves as an interface between the software and the hardware. The driver enables the operating system to communicate with the NIC, which connects the physical data transmission media. Drivers can be used to handle I/O interrupts during a data transmission process. In addition to interacting with the operating system, drivers also interact with buffers, network protocols, and network adapters.

A network adapter is a piece of hardware that connects the physical media to a computer on the network. During data transmission, a network adapter communicates with its peer network adapter installed on another computer. Network adapters may be a wired Ethernet NIC, or it can also be a wireless network device. A network adapter serves as an interface between the operating system kernel and the physical media. Electrical signals are framed in a network adapter. The frame specifies the transmission rate and the shape and strength of the binary signals. By using a network adapter, the binary electric signals are sent to or received from physical transmission media. The network adapter is able to locate its peer network adapter through the hardware address. Once the data arrive at the receiving network adapter, the receiving network adapter informs the operating system to get ready to process the incoming binary signals.

The physical medium links two network hosts such as computers or network devices. The electric signals representing the binary bits are transmitted through the physical media such as copper cables, fiber glass, radio waves, etc. The physical media may also include network devices used to pass the electric signals to a particular destination.

A network can be presented in two different network architectures. The first one is the Open Systems Interconnection (OSI) architecture developed by the International Organization for Standardization (ISO). OSI is a network architecture that defines the communication process between two computers. OSI categorizes the entire communication process into seven layers as shown in Figure 1.19. The second one is the Internet architecture. This architecture is built around the Transmission Control Protocol and Internet Protocol (TCP/IP). Therefore, the Internet architecture is also called the TCP/IP architecture, which includes four layers as shown in Figure 1.20.

In the OSI network architecture, the top layer is the application. The protocols in the application layer are provided by application software. The application layer protocols handle requests from users for file transfer, database query, message exchange, and so on. The protocols in the application layer communicate with the protocols in the presentation layer.

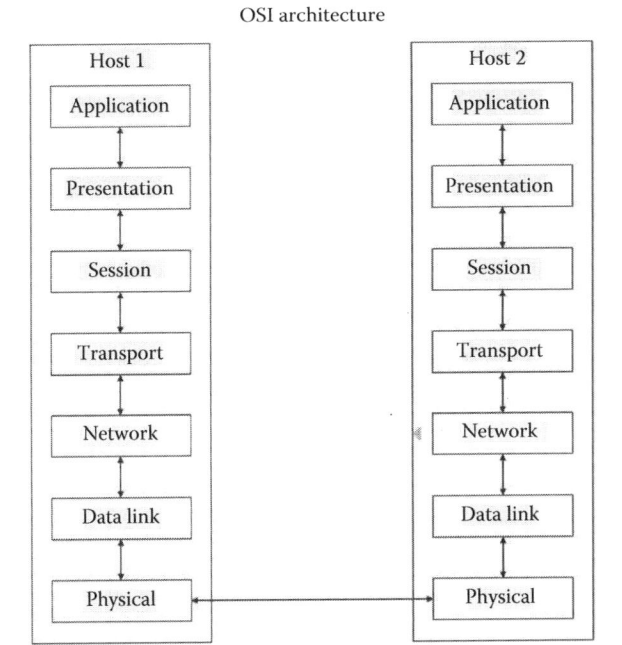

Figure 1.19   OSI architecture diagram.

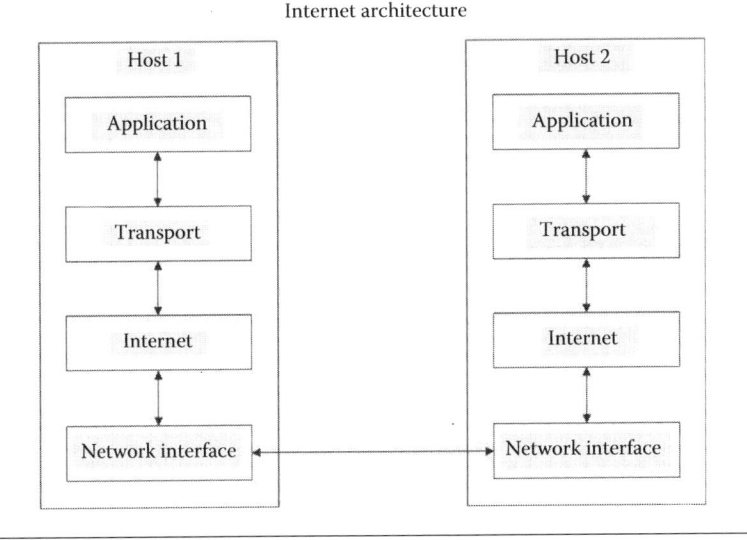

Figure 1.20   Internet architecture diagram.

The protocols in the presentation layer format the data so that the data meet certain transmission requirements. The tasks to be handled by this layer can be data compression, data encryption, video streaming, data format conversion, and so forth.

The protocols in the session layer establish the communication session between two applications such as a conference call or remote connection to a database server. These protocols can be used to start, manage, and terminate a communication session.

They also perform tasks such as requesting and responding during a data transmission process between applications.

The protocols in the transport layer establish and manage the connection between two hosts on the network. This layer handles tasks such as detecting transmission errors; controlling network flow; transporting data; and establishing, managing and terminating connections.

The protocols in the network layer can identify the destination network and establish the data transmission route to a destination host. This is the layer that works with routers and network logical address configuration tools. The routing protocols are able to calculate the shortest path to the destination host and update the routing table periodically.

The data link layer is often implemented in the network card driver. This layer defines the beginning and ending of a binary data transmission frame. It also defines data types. During the process of sending and receiving binary code, this layer also detects and corrects errors in the binary code.

The physical layer transmits electrical binary signals over the physical media that link two hosts. It also defines the shape of electronic signals. When an electrical binary signal arrives from the physical media, the physical layer passes the binary signal up to the data link layer.

Another commonly used network architecture, the Internet architecture, is designed for modeling data exchange through the Internet. The application layer in the Internet architecture includes the application layer, the presentation layer, and the session layer of the OSI architecture. The transport layer of the Internet architecture is equivalent to the transport layer of the OSI architecture. The Internet layer of the Internet architecture is similar to the network layer of the OSI architecture. The network interface layer of the Internet architecture includes data link layer and the physical layer of the OSI architecture. Figure 1.20 shows the diagram of the Internet (TCP/IP) architecture.

The OSI network architecture is the standard adopted by the U.S. government. Therefore, the hardware and software companies working for the U.S. government need to follow the OSI network architecture. On the other hand, many private companies have been traditionally using the TCP/IP architecture, which matches the network architecture used by the Berkeley UNIX operating system. The Microsoft Windows Server operating system uses the TCP/IP architecture to describe its network system.

Both Linux and Windows network systems can be implemented by closely following the TCP/IP network architecture. Comparing the network components in Figure 1.18 with the TCP/IP network architecture, one can see that the application layer in the TCP/IP network architecture matches the component of application software in Figure 1.18. Application software often carries out tasks such as data compression, data encryption, video streaming, and data format conversion. The application software component also includes network management tools. These tools are used to handle tasks related to session establishment, maintenance, and termination. The operating system kernel manages protocols such as TCP and IP around which the TCP/IP architecture is constructed. The combination of network drivers, network adapters, and physical media in Figure 1.18 matches the network interface layer in the TCP/IP architecture.

Earlier, we briefly discussed the network architecture, which shows how data communication is carried out between applications over a network. The network architecture models the data communication process. In later chapters, more detailed discussion about each layer of the network architecture will be given.

Activity 1.1: Preparing for Hands-On Activities

To carry out the lab activities covered in this book, we need to install the operating system and virtualization software. We also need to prepare the cloud environment for the hands-on practice. As for the public cloud provider, we will choose Microsoft Windows Azure since it has a free trial period, academic support, and it supports both Linux and Windows operating systems. To develop virtual networks, we can use Microsoft Azure, or use Hyper-V if Windows Server 2012 or Windows 8, or use VMware Workstation, which can work with various desktop operating systems. The following tasks will be performed on Microsoft Azure.

Getting Started with Microsoft Azure

To be able to use Microsoft Azure, you need to first create a free account. You also need to create a storage account and virtual network on Microsoft Azure. Then, you will create a virtual machine on Microsoft Azure as shown in the following steps:

1. Assume that you have established the free trial account or academic account. First, you need to go to the following Web site to log on to Microsoft Azure (Microsoft Azure, The cloud for modern business, May, 2015): http://azure. microsoft.com/en-us/.
2. Log on to your Microsoft Azure Management Portal with your user name and password.
3. In the lower left-hand corner of your screen, click **New**. Then, click **NETWORK SERVICES**, and then click **VIRTUAL NETWORK**. Click **CUSTOM CREATE** as shown in Figure 1.21.
4. On the Virtual Network Details page, enter the information about the name and location as shown in Figure 1.22, and then click the **Next** arrow at the lower right corner.
5. On the DNS Server and VPN Connectivity page, leave DNS server blank as shown in Figure 1.23. Then, click the **next arrow** on the lower right.

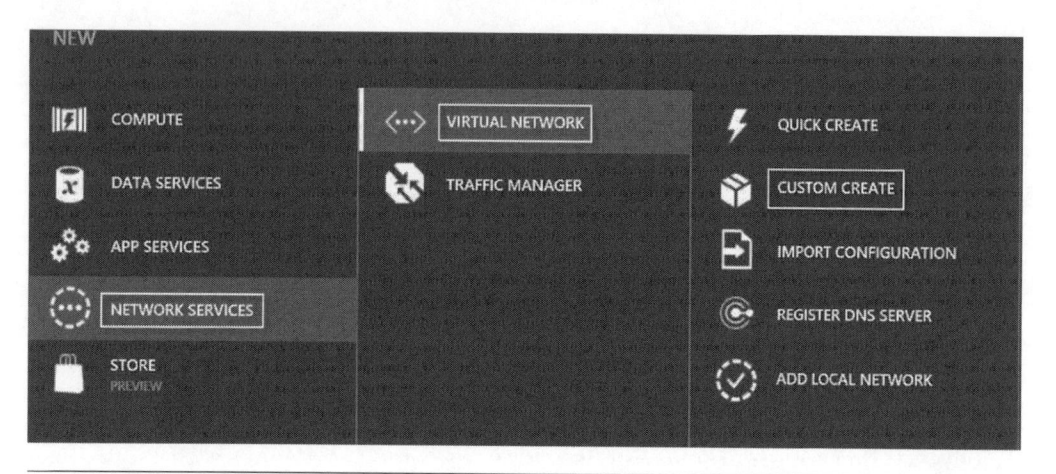

Figure 1.21   Creating new virtual network.

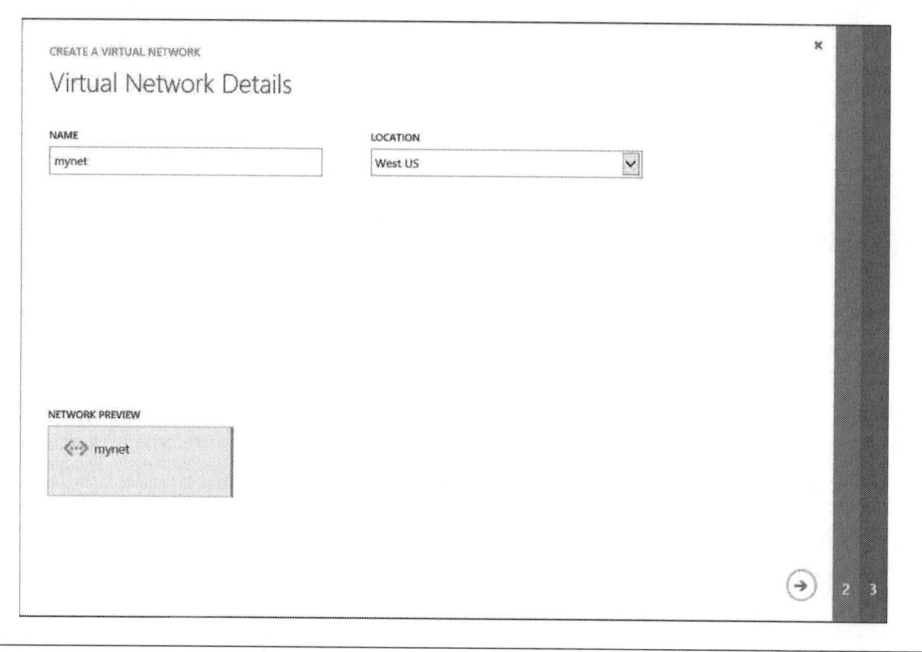

Figure 1.22   Virtual network configuration.

6. On the Virtual Network Address Spaces page, click **add subnet** button to create a subnet as shown in Figure 1.24. Then, click the **check mark** on the lower right.

7. In addition to the virtual network, you may create a storage account that provides the namespace for data storage. At the lower left-hand corner of the screen, click **New**.

8. In the navigation pane, click **DATA SERVICES, STORAGE,** and then **QUICK CREATE**. Specify the URL and Affinity group as shown in Figure 1.25. Then, click the **CREATE STORAGE ACCOUNT** check mark on the lower right.

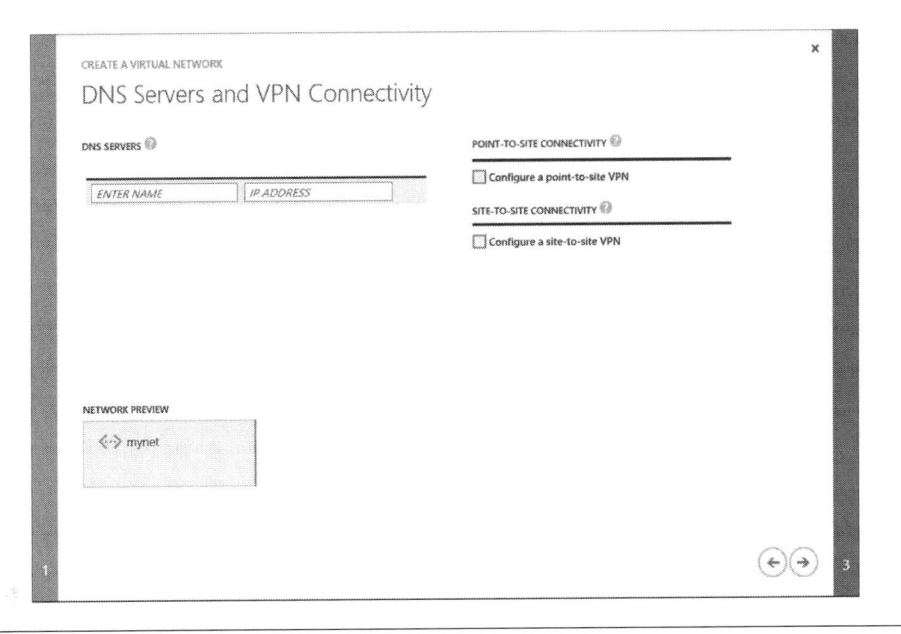

Figure 1.23 DNS server configuration.

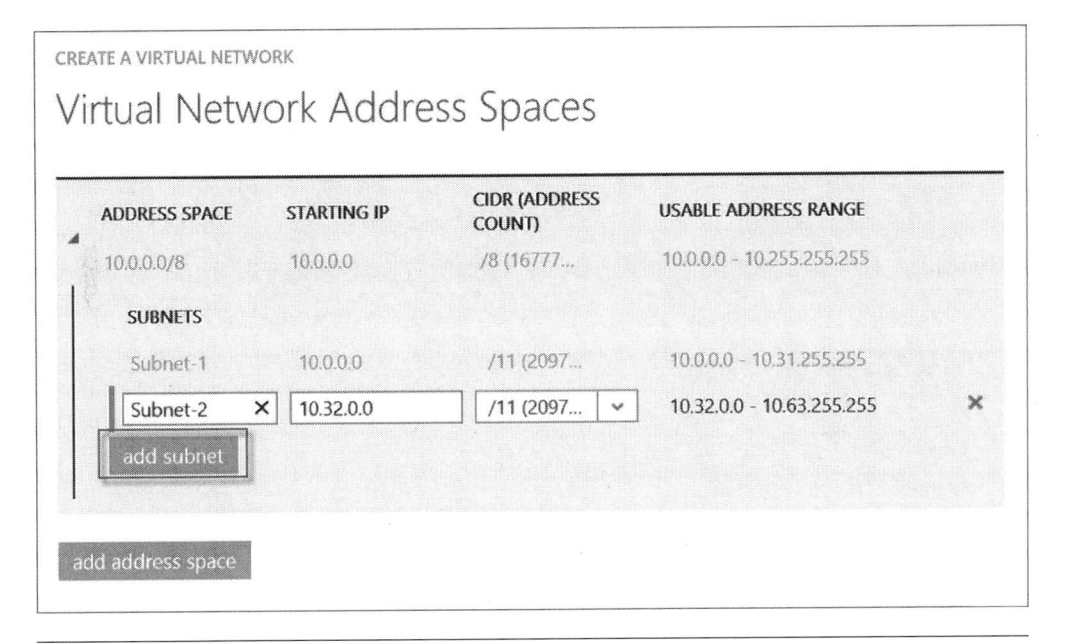

Figure 1.24 Adding virtual subnet.

9. Your next step is to create a virtual machine installed with Windows Server 2012. To do so, at the lower left-hand corner of your screen, click **New**. Then, click **COMPUTE, VIRTUAL MACHINE, FROM GALLERY** as shown in Figure 1.26.

10. On the Select virtual machine operating system page, click **Windows Server 2012 R2 Datacenter** (Figure 1.27) and then click the **Next** arrow on the lower right.

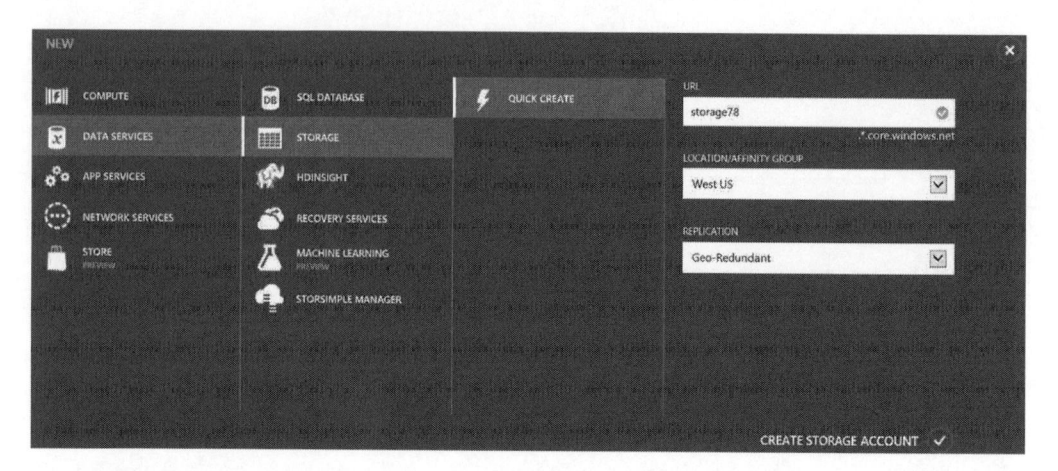

Figure 1.25   Creating storage account.

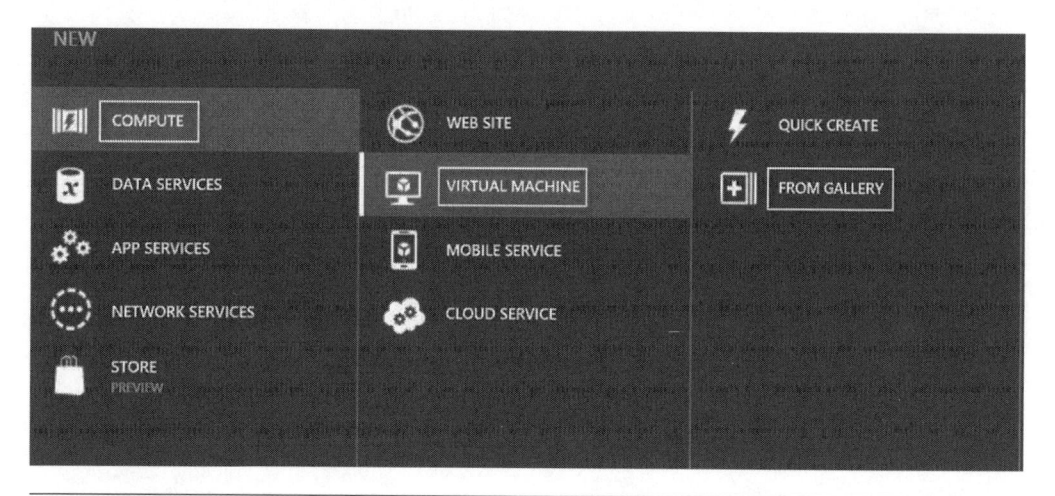

Figure 1.26   Selecting virtual machine.

11. On the Virtual machine configuration page, enter your virtual machine name **servera**, the user **student** and the password, confirm the password, and select the size of your virtual machine as shown in Figure 1.28. The A1 size is adequate for the hands-on activities in this book. Then, click the **Next** arrow.
12. On the Virtual machine configuration page, specify the virtual machine as shown in Figure 1.29.
13. Depending on the needs, you may add a few more communication protocols as shown in Figure 1.30. Then, click the **Next** arrow.
14. On the Virtual machine configuration page, click the **check mark** at the lower right corner to create the virtual machine.
15. After the virtual machine is created, click the **CONNECT** link at the bottom of your screen. Select the option **Use another account**. Enter the user name as **student** and the password for the user and then click **OK** to log on to the virtual machine (Figure 1.31).

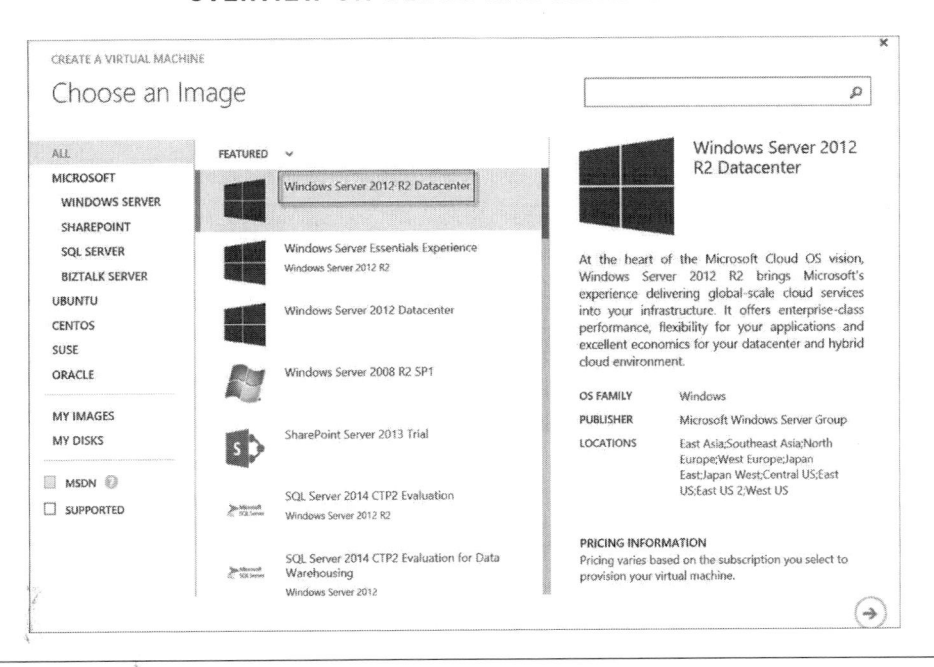

Figure 1.27 Selecting operating system.

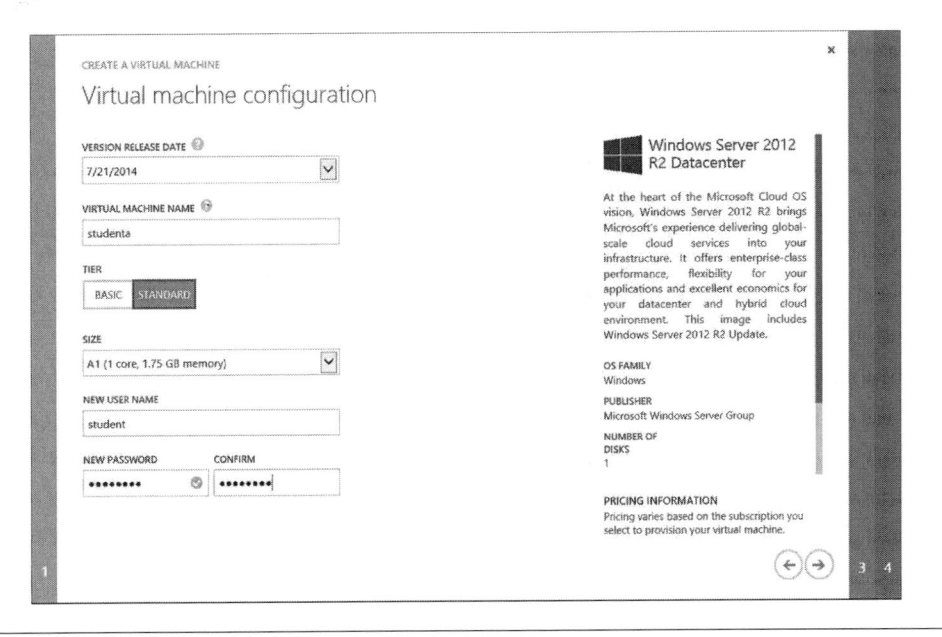

Figure 1.28 Configuring virtual machine.

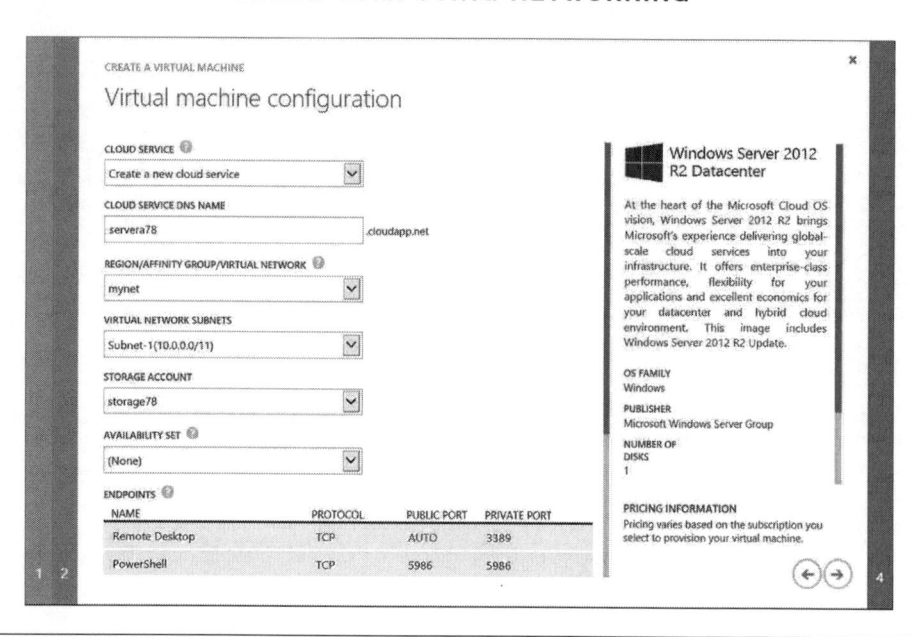

Figure 1.29   Virtual machine configuration.

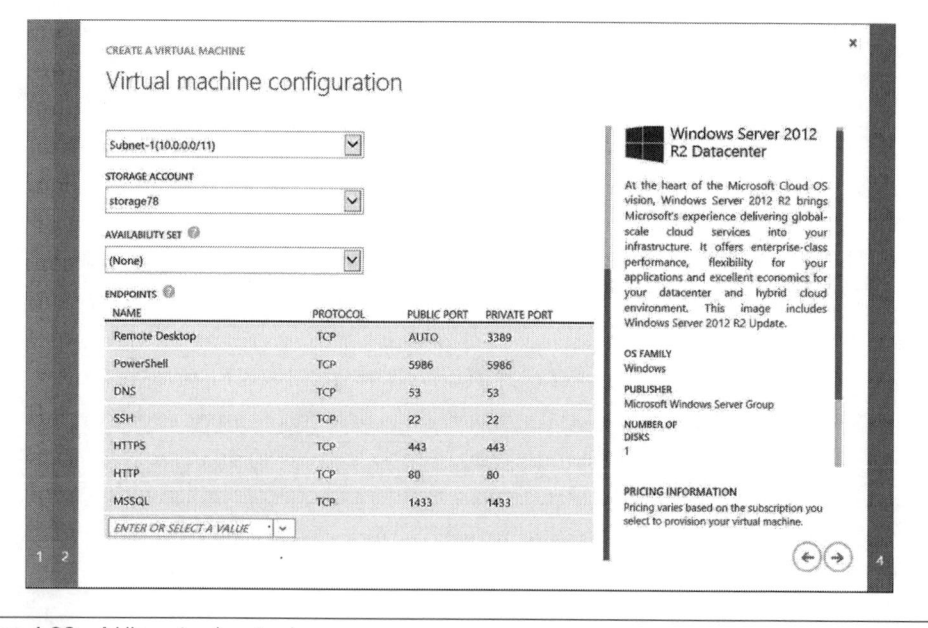

Figure 1.30   Adding network protocols.

16. After logging on to the virtual machine, you should be able to see Server Manager as shown in Figure 1.32.

17. For networking, you need to create another virtual machine. Assume that you are still logged on to the Microsoft Azure Management Portal. Click **NEW** at the bottom of the screen. Click **FROM GALLERY** and select **Windows Server 2012 R2 Datacenter**. Enter the virtual machine **serverb** and user

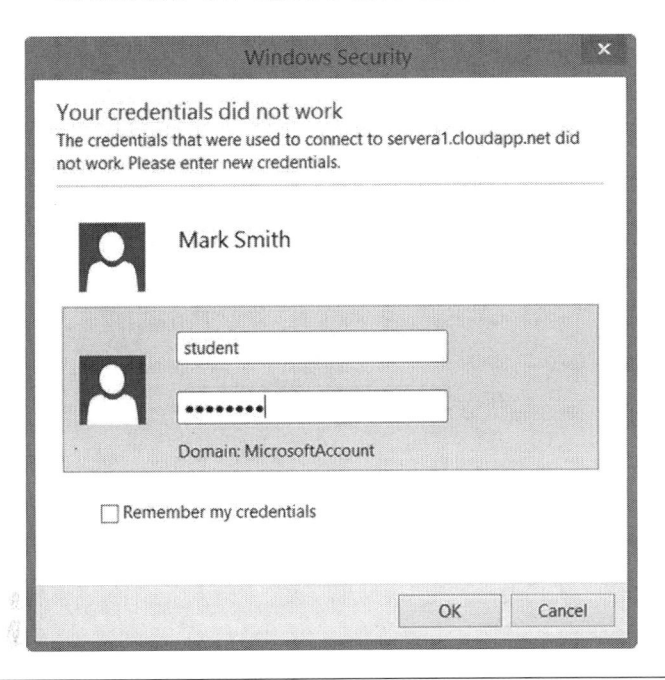

Figure 1.31 Remotely logging on to virtual machine.

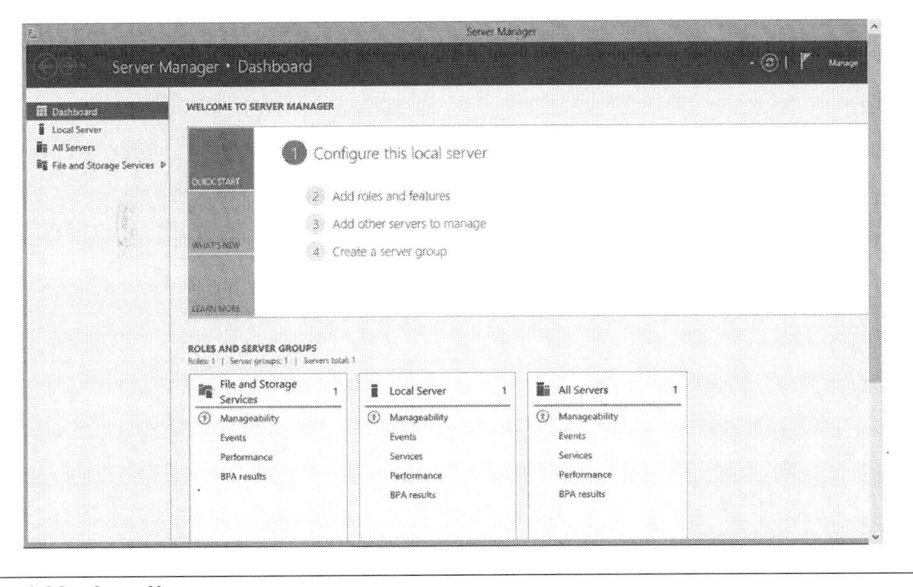

Figure 1.32 Server Manager.

name **student**. Enter your password as shown in Figure 1.33 and click the **Next arrow**.

18. On the Virtual Machine Configuration page, specify the virtual machine as shown in Figure 1.34. Similarly, add some network protocols as shown in Figures 1.30. Then, click the **Next arrow**.

19. On the Virtual machine option page, click the **check mark** at the lower right corner to create the virtual machine.

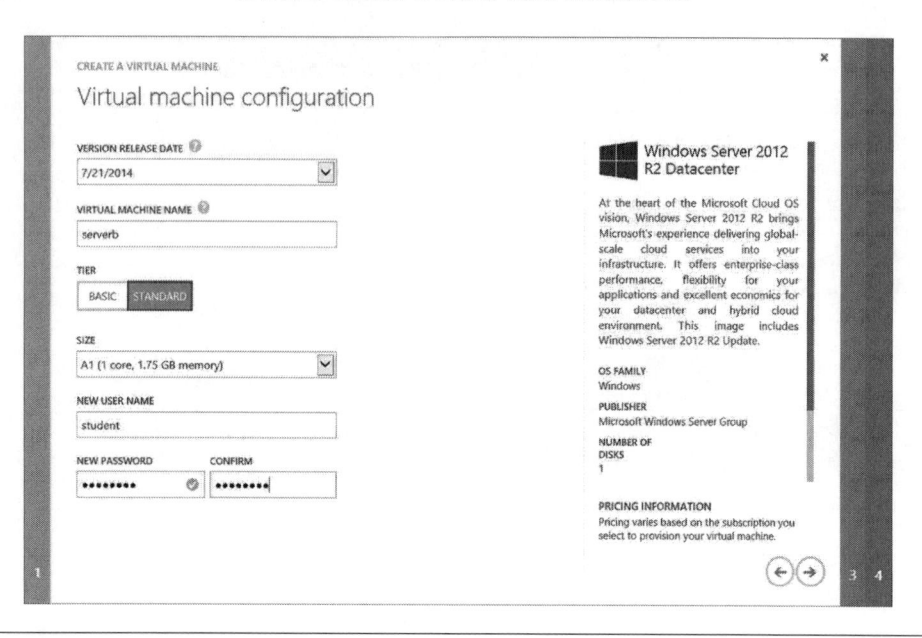

Figure 1.33 Configuring virtual machine server.

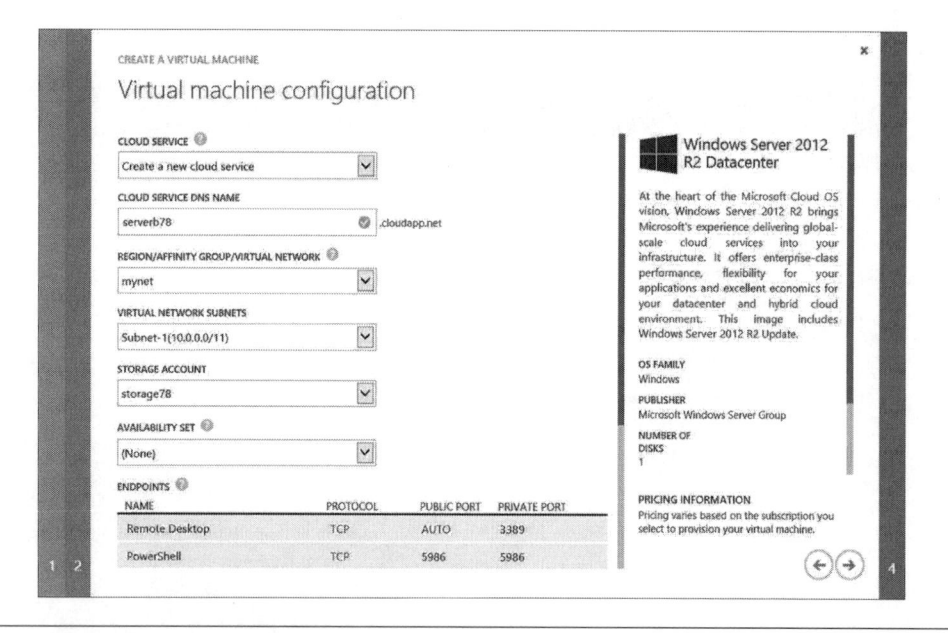

Figure 1.34 Configuring virtual machine.

20. Due to the spending limit on Azure, make sure to shutdown the virtual machines whenever you are not using them. In the Microsoft Azure Management Portal, you should shutdown both servera and serverb before exiting the Microsoft Azure Management Portal.

So far, you have created two virtual machines on Microsoft Azure. Later, you will perform networking on these two virtual machines.

1.5 Summary

This chapter introduces networking. It first provides an overview of networks. Then, it discusses network operating systems. It also provides information on how the operating systems handle virtualization and support cloud computing. This chapter reviews network architectures. Two abstract network architectures, the OSI network architecture and Internet network architecture, are introduced. The chapter then describes the role of operating systems in developing network systems.

To prepare the computing environment for the hands-on practice in later chapters, the activity of this chapter walked the reader through a process of creating virtual machines and installing a guest operating system on the virtual machines. Once the virtual machines are created, we are ready to discover how these virtual machines are used to accomplish various networking tasks.

Review Questions

1. What are hosts?
2. What is LAN?
3. What is WAN?
4. Describe the Internet.
5. What is POP?
6. What is NAP?
7. Which operating system mentioned in this chapter is designed for the cloud platform?
8. Which operating system mentioned in this chapter provides the virtualization tool, Hyper-V?
9. What do you do with Hyper-V?
10. What are cloud services provided by Microsoft Azure?
11. What is vSphere?
12. Name five hypervisors supported by OpenStack.
13. Describe the application layer in the OSI network architecture.
14. What tasks can be handled by the transport layer in the OSI network architecture?
15. What tasks can be handled by the network layer in the OSI network architecture?
16. Which layers in the OSI network architecture are included in the application layer of the TCP/IP network architecture?
17. Which layers in the OSI network architecture are included in the network interface layer of the TCP/IP network architecture?
18. What tasks can be accomplished by the TCP in the transport layer?
19. IP is in which layer of the TCP/IP network architecture?
20. Network drivers are in which layer of the TCP/IP network architecture?

2

NETWORK PROTOCOLS

Objectives

- Learn about commonly used protocols in the Internet architecture.
- Understand the relationships among the protocols.
- Explore network tools.

2.1 Introduction

As described in Chapter 1, a networking process involves various protocols, which are used as communication languages. In a network, the data transfer is accomplished by multiple protocols; each protocol carries out a specific task. Various protocols will be used in later chapters. To enhance the understanding of how network devices communicate with each other, it is necessary to understand how the protocols are designed, what the responsibilities of these protocols are, and how these protocols are related. In this chapter, the commonly used protocols in cloud computing will be discussed in detail. Due to the fact that the network architecture used by Windows and UNIX-like operating systems is the Internet architecture (or Transmission Control Protocol/Internet Protocol [TCP/IP] architecture), the protocols introduced in this chapter will be grouped based on the TCP/IP architecture.

There are four layers in the TCP/IP network architecture: application layer, transport layer, Internet layer, and network interface layer. Each layer in the TCP/IP architecture may include dozens or even hundreds of protocols. In this chapter, a few commonly used protocols in each layer will be introduced. In the hands-on practice, some of the networking tools will be used to illustrate the protocols used in cloud computing.

2.2 Application Layer Protocols

Protocols in the application layer handle the communication of application software. They can carry out tasks such as responding to requests from web browsers, making conference calls, or connecting to remote database servers. Some of the protocols can be used to set up user authentication. Others can be used to set up agreements on data resources, data integrity, and data syntax rules. The protocols included in this layer can be used to establish, terminate, and manage sessions that handle requests and responses between hosts. In the application layer of the TCP/IP architecture, the protocols also perform tasks such as data compression, data encryption, video streaming, and data format conversion.

There are hundreds of protocols included in this layer. Some of the well-known application protocols are Hypertext Transfer Protocol (HTTP), Domain Name System (DNS), Dynamic Host Configuration Protocol (DHCP), Simple Mail Transfer Protocol (SMTP), Post Office Protocol Version 3 (POP3), Internet Message Access Protocol (IMAP), Telecommunication Network (Telnet), Secure Shell (SSH), Lightweight Directory Access Protocol (LDAP), Secure Sockets Layer (SSL), Secure Shell (SSH), Secure Socket Tunneling Protocol (SSTP), and Simple Network Management Protocol (SNMP).

An application protocol communicates through a dedicated port number. For example, HTTP communicates through the port 80, DNS communicates through the port 53, and DHCP communicates through the port 67.

The following gives general descriptions of the commonly used protocols in the application layer. In later chapters, more specific application protocols will be introduced.

Hypertext Transfer Protocol (HTTP): The protocol HTTP is used for transferring data between web browsers and web servers. HTTP can carry data in various formats such as text, graphic images, sound, video, and other multimedia files. To manage data transferring, HTTP provides a set of commands. With these commands, HTTP handles how a web browser requests data stored on a web server and how the web server responds to the request from the web browser. HTTP also handles how a web browser uploads files to a web server and how the web server executes scripts to support a dynamic web page. For example, suppose that a user enters a URL in a web browser. After the user presses the Enter key, HTTP carries the GET command to the web server through Port 80. By executing the GET command, the web server finds the requested web page. Then, HTTP carries the web page back to the web browser. If the user uploads a file to the web server, HTTP sends the web page and the PUT command to the web server. By executing the PUT command, the web server stores the web page in a proper place. In addition to telling the web server how to respond to a request from a client, HTTP can instruct the web server to place requested data in an application. It can also instruct the web server to run scripts.

Domain Name System (DNS): DNS is a protocol used to find the corresponding IP address for a given host name, or vice versa. It communicates with UDP through Port 53. In a network, each host needs to have an IP address for data communication. However, it is not easy for a user to remember the host's IP address. The host in a network needs a user-friendly name such as www.windowsazure.com. When accessing a web server, the data communication process needs the web server's IP address to contact the web server. DNS works like finding a phone number in a telephone directory. Based on the URL entered by the user, DNS finds the corresponding IP address in a

DNS server. Then, it returns the IP address to the host with the web browser installed for connecting to the web server.

DNS is implemented with two components, the DNS client and DNS server. The DNS client is the host that requests the IP address. The DNS server stores a database that contains pairs of host names and corresponding IP addresses. As you can imagine, for all the hosts on the Internet, the DNS database can be a really large one. Therefore, the database has to be distributed to many DNS servers; each of them stores only part of the database.

Dynamic Host Configuration Protocol (DHCP): As described earlier, each host in a network needs to have a unique IP address. It can be a tedious task to manually assign each host an IP address. DHCP is a protocol that can be used to automatically assign an IP address and other network parameters to a computer or a network device. In addition to assigning IP addresses, DHCP can also be used to deliver network parameters such as the subnet mask, the IP address of the router used as the default gateway, and the DNS server, and so on. Later chapters will provide more information about these parameters. DHCP greatly reduces the amount of configuration time spent on these network hosts such as computers and network devices.

Here is an example to illustrate how DHCP works. If a computer is configured to automatically receive an IP address and other network parameters from a DHCP server, as the computer is booted up, it sends out a broadcast message to look for the DHCP server on a network. Once the DHCP server receives the request broadcasted by the client computer, it offers an IP address and a set of network parameters to the client computer. When the client computer receives the offer from the DHCP server, it accepts the offer by sending a response to the DHCP server. If the DHCP client receives multiple offers from multiple DHCP servers, the client computer will inform the DHCP servers to let them know which offer has been accepted. Then, the chosen DHCP server sends an acknowledgment to the client computer and informs the client computer that the IP address and other network parameters are ready for data communication.

Simple Mail Transfer Protocol (SMTP): Sending and receiving e-mail message need different protocols. SMTP is a protocol used to send messages to e-mail servers. It can also be used to deliver e-mail messages between two e-mail servers. However, SMTP is not used to receive messages from e-mail servers for reading due to its limited ability on user authentication and queuing messages at the receiving end.

As a simple text-based protocol, SMTP has about 10 commands in order to reduce bandwidth and improve performance. SMTP has no authentication measure to verify who is sending the message. Therefore, it cannot tell if the message is sent by a real sender or a hacker. SMTP communicates through Port 25. To improve security and performance, the Enhanced Simple Mail Transfer Protocol (ESMTP) has been developed to enforce security. ESMTP adds many features for authentication, reduces bandwidth, and does error recovery.

Post Office Protocol Version 3 (POP3): POP3 is one of the protocols used for receiving e-mail messages. It can check the mail box on an e-mail server and download the e-mails from the server. It has the user authentication mechanism so that only the qualified user can receive the e-mails that belong to that user. POP3 is included in most of the e-mail client software and web browsers. The disadvantage of POP3 is that it only supports a single inbox, so the user cannot place related e-mails into different folders. POP3 communicates through Port 110.

Internet Message Access Protocol (IMAP): IMAP is another protocol used for receiving e-mail messages. Unlike POP3, IMAP supports multiple folders on the server side. These folders can be used for organizing e-mail messages. IMAP allows users to select which messages to download. It uses Port 143 to download e-mail messages from an e-mail server.

Secure Sockets Layer (SSL): SSL is a security protocol used for protecting sensitive information transferred between a web server and a web browser. When a web browser connects to an SSL server hosted by a web server, it requests the server to provide a digital Certificate of Authority (CA). The CA is usually validated by a third party authority agency such as VeriSign. This CA is used to authenticate the SSL server to make sure that the server is not a hacker. The web browser also checks if the name of the server matches the domain name provided by the CA and if the digital signature is valid. When a web browser uses the URL starting with https, it means that the SSL protocol is used to connect to the SSL server. Sensitive information will be protected during data communication. For web applications, SSL runs on the port number 443. However, for other applications, SSL runs on different ports. Also, the network administrator can choose to run SSL on a different port number.

Secure Shell (SSH): SSH is another protocol used to secure the access of a remote network host. With SSH, a user can securely log on to a remote computer to carry out tasks such as executing commands and transferring files. With the built-in authentication and encryption mechanism, SSH can protect the network from attacks such as IP spoofing or IP source routing. The authentication mechanism only allows the connection from trusted hosts. The encryption mechanism encrypts SSH commands and passwords for confidentiality. During transmission, SSH establishes a secure channel between two hosts on the network. By default, SSH uses the port 22 for information exchange.

Secure Socket Tunneling Protocol (SSTP): SSTP is a protocol designed to allow two application programs to engage in bidirectional, asynchronous communication. For example, it can be used to establish a virtual private network (VPN), which is a private network constructed over the public Internet. Even though the data communication is carried out in the public network, the communication between two hosts in the private network is protected by using encryption and authentication mechanisms. SSTP depends on SSL to provide the security mechanism. SSTP uses TCP Port 443 for relaying SSTP traffic. In later chapters, SSTP is used to connect a host on a home network to a virtual network on a cloud. The advantage of SSTP is that it is not blocked by the firewall, so the virtual machine on the cloud can communicate with the hosts behind the router in your home network.

Lightweight Directory Access Protocol (LDAP): A directory service is used to store and organize the authentication information about network resources such as users, groups, computers, printers, files, domains, and organization units. LDAP is a protocol used to manage the directory service. With LDAP, the network administrator can perform tasks such as implementing centralized user authentication, arranging users according to an organization's structure, and configuring group policies. LDAP is often used by other services, such as web service and e-mail service for authentication.

Simple Network Management Protocol (SNMP): SNMP is a protocol for network management. It can be used to improve network performance, detect and correct network problems, and monitor network activities. The commands provided by SNMP are used to perform management tasks such as obtaining information from network devices and controlling the behavior of network devices. To accomplish the management tasks, SNMP needs information about the network devices and software that is stored in a management information base (MIB). In the MIB, the names of network objects and the information about their locations are stored on a tree structure and are coded in the Abstract Syntax Notation One (ASN.1) language. SNMP provides the security measures called SNMP Community Strings to protect the data being transmitted.

Earlier, a few commonly used application protocols were introduced. More application protocols will be introduced in later chapters. The list of application protocols introduced in this book is far from complete. There are about 100 known application protocols available. Also, there is no consistent definition on which protocol should be qualified as an application layer protocol.

2.3 Transport Layer Protocols

Protocols in the transport layer transfer data from one application to another. To prepare data transferring, protocols in the transport layer break the data into small units called packets. The transport layer protocols also handle tasks such as data transmission error checking; network flow control; and establishing, managing, and terminating a connection between hosts. The transport protocols process requests from the application layer protocols and issue the requests to the protocols in the Internet layer. While communicating with the protocols in the application layer, the transport layer protocols have the ability to identify the ports in the destination hosts. In such a way, the packets can be delivered to the proper ports of the destinations. The two commonly used transport layer protocols are Transmission Control Protocol (TCP) and User Datagram Protocol (UDP).

2.3.1 Transmission Control Protocol

TCP is a well-known transport layer protocol. It controls and manages data communication between ports. The following TCP features make TCP a core protocol in the TCP/IP architecture:

- *Connection orientation*: Once TCP receives a connection request from an application layer protocol, it establishes a reliable connection between the hosts that have agreed to communicate. Before the data communication begins, this feature makes sure that the application layer ports on the hosts are properly linked.
- *Point-to-point communication*: TCP views ports as connection end points. Data communication takes place between two end points.
- *Complete reliability*: This feature guarantees no data missing during transmission.
- *Full duplex communication*: TCP allows simultaneous communication in both directions just like a 2-way street.
- *3-Way handshake connection*: To initiate and terminate a connection, TCP uses a 3-way handshake process, which guarantees that the connection is reliable and the termination is graceful.

The aforementioned features can be implemented by accomplishing the following tasks:

- TCP divides a data file to be transmitted into small units called packets.
- A reliable TCP connection is established by using the 3-way handshake process.
- The termination of a TCP connection is also done through the 3-way handshake process.
- The 3-way handshake is implemented with a three-packet process.
- During the transmission process, a window mechanism is used to control the packet transmission flow.
- Based on the network capacity, TCP determines the proper packet transmission rate to avoid network congestion.
- TCP tracks packets to make sure that all the packets arrive at the destination host.
- TCP keeps the transmitted packets in order so that the packets can be reassembled back to the original file.
- TCP creates checksum used for detecting any transmission error.
- TCP resends the packets that are lost or that have transmission errors detected during the transmission.
- TCP discards duplicated packets.

To see how TCP can accomplish the aforementioned tasks, read the next few paragraphs for detailed descriptions.

The reasons for TCP to break a data block to be transmitted over a network into small units are listed:

- It needs some time to coordinate the protocol and hardware involved in a data transmission process.
- When the network transmission media are shared by multiple computers, the use of packets allows these computers transfer data in turns.

Packets are formed by combining each small data unit with a header and a trailer. In a packet, the small data unit is called a payload. The header includes information about the data to be transferred. It also includes information about the network used to carry out the transmission. It general, the header may include the following:

- The header includes the source and destination information for delivering a packet to the destination host and for receiving response from the destination host.
- It contains a packet sequence number used as the packet identification.
- It contains a synchronization bit, which can be turned on and off to synchronize network transmission.
- It has a packet type indicator to identify the type of information to be carried by the packet.
- It also has the information about the packet length, which is the size of the packet.

In practice, the header of a protocol may include more or less information than the basic information listed earlier. As a complicated protocol, TCP has much more information in its header. The following is the diagram of a typical TCP header (Figure 2.1).

In the diagram, each row represents a unit of 32 binary bits transmitted through a network. The following briefly describes each field in the diagram:

- Source and Destination Ports: These two fields identify the end points of a TCP connection for delivering and receiving packets.
- Sequence Number: Assigned to the outgoing packet, this number is used for reordering packets and calculating the acknowledgment number(s).

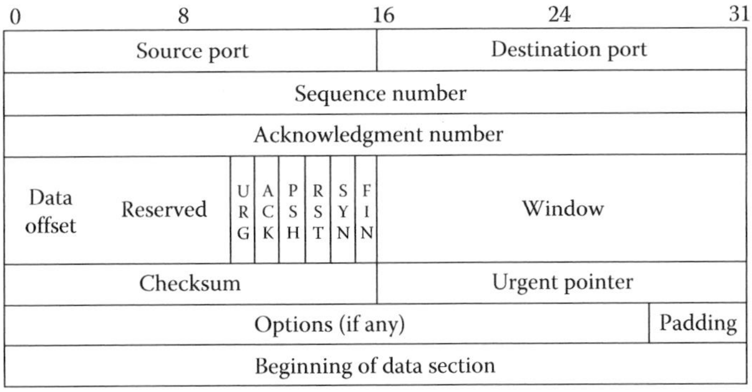

Figure 2.1 TCP header diagram.

- Acknowledgment Number: The acknowledgment number is used by the receiving host to inform the sending host that the transmitted data have been received successfully. This number is expected to be sent after the sequence number.
- Data Offset: This field specifies the number of 32-bit words in the header. The minimum size is five words. Each word has 32 bits, which are equal to 4 bytes. Therefore, the smallest TCP header contains 20 bytes of information.
- Reserved: This field is reserved for future use.
- Control Bits: This field has 6 information control bits described in the following list:
  - URG: This flag is used for validating the urgent pointer.
  - SYN: This flag synchronizes the sequence of numbers that is used to indicate the beginning a 3-way handshake connection process.
  - ACK: This flag is a signal to acknowledge the receipt of data. It can be used for establishing a 3-way handshake connection.
  - PSH: This flag indicates that the data must be pushed out immediately.
  - RST: This is the reset flag.
  - FIN: This flag means that there are no more data from the sender.
- Window: This field specifies the size of the receiving window, which limits the sender to send up to n bytes of data before waiting for the acknowledgment from the receiver. The size of the receiving window is determined by the buffer space available for the incoming data.
- Checksum: Checksum is used to verify if the header is damaged during transmission.
- Urgent Pointer: This field contains a pointer that points to the data that needs to be processed as soon as possible. The data will be processed if the URG control bit is turned on.
- Options: This field can be used to deal with various TCP options such as the maximum segment size and the window scale.
- Padding: The padding field is used to create a 32-bit boundary between the header and the data section.

The data section is placed after the header. The data section typically contains 1000–1500 bytes of message. It is also called the payload or packet body. Depending on the size of the data, the length of the data section may vary. If a packet is set to have a fixed length, the data section will be padded with blanks.

The packet trailer is placed after the data section. It is used to indicate the end of a packet. The error checking mechanism called Cyclic Redundancy Check (CRC) may be included in the packet trailer. During transmission, binary signals can be wrongly altered by outside interference. CRC can be used for detecting this type of transmission error. It can also be used to detect damaged binary signals caused by hardware failure.

Host A   Host B

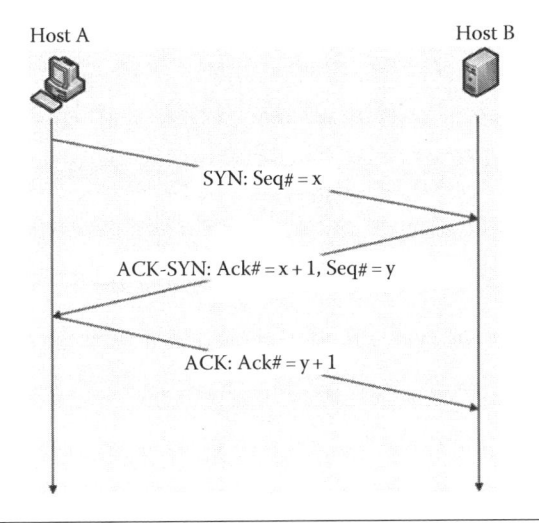

SYN: Seq# = x

ACK-SYN: Ack# = x + 1, Seq# = y

ACK: Ack# = y + 1

Figure 2.2 3-Way handshake process.

A reliable TCP connection is established through a 3-way handshake process. As illustrated in Figure 2.2, the 3-way handshake is implemented with three packets. The following are the steps used by the 3-way handshake process:

- To establish a reliable connection, the 3-way handshake process is started by the sender Host A. Host A first sends a packet to Host B with the control bit SYN turned on. When the SYN bit is turned on, it means that this packet is asking for a connection negotiation. In addition to turning on the SYN bit, the first packet also contains several network connection parameters such as the sequence number, say x, called the Initial Send Sequence (ISS). Therefore, the first packet is sometimes called the SYN packet.
- Once Host B receives the SYN packet, it responds with a packet with both the ACK and SYN control bits turned on. The turned on ACK bit is used as the acknowledgment of the connection negotiation request from Host A. The second packet also contains an acknowledgment sequence number x+1, which is the increment of the sequence number in the first packet. In addition to the acknowledgment sequence number, the second packet includes several network connection parameters such as another sequence number, say y. Therefore, the second packet is also called the ACK- SYN packet.
- When Host A receives the ACK- SYN packet and if it accepts the negotiation parameters, Host A will return a packet with the ACK bit turned on and the acknowledgment sequence number, which is updated to y + 1. Once the third package arrives at Host B, the 3-way handshake process is completed and the data transmission process can be started.

Similarly, the 3-way handshake process is also used in the process of terminating a connection. It makes sure that the communication between two hosts is terminated in a graceful way.

After sending out a packet, the sender waits for the acknowledgment from the receiver. When a packet gets lost or delayed during the transmission, a retransmit mechanism provided by TCP will resend the packet. If TCP waits for the acknowledgment from the receiver long enough, it will resend the same packet to the receiver. The waiting period is estimated by TCP according to the network transmission rate. TCP collects the round-trip time for sending a packet and getting the acknowledgment back. Based on the collected round-trip time, TCP then calculates the estimated mean and standard deviation of the round-trip time. The waiting period for retransmission can be determined by the following rules:

- When the measures of the round-trip time remain close to the mean, it means that the round-trip time is relatively consistent. In such a case, the waiting period for retransmission can be a time period value that is slightly longer than the mean. With such a length of waiting time, TCP waits long enough for most of the sending–receiving round trips to complete before retransmission.
- When the measures of the round-trip time vary significantly from the mean, it means that the round-trip time is not consistent. The waiting period value should be set as the mean plus two times the standard deviation. According to the statistics theory, such a waiting period is long enough for 95% of the round-trip transmissions to complete their journeys. In fact, such a calculated waiting period is suitable to any type of network traffic environments.

After the waiting period is over, TCP assumes that the packet is lost and resends the packet.

During packet transmission, there could be a situation where the sender sends more packets than the receiver can handle. To prevent this from happening, TCP uses a window mechanism to control the traffic flow so that the receiver is not overwhelmed. Once the incoming data arrive, the receiver uses a buffer to store the incoming data. The available buffer is also called the window. To not over feed the receiver, it is necessary for the sender to adjust the packet transmission rate according to the receiver's window size. Before the data transmission starts, the receiver sends out a notification about its buffer size. This notification is also called the window advertisement. According to the window advertisement, the sender delivers packets. When the receiver receives the packets from the sender, it will recalculate its window advertisement. Then, it sends the updated window advertisement to the sender with the acknowledgment. When the buffer is full, the receiver will send a zero window advertisement to inform the sender to stop sending packets. After the receiver informs the sender with a positive window advertisement, the sender can restart the data sending process.

When a packet transmission gets too crowded in one section of a network, the delivery of packets may be delayed. Some of the packets may even get lost. Such a phenomenon is called network congestion. When network congestion occurs, TCP's resending mechanism will resend those packets that get delayed or lost. Resending the packets will add more traffic on the network. In the end, little or no meaningful communication can be carried out by the network. Such a phenomenon is called network congestion collapse. To prevent the network congestion collapse, TCP provides several congestion control mechanisms. TCP is able to adjust the packet transmission rate according to the packet loss rate. When many packets get lost or delayed in a short time, instead of resending all the missing packets immediately, TCP will resend one packet first. If no packet gets lost during the transmission, the sender will get the acknowledgment back from the receiver. In such a case, TCP will double the retransmission rate. If there is still no packet that is lost during the transmission, TCP will double the retransmission rate again. By doing this, the retransmission rate will increase exponentially. The retransmission can quickly reach about half of the advertised window size. After that, if there is still no packet lost, TCP will increase the retransmission rate one packet at a time until the whole retransmission process is done. In such a way, TCP can control how much traffic to add to the network and thereby avoid a network congestion collapse.

This section describes some of the main TCP features during packet transmission. In addition to TCP, UDP is another important protocol in the transport layer. A brief discussion of UDP is given in the next section.

2.3.2 User Datagram Protocol

Like TCP, UDP is a transport layer protocol used for sending and receiving packets between ports. Unlike TCP, UDP does not provide mechanisms to establish a reliable connection between network hosts. Also, it does not provide transmission control mechanisms such as the error correction mechanism and packet resending mechanism. The way that UDP delivers packets resembles mail delivery. It delivers a packet without the permission of the receiver. With UDP, packets are sent out without establishing a connection first. Therefore, UDP is said to be a connectionless network protocol. The advantage of UDP is that it has better performance than TCP. On the other hand, UDP is a less reliable protocol. Therefore, UDP is suitable for a situation that requires high performance but not high reliability in packet delivering. UDP is commonly used in delivering multimedia content such as streaming media in online digital games, Voice over IP (VoIP), and IP Television (IPTV). Due to its high performance feature, UDP is also used by some network protocols, applications, and services such as Trivial File Transfer Protocol (TFTP), Domain Name System (DNS), and broadcasting messages over the network.

TCP and UDP are two main transport layer protocols. In addition to TCP and UDP, there are a few dozen other less known transport layer protocols. In the TCP/IP architecture, transport protocols handle service requests from application protocols. Based on the requests from the protocols in the application layer, the transport protocols instruct the protocols in the Internet layer to prepare packet delivery to the destination hosts. In the next section, we will discuss the protocols in the Internet layer.

2.4 Internet Layer Protocols

In the TCP/IP architecture, protocols in the Internet layer are used to deliver packets from a source host to a destination host across a network. The IP is a well-known Internet layer protocol. It is the core protocol in the TCP/IP architecture. IP is the protocol that carries packets to the destination host. The journey may cross various types of networks. Another significant Internet layer protocol is the Internet Control Message Protocol (ICMP) used by network operating systems to get responses from remote hosts. The Address Resolution Protocol (ARP) relates an IP address with its hardware address, and IP Security (IPSec) is for securing IP communication. There is an argument on which layer the routing protocols should belong to. Since BGP and RIP use UDP in data transmission, some authors think BGP and RIP should belong to the application layer. Since OSPF uses IP in data transmission, some authors believe OSPF should belong to the transport layer. Sometimes, OSPF is listed in the network interface layer. Also, some authors think ARP should belong to the network interface layer. So far, there is no convincing answer to the argument. Here, for convenience, these protocols will be described in the Internet layer.

2.4.1 Internet Protocol

IP relies on TCP to establish a reliable connection. It also relies on TCP to provide mechanisms to control the transmission flow and check for transmission errors. IP depends on TCP to provide connection-oriented service to accomplish packet delivery tasks. IP's main function is to deliver packets from one host to another host. Therefore, IP should be able to keep track of the destination host's IP address. IP should also be able to find the destination host. IP formats packets, called Internet packets, so that these packets can be delivered across the Internet. An Internet packet is also called a datagram.

Currently, there are two versions of IP, IPv4 and IPv6, used on the Internet. IPv4 has been widely deployed for delivering data across the Internet. IPv4 uses a 32-bit binary number to specify the address of a network host. This means that IPv4 can identify at most 2^{32} = 4,294,967,296 network hosts uniquely. However, not all the 32-bit numbers are available for identifying hosts. Some of the 32-bit numbers are used for indentifying networks and others are used for broadcasting and multicasting, and also some of the numbers are reserved for testing or experiments. On the other hand, the number of hosts on the Internet grows exponentially. Nowadays, we are facing a shortage of 32-bit numbers to address the hosts on the Internet.

Originally, IPv4 is designed as a data-oriented protocol. It is not able to provide a high quality path for transmitting audio and video signals. In many ways, IPv4 is not very efficient for delivering packets in a large network. For example, IPv4 uses a broadcasting process to contact an unknown host in a network. During the broadcasting process, IPv4 delivers the packets to every host in the network. This can create a large amount of network traffic in the network.

Header	Data section

Figure 2.3 Internet packet.

The next generation IP protocol IPv6 is designed to overcome the limitations of IPv4. To make sure that we do not run out of IP addresses for many years to come, IPv6 uses 128-bit binary numbers to identify the hosts on the Internet. The set of 2^{128} binary numbers is large enough so that each atom on the surface of the earth can be assigned an IP address. IPv6 is also designed to be able to establish an optimized path to transmit the audio and video signals over the Internet. IPv6 is more efficient by eliminating the broadcast. It is also designed to simplify the network configuration and management tasks.

The Internet packet or datagram is formed with a header and a data section (Figure 2.3).

The header contains information used to send data across a network. The size of the data section may vary depending on the specification of an application. For IPv4, the maximum size of an Internet packet is 64K bytes including both the data and the header.

Since IP is designed to carry data across the Internet, it must be able to deliver a packet through heterogeneous networks. To accommodate heterogeneity, IP must accomplish the following tasks:

- Format packets with an addressing scheme.
- Pass data from one type of network to another type of network.
- Fragment packets into smaller packets to pass through the networks with low data transmission rates and reassemble the fragments at the ultimate destinations.

IP formats packets with both the destination IP addresses and source IP addresses. It must format the packets with the destination addresses so that it will know where to deliver the packets. Also, IP must format a packet with the sender's address called the source address in order to get response from the receiver. Both the source and destination addresses are included in the header of the IP packet. An IP address is assigned to each network interface device, such as a network interface card. The IP address for each host on the Internet must be unique.

In order for an Internet packet to be transmitted through a network, the Internet packet needs to be enclosed in a frame, which is a sequence of bits or symbols used to define the beginning and end of an Internet packet. The frame is formed by a specific network hardware technology in the network interface layer. Different types of networks form different types of frames. The process to load a datagram to a frame is called encapsulation. Figure 2.4 illustrates the encapsulation process.

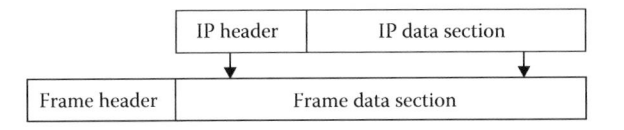

Figure 2.4 Encapsulation.

If the destination host is located within the same network, the frame will carry the Internet packet or datagram to its destination directly. However, if the destination host is located in a different type of network, the frame can only carry the datagram to the border between the two networks where the datagram will be reloaded to a different type of frame formed by a different type of network technology. This is how the datagram can be carried through different types of networks.

When a datagram is delivered across the Internet, it may need to travel through multiple networks to get to the destination. Different networks may have different data transmission rates. The data transmission rate is specified by the parameter Maximum Transmission Unit (MTU). The MTU refers to the maximum amount of data that a frame can carry. It may happen that the MTU of a network in the middle of the delivery path is less than that of the network which the sender belongs to. In such a case, the amount of data originally loaded in the frame formed by the sender's network is too much to be carried by the frame formed by the network with the lower MTU. Therefore, the originally loaded data unit needs to be divided into smaller units so that they can be carried by the frame formed by the network with the lower MTU. The process of dividing the original data unit into several small units is called fragmentation. The header of each fragment is so constructed that all the fragments can be reassembled back to the original datagram. As the fragments may be transmitted through different routes to the ultimate destination, it is difficult to reassemble them in the middle of the delivery path. Also, the fragments may need to be further fragmented if there is a network with an even smaller MTU in the delivery path. Therefore, the fragments are reassembled at the ultimate destination.

An IP header is constructed to accomplish the aforementioned tasks. Figure 2.5 illustrates an IP header's structure.

The following briefly describes the main fields in the IP header:

- H. Len: This field specifies the length of the IP packet header. The minimum length of an IP header is five words and each word contains 32 bits. Therefore, the smallest IP header contains 20 bytes of information.

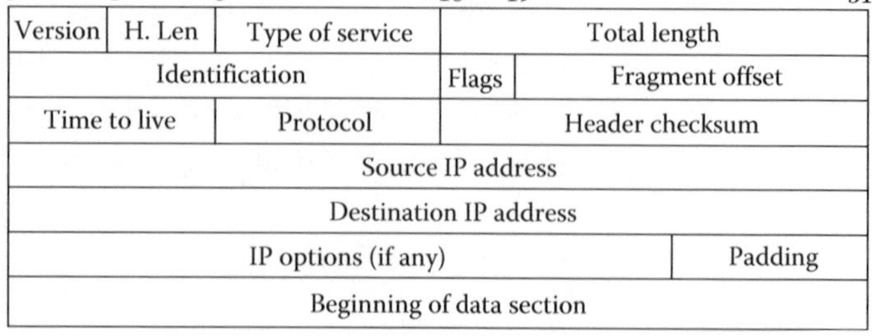

0	4	8	16	19	31
Version	H. Len	Type of service	Total length		
Identification			Flags	Fragment offset	
Time to live		Protocol	Header checksum		
Source IP address					
Destination IP address					
IP options (if any)				Padding	
Beginning of data section					

Figure 2.5 IP header.

- Type of Service: This field is used to specify if a datagram passes through a route with the minimum delay, the maximum throughput, the maximum reliability, or the minimum cost.
- Total Length: This field specifies the length of a datagram, including both the header and the data section.
- Identification: This field is used to identify the datagram to which the fragments belong. Together with the source address, the value in the identification field can be used to reassemble the fragments back to the original datagram.
- Flags: This field is used to set and display fragment-related properties.
- Fragment Offset: The content of this field is used to instruct the receiver how to reassemble a fragmented datagram.
- Time to Live (TTL): The value in this field represents the lifetime of a datagram. Each time a datagram passes through a network, the lifetime number will be reduced by one. When the lifetime number is down to zero, the datagram is discarded. TTL is used to prevent a datagram from traveling in an infinite loop.
- Protocol: This field specifies the protocol to be encapsulated.
- Header Checksum: This field contains an IP header checksum, which is used to detect transmission errors in the IP header.
- Source Address: This field contains the sender's IP address.
- Destination Address: This field contains the receiver's IP address.
- Options: This field specifies various IP options such as MTU replay and experimental flow control.
- Padding: This field is used to create a 32-bit boundary between the header and the data section.

In the TCP/IP architecture, TCP and IP are the core protocols. During data transmission, these two protocols work together and are often denoted as TCP/IP. In addition to IP, the Internet layer also includes several other protocols, which are introduced next.

2.4.2 *Internet Control Message Protocol*

ICMP is a protocol used to report network operation status and network errors. The following are some of the tasks accomplished by ICMP:

- Report Network Status: ICMP can be used to send an echo request message to the receiver. Then, it carries the reply of the receiver back to the sender. ICMP can also be used to report how packets are redirected to different networks.
- Report Network Errors: ICMP can be used to report network problems such as an unreachable host or network. It also carries network parameters that may reveal an improperly functioning network.

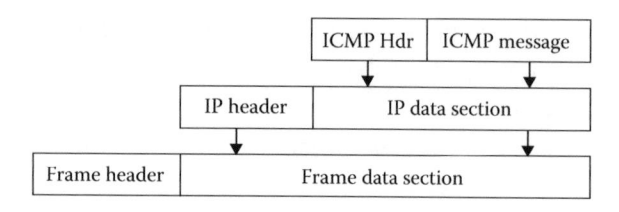

Figure 2.6   Encapsulation of ICMP.

- Report Network Congestion: When a receiving device on a network cannot process the incoming data fast enough, ICMP will deliver a source quench message to the sender for adjustment. ICMP can also be used to probe the MTU of a network and send the result back to the sender.
- Assist Network Troubleshooting: ICMP can be used with network trouble-shooting commands. When used with a network management command such as ping, ICMP reports if a packet can be sent to a dedicated destination. ICMP can also report the round-trip time and the percentage of packet loss during the transmission. When used with the tracert command, ICMP reports what networks the packet has passed through. The report also includes the TTL value. A time expired message will be returned by ICMP when TTL drops to zero.

To deliver an ICMP message through different networks, a network device creates an IP datagram first and then encapsulates the ICMP message in the IP datagram as shown in Figure 2.6.

2.4.3 Address Resolution Protocol

For the data communication between two hosts, the IP header includes the source and destination IP addresses. However, a frame uses the hardware address (also called MAC address) to deliver packets. When the frame reaches the destination network, each host in the destination network compares its hardware address with the destination hardware address included in the frame. If there is a match, the frame will be processed by the destination host. Therefore, the destination IP address in the datagram needs to be correctly converted to the hardware address. Otherwise, the frame will not be able to find its destination. ARP is the protocol used to resolve the IP address to the hardware address.

The commonly used address resolution scheme is called message exchange, which can be accomplished in three steps. When a host needs to resolve a destination IP address, it first broadcasts an ARP request to ask which host in the destination network has the IP address that matches the destination IP address. After the destination host discovers that its IP address matches the destination IP address, it will respond with an ARP reply, which contains the corresponding hardware address to the host that issued the ARP request. After the ARP reply arrives, the host that issued the

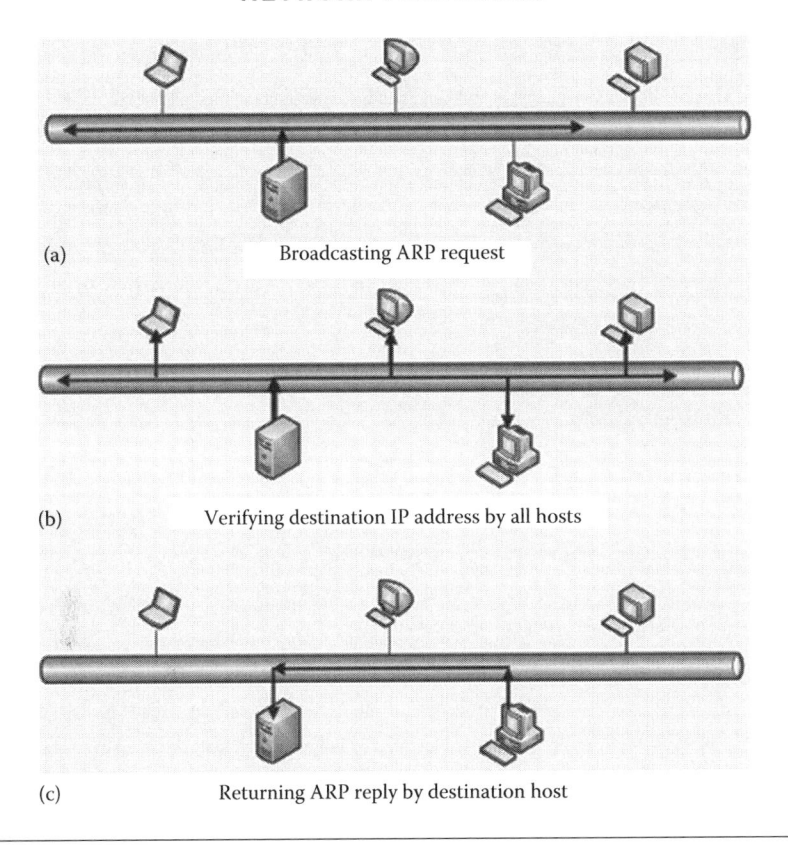

(a)   Broadcasting ARP request

(b)   Verifying destination IP address by all hosts

(c)   Returning ARP reply by destination host

Figure 2.7   Address resolution process.

ARP request places the destination hardware address to the frame. Now, the frame is ready to be sent. Figure 2.7 illustrates the three-step process.

To make the address resolution process more efficient, the host operating system saves the pair of the IP address and its matching hardware address in a cache. Next time, if the host needs to resolve a destination IP address to a hardware address, it will search the cache first. If there is no match in the cache, then the host will start the message exchange process.

2.4.4 IP Security

While traveling across a network, packets can be captured by unauthorized individuals or hackers. The unauthorized individuals can read or intentionally alter the data content in the packets. IPSec is a protocol that provides protection against hackers. It provides authentication, encryption, and digital signature mechanism for securing TCP/IP communication. The authentication mechanism is used to make sure that the computers or network devices on both ends of a communication path are trusted. After a secure connection is established, IPSec hides the IP address. The encryption mechanism is used to make the content carried by IP packets unreadable. With IPSec, even if the packets are captured by hackers during the transmission, the hackers cannot figure out the data content. The IPSec digital signature is used to make sure that the content of an IP packet is not altered during the transmission. Since IPSec is an Internet layer protocol, it can protect all the protocols in the transport layer and application layer so that those protocols do not have to have their own protection. The disadvantage of IPSec is that it slows down the network traffic. Later chapters will show how IPSec is used to connect an on-premises network to a virtual network on a cloud. The advantage of IPSec is that the data communication between two networks is highly secured.

2.4.5 Internet Routing Protocols

Routing protocols such as Routing Information Protocol (RIP), Open Shortest Path First (OSPF) protocol, and Border Gateway Protocol (BGP) are used to create and update routing tables. A routing table stores information about the routes from one network to other networks. The routing protocols can also be used to calculate the shortest path from one network to another.

BGP is a protocol used to manage routes among autonomous systems. An autonomous system is a heterogeneous network system typically governed by a large organization such as an Internet service provider (ISP). Each ISP may create its own autonomous system. The networks included in an autonomous system adopt the same routing policy. BGP is often used by ISPs to establish routes among them. The Internet routing protocol that manages routes among autonomous systems is also called Exterior Gateway Protocol (EGP). The Internet routing protocol that manages routes within an autonomous system is called Interior Gateway Protocol (IGP). To accomplish the routing management tasks, BGP has the following features:

- BGP is a type of EGP as well as IGP.
- BGP allows the sender and the receiver in different autonomous systems to negotiate routing policies.
- BGP uses the reliable TCP to update the routing table.
- With BGP, an autonomous system can be defined as a transit system, which allows the network traffic to pass through, or can be defined as a stub system, which blocks the network traffic from passing through.
- BGP can be used to dynamically update the routing tables of neighboring autonomous systems.
- BGP can be used to program routing policies and route filters.
- BGP allows network administrators to inject specific routes into the routing table.

RIP is used as an Internet routing protocol within an autonomous system. RIP is a simple protocol and requires very little configuration. However, RIP is not suitable for large networks since it can only manage up to 15 subnetworks and it takes a lot of network resources to update routing tables. Therefore, RIP is usually used in small network systems or used for education purposes. The following are some of the RIP features:

- RIP is used as IGP.
- RIP uses UDP to update routing tables, which is faster but less reliable.
- RIP does not check transmission faults while updating routing tables.
- RIP uses broadcasting to update routing tables. Although the use of broadcasting may take less effort, it is much less efficient.
- RIP measures the distance of a route by counting the number of networks the route traverses. RIP can only count up to 15 networks. This feature makes RIP a protocol that updates routing tables locally.
- To update routing tables, RIP broadcasts a packet that contains a complete routing table every 30 s. The broadcasted routing table is used by other routers to update their own routing tables. Broadcasting routing tables to one another every 30 s can significantly slow down network performance if there are many routers used in the network. Therefore, RIP is not designed for large networks.

The OSPF protocol is designed to handle the routing needs of large companies and ISPs. It has the following features:

- OSPF is used as IGP.
- OSPF has a hierarchical structure. With the hierarchical structure, OSPF can divide a large autonomous system into areas and update the routing tables within an area. The use of areas can significantly reduce the size of a routing table.
- OSPF uses Dijkstra's algorithm to find the shortest path inside each area. OSPF allows the network administrator to define the criteria of the shortest path.
- By using OSPF, more IP addresses are available to be assigned to networks and hosts in a network.
- OSPF provides the authentication mechanism to secure the updating of routing tables.
- OSPF can import routes created by other routing protocols.
- Instead of using broadcasting, OSPF uses multicasting within an area for routing table updating. Multicasting is more efficient than broadcasting.
- When updating a routing table, instead of sending out the entire routing table, OSPF only sends out what has been changed in the routing table to other routing tables in an area. Changes are sent only when they occur, not every 30 s.

With the aforementioned features, OSPF is a more sophisticated Internet routing protocol. The disadvantages of OSPF are the complexity in configuration, which takes more time for one to learn how to configure the protocol.

2.5 Network Interface Layer Protocols

Protocols in the network interface layer are implemented by combining the hardware and software. In some of the textbooks, the network interface layer is broken into two layers. One is the network interface layer, which contains protocols that are used to form frames. The other layer is the physical layer, which includes the network hardware. Here, for convenience, the hardware and the protocols are all combined into a single network interface layer. There are more than a dozen protocols and network technologies included in this layer. The commonly used protocols and network technologies in the network interface layer are Point-to-Point Tunneling Protocol (PPTP), Layer 2 Tunneling Protocol (L2TP), Point-to-Point Protocol (PPP), Ethernet, Wireless Fidelity (Wi-Fi), Worldwide Interoperability for Microwave Access (WiMAX), the network interface card, twisted pair cable, optical fiber, electromagnetic radio wave, and so forth.

The network interface layer protocols convert packets into raw binary bits and transport the binary bits across the network media. The binary bits are then formed into code words. After that, the code words are converted into physical electric signals. Through the network media, the electric signals are then transmitted to the destination host. Once the electric signals arrive at the destination host, they are reorganized into packets for protocols in the upper layers to process. Some of the protocols in the network interface layer have the mechanism to verify if the physical electric signals have been correctly transferred to the destination.

Point-to-Point Tunneling Protocol (PPTP): PPTP is sometimes listed as the application layer protocol. Again, there is no convincing answer to this. PPTP is also a protocol used for VPN connections. PPTP was jointly developed by several companies such as Microsoft, 3COM, US Robotics, and others. By using PPTP, users can securely remotely access their companies' or universities' network devices and computers through the Internet. PPTP provides both user authentication and encryption to secure the communication on the Internet. It is relatively easy to configure PPTP. The disadvantage of PPTP is that it only authenticates users but not network hosts. This means that the users are able to access the VPN server through any host, which may cause some security concern. For better security, one can consider using L2TP.

Layer 2 Tunneling Protocol (L2TP): L2TP can also be used to support VPN connections. The data to be transmitted are encapsulated into L2TP packets. To protect the data's confidentiality, L2TP relies on IPSec to provide the encryption mechanism. In order to do so, the L2TP packet is encapsulated into an IPSec. Then, the IPSec packet is delivered over the public Internet. The L2TP/IPSec pair requires more configurations. Both the VPN client and VPN server are required to use the IPSec authentication. L2TP/IPSec improves authentication by providing both the user level authentication and the computer level authentication.

Point-to-Point Protocol (PPP): PPP is a protocol commonly used for transferring Internet packets over a serial link such as a telephone line or an optical link. TCP/IP protocols do not work well over a serial link. Therefore, PPP is designed for this purpose. For example, since IP packets cannot be transmitted through a modem line on their own, an ISP uses this protocol to connect their customers to the Internet. PPP also provides error checking and authentication mechanisms.

Ethernet: The Ethernet technology does two tasks. The first task specifies the format of a frame to be transmitted across a network. The second task defines the wiring and signaling standards. In an Ethernet network, the network media such as cables are designed according to the Ethernet standards. The network hardware used to connect to cables, such as cable plugs and network interface cards, is also designed to follow the Ethernet wiring and signaling standards. The Ethernet technology is widely used in both the wired networks and wireless networks. Originally, the transmission rate supported by the Ethernet technology was 10 megabits per second (Mbps). Later, the Fast Ethernet technology supported the transmission rate of 100 Mbps. The Gigabit Ethernet technology can support the transmission rate up to 1000 Mbps. Recently, 10G Gigabit Ethernet has become available. All these Ethernet technologies are designed to share the same frame format; this makes the current Ethernet technology backward compatible with the early versions of Ethernet.

Wireless Fidelity (Wi-Fi): Wi-Fi is well known for short distance wireless communication. It is commonly used in local area networks, cordless phones, video games, and so on. Wi-Fi network devices are widely installed in laptop computers and mobile devices. In a data communication process, a Wi-Fi adapter converts the binary code into radio signals, and then transmits the radio signals through an antenna. When a Wi-Fi access point receives the radio signals, it converts the radio signals back to the binary code and transmits the code through a wired network media. A Wi-Fi access point is typically available in a home network. It may also be available in many public locations such as student dormitories, restaurants, airports, and hotels. The Wi-Fi technology makes networking more flexible by avoiding the cabling process. Without cabling, Wi-Fi also reduces the cost on network deployment. The main disadvantage of Wi-Fi is the short communication range. It may also cause some security concerns.

Network Interface Card (NIC): Physically, an NIC connects the bus system in a computer and the network media. A computer bus is an array of wires with a connector on each end of the bus. The computer bus shared by different electric devices is used to transmit binary signals from one device to another device inside a computer. Through NICs, binary signals can be passed on to the network media such as the copper wire, fiber optic cable, or radio wave for wireless networks. Each NIC has a unique serial number, which is often used as the hardware address. In a data transmission process, after a frame is formed, the CPU sends the frame through the computer bus to the NIC and instructs the NIC to forward the frame to the network media. The NIC handles all the details of frame transmission and reception. After the frame reaches the receiver, the receiving computer's CPU allocates buffer space in the memory and tells the receiving computer's NIC to read the incoming frame. After all parts of the frame have been received, the NIC verifies the checksum.

If there is no error, the NIC will compare the destination address in the received frame with its own hardware address. If there is a match, the NIC will inform the CPU to make a copy of the frame in the memory and begin to process the frame. If the hardware address does not match the destination address, the received frame will be discarded. The communication between the NIC and CPU is handled by the network card driver, which handles the interaction between the computer and the attached hardware.

Twisted pair cable: A twisted pair cable is a type of network media. It is a type of wire used to transmit electric signals to the destination host through a pair of copper wires. The pair of insulated copper wires is twisted together to minimize the electric interference. The use of the copper wire is due to its low resistance to electric currents.

Optical fiber: Optical fiber is another type of network media. It is made with flexible glass fiber that can be used to transmit data to a remote destination. To transmit data over optical fiber, the sender first converts the binary signals into light pulses and then transmits the light pulses by using a light emitting diode (LED). When the light pulses reach the destination, the receiver uses a phototransistor to detect the light pulses and converts them into electric currents. Then, the network adapter converts the electric currents to binary code. Compared with the copper wire, optical fiber has the following advantages:

- The light pulses transmitted by optical fiber are not susceptible to electric interference.
- The transmission of light pulses in optical fiber is much faster than the transmission of electric signals in a copper wire.
- Optical fiber can transmit data over much longer distance than what a copper wire can do. During long distance travel, a light pulse has very little loss.
- Light pulses can be encoded with much more information than electric currents.

The disadvantage is that it is difficult to install and repair optical fiber.

Electromagnetic radio wave: An electromagnetic radio wave is a type of wireless network transmission media. It can be used to transmit data over the air. With radio waves, senders and receivers send and receive data through antennae. Radio waves can be converted into binary signals or vice versa. Different sections of radio wave frequencies are reserved for different types of wireless technologies. For example, Wi-Fi uses radio frequencies between 2.4 and 5.6 GHz. The higher the frequency, the faster the transmission rate is.

This section has briefly introduced some of the network interface layer protocols and technologies. Some of the protocols and technologies in the network interface layer are responsible for physically transferring data between hosts. Some of them are also responsible for interacting with the protocols in the Internet layer. In the next section, we will take a closer look at how these protocols relate to each other.

2.6 Network Protocol Graph

In this section, a protocol graph will be used to illustrate the relationships among the protocols. The protocols in the application layer handle data communication requests and responses by application software. However, the protocols in the application layer cannot deliver or receive data through a network by themselves. To deliver the data to a destination host in a network, the data block needs to be chopped into small units and carried by the IP protocol to the destination host. To reach the destination host, one needs a protocol such as TCP to create a connection between two hosts on the network. Also, other protocols may be needed to convert IP packets to electric signals so that they can be physically transmitted over the network media. Therefore, data transmission over a network is accomplished by multiple protocols working together. Figure 2.8 illustrates the relationships among these protocols.

As shown in Figure 2.8, when a client needs certain information from the server, the request is initiated by an application layer protocol. The request will be passed on to a transport protocol such as TCP through a dedicated communication port. Then, TCP will establish a reliable connection to the port dedicated to the application on the server.

IP delivers packets to destination hosts across the Internet. IP itself does not create a connection to a remote host. It relies on TCP to establish the connection and control the data flow. ICMP is used to get error messages from remote hosts. Protocols such as ICMP and ARP are encapsulated in IP so that messages can be delivered through different types of networks. To deliver an Internet packet or datagram, IP depends on the protocols or technologies in the network interface layer. For example, to transmit an Internet packet across an Ethernet network, the

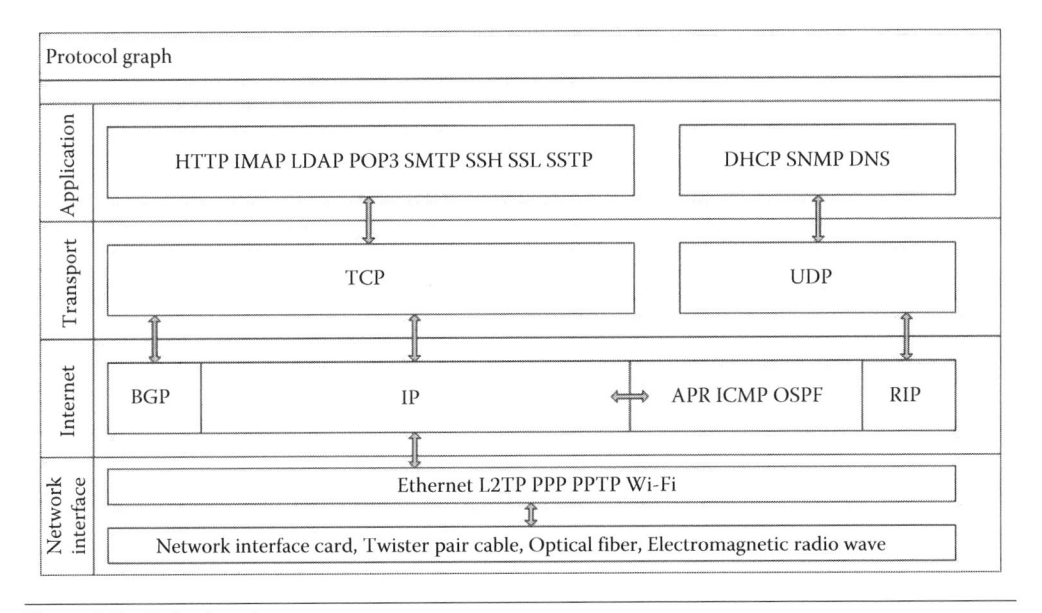

Figure 2.8 Protocol graph.

Table 2.1   Communication Ports

APPLICATION LAYER PROTOCOL	PORT NUMBER	TRANSPORT LAYER PROTOCOL
HTTP	80	TCP
IMAP	143	TCP
LDAP	389	TCP
POP3	110	TCP
SMTP	25	TCP
SSH	22	TCP
SSTP	443	TCP
DHCP	67	UDP
SNMP	161	UDP
DNS	53	UDP

Internet packet will be carried by a frame formed by the Ethernet technology. By using a network interface card, the frame is then converted to binary signals and is transmitted by electric currents, light pulses, or electromagnetic radio waves to the remote destination. Once the binary signals reach the destination host, the network interface card on the destination host will verify the destination address with its own hardware address. If there is a match, the binary signals will be reassembled to get the Internet packet back. At the destination, TCP will perform error checking and decide if a resend is necessary. If there is no error, the TCP on the destination host will pick up the request and forward the message to the protocol related to the server side application through the corresponding port. Table 2.1 lists the port numbers used by the application layer protocols for communicating with the transport layer protocols mentioned in Figure 2.8.

Earlier, we have examined the relationships among some commonly used protocols in each layer of the TCP/IP architecture through a graph. Next, we are going to explore some networking tools and view some of the protocols through hands-on activities.

Activity 2.1: Exploring Windows Server 2012

The objective of this activity is to get familiar with the networking tools provided by Windows Server 2012.

Task 1: Exploring Windows Server 2012 Operating System

1. Log on to the Microsoft Azure Management Portal with your user name and password.
2. Select your virtual machine **servera** and click **CONNECT**.
3. Log on to your **servera** server as **student** with your password.
4. Click **Local Server,** you should be able to see the configuration of the local server shown in Figure 2.9. In Figure 2.9, you can find the computer name,

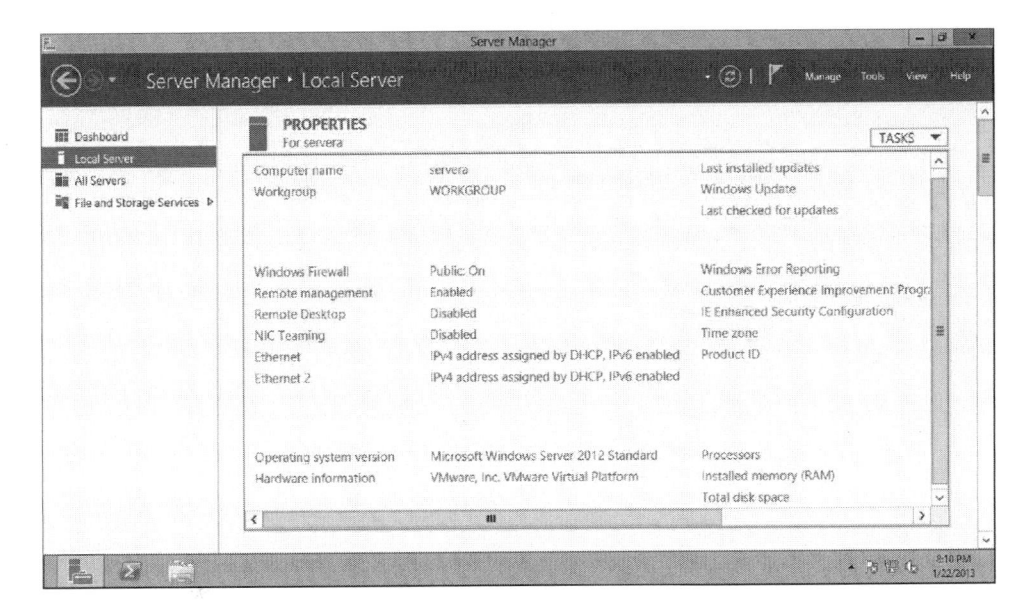

Figure 2.9 Information about local server.

workgroup name, firewall status, information about the Ethernet cards, and the version of your operating system.

5. You can configure the name of the local server. Click **servera**, you will see the **System Properties** dialog where you can configure the computer name and workgroup as shown in Figure 2.10. Click **Cancel** to close the System Properties dialog.

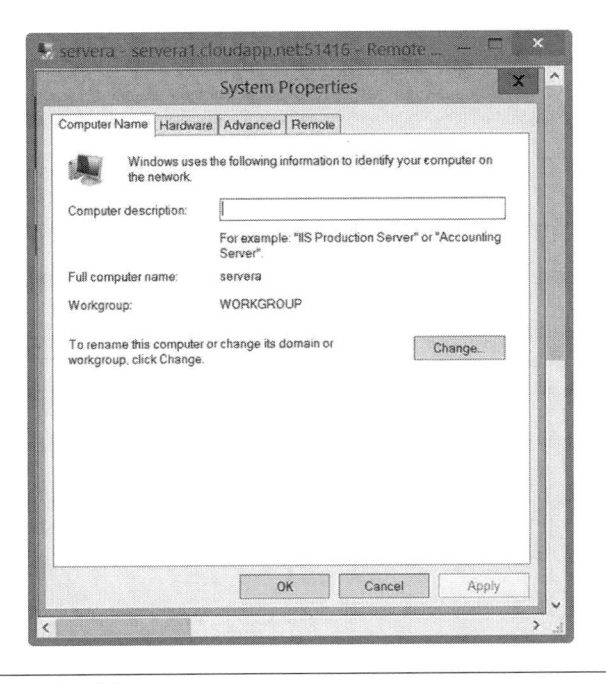

Figure 2.10 System properties dialog.

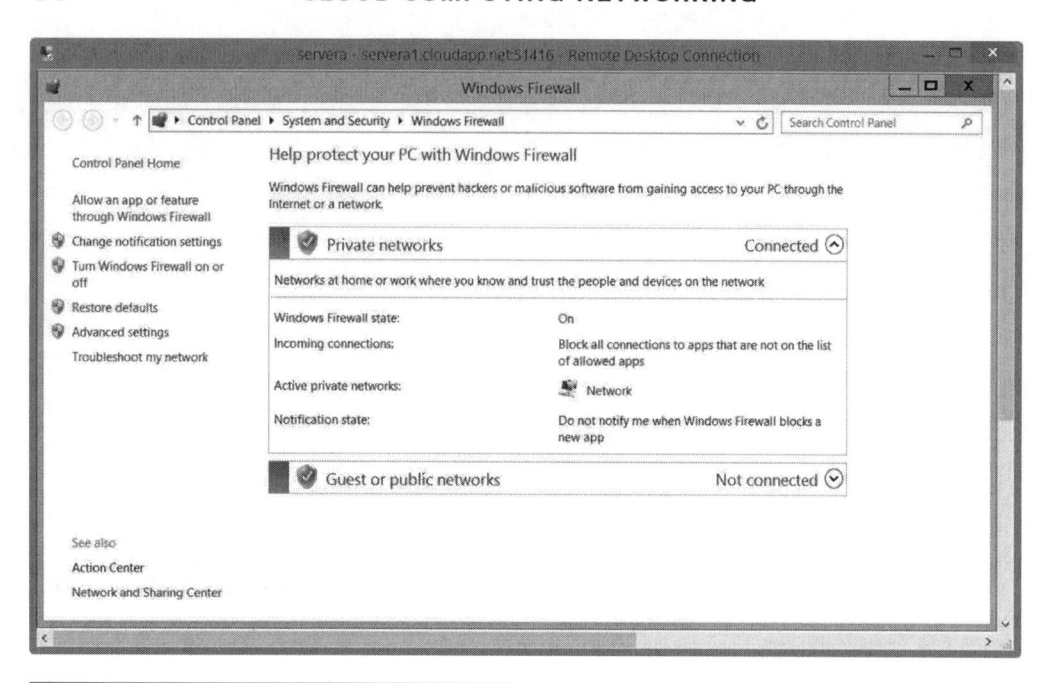

Figure 2.11   Windows firewall dialog.

6. For firewall configuration, click the link **Public: On**. You should be able to see the Windows Firewall dialog shown in Figure 2.11. You can change the firewall settings in the Windows Firewall dialog. Close the **Windows Firewall** dialog.

7. To configure the network adapter, click the link **IPv4 address assigned by DHCP, IPv6 enabled**. Right click the **Ethernet** icon and select **Properties**. Select **Internet Protocol Version 4 (TCP/IPv4)** and click the **Properties** button. You should be able to see the **Internet Protocol Version 4 (TCP/IPv4) Properties** dialog shown in Figure 2.12.

8. To be able to access the Internet from your virtual machine, click the option **Use the following DNS server addresses** as shown in Figure 2.13. Enter a public know DNS server IP address such **8.8.8.8** and click **OK**.

9. You should be able to see the **Internet Protocol Version 6 (TCP/IPv6) Properties** dialog shown in Figure 2.14. Click **Cancel** to close the dialog.

Task 2: Viewing Ethernet Properties

1. Assume that you have logged on to your Windows Server 2012. Click the link **Local Computer**. Then, click **IPv4 address assigned by DHCP, IPv6 enabled**.

2. Right click the **Ethernet** icon and select **Properties.** In the Ethernet Properties dialog, as you can see, the network protocols TCP/IPv4 and TCP/IPv6 are installed. Click the **Install** button (Figure 2.15).

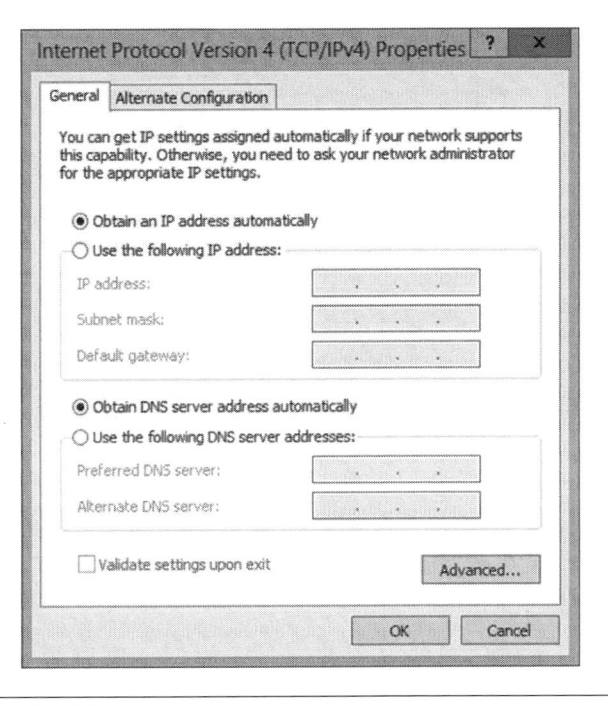

Figure 2.12 IPv4 properties dialog.

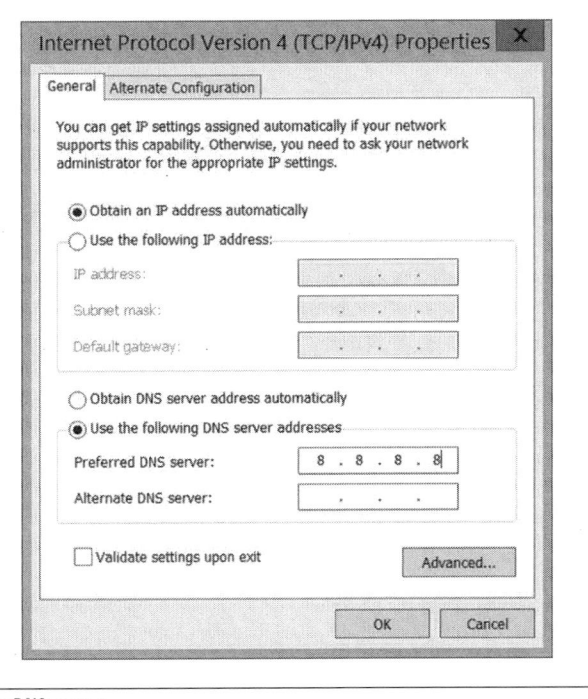

Figure 2.13 Specifying DNS server.

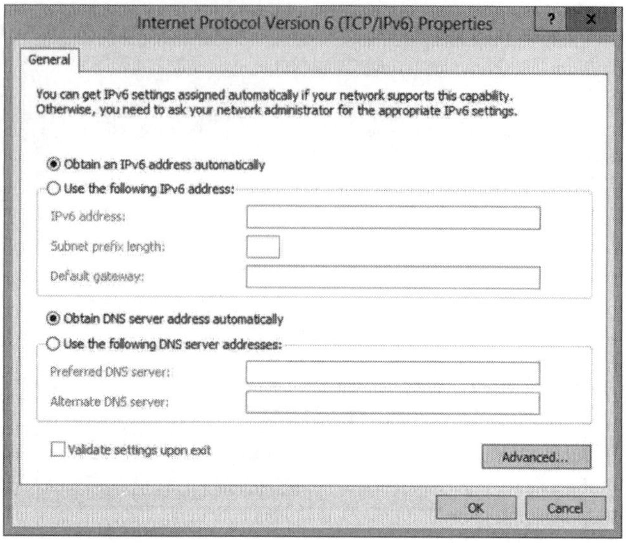

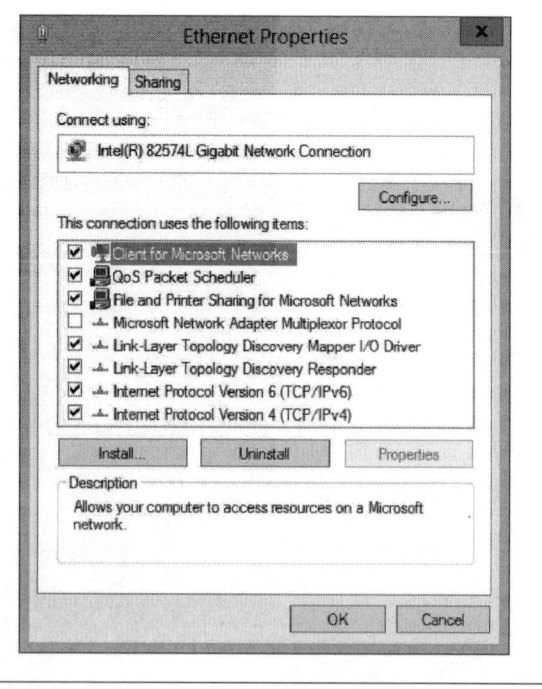

Figure 2.14   IPv6 properties dialog.

Figure 2.15   Ethernet properties.

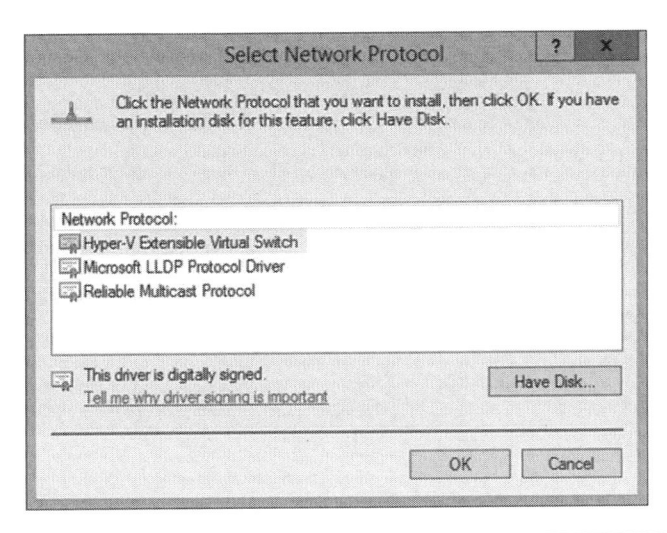

Figure 2.16   Available network protocols.

3. To see more protocols available to install, in the Select Network Feature Type dialog, select **Protocols** and click the **Add** button. You will see a few protocols available for installation as shown in Figure 2.16.
4. After you have viewed the protocols, click the **Cancel** button.

Task 3: Viewing Available Roles and Features

You will be using ICMP to test the connection between two virtual machines. By default, the ICMP protocol is blocked by the firewall. You need to enable ICMP. The following are the steps to enable ICMP:

1. Log on to your Microsoft Azure Management Portal with your user name and password.
2. Select your virtual machine **servera** and click **CONNECT**.
3. Log on to your **servera** server as **student** with your password.
4. In Server Manager, click the **Tools** menu and select **Windows Firewall with Advanced Security** as shown in Figure 2.17.
5. After the configuration dialog is opened, click **Inbound Rules** on the left-hand side of your screen. Use the **Ctrl** key to select **File and Printer Sharing (Echo Request - ICMPv4-In)** and **File and Printer Sharing (Echo Request - ICMPv6-In)**. Right click the selected items and click **Enable Rule** as shown in Figure 2.18.
6. In the configuration dialog, click **Outbound Rules** on the left hand side of your screen. Use the Ctrl key to select **File and Printer Sharing (Echo Request - ICMPv4-Out)** and **File and Printer Sharing (Echo Request - ICMPv6-Out)**. Right click the selected items and click **Enable Rule** as shown in Figure 2.19. After the outbound rules are configured, close the configuration dialog.

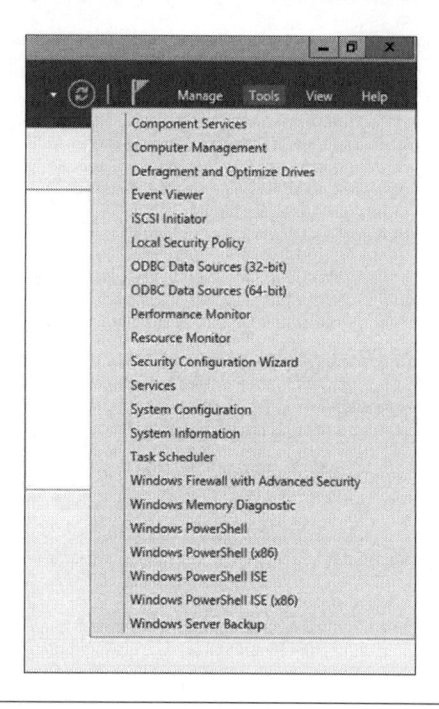

Figure 2.17   Configuring firewall.

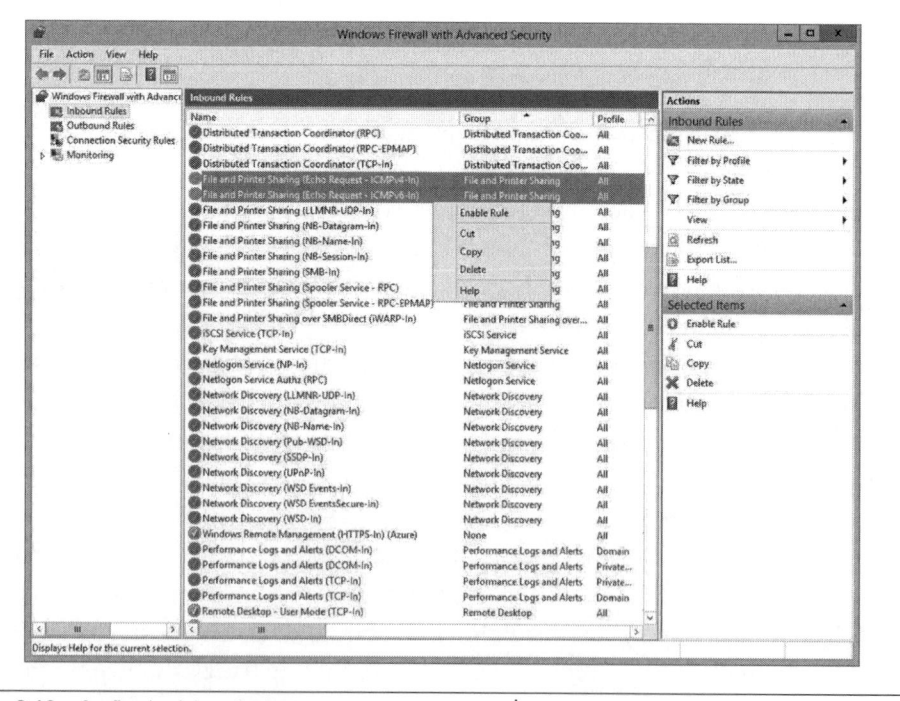

Figure 2.18   Configuring inbound rules.

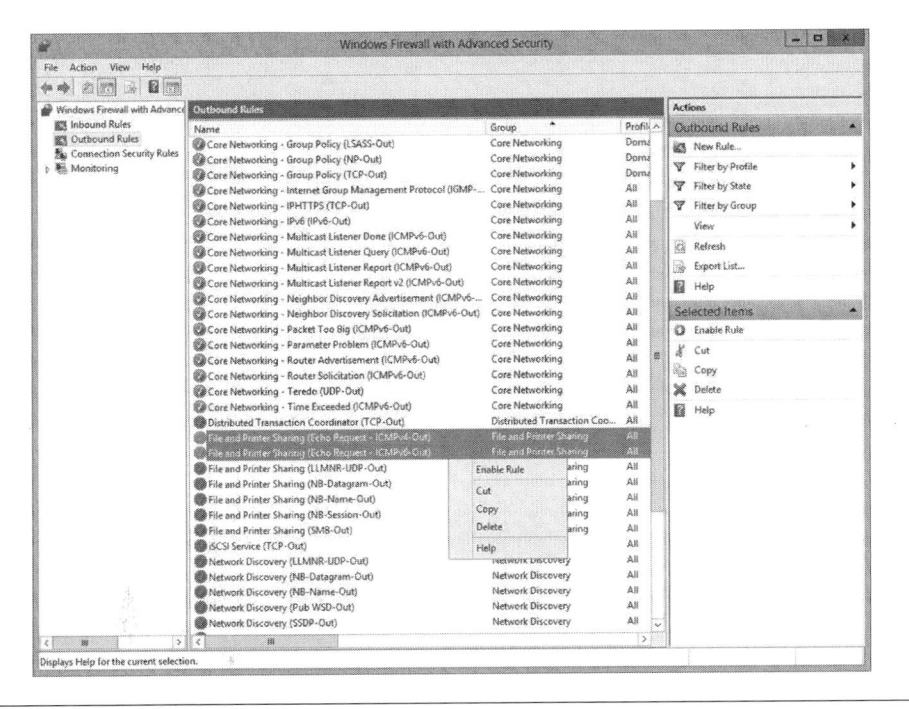

Figure 2.19 Configuring outbound rules.

7. Similarly, enable ICMP in serverb.
8. Assume that you have logged on to your Windows Server 2012. To view the available roles, on the Server Manager page, click the link **Dashboard**.
9. On the Dashboard, click the link **Add roles and features** as shown in Figure 2.20.

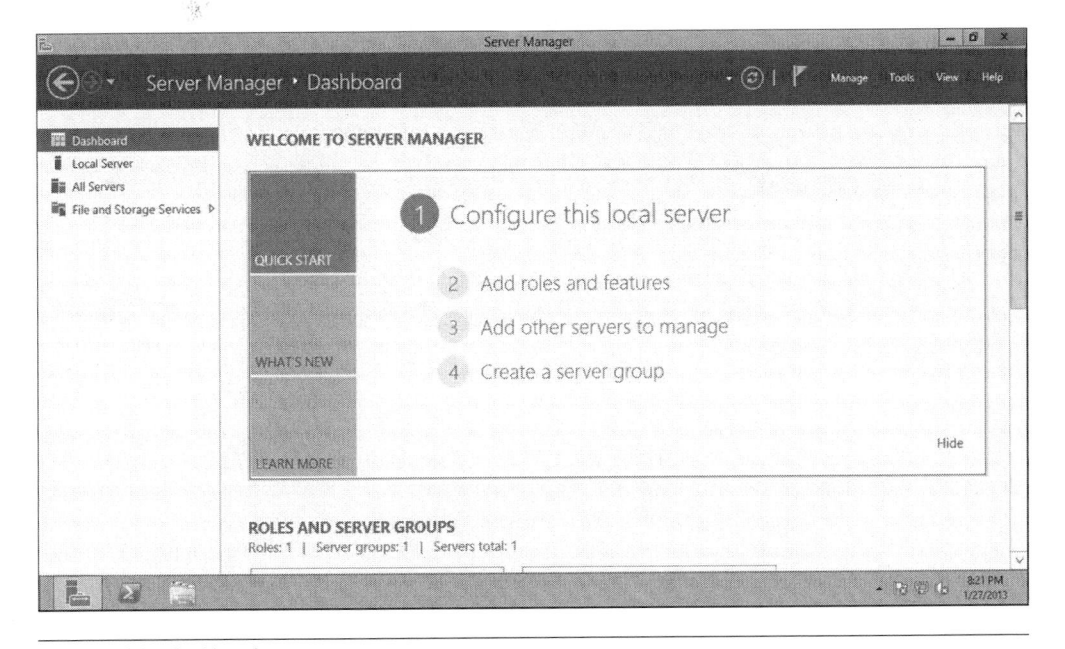

Figure 2.20 Dashboard.

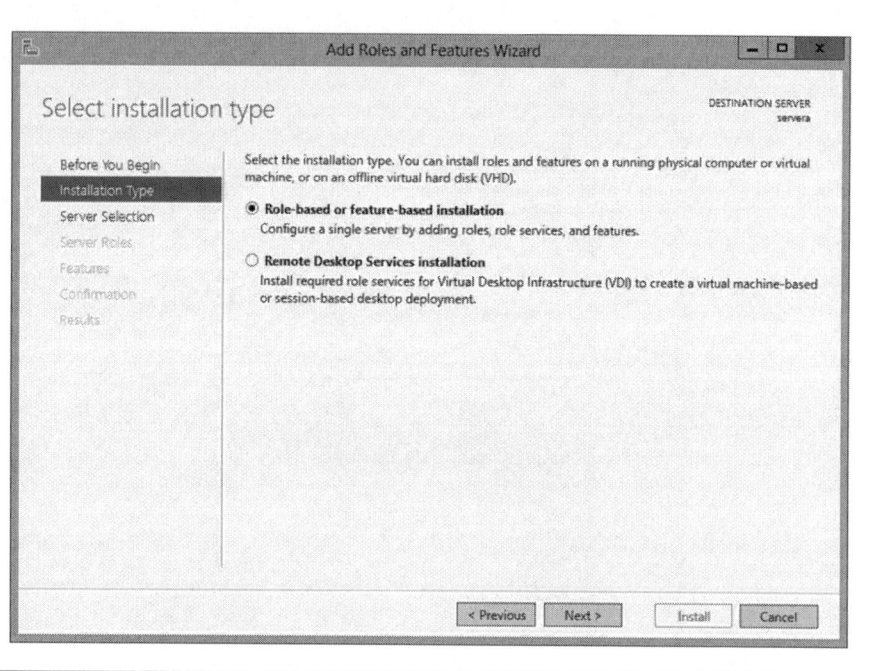

Figure 2.21   Select installation type page.

10. After the Add Roles and Features Wizard is opened, click the **Next** button.
11. On the Select installation type page, select the option **Role-based or feature-based installation** and click the **Next** button as shown in Figure 2.21.
12. On the Select destination server page, select your server as shown in Figure 2.22, and then click the **Next** button.

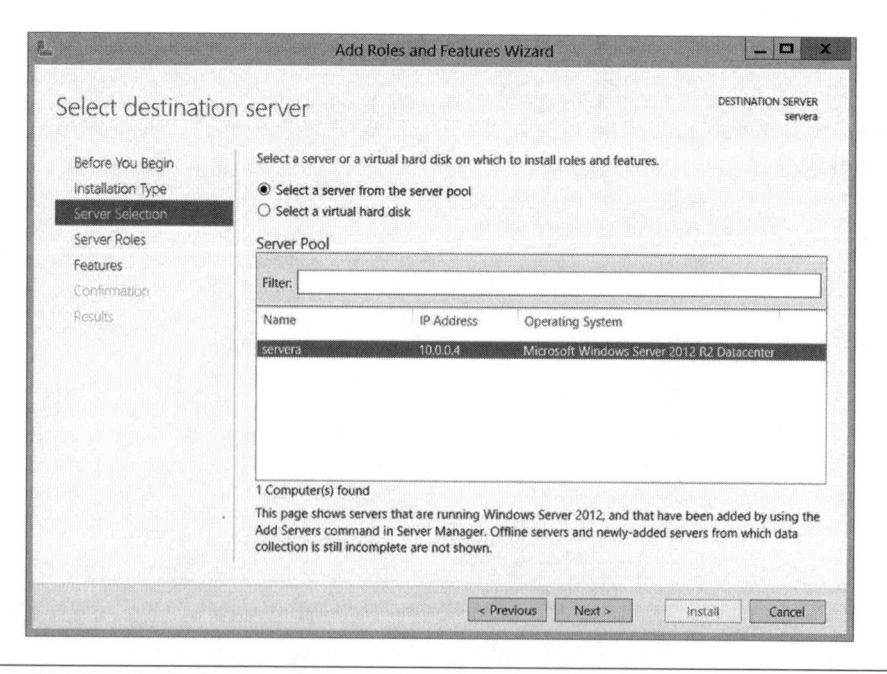

Figure 2.22   Select destination server page.

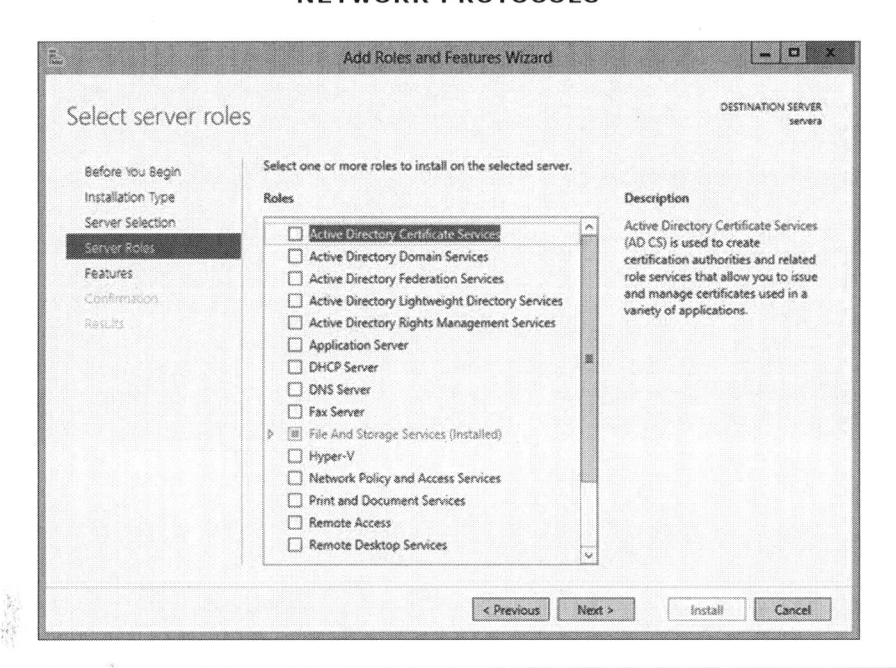

Figure 2.23 Select server roles page.

13. On the Select server roles page, you can see a number of service roles available for installation as shown in Figure 2.23. Then, click the **Next** button.
14. On the Select features page, you can see a number of features available for installation as shown in Figure 2.24. After viewing the features, click the **Cancel** button.

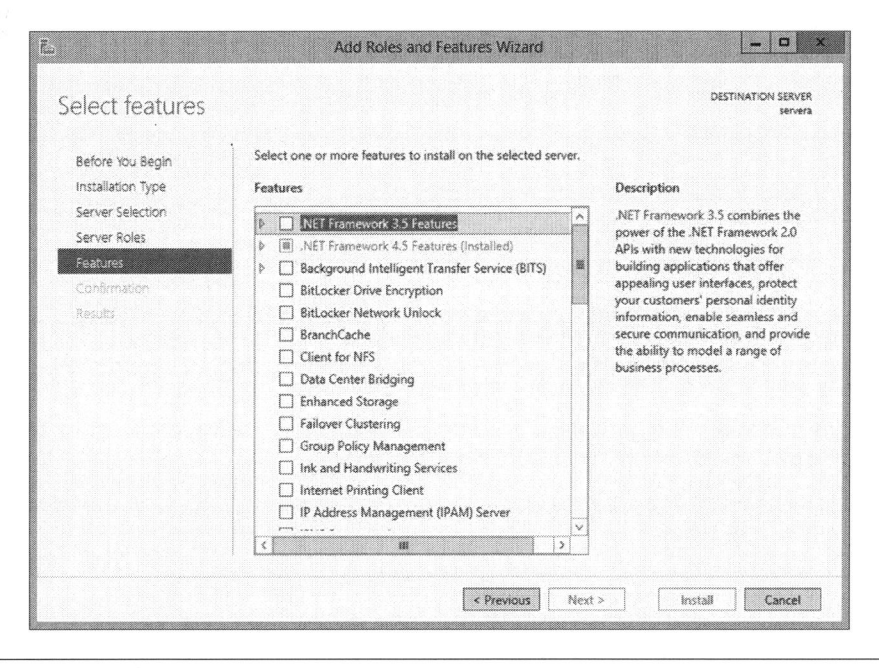

Figure 2.24 Select features page.

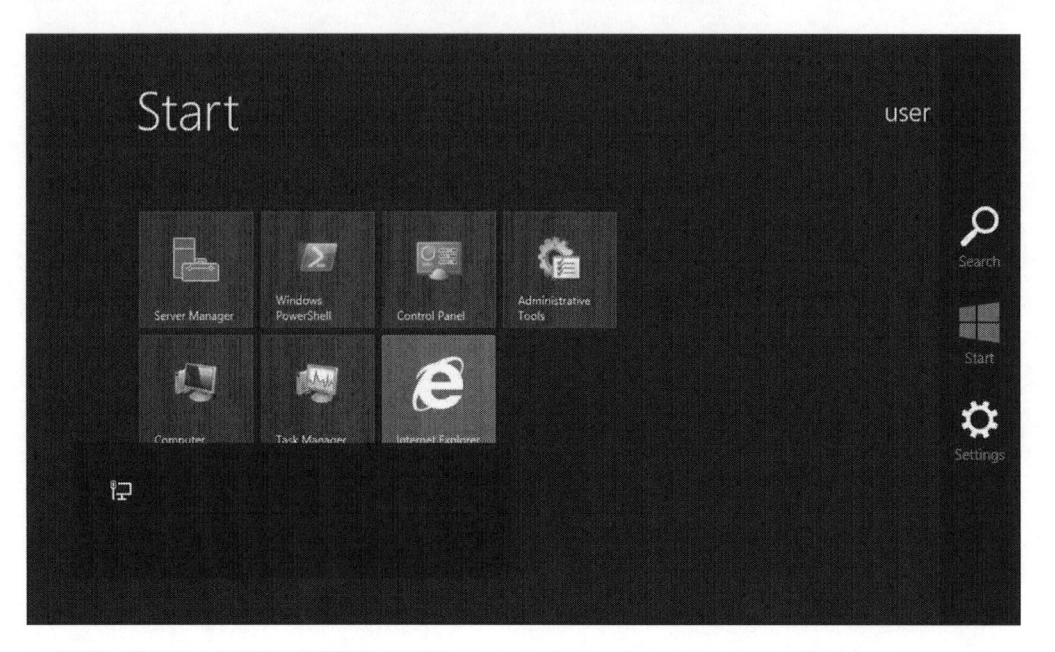

Figure 2.25   Pop-up start screen.

Task 4: Viewing Installed Roles and Features

To view the installed services on Windows Server 2012, you may follow the steps given here:

1. Move the mouse along the border at the lower right corner of your Windows Server screen. After the pop-up menu is displayed on the screen, click the **Start** icon as shown in Figure 2.25. You may also get the Start menu by clicking the **Start** icon on the task bar.
2. On the Settings menu, click **Administrative Tools** tile.
3. On the Administrative Tools page, double click **Services**. Then, you will see the installed services shown in Figure 2.26.
4. After you have viewed the installed services, close the Services window.

Activity 2.2: Viewing IP Configuration in the Command Prompt Window

In this activity, you will use the Command Prompt window to view IP configuration:

1. If you have not done so, log on to your Microsoft Azure account and connect to your virtual machine servera.
2. Press the **Windows logo** key. Type **cmd** and then click the **Command Prompt** tile as shown in Figure 2.27.
3. In the Command Prompt window, enter the command **ipconfig/all** as shown in Figure 2.28 and press **Enter**. From the printout, you can find the information about the Windows IP configuration and Ethernet Adapter configuration.

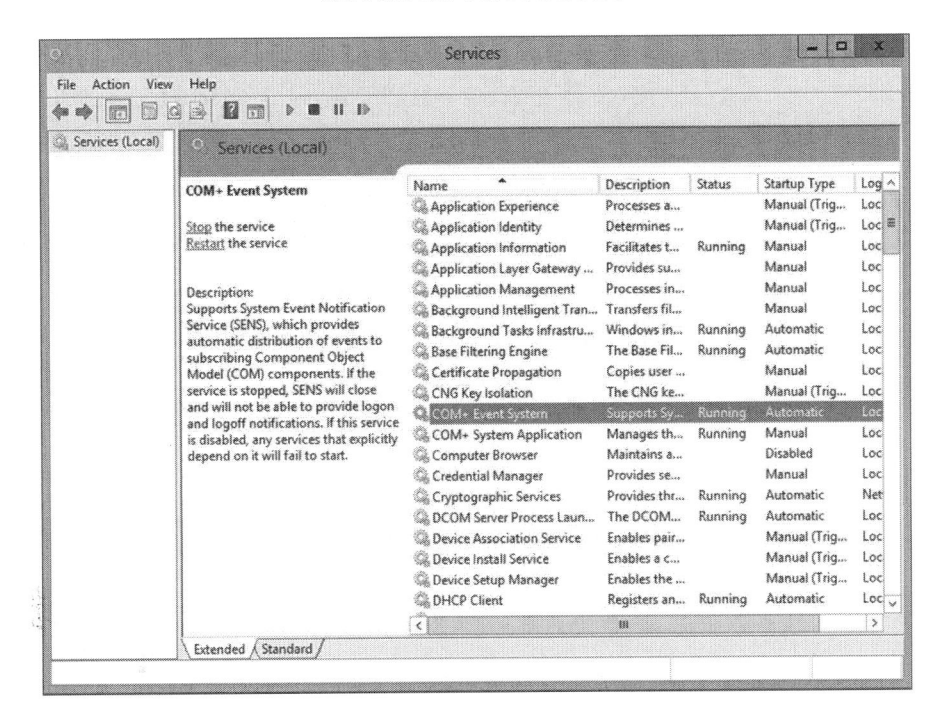

Figure 2.26 Installed services.

Figure 2.27 Open command prompt.

4. As shown in Figure 2.29, the information about Ethernet Adaptor 2 of servera is displayed. The information includes the IPv4 IP address and IPv6 IP address.

5. Close the command prompt window.

6. Similarly, you can get the IP information from serverb as shown in Figure 2.30.

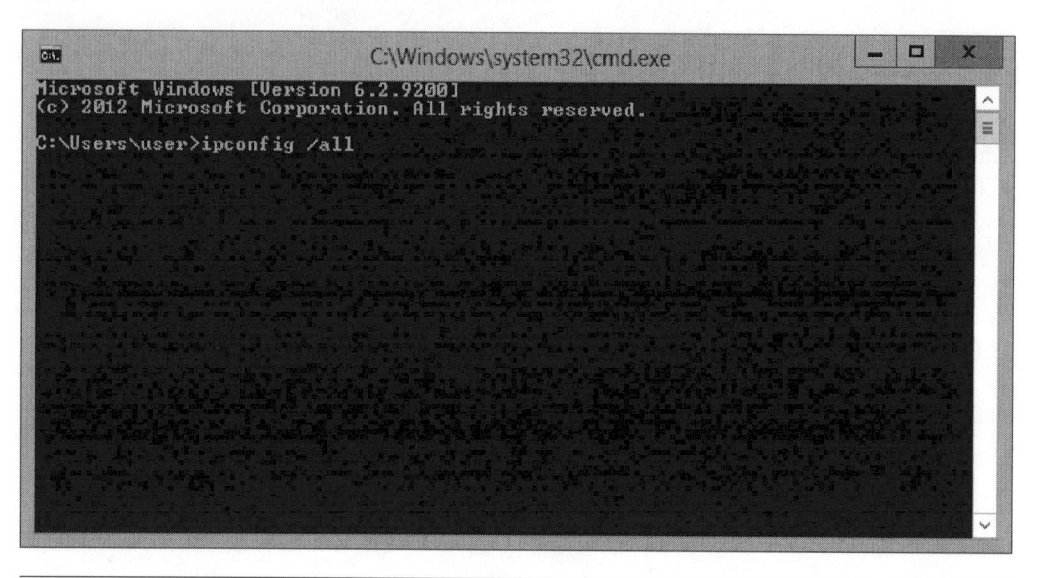

Figure 2.28   Command prompt.

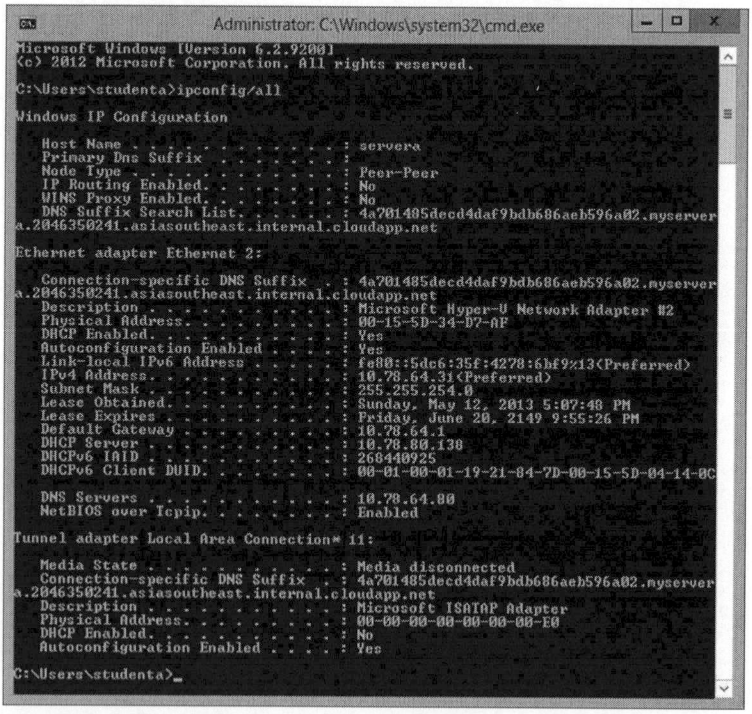

Figure 2.29   IP Information from servera.

Figure 2.30 IP Information from serverb.

As shown in Figures 2.29 and 2.30, the private IP address for servera is 10.78.64.31 and the IP address for serverb is 10.78.30.82. Note that your IP address should be different from the ones illustrated in Figures 2.29 and 2.30.

Activity 2.3: Viewing Protocols with Network Monitor

The goal of this activity is to install the Network Monitor. Then, use Network Monitor to view some of the protocols introduced in this chapter.

Task 1: Installing Network Monitor

1. Assume that you have logged on to **servera**.
2. Click the **Start** icon on the Taskbar to open the Start menu. Then, click **Internet Explorer**.
3. After the browser is opened, click **Tools** icon and **Internet options**.
4. After the Internet Options dialog is opened, click the **Security** tab and click the **Internet** icon.
5. Click the **Custom level** button. Find the **File download** node on the list of security settings. Click the **Enable** option as shown in Figure 2.31.
6. Click **OK** twice to complete the configuration of Internet options.

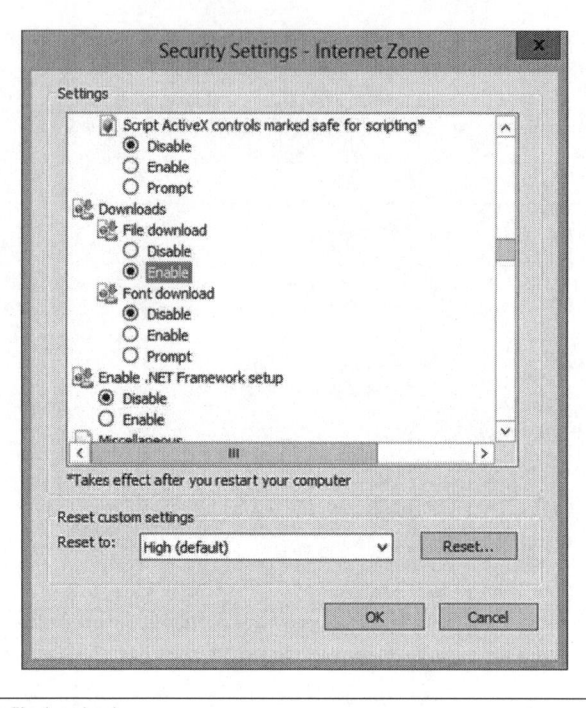

Figure 2.31 Enabling file download.

7. You may also need to temporarily turn off the IE Enhanced Security Configuration. To do so, On the Server Manager page, click **Local Server**. Then, turn off **IE Enhanced Security Configuration**.

8. You can now download Network Monitor from the following website (Microsoft Azure, Download Center, May, 2015). http://www.microsoft.com/en-us/download/?id%20=%204865.

9. From the website, download the **NM34_x64.exe** file. Then, **run** the file to install the **Typical** version of Microsoft Network Monitor.

10. Double click the icon of **Microsoft Network Monitor 3.4** on Desktop.

11. Network Monitor will be opened as shown in Figure 2.32. Then, close the Network Monitor window.

Task 2: Viewing TCP and HTTP

1. On your desktop, right click the **Network Monitor** icon and select **Run as administrator**.

2. Make sure **Ethernet** is checked as shown in Figure 2.33.

3. Click the link **New Capture** tab. Then, click **Start** on the menu bar (Figure 2.34).

4. Assume that Internet Explorer is still open, type the URL **http://go.microsoft.com**.

5. In the Network Monitor window, click the **Stop** menu.

6. Select the first **HTTP** packet under the Protocol Name column as shown in Figure 2.35.

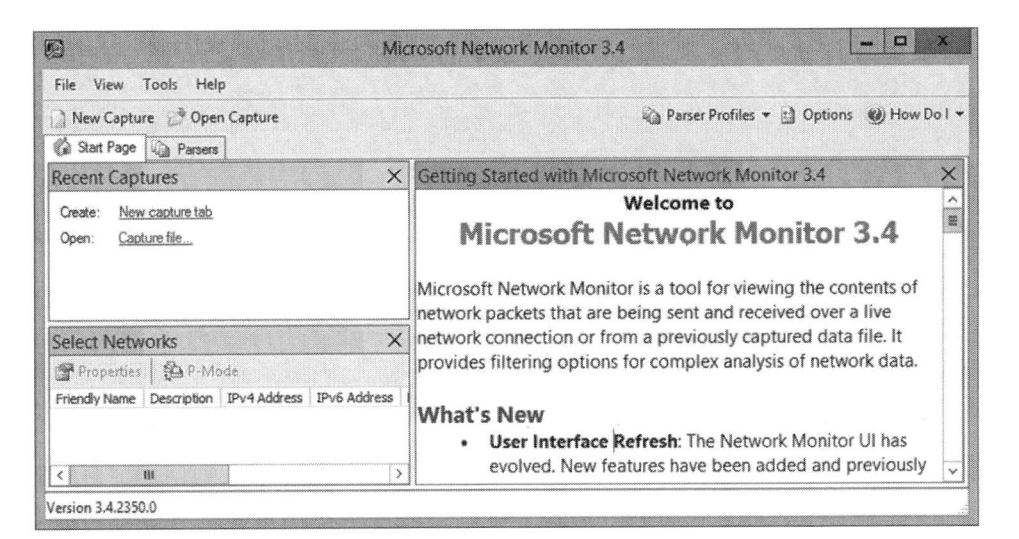

Figure 2.32 Network monitor.

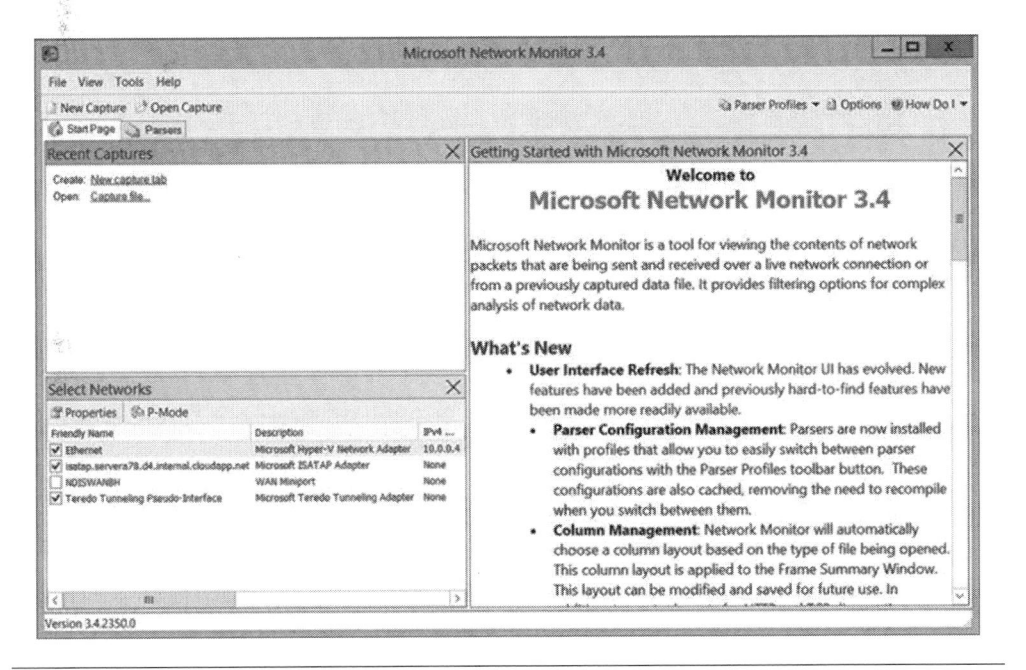

Figure 2.33 Checking exterior NIC for monitoring.

7. Then, expand the **HTTP** node in the Frame Details pane. As you can see in Figure 2.35, the protocol HTTP sends a requested file to the web server and the command GET is used to retrieve the data requested by the HTTP client.

8. In the Frame Summary pane, click the first **TCP** after HTTP under the Protocol Name column. Then, expand the **TCP** node in the Frame Details pane. As shown in Figure 2.36, the source port number is HTTP(80), and the destination port number is 49162. In the Frame Details pane, you can also find information of other items included in the TCP header.

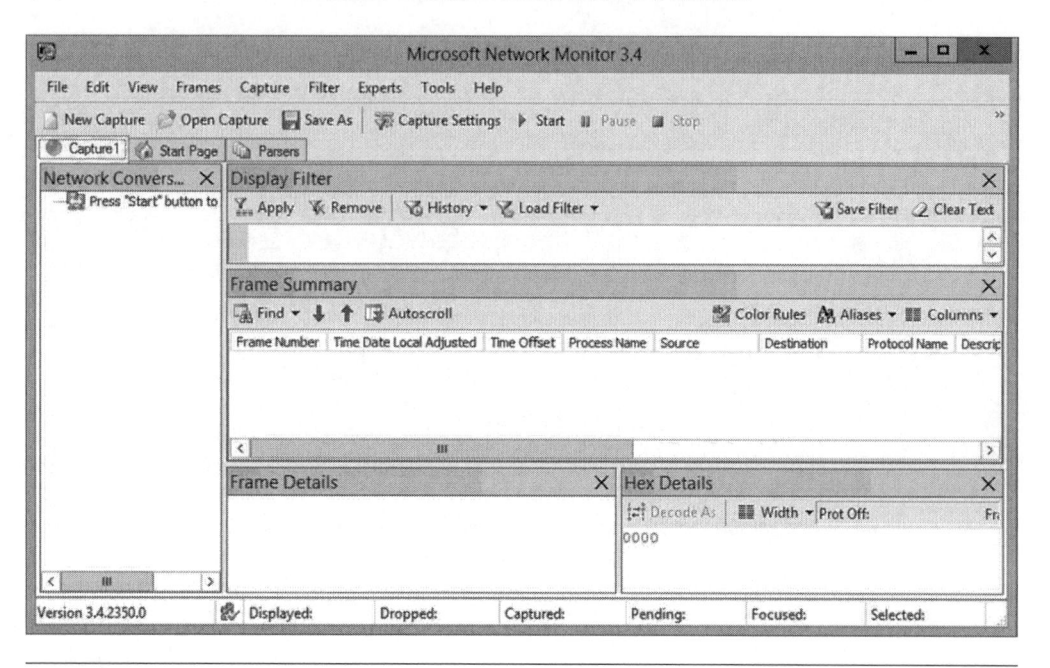

Figure 2.34   Starting to capture packets.

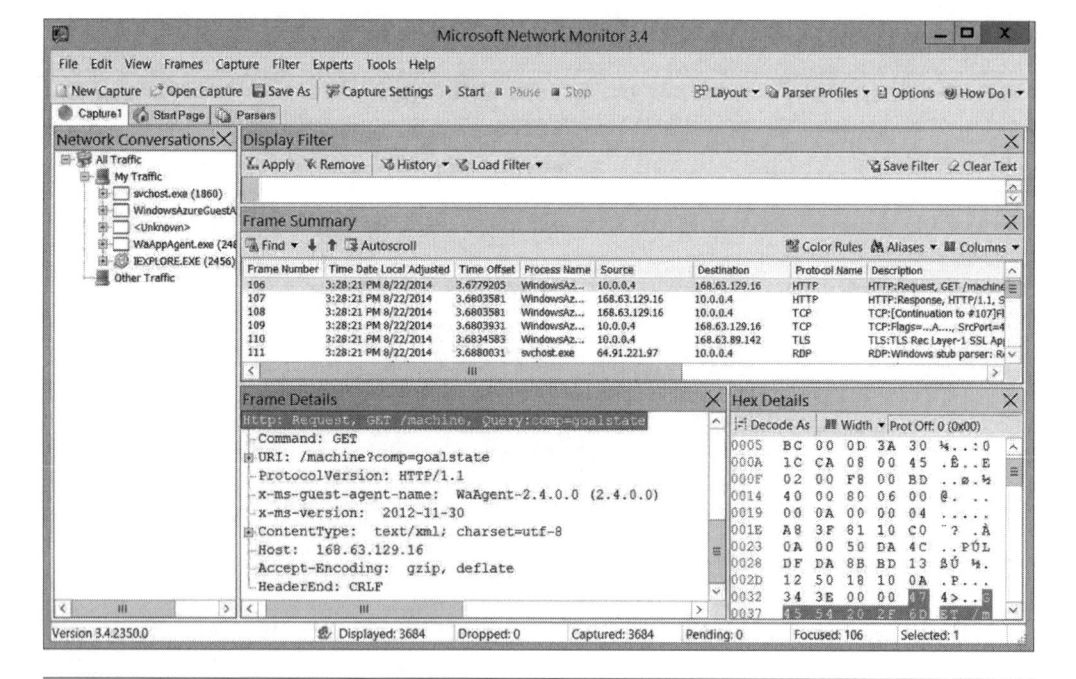

Figure 2.35   HTTP protocol.

Task 3: Viewing ARP and ICMP

1. To start the Command Prompt window, press the **Windows logo + r** key combination. In the Run dialog box, type **cmd** and then click **OK**.
2. In the Network Monitor window, click **Start** on the menu bar.

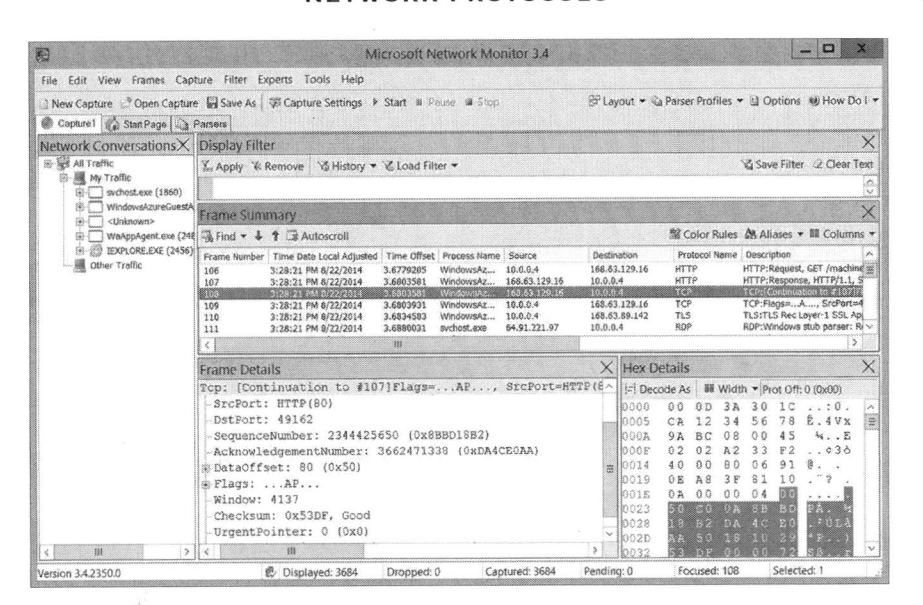

Figure 2.36 TCP protocol.

3. In command prompt window, type **ping 10.0.0.5**. Then, in the Network Monitor window, click the **Stop** menu.
4. Expand the ARP node as shown in Figure 2.37. The IP address has a corresponding MAC address (hardware address or physical address). Note that your IP address should be different from the one illustrated in Figure 2.37.
5. To view the ICMP protocol, click the **ICMP** packet under the Protocol Name column. Expand the **Icmp** node in the Frame Details pane. As shown in Figure 2.38, the message type is Echo Request Message.

Task 4: Viewing IP and UDP

1. To view the IP protocol, in the Network Monitor window, click **Start** on the menu bar. In Internet Explorer, enter the URL **http://go.microsoft.com**. In the Network Monitor window, click the **Stop** menu.
2. Click the first **DNS** packet under the Protocol Name column. Expand the **Ipv4** node in the Frame Details pane. As shown in Figure 2.39, the source IP address and destination IP address are specified in the IPv4 protocol. In the Frame Details pane, you can also view the configuration of other items in the IP header.
3. To view the UDP protocol, expand the **Udp** node in the Frame Details pane. As you can see, the UDP protocol communicates through the source port 62215 and the destination port 53 (Figure 2.40).
4. Close the Network Monitor window. When prompted to save the captured packets, click **No**.
5. In the Microsoft Azure Management Portal, shutdown both servera and serverb before exiting the Microsoft Azure Management Portal.

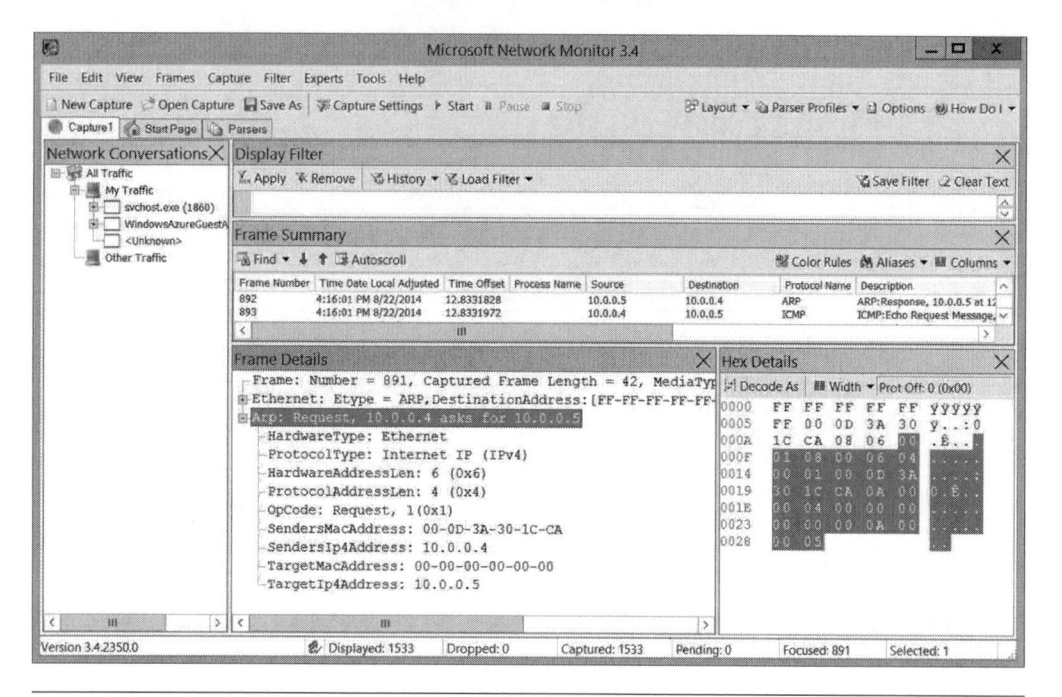

Figure 2.37   ARP protocol.

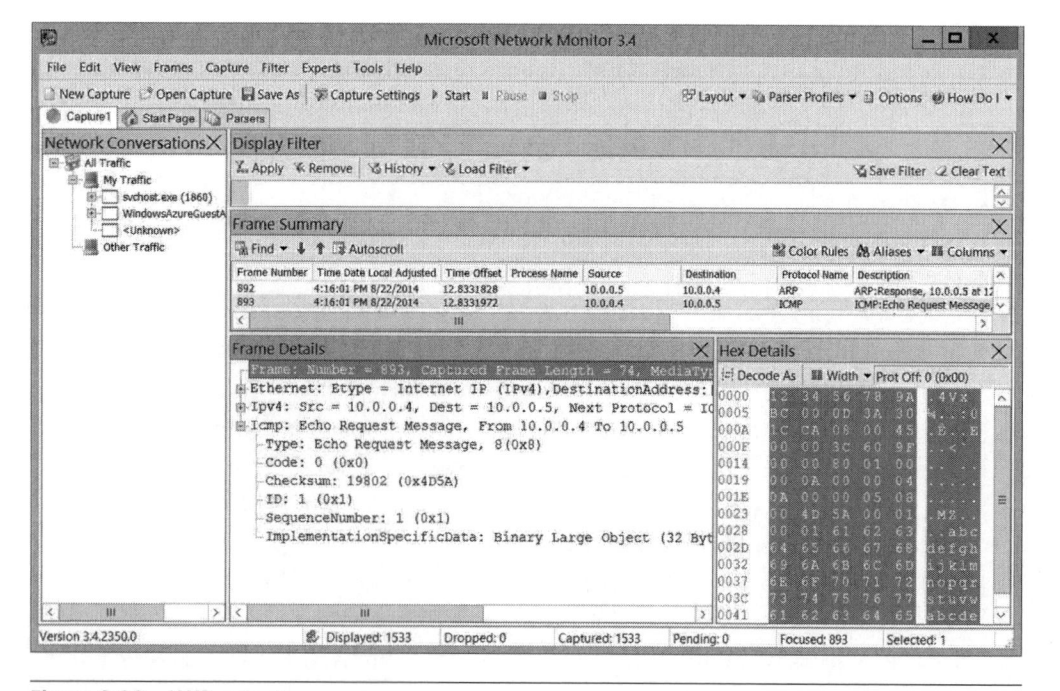

Figure 2.38   ICMP protocol.

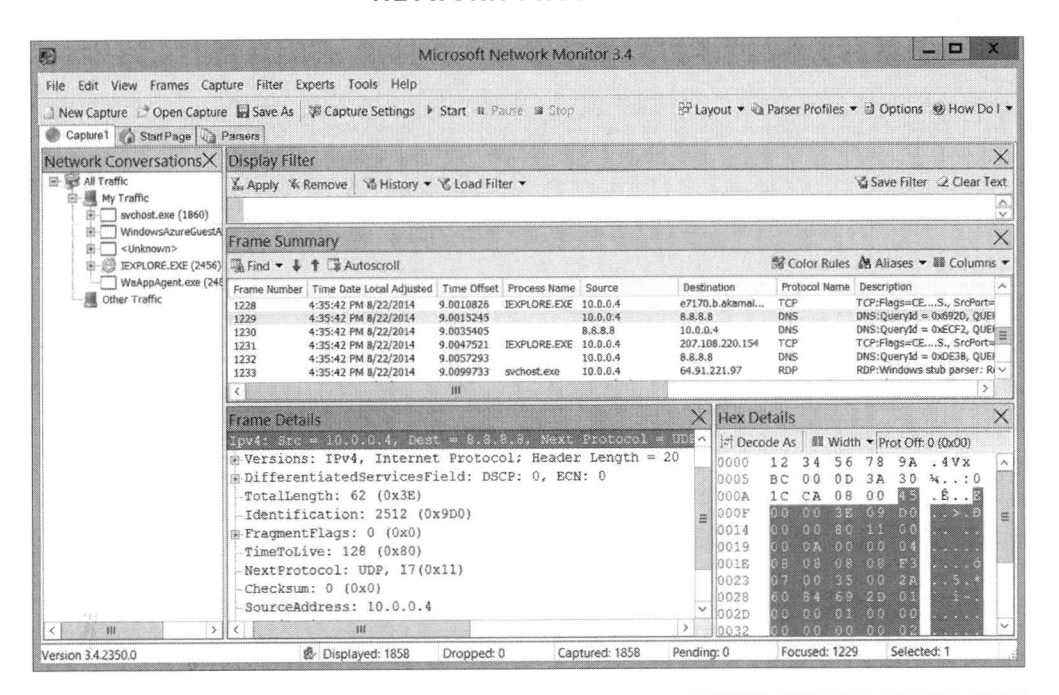

Figure 2.39 IPv4 protocol.

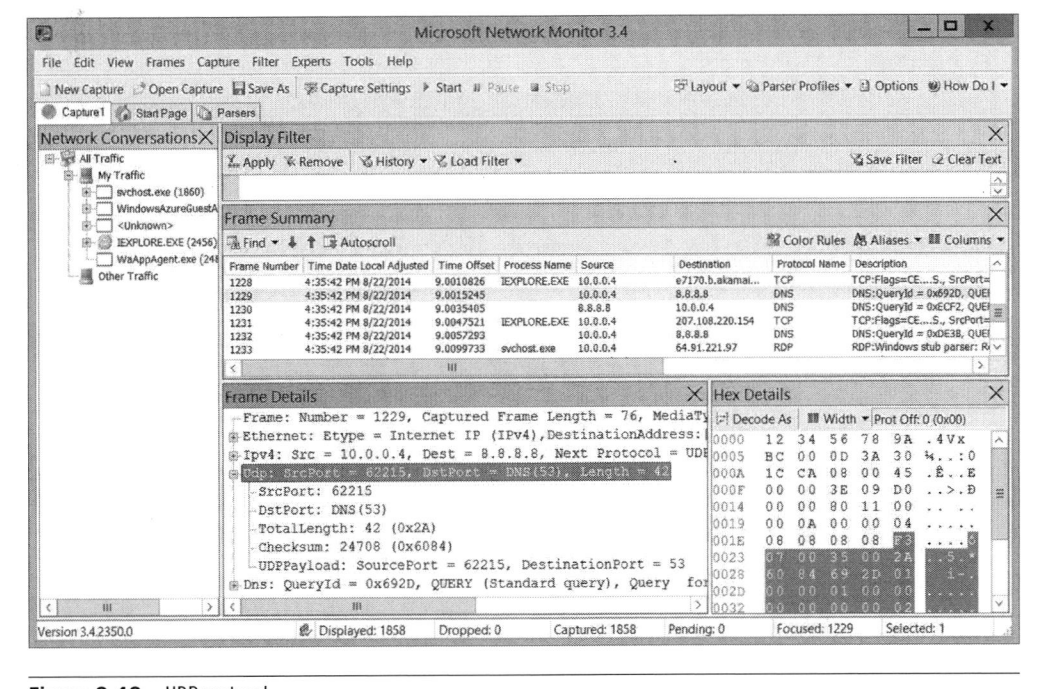

Figure 2.40 UDP protocol.

2.7 Summary

This chapter introduces some of the commonly used protocols in the TCP/IP architecture. Protocols are used to handle data communication between network hosts. This chapter shows how different protocols work together to deliver or receive data across networks. The relationships among these protocols are also illustrated through a protocol graph. The hands-on activities in this chapter explore various network management tools such as Server Manager, Command Prompt, and Network Monitor. The knowledge of protocols and network management tools covered in the next chapter will help design and develop networks.

Review Questions

1. What are the core protocols in the TCP/IP architecture?
2. What is HTTP used for?
3. What is DHCP used for?
4. The protocols SMTP, POP3, and IMAP are e-mail-related protocols. What are the differences among these protocols?
5. What makes SSH safer?
6. What can the network administrator do with LDAP?
7. What are the TCP features mentioned in this chapter?
8. What tasks discussed in this chapter can be handled by TCP?
9. What makes a TCP connection reliable?
10. How does TCP decide the waiting time before resending a packet?
11. What is the difference between UDP and TCP?
12. What is ARP used for?
13. Why do we need to replace IPv4 with IPv6?
14. What tasks mentioned in this chapter can be accomplished by IP?
15. What is encapsulation?
16. How can ICMP packets be transmitted across heterogeneous networks?
17. Describe the differences among the IP routing protocols: RIP, OSPF, and BGP.
18. What is the concern when we use PPTP for a VPN?
19. How does Ethernet work?
20. Compared with the copper wire, what are the advantages of optical fiber?

NETWORK CONCEPTS AND DESIGN

Objectives

- Understand network concepts and technologies.
- Design a network with subnetting.
- Construct local area networks.

3.1 Introduction

In Chapter 2, we discussed the protocols in each layer of the Transmission Control Protocol/Internet Protocol (TCP/IP) architecture. In this chapter, we will first explore various types of networks. We will examine network devices and network media. We will also take a closer look at network interface cards (NICs), switching devices, and network routing devices. We will see how these devices are put together to physically construct a network.

Before network hosts including computers and network devices can be physically connected, each host on a network should be properly assigned an IP address. One needs to know how to configure a group of hosts so that they can exchange information within the group. One also needs to know how the hosts in different groups communicate with one another. The process to group a set of hosts is called subnetting. Distributing IP addresses and subnetting are part of network design. This chapter covers issues related to network design. This chapter provides examples to illustrate the calculation of subnets. This chapter also discusses the issues related to the coexistence of IPv4 and IPv6.

For hands-on practice, step-by-step instructions are given to help you create a simple virtual network in the cloud. The virtual technology will be used to realize virtual machines and network media. These virtual machines will be configured in a way that they can communicate with each other on the virtual network. Networking tools illustrated in the previous chapter are used to accomplish the configuration tasks.

3.2 Network Types

Based on the network scales and technology used, networks can be categorized as a local area network (LAN), wide area network (WAN), and the Internet. In addition to the fact that a WAN is a large-scale network, its network devices and network media may also be different from those of a LAN. Depending on where a WAN is implemented, a WAN may also be called a campus area network (CAN) or a metropolitan area network (MAN). When radio waves are used as network media, a network can be implemented as a wireless network. In the following, we will look into the details of the LAN, WAN, Internet, and the wireless networks.

3.2.1 Local Area Network

Normally, a LAN is a small-scale network with each network hosts located in a building or a room. The hosts in a LAN are usually linked with twisted-pair cables. The electrical pulses are delivered to other network hosts through the network media. The goal of the LAN is to allow a group of network devices and computers to share the resources in a room or in a building.

The network devices in a LAN are relatively less expensive. A LAN mainly uses the Ethernet technology for data transfer.

3.2.1.1 Ethernet   Ethernet is the most popular and most widely deployed LAN network technology. As a protocol, it is used to format frames and check errors in data transfer. The hardware built around Ethernet can be used to connect a network host to network media. For a wired network, the twisted-pair network cable is able to carry Ethernet frames. Ethernet can transmit data with various transmission rates over twisted-pair wires. Table 3.1 lists the Ethernet technologies and their transmission rates.

In a LAN, two network hosts are linked by a twisted-pair cable that is plugged into a RJ45 network connector built in the network interface adapter. Ethernet supports twisted-pair cables in various transmission rates. Twisted-pair cables can be classified into several categories. Table 3.2 lists some of the cable categories.

In the early days, an Ethernet network was constructed on a bus system shown in Figure 3.1.

To transmit data to a receiver on the bus, the sender places electrical signals to the bus through a transceiver that converts the binary signals to analog signals used by the hardware or *vice versa*. When the electrical signals reach the end of the bus, two terminators are used to absorb the electrical signals to prevent the electrical signals from bouncing back to collide with other electrical signals. The electrical signals will be delivered to all the hosts on the bus. Only the host with the IP address that matches the destination address receives the delivered data. After years of improvement, a small

Table 3.1 Transmission Rates of Ethernet Technologies

ETHERNET	TRANSMISSION RATE (MBPS)
10Base-T	10
100Base-T	100
1000Base-T or Gigabit Ethernet	1,000
10 Gigabit Ethernet	10,000

Table 3.2 Twisted-Pair Cable Categories

CATEGORY	BANDWIDTH (MHZ)	USAGE
5	100	Can be used on 10Base-T and 100Base-T Ethernet networks. May not be suitable for Gigabit Ethernet.
5E	100	Can be used for 10Base-T, 100Base-T, and Gigabit Ethernet networks.
6	250	Can be used for 10Base-T, 100Base-T, Gigabit Ethernet networks and 10 Gb Ethernet networks with limited distance.
6a	500	Can be used for 10Base-T, 100Base-T, Gigabit Ethernet networks and 10 Gb Ethernet networks up to 100 m.
7	600	This is a feature of the 10 Gigabit Ethernet technology designed for 10 Gb Ethernet networks over 100 m. Its transmission rate can possibly reach 100 Gbps over 70 m.

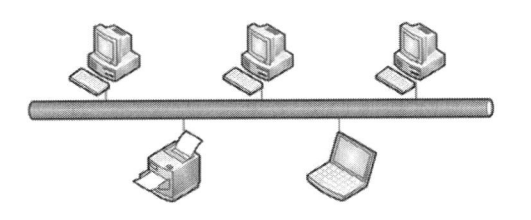

Figure 3.1 Ethernet.

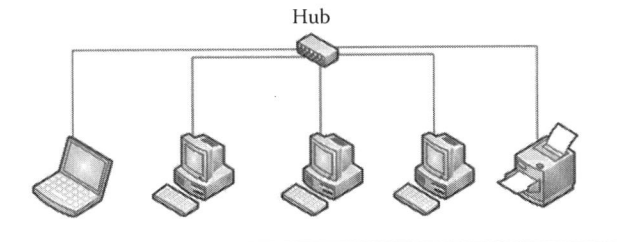

Figure 3.2 Hub.

network device called a hub is used to replace the original bus system. The transceivers and terminators are all built into the hub. Figure 3.2 illustrates how computers and network devices are linked to a hub with twisted-pair cables.

In a bus system, to send a frame across a bus or hub, the sender first checks if another host is sending a frame. If another host is sending a frame, the sender waits until the other host completes the process. The technology that determines when a host is allowed to send a frame is called Carrier Sense Multiple Access (CSMA). In practice, even with the CSMA technology, there is still a small chance that two hosts are sending their frames simultaneously without knowing that the other one is sending a frame too. When sending frames simultaneously in the bus system, a collision occurs, which harms both frames. The technology to detect a collision is called Collision Detect (CD). To fix the collision problem, each host will take a random delay and then try to resend its frame at a different time.

A frame is used to carry IP packets across a network. It is technology specific. Different types of networks use different technologies to form frames. The most

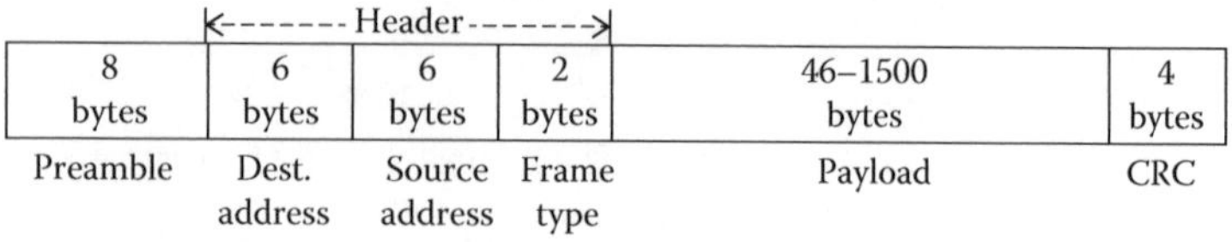

8 bytes	6 bytes	6 bytes	2 bytes	46–1500 bytes	4 bytes
Preamble	Dest. address	Source address	Frame type	Payload	CRC

|←------- Header ------→|

Figure 3.3 Ethernet frame.

commonly used technology to form frames in a LAN is Ethernet. The frame formed with Ethernet is shown in Figure 3.3.

An Ethernet frame consists of preamble, header, payload, and CRC sections. These sections are described as follows:

- *Preamble*: The preamble section in Figure 3.3 is 8-byte long or 64-bit long. It provides a pause time so that the receiver's hardware can get ready for the incoming signal. In this section, 64 bits of 1s or 0s are used to synchronize the signal frequency before the transmission of the data in the header.
- *Header*: The header section contains three parts, destination hardware address, source hardware address, and frame type. Each hardware address is 6-byte or 48-bit long. The frame type part is used to identify the type of the content. The frame type part has 2 bytes (or 16 bits), which can be used to identify thousands of data content types.
- *Payload*: The payload section is used to carry data. Depending on the size of data, it is 46–1500 bytes long.
- *Cyclic Redundancy Check (CRC)*: The CRC section contains 4 bytes of CRC code used to check data transmission errors.

There are some other versions of the Ethernet technology designed to overcome some of the difficulties in the original Ethernet technology. It may be difficult to put the frame type into practice. The frame type code definition may vary from one organization to another organization. Therefore, some of the Ethernet versions do not have the frame type section. Instead, they use the first few bytes of the payload section to identify the content type. IEEE 802.2 LLC/SNAP is this type of frame. In an IEEE 802.2 LLC/SNAP frame, LLC stands for Logical Link Control used to indicate that a type field follows. SNAP stands for SubNetwork Attachment Point, which contains two fields. The first field identifies the organization and the second field identifies the content type defined by the organization. Figure 3.4 illustrates the fields in the IEEE 802.2 LLC/SNAP frame header.

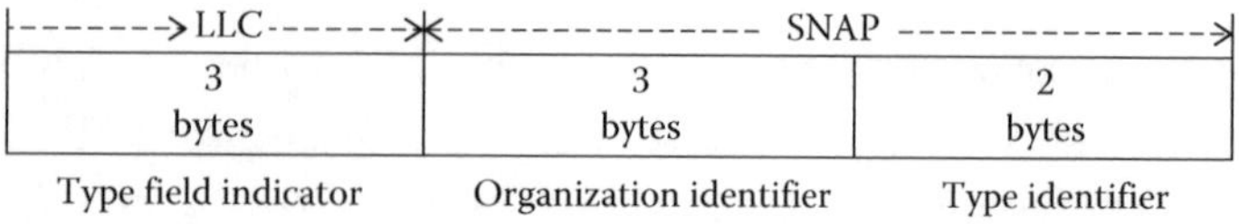

3 bytes	3 bytes	2 bytes
Type field indicator	Organization identifier	Type identifier

|------→ LLC ------→|←------------- SNAP --------------→|

Figure 3.4 IEEE 802.2 LLC/SNAP.

This version of Ethernet is widely accepted in the LAN technology. It is the dominant LAN technology for wired networks. The Ethernet technology can also be used to transmit data over a wireless network such as Wi-Fi. In addition to Ethernet, there are some newly developed LAN technologies such as Fibre Channel, which is discussed in the next section.

3.2.1.2 Fibre Channel   Fibre Channel is a LAN technology designed for mass data transition. Fibre Channel is able to reach a data transmission rate as high as 32 Gbps. It is often used to connect a network server to a network storage device such as a storage area network (SAN). When optical fiber is used as the network media, Fibre Channel can be used to transmit data between two network hosts that are 10 km apart. Fibre Channel can also work with other network media such as the TV cable and twisted-pair cable. When implemented over twisted-pair cables, Fibre Channel can only reach the hosts in a short distance.

Data communication among the devices linked through Fibre Channel can be done in three ways. Fibre Channel supports the point-to-point connection between network hosts such as a network server and a network device, for example, an external hard drive array, a SAN storage device, or a printer.

Data communication can also be carried out through an arbitrary loop. Before a host sends data out, it sends an arbitrary frame, which is used to inform other hosts on the network. The host can begin to send data only when the arbitrary frame loops back to the host. If multiple hosts send arbitrary frames at the same time, the sender with the lowest hardware address wins the competition. When a sender wins the arbitration, it is allowed to send data and then waits for all other hosts in the competition to get their chance to send data before it can send data again. The arbitrated loop only allows one pair of ports to communicate concurrently. Typically, the Fibre Channel arbitrated loop mechanism allows as many as 126 devices to be connected to the network.

Data communication can also be done through the switched-fabric mechanism. The switched-fabric technology is flexible; various network devices and computers are connected to Fibre Channel switches. The switched-fabric mechanism allows multiple pairs of ports to communicate simultaneously in the fabric. When fiber optic cables are used as network media, the switched-fabric mechanism allows over 16 million devices to be linked to the network. However, switches are expensive. A disadvantage of Fibre Channel is the lack of compatibilities among Fibre Channel manufacturers.

3.2.1.3 LAN Segment   A hub or a switch is used to link the hosts in a LAN segment so that a host can communicate with another host in the same LAN segment. Figure 3.5 shows a simple LAN segment. It consists of desktop computers, a server, a laptop computer, and a network printer. A hub is used to link the computers and

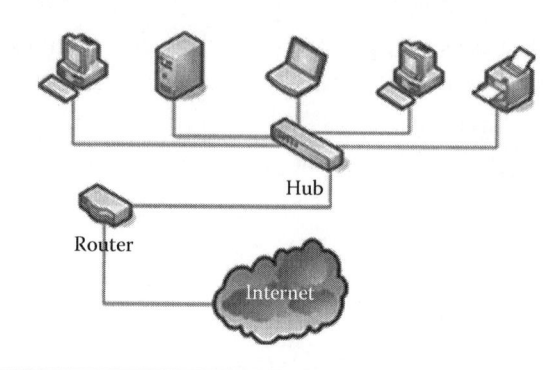

Figure 3.5   LAN segment.

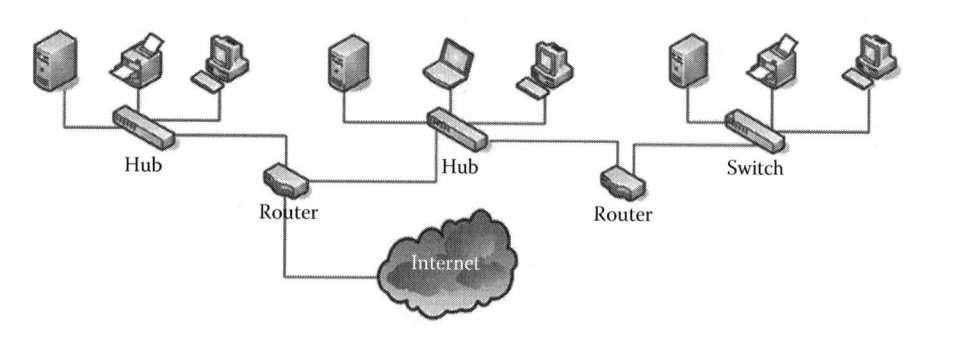

Figure 3.6   LAN segments.

network devices together. As a network device, a switch can be used to link computers and network devices like the hub does.

In practice, hosts in one LAN segment needs to communicate with hosts in another LAN segment. A hub or a switch provides an uplink port through which two network LAN segments can be connected through a network device called router. A router is used to connect networks. By using a router, a LAN segment is also able to be connected to the Internet. More discussion about switches and routers will be given later in this chapter. Figure 3.6 shows three LAN segments that are linked by two routers.

Multiple LAN segments may be linked to a large network. The large network may include multiple switches, hubs, routers, and other network devices.

3.2.2 *Wide Area Network*

A network with large scalability is called a WAN. A WAN can be scaled to a large geographical area. It may include multiple sites, each of which has a large number of hosts. The WAN allows a large number of hosts to communicate with one another simultaneously. Scalability is a key factor of the WAN. If a network can link hosts that locate in a large geographical area but is only limited to a few hosts, it may not be qualified as a WAN.

3.2.2.1 WAN Technology   To allow multiple sites to communicate simultaneously in a long distance, WANs depend on telephone companies or Internet service providers (ISPs) to carry out telecommunication services. The telecommunication uses different technologies from those used in a LAN. The long distance communication among sites can be carried out through four telecommunication technologies, leased line, circuit switching, packet switching, and cell relay. The following briefly describes these four technologies:

1. *Leased telephone line*: An organization can link its sites located in a large geological area by leasing the lines from a telephone company. The connection is exclusive and expensive. Protocols such as Point-to-Point Protocol (PPP) are used for data communication. The wire and the equipment at each end of the connection are provided by the telephone company. PPP is a protocol commonly used in establishing a direct connection between two network nodes. The protocol can be used on various network media such as the phone line, radio wave, and optical fiber.

2. *Circuit switching*: Unlike the leased telephone line connection, which is exclusive, this kind of connection can be initialized based on a request. When data transmission is requested by the sender, a call to the receiver's number is dialed. A connection is then established between the sender and receiver. Once the data transmission is completed, the connection will be terminated. Protocols such as Point-to-Point Protocol (PPP) and Integrated Services Digital Network (ISDN) are used for data communication in circuit switching. When used for the communication between two WAN sites, ISDN is very much like a digital telephone technology.

3. *Packet switching*: Different from circuit switching, packet switching has its end nodes connected all the time so that data can be sent at any time. Like the packet transmission in a LAN, packet switching used in a WAN transmits data formed as packets constructed by telecommunication companies. Therefore, packet switching is used by the Internet as well as LANs. When the packets reach to the end of a connection, they are transmitted through a network device called a packet switch, which links multiple hosts on a LAN. A packet switch has two sets of ports. One set is used to link to other packet switches in a WAN and the other set is used to link to the hosts on the LAN segment attached to the packet switch. When packets arrive at a packet switch, they are queued or buffered. Based on the destination address carried by a packet, the packet switch determines if the packet should be sent to the attached LAN segment or be forwarded to another packet switch. By efficiently sharing a network, packet switching can lower the operating cost when compared with other types of WAN technologies. Data communication in packet switching can be handled by protocols such as X.25, frame relay, and Synchronous Optical Network (SONET). X.25 is an early WAN protocol

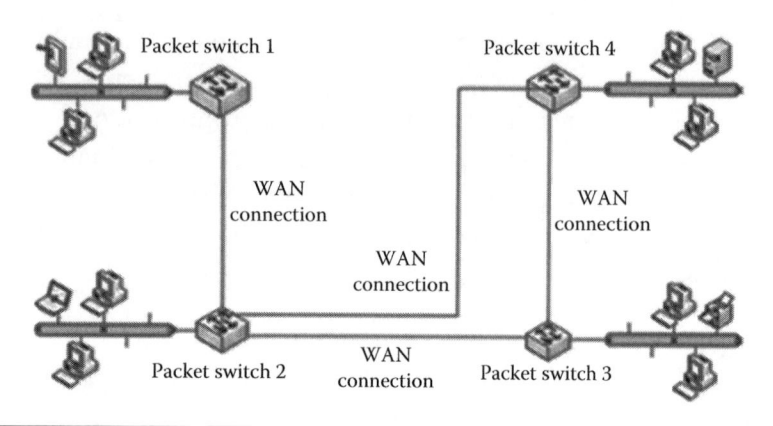

Figure 3.7 Packet switching.

created even before personal computers. In today's standard, X.25 is a low-performance protocol. As the name indicates, frame relay is a WAN technology that relays frames from one LAN segment to another remote LAN segment. Its data transmission rate can reach to 100 Mbps. SONET is a WAN technology designed for data communication over fiber optic cables. SONET has a high data transmission rate ranging from 51.84 Mbps to 40 Gbps. One of the features of SONET is that it is able to combine packets with different formats into a frame used by fiber optic cables. A large company with its data service handled by multiple WAN technologies can take advantage of this feature. SONET simplifies packet transmission between two different WAN technologies. The packet switch mentioned here is this type of device. Figure 3.7 illustrates packet switching in a WAN.

4. *Cell relay*: Like packet switching, cell relay delivers fixed-length packets called cells through a WAN connection. The advantage of cell relay is that it can transmit voice and data simultaneously. The disadvantage is that it has a considerable large overhead. In cell relay, the protocols Switched Multimegabit Data Services (SMDS) and Asynchronous Transfer Mode (ATM) are used for data transmission. SMDS is designed for data transmission in both the LAN and WAN. It can transmit a frame that contains 53 bytes of data. Its data transmission rate is faster than that of frame relay. ATM is another WAN or LAN technology designed to handle telecommunication services as well as data transmission on a LAN. ATM is a hardware-based technology; therefore, it can achieve a high transmission rate. In theory, the transmission rate of ATM may reach as high as 10 Gbps. On the other hand, it requires a new set of hardware and software, which can be expensive for many users.

3.2.2.2 Modulation   A message transmitted in a LAN cannot travel very far, say, not more than 200 m. In a LAN, network hosts transmit data in the binary form. On a telecommunication line, analog electrical signals or lights are used for long distance

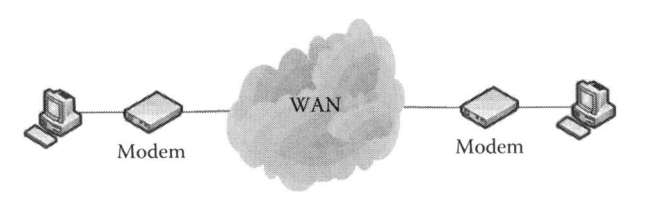

Figure 3.8 Modem.

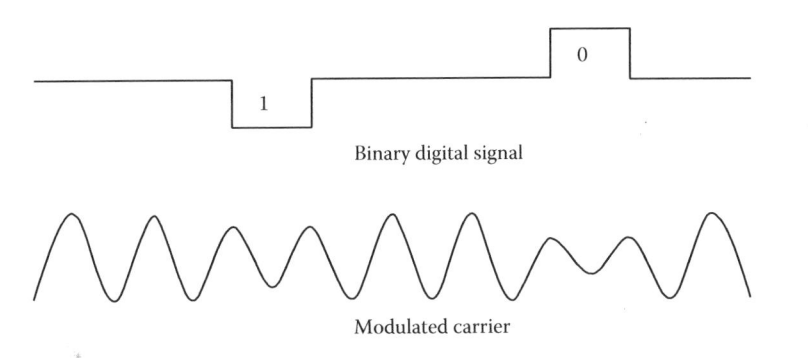

Figure 3.9 Illustration of amplitude modulation.

data communication. A modem is such a network device used to convert binary signals to analog signals transmitted by telephone lines. At the destination, the analog signals will be converted back to binary signals by the modem for the computer to use. Figure 3.8 illustrates the usage of modems.

For long distance transmission, a carrier, which is a continuously oscillating electric current, is used to carry binary signals. The continuously oscillating electrical current is known for being able to propagate long distance without losing much of its energy. To represent a binary signal, the continuously oscillating electrical current needs to be modified either to its amplitude, or its frequency, or its phase so that the zeros and ones have distinguished representations. Such modification of a carrier is called modulation. Figure 3.9 illustrates an amplitude modulation process.

Another way to represent the zeros and ones in the binary signals is to change frequency. Figure 3.10 illustrates the idea of frequency modulation.

Changing the phase of the carrier's waves can also represent the binary signals.

3.2.2.3 Multiplexing The continuously oscillating electric current can be formed with different frequencies. By using these carriers with different frequencies, multiple pairs of senders and receivers can communicate simultaneously. The process of sharing a single medium by using multiple carriers with different frequencies is called frequency division multiplexing. Using frequencies is not the only way to distinguish carriers. When optical fiber is used for data transmission, colors can be used to distinguish different carriers. Such a process is called color division multiplexing or technically called wavelength division multiplexing. Another way to implement multiplexing is

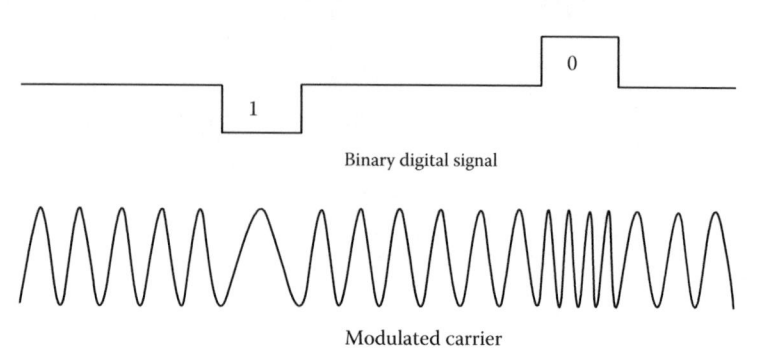

Binary digital signal

Modulated carrier

Figure 3.10 Illustration of frequency modulation.

to let multiple carriers take turns in data communication. Such a process is called time division multiplexing. By using multiplexing, telecommunication can be made much more efficient.

3.2.2.4 WAN Network Media The digital telephone circuit called T-series is commonly used as the network media for long distance data communication. T-series lines are made of optical fiber and can carry much more data than traditional copper telephone lines. The well-known T-series connections are T1, T2, and T3. The data transition rate ranges from 1.544 Mbps for T1 to 44.736 Mbps for T3. The features of T-series are listed in Table 3.3.

For data communication among the sites in a WAN, a digital-interface device unit called Channel Service Unit/Data Service Unit (CSU/DSU) is used to connect a router on a LAN segment to the T-series line. CSU/DSU converts a LAN frame to a frame that meets the T-series standards and vice versa. The frame conversion task is done by DSU. CSU is used to send data to or receive data from T-series lines and provides loopback signals for testing. Figure 3.11 illustrates the usage of CSU/DSU in the implementation of a WAN.

Table 3.3 T-Series Standards

NAME	TRANSMISSION RATE (MBPS)	NUMBER OF VOICE CIRCUITS SUPPORTED
T1	1.544	24
T2	6.312	96
T3	44.736	672

Figure 3.11 T-series.

Table 3.4 OC Standards

NAME	TRANSMISSION RATE (MBPS)	NUMBER OF VOICE CIRCUITS SUPPORTED
OC-1	51.840	810
OC-3	155.520	2,430
OC-12	622.080	9,720
OC-24	1,244.160	19,440
OC-48	2,488.320	38,880
OC-192	9,953.280	155,520
OC-768	39,813.12	622,080

Figure 3.12 ISDN.

As the amount of data is growing exponentially, the T-series standards are not able to meet the needs of today's data communication. The new standards called Optical Carrier (OC) have been created for OCs. The data transmission rates in the OC standards can reach as high as 40 Gbps. The features provided by the commonly used OC standards are listed in Table 3.4.

As an older technology, the digital telephone technology ISDN can also be used to connect the sites in a WAN. ISDN has the data transmission rate of 64 Kbps, which is much slower than those of the T-series standards and DC standards. However, ISDN can deliver data through the traditional copper telephone lines. ISDN uses terminal adapters to connect a frame on a LAN segment to the frame used on a telephone line. The usage of ISDN terminal adapters is illustrated in Figure 3.12.

WANs and LANs can be interconnected to form an even larger network called the Internet. The next section describes the Internet.

3.2.3 Internet

WANs and LANs are created with different types of technologies. It is difficult for these WANs and LANs with different technologies to communicate directly with each other. For worldwide data communication, it is necessary to create a uniform network technology to allow the hosts worldwide to share the same network. The Internet is this type of worldwide network that interconnects a large number of heterogeneous WANs and LANs. The Internet is a public network that is accessible to network hosts anywhere and anytime. To deal with heterogeneous network technologies, routers are used to deliver packets from one type of network to another type of network. Also, the protocols TCP and IP are used to hide complicated details from application software. By doing so, application software can treat the Internet as a uniform network and let TCP/IP deal with the differences in network technologies. The application layer protocols such as HTTP and DNS all rely on TCP/IP to communicate over the Internet. The combination of the router and TCP/IP makes the Internet possible.

Suppose that two home networks (LANs) are linked to the Internet. To illustrate how a computer in a home network communicates with another computer located in a different home network, the home networks need to be connected to the Internet through ISPs. First, a packet sent by the computer on the home network will be delivered to the ISP. Through an access point called Point of Presence (POP), the ISP connects the home network to another POP. A POP can be a telecommunication facility rented by an ISP for accessing the Internet, or it can be any facility used to access the Internet such as a dial-up server, router, or ATM switch. An ISP may have thousands of POPs to keep up with the demand for Internet access. Computers within each ISP are able to communicate with each other through the interconnected POPs. Some of the large enterprise can also have their own POPs for accessing the global network.

Data communication among ISPs requires a higher level connection. ISPs communicate through the network access point (NAP), which is a major Internet interconnection point. The major Internet interconnection or the global network is able to reach other NAPs throughout the world. In such a way, every computer on the Internet is able to communicate with every other computer. Through the global network, packets will be delivered to the destination NAPs. From there, these packets will be delivered to the ISPs on the receiving side. Through the POPs owned by the receiving ISPs, the packets will be delivered to the destination home networks. Figure 3.13 is an overview of the Internet structure.

Fiber optic cables are used to construct the backbone of the global network, which either follows the T-series standards or the faster OC standards. In the early days, the backbone of the global network was jointly developed by the National Science Foundation (NSF), IBM, MCI, and Merit. Nowadays, many international enterprises such as AT&T, Sprint, MCI, CenturyLink, and many others also own some of the Internet backbone networks. These backbone connections are linked through NAPs. However, no one owns the entire Internet. Once a computer in a LAN is connected to the Internet through a POP, the computer and the LAN become part of the Internet. Although the LAN becomes part of the Internet, no one else owns this part of the Internet except the local owner.

As more and more WANs and LANs participate in the Internet, the size of the Internet is growing exponentially. Due to the lack of centralized control on the Internet and the openness of Internet protocols, the Internet has changed the way of data communication. From anywhere and at anytime, users can access Internet-based application software such as World Wide Web, e-mail, online chats, online games, text messaging, file transfer, web logging, Internet phones, Internet TVs, and so on. Social network software has greatly impacted the form of social life as well.

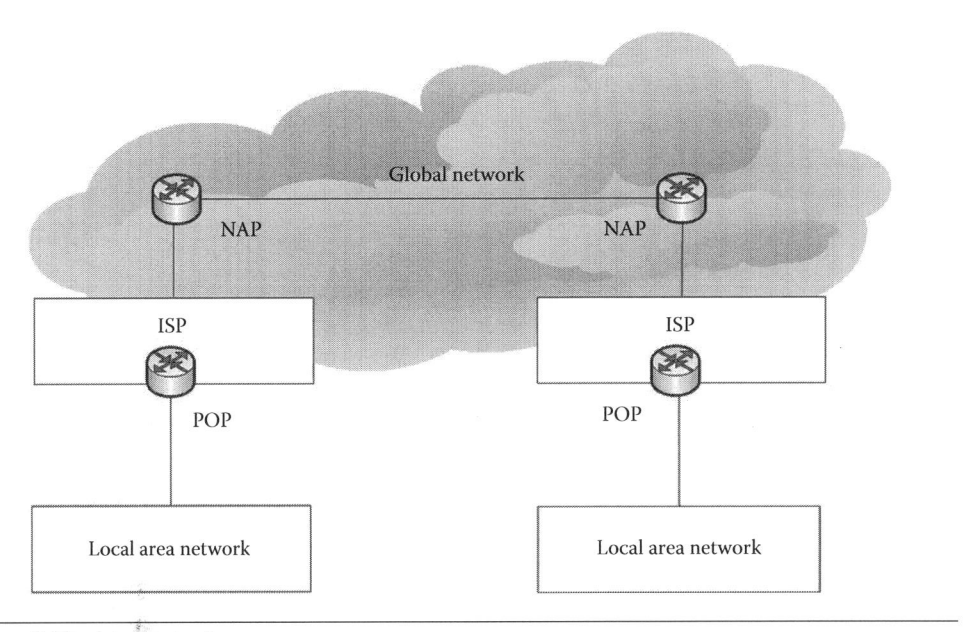

Figure 3.13 Internet structure.

3.2.4 Wireless Network

Due to its flexibility, mobility, maintainability, and scalability, wireless networks are becoming more and more popular. Because no cabling is necessary, a wireless network can significantly reduce the cost of network construction. As wireless network technologies improve, the speed of wireless data transmission is as fast as the data transmission rate of a copper wire. The wireless network can use radio waves, microwaves, and infrared to transmit data. Based on these transmission media, different wireless technologies such as Wi-Fi, WiMAX, infrared, and Bluetooth have been developed. The following briefly describes these commonly used wireless technologies.

3.2.4.1 Wi-Fi Technology In a Wi-Fi wireless network, a wireless network adapter is used to convert binary signals into radio signals. These radio signals are transmitted into the air through an antenna. A wireless device communicates with other network hosts in two different ways, infrastructure mode and ad hoc mode. In the infrastructure mode, the radio signals are delivered to a device called an access point. The access point has a built-in antenna and a radio transmitter for transmitting the radio signals. The access point broadcasts the access information, such as the service set identifier (SSID), repeatedly. When a wireless device comes to the receiving range of the access point, the wireless device sends a request to the access point to initiate a connection. When the access point receives the request, it compares its SSID with the SSID of the request. If there is a match, the access point will respond with a synchronization message and the information about its traffic load. After the wireless device receives the response, it will calculate the distance between itself and the access point. Based on the distance, the wireless device will estimate the traffic load and the quality of the transmission.

After the connection is established between the wireless device and access point, at the access point, the radio signals will be converted back to electrical signals so that the electrical signals can be forwarded to the Internet through a wired connection. The electrical signals on the Internet are sent to an access point. At the access point, the electrical signals are converted to radio signals and are transmitted into the air. When a wireless NIC of the receiving end receives the radio signals, it converts the radio signals into the binary signals. One access point can communicate with as many as 255 mobile devices. Figure 3.14 illustrates a wireless network that operates in the infrastructure mode.

Another way of communication among wireless devices is to use the ad hoc mode, which delivers the radio signals to each other directly without using an access point. This is why the ad hoc mode is also called the peer-to-peer mode. Since no access point is used, the setup of a wireless network in the ad hoc mode is less complicated. The disadvantage of the ad hoc mode is its weak scalability. Figure 3.15 illustrates the ad hoc mode.

The Wi-Fi technology is defined by the IEEE 802.11 standards, which set the data transmission rates and other properties for low-level operations. Table 3.5 lists some commonly available Wi-Fi standards.

The transmission rate and coverage range may vary from one hardware vendor to another. Running at 5 GHz, 802.11ac has a much faster data transmission rate. On the other hand, it is not backward compatible with 802.11g, which only runs at 2.4 GHz.

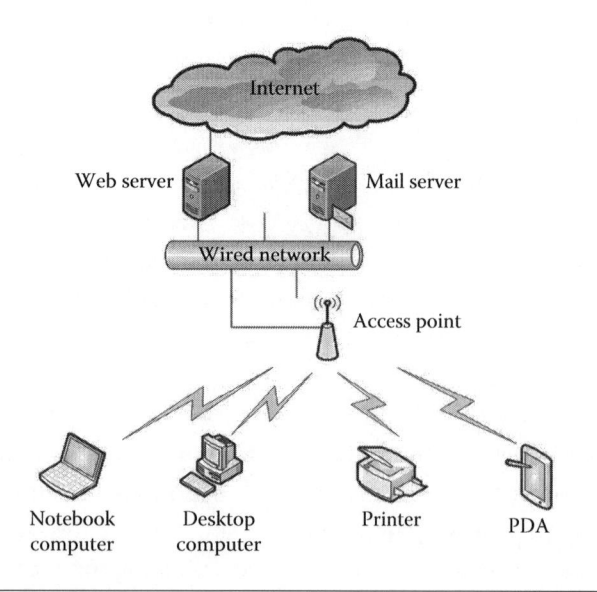

Figure 3.14   Infrastructure mode.

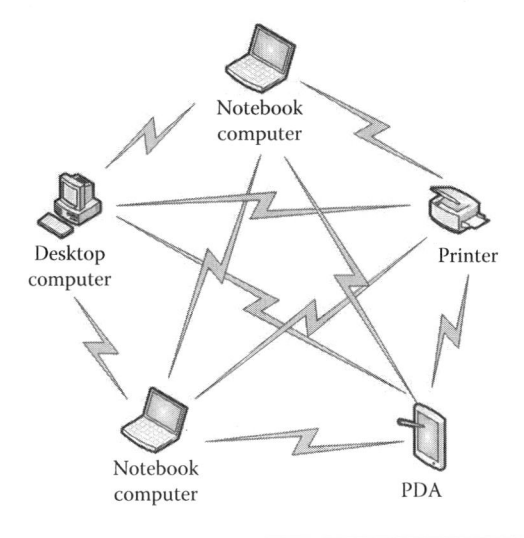

Figure 3.15 Ad hoc mode.

Table 3.5 Wi-Fi Standards

STANDARD	FREQUENCY	MAX TRANSMISSION RATE	MAXIMUM RANGE
802.11g	2.4 GHz	54 Mbps	38 m (indoor) 140 m (outdoor)
802.11n	2.4 GHz 5 GHz	450 Mbps	70 m (indoor) 250 m (outdoor)
802.11ac	5 GHz	1.3 Gbps at 80 MHz 2.6 Gbps at 160 MHz	95 m (indoor) with three antennas

3.2.4.2 WiMAX Technology Worldwide Interoperability for Microwave Access (WiMAX) runs on microwaves that have a much higher frequency than that of radio waves. The high frequency allows for a high data transmission rate, low interruption, as well as a long transmission distance. The microwave is the network medium suitable for long distance data transmission. The data transmission rate between two microwave transmission towers can run on a frequency as high as 66 GHz. On the other hand, the data transmission between network devices and a microware tower uses a lower frequency ranging from 2 to 11 GHz. With the lower frequency, electrical signals can easily get around physical objects such as buildings. By using the microwave, the data sent by a transmission tower can reach another tower 50 km away. While Wi-Fi changes the way of delivering messages for the last 100 ft of a network, the microwave changes the way of delivering messages for the last mile. WiMAX has the proposed downloading rate of 75 Mbps and uploading rate of 25 Mbps. The rates may vary depending on the distance and the number of users accessing the transmission center. Figure 3.16 illustrates a WiMAX system.

The WiMAX technology is defined by the IEEE 802.16 standards. Table 3.6 lists some commonly available WiMAX standards.

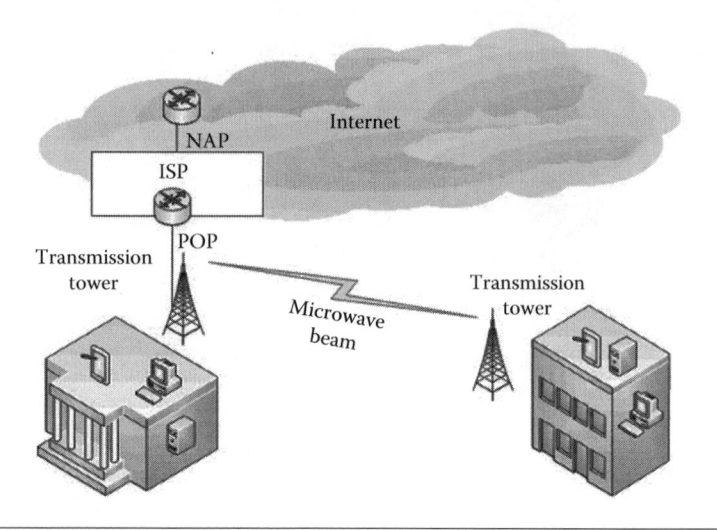

Figure 3.16   WiMAX network.

Table 3.6   WiMAX Standards

STANDARD	FREQUENCY	USAGE
802.16	10–66 GHz	Supports point-to-point delivery between transmission towers
802.16a	2–11 GHz	Supports point-to-multipoint delivery between a transmission tower and individual receivers on network devices
802.16e	2–6 GHz	Supports mobile connection and fixed connection
802.16m	Supports multiple frequency bands	Supports mobile connection and fixed connection

Although WiMAX is the technology that brings high data transmission speed to a wireless network, it is a brand-new technology. The requirement for new equipment in the construction of a WiMAX network will increase the cost. Therefore, the market share of WiMAX is much smaller than that of Wi-Fi and that of Long Term Evolution (LTE), which is a technology used in 4G mobile networks.

3.2.4.3 Infrared   Infrared is a wireless network media used for data transmission in a short distance. It is often used by cordless computer keyboards and mice, LCD projector remote controls, and so on. As a point-to-point connection wireless technology, infrared requires two devices to aim at each other. This feature makes infrared more secure but less convenient since it cannot communicate with multiple network devices at the same time.

3.2.4.4 Bluetooth   Bluetooth is also a wireless technology for short distance communication. Unlike infrared, Bluetooth uses radio waves as the network media. The radio wave frequency used by Bluetooth is from 2.402 to 2.480 GHz. Compared with the Wi-Fi technology, the Bluetooth technology is more user friendly, less expensive, and has much less power consumption. On the other hand, Bluetooth has a lower data transmission rate and travels in a much shorter distance than Wi-Fi. Bluetooth is suitable for a network inside a car or in a small room. This type of network is some-times called a personal area network (PAN), which can usually reach a distance less than 10 m.

The advantage of Bluetooth is that it needs much less user attention during data transmission. The Bluetooth network can deal with a variety of mobile devices such as mobile phones, notebook computers, printers, GPS receivers, televisions, digital cam-eras, PDAs, and video game consoles. Bluetooth has a user-friendly feature, which does not require the user to initiate the connection between the Bluetooth-enabled network devices. In a Bluetooth-enabled network, there is no need to configure the network devices for data transmission. After a Bluetooth-enabled device is turned on, the device sends out signals to search and see if there is another Bluetooth-enabled device within its range. If another Bluetooth-enabled device comes to the coverage range of the Bluetooth device, these two devices automatically exchange information. Once the connection is established, it cannot be broken by other devices.

Each of the Bluetooth-enabled devices has a Bluetooth transmitter preconfigured by the manufacturer. The Bluetooth transmitter can also be plugged to a device to make it a Bluetooth-enabled device. Bluetooth can communicate with up to eight network devices simultaneously. To prevent the Bluetooth-enabled devices from inter-fering with each other, a technology called spread-spectrum frequency is used so that the Bluetooth devices do not use the same frequency at the same time.

Bluetooth automatically establishes a connection between network devices, which makes it user friendly. On the other hand, the convenience introduces some secu-rity concerns. A hacker can take advantage of this feature to connect to a Bluetooth device. Through the connection, a hacker can send some harmful data to the device. To solve this problem, a Bluetooth authentication mechanism is added to a Bluetooth device. The authentication mechanism checks if the connection is allowed.

3.2.5 Virtual Network

A virtual network is a software-based network. Software is used to emulate the net-work architecture and functions of a physical network. There are two different types of virtual network technologies, the protocol-based virtual network and the device-based virtual network.

The virtual LAN (VLAN) and virtual private network (VPN) are two well-known protocol-based virtual network technologies. It may not be easy to manage a large net-work physically. For better resource management of complicated large networks, one may consider the virtual LAN (VLAN) technology. Through the VLAN technology, a set of network hosts can be configured to be in the same virtual network even if the hosts belong to different LAN segments physically. On the same virtual network, hosts communicate with one another as if they were on the same network. With the VLAN technology, multiple virtual LAN segments can be created on a physical LAN segment. In this way, the network traffic on a large physical network can be limited to a specific virtual LAN segment. When a network structure is changed, it is a tedious task to reconnect the physical network to meet the requirements. The VLAN technology provides the flexibility of reconfiguring the network structure without physically relocating the network hosts. The VLAN technology can also be used to improve network security and manageability.

The VPN technology creates a secure private network over the public network such as the Internet. A VPN can use the public Internet to deliver private data by using the authentication and encryption mechanisms. It can work with the broadband Internet technology to achieve a high data transmission rate. Since the VPN uses the existing network technology such as NICs and network media, there is no extra network equipment required. This makes the management of the VPN server relatively easy. Due to these advantages, the VPN technology is commonly used by large corporations and educational institutions to enable users to securely connect to a private network remotely.

Instead of using physical network devices, a virtual device–based virtual network can be constructed with virtual network resources such as virtual NICs, virtual machines, and virtual switches. On a physical server, a virtual machine can be created inside a hypervisor, which is a virtualization management software program. The hypervisor manages virtual networks, virtual NICs, virtual switches, virtual machines with virtual processors and memory, and other resources. Inside a hypervisor, the network traffic between virtual servers are routed through virtual routers and virtual switches. Virtual firewalls are also configured for blocking certain network traffic.

Since a virtual device–based virtual network connects a group of virtual machines hosted by the hypervisor, it can connect a virtual machine to a physical network. Through a virtual network, a virtual machine can provide network services to a physical network. A virtual network is compatible with nonvirtual network technologies such as Ethernet. The virtual technology also supports nonvirtual devices such as CD-ROM drives and USB devices.

The virtualization technology has been supported by major server operating system vendors including Microsoft and VMware. Windows Server provides a virtualization technology called Hyper-V. Hyper-V supports up to 64 processors and 1 terabyte of memory, and a virtual hard disk with up to 64 TB of capacity. vSphere is the virtualization solution provided by VMware. vSphere is a software suite including the components of ESXi, vCenter, and many others. ESXi is a virtualization server, which is the most important part of vSphere. Virtual machines and virtual networks are installed on the ESXi server. The vCenter server is a centralized management application, which allows a user to manage ESXi remotely. Both Hyper-V and vSphere are built to support cloud computing.

Now that you have learned the technical details of LANs, WANs, the Internet, wireless networks, virtual networks, and how data are transmitted in these networks, the next task is planning and configuring a network so that the computers in the same network can communicate with each other.

3.3 IP Addressing

It is well known that each computer on the Internet must have an IP address. A router must have two or more IP addresses to connect two or more networks. For the computers in a network to be able to communicate with each other, we need to resolve some issues such as how to assign an IP address to a computer, how to distribute a set of IP addresses to a group of computers, how to configure the computers in a LAN segment so that they can exchange information within the segment, how to determine the size of a LAN segment, and so on. In this section, we will first take a closer look at the issues related to the IP address assignment to meet the requirements of a network infrastructure.

3.3.1 Network Planning

Before a network can be physically built, it must be carefully planned, especially for a large-scale network project. The following are some of the major tasks commonly accomplished in the planning phase:

- First, we need to examine the requirements for the future network.
- Develop a logical network model, the blueprint for future network. The logical network should include specifications of the protocols, network media, and network devices to be used in the future network.
- Draft the IP address distribution sketch.
- Outline a security policy.
- Make a plan for the physical implementation of the network.

Through the investigation of the requirements, we are able to find out what network services should be provided by the network and what type of network to be built to meet the requirements.

After the needs for the future network have been identified, our next task is to create a blueprint to represent the future network. In the blueprint, we can specify the network technology, network devices, network operating system, and network media so that they can meet the requirements on the network's performance, reliability, scalability, and security. In the network blueprint, we can specify the model, feature, and capacity of these devices. We decide how to use these devices to define a broadcasting domain and how to restrict certain network traffic. We can also implement some security measures through these devices.

In the blueprint, we can specify network routing protocols such as RIP or OSPF based on the requirements for scalability and performance. Often, the network operating system that hosts the network management software can also be specified in the blueprint. Security application software such as antivirus software and firewall systems are also specified in the blueprint.

In the blueprint, network hosts such as personal computers and printers can also be specified. We can decide what desktop operating system edition and mobile devices to be used in the future network. Also, network-based application software such as the database client and VPN client should also be specified in the blueprint.

One of the planning tasks is to work out a user authentication and authorization plan. We need to identify user groups and privileges to be assigned to those groups. We also need to consider measures to prevent virus infection and block hackers from penetrating the private network. It requires team work to create a security policy. The team may include user representatives, network managers, and the organization's administrators. The issues related to data confidentiality, integrity, and availability should be addressed in the security policy. For confidentiality, the methods of authentication and encryption should be specialized in the security policy. To protect data integrity, we need to identify the secure protocols for data transmission and the mechanisms such as digital signature to prevent the data from being altered by unauthorized individuals. To make the data available to qualified users is another issue to be addressed in the security policy. We should specify which group users can access which part of the network. We also need to consider adding redundancy to reduce down time. Cloud computing is another choice for improving availability.

During network planning, the project manager needs to allocate the budget, organize the development team, identify product suppliers, contact consulting companies, and seek support from the administrators. Often, the project manager needs to balance the needs and the cost. If there is a limitation on the budget or other resources, it is necessary to revise the blueprint to lower the cost. If the cost is a concern, the virtual network technology and cloud-based solution should be considered. We also need to balance the security and the needs. Often, it may take several rounds of modification before a satisfactory result can be achieved.

After the blueprint is accepted, a project implementation plan should be drafted. The following tasks should be included in the implementation plan:

- A timeline should guide the network implementation process. The timeline tells when each implementation task should be completed. It also indicates what tasks can be done simultaneously.
- Form a network construction team and specify the job assignment for each of the team members so that everyone in the construction team is clear about his/her responsibilities.
- If a wired network is to be implemented, there should be a floor plan for wiring.
- After the network servers, switches, and routers are put into place, technical details on the configuration of network hosts should be documented.
- Lastly, the plan should include regulations on the network testing process.

The team project manager also needs to make sure that the members of the network construction team have adequate knowledge to handle the job.

3.3.2 IP Addressing Strategy

An enterprise-level network often includes a large number of computers, LAN segments, and Internet connections. The network designers need to come up with an IP address strategy to decide how IP addresses should be assigned to the LAN segments and network hosts. Decisions should be made based on the following options:

- Decide if to assign a public or private IP address to a network host or a subnet.
- Make decisions on how many subnets to be created and how many hosts can be connected to a subnet.
- Choose whether to use classless IP addresses or classful IP addresses.
- Determine if to use VLANs or virtual networks.
- Work on subnet masks to design the subnets.
- Determine if to use a private or public cloud.
- Decide if to assign a host a static IP address or a dynamic IP address.
- Make a decision on the range of static IP addresses to be assigned to the servers and routers.

Many of the IP addressing–related topics will be discussed later in this chapter.

3.3.3 IP Addressing

By nature, the Internet is a combination of networks with various technologies. Hardware addresses are not sufficient to identify the hosts on the Internet since they are coded differently in different technologies. To be consistent, we must come up with a unified addressing scheme, which is independent of various physical structures. Therefore, IP addressing is a unified addressing scheme. In this section, you will find out how an IP address is formed and how IP addresses are classified. You will also learn about some specially defined IP addresses.

3.3.3.1 IPv4 IP Addressing   In IPv4, an IP address is represented with a unique 32-bit binary number. With 32 bits, IPv4 is able to provide 2^{32} unique addresses. The 32 binary bits in an IP address are divided into two parts. The first part is called the prefix, which is used to identify a network. The second part is called the suffix, which is used to identify the hosts in a network.

Although the Internet consists of hundreds and thousands of networks, a few of them are very large networks such as those networks run by ISPs. Most of the networks on the Internet are small networks such as those networks run by small companies. For a large network, which is designed to have a large number of hosts, an IP address should be formed with more bits in the suffix and fewer bits in the prefix. On the other hand, for a small network, which is designed to have a small number of hosts, an IP address should be formed by using fewer bits in the suffix section and more bits in the prefix section.

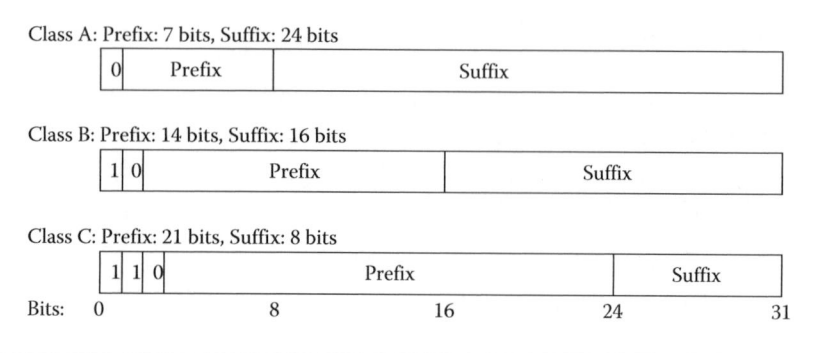

Figure 3.17 Classes of IPv4 addresses.

To efficiently use IP addresses, the IPv4 IP addresses are categorized into different classes for different-sized networks. The IP addresses in Class A are used by large networks, The IP addresses in Class B are used for medium-sized networks, and the IP addresses in Class C are used for small networks. Figure 3.17 shows how the prefix and suffix are divided in each class. In Figure 3.17, the binary code in front of the prefix is used to identify the class type. That is, if an IP address starts with the bit 0, it is a Class A IP address. Similarly, if an IP address starts with the bits 10, it is a Class B IP address, and if an IP address starts with 110, it is a Class C IP address. IPv4 also includes Class D and Class E IP addresses. The IP addresses in Class D are used for multicasting. The IP addresses in Class E are reserved for future use. Since both Class D and Class E are not widely used, they are less known by users. Since this type of IP addressing scheme categorizes IP addresses into classes, it is called classful IP addressing.

Class A uses the first octet as the prefix. Among the 8 bits of the first octet, the first bit is used for class identification. Therefore, only 7 bits in the first octet is used for network identification. Since the range of 7-bit binary numbers is from 0000000 to 1111111. This means that Class A can only identify $2^7 = 128$ networks. The rest of the bits (24 bits) in an IP address are used to identify network hosts. Therefore, each Class A network can have as many as $2^{24} = 16,777,216$ network hosts.

The Class B uses the first two octets as the prefix. In the first two octets, there are 16 binary digits. Since a Class B IP address uses the first two binary digits as the class identifier, this leaves 14 digits available for network identification. Therefore, Class B can identify $2^{14} = 16,384$ networks.

The Class C uses the first three octets as the prefix. In the first three octets, there are 24 binary bits. The first three of them are used as the class identifier. This leaves 21 bits to be used to identify networks. Therefore, Class C has $2^{21} = 2,097,152$ networks. Table 3.7 lists the number of networks and the number of hosts that can be identified by each of the three primary classes.

An IP address has a 32-bit binary numbers; it is difficult for humans to use. For the convenience of humans, decimal numbers are used when configuring the IP address of a network host. To represent an IP address with decimal numbers, the 32 binary

Table 3.7 Number of Networks and Hosts Identified by Each Class

CLASS	NUMBER OF NETWORKS	NUMBER OF HOSTS
Class A	$2^7 = 128$	$2^{24} = 16,777,216$
Class B	$2^{14} = 16,384$	$2^{16} = 65,536$
Class C	$2^{21} = 2,097,152$	$2^8 = 256$

Table 3.8 Decimal Value for Each Bit of 1 in an Octet

Octet column	7	6	5	4	3	2	1	0
Decimal value	$2^7 = 128$	$2^6 = 64$	$2^5 = 32$	$2^4 = 16$	$2^3 = 8$	$2^2 = 3$	$2^1 = 2$	$2^0 = 1$

bits are equally divided into four groups called octets. Each 8-bit octet is represented by a decimal number. An IP address can be represented with four decimal numbers such as 192.168.1.1. The decimal number for one octet is ranging from 0 to 255. The conversion of the binary octet can be done by using Table 3.8, which shows the corresponding decimal value for each bit of 1 in an octet.

As an example, let us consider converting the binary octet 10110011 in an octet to a decimal number. To do so, let us multiply the binary value with its corresponding decimal value as follows. Then, sum the products to get the corresponding decimal value:

$$1 \times 2^7 + 0 \times 2^6 + 1 \times 2^5 + 1 \times 2^4 + 0 \times 2^3 + 0 \times 2^2 + 1 \times 2^1 + 1 \times 2^0$$

$$= 128 + 0 + 32 + 16 + 0 + 0 + 2 + 1$$

$$= 179$$

The largest binary value in an octet is 1111111. By using Table 3.8, we can find that the corresponding decimal value is 255. That is, the decimal value for an octet cannot go beyond 255. The smallest binary value in an octet is 00000000. Based on Table 3.8, we have the corresponding decimal value 0.

By using a decimal number to represent an octet, a 32-bit IP address can be represented by four decimal numbers separated by three dots. Table 3.9 gives some examples of IP addresses in both binary numbers and decimal numbers.

For Class A IP addresses, the first decimal number is used to identify networks. Since seven binary digits in a Class A IP address are used to identify networks, the range of 7-bit binary numbers is from 0000000 to 1111111, which has the range from 0 to 127 in decimal numbers.

Table 3.9 Binary and Decimal Representations of IP Addresses

32-BIT BINARY IP ADDRESS	DECIMAL IP ADDRESS
00001010 00010000 00000000 00000000	10.16.0. 0
10101100 00000100 10011011 00000110	172.4.155.6
11000000 10101000 00010000 00000001	192.168.16.1

Table 3.10   Range of Decimal Values of First Number

CLASS	RANGE OF VALUES IN THE FIRST NUMBER
Class A	0–127
Class B	128–191
Class C	192–223

Similarly, the first octet in Class B IP addresses has six binary digits available for network identification. Therefore, the six digits range from 000000 to 111111 in binary. In decimal numbers, the corresponding range is from 0 to 64. Thus, following the decimal numbers used by Class A IP addresses, the first decimal number in a Class B IP address has the range from 128 to 191.

In Class C, the first octet has five binary digits ranging from 00000 and 11111. In decimal numbers, the corresponding range is from 0 to 32. Similarly, the first decimal number in a Class C IP address has the range between 192 and 223. Table 3.10 lists the range of decimal values used by the first number of an IP address for each class.

By looking at the first decimal number in the IP address, we can easily identify the class the IP address belongs to. For example, we can easily tell the IP address 192.168.1.16 is a Class C IP address, and 10.4.155.0 is a Class A IP address.

3.3.3.2 Special IP Addresses   In IPv4, some of the IP addresses are reserved for special purposes. These special IP addresses are for network IDs, broadcasting, loopback IP addresses for testing, and computer IP addresses for booting computers. These special IP addresses should not be assigned to regular network hosts.

For a Class A IP address, the network ID is formed by setting all the digits in the suffix to 0 and keeping the prefix unchanged. For example, for the Class A IP address 10.1.1.11, its network ID is 10.0.0.0. Similarly, network IDs for Class B and Class C IP addresses are formed by keeping the digits in the prefix unchanged and setting the digits in the suffix to 0. Table 3.11 illustrates the network IDs for Class A, Class B, and Class C IP addresses.

A network ID is used by a router to identify a destination network for data delivery. It should not be assigned to a regular network host. Although there is a nice pattern to figure out the network ID for class A, Class B, and Class networks, in general, network IDs of subnets do not follow the nice pattern shown in Table 3.11. Many network IDs of subnets look like IP addresses used by network hosts. When dealing with the network ID of a subnet, extra caution is needed for not assigning the network

Table 3.11   Network IP Addresses

CLASS	IP ADDRESS	NETWORK IP ADDRESS
Class A	10.2.123.101	10.0.0.0
Class B	172.168.62.201	172.168.0.0
Class C	192.168.2.6	192.168.2.0

ID of a subnet to a regular host. Later, the subnetting of Class A, Class B, and Class C will be introduced.

Broadcasting is a process to send a message to all the hosts in a network. Broadcasting can be used to find a network host, which provides some services. To broadcast to a specific network, a dedicated broadcast IP address is used. For the three primary classes, broadcast IP addresses can be formed by keeping the digits in the prefix unchanged and filling the suffix with the number 255. The decimal number 255 represents an octet with all its binary values as 1. If the broadcast IP address has no specified network ID in the prefix and instead it has 255 for both the prefix and suffix, the message is broadcasted to the local network. Table 3.12 shows how these broadcast IP addresses are formed.

Like network IDs, broadcast IP addresses should not be assigned to a regular host. The broadcast IP address pattern shown in Table 3.12 only applies to IP addresses in the three primary classes. For the subnets of the primary classes, the broadcast IP addresses may not follow the pattern shown in Table 3.12.

During a computer's startup process, the computer uses the local broadcast IP address 255.255.255.255 to find the network services on the local network. To communicate with other hosts on the network, a source IP address needs to be specified. During the startup process, the computer does not know its own IP address yet. In this case, the IP address 0.0.0.0 is assigned to "this" computer so that the computer can complete its startup process. When used in a routing table, 0.0.0.0 represents "this" network.

For testing network-based application software, it usually requires two computers; one is used as the client and the other is used as the server. However, by using a specially assigned loopback IP address, the test can be done on a single computer. The loopback IP address starts with the number 127. For example, the commonly used first loopback IP address is 127.0.0.1. The loopback IP address has a reserved name called localhost. When testing the default web page on a computer, one can enter the URL http://localhost in the web browser. The word localhost is then translated to 127.0.0.1. The user should be able to see the computer's default web page displayed on screen.

A computer can be configured to receive an automatically assigned IP address from a DHCP server. Sometimes, due to network or DHCP server problems, the computer may not be able to obtain an IP address from the DHCP server. In such a case, the computer will be automatically assigned an Automatic Private IP Addressing

Table 3.12 Broadcast IP Addresses

CLASS	IP ADDRESS	BROADCAST IP ADDRESS
Class A	10.2.123.101	10.255.255.255
Class B	172.168.62.201	172.168.255.255
Class C	192.168.2.6	192.168.2.255
Local	—	255.255.255.255

(APIPA) IP address. APIPA includes IP addresses ranging from 169.254.0.1 to 169.254.255.254. Since APIPA IP addresses have a different network ID from the local network, they cannot be used for data communication on the local network. The APIPA IP addresses are also not recognizable on the Internet. Once the network or DHCP server problem is fixed, the APIPA IP addresses will be automatically replaced by the dynamic IP addresses provided by the DHCP server.

Like network ID and broadcast IP addresses, none of the special IP addresses should be assigned to regular hosts. Also, each type of the special IP addresses is designed to accomplish a special task. One type of special IP address cannot be used to accomplish other tasks.

3.3.3.3 Private and Public IP Addressing   To be able to communicate on the Internet, the IP addresses assigned to network hosts should be publically accessible. This type of IP address is known as the public IP address. On the other hand, many institutions have their own Intranets, which are not supposed to be accessible to the public. In such a case, some of the IP addresses are reserved for the internal network. This type of IP address is known as the private IP address. Three blocks of IP addresses are reserved as private IP addresses for internal use. Table 3.13 lists the three blocks of private IP addresses.

Private IP addresses are not recognized on the Internet. Therefore, they can be used inside a company without the company worrying about its private IP addresses conflicting with those of other companies. For example, in a home network, 192.168.1.0 is the commonly used network ID. It does not conflict with the network ID 192.168.1.0 used in another student's home network. For a computer with a private IP address on a home network to access the Internet, the private IP address needs to be translated to the public IP address assigned by an ISP. Network Address Translation (NAT) is the technology to accomplish this task.

The preceding discussions are based on IPv4. IPv6 will be covered in the next section.

3.3.3.4 IPv6 IP Addressing   As mentioned previously, IPv4 is about to run out IP addresses for network hosts on the Internet. To solve the problem, IPv6 is developed. An IP address in IPv6 is a unique 128-bit binary number. IPv6 supports 2^{128} distinguished IP addresses, which are such a large number so that we do not need to worry about running out of IP addresses in many generations to come.

Table 3.13 Private IP Addresses

BLOCK	BLOCK RANGE	NUMBER OF AVAILABLE IP ADDRESSES
Class A Block	10.0.0.0–10.255.255.255	16,777,216
Class B Block	172.16.0.0–172.31.255.255	1,048,576
Class C Block	192.168.0.0–192.168.255.255	65,536

Since an IP address in IPv6 has 128 binary bits, it is not convenient to represent such a large number even with decimal numbers. Therefore, an IPv6 IP address is represented with eight hexadecimal numbers separated by the character ":". For example, an IPv6 IP address may look like

49AB: 84FE:0000:0000:0000:0000:0000:12CB

Even represented in the hexadecimal system, an IPv6 IP address is still not convenient to use. To further simplify the IPv6 IP address, the consecutive zero sets can be compressed as follows:

43AC:84EF::12CB

In addition to providing more IP addresses, IPv6 has other desired features designed for the Internet. The following are some of the IPv6 features:

- IPv6 has a flexible header. The header can minimize header overhead and increase the size of payload.
- IPv6 supports hierarchical addressing and routing infrastructure, which can reduce the traffic on backbone routers.
- IPv6 does not support broadcasting, which may make a network less efficient. Instead, it supports the more efficient multicast, unicast, and anycast.
- For transmitting multimedia content, IPv6 can establish a high-quality path between the sender and receiver.
- IPv6 has the built-in encryption service for data security.

An IPv6 packet has a 40-byte base header. Additional extension headers can be added when additional protocols are used in data communication. For example, to transmit TCP data, IPv6 simply adds a TCP header to the base header as shown in Figure 3.18. With such a flexible header structure, IPv6 simply adds one or more extension headers to support new features once they become available.

IPv6 organizes IP addresses into a hierarchical system to enhance routing and scaling. Similar to a telephone number system that starts with the country code, area code, prefix, and line number, an IPv6 address has three levels, public topology, site topology, and interface identifier as shown in Figure 3.19.

Base header 40 bytes	Optional extension header 1	...	Optional extension header N	Payload

Figure 3.18 Flexible IPv6 header structure.

Public topology	Site topology	Interface identifier
48 bits Global routing prefix	16 bits Subnet ID	64 bits Interface ID

Figure 3.19 Three-level hierarchical system.

- Public Topology: The leftmost 48-bit section of an IPv6 IP address is the public topology. The public topology is assigned by ISPs to provide access to the IPv6 Internet.
- Site Topology: The 16-bit section is the site topology. The site topology is used to identify the subnets within an organization.
- Interface Identifier: The 64-bit section is the interface identifier, which identifies an NIC. The interface identifier can be either automatically assigned based on the NIC's hardware address or manually configured by the user.

The three-level hierarchical system makes IP addressing more efficient and can reduce the latency for routing lookup.

In IPv6, instead of using broadcasting, IPv6 uses three types of addresses: unicast, multicast, and anycast.

3.3.3.4.1 Unicast IP Addresses   Unicast IP addresses are used for individual network hosts in a network. There are five types of unicast IP addresses, the global unicast address, link-local address, site-local address, special address, and compatibility address.

Like the public IP addresses in IPv4, the global unicast addresses in IPv6 are IPv6 Internet accessible IP addresses. For a unicast IP address, the three-level hierarchical system can be specified as shown in Figure 3.20.

The prefix code 001 is used to indicate that the IP address is a global unicast address. For a global unicast address, the size of the global routing prefix is 45 bits. It has 16 bits for the subnet ID, and 64 bits for the interface identifier.

Similar to the APIPA IP addresses in IPv4, the link-local addresses in IPv6 are structured as shown in Figure 3.21. In case a host is not assigned an IP manually or by DHCP, a link-local address is assigned to the network host.

Similar to the private addresses in IPv4, the site-local addresses in IPv6 are used for the Intranet and are not accessible on the Internet. The site-local addresses can also be used in the subnets of an internal network. The structure of a site-local address is given in Figure 3.22.

	Public topology	Site topology	Interface identifier
001	45 bits Global routing prefix	16 bits Subnet ID	64 bits Interface ID

Figure 3.20   Global unicast hierarchical system.

1111 1110 10	54 zero bits 0000000000...0000000000	64 bits Interface ID

Figure 3.21   Link-local address structure.

1111 1110 11	54 zero bits 0000000000...0000000000	64 bits Interface ID

Figure 3.22 Site-local address structure.

Like the special IP addresses in IPv4, IPv6 reserves some special addresses including the loopback address and unspecified address.

- Loopback Address: Similar to the loopback address in IPv4, the IPv6 loopback address looks like ::1 or 0:0:0:0:0:0:0:1.
- Unspecified Address: Similar to the IP address 0.0.0.0 in IPv4 used for "this" computer, the IPv6 unspecified address looks like :: or 0:0:0:0:0:0:0:0.

To help the migration from IPv4 to IPv6, the compatibility addresses are compatible with both IPv4 and IPv6 standards. Table 3.14 lists some types of compatibility addresses.

With these compatibility addresses, IPv6 can work with the existing IPv4 Internet without reconfiguration.

3.3.3.4.2 Multicast The communication between a single sender and multiple receivers is called multicast. The group of receivers can be identified by a multicast address. Hosts can join or leave a multicast group at any time. In IPv6, the packet in the multicast traffic use the multicast address as its destination address. The packet is delivered to all the hosts identified by the multicast address. The structure of a multicast address is shown in Figure 3.23.

The 4-bit flag field in Figure 3.23 defines the transient flag or T flag. The T flag can be set to 0, which indicates that the multicast address is assigned by the Internet Assigned Numbers Authority (IANA) permanently. When the T flag is set to 1, it

Table 3.14 Compatibility Addresses

ADDRESS NAME	EXPRESSION	USAGE
IPv4 Compatible Address	0:0:0:0:0:0:w.x.y.z or ::w.x.y.z	Used by IPv6 or IPv4 hosts to communicate with the IPv4 router. w.x.y.z is the 32-bit IPv4 address.
IPv4-Mapped Address	0:0:0:0:0:FFFF:w.x.y.z or ::FFFF:w.x.y.z	Used internally to represent IPv4 addresses to IPv6 applications. w.x.y.z is the 32-bit IPv4 address.
6 to 4 Address	2002:wwxx:yyzz:[subnetId]: [interfaceId]	Allow IPv6 packets to be transmitted over an IPv4 network. wwxx:yyzz is the embedded IPv4 address in the HEX format.
ISATAP Address	::0:5EFE:w.x.y.z	Used by two IPv6 or IPv4 hosts to communicate over an IPv4 intranet. w.x.y.z is the 32-bit IPv4 address.
Teredo Address	2001:0000:[serverId]:[flag]:[UDP port number]:[public IPv4 address]	Used by IPv6/IPv4 hosts located behind IPv4 NAT devices. All values are in the HEX format.

1111 1111	4 bits	4 bits	112 bits
	Flag	Scope	Mulitcast group address

Figure 3.23   Multicast addresses structure.

Table 3.15   Scope Definitions

SCOPE VALUE	DEFINITION
1	Node-local scope
2	Link-local scope
5	Site-local scope
8	Organization-local scope
14	Global scope

indicates that the multicast address is assigned temporarily by the IANA. The 4-bit scope field defines the scope that a multicast address can cover. The commonly defined scope values are defined in Table 3.15.

There are several special multicast group addresses. For example, the multicast group address FF02:0:0:0:0:0:1 is the multicast address for "all hosts" in the link-local scope and FF05:0:0:0:0:0:2 is the multicast address for "all routers" in the site-local scope.

3.3.3.4.3 Anycast   The communication between any sender and one of the receivers in a group of hosts is called anycast. Anycast is used in a situation where each of the hosts in the group can handle the job equally well and the sender has no preference on which host to handle the task. In anycast, the sender selects the host that is the easiest to reach.

As the destination address in a packet, the anycast address is often assigned to a router, which serves as the gateway of a group. The anycast address is chosen from the unicast address pool. When a unicast address is assigned to a group of devices, the anycast address is created automatically.

3.3.4 Subnets

The process of dividing a network into several smaller networks is called subnetting. In a subnetting process, a physical network can be logically divided into logical units called subnets. Within a subnet, all the hosts have the same network ID and they can directly communicate with each other. The local broadcasting is limited to the subnet. There are several reasons for us to divide a network into subnets.

3.3.4.1 Reasons for Using Subnets   As previously mentioned, a network in Class A can have as many as 16,777,216 hosts, a Class B network can have as many as 65,536 hosts, and a Class C network can have as many as 256 hosts. In practice, the size of a network may vary depending on its required size. For example, a network has 5500 hosts, which is larger than the size of a Class C network and is much less than the size of a Class B network. In such a case, if the company uses a Class B network, there will be about 60,000 IP addresses unused. Therefore, subnets are often used to reduce the number of unused IP addresses.

In addition to reducing unused IP addresses, there are more reasons to use subnets. Subnets can also be used to improve network performance. The chances of collisions can be increased dramatically when a network has a large number of hosts. The use of subnets can restrict the network traffic in each subnet, which can prevent a packet from running into the packets in other subnets. Broadcasting is a process of sending packets to every host in a network. A broadcasting process will generate a large amount of network traffic, especially when a network has a large number of hosts. As subnetting reduces the number of hosts in a subnet, the broadcasting caused network traffic can be reduced significantly.

Another usage of subnets is to strengthen the network security control. As subnetting divides a network into several smaller subnets, if a security problem happens in one subnet, it can be limited to the local subnet. In such a way, only the hosts in the local subnet will be affected by the security problem.

The router that connects two subnets can also be configured to control network traffic. The router can be configured to block certain protocols or certain hosts from accessing certain networks. In such a way, subnets can be used to protect a group of hosts from being hacked.

A subnet can be further divided into several smaller subnets. Such a hierarchical structure can be used by large organizations to match their organization's infrastructure. A large company may be structured with the multiple sites, buildings, departments, and offices. The company's network can be designed according to the company's physical and geological structures. In such a case, a hierarchical subnet structure can be used to implement the network structure at the site, building, department, and office levels.

By using subnets, a set of computers on the network at home can share one public IP address to access the Internet. By sharing the public IP address, the home computers do not have to pay the ISP for multiple public IP addresses.

Subnetting requires some calculation on the subnet IP address, subnet ID, and the size of the subnet. During the subnetting process, the size of the prefix and suffix in the IP address will be recalculated. It also needs to reconfigure the networks so that the routers are able to recognize the new subnets. The following are some of the topics related to subnet calculation. Let us start with subnet masks, which are used in the calculation of subnets.

3.3.4.2 Subnet Masks   A subnet mask is a string of 32-bit binary code used to determine the prefix and suffix in an IP address. Table 3.16 shows examples of binary and decimal subnet masks.

Table 3.16   Examples of Subnet Masks

BINARY SUBNET MASK	DECIMAL SUBNET MASK
11111111 00000000 00000000 00000000	255.0.0.0
11111111 11111111 00000000 00000000	255.255.0.0
11111111 11111111 11111111 00000000	255.255.255.0
11111111 11111111 11110000 00000000	255.255.240.0
11111111 11111111 11111111 11111000	255.255.255.248

Table 3.17   Invalid Subnet Masks

BINARY	DECIMAL
11111111 00000001 00000101 00000000	255.1.5.0
11111111 11111110 11110000 00000000	255.254.240.0
10000000 00000111 11111111 00000000	128.7.255.0
11111111 11111111 11111111 11100010	255.255.255.226

Table 3.18   Subnet Masks for Primary Classes

CLASS	BINARY SUBNET MASK	DECIMAL SUBNET MASK
Class A	11111111 00000000 00000000 00000000	255.0.0.0
Class B	11111111 11111111 00000000 00000000	255.255.0.0
Class C	11111111 11111111 11111111 00000000	255.255.255.0

The leftmost bits in a subnet mask must be a sequence of consecutive 1s, which are used to define the prefix section of an IP address. The rightmost bits must be consecutive 0s, which are used to define the suffix of an IP address. Table 3.17 gives a few examples of invalid subnet masks.

As mentioned earlier that the consecutive 1s in a subnet mask are used to define the prefix section, the subnet masks for the primary Class A, Class B, and Class C are defined in Table 3.18. Since Class A uses the first octet as the prefix, the subnet mask for Class A sets all the bits of the first octet to 1 and sets the rest of the bits to 0 to form the suffix section. Similarly, the subnet mask for Class B sets all the bits in the first two octets to 1, and the subnet mask for Class C sets all the bits in first three octets to 1.

For other subnets of the primary class networks, the subnet masks have no nice pattern as shown in Table 3.18. It often requires the user to manually calculate the subnet mask so that the prefix section and the suffix section are properly defined. The number of bits in the suffix section decides the maximum numbers of hosts in a subnet. For example, to support a subnet that is able to host 1700 computers and other network devices, the suffix needs to have 11 bits so that it can have $2^{11} = 2048$ hosts in the subnet. This means that the subnet mask has eleven 0s in the suffix section as shown in Table 3.19.

Subnet masks can be used to identify network IDs through the AND operation on binary numbers. Table 3.20 illustrates how the AND operation is performed.

Table 3.19   Subnet Mask for Subnet with Maximum of 2048 Hosts

BINARY	DECIMAL
11111111 11111111 11111000 00000000	255.255.248.0

Table 3.20   AND Operation

BIT 1	BIT 2	AND OUTPUT
0	0	0
0	1	0
1	0	0
1	1	1

Table 3.21   Extracting Network ID with Subnet Mask and AND Operation

	BINARY	DECIMAL
IP Address	11000000 10101000 00000010 00001010	192.168.2.10
Subnet Mask	11111111 11111111 11111111 00000000	255.255.255.0
AND Result	11000000 10101000 00000010 00000000	192.168.2.0

That is, 0 AND 0 = 0, 0 AND 1 = 0, 1 AND 0 = 0, or 1 AND 1 = 1. With the AND operation, one can extract the network ID out of an IP address.

The following is an example that is used to show how to get the network ID from a given IP address by using the subnet mask. Suppose that the Class C IP address is 192.168.2.10 and the subnet mask is 255.255.255.0. The result of the AND operation is given in Table 3.21.

As expected, the result of the AND operation is 192.168.2.0, which is the network ID for the IP address 192.168.2.10. From Table 3.21, we can see that, if any binary bit is ANDed with a 1 bit, the result will be the original bit unchanged. Any bits ANDed with 0-bit digits will be changed to 0. This is how the network ID is extracted from an IP address.

3.3.4.3 Network Subnetting   To subnet a network in Class A, Class B, or Class C, one needs to turn some of the 0-bit digits in a subnet mask into 1-bit digits. By doing so, the number of 0-bit digits is reduced so that there will be fewer hosts in each subnet. Also, as the number of 1-bit digits is increased in the subnet mask, there will be more subnets to be created. The following are some of the examples to demonstrate the subnetting process.

Example 3.1

Suppose that you have a Class B network with the network ID 172.10.0.0. You want to divide this Class B network into eight possible subnets. The subnetting process is summarized in Table 3.22.

Table 3.22   Subnetting Class B Network

	BINARY	DECIMAL
Original Network ID	10101100 00001010 00000000 00000000	172.10.0.0
Original Subnet Mask	11111111 11111111 00000000 00000000	255.255.0.0
New Subnet Mask	11111111 11111111 11100000 00000000	255.255.224.0
New Subnet IDs	10101100 00001010 00000000 00000000	172.10.0.0
	10101100 00001010 00100000 00000000	172.10.32.0
	10101100 00001010 01000000 00000000	172.10.64.0
	10101100 00001010 01100000 00000000	172.10.96.0
	10101100 00001010 10000000 00000000	172.10.128.0
	10101100 00001010 10100000 00000000	172.10.160.0
	10101100 00001010 11000000 00000000	172.10.192.0
	10101100 00001010 11100000 00000000	172.10.224.0

As shown in Table 3.22, to divide a Class B network into eight possible subnets, we need to turn the first three leftmost zeros in the suffix to three ones. The reason to turn the three 0-bit digits to 1-bit digits is that $8 = 2^3$. The exponential value is the number of bits that should be altered.

Notice that there will be eight possible subnets. The word possible means that we may not have all 8 subnets. In the classful IPv4 IP address system, the first subnet ID 172.10.0.0 and the last subnet ID 172.10.224.0 are reserved to avoid the conflict with the original network ID and broadcast IP address. These two subnet IDs should not be assigned to any of the subnets. In such a case, only six subnets are actually available. Therefore, the formula

$$2^n - 2$$

is often used to calculate the number of subnets; here n is the number of 0-bit digits, which are changed to 1-bit digits. Since n = 3 in our example, then $2^3 - 2 = 6$ subnets are actually formed for the classful IPv4 network.

The formula $2^n - 2$ is also used to calculate the number of hosts in each subnet. The number n is the number of zeros in the new subnet mask. In our example, the new subnet mask has 13 zeros. Therefore, the number of hosts in each subnet is

$$2^{13} - 2 = 8190$$

Example 3.2

For a given IP address 192.168.2.130 and the subnet mask 255.255.255.224, determine the network ID and broadcast IP address for the subnet that contains the given IP address. Also, find how many subnets and how many hosts in each subnet can be specified by the subnet mask 255.255.255.224.

Since the IP address 192.168.2.130 starts with the decimal number 192, this IP address belongs to Class C. The subnet mask for the primary Class C network has all the 0s in the fourth octet. Therefore, some of the 0-bit digits in the fourth octet of the subnet mask should be changed to 1-bit digits. The subnetting process is summarized in Table 3.23.

Table 3.23 Subnet Identified by the Fourth Octet

	BINARY	DECIMAL
IP Address	11000000 10101000 00000010 10000010	192.168.2.130
Subnet Mask	11111111 11111111 11111111 11100000	255.255.255.224
Subnet ID	11000000 10101000 00000010 10000000	192.168.2.128
Broadcast	11000000 10101000 00000010 10011111	192.168.2.159

From the subnet mask, we can see that the rightmost 5 bits are 0-bit digits; this means that the number of hosts in each subnet is

$$2^5 - 2 = 30$$

Compared with the standard Class C subnet mask, the given subnet mask has three 1-bit digits in the last octet, the number of subnets can be calculated with the following formula:

$$2^3 - 2 = 6$$

To calculate the subnet ID for the subnet that contains the given IP address 192.168.2.130, one can AND the IP address with the subnet mask. The result of the IP address ANDing the subnet mask is

$$11000000 \quad 10101000 \quad 00000010 \quad 10000010$$

$$\text{AND } 11111111 \quad 11111111 \quad 11111111 \quad 11100000$$

$$\overline{11000000 \quad 10101000 \quad 00000010 \quad 10000000}$$

When representing the AND result in decimal, the ID of the subnet that contains the IP address 192.168.1.131 is 192.168.1.128.

Broadcasting uses the IP address whose bits in the suffix are all 1-bit digits. Since the rightmost 5 bits belong to the suffix, we then have the following broadcast IP address in binary:

$$11000000 \ 10101000 \ 00000010 \ 10011111$$

The corresponding decimal broadcast IP address is 192.168.1.159.

Note that the subnet ID 192.168.2.128 does not have the nice pattern shown in Table 3.20, where a network ID has all its digits corresponding to the suffix set to zero. Similarly, the broadcast IP address 192.168.1.159 does not necessarily have all the bits corresponding to the suffix set to 1-bit digits or 255 in decimal.

Example 3.3

For a given IP address 172.16.9.170 and the subnet mask 255.255.252.0, determine the network ID and broadcast IP address for the subnet that contains the given IP address. Also, find how many subnets and how many hosts in each subnet can be specified by the subnet mask 255.255.252.0.

Since the IP address 172.16.9.170 starts with the decimal number 172, it belongs to Class B. The subnet mask for the primary Class B network has all the 0s in the third and fourth octets. Therefore, some of the 0-bit digits in the third octet of the

Table 3.24   Subnet Identified by Third Octet

	BINARY	DECIMAL
IP Address	10101100 00010000 00001001 10101010	172.16.9.170
Subnet Mask	11111111 11111111 11111100 00000000	255.255.252.0
Subnet ID	10101100 00010000 00001000 00000000	172.16.8.0
Broadcast	10101100 00010000 00001011 11111111	172.16.11.255

subnet mask should be changed to 1-bit digits. The subnetting process is summarized in Table 3.24.

From the subnet mask, we can see that the rightmost 10 bits are 0-bit digits; this means that the number of hosts in each subnet is

$$2^{10} - 2 = 1022$$

Compared with the standard Class B subnet mask, there are six 0-bit digits in the third octet that are turned into 1-bit digits; the number of subnets can be calculated with the following formula:

$$2^6 - 2 = 62$$

To calculate the subnet ID for the subnet that contains the given IP address 172.16.9.170, you may need to AND the IP address with the subnet mask just like what you did in the previous example. The result of the IP address ANDing the subnet mask is as follows:

$$10101100 \quad 00010000 \ 00001001 \quad 10101010$$
$$\text{AND } 11111111 \quad 11111111 \quad 11111100 \quad 00000000$$
$$\overline{}$$
$$10101100 \quad 00010000 \ 00001000 \quad 00000000$$

Converting the preceding result to a decimal number, we have 172.16.8.0 as the ID of the subnet that contains the IP address 172.16.9.170.

To obtain the broadcast IP address, we need to change all the bits in the suffix of the given IP address to 1-bit digits. Since the rightmost 10 bits belong to the suffix, we then have the following broadcast IP address in binary:

$$10101100 \ 00010000 \ 00001011 \ 11111111$$

The corresponding decimal broadcast IP address is 172.16.11.255.

Example 3.4

For a given IP address 10.33.1.11 and the subnet mask 255.224.0.0, determine the network ID and broadcast IP address for the subnet that contains the given IP address. Also, find how many subnets and how many hosts in each subnet can be specified by the subnet mask 255.224.0.0. Since the IP address 10.33.1.11 starts with the decimal number 10, it belongs to Class A. The subnetting process will create several subnets under a standard Class A network. Therefore, some of the 0-bit digits in the second octet of the standard Class A subnet mask will be changed to 1-bit digits. The subnetting process is summarized in Table 3.25.

Table 3.25 Subnet Identified by Second Octet

	BINARY	DECIMAL
IP Address	00001010 00100011 00000011 00001010	10.35.3.10
Subnet Mask	11111111 11100000 00000000 00000000	255.224.0.0
Subnet ID	00001010 00100000 00000000 00000000	10.32.0.0
Broadcasting	00001010 00111111 11111111 11111111	10.63.255.255

From the subnet mask, we can see that the rightmost 21 bits are 0-bit digits; this means that the number of hosts in each subnet is as follows:

$$2^{21} - 2 = 2097150$$

Compared with the standard Class A subnet mask, there are three 1-bit digits in the second octet; the number of subnets can be calculated with the following formula:

$$2^3 - 2 = 6$$

To calculate the subnet ID for the subnet that contains the given IP address 10.35.3.10, you may need to AND the IP address with the subnet mask just like what you did in the previous examples. The result of the IP address ANDing the subnet mask is as follows:

$$00001010 \quad 00100011 \quad 00000011 \quad 00001010$$

$$AND \; 11111111 \quad 11100000 \quad 00000000 \quad 00000000$$

$$00001010 \quad 00100000 \quad 00000000 \quad 00000000$$

Converting the preceding result to a decimal number, we have 10.32.0.0 as the ID of the subnet that contains the IP address 10.35.3.10.

To obtain the broadcast IP address, we need to change all the bits in the suffix of the given IP address to 1-bit digits. Since the rightmost 21 bits belong to the suffix, we then have the following broadcast IP address in binary:

$$00001010 \; 00111111 \; 11111111 \; 11111111$$

The corresponding decimal broadcast IP address is 10.63.255.255.

Example 3.5

Create a subnet under a standard Class B network so that the subnet is large enough to include both the IP addresses 172.21.24.17 and 172.21.31.224.

Since the IP address 172.21.21.17 starts with the decimal number 172, it belongs to Class B. To create subnets under a primary Class B network, some of the 0-bit digits in the third octet of the Class B subnet mask should be converted to 1-bit digits. On the other hand, the third octet should have enough 0-bit digits so that the IP addresses 172.21.24.17 and 172.21.31.224 are included in the same subnet. The difference between 31 and 24 is 7. We need to determine the number of 0-bit digits in the third octet to cover the difference in the third octet of the two IP addresses 172.21.24.17 and 172.21.31.224. Since $2^3 = 8 > 7$, in the subnet mask, we need to assign three 0-bit digits to the third octet. The subnetting process is summarized in Table 3.26.

Table 3.26   Subnet Including Both 172.21.24.17 and 172.21.31.224

	BINARY	DECIMAL
IP Address	10101100 00010101 00011000 00010001	172.21.24.17
IP Address	10101100 00010101 00011111 11100000	172.21.31.224
Subnet Mask	11111111 11111111 11111000 00000000	255.255.248.0
Subnet ID	10101100 00010101 00011000 00000000	172.21.24.0

When ANDing both the IP addresses

$$10101100\ 00010101\ 00011000\ 00010001$$

$$10101100\ 00010101\ 00011111\ 11100000$$

with the subnet mask

$$11111111\ 11111111\ 11111000\ 00000000$$

we have the same subnet ID:

$$10101100\ 00010101\ 00011000\ 00000000$$

This means that both the IP addresses 172.21.24.17 and 172.21.31.224 belong to the same subnet with the network ID 172.21.24.0.

Example 3.6

If you want to create a subnet that includes the IP address 192.21.9.33 with the subnet mask 255.255.255.224, what is the range of IP addresses in the subnet?
    Converting the IP address 192.21.9.33 to the binary format, we have

$$11000000\ 00010101\ 00001001\ 00100001$$

The binary representation of the subnet mask 255.255.255.224 is

$$11111111\ 11111111\ 11111111\ 11100000$$

AND the IP address with the subnet mask, we have

$$11000000\ 00010101\ 00001001\ 00100001$$
$$\text{AND } 11111111\quad 11111111\quad 11111111\quad 11100000$$
$$\overline{\hspace{6cm}}$$
$$11000000\ 00010101\ 00001001\ 00100000$$

Thus the subnet ID is

$$11000000\ 00010101\ 00001001\ 00100000$$

The subnet ID is the first IP address included in the subnet. The decimal representation of the subnet ID is 192.21.9.32. The fact that there are five 0-bit digits in the fourth octet of the subnet mask indicates that there are $2^5 = 32$ values in the third octet that can be used for hosts. Starting with the number 32, count 32 times, we have the last number as 63. Thus, the range for the fourth octet is from 32 to 63. In a subnet, the first IP address is the network ID and the last IP address is the broadcast IP address. In our example, the binary form of the broadcast IP address is

$$11000000\ 00010101\ 00001001\ 00111111$$

The corresponding decimal broadcast IP address is 192.21.9.63. Therefore, the subnet has IP addresses ranging from 192.21.9.32 to 192.21.9.63.

3.3.4.4 Classless Inter-Domain Routing Classless Inter-Domain Routing (CIDR) is another way to allocate IP addresses for a subnet with a more flexible prefix section. The traditional Class A, Class B, and Class C use the fixed 8-bit, 16-bit, and 24-bit prefixes. As a flexible alternative, CIDR uses prefixes anywhere from 0 bit to 32 bits. That is, CIDR can define networks that may have $0-2^{32}$ hosts. By doing so, the number of hosts in a network can precisely match the need of an organization.

CIDR defines a network with the combination of an IP address and a network mask as follows:

$$xxx.xxx.xxx.xxx/N$$

The xxx.xxx.xxx.xxx is an IP address and N is the number of bits used by the prefix. For example, 10.0.0.1/24 and 192.168.2.31/28 define two networks. The first network uses a 24-bit prefix and the second one uses a 28-bit prefix. This means that the suffix in the first network has 8 bits. Therefore, the first network can have $2^8 = 256$ possible hosts. Similarly, the second network may have $2^4 = 16$ possible hosts. For an IP address, if all its bits corresponding to the suffix section are turned to 0, we have the network ID. For example, the IP address 10.0.0.1/24 has the 8-bit suffix. Therefore, by turning the value in the fourth octet to zero, we have the network ID 10.0.0.0. Similarly, if all the bits corresponding to the suffix section are turned to 1, we have the broadcast address. For example, for the IP address 10.0.0.1/24, by turning the value in the fourth octet to 255, which is 11111111 in binary, we have the broadcast address 10.0.0.255.

The network mask N is closely related to the subnet mask. For example, for the IP address 192.168.2.0 with the subnet mask 255.255.255.0 and its binary equivalent

$$11111111\ 11111111\ 11111111\ 00000000$$

which has 24 1-bit digits, the corresponding CIDR notation is 192.168.2.0/24. Conversely, one can easily find the subnet mask for a given CIDR notation. For example, for the given CIDR notation 172.5.10.17/19, the corresponding subnet mask is 255.255.224.0 with its binary equivalent

$$11111111\ 11111111\ 11100000\ 00000000$$

The number of 1-bit digits in the prefix is exactly 19.

CIDR is flexible and efficient. Therefore, network devices such as routers are built to support CIDR notations. CIDR addressing allows route aggregation, which organizes a routing table in a hierarchical way. By doing so, the routing table can be simplified by summarizing the routes across the Internet.

Activity 3.1: Implementing Simple Network

In this activity, you will connect two virtual machines in the virtual network. If you have a free trial or academic pass account on Microsoft Azure, you can make two virtual machines on the same virtual network to communicate with each other.

To use a server to host DNS or Active Directory, the server needs to be configured to have a fixed IP address. The task to retain the IP address assigned to your server can be accomplished with Microsoft Azure PowerShell:

1. Log on to the Microsoft Azure Management Portal with your user name and password.
2. Select your virtual machine **servera** and click **CONNECT**.
3. Log on to **servera** with your username and password.
4. Press the **Windows logo** key and click the **Internet Explorer** tile.
5. To start the Microsoft Web Platform Installer, browse to the following website (Microsoft/Web, Microsoft Web Platform Installer 5.0, May, 2015): http://www.microsoft.com/web/downloads/platform.aspx
6. When prompted, click Save and then click Run.
7. After the Microsoft Azure PowerShell page is opened as shown in the Figure 3.24, click the Install button.
8. Once Microsoft Azure PowerShell is installed, to view Microsoft Azure PowerShell, press the **Windows logo** key and type **Power**. You should be able to see the Microsoft Azure PowerShell tile. Right click the tile and select **Run as administrator** to open Azure PowerShell as shown in Figure 3.25.

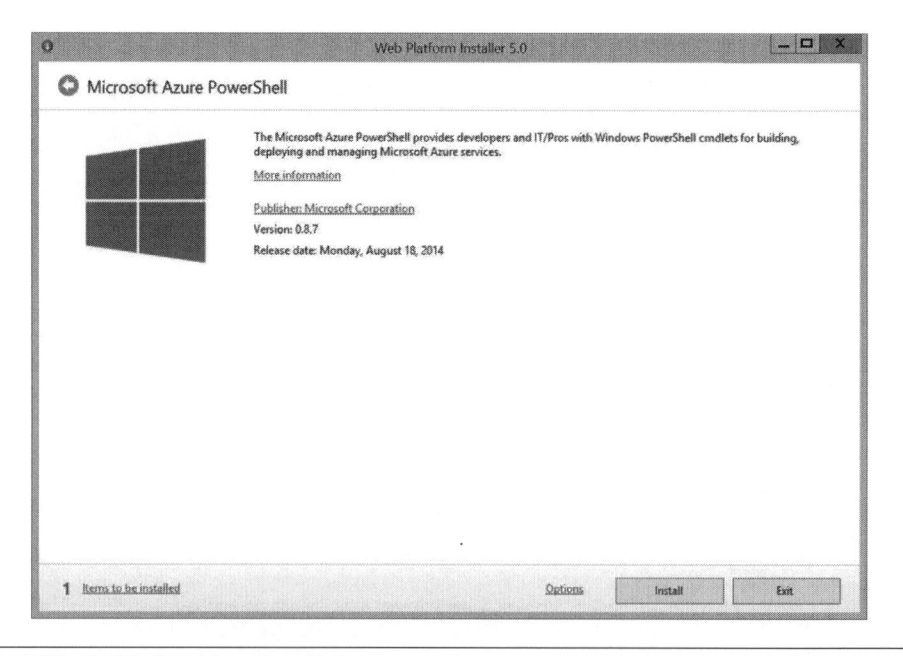

Figure 3.24   Installation of Azure PowerShell.

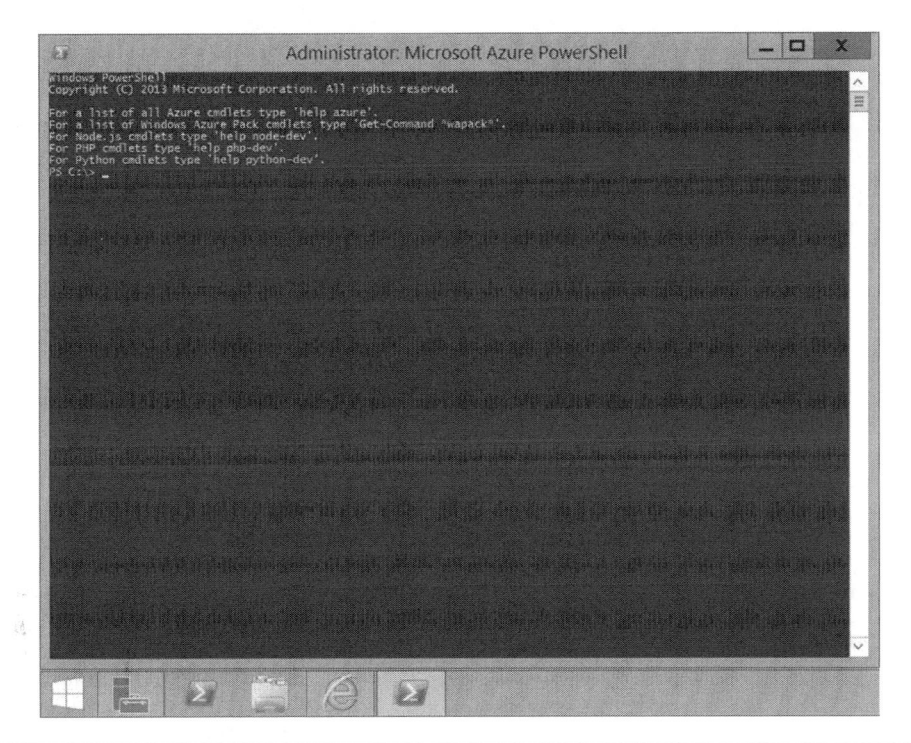

Figure 3.25 Microsoft Azure PowerShell.

9. To make your account information available in Azure PowerShell, run the following cmdlet.

```
Add-AzureAccount
```

10. When prompted, enter the email address and password used to log into the Microsoft Azure Management Portal.

11. To retain the IP address for your virtual machine servera, execute the following cmdlet.

```
Get-AzureVM -ServiceName servera78 -Name servera | Set-
AzureStaticVNetIP -IPAddress 10.0.0.4 | Update-AzureVM
```

Note that the aforementioned cmdlet should be entered as a single line in Azure PowerShell. Also, your cloud service name may be different from the one entered in this cmdlet.

12. Similarly, log on to serverb, turn off **IE Enhanced Security Configuration**, open the web browser, and configure the Internet option to enable file download.

13. In the web browser, enter the following URL (Microsoft/Web, Microsoft Web Platform Installer 5.0, May, 2015). http://www.microsoft.com/web/downloads/platform.aspx

14. **Save** and **Run** the Microsoft Web Platform Installer to install Microsoft Azure PowerShell on serverb.

15. Click the **Start** icon on Taskbar and type **Power**. Right click the tile **Microsoft Azure PowerShell** and select **Run as administrator**.

16. After Azure PowerShell is opened, enter the cmdlet:

    ```
    Add-AzureAccount
    ```

17. When prompted, enter the email address and password used to log into the Microsoft Azure Management Portal.

18. To retain the IP address for your virtual machine serverb, execute the following cmdlet.

    ```
    Get-AzureVM -ServiceName serverb78 -Name serverb | Set-
    AzureStaticVNetIP -IPAddress 10.0.0.5 | Update-AzureVM
    ```

19. Note that the aforementioned cmdlet should be entered as a single line in Azure PowerShell. Also, your cloud service name may be different from the one entered in this cmdlet.

20. To verify the connection between servera and serverb, on servera, press the **Windows logo key + r** combination. Enter **cmd** and click **OK** to open the **Command** window. Once the command prompt window is opened, enter the command:

    ```
    ipconfig
    ```

21. Record the IP address for the Ethernet 2 adapter and the IP address for the gateway as shown in Figure 3.26. For example, on this screen, you should record the IPv4 address 10.0.0.4 and the gateway IP address 10.0.0.1.

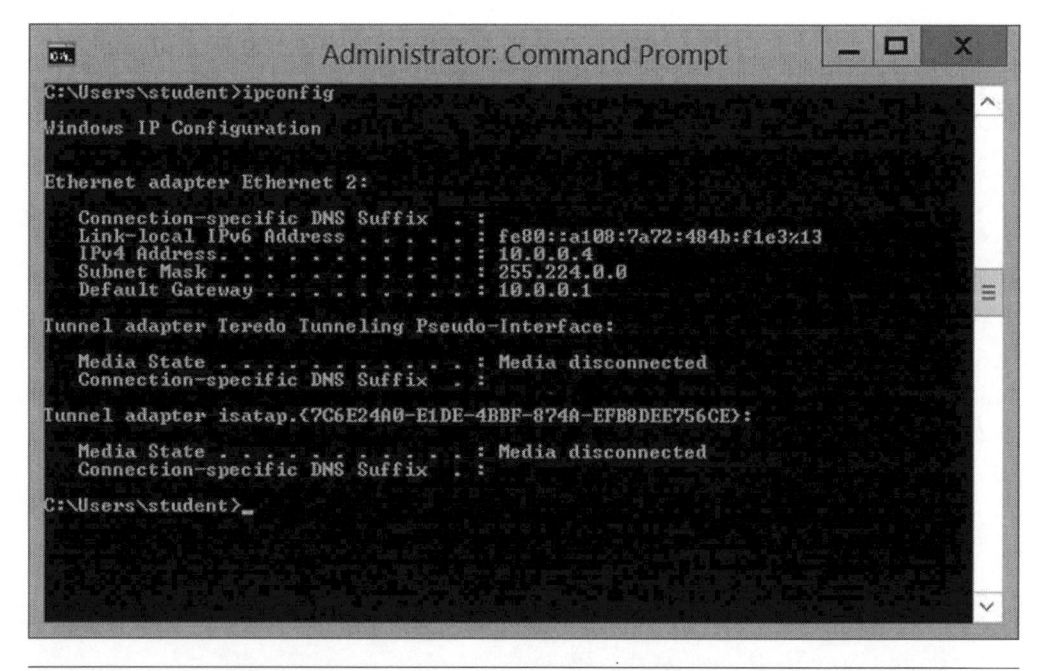

Figure 3.26 IP address of servera.

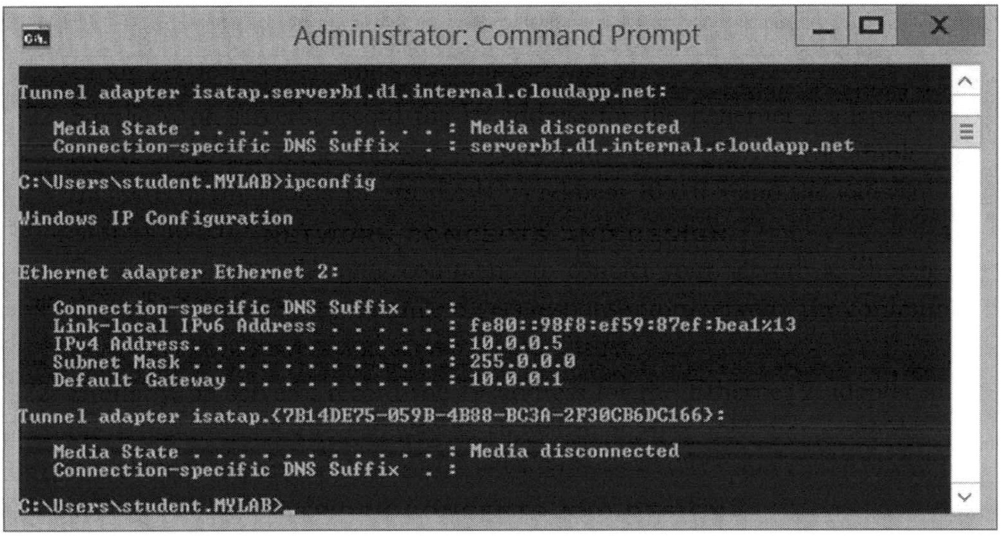

Figure 3.27   IP address of serverb.

22. Similarly, on serverb, record the IP address for the Ethernet 2 adapter and the IP address for the gateway as shown in Figure 3.27. For example, on this screen, you should record the IPv4 address 10.0.0.5 and the gateway IP address 10.0.0.1.

On servera, enter the ping command to contact your serverb as shown in Figure 3.28. If the ping command gets response from serverb, the communication between servera and serverb is established.

ping 10.0.0.5

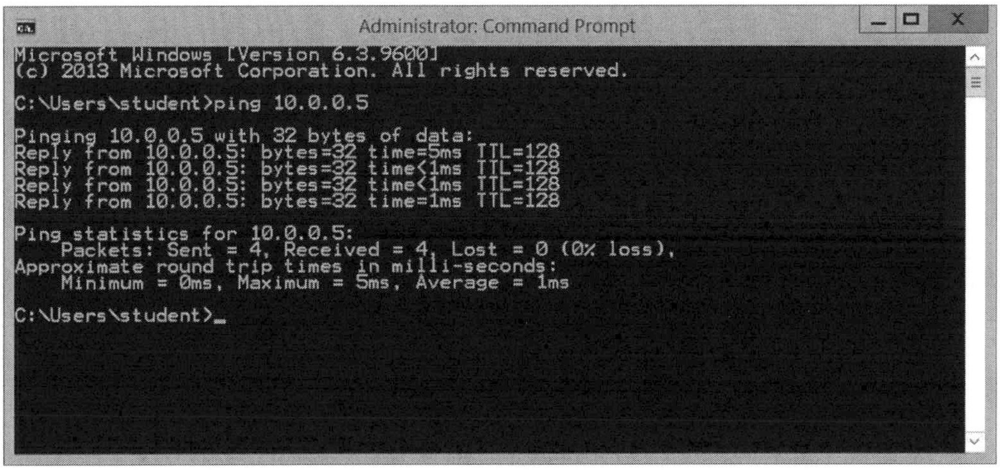

Figure 3.28   Verifying connection between servera and serverb.

So far, you have created a simple network with two virtual machines. In later chapters, more hosts will be added to the network. You will create some network services on this network. Make sure that the network is working properly before you move on to the next project.

23. In the Microsoft Azure Management Portal, shutdown both servera and serverb before exiting the Microsoft Azure Management Portal.

3.4 Summary

In this chapter, we have examined the network technology and IP addressing. The knowledge covered in this chapter prepares network developers to get ready to build a simple network. This chapter provides the information about various types of networks and explains how each type of network works. It describes various types of network media such as twisted wire, optical fiber, radio wave, and infrared. The chapter shows that a successful network relies on a good network development plan and design. To implement data communication on a network, network developers should come up with a network addressing plan so that each host can be properly assigned a unique address. The chapter discusses both IPv4 and IPv6 addressing schemes.

To be able to use network resources more efficiently, the method of subnetting is introduced.

This chapter explains how to do subnetting. Through several examples, this chapter demonstrates how to calculate a subnet mask, network ID, broadcast address, and the size of a subnet. Through the hands-on practice provided in this chapter, a simple network can be created in the cloud environment or in the virtual environment on a local computer. Our next task is to develop some network services. In the next chapter, you will learn how to create some network services.

Review Questions

1. Describe the most popular LAN technology.
2. Describe the Ethernet frame.
3. What are the two key technologies that make communication on the Internet possible?
4. Describe three types of commonly used wireless technologies.
5. What is the virtual network?
6. Why do we need modulation?
7. What is prefix and what is a suffix?
8. How many networks can be specified by each of the primary classes?
9. How many hosts can be specified in each of the primary classes?
10. For a given binary number 10010101, find its corresponding decimal value.

11. For a given binary IP address 10001011 00101101 10001010 01001010, what is the corresponding decimal IP address?

12. What are the network IDs for the IP addresses 10.3.55.120, 172.16.48.110, and 192.168.1.31?

13. What are the dedicated broadcast IP addresses for the IP addresses 10.3.55.120, 172.16.48.110, and 192.168.1.31?

14. What are the subnet masks for the three primary classes?

15. For the IP address 192.168.1.34 and the subnet mask 255.255.255.252, determine the network ID and broadcast IP address for the subnet that contains the given IP address. Also, find how many subnets and how many hosts in each subnet can be specified by the subnet mask 255.255.255.252.

16. For the IP address 172.6.24.60 and the subnet mask 255.255.248.0, determine the network ID and broadcast IP address for the subnet that contains the given IP address. Also, find how many subnets and how many hosts in each subnet can be specified by the subnet mask 255.255.248.0.

17. For the IP address 10.3.54.11 and the subnet mask 255.224.0.0, determine the network ID and broadcast IP address for the subnet that contains the given IP address. Also, find how many subnets and how many hosts in each subnet can be specified by the subnet mask 255.224.0.0.

18. Create a subnet under a standard Class B network so that the subnet is large enough to include both the IP addresses 129.8.138.16 and 129.8.129.12. What is the ID for the subnet that includes these two IP addresses?

19. For the IP address 192.168.225.54 and subnet mask 255.255.255.240, what is the equivalent CIDR expression?

20. For the CIDR expression 129.20.3.11/19, find the equivalent subnet mask.

4

NETWORK DIRECTORY SERVICES

Objectives

- Understand directory services.
- Examine the functions of directory services.
- Install and configure Active Directory.
- Manage Active Directory.

4.1 Introduction

A large organization's network may have thousands of network hosts, many different types of software, and a large number of users. The management of these network hosts, software, and users can be a tedious task. Directory services centralize the administration of network hosts, software, and users. Centralized services eliminate the visits to each individual computer by a network administrator. On a server installed with directory services, the network administrator can perform the following the tasks:

- Implement an authentication and authorization strategy for sharing network resources.
- Grant or remove permissions for remotely accessing certain network resources.
- Group users and computers so that different security policies can be applied to them.
- Store information about network resources such as users, computers, network devices, and application specific data.

By integrating user authentication, a directory service is able to identify a user with the user name and password combination anywhere on a local network. The directory service allows the users to log on to any computer in the organization's network and still keep their personal data secure. The directory service can be critical for managing any medium-sized or large organization. It is necessary for a network administrator to understand how the directory service work and have the hands-on skills to manage the directory service. In this chapter, we will take a closer look at this important network service. The directory service is supported by many server operating systems. In particular, Active Directory Domain Services (AD DS) or simply Active Directory (AD) is the directory service provided by the Windows operating system.

4.2 Active Directory Logical Structure

Active Directory serves as a distributed database to store information about network users, computers, shared directories, and other network services. Like a database that can be represented by a logical model, Active Directory can be represented by a logical model called Active Directory Logical Structure. The logical structure provides a number of benefits for deploying, managing, and securing network services and resources. It provides the overview of an Active Directory service. It shows how the users, computers, and other network resources are distributed. It can be used to display the structure of the Active directory service. The logical structure reveals the relationships among the components in Active Directory. It can also be used to facilitate the implementation of other network services such as Domain Name Service (DNS) and email service.

If a user needs to access a network service or a resource, the authentication information will be forwarded to a server called domain controller or an Active Directory server, which contains valid user information. If the authentication information is matched, the user will be permitted to access the service in the network. The domain controller also provides information about the network service. When a computer requests to join the network, it will check with the domain controller. If the request is permitted, the computer will become a member of the network. If not, the computer is an independent computer and will not see the services provided by the network (Figure 4.1).

Like a database, which consists of entities and each entity is characterized by its attributes, the logical structure of Active Directory also consists of objects and each object is characterized by its attributes. In Active Directory, a schema is used to define an object and its attributes. The schema can be used to create attributes to extend the existing object. It can also be used to create new objects.

There are two types of objects, the leaf object and container object. The leaf object has no child object. The container object contains other objects. In Active Directory,

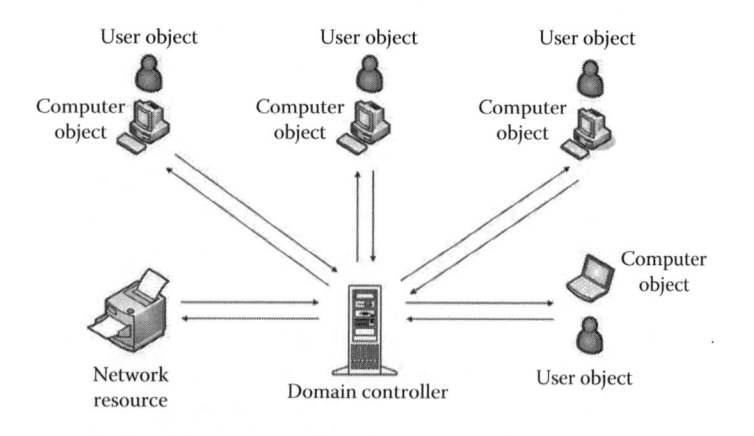

Figure 4.1 Network with centralized control.

the user object is an example of the leaf object. The commonly known container objects are forest, domain, organizational unit (OU), and so on. Briefly, the commonly used objects are described in the following. The leaf objects—user object, computer object, contact object, and group object—will be introduced. Then, we will discuss the container objects such as the OU, domain, tree, and forest.

User object: A user object stores information about users. Each instance of the user object represents an individual user account. The attributes of the user object are the user name, password, and so on. In Active Directory, there are two types of built-in user accounts, administrator and guest accounts.

Computer object: A computer object stores information about computers. Each instance of the computer object is an individual computer account.

Contact object: A contact object stores contact information about an organization's contractors, suppliers, and other people who have connection with the organization. The people listed in the contact object have no permission to access the organization's network.

Group object: A group object stores a group of user accounts, computer accounts, and information about other groups. There are two types of groups, the security group and the distribution group. With different levels of restrictions, security groups are configured for accessing network resources. Distribution groups are used for data communication.

Organizational unit object: An OU is a container object that can be used to group objects. As a container object, an OU object contains leaf objects, such as users, computers, and network devices. It may also contain information about other OU projects. In a hierarchical structure, an OU object is the lowest level container object. By including leaf objects in the OU object, the OU object can be used to support business activities. For example, according to the group policy, the user objects in the OU object can have a specially designed desktop. By using the OU, a group of users can also be granted permission to access a server specially configured for this group of users. The OU can also be used to include a group of users whose passwords should be changed in a predefined time period such as every 6 months.

Domain object: A domain object is a container project that may contain leaf objects and OU objects. The leaf objects in a domain are not included in OUs. In addition to these physical objects, the domain also contains objects that are used to help with communication among domains such as trusted domain objects (TDOs) and site link objects. In the domain, these leaf objects and OU objects are authenticated by the same Active Directory (AD) servers. That is, each domain is an administrative boundary for objects. The administrative control can be designated to other AD objects such as user objects. In that way, the user may have some or full administrative privilege. If an organization wants to construct a centralized network, it should create a domain for organization-level administration and use OUs for the management of departments. Figure 4.2 illustrates the domains in the Internet.

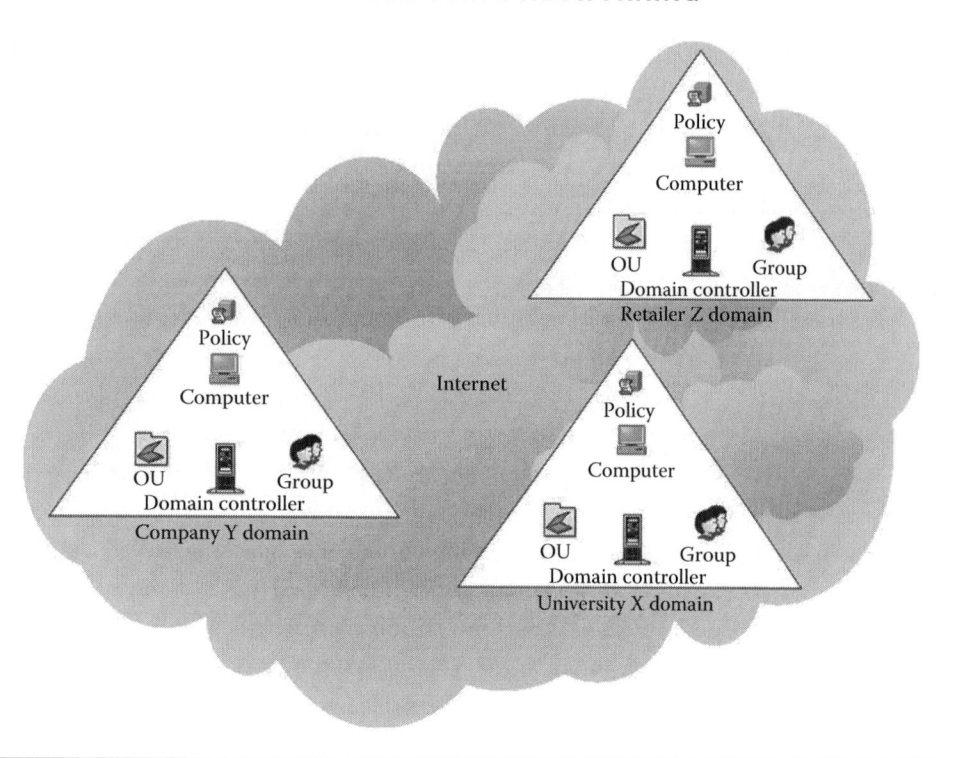

Figure 4.2   Domains in the Internet.

Domain tree object: A domain tree is a collection of domains. In a domain tree object, the domains are grouped in a hierarchical structure. A domain may have subdomains in it. A domain with subdomains is called parent domain. A domain that has no parent domain is called a root domain. When a domain is added to a domain tree, it becomes a child domain of the root domain. The child domain can also have its own subdomain. Figure 4.3 shows a domain tree with three domains, jsu.edu and its two subdomains westcampus.jsu.edu and eastcampus.jsu.edu.

Forest object: A forest object is the top-level container object. It contains one or more domains or domain trees. The forest is also known as a collection of domains. The objects of Active Directory are saved in a distributed data repository called a global catalog. The global catalog stores all Active Directory objects for its host domain and a partial copy of all objects for all other domains in the forest. In a forest, a global catalog is created automatically on the first domain controller.

For the domains that are not suitable to be in a hierarchical structure, they cannot be placed in a domain tree object. In that case, these domains can be placed in a forest object. The domains in a forest have two-way transitive relationships. Since the Active Directory information can be shared by the domains in a forest, the forest can be considered the boundary of Active Directory. As an example, suppose that jsu and isu are partners. However, these two universities are not suitable to be in a hierarchical structure. In such a case, a forest can be created to include both domain trees as shown in Figure 4.4.

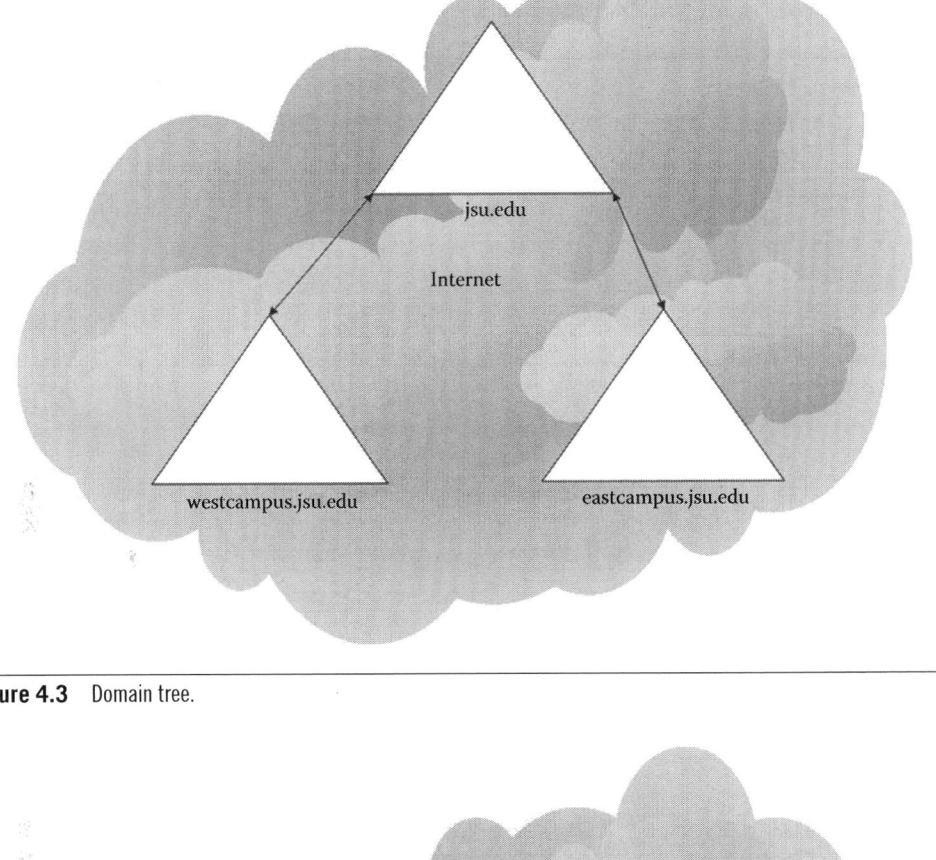

Figure 4.3   Domain tree.

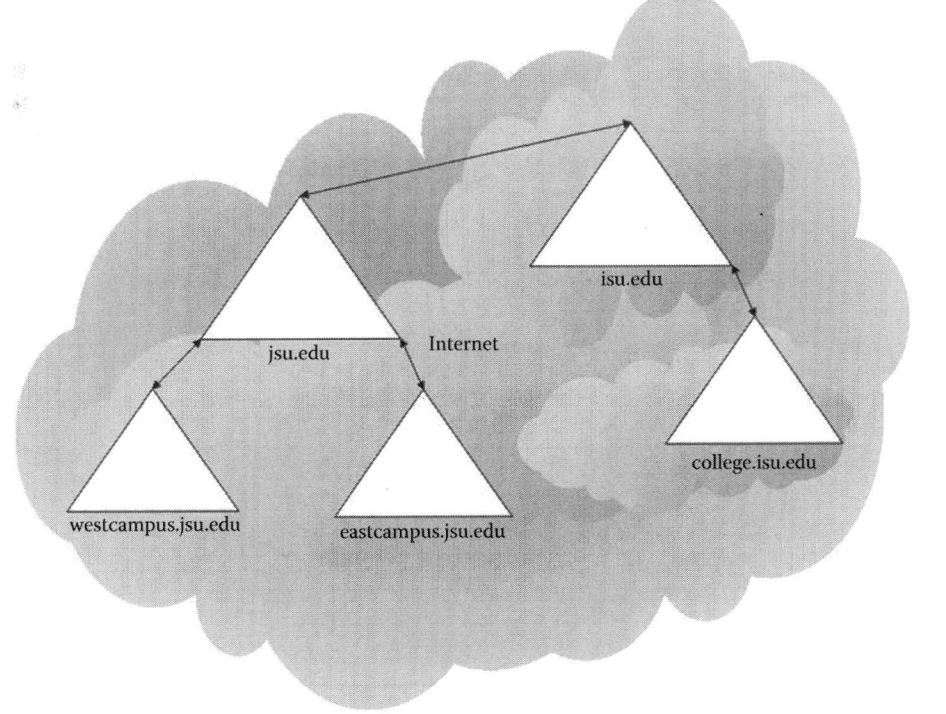

Figure 4.4   Forest with two domain trees.

Site object: A site object represents the physical structure of a network. For example, a site can be a geographic location where a subnet is constructed. In a forest, the site objects and their contents are replicated to all Active Directory servers. When the sites are connected through a WAN, which has relatively slow but more expensive connections, the data are compressed before a replication process begins. Sites are often connected through a WAN or through the Internet with the VPN technology. The communication between network hosts and the domain controller on a WAN can be slow and expensive. However, it is not a problem on a LAN. If an organization is physically located in multiple sites, which are far away from each other, the use of site objects provides the solution on Active Directory replication. The computers joined to a domain are assigned to different sites based on their physical locations. At each site, subnets are constructed to physically connect network hosts including the domain controller. The subnet has adequate bandwidth for the communication between network hosts and the domain controller. The domain controllers at different sites replicate the Active Directory database regularly (Figure 4.5). To improve performance, the Active Directory replication uses the compressed replication data and communicates through the route with the lowest cost.

Active Directory is designed to store and manage a large amount of information. A domain controller is able to manage 2 billion objects. For such a large-scale project, a careful design is necessary before Active Directory can be implemented.

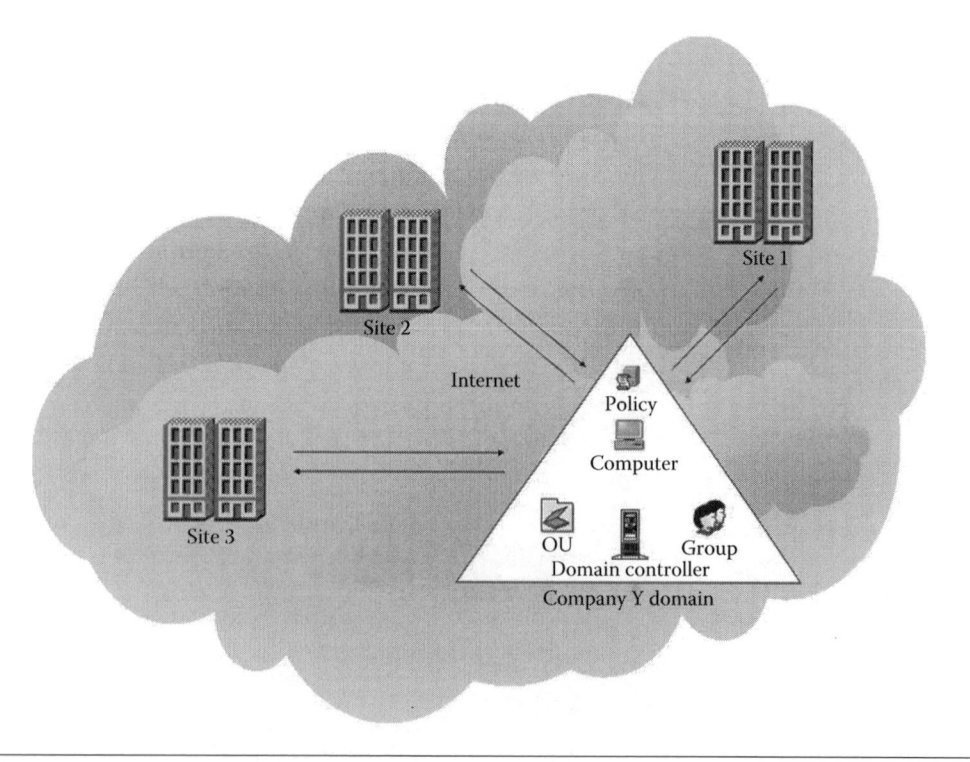

Figure 4.5   Sites.

4.3 Active Directory Design

As Active Directory is used for organizing network objects, it is critical for running a successful business. The goal of the Active Directory design is to construct Active Directory that is cost efficient, easy to use, secure, scalable, robust, and reliable. Therefore, we must carefully design and plan Active Directory before putting it to use. As the centralized administrative service, Active Directory should be built so that it is able to authenticate and authorize users, computers, network devices, and other network resources. It should provide network services and enforce security policies. The information stored in Active Directory should be available to qualified users.

4.3.1 Requirement Analysis

Well-built Active Directory should meet the needs of network management. The designer needs to be able to answer some questions such as

- How to use Active Directory to meet the requirements of an organization?
- How to organize objects into groups?
- What the capacity of a domain controller is?
- What the role of Active Directory is?
- Who owns the data stored in Active Directory?
- Whether the delegation of authority is needed?
- How to select the locations of sites?
- What the relationships among domains are?

To answer these questions, the designer needs to investigate the requirements and to structure the AD objects to meet the requirements. These tasks can be accomplished through the requirement analysis, logical design, and physical design.

The requirement analysis provides administrators and project developers with a clear vision, which will be the foundation for the planning and design. One way to get the requirement information is to interview the key players who are involved in the business process. Through the interviews, the designer can discover what works and what does not work in the current business process and the requirements for the future Active Directory. The key players may include the following:

- Administrators of an organization
- Managers of human resources, finance, and IT service
- Employees who will be using the future Active Directory
- Customers or students

The interviews set the stage for finding out the answers to the questions listed earlier. The key players at different levels should be asked about the goals and constraints of the project. The designer should ask the expected timeline and the resources available for the project. In addition to interviewing the key players, the designer can also collect information from related documents and observe the origination's daily operation.

4.3.2 Structure Specification

Before physically implementing the Active Directory, we need to specify a logical model that represents the future Active Directory. To specify the Active Directory's logical structure, the designer's first task is to identify the boundary for the forest, then the boundary for the domains. The designer needs to decide where the sites will be located and decide on how many domains to create. Once the domains are defined, the designer should consider the names of the domains and determine how the domains and their objects are related and how the services are provided. The owners of the domain objects should be identified. In the end, the designer should consider how to divide a domain into OUs and indicate how the objects such as users, computers, and groups are distributed in the OUs and domains.

Forest specification: Once all the information is collected, the designer needs to specify the forest. A forest is an instance of Active Directory. That is, every time you install a new Active Directory, a forest is created. Each Active Directory contains four partitions: The domain partition contains all the Active Directory objects in that domain, the schema partition contains the configurations of the Active Directory, the configuration partition contains the settings of the forest, domain, and domain controller, and the application partition contains information about applications if there is any.

Defined by the security boundary, a forest serves as the container of Active Directory objects. The security boundary is so created that no one else can control the objects in the container without the permission of the administrator of the forest. All domains in a forest will share the following security information:

- Common configuration information about the forest infrastructure, domains, sites, and so on
- Global catalog, which enables user search for object information throughout all domains in the forest
- The information about trust relationships

An entire organization can be represented by a forest. For example, a university system with multiple branch campuses can be represented by a forest in Active Directory. Everyone to access the university's network must have permission from the forest administrator. Usually, a forest is adequate for an entire organization. In the situation that one part of the company requires complete isolation from other parts of the company, two forests can be considered. Also, in the case that two merged companies have independent administrative units, two forests can also be considered and a trust relationship can be created between these two forests.

Domain specification: A domain is defined by an administrative boundary. The domain is designed to meet the administrative requirements of an organization. The administrator of a domain can create, modify, and delete Active Directory objects in the domain. The domain administrator can configure the service and user authentication, and can specify user groups and control the access to network resources. The domain administrator decides which computer can join the domain, how to divide the domain into OUs, and how to apply group policies. A group policy is applied to the domain so that the domain in a forest can behave differently from other domains. To specify the domains in a forest, the designer needs to identify administrative boundaries. For example, if a university with multiple branch campuses requires each branch campus to manage its own students, employees, and computers, the designer should create a domain for each campus.

To simplify domain management, a single domain is recommended. With the single domain, it is easier for the network administrator to delegate authorities and apply group policies. The single domain also uses less network resources. The decision on creating multiple domains depends on the following factors:

- Each branch of an organization wants to manage their own users and network objects.
- It is too costly to replicate the entire Active Directory over a slow WAN network.
- Each branch of the organization must have a different set of Active Directory configurations.

In such a case, the designer may consider creating multiple domains in a forest. Once the decision about domains is made, the network task is to determine the relationships between the domains. For example, the domains can be grouped together. Some domains may have subdomains. The related domains can make up domain trees in the forest. For instance, if one of the branch campuses has overseas subcampuses, the designer may consider creating a subdomain for the overseas campuses. A trusted relationship between a domain and its subdomains should be specified. The domain replication scheme should also be addressed.

Trusted relationship: Sometimes, a domain may use information provided by another domain or another object such as a person or a domain controller. The identification of the trusted objects is also a task to be accomplished during the design of Active Directory. In a forest, trusts are created among domains. Two domains can be trusted in a one-way or two-way relationship. The first domain created in a forest is called the root domain. Once created, the forest root domain cannot be deleted. By default, the root domain contains the Enterprise Admins and Schema Admins groups, which have the forestwide administrative credentials. In a forest, optional domain tree roots can also be created. A two-way trust is automatically established between a parent domain and its child domain. If in a situation where the administrators of the child domain should not be allowed to access the resources of the parent domain, the trust can be reconfigured to a one-way trust.

When a domain is trusted, the users of the trusted domain can access the objects and services from the trusting domain. For example, the domain of a branch campus is trusted by the domain of the main campus of a university, the users of the branch campus can access the services provided by the main campus. By using the branch campus domains, the administrators of the main campus domain do not have to manage the students enrolled in the branch campuses. They do not have to set the policies for the branch campus domains. This can reduce their responsibilities. On the other hand, this may cause some security concerns since the users of the branch campuses are not under the control of the domain administrators of the main campus domain. Therefore, it is safer to get all the users and services managed in a single domain.

When a domain is trusted by another domain, the administrators of the trusted domain may have the power to alter the container of the Active Directory in the trusting domain. This leads to the consideration of which person should be trusted. One should carefully select the administrators in the trusted domain. Once trusted, the administrators of the trusted domain should be considered the members of the trusting domain. Here, it shows the difference of a forest and a domain. A domain is not a security boundary, and therefore an administrator of a trusted domain is able to control the objects of the trusting domain although by default the administrative rights do not flow across domain boundaries. On the other hand, a forest does not allow the domain administrators of another forest to access the objects in its own domains.

Domain name specification: The next task is to specify the name for each domain. A good domain name should be meaningful and proper. For the Internet computing environment, a domain should be named by following the convention of Domain Name System (DNS). A domain is named in a hierarchical structure based on the names of an organization, sites, departments, and offices. By the rules of DNS, the domain name is a sequence of names separated with periods. For example,

myhost.department.collge.unniversity.edu

In the hierarchical structure shown in this example, the name on the right has more general use than the one on the left. The right most name is called the top-level domain. Top-level domains are generic domains, which are managed by the Internet Corporation for Assigned Names and Numbers (ICANN). There are only a limited number of top-level domains, each representing a main segment of the naming system. There are about 100 such domains. The commonly used top-level domains are listed in Table 4.1.

In the Internet computing environment, a domain name should include a top-level-domain. By doing so, the domain becomes part of the Internet. The first task of naming a domain is to decide which top-level domain to join. Once the top-level domain is selected, the other part of the domain name can be named according the organization's structure. The organization's main domain is in front of the top-level domain name separated by a dot. The subdomain name is in front of main domain

Table 4.1 Commonly Used Top-Level Domains

DOMAIN NAME	CATEGORY
.com	Commercial
.edu	Education
.gov	Government
.org	Nonprofit Organization
.mil	Military
.net	Network Organization
.name	Individual user

name, and so on. It will cost the organization for registering to the top-level domain. After the organization has registered its name in one of the top-level domains, it can add more layers to the hierarchical name system. The organization can add layers for all its departments, offices, and individual hosts under its name for free. There are up to 127 layers that can be created. Therefore, computers and other network devices can have their own names, which are added to in the organization's domain name and the top-level-domain name.

OU specification: For the convenience of management, the objects in a domain can be partitioned into organization units (OUs) according the department structure in an organization. If a domain contains a large number of objects, OUs can be used to facilitate domain management. Although an OU is not an administrative object, the domain administrator can delegate some of the authority duties to the OU. Once the OU is given authority duties, trusted users will have permission to perform management tasks.

Instead of using a trusted domain, one can use OUs as a securer solution. After the Active Directory objects are grouped into OUs, each OU can be assigned a group policy to implement the special requirements to the objects in that OU. For example, each branch campus can have its own OU. The users, computers, and services of that campus can be included in the campus OU. The administrators of the domain in the main campus can delegate some of the authorities and permissions to the system administrators of the branch campuses.

A group policy can be created to an OU to meet the needs of the campus. It can be applied to a site, domain, or OU. Note that a group policy cannot be applied to an individual user, a computer, or a group. The settings of the group policy are stored as Group Policy objects (GPOs) in Active Directory. Some policies can be set at the OU level and others can be set at the domain level. For example, the following policies can be set at the domain level:

- Account-related policies such as rules about passwords and account logouts
- Certification-related policies such as rules related to the public key and Kerberos ticket

All other policies can be specified at the OU level.

An OU can have sub-OUs. Different group policies can be assigned to different sub-OUs. For example, each branch campus can use sub-OUs for each department The HR department can have an OU that can be delegated some of the authorities to make HR a data owner but not a service owner. By doing so, the HR department can perform tasks such as creating user objects.

When designing OU structures, the designer should define an OU in a way that a specific group policy can be applied to it. As one of the purposes of the OU is to facilitate the management of domain objects, the designer should define the OU structure so that it can make administrative tasks easier. The designer should also make a group of trusted users have the permission to manage the objects of the OU.

Data ownership: As an Active Directory reflects an organization's infrastructure, the information stored in the Active Directory may belong to multiple departments in the organization. The ownership of the information should be clearly defined. The Active Directory has two types of ownerships: the data owner and service owner. The data owner has both the control and responsibility of information. The data owner does data management such as creating, modifying, and deleting objects in the Active Directory. The information control can be implemented through setting up group policies. The service owner is in charge of the operation of Active Directory services. The tasks performed by the service owner are creating domains and sites, modifying domains and sites, deleting domains and sites, managing domain controllers, and monitoring the operation of the Active Directory. As an example, let us consider the structure of a university. Under the president, the university has two vice presidents, one is in charge of the academic division and the other one is in charge of the business division. The users in the academic division are faculty members, students, and staff members. The users in the business division are employees who take care of daily operations to keep the university running (Figure 4.6).

In this example, the staff members of the Admissions and Registration office are the student data owner. They can create, modify, and delete student objects. The people who work in the Human Resources office can create, modify, and delete employee objects. Therefore, they are the employee data owner. The domain controller's administrator in the IT service department is the service owner who can create and manage domains.

Site specification: When an organization has multiple geographic locations, a site structure can be specified to represent the organization's subnets at those geographic locations. The designer needs to specify the number of sites and the locations of the sites. The specification of the domain controller at each site should also be specified. A domain is a unit of replication. It is the smallest unit of replication that can be administered within a forest. The objects located within a domain container can be replicated to other domain controllers within that same domain over either a LAN or even a WAN connection. A domain controller in the forest is also specified to replicate forestwide data.

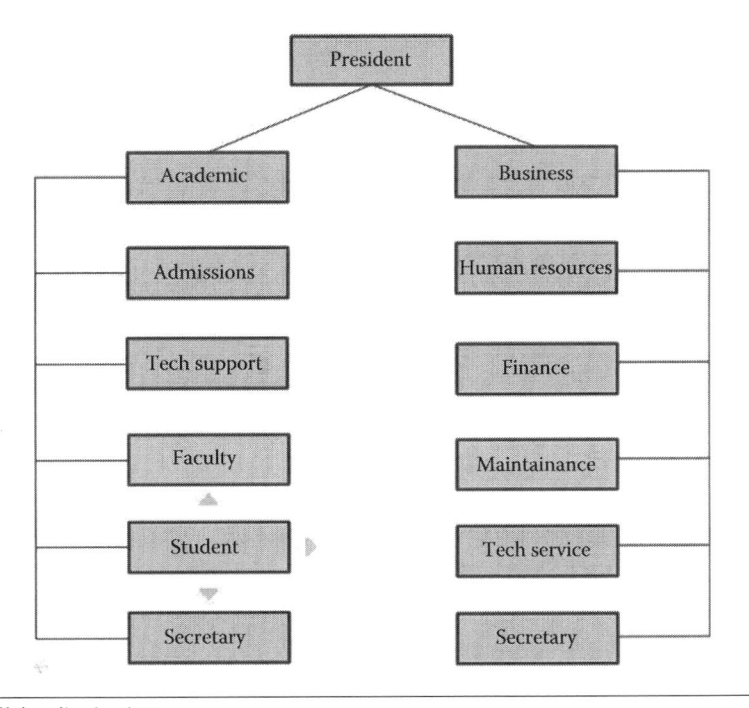

Figure 4.6   University structure.

The designer should also specify the replication scheme among these sites. Therefore, replication often occurs within sites and between sites to keep domain and forest data updated. In a replication scheme, the designer needs to address questions such as what to replicate, when to replicate, and how to replicate.

For example, the network media linking the sites can often have a bottleneck during replication. In such a case, one may consider to schedule replication during off-peak hours. Computers served as domain controllers should also be powerful enough to handle the operation and replication of Active Directory distributed among multiple sites. The designer should also make the domain controllers among different sites able to communicate with each other.

Schema specification: Each forest has a schema that contains formal definitions of all objects and attributes. The default schema contains the definitions of objects such as user accounts, computer accounts, groups, domains, OUs, and security policies. More definitions can be added by the administrator. The schema partition is replicated across the entire forest. All the objects created in the forest have to follow the rules set in the schema. When creating an Active Directory object, the schema is used to determine the attributes of the object. The specifications of the attributes should be consistent with the rules defined in the schema partition. For example, if the schema decides that a user's first name, last name, and student ID are required when creating a user object, the user object must specify the attributes of the first name, last name, and student ID. In addition to the required attributes, other attributes such as major and email address can also be specified.

4.4 Active Directory Implementation

After the logical model is specialized, the next task is to physically implement the Active Directory. The development process starts by forming a development team. Based on the areas of expertise, the roles of the team members are clearly defined. The development team may need to accomplish the following tasks during the development process:

- Investigate the existing computing resources and make a decision on whether an upgrade to newer technology is necessary.
- Find out resource constraints that may impact the deployment. The team should check potential problems due to the constraints of resources.
- Indentify users who may be affected by the implementation.
- Draft a timeline for the project to be completed.

During the implementation process, the first thing is to implement the network infrastructure and install the server operating systems on the domain controllers. The following are some of the general strategies that may be considered for the implementation of the subnets and domain controllers.

Domain controller: During the installation of Active Directory, you need to specify the forest functional level. By specifying the forest functional level as Windows Server 2012, the Active Directory is supported by Windows Server 2012 domain controllers. Once the forest functional level is selected, domain controllers running earlier versions of operating systems will not be able to participate in the forest.

When the first domain controller is created, the first forest along with the root domain is created. The name of the root domain should be the one specified in the design phase. To avoid compatibility issues, the version of the operating system installed on the domain should be consistent. Each domain controller is used to hold a single Active Directory. It is advisable to install at least two domain controllers in each domain for redundancy. In case that one of the domain controllers crashes, we have another to keep the daily operation running.

Subnet: A subnet is used to connect all the domain controllers and other network objects in a site. All domain controllers and computers are configured in the same LAN. By doing so, the domain controllers can efficiently communicate with the network objects. The subnet is used to reduce the latency on the replication of Active Directory. The bandwidth of the subnet should be adequate for the frequent replication of domain controllers.

Replication: To control replication, the Active Directory data are divided into four partitions:

1. The domain partition, which contains the object data
2. The schema partition, which contains the rules
3. The configuration partition, which contains the settings of the forest, domain, and other objects
4. The application partition, which contains the application data

Stored in the domain partition, the domain partition data are replicated to the other domain controllers in the same domain. All the changes made to the domain partition data on one domain controller will be replicated to all the other domain controllers in the same domain. The domain controllers also have two nondomain directory partitions: the schema partition and application partition, which store forestwide data. The schema is replicated to all the domain controllers in the forest. As the optional application partition can be generated by one or more applications, it can be used for redundancy, availability, or fault tolerance of application data. This partition does not have to be replicated to all the domain controllers in the forest.

For a large organization, the network infrastructure may be physically across multiple locations and thousands of users may log on to the network simultaneously. In such a case, cloud computing can provide a better solution. Instead of creating multiple subnets and installing servers as domain controllers, the domain controllers can be implemented in the cloud environment. The implementation can be done with a short time. The domain controllers can be highly scalable and available. Implementing the domain controllers in the cloud environment can help the organization smoothly expand their on-premises computing environment to the cloud environment.

The Active Directory implemented in the cloud environment can provide the authentication service for both the on-premises and cloud applications. The cloud-based Active Directory can be integrated with the on-premises Active Directory so that the users can access the applications on both the cloud and on the premises with a single user name and password. When the organization deploys the cloud-based application software, the authentication for the worldwide access to the application software can be handled by the cloud-based Active Directory. With the cloud-based Active Directory, the domain administrators are able to manage the objects with GUI tools anytime and anywhere around the world. The cloud environment provides a highly available application developing platform for application developers. Through the cloud-based Active Directory, the application developers can be authenticated with credentials provided by an organization.

4.5 Active Directory Deployment

The deployment process starts with testing the implementation. The design specifications and features will be tested to verify if the design goals have been achieved. The testing may include the following:

- Authentication and authorization tests
- Domain name test
- Remote access test
- Connections of sites
- Performance of domain controllers
- Active Directory replication

- Applications, such as email service, deployed through Active Directory
- Encryption and Certification implementation
- Services, such as storage area network (SAN) deployment, file distribution, fault tolerance, and disaster recovery, deployed through Active Directory
- Application availability, scalability, and compatibility with the Active Directory to be deployed
- Group policies and the delegation of authority

Once the testing is completed, the deployment team may conduct a pilot study to make sure that everything works as expected. The pilot study should be done on a small group of computers that are not critical to the organization's daily operation. The pilot study can also be used as a platform for training so that the deployment team members know exactly what to do during the deployment process.

Once the pilot study is completed and problems are fixed, the deployment process can begin. Before rolling out the newly developed Active Directory, the administrators of the organization should be informed. The deployment team needs to inform the users about the domain change and provide instruction on how to deal with the change. During the deployment, the deployment team needs to find a way to collect, store, and migrate the network objects to the Active directory. As the new system is deployed, the deployment team needs to prepare for the technical support. The support team's contact information and work schedule should be available to the users. Answers for commonly asked questions should be documented and published. For project evaluation, the entire development process should be reviewed. The problems encountered, the methods used for problem solving, and the experience gained in the project development should all be documented for future use.

Activity 4.1: Active Directory Domain Services

In this activity, you will perform four tasks:

> *Task 1*: Installing Active Directory Domain Services on servera
> *Task 2*: Joining serverb to Active Directory Domain
> *Task 3*: Configuring serverb as Replica Domain Controller
> *Task 4*: Creating and Viewing Active Directory Objects

Task 1: Installing Active Directory Domain Services on servera

1. To install the Active Directory domain server, log on to the **Microsoft Azure Management Portal** and connect to servera by clicking **CONNECT**.
2. After you have connected to servera, to open **Add Roles and Features Wizard** in Server Manager, click **Manage** menu and then click **Add Roles and Features** as shown in Figure 4.7.

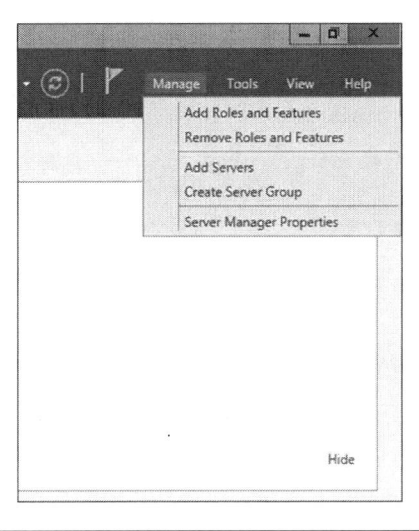

Figure 4.7 Adding roles and features.

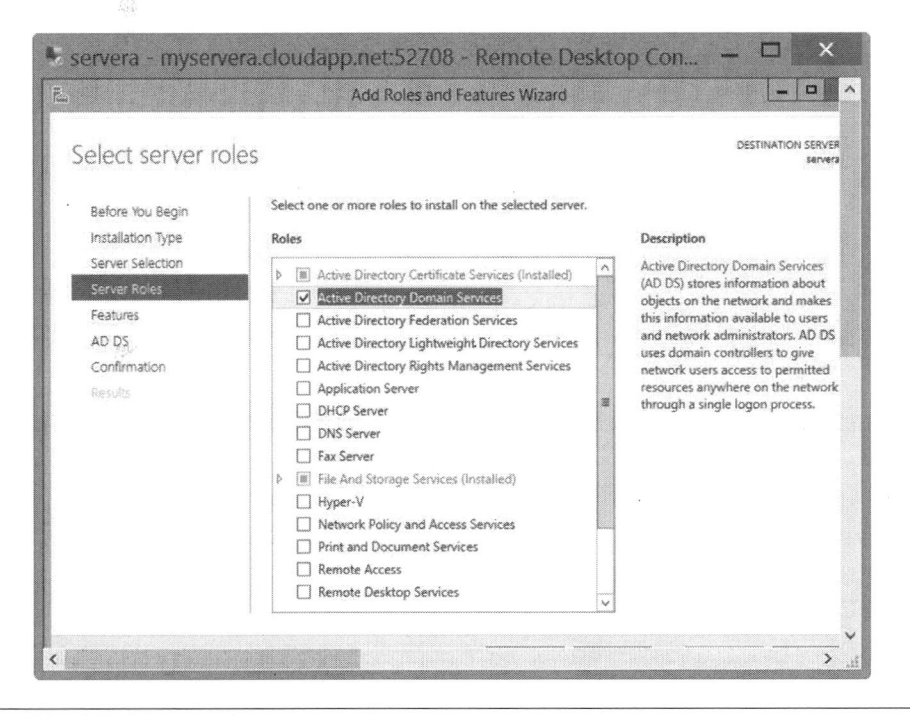

Figure 4.8 Selecting server roles.

3. Click **Next** a few times to go to the **Select server roles** page. Click **Active Directory Domain Services** as shown in Figure 4.8.
4. In Add features that are required for Active Directory Domain Services dialog, click **Add Features** as shown in Figure 4.9. Then, click **Next**.
5. On the **Select features** page, click **Next** several times to go to the **Confirm installation selections** page. Check the check box **Restart the destination**

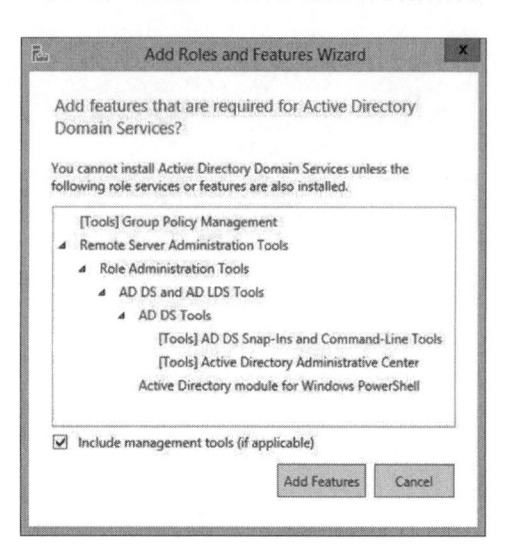

Figure 4.9   Adding features.

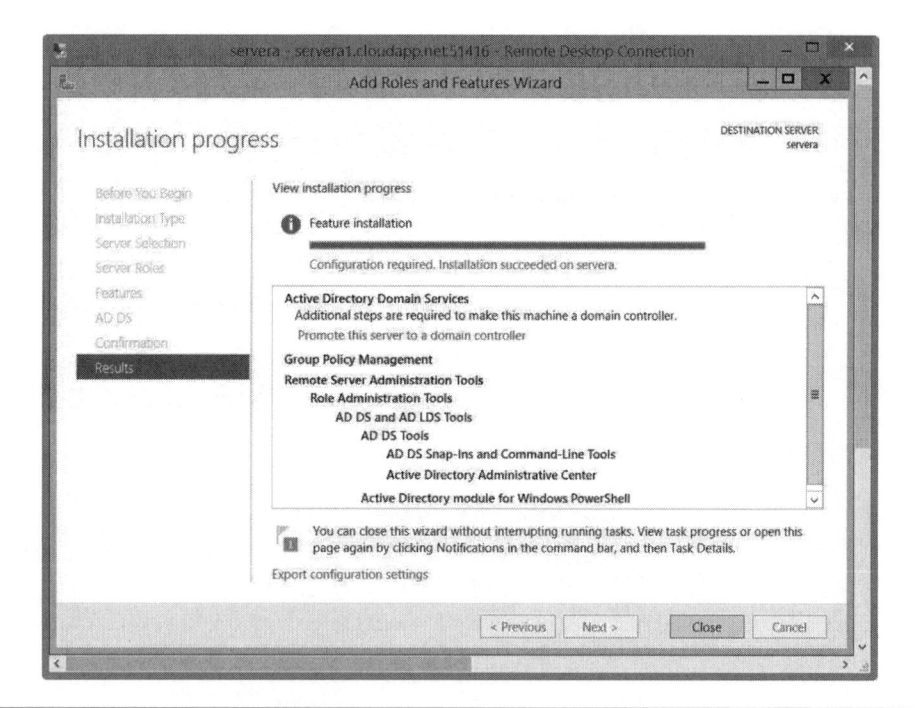

Figure 4.10   Viewing installation progress.

server automatically if required and click **Install**. The Installation progress page displays the status during the installation process as shown in Figure 4.10.

6. When the process completes, in the message details, click **Promote this server to a domain controller** and the Active Directory Domain Services Configuration Wizard will open.

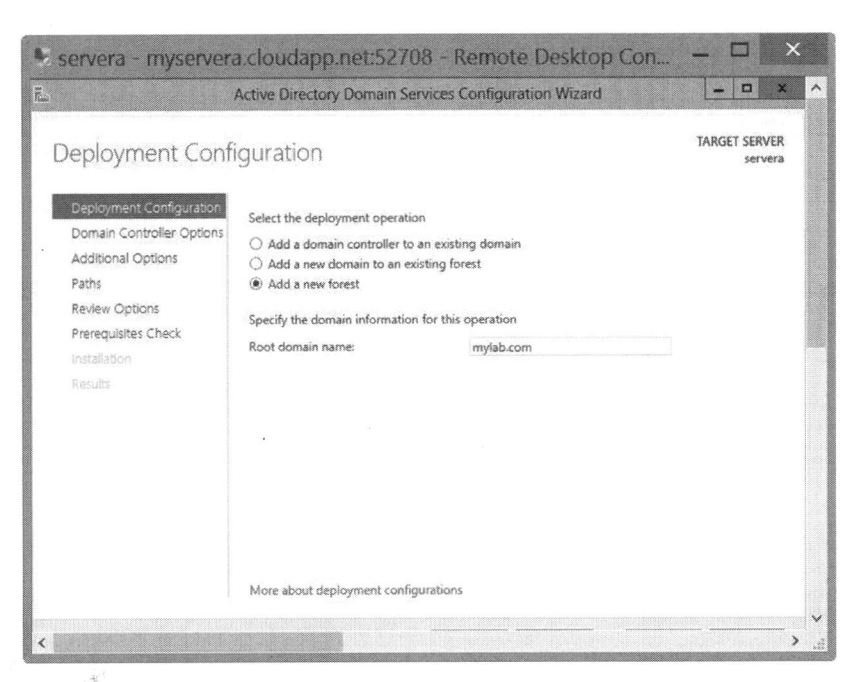

Figure 4.11   Adding new forest.

7. On the **Deployment Configuration** page, select **Add a new forest** as shown in Figure 4.11. For the **Root domain name**, type the fully qualified domain name (FQDN) for your domain. For example, if your FQDN is mylab.com, type **mylab.com**. Click **Next**.

8. On the **Domain Controller Options** page, type the password of your choice and confirm it (Figure 4.12); click **Next**.

9. On the **DNS Options** page, click **Next** several times until you get to the **Review Options** page.

10. On the **Review Options** page, review your selections. If you want to export settings to a Windows PowerShell script, click **View script**. The script opens in Notepad, and you can save it to the folder location of your choice. Click **Next**.

11. On the **Prerequisites Check** page, your selections are validated (Figure 4.13). When the check completes, click **Install**.

12. Once the installation is complete, you will see that AD DS is added to the Dashboard list (Figure 4.14).

Task 2: Joining serverb to Active Directory Domain

1. In the Microsoft Azure Management Portal, select the virtual machine **serverb** and click **CONNECT**.

2. Log on to the **serverb** virtual machine. Click the **Local Server** link on the left-hand side of your screen. Then, click **IPv4 address assigned by DHCP, IPv6 enabled** as shown in Figure 4.15.

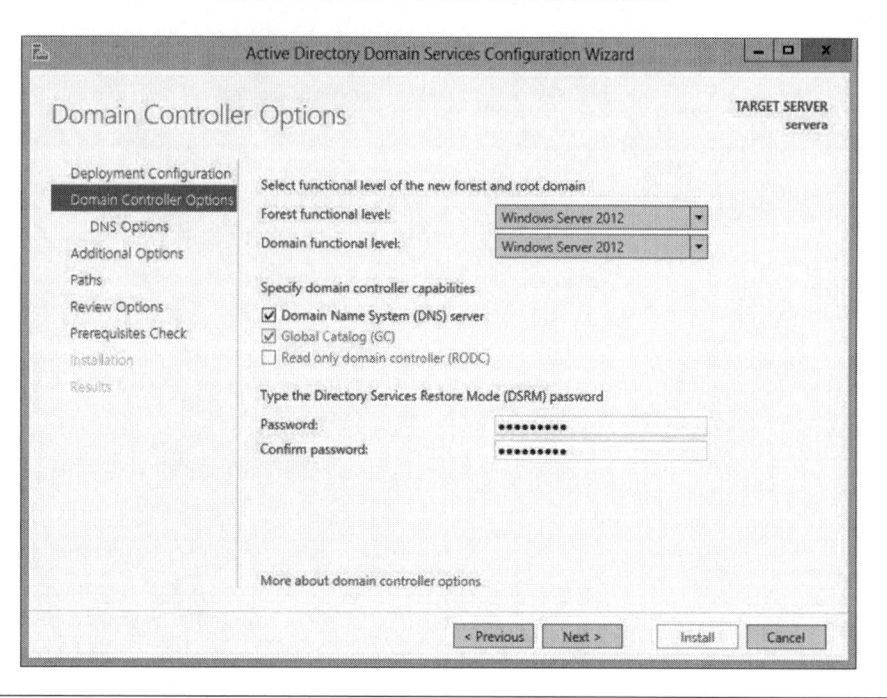

Figure 4.12 Domain controller options.

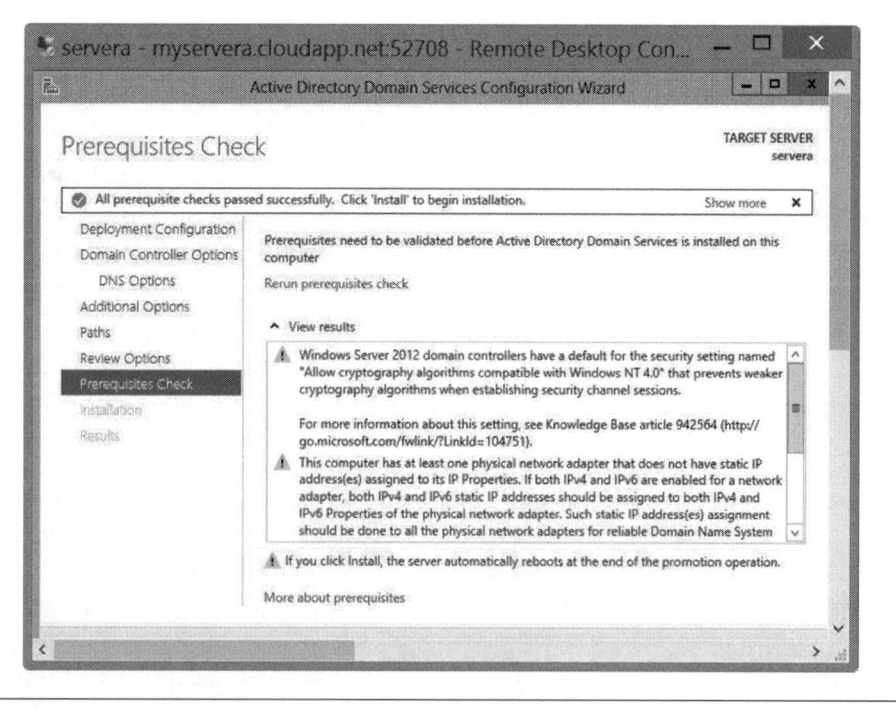

Figure 4.13 Prerequisites check.

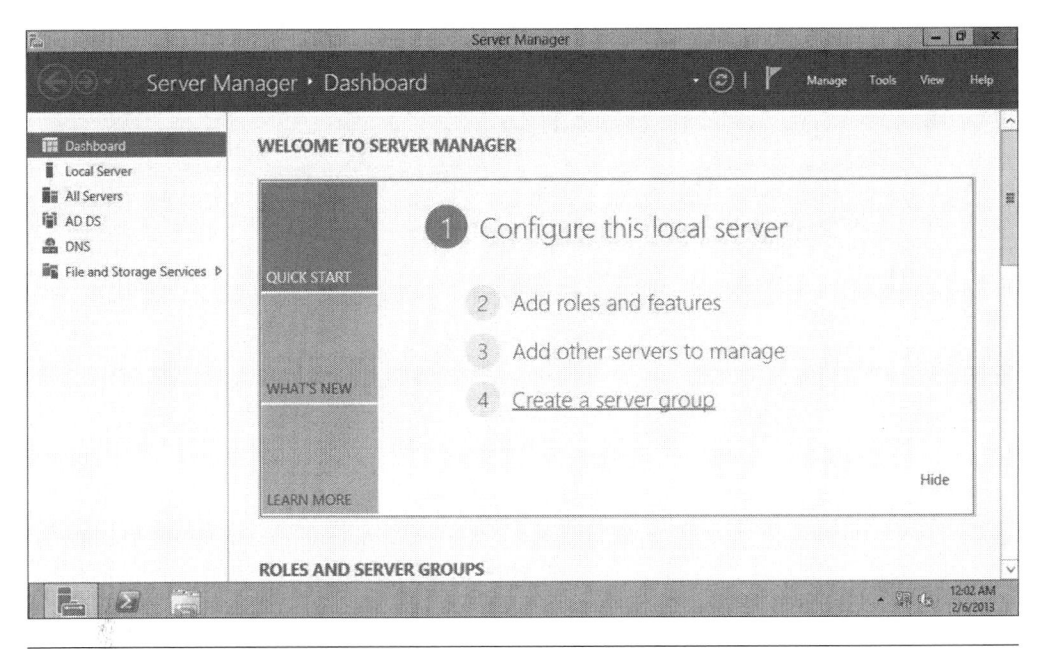

Figure 4.14 AD DS added to dashboard list.

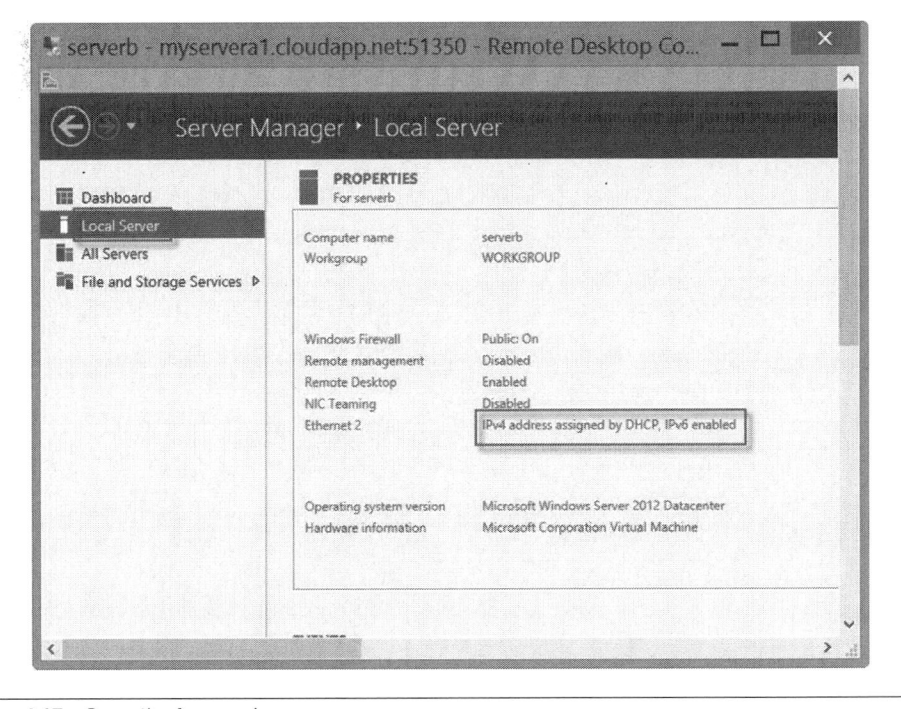

Figure 4.15 Properties for serverb.

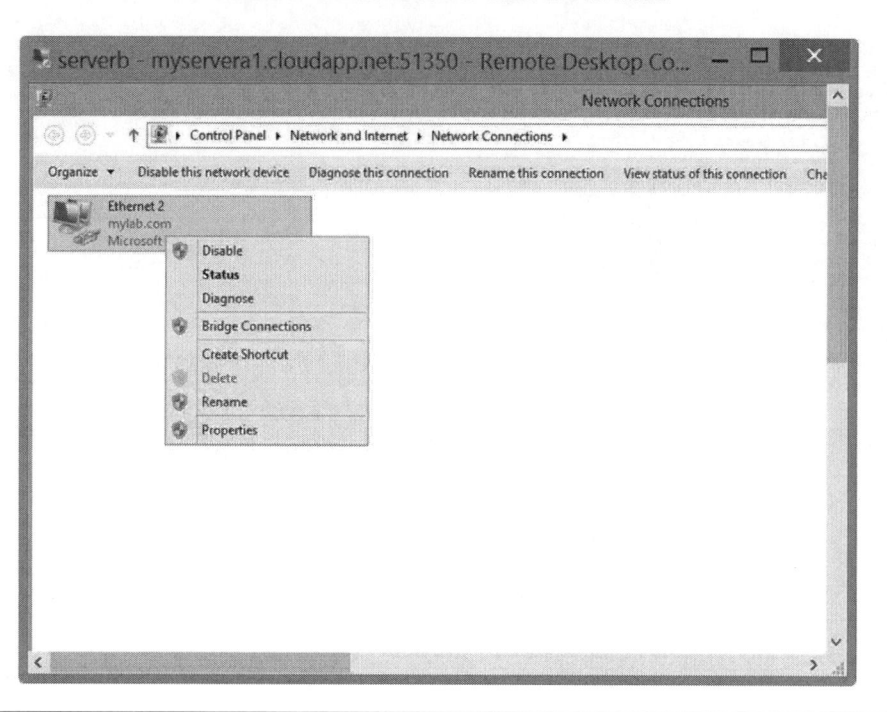

Figure 4.16   Configuring Ethernet 2.

3. Before you can join serverb to the domain mylab.com, you need to make sure that the network interface card is configured to use servera as the DNS server. To do so, right click **Ethernet 2** and select **Properties** as shown in Figure 4.16.

4. Check **Internet Protocol Version 4 (TCP/IPv4)** and click **Properties** as shown in Figure 4.17.

5. In the Internet Protocol Version 4 Properties dialog, enter the IP address of servera for the Preferred DNS server as shown in Figure 4.18. Then, click **OK**. (Note: your servera IP address may be different from the one shown in Figure 4.18.)

6. Once you are done with the configuration of your NIC, go back to the Local Server page. Click the **WORKGROUP** link as shown in Figure 4.19.

7. Once the configuration of the network interface card is complete, click the **Change** button in the System Properties dialog as shown in Figure 4.20.

8. On the Computer Name/Domain Changes dialog page, check the **Domain** option and type the domain name **mylab.com** as shown in Figure 4.21. Then, click **OK**.

9. You will be prompted to enter servera's user name and password. Type in the username with the domain prefix and the password as shown in Figure 4.22.

10. If successful, you should be able to see a welcome message shown in Figure 4.23. Close the configuration dialogs and restart the virtual machine.

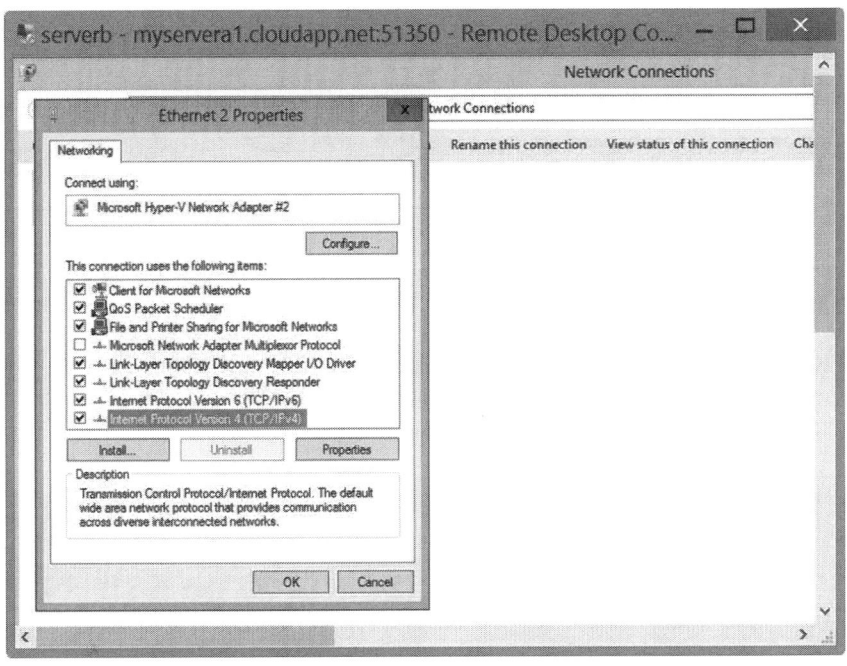

Figure 4.17 Ethernet 2 properties.

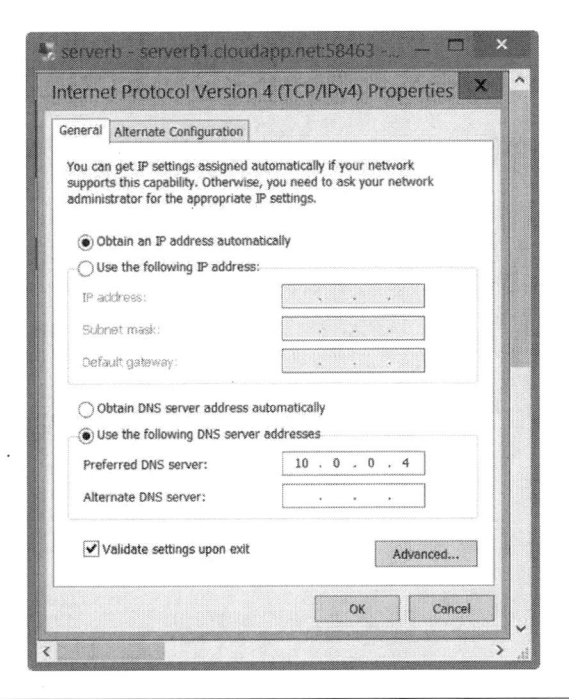

Figure 4.18 Entering IP address of servera.

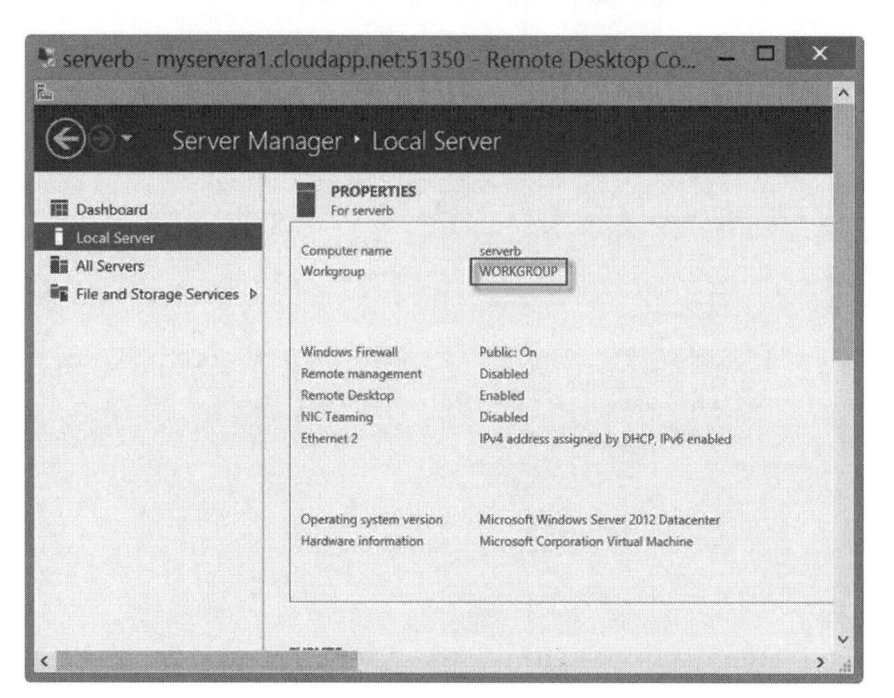

Figure 4.19   Workgroup.

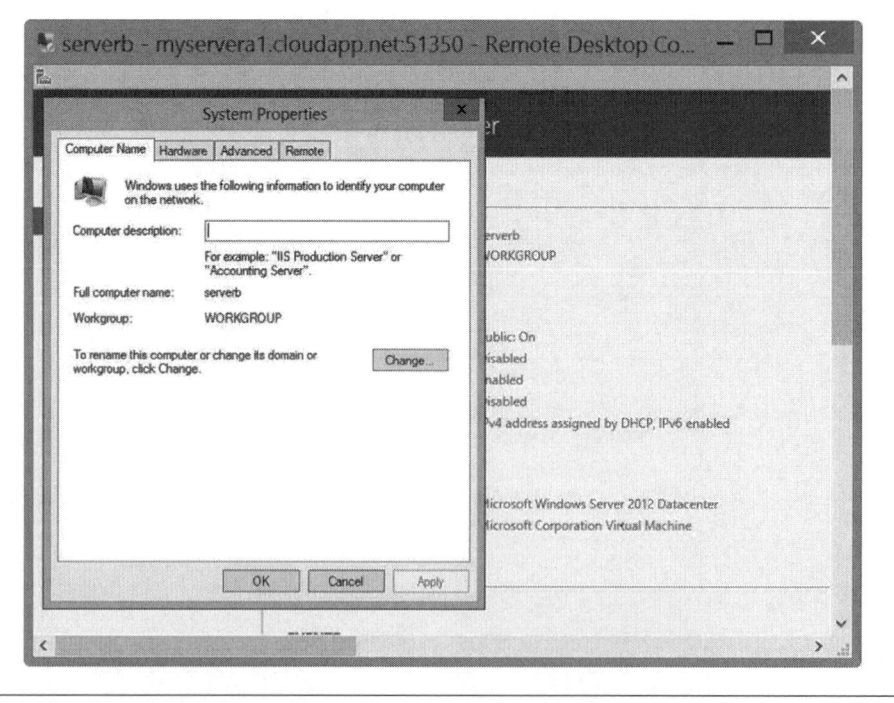

Figure 4.20   Changing system properties.

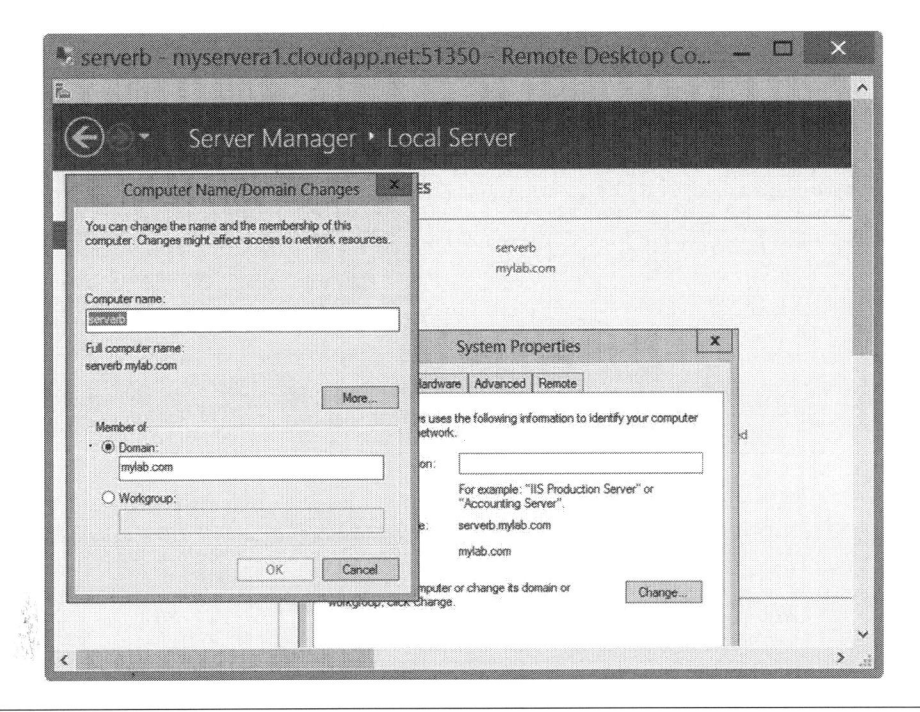

Figure 4.21 Domain name.

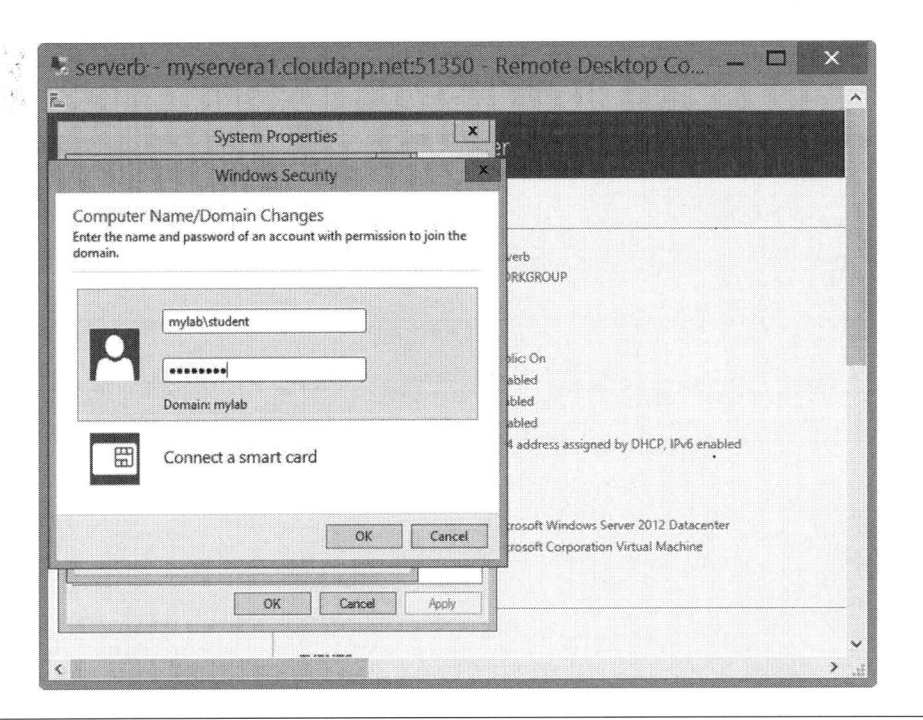

Figure 4.22 Entering user name and password.

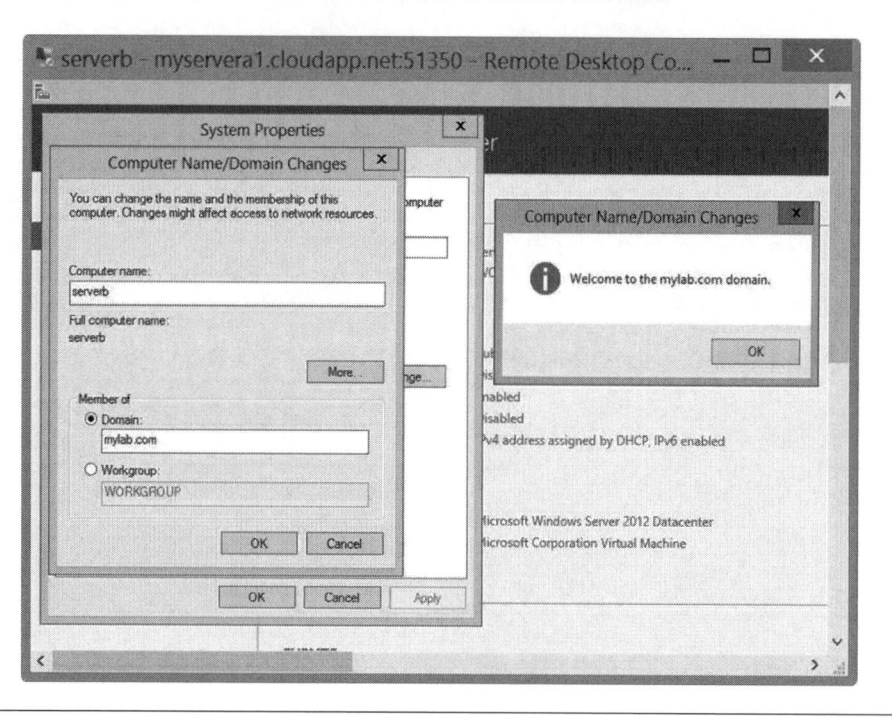

Figure 4.23   Welcome message.

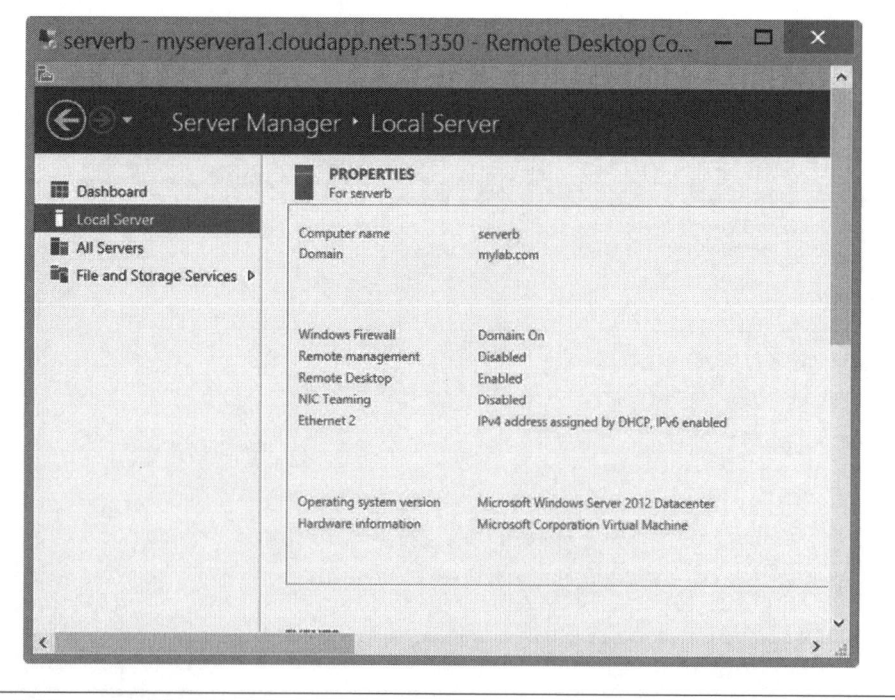

Figure 4.24   serverb joined domain.

11. Once the virtual machine is rebooted, in the Microsoft Azure Management Portal, reconnect to **serverb**. Through another user option, log in with the username, which has the domain prefix such as mylab\xxx where xxx is your user name. Click the **Local Server** link; you should be able to see that serverb has joined the domain as shown in Figure 4.24.

Task 3: Configuring serverb as a Replica Domain Controller

In case that the domain controller fails, the replica domain controller continues to perform the centralized authentication service. It provides fault tolerance and load balancing.

1. Log on to **serverb**. Click the **Manage** menu and select **Add Roles and Features**.
2. Once the Add Roles and Feature Wizard is opened, click **Next** several times until you get to the **Select server roles** page.
3. Check the option Active Directory Domain Services as shown in Figure 4.25.

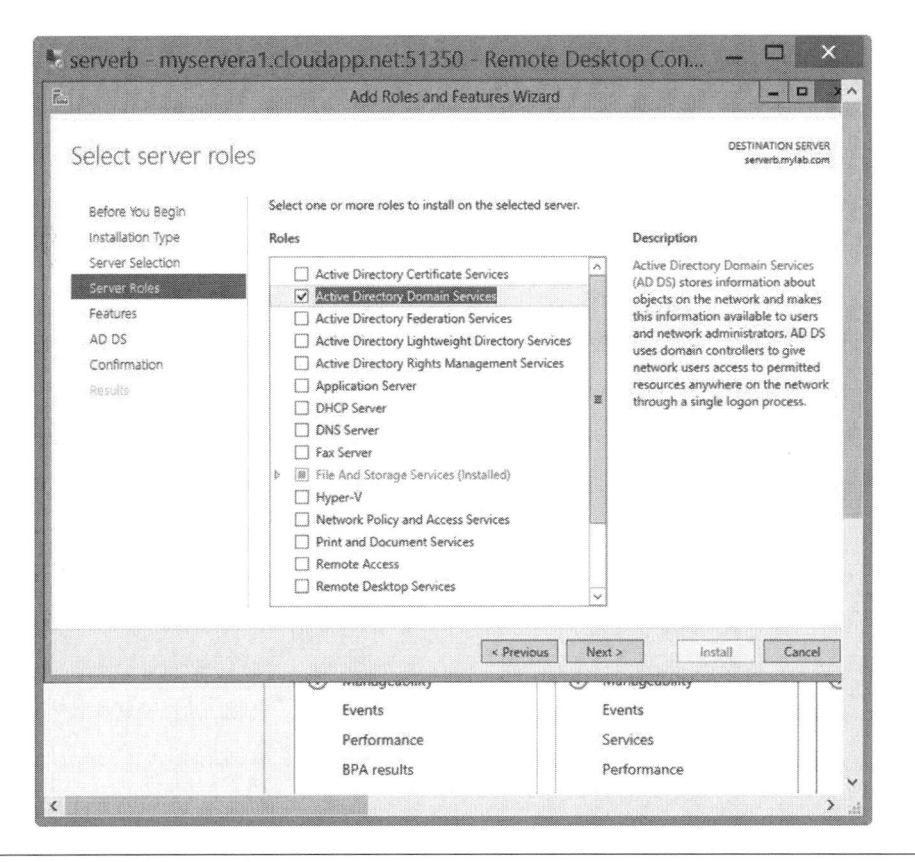

Figure 4.25   Selecting server roles.

4. When prompted to add additional features, click **Add Features**. Then, click **Next** until you get to the **Confirm installation selection** page. Check the check box **Restart the destination server automatically if required** and click **Install**.

5. Once the installation is completed, click the **Promote this server to a domain controller** link as shown in Figure 4.26.

6. In the Active Directory Domain Services Configuration Wizard, check the option **Add a domain controller to an existing domain**. Type in the domain name as **mylab.com** as shown in Figure 4.27.

7. Click the **Change** button to open the Windows Security dialog. Enter the user name as mylab\xxx where xxx is your user name (Figure 4.28). Then, click **OK**.

   Note that, if there is an error and you cannot contact the domain controller, you may need to reconfigure your Ethernet 2 network card to use the IP address of servera as the preferred DNS server (Figure 4.29).

8. As shown in Figure 4.30, the credential has been changed to add the domain prefix to the user name. Then, click **Next**.

   Note: If you cannot log onto the domain with the student account, change it to the administrator's account.

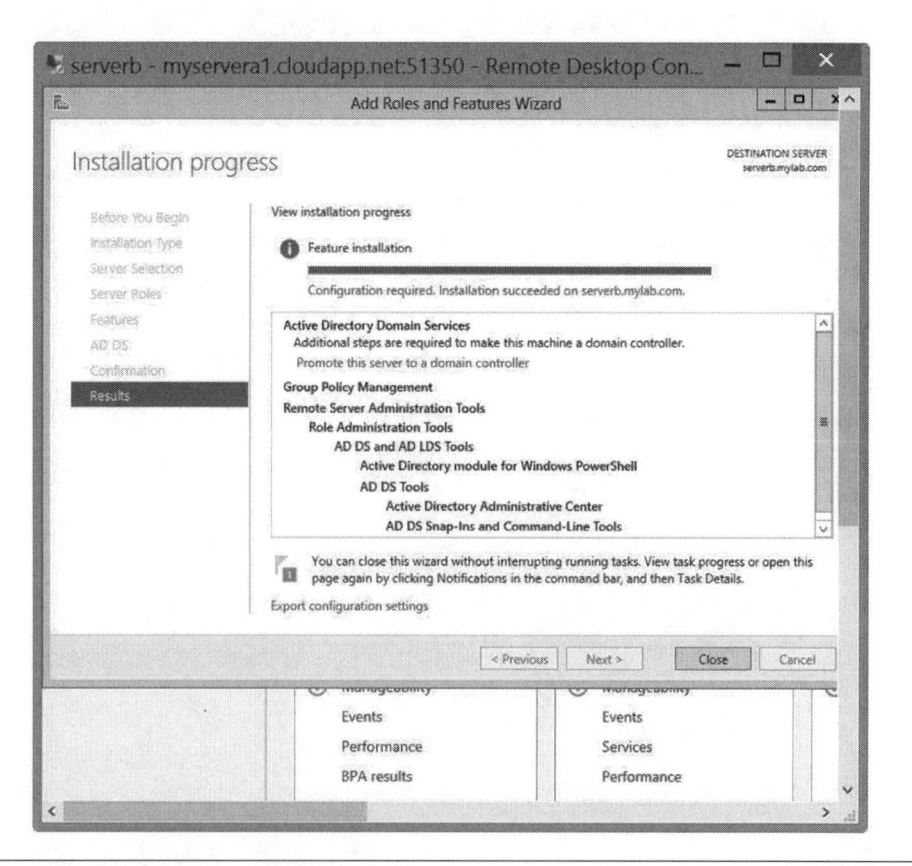

Figure 4.26   Promoting server to domain controller.

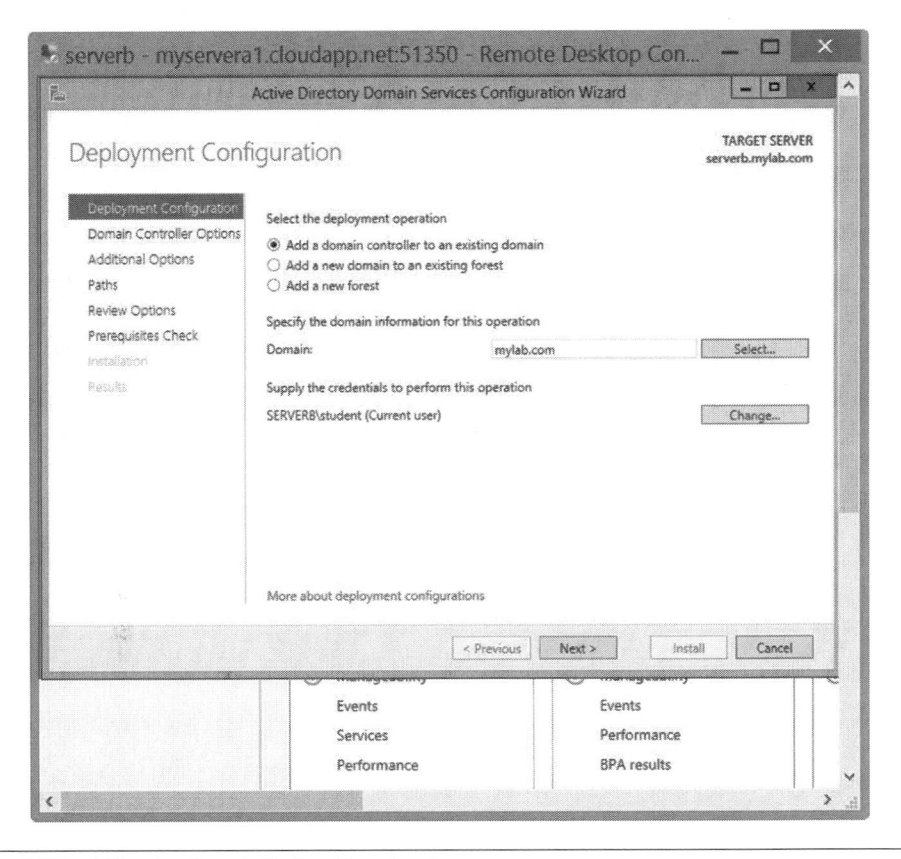

Figure 4.27 Adding domain controller to existing domain.

9. Click **Next** until you get to the Domain Controller Options page. Enter the password as shown in Figure 4.31.
10. Click **Next** until you get to the Prerequisites Check page. Then, click **Install** as shown in Figure 4.32.
11. After reboot, reconnect to serverb. Enter the user name mylab\student and password (Figure 4.33). Then, click **OK**.
12. After logging on to serverb, you can see that a new AD DS is added (Figure 4.34).

Task 4: Creating and Viewing Active Directory Objects

In this task, you are going to create an OU and a sub-OU. You will also view the domain controllers installed in this domain.

1. Suppose that you have logged to the **servera** virtual machine. In Server Manager, click the **Tools** menu. Then, click **Active Directory Users and Computers**.
2. In the Active Directory Users and Computers dialog, select your domain such as **mylab.com**. Click the **Action** menu, select **New**, and then choose **Organizational Unit** as shown in Figure 4.35.

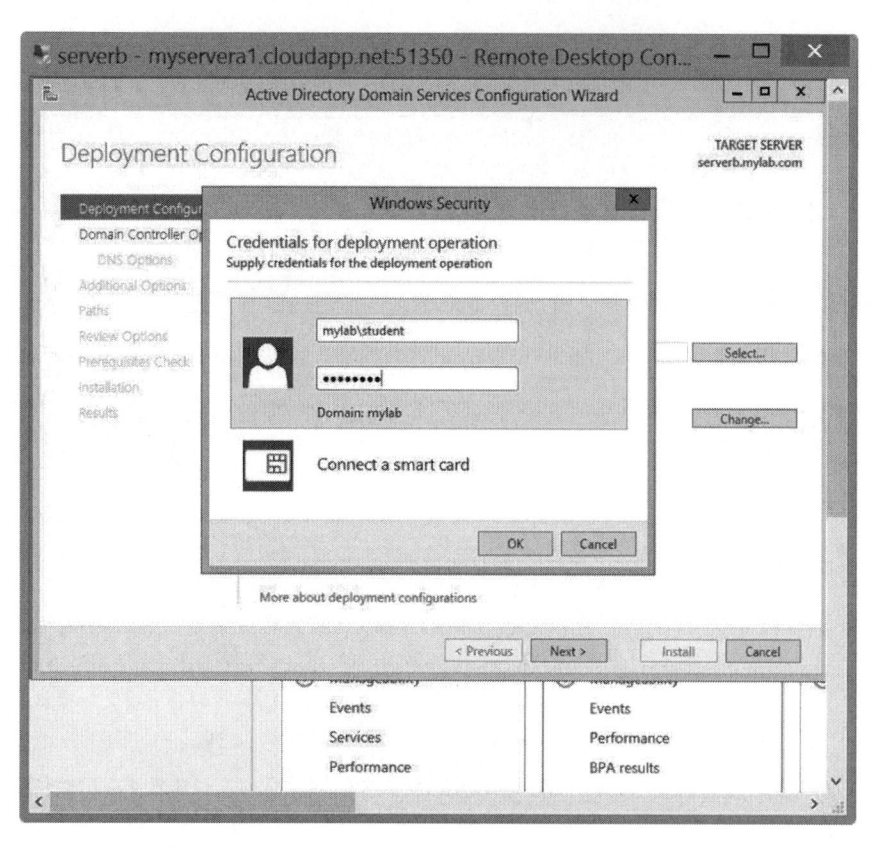

Figure 4.28   Entering user name and password.

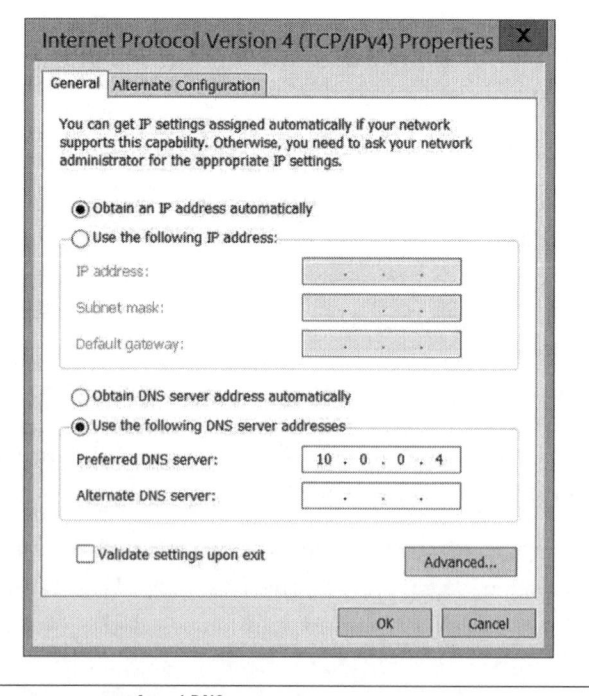

Figure 4.29   Specifying servera as preferred DNS server.

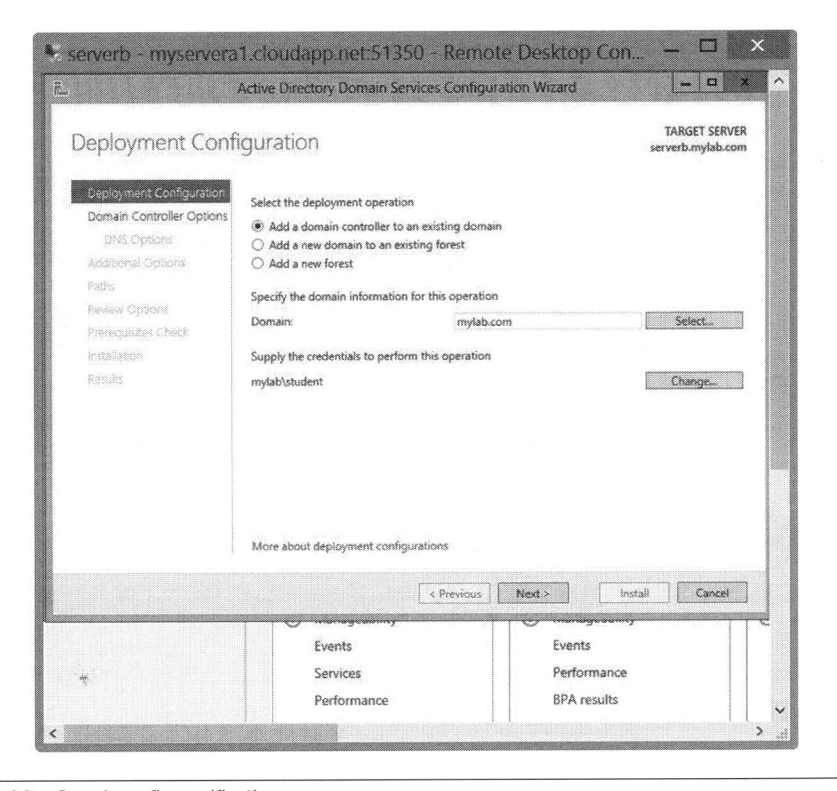

Figure 4.30 Domain prefix specification.

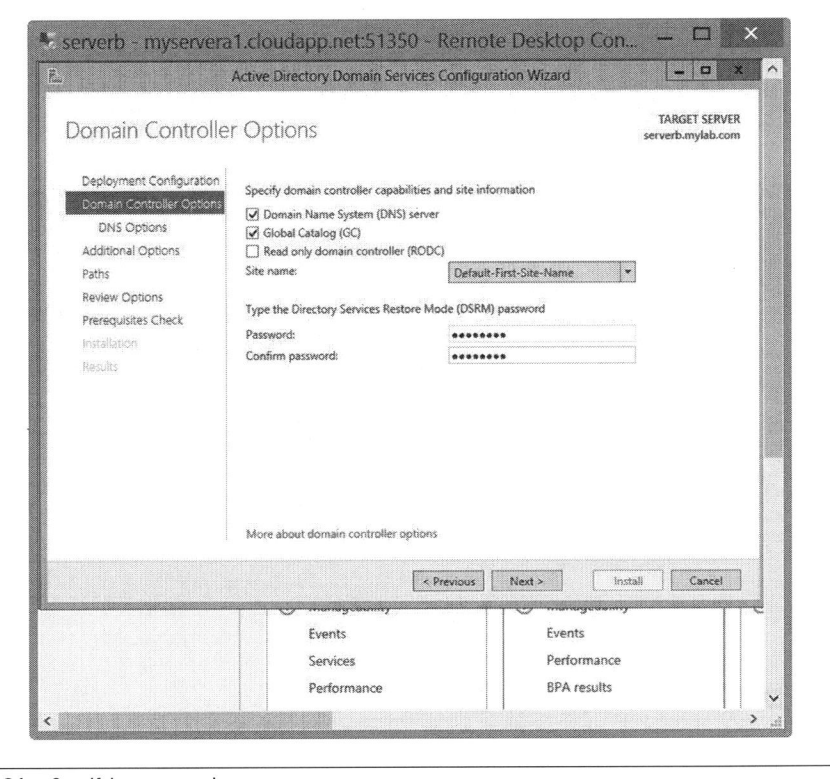

Figure 4.31 Specifying password.

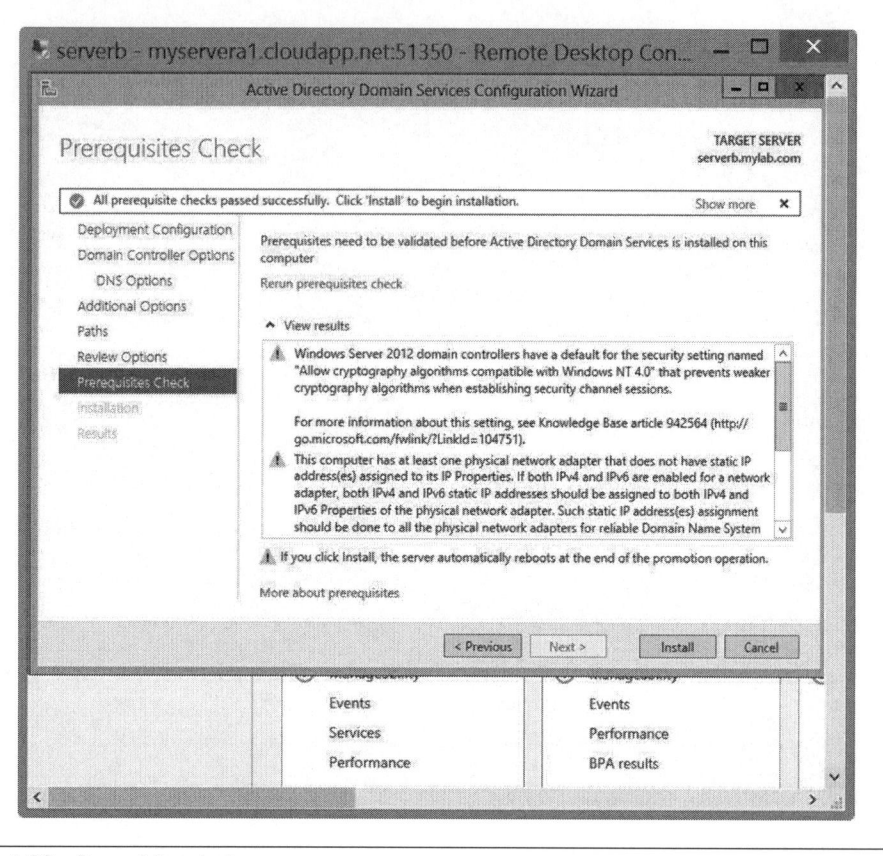

Figure 4.32   Prerequisites check page.

Figure 4.33   Entering credentials.

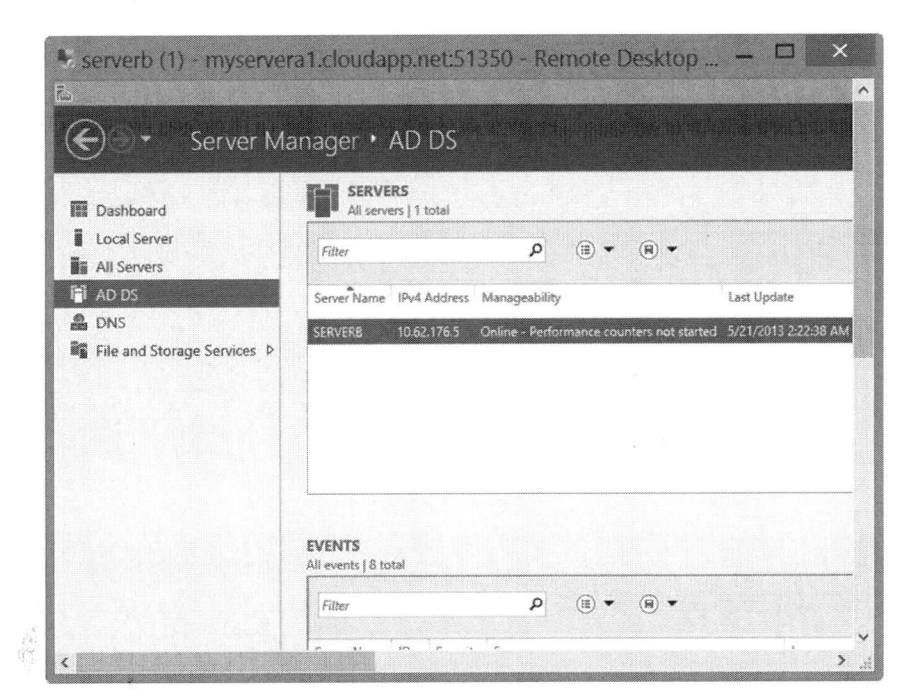

Figure 4.34 New AD DS.

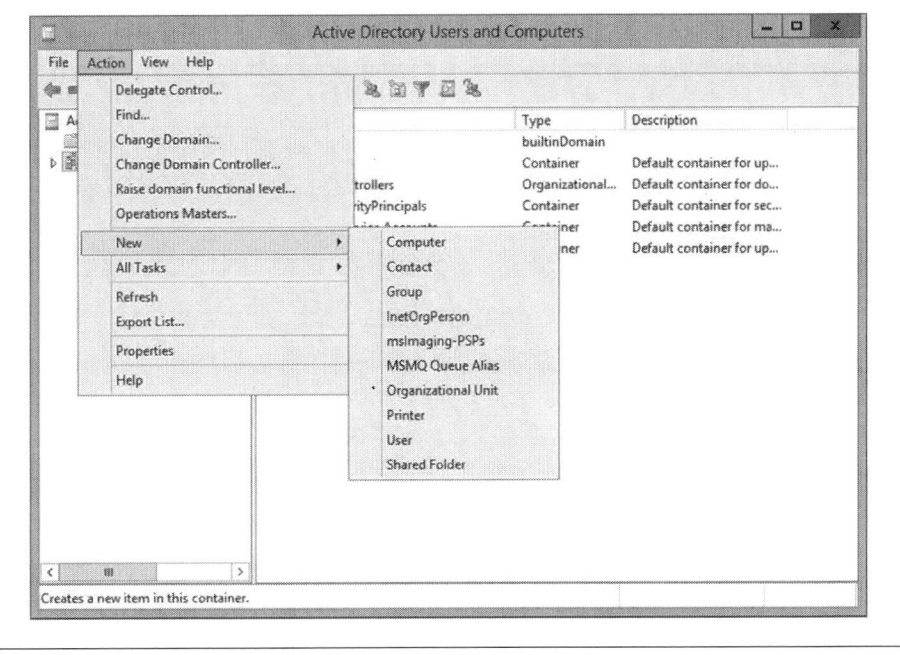

Figure 4.35 Creating OU.

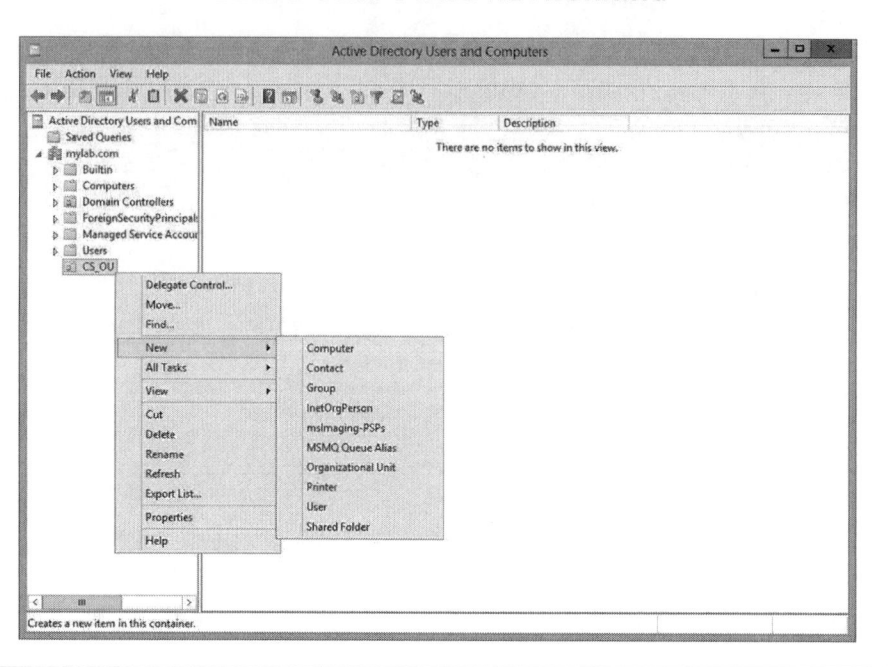

Figure 4.36 Creating sub-OU.

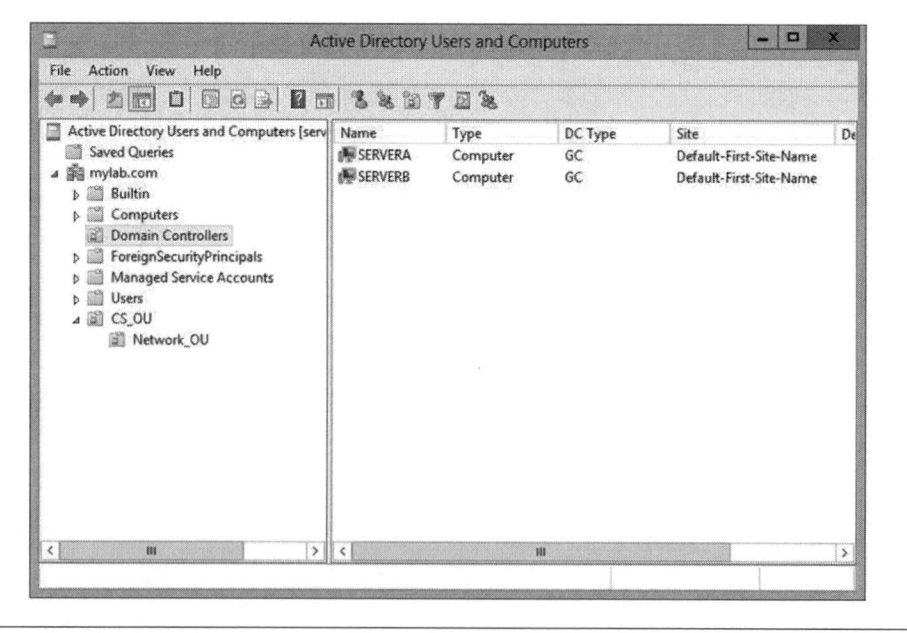

Figure 4.37 Domain controllers.

3. Provide a name to your OU such as **CS_OU** and then click **OK**.

4. To create a sub-OU, right click the newly created OU **CS_OU** in Active Directory Users and Computers. Click **New** and select **Organizational Unit** as shown in Figure 4.36.

5. Name the sub-OU as **Network_OU** and then click **OK**.

6. To view other Active Directory objects such as the domain controllers created in the previous steps, click the **Domain Controllers** node. You should be able to see the two domain controllers, SERVERA and SERVERB as shown in Figure 4.37.

7. In the Microsoft Azure Management Portal, shutdown both servera and serverb before exiting the Microsoft Azure Management Portal.

4.6 Summary

This chapter deals with Active Directory–related topics. Through a logical model, Active Directory components such as forests, domains, domain trees, OUs, and other Active Directory components are described in detail. The Active Directory development process consists of four stages, requirement analysis, logical model specification, implementation of Active Directory, and deployment of Active Directory. This chapter describes how the tasks in each stage can be accomplished. To enhance the understanding of Active Directory, a hands-on activity is provided. The hands-on activity implements Active Directory services on the virtual machines created on the Microsoft Azure cloud platform. Through the hands-on activities provided in this chapter, readers can create a forest, domains in the forest, OUs, and other Active Directory objects. The hands-on practice demonstrates how to use the authentication service provided by Active Directory. Our next task is to develop some network services. You will find more network services in the next chapter.

Review Questions

1. What tasks can be accomplished with directory services?
2. What is the directory-service supported Windows operating system?
3. What are the benefits of using the logical structure of Active Directory?
4. Explain the term schema of Active Directory.
5. Describe the user object in Active Directory.
6. Describe the computer object in Active Directory.
7. Describe the group object in Active Directory.
8. What tasks can be accomplished by an OU object?
9. Name the objects contained in a domain object.
10. What boundary can be formed by a domain object?

11. What type of Active Directory object should be created for organization-level administration?
12. What objects are contained in a forest object?
13. In a forest, where are the Active Directory objects stored?
14. Name some of the questions that may be asked for the requirement analysis.
15. Name some top-level domains.
16. What policies can be set at the domain level?
17. Name the objects to which a group policy cannot be applied.
18. Describe the data owner and service owner.
19. Why do we need to install at least two domain controllers?
20. What tasks should be accomplished before rolling out an Active Directory?

5

DYNAMIC HOST SERVICE AND NAME SERVICE

Objectives

- Install and configure the DHCP service.
- Install and configure the Domain Name System (DNS) service.

5.1 Introduction

In addition to Active Directory services, there are some other important network services such as the Dynamic Host Configuration Protocol (DHCP) service and Domain Name System (DNS) service. In this chapter, we will discuss these two services. To be able to communicate with one another, each network host must have an IP address. If a network has only a few network hosts, we may manually assign an IP address to each host. However, when a network has a large number of hosts, it may not be practical to assign IP addresses manually. Especially, when working in the wireless environment, network hosts such as mobile devices come in and out of a network randomly. In such a case, it is impossible for network administrators to manually assign an IP address to each mobile device that joins the network. To be more efficient on assigning IP addresses, this chapter introduces the DHCP service, which automates the IP address assignment process. DNS service is another key network service. For example, to access a website, we must provide the name of the web server. However, network hosts communicate through IP addresses. Therefore, we must have a service that is able to convert the name of a server to its corresponding IP address so that the web server and client computer can communicate with each other. This chapter will teach the configuration and management of DNS, which is used to resolve the IP address for a given name or vice versa. This chapter will provide hands-on practice on both the DHCP service and DNS service.

5.2 Dynamic Host Configuration Protocol

During a computer's boot process, the DHCP service assigns an IP address that is able to communicate with other network hosts on the local network. In addition to assigning the IP address, the DHCP service can also deliver other network parameters, such as the IP addresses of a DNS server and subnet masks, to the computer during the boot-up time. All the assignments are done automatically without requiring the network administrator to configure the IP addresses. In this section, your first task is to understand how the DHCP service does the job of assigning IP addresses. After that, you will learn how to configure the DHCP service.

5.2.1 Dynamic IP Address Assignment Process

A client–server approach is used by the DHCP service to assign IP addresses. During the IP address assignment, one or more preconfigured DHCP servers should be reachable in the network. When a computer that is the DHCP client boots up, it searches for a DHCP server by broadcasting a DHCP discovery packet called DHCPDISCOVER. The broadcast address 255.255.255.255 is used by the DHCP service to reach each network host in the local network. Once the DHCP server receives the DHCP discovery packet, the DHCP server responds by broadcasting a packet called DHCPOFFER, which contains the IP address, the IP address lease time, the subnet mask, and the information about the default gateway. If there are multiple DHCP servers in the local network, the DHCP client will receive multiple responses from these DHCP servers. Usually, the DHCP client takes the first offer. Once the DHCP server is chosen, the DHCP client will send the broadcast packet DHCPREQUEST to inform all the servers about which DHCP server has been accepted. The chosen DHCP server broadcasts a packet DHCPACK back to the DHCP client to inform it that it can now use the IP address for communication. The dynamic IP address assignment process is illustrated in Figure 5.1.

If the DHCP server is not reachable during the IP address assignment process, the DHCP client will not get an IP address useful for communication in the local network. Instead, the DHCP client will get an Automatic Private IP Addressing (APIPA) IP address. APIPA IP addresses range from 169.254.0.1 to 169.254.255.254, which cannot be used to join the local domain. However, the computer assigned with the APIPA IP address can communicate with other computers assigned with APIPA IP addresses. Once the DHCP is available, the APIPA IP address will be automatically replaced by the IP address assigned by the DHCP server.

After a dynamic IP address is assigned to a computer, it needs to be renewed before a predefined lease time expires. The default DHCP lease time is 8 days. The lease time can be specified during the configuration of a DHCP server. The dynamic IP address is automatically renewed after half of the lease time expires. Once half of the lease time is reached, the DHCP client will issue a new request to the DHCP server to renew the IP address. The new request is issued by sending a DHCPREQUEST packet directly to the DHCP server. Once the DHCP server is reached, it will respond with a DHCPACK packet if the renewal is successful or a DHCPNACK packet if the renewal is not successful. In case that the original DHCP server is not available due to failure or maintenance, the computer may contact other DHCP servers for a new IP address. The expired IP address can be recycled and assigned to another computer (Figure 5.2).

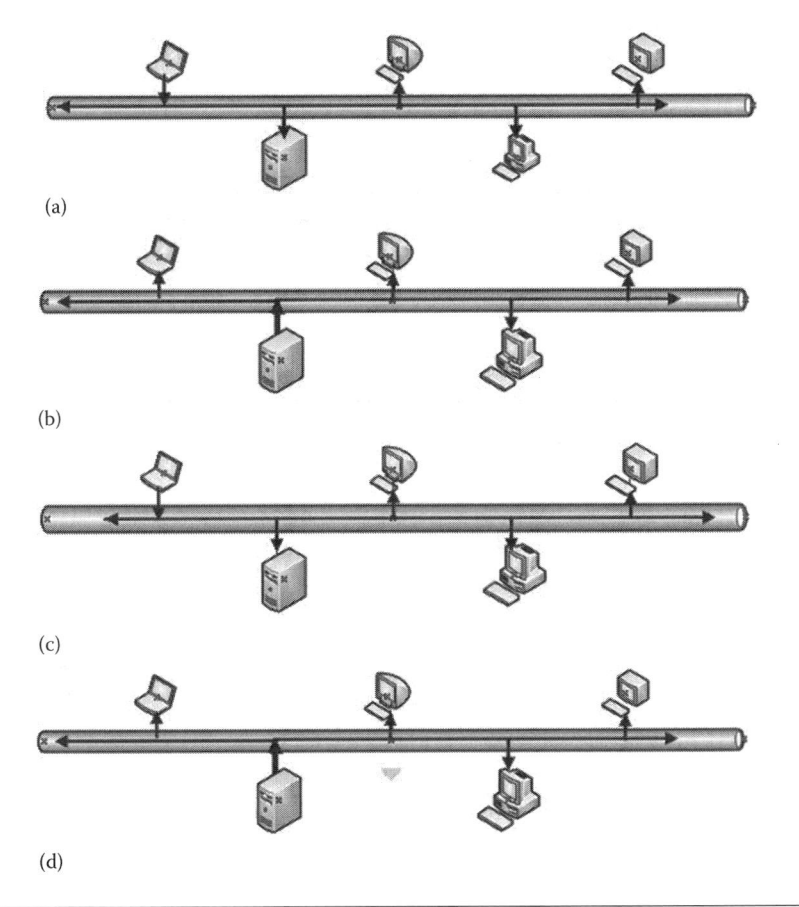

Figure 5.1   Dynamic IP address assignment process. (a) Broadcasting DHCPDISCOVER packet from client (b) Responding with DHCPOFFER packet from DHCP server (c) Broadcasting DHCPREQUEST packet from DHCP client (d) Responding with DHCPACK packet from DHCP server.

Usually, the dynamic IP address assigned to a computer is not permanent unless it is specifically configured as a permanent IP address. Although a dynamically assigned IP address is just fine for most of the computers, there are some situations where a computer may need a permanent IP address. For example, in the situation where a computer is so configured that it is accessible remotely, this computer needs a permanent IP address. With the permanent IP address, the other network hosts can be configured with the remote connection dedicated to this computer. If a network administrator needs to assign a computer a permanent IP address, he or she can assign a fixed IP address or assign a reserved dynamic IP address to that computer by relating a specific IP address to the hardware address of that computer. This can be done during the configuration of the DHCP service.

When a DHCP client broadcasts a packet to search for a DHCP server, the broadcasted packet cannot be forwarded through a router. Therefore, each subnet should have its own DHCP server. Or, we can configure a router so that the broadcasted packet can be forwarded to another subnet. By doing so, the DHCP client is able to

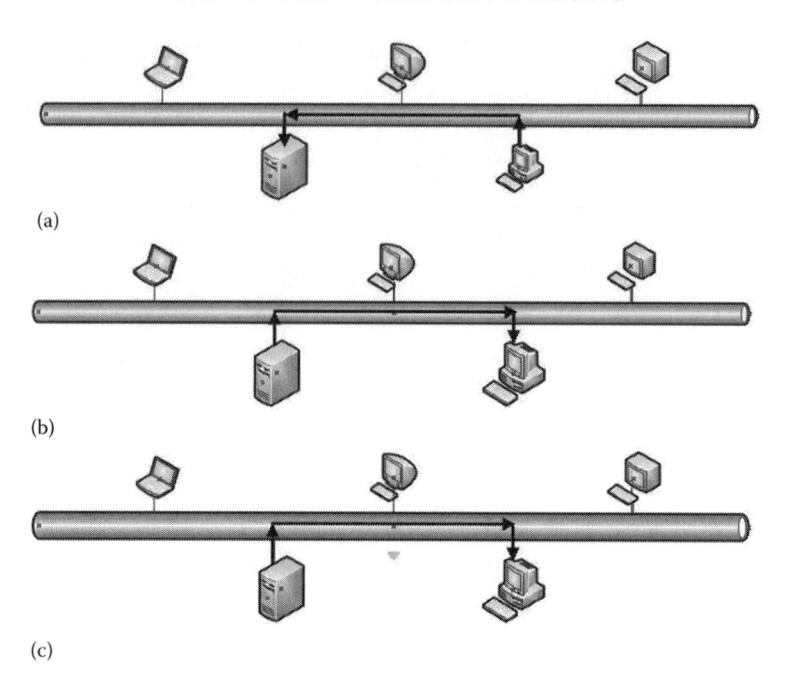

Figure 5.2   DHCP renewal process. (a) Client sends DHCPREQUEST packet to DHCP server (b) DHCP server responses with DHCPACK packet if successful (c) DHCP server responds with DHCPNACK packet if unsuccessful.

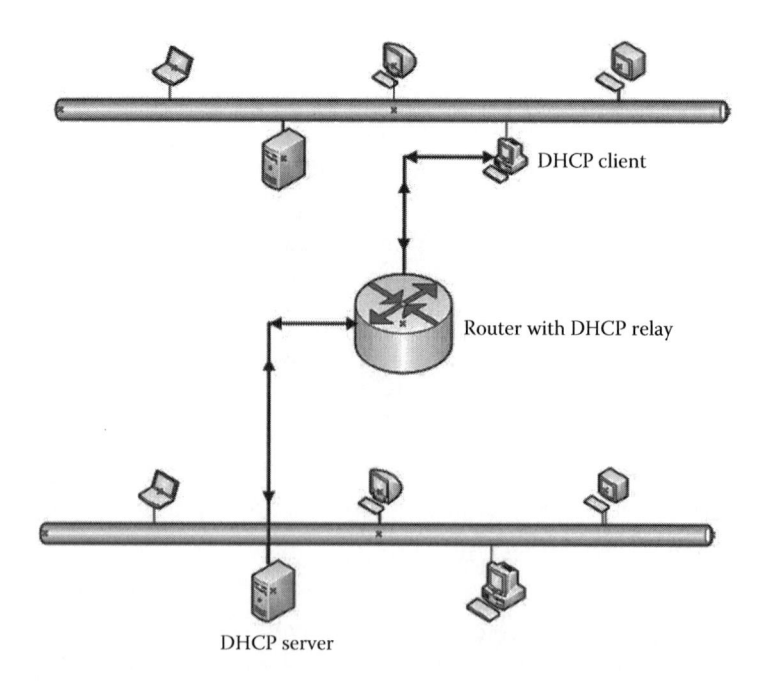

Figure 5.3   DHCP relay.

get a dynamic IP address from the DHCP server in another subnet. This can be done through the service called a DHCP relay. Using a DHCP relay is a more cost-efficient way to assign IP addresses to computers in multiple subnets.

If a router is configured as a DHCP relay, it will pass DHCP request packets to another network. The router is so configured that it can find a DHCP server in a different network and forward DHCP requests to that DHCP server. When the DHCP server responds with a broadcasted packet, the router with the DHCP relay gets the packet and forwards it to the DHCP client in another network as shown in Figure 5.3.

Offering dynamic IP addresses to other network hosts in the network can cause a security problem. A hacker can set up a DHCP server in a network to offer IP addresses to network hosts so that these hosts are unable to access resources in the network. Therefore, the DHCP server should be authorized by the network administrator before it can start the DHCP service.

5.2.2 DHCP Configuration

Before we can configure the DHCP service, we need to install the DHCP role with Server Manager provided by Windows Server 2012. The installation has the prerequisites as follows:

- The user who performs the installation needs to be a domain user with the local administrative privilege.
- In a production environment, the server with the DHCP role installed should have a static IP address.

Each subnet is designed to have its own IP address range. The scope is defined according the IP address range for the subnet. A scope can be specified with the following properties:

- The range of IP addresses to be handed out by the DHCP server
- A subnet mask that is used to define the prefix/suffix of the IP addresses to be handed out by the DHCP server
- A scope name given by the network administrator
- The lease time for a handed-out IP address
- Additional information to be handed out with the IP addresses, such as the name server IP address and the subnet gateway IP address
- A list of reserved IP addresses used to make a DHCP client always receive the same IP address

The scope can be defined with two strategies. The first strategy is to define the scope to include all the available IP addresses in the network. Then, exclude the IP addresses that will be used as reserved IP addresses and static IP addresses. The second strategy is to define the scope by using some of the available IP addresses in the network.

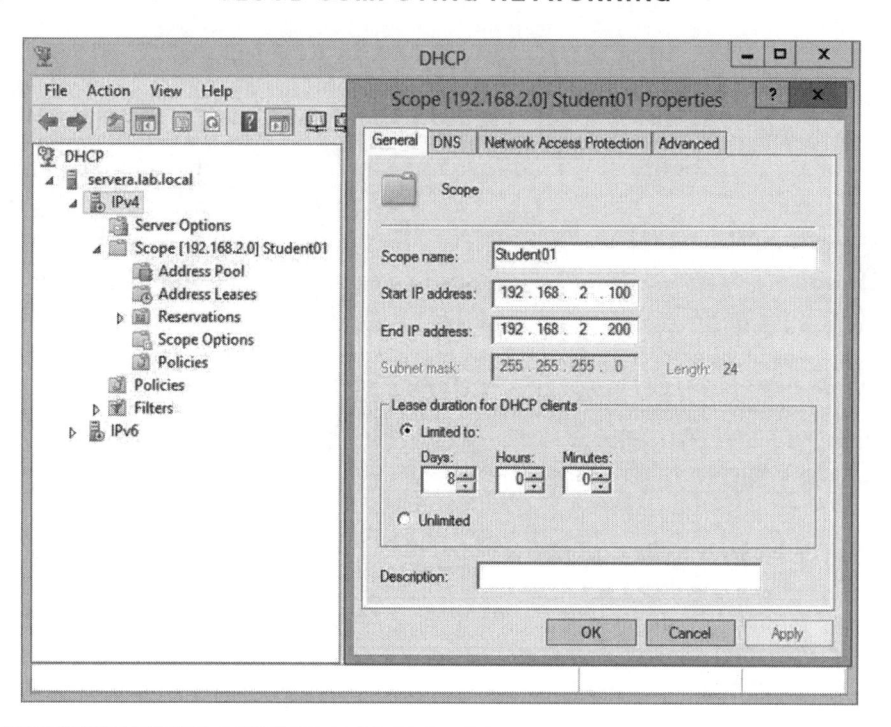

Figure 5.4 Scope configuration.

With this strategy, the scope can be defined by specifying a range with a start IP address and an end IP address as shown in Figure 5.4.

As seen in Figure 5.4, after the range of IP addresses is specified, the DHCP service provides a default subnet mask. In Figure 5.4 the default subnet mask is 255.255.255.0, which is given based on the IP address 192.168.2.100 entered in the configuration. The default subnet mask works if the network is so defined that it belongs to one of the primary classes. However, in a situation where a primary class is divided into multiple subnets, the network administrator needs to enter the subnet masks in the DHCP configuration to define the subnets. The IP addresses to be assigned to the computers on a subnet will be assigned the same subnet mask.

To reserve some of the IP addresses for some of the DHCP clients so that they can always receive the same IP addresses, the network administrator can create an exclusion range in the DHCP scope. The IP addresses within the exclusion range will not be automatically assigned to computers. They can only be manually assigned to DHCP clients. When specifying the exclusion range, the network administrator needs to consider potential growth of the network. The exclusion range should include some extra IP addresses for future use on routers, DHCP servers, DNS servers, and other network devices such as printers and network storage devices. From the example shown in Figure 5.4, the scope includes the IP addresses between 192.168.2.100 and 192.168.2.200. This leaves the exclusion range from 192.168.2.1 to 192.168.2.99 and from 192.168.201 to 192.168.2.254.

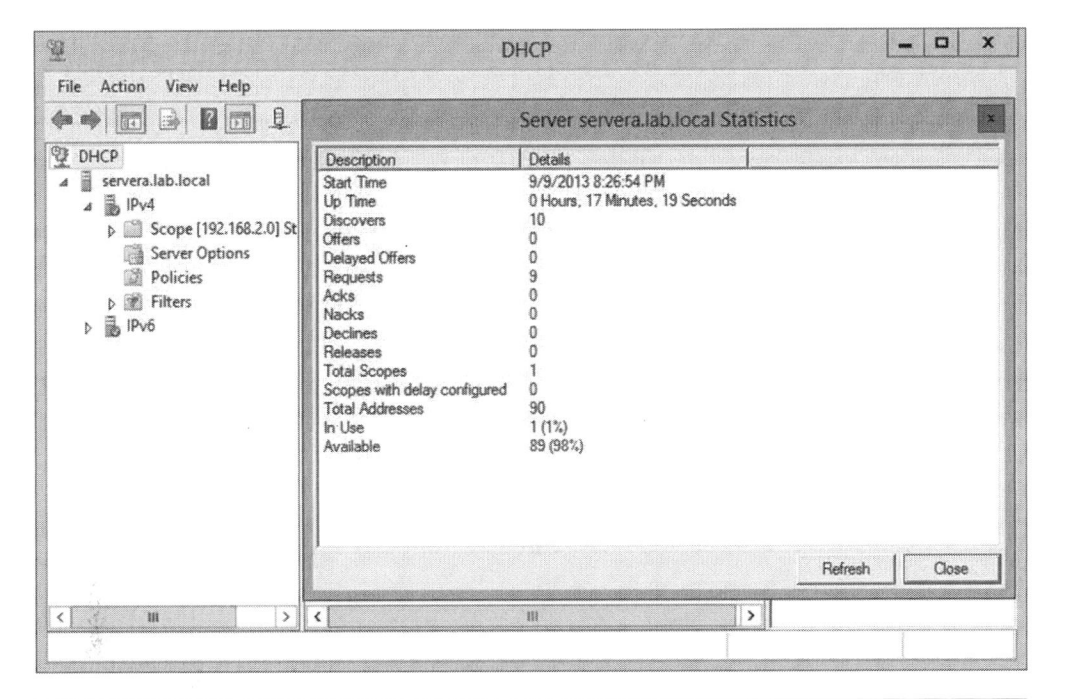

Figure 5.5 DHCP statistics.

Step-by-step instructions on DHCP service configuration will be given in Activity 5.1. Once IP addresses are handed out to DHCP clients, IP address–related information will be recorded in the database file Dhcp.mdb. As a database, the file is automatically backed up every 60 min. In case of failure, the backup file will be used in the database recovery. The DHCP service automatically tracks the operations. The tracked information can be displayed through a GUI interface as shown in Figure 5.5.

5.3 Domain Name System

As you have learned, each network host needs an IP address for data communication. However, the IP address is not easy for a user to remember. Users prefer to have a meaningful name for a network host so that it reflects what the host can do or where the host is located. A name service resolves host names to IP addresses and vice versa. Name services are essential for large organizations. For a large organization, its hierarchical system can be represented by an Active Directory system. The naming of domains and other Active Directory objects is based on the names of the organization, sites, departments, offices, and each individual computer and network device. To be able to access these Active Directory objects such as a domain controller, the naming service can be used to convert the names used in the Active Directory to the corresponding IP addresses. In today's Internet computing environment, each web server has a distinct name representing the host organization. By doing so, users can easily remember them during web surfing. It is necessary to resolve a web server name to the corresponding IP address, so the web server can communicate with computers installed with the web browser. Also, all e-mail servers have meaningful names so that users can easily identify e-mail senders and receivers. Again, the name service is required to resolve the names of e-mail servers and the corresponding IP addresses. In summary, the name service is a critical component for supporting the daily operation of an organization.

The DNS is a name service protocol, which is widely used for name services. DNS works like a distributed database, which contains the pairs of names and IP addresses. When a client requests the IP address for a given name, DNS searches the corresponding IP address in the distributed database. Once the IP address is found, DNS returns the IP address to the client. Reversely, DNS can find the corresponding name for a given IP address. Later, in the hands-on practice, you will learn how to install and configure a DNS service and how to manage the DNS server.

5.3.1 Naming Hierarchy

The naming of a network host uses the naming convention of Active Directory. For example, myhost.mydepartment.mycollege.myuniversity.edu.

The host name is a sequence of names separated with periods. This name represents the hierarchical structure of a university. The name on the right has more general use than the one on the left. The right most name is the most general name that is provided by the top-level domain. There are only a limited number of such domains that are managed by the Internet Corporation for Assigned Names and Numbers (ICANN). The commonly used top-level domains are listed in Table 5.1. Each of the names in the top-level domain represents a main category of the naming system.

The top-level domains can also be listed based on the country code. Table 5.2 illustrates some of the country-code-based top-level domains.

Table 5.1   Examples of Category-based Top-Level Domains

DOMAIN NAME	CATEGORY
.biz	Business
.com	Commercial
.edu	Education
.gov	Government
.info	Information
.int	International use
.mil	Military
.museum	Museums
.net	Network Organization
.org	Nonprofit Organization

Table 5.2 Example of Country-Code-Based Top-Level Domains

DOMAIN NAME	CATEGORY
.us	United States
.au	Australia
.ca	Canada
.cn	China
.de	Germany
.ru	Russia
.uk	United Kingdom
.tv	Tuvalu
.ws	Samoa

Many of the small countries such as Tuvalu and Samoa allow the public to register in their top-level domains. For example, the top-level domain.tv has been registered by many television companies.

To be able to connect to the Internet, it is necessary for an organization to register to one of the top-level domains. The organization needs to submit its name to ICANN for approval. Once the name is approved by ICANN, the organization's name is registered under a selected top-level domain. After it is registered in the top-level domain, the organization can add more lower level names under the top-level domain name. According to the hierarchical structure of the organization, department names and host names can all be added to the organization's name. Under the organization's name, one can add up to 127 layers of names. It is required that the host names within the same domain must be unique. If the organization has multiple servers running at the same time, it can distinguish these servers by naming them according to their functions such as mail, www, and learning.

5.3.2 DNS Server Hierarchy

As we know, the Internet connects billions of the hosts. Therefore, there are billions of unique names and IP addresses related to these names. DNS needs to handle the name resolution of billions of hosts on the Internet. For such a gigantic task, it is not practical to handle the job by using one database and one server. The database would have billions of records and the server that hosted the database would need to handle billions of requests every day. In case that the server had a problem, the entire Internet would shut down. Therefore, DNS databases are distributed to many DNS servers. In the DNS server hierarchical system, the root server hosts the top-level domain, which stores the IP address and name records such as com and edu. Under the root DNS server, there are top-level DNS servers for a top-level domain. Each top-level DNS server hosts a database that contains the name–IP address pairs of the organizations registered to the top-level DNS server. Under the top-level DNS server, organizations may have their own DNS servers, each of which stores its own IP address and name pairs. Many organizations create their own name service for better security and performance. For some large organizations, they may have lower level DNS servers for their sites and departments.

Searching for records in such a distributed database can be a complicated task. One needs to know where to find the DNS server hosting the database that has the requested records. The next section illustrates how to search for a record in a hierarchical distributed DNS database.

5.3.3 Name Resolution Process

The process to match the IP address for a given domain name is called a forward lookup process. Reversely, the process to match the domain name for a given IP address is called a reverse lookup process. The following is an example of a forward lookup process. Suppose that a student needs to remotely access the lab server from home. The student enters the following URL in a web browser: lab.cis.myuniversity.edu.

After the student presses the Enter key, the operating system first checks the file named HOSTS for the related IP address. If the file HOSTS does not have the matching IP address for the name entered in the URL, the operating system will check the DNS cache to see if there is a matched IP address. If not, the operating system on the client computer issues a name resolution request to the local DNS server whose IP address is specified during the configuration of the network interface card. If there is no matched IP address in the database hosted by the local DNS server, the request will be forwarded to the root server since each DNS server knows the root server's IP address. The root server contains the IP addresses of all the major categories of domain names such as com, edu, or org. The root server returns to the local DNS server the IP address that matches the top-level domain name in the URL; it is edu in this example. Once the local DNS server gets the IP address of the top-level domain edu, the local DNS server will issue a request to the edu DNS server. The edu DNS server will search for the IP address that matches the university name in its database. If there is a match, the edu DNS server will send the IP address that matches the university's DNS server back to the local DNS server. By using the returned IP address, the local DNS server will send the request to the university's DNS server. Once the university's DNS server gets the request, it will search for the IP address of the CIS department DNS server. If there is a match, the matched IP address will be returned back to the local DNS server. The local DNS server will then send the request to the cis DNS server for the IP address of the lab server. After the cis DNS server receives the request, it searches its database for the IP address of the lab server. If there is a match, the IP address of the lab server will be returned back to the local DNS server. After receiving the IP address, the local DNS server will send the IP address to the client computer. With the IP address of the lab server, the client can now communicate with the lab server. Figure 5.6 illustrates the name resolution process in the hierarchical system.

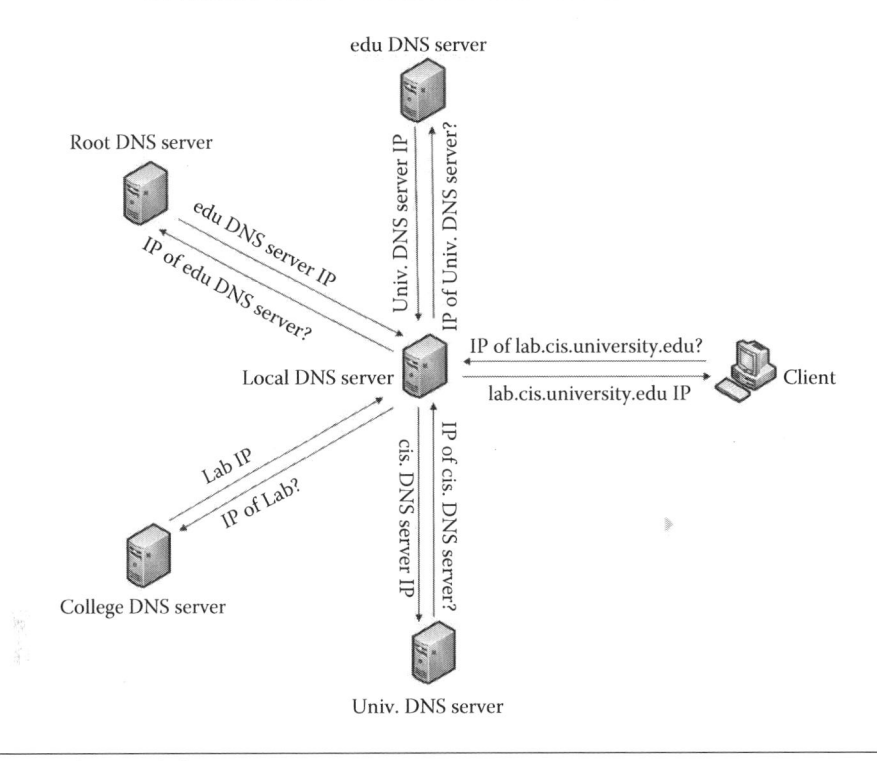

Figure 5.6 Name resolution process.

Once the client computer gets the IP address for a given name, it caches the IP address with the given name. Next time, to search for the IP address of the same host, the client computer will check the cache first. If there is a match, it gets the corresponding IP address from the cache in no time. In such a case, the client computer does not need to send a request to the local DNS server.

5.3.4 DNS Zones

As the entire DNS database is distributed to millions of DNS servers, each DNS server only hosts a small portion of the entire DNS namespace. Such a portion managed by a DNS server is called a DNS zone. After a DNS server is installed, the network administrator can create one or more DNS zones to store DNS records. There are two types of zones. One is used to store the records for forward lookup and the other one is used to store the records for reverse lookup. A forward lookup zone can be used to query another IP address for a given host name. With the DNS reverse zone, one can look up a host name for an IP address. The network administrator can manually create a forward zone on a DNS server. On a primary DNS server, a forward zone can be automatically created during the installation of a DNS server if DNS is integrated with Active Directory. When a reverse lookup zone is created, the standard domain name in-addr.arpa is used for the reverse lookup zone. For example, to create a reverse lookup zone on a computer with the IP address 192.168.2.1, the reverse lookup zone name should be

2.168.192. in-addr.arpa

where 2.168.192 is the reverse order of the numbers in the dotted-decimal notation of IP addresses as shown in Figure 5.7. The in-addr.arpa domain name applies to all IPv4 networks.

Like a database, the zone files can be backed up or replicated to many other servers for fault tolerance. The copies of a zone file can be distributed to other DNS servers at different physical locations to reduce network traffic. The originally created zone is called the master zone (or the primary zone) and the copy of the master zone is called the slave zone (or the secondary zone). During a replication process, the master zone and slave zones are automatically synchronized.

For better security and management, the DNS zone can be stored in the Active Directory. The DNS zone can be stored in two areas, the domain directory partition and the application directory partition, in the Active Directory. Stored in the Active Directory, the DNS zone can be automatically backed up and replicated to domain controllers for fault tolerance. As the Active Directory is highly protected with various security measures, the DNS zones stored in the Active Directory are also protected by these security measures.

A domain directory partition contains Active Directory objects such as users and computers. The content of the domain directory partition is replicated to all domain controllers within the domain. This means that the DNS zones stored in the domain directory partition will also be replicated to all domain controllers even if some of the domain controllers are not configured as DNS servers. Therefore, storing DNS zones

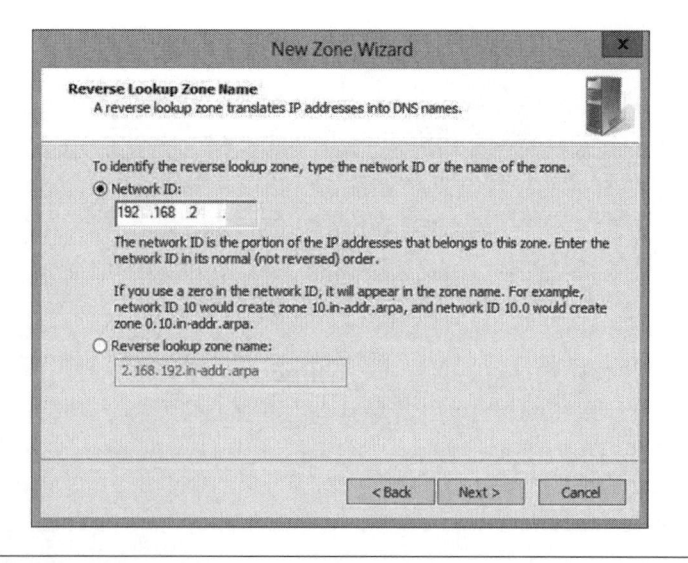

Figure 5.7   Reverse lookup zone name.

in the domain directory partition is less efficient. The application directory partition stores the application-specific data. Unlike the domain directory partition, which replicates content to all domain controllers in a domain, the application directory partition can replicate its content only to specific domain controllers. In such a way, the replication of a DNS zone stored in the application directory partition can be more efficient. There are three options for storing DNS zones in the application directory partition. One can choose to store DNS zones to all DNS servers in a forest, or to store the DNS zones to all DNS servers in a domain, or to store the DNS zones to the DNS servers in a predefined scope. By doing so, the replication of DNS zones can be limited to a few domain controllers. When creating a new zone, the network administrator can specify how the replication can be done. Figure 5.8 illustrates the available replication options.

In summary, when creating a new DNS zone with the New DNS wizard, it is recommended that the network administrator use the configuration options shown in Table 5.3.

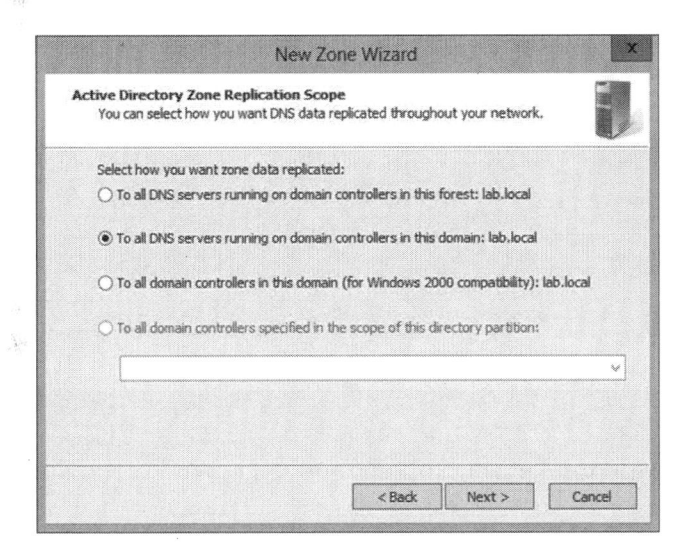

Figure 5.8 Replication options.

Table 5.3 Configuration of New DNS Zone

CONFIGURATION PAGE	CONFIGURATION OPTIONS
Zone Type page	Select the options **Primary zone** and **Store the zone in Active Directory**
Active Directory Zone Replication Scope page	Select the option **To all DNS servers running on domain controller in this domain** (Figure 5.8)
First Reverse Lookup Zone Name Wizard page	Select the option **IPv4 Reverse Lookup Zone**
Second Reverse Lookup Zone Name Wizard page	Enter network ID, for example, Network ID = 192.168.2. (Figure 5.7)
Dynamic Updates page	Select the option **Allow only secure dynamic updates** (Figure 5.10)

5.3.5 *Types of DNS Records*

DNS records are created for different services. Some of them are used to bind a domain name to an IP address, some of them are used to match an IP address to an e-mail server, some are used to match an IP address to local DNS servers, some are used for the reverse lookup, and some are used to create aliases for other domain names. The types of DNS records are summarized in Table 5.4.

5.3.6 *Stub Zone*

Sometimes, a subdomain is not registered to the top-level domain. The type of host name in such a subdomain can be used internally. To search for IP addresses of hosts outside the internal subdomain, the subdomain can use a specific DNS zone called a stub zone, which contains the records of DNS servers outside this subdomain. The stub zone can also be used in a situation where two organizations are merged. One organization has no DNS records of the other. Thus, it can set up a stub zone, which contains the records of the DNS servers of the other organization.

By using the name servers listed in a stub zone, a request from a host in one domain can be forwarded to a DNS server outside of the current domain. Once the DNS server outside of the current domain finds the IP address, it returns the IP address to the stub zone and from there the IP address is returned to the host that made the request. Figure 5.9 illustrates the name resolution process with a stub zone.

5.3.7 *Dynamic DNS*

When creating a DNS zone, records can be entered by the network administrator manually. Entering DNS records manually can be a tedious task. Dynamic DNS is such a service that it can update DNS records automatically. Dynamic DNS enables DNS client computers to register and dynamically update their records whenever changes in the IP addresses occur. When a DNS client uses DHCP or frequently

Table 5.4 Types of DNS Records

TYPE	USAGE
A	This type of record is used to resolve a host name to an IPv4 IP address.
AAAA	This type of record is used to resolve a host name to an IPv6 IP address.
CNAME	This type of record is used to assign an alias to a host name.
MX	This type of record is used to bind an IP address to a specified mail server.
NS	This type of record is used to bind an IP address to a specified DNS server.
PTR	This is the Pointer type of record used to resolve an IP address to a host name.
SOA	This is the Start of Authority type of record that contains the configuration information about the domain that this DNS server is responsible for.
SRV	This is the Service type of record that is used to store the locations of domain controllers.

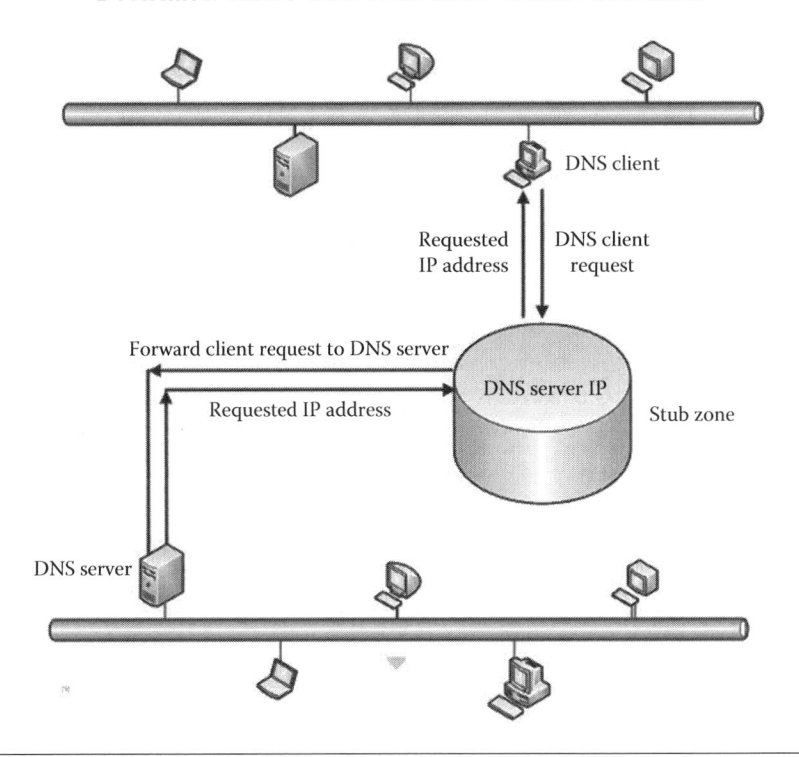

Figure 5.9 Name resolution with stub zone.

changes its location, its IP address gets altered as well. In such a case, Dynamic DNS can be used to reduce the workload of the network administrator. With the dynamic DNS service, DNS clients register themselves in a DNS server. There is no need for the network administrator to manually enter the records into a DNS zone. For the DNS zone, the network administrator can enable or disable dynamic updates. By default, dynamic updates are applied to Type A DNS records. The network administrator can configure a DNS zone to be dynamically updated securely or nonsecurely. A DNS zone can also be configured to not allow dynamic updates. The configuration can be done while creating a new zone. Figure 5.10 illustrates the dynamic update options when creating a new zone.

5.3.8 DNS Server Management

Through the GUI tools provided by the Windows Server operating system, the network administrator can accomplish the following DNS management tasks:

- Management of DNS records aging and scavenging
- Management of DNS cache
- Management of server binding
- Management of root hints
- Management of forwarding

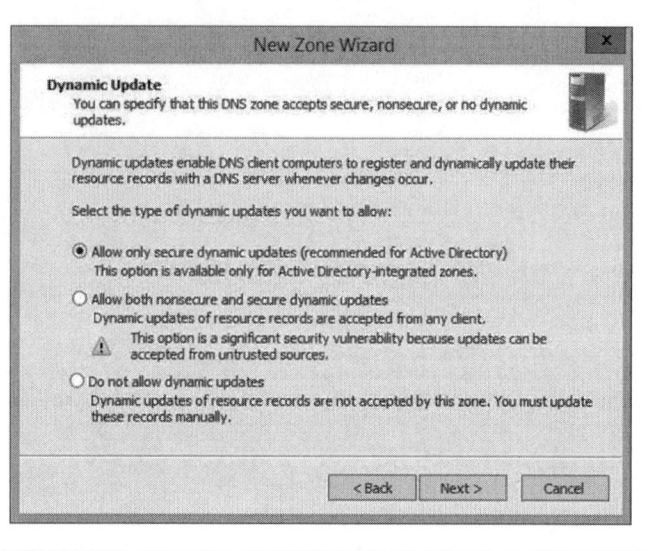

Figure 5.10 Dynamic update options.

Management of DNS records aging and scavenging: When DNS records become out of date, they can be removed from a DNS zone. Aging and scavenging is this type of service. For each zone, the network administrator can enable automatic scavenging and define the scavenging time period. Figure 5.11 shows the configuration of the aging and scavenging service.

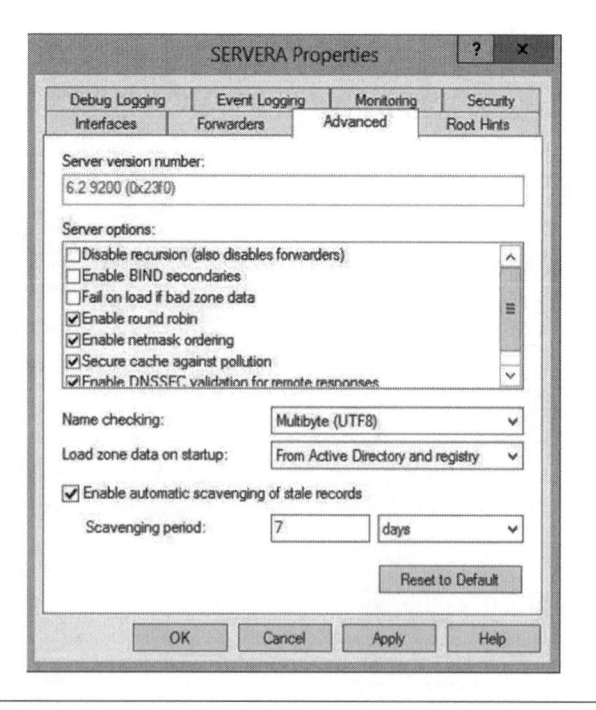

Figure 5.11 Aging and scavenging.

Management of DNS cache: To improve performance, the results of DNS lookups are automatically cached. Since the DNS server looks at the cache first, the cached records will be used repeatedly for subsequent IP address lookups. Sometimes, the cached records may be out of date or have errors. To make the DNS server have a new lookup, the network administrator needs to clear the cache first. The network administrator can also lock down the DNS cache to prevent the DNS records from being altered frequently.

Management of server binding: Often, a DNS server may be installed with multiple NICs to handle DNS requests. By default, the DNS server lists all the IP addresses. To free up some IP addresses for other services such as web service, the network administrator can block some of the IP addresses from DNS requests. The network administrator can specify which IP addresses can be used to handle DNS requests for name resolution. Figure 5.12 shows that only one IP address is configured to handle DNS requests.

Management of root hints: Root hints contain the names and IP addresses of the DNS root servers on the Internet. When a local DNS server cannot find a requested record, it will forward the request to a root server. By using root hints, the DNS request is forwarded to the root server for resolving a public host name. When there is no need for public host resolution, the network administrator can specify the root hints to point to an internal DNS server. By doing so, the private network information will not be forwarded to the Internet. Figure 5.13 shows that the root hints are configured to point to an internal DNS server.

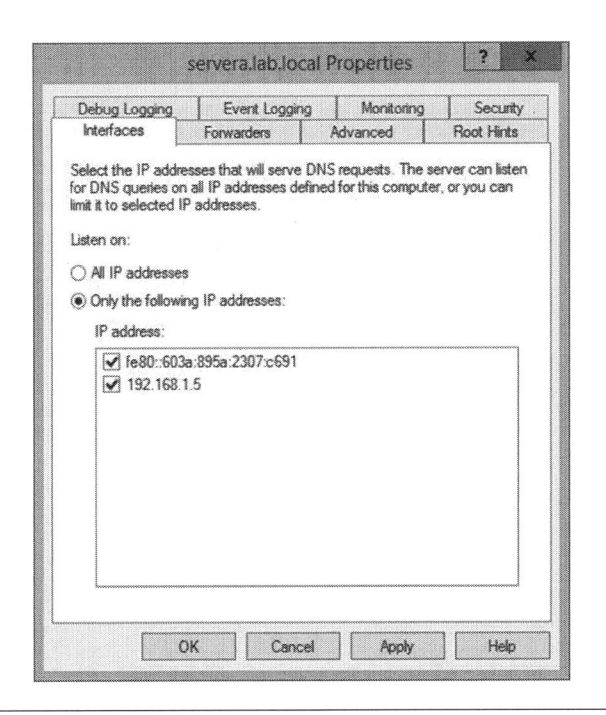

Figure 5.12 Specifying IP address for handling DNS requests.

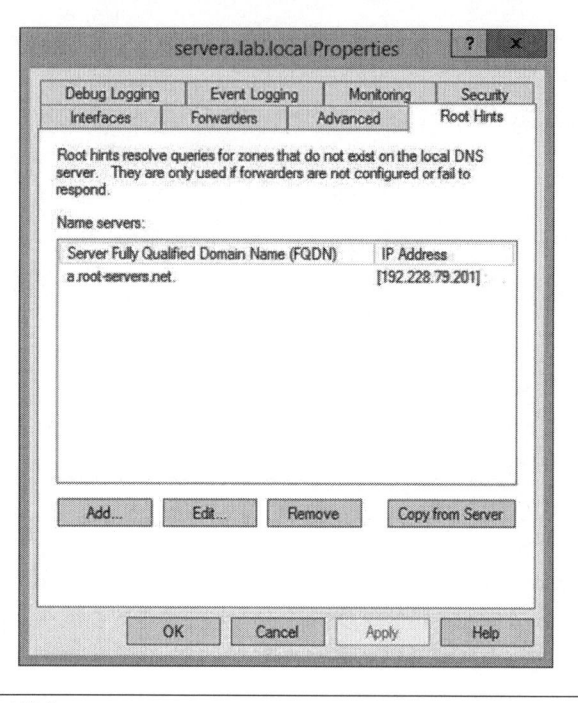

Figure 5.13 Private root hints.

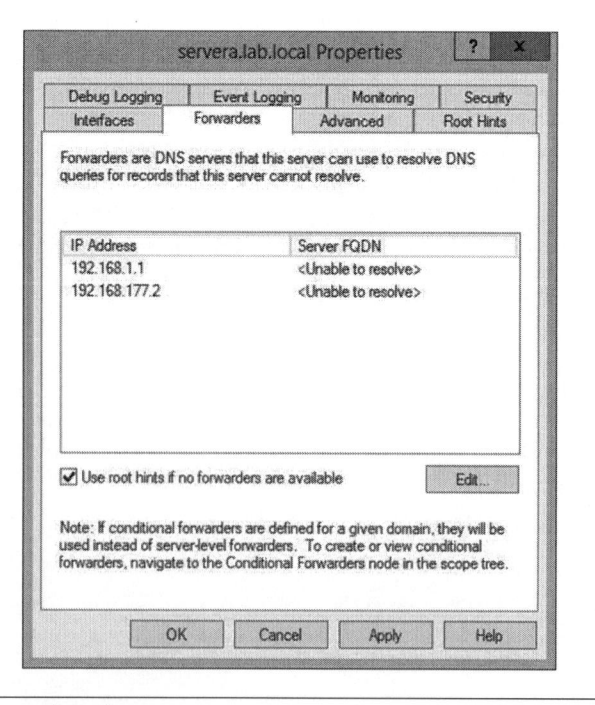

Figure 5.14 Forwarding configuration.

Management of forwarding: When a local DNS server does not have the required records, the forwarding service will forward a request to another DNS server. By default, DNS will attempt to forward the DNS request to the root server. The forwarding service can be configured to forward the DNS request to a specific DNS server. Figure 5.14 shows that DNS requests are forwarded to two internal DNS servers.

5.3.9 DNS Security

Working in the Internet environment, DNS is vulnerable to hackers who can disable a DNS service by flooding the DNS service with fake DNS responses or requests, stealing information about network resources by misusing the zone files, finding out the IP address bound to a host name by capturing IP packets on a network, or redirecting DNS queries to a phony DNS server by compromising the dynamic updates.

A network host can be configured to dedicate a machine as its DNS server so that the host can send all its DNS requests to that DNS server. Once the DNS server receives the DNS requests, it processes the requests without verifying the source of the requests. This opens the door for hackers who can dedicate a DNS server and flood the DNS server with hundreds and thousands of DNS requests in a short time until the DNS server is disabled.

If a hacker logs on to a DNS server, it is really easy for the hacker to explore the DNS zones. The network administrator should limit the access to the DNS server by only a few qualified network administrators through dedicated computers. Only the network administrators should be authorized to operate on DNS zones. Once a suspected network host is identified, the host name can be added to the Global Query Block List, which contains the names that will not get responses from the DNS server.

When a DNS client is sending a request to a DNS server, the IP packet carrying the message can be captured by a hacker on the Internet. Through the captured packet, the hacker can figure out the IP address and name of the DNS server and other server information. Also, when the DNS server is replicating DNS zones to other DNS servers, the content may also be caught by hackers on the Internet. The hackers can download the entire DNS zones to their own machines. With the collected information, the hackers are able to set up replication servers. In that way, the hackers can get all the DNS replications. To avoid hacker attacks, the network administrator should consider using an internal DNS server to handle all the internal network host name resolution. For all the external name resolution, use a separate DNS server. Then, create a forward zone on this DNS server for the web servers to resolve the names of the internal network hosts. The network administrator may let the Internet Service Provider (ISP) host the external DNS server or create a neutral network between the Internet and the organization's private network called a demilitarized zone (DMZ).

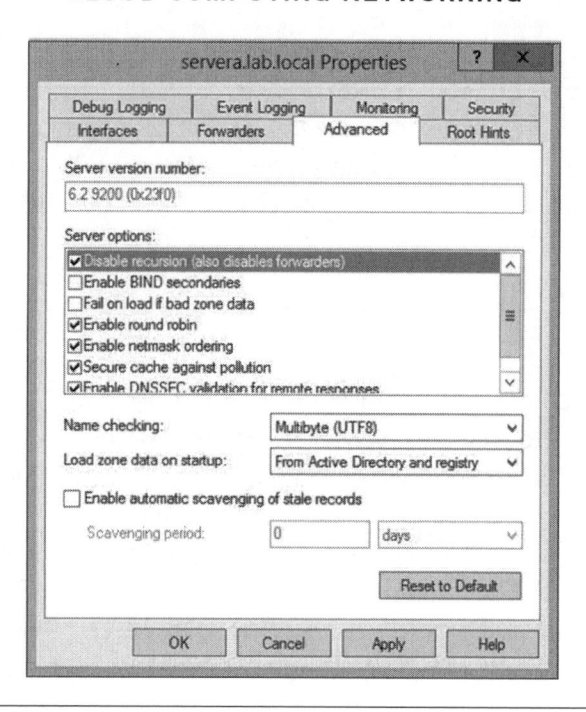

Figure 5.15   Disabling DNS recursion.

To prevent the spread of hackers' DNS requests, the network administrator can disable the recursion option to stop forwarding the DNS requests to other DNS servers. Figure 5.15 shows that the DNS recursion is disabled.

By default, zone transfers are not enabled. In case that a zone transfer is necessary, it is recommended to use the option only to the server shown in Figure 5.16.

DNS data files can be updated manually with the DNS management GUI tool. During a manual update, all the changes made in memory are written to the DNS zone files. Dynamic DNS updates automate the insertion and update of DNS records. On the other hand, they also introduce vulnerability to the DNS service. If a DNS server allows a nonsecure update, any network host is able to register itself to the DNS zone. Therefore, the network host can join the domain and the hacker who owns that host can make significant damage to the domain by altering or deleting the DNS records in the zone. With Active Directory, a dynamic update can be configured to only handle the requests from the domain members and block the requests from nondomain members. The network administrator can also control which network host can register and change the content in the DNS zone with the discretionary access control lists (DACLs). Figure 5.17 shows that the dynamic updates are configured as "Secure only," which only handle DNS requests from domain members.

In addition to aforementioned security measures, network administrators can improve the security of DNS by enforcing encryption and authentication. The topic related to encryption and authentication will be discussed in later chapters.

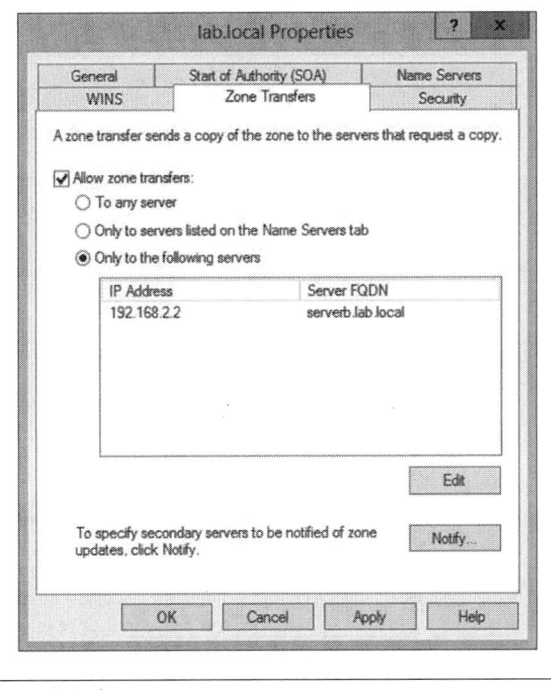

Figure 5.16 Configuring zone transfer.

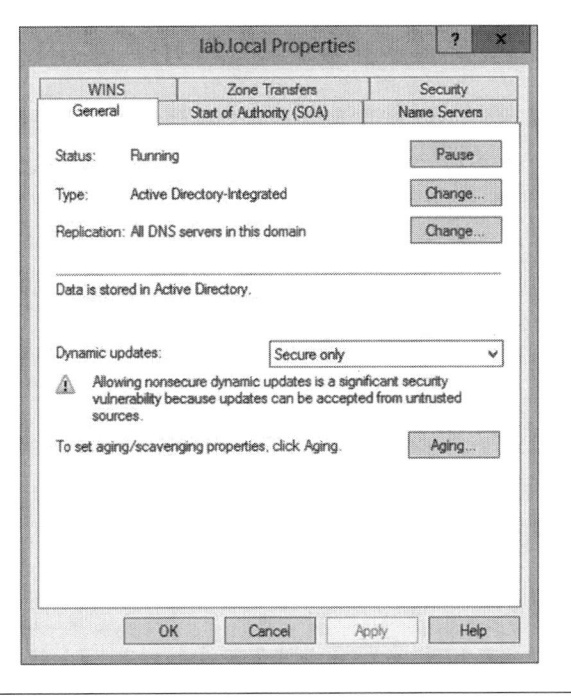

Figure 5.17 Secure dynamic update.

Activity 5.1: Network Services

In this activity, you are going to develop network services such as DNS and DHCP services in the Microsoft Azure environment:

> *Task 1*: DNS Service Development
> *Task 2*: DHCP Service Development

DNS is a service that automatically converts the name of a host to a corresponding IP address for data communication. DHCP is a service that automatically assigns an IP address to a host in the network. It may also be used to assign other network parameters such as the IP address of a gateway and the name server for a host.

Task 1: DNS Service Development

After Active Directory is installed, the DNS is installed with it. To verify the installation, follow the given steps:

> *Creating primary zone*: First, let us create a primary zone on servera.

1. Log on to **servera** with the mylab\student account. In System Manager, click **Tools** and **DNS** to open DNS Manager.
2. Expand the **SERVERA** node, **Forward Lookup Zones**, and **maylab.com**. In Figure 5.18, you should be able to see the records of servera and serverb registered under the DNS node.

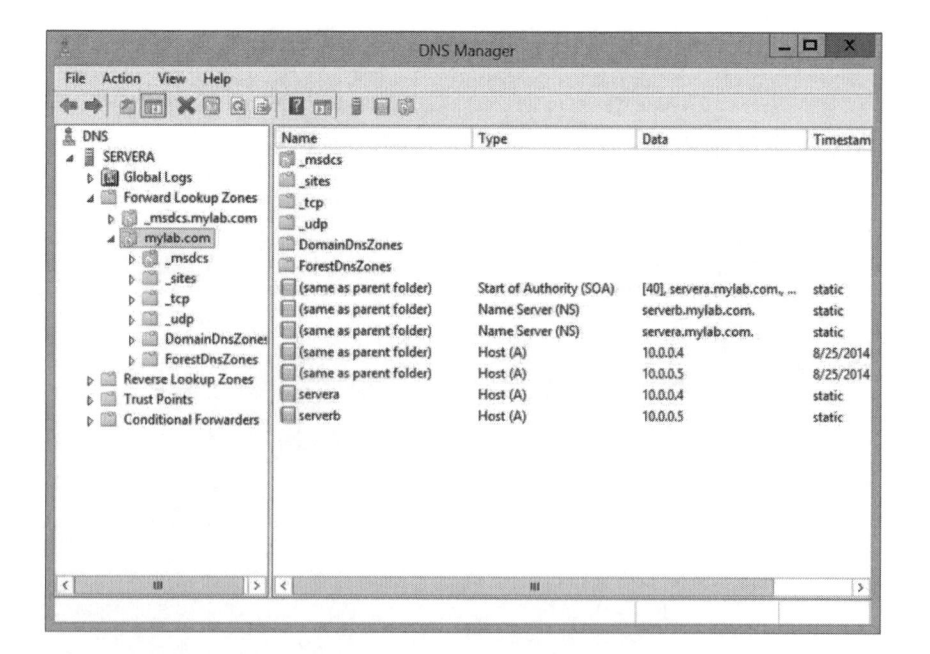

Figure 5.18 DNS records.

3. Although a forward lookup zone is automatically generated during the installation of Active Directory, a reverse lookup zone is not. To create a reverse lookup zone, double click **Reverse Lookup Zones** and then right click **Reverse Lookup Zones**, and select **New Zone** to open the New Zone Wizard.

4. Click **Next** in **Welcome to the New Zone Wizard**. Then, select **Primary zone** for the zone type. Then, click **Next**.

5. In Active Directory Zone Replication Scope, select **To all DNS servers running on domain controllers in this domain: mylab.com**. Then, click **Next**.

6. On the first Reverse Lookup Zone Name page, select **IPv4 Reverse Lookup Zone**. Click **Next**.

7. On the second **Reverse Lookup Zone Name** page, type the **network ID** of your subnetwork. In our case, type your subnet ID. (Use the starting IP address for subnet_1 in Figure 1.24) In **Reverse Lookup Zone Name**, take the automatically generated name as shown in Figure 5.19. Click **Next**.

8. In **Dynamic Update**, click **Next**. Then, click **Finish**.

9. Click the **Reverse Lookup Zones** node to expand it. Double click the node **0.0.10.in-addr.arpa**. You should be able to see the reverse lookup records shown in Figure 5.20.

Creating secondary zone: To reduce network traffic, you may create a secondary zone on a local server so that your server does not need to resolve a host name on a remote server. As an illustration, on serverb, let us make a secondary zone of the reverse lookup zone created previously.

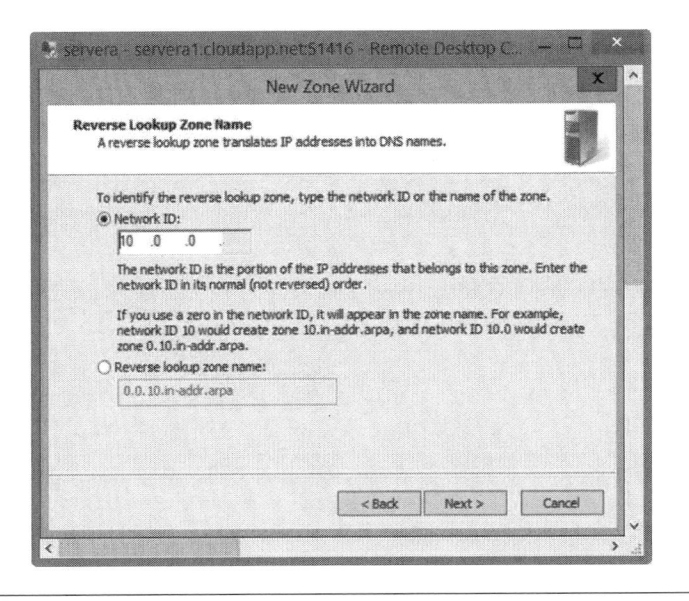

Figure 5.19 Reverse lookup zone.

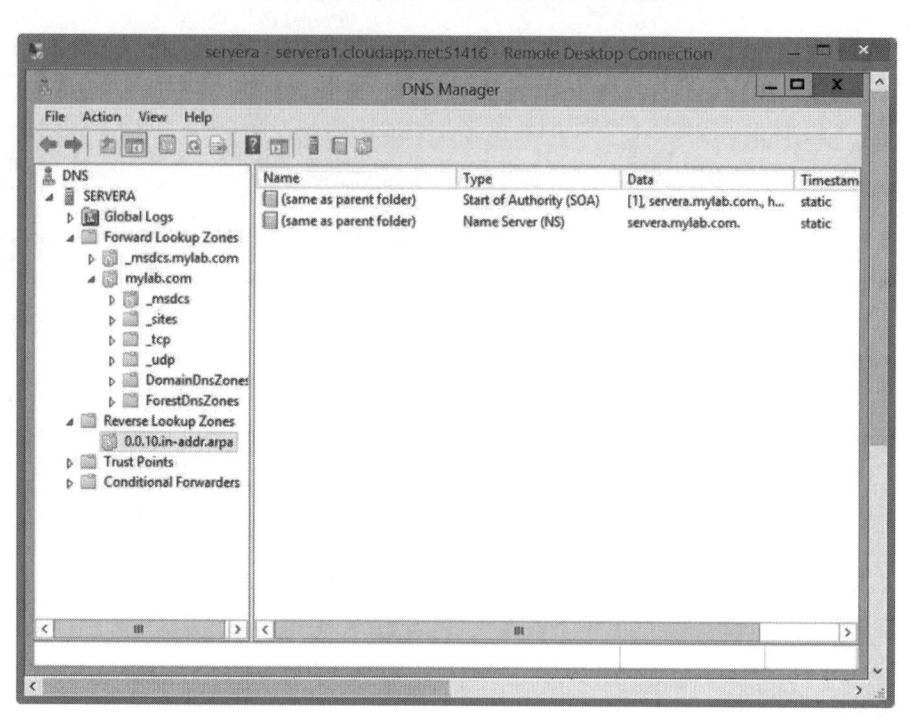

Figure 5.20   Reverse lookup records.

1. Assume that you are still logged on to **servera**. In System Manager, click **Tools** and **DNS**.
2. Expand the **Reverse Lookup Zones** node. Right click the **0.0.10.in-addr. arpa** node and select **Properties** (Figure 5.21).
3. Click the **Zone Transfers** tab. Check the option **Allow zone transfers** and make sure that **To any server** is selected as shown in Figure 5.22. Then, click **OK**.
4. Log on to **serverb** with the mylab\student account.
5. In System Manager, click **Tools** and **DNS** as shown in Figure 5.23.
6. Double click **Reverse Lookup Zones** to open the reverse lookup node as shown in Figure 5.24.
7. Double check **0.0.10.in-addr.arpa** as shown in Figure 5.25. You should see the reverse lookup records.

Configuring aging and scavenging: When the DNS records have been updated or refreshed after the update or refresh interval has expired, they will be scavenged. The following are the steps to configure aging and scavenging.

1. Log on to **servera** with the mylab\student account. In System Manager, click **Tools** and **DNS**.
2. Right click **SERVERA** and select **Properties** (Figure 5.26).

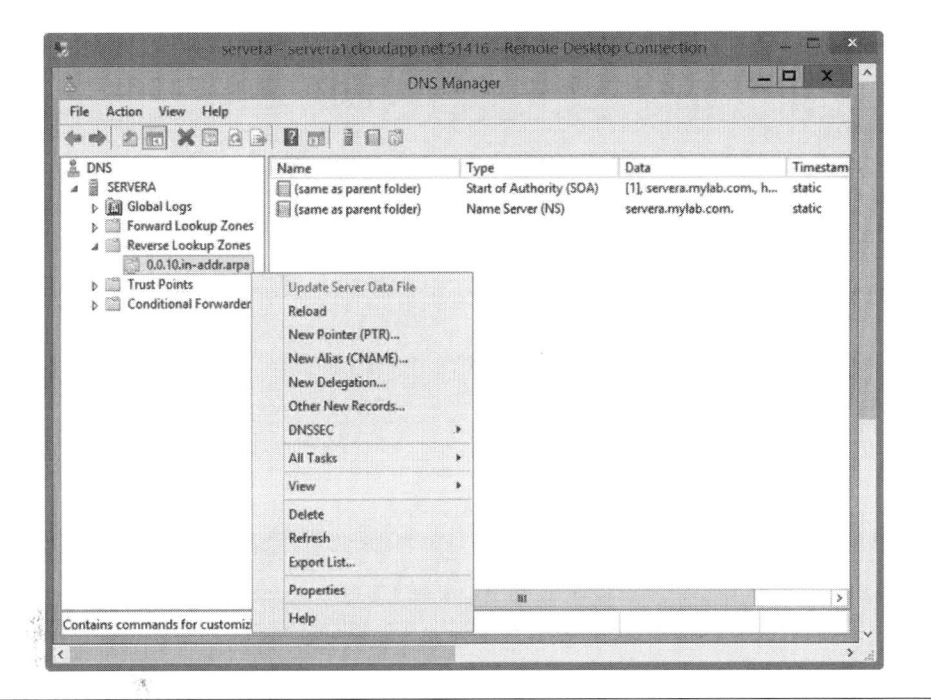

Figure 5.21   Configuring reverse lookup zone.

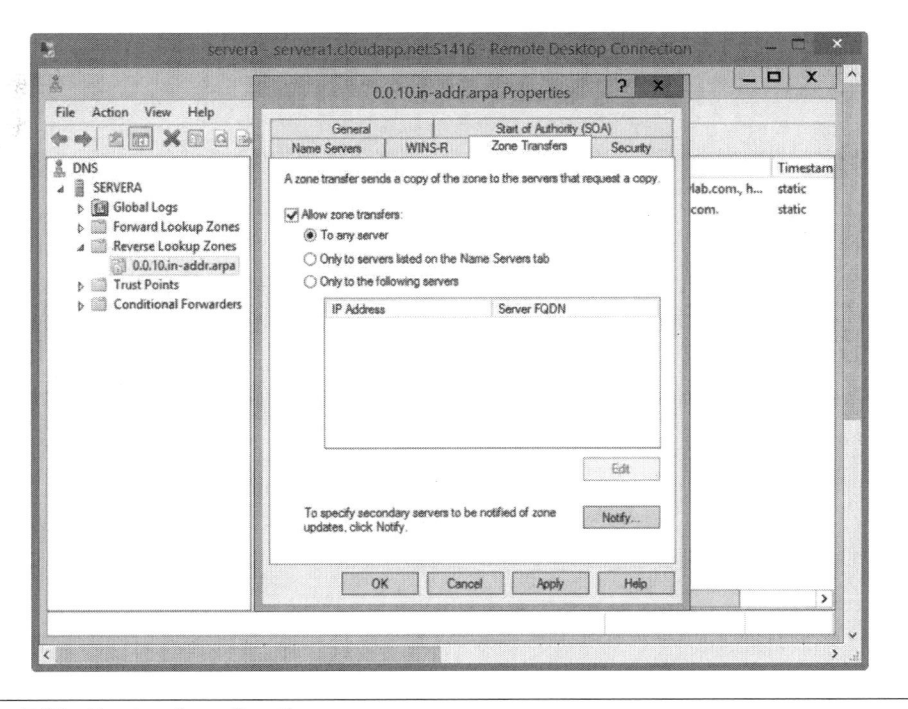

Figure 5.22   Zone transfer configuration.

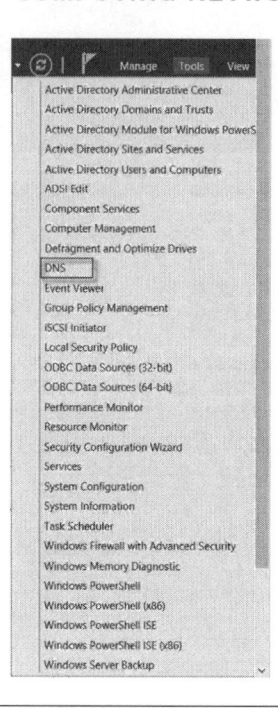

Figure 5.23   Opening DNS.

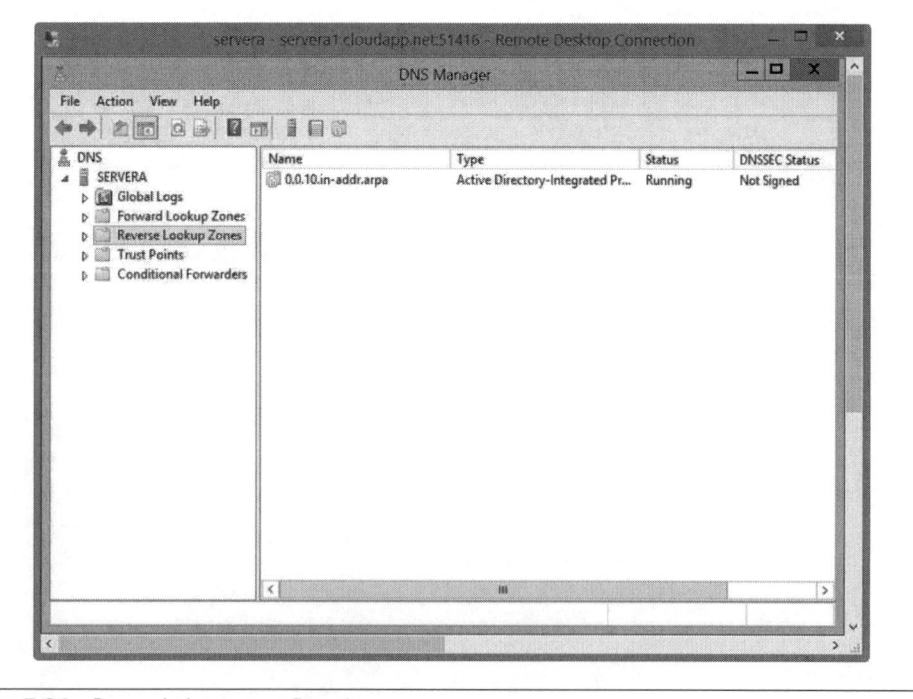

Figure 5.24   Reverse lookup zone configuration.

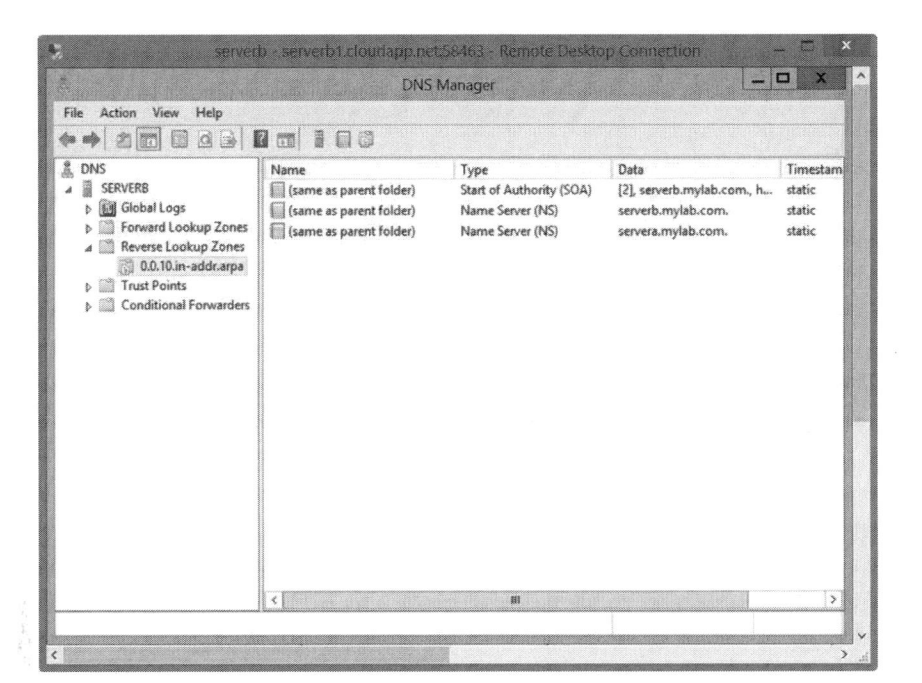

Figure 5.25 Secondary zone type.

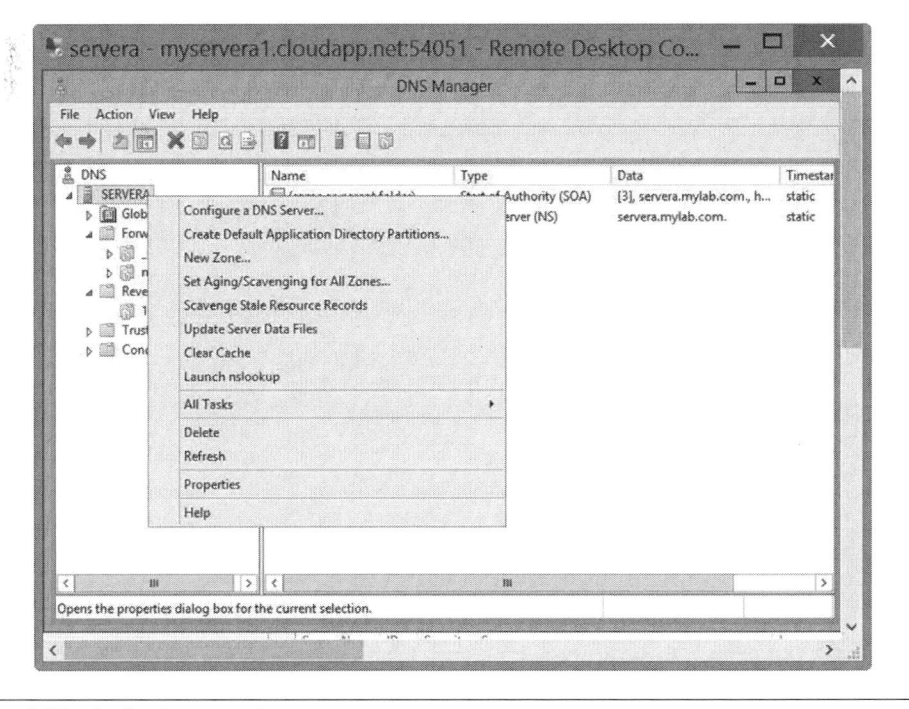

Figure 5.26 Configuring scavenging.

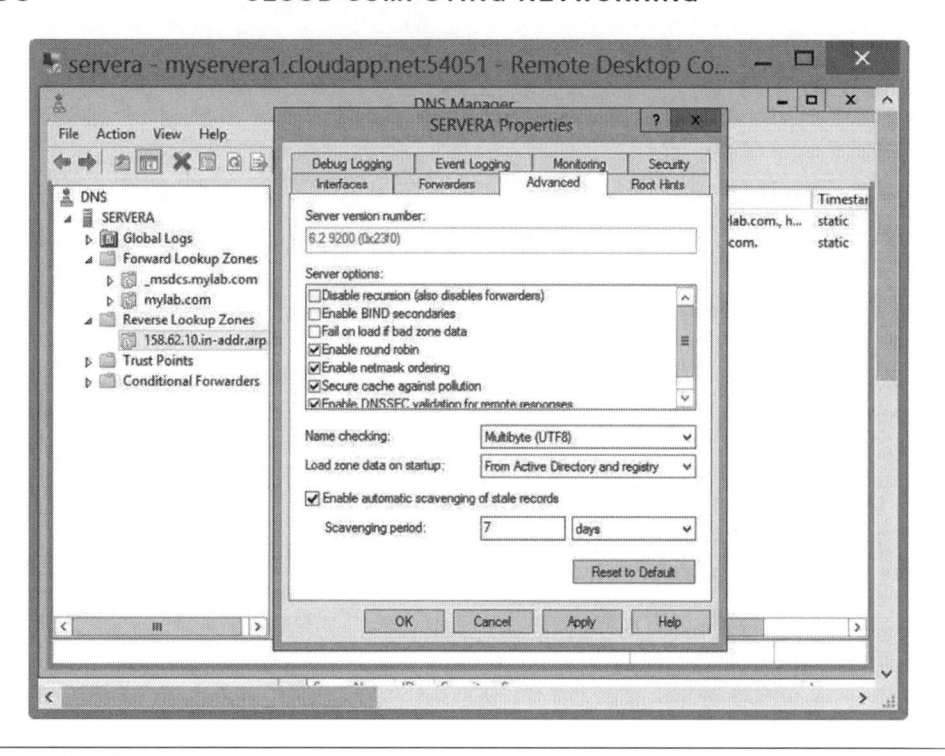

Figure 5.27   Enabling automatic scavenging.

3. Click the **Advanced** tab and click **Enable automatic scavenging of stale records**. Then, click **OK** as shown in Figure 5.27.
4. Double click **Forward Lookup Zones** to expand the node. Right click the zone **mylab.com** and select **Properties** (Figure 5.28).
5. Click the **Aging** button to open the Zone Aging/Scavenging Properties dialog as shown in Figure 5.29.
6. Check **Scavenge stale resource records**. Keep the default No-refresh interval as **7 days** and change the Refresh interval to **200 days** (Figure 5.30). Then, click **OK** twice. The configuration indicates that the dynamic DNS records will be scavenged after 207 days.

NSLOOKUP: NSLOOKUP is a utility that can be used to query DNS records. It can be used to verify if the DNS server is properly configured and can be used to do troubleshooting tasks. In the following practice, you will use NSLOOKUP to check if the stub is configured properly.

1. Log on to serverb. Press the **Windows logo** key + **r** combination. Type **nslookup** and press the **Enter** key (Figure 5.31).
2. Type **set type = a** as shown in Figure 5.32 and press the **Enter** key.
3. Now, type **servera.mylab.com** and press the **Enter** key (Figure 5.33).
4. Type **exit** and press the **Enter** key to complete the task.

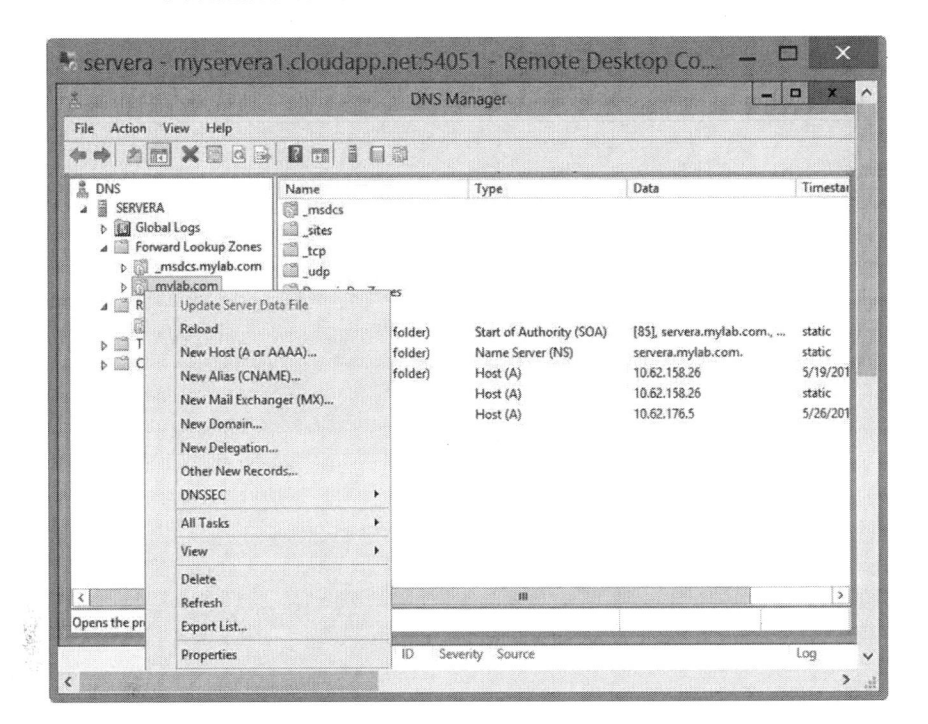

Figure 5.28 Configuring aging.

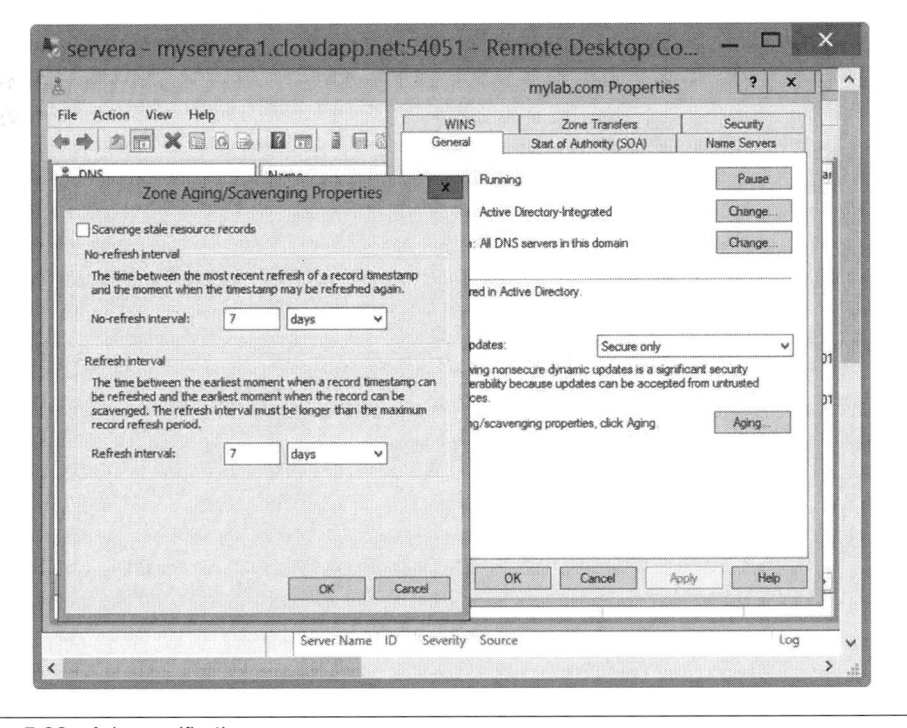

Figure 5.29 Aging specification.

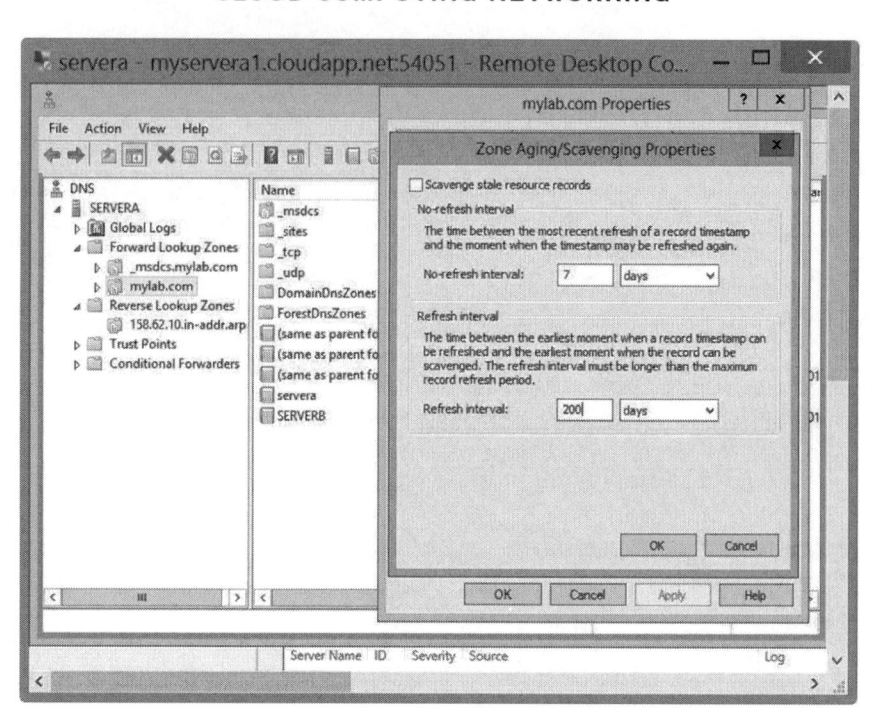

Figure 5.30   Specifying refresh interval.

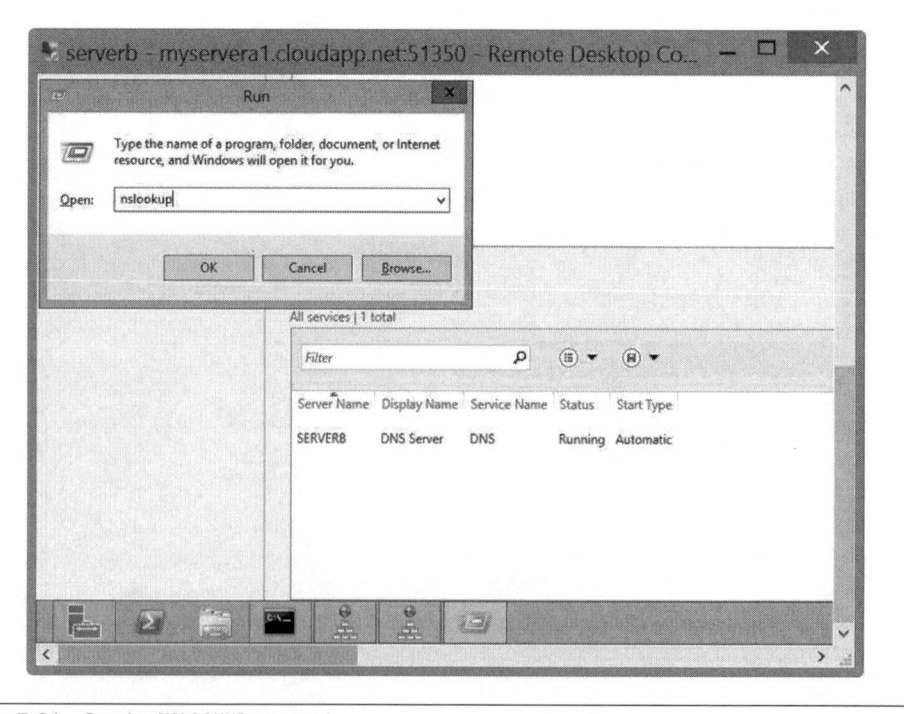

Figure 5.31   Running NSLOOKUP command.

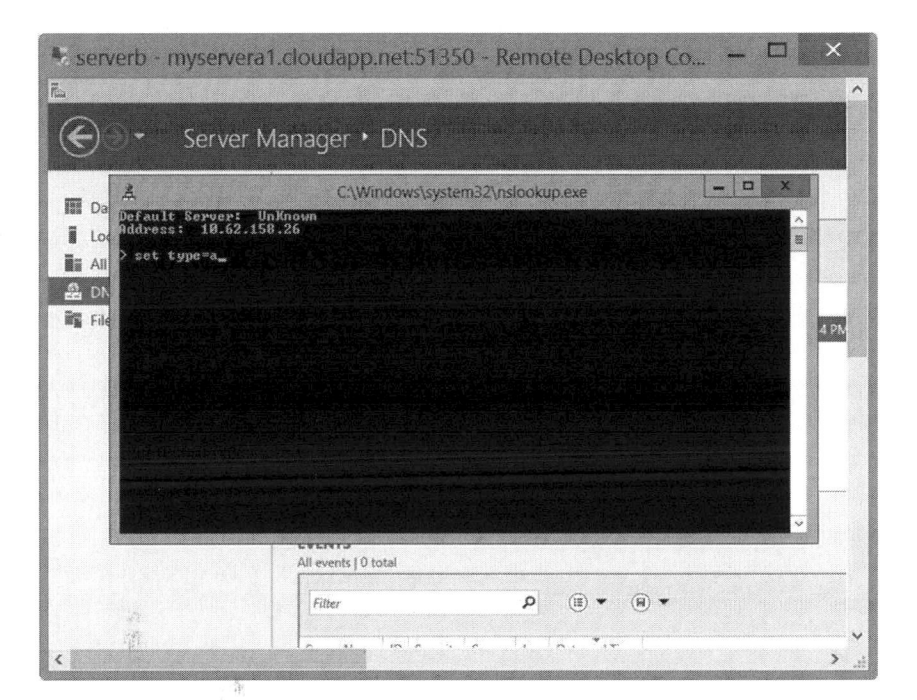

Figure 5.32 Setting record type.

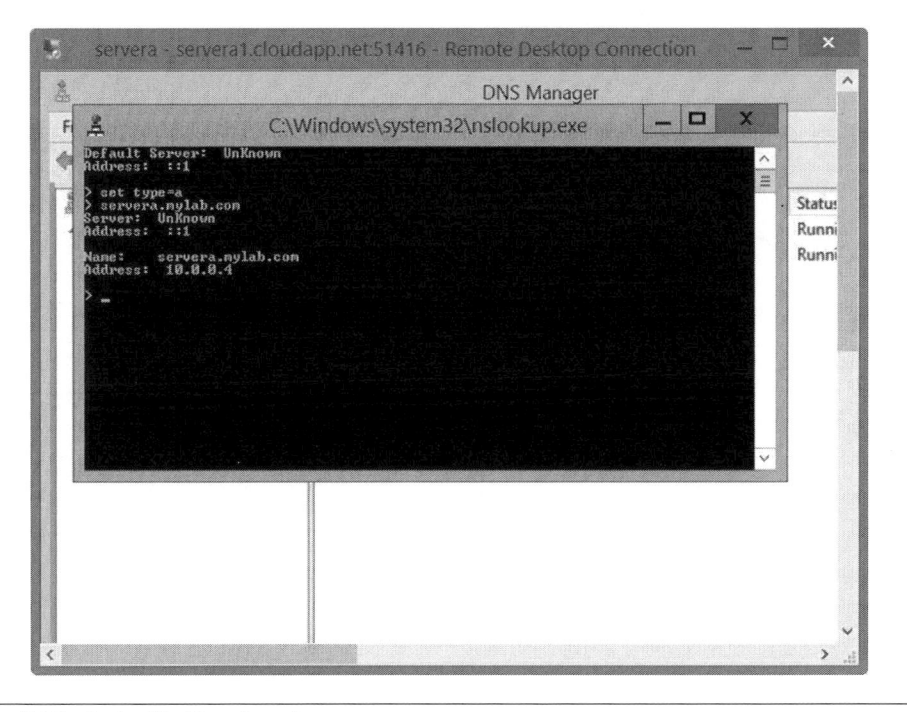

Figure 5.33 Lookup IP address for a given name.

Task 2: DHCP Service Development

To install DHCP service,

1. Sign on to **servera** using the mylab\student account with your password.
2. In Server Manager, click **Add Roles and Features**.
3. In the Add Roles and Features Wizard, click **Next** three times. On the **Select server roles** page, click the **DHCP Server** checkbox.
4. When you are prompted to add required features, click **Add Features** as shown in Figure 5.34.
5. Click **Next** three times, and then click **Install**.
6. Wait for the installation process to complete. In the Add Roles and Features Wizard, click **Complete DHCP configuration** as shown in Figure 5.35.
7. In the DHCP Post-Install configuration wizard, click **Next** and then click **Commit** as shown in Figure 5.36. Then, click **Close**.
8. On the Server Manager menu bar, click **Tools** and then click **DHCP** (Figure 5.37). The DHCP console will open.
9. On the DHCP console tree, navigate to **IPv4**. Right click **IPv4** and then click **New Scope** (Figure 5.38). The **New Scope Wizard** will open.
10. Click **Next** and then type a name, such as **lab-scope**, for the new scope next to Name (e.g., lab-scope in Figure 5.39).

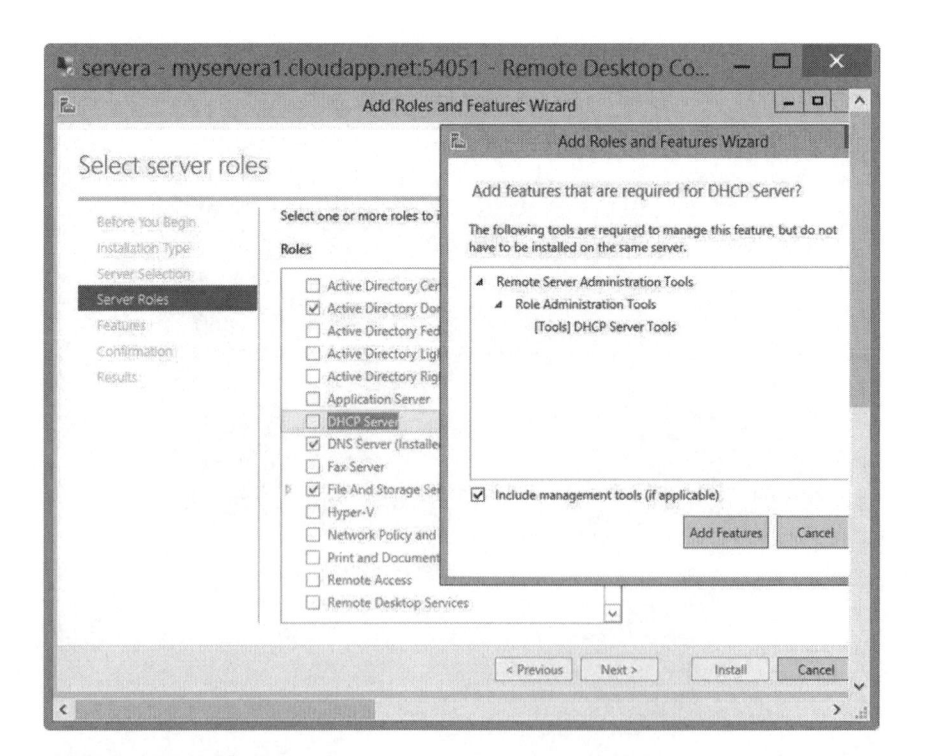

Figure 5.34   Installing DHCP role.

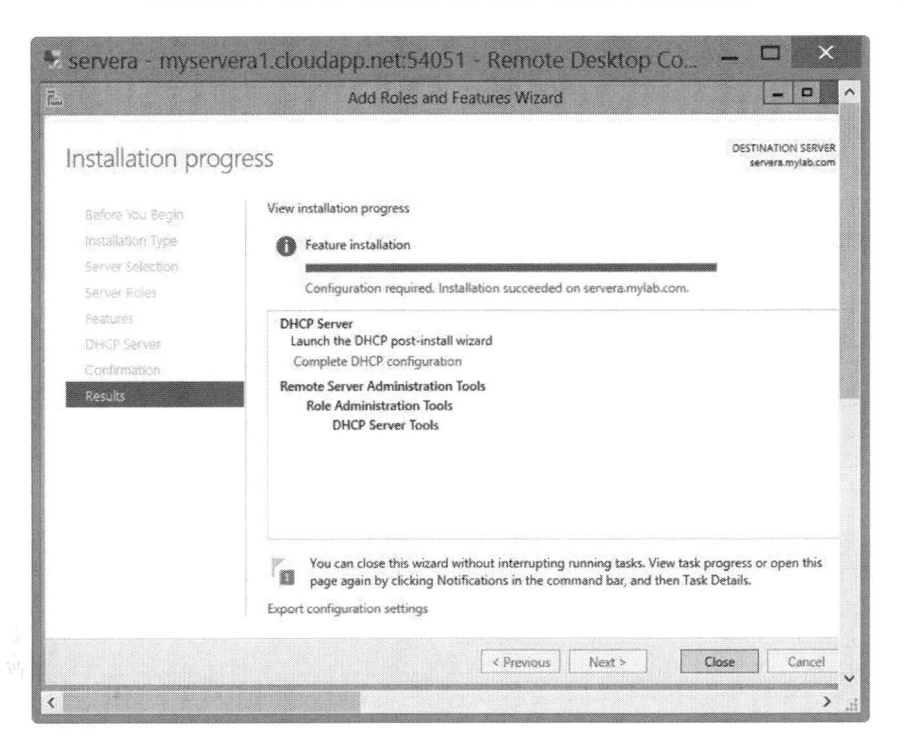

Figure 5.35 Completing DHCP configuration.

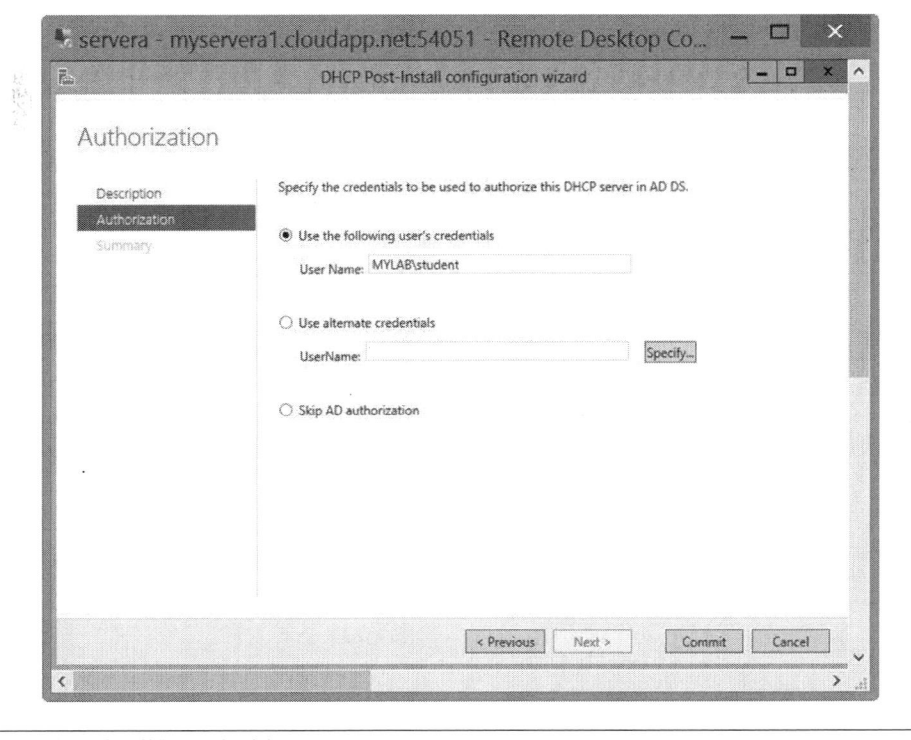

Figure 5.36 Specifying credentials.

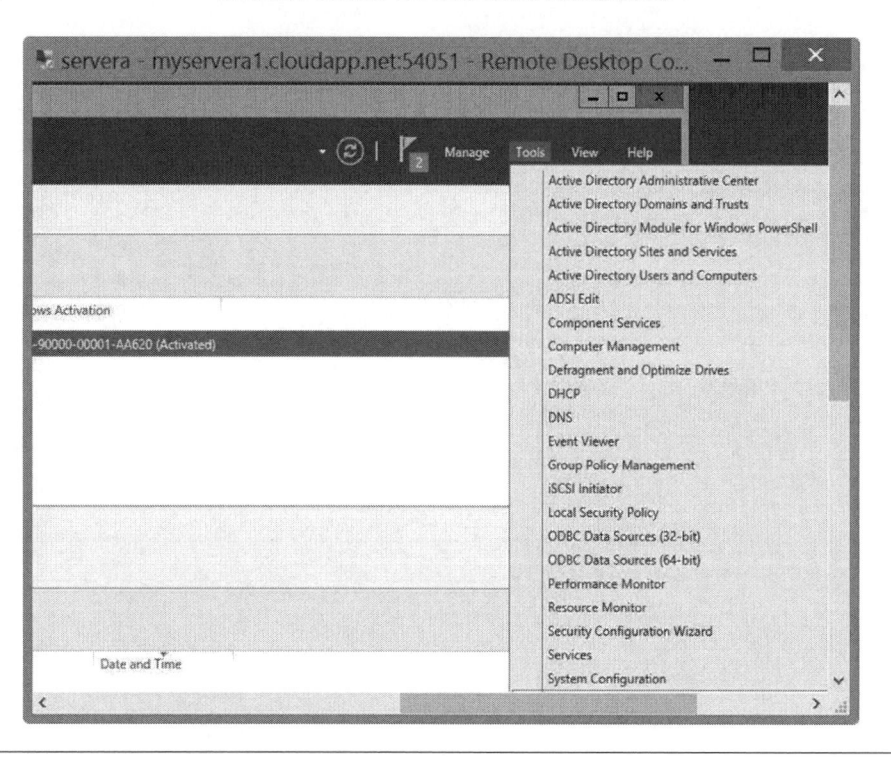

Figure 5.37   Selecting DHCP service.

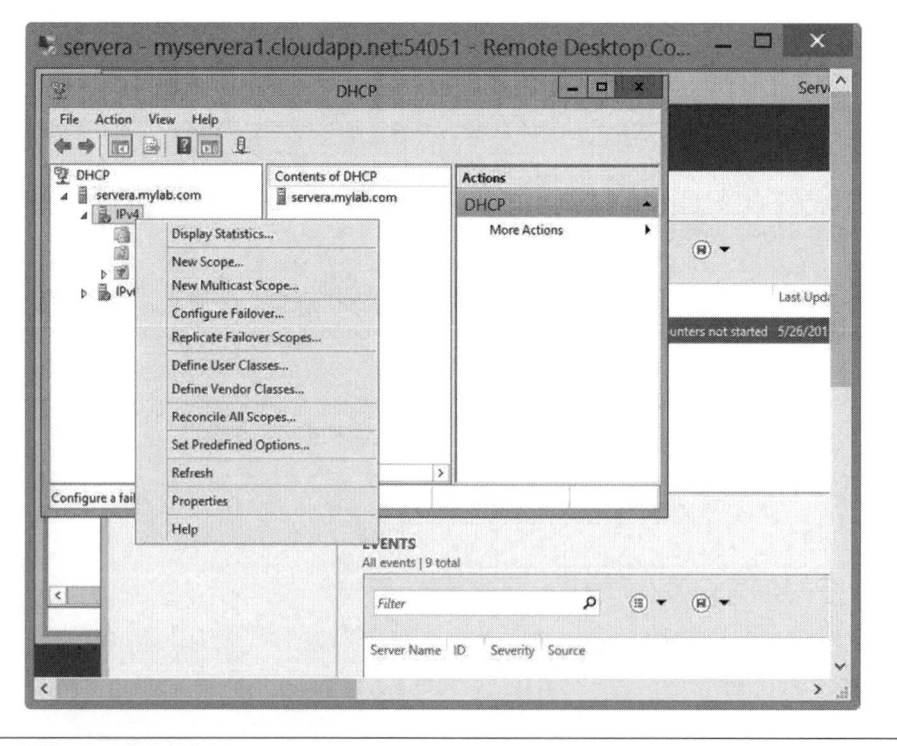

Figure 5.38   Creating new scope.

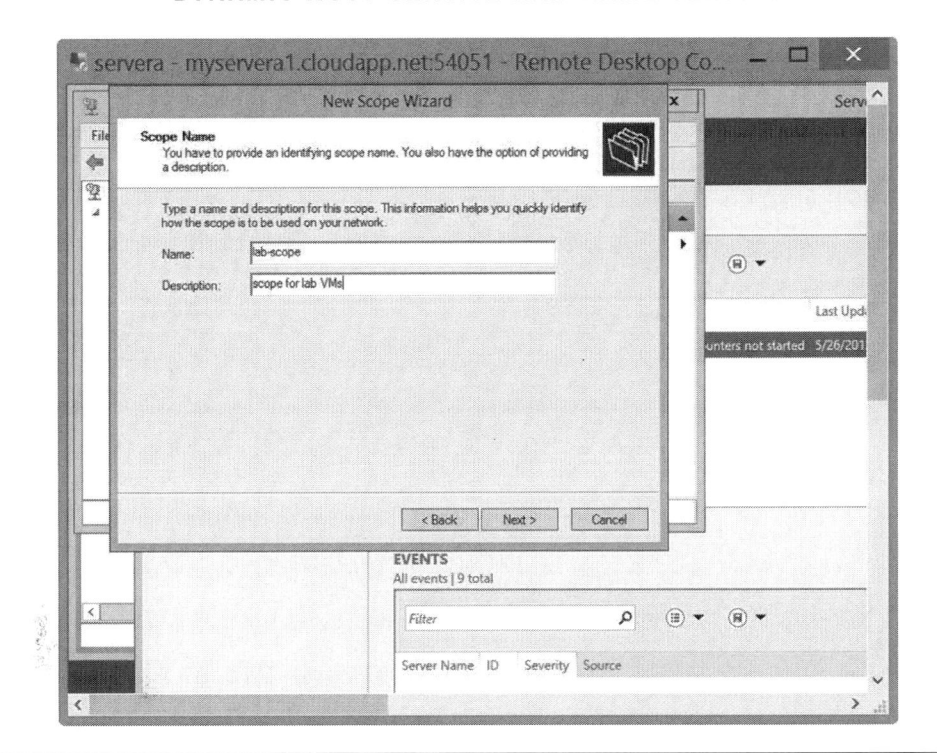

Figure 5.39   Scope name.

11. Click **Next**. Then, for the IP address range, type **10.0.0.10** next to **Start IP address**, type **10.0.0.20** next to **End IP address**, and type **8** next to **Length**. The value of the subnet mask will change automatically to **255.0.0.0** (Figure 5.40).

12. Click **Next**. Then, in **Add Exclusions and Delay,** type **10.0.0.15** under **Start IP address**, type **10.0.0.16** under **End IP address**, and then click **Add** (Figure 5.41).

13. Click **Next** and then in Lease Duration, take the default.

14. Click **Next**. In the Router page, enter the default gateway IP address **10.0.0.1** and click **Add** as shown in Figure 5.42.

15. Click **Next**. In **Domain Name and DNS Servers**, verify that the **Parent domain** is **mylab.com** and **10.0.0.4** is listed as the only DNS server IP address (Figure 5.43). (Your DNS server IP address may be different.)

16. Click **Next** twice, and then in Activate Scope, select **Yes, I want to activate this scope now**.

17. Click **Next**, and then click **Finish**.

18. Refresh the view in the DHCP console and verify that IPv4 is checked and lab-scope is active (Figure 5.44).

Reservation: You may reserve an IP address for a specific computer by matching the IP address with the hardware address of that computer.

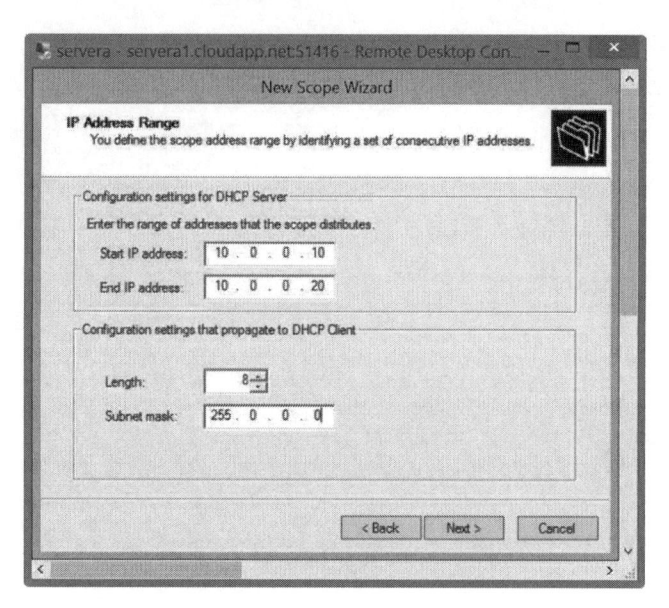

Figure 5.40   Specifying scope range.

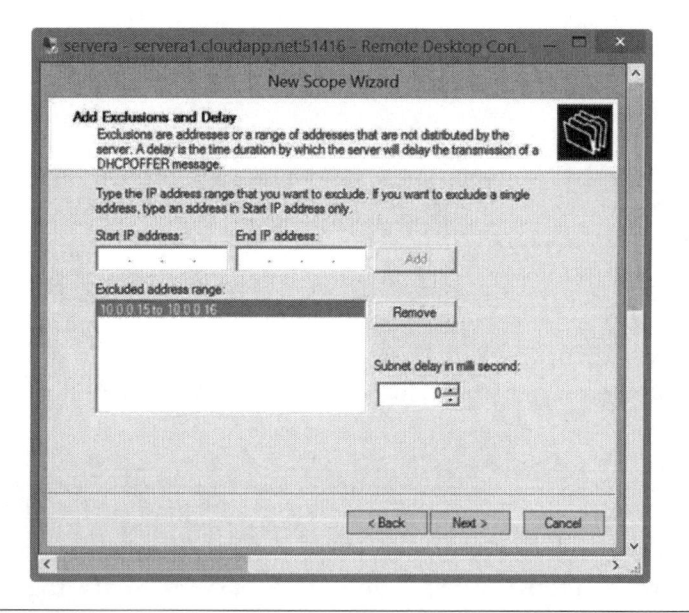

Figure 5.41   Configuring exclusions.

1. Log on to **serverb**, press the **Windows logo** key + **r** combination to open the **cmd** window. Run the command:

   ipconfig/all

2. Record the hardware address for the private NIC Ethernet 2.

3. Log on to **servera** as the user **mylab\student**. Click **Tools** and **DHCP** to open the DHCP configuration dialog. Double click the **Reservations** node. Right click the **Reservations** node and select **New Reservation** (Figure 5.45).

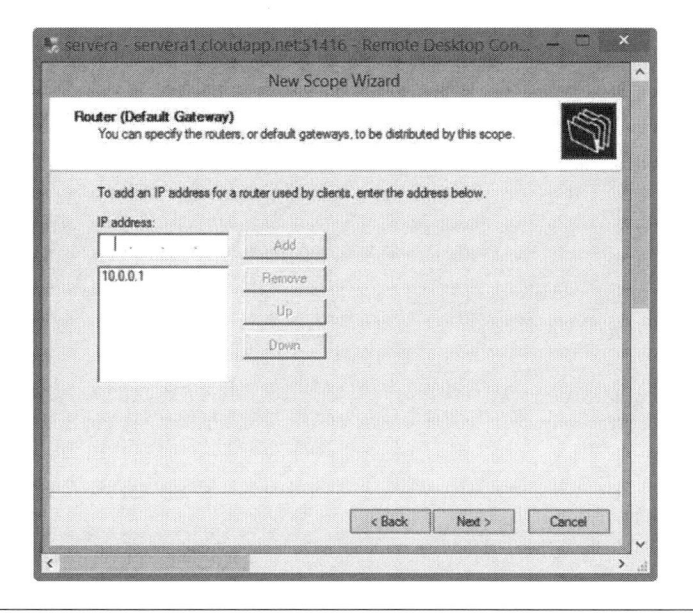

Figure 5.42 Specifying router.

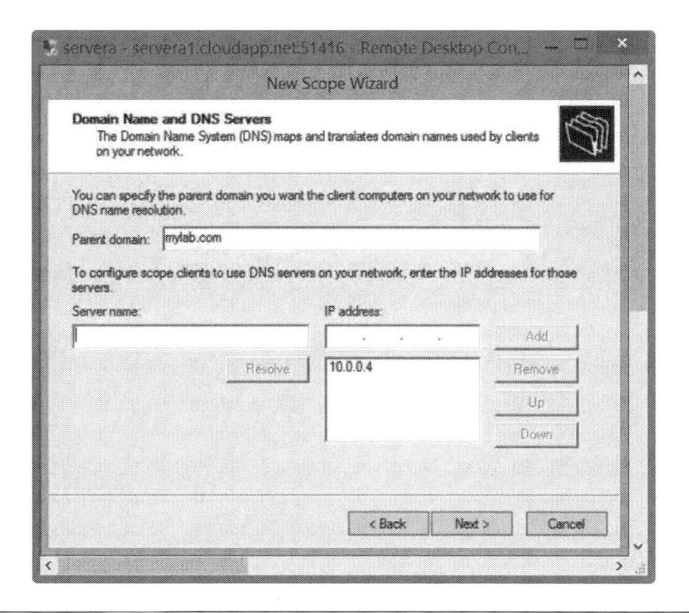

Figure 5.43 Specifying parent domain.

4. Enter the reservation name; reserve the IP address 10.0.0.5 for studentb server as shown in Figure 5.46. (The MAC address of your virtual machine should be different.)

5. Click **Add** and then **Close**. You will see that the new reservation is added as shown in Figure 5.47.

6. In the Microsoft Azure Management Portal, shutdown both servera and serverb before exiting the Microsoft Azure Management Portal.

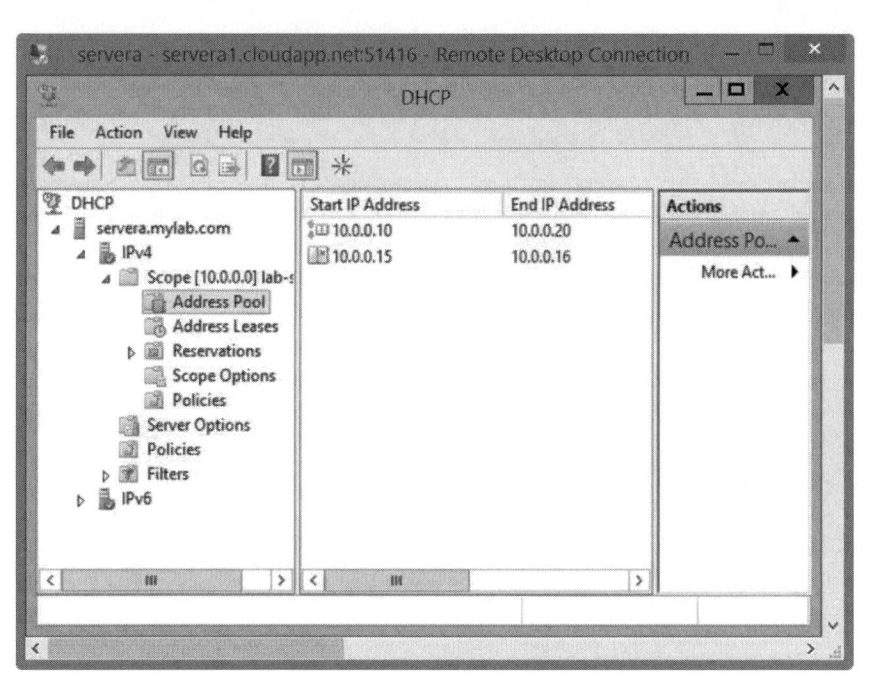

Figure 5.44   Activated scope.

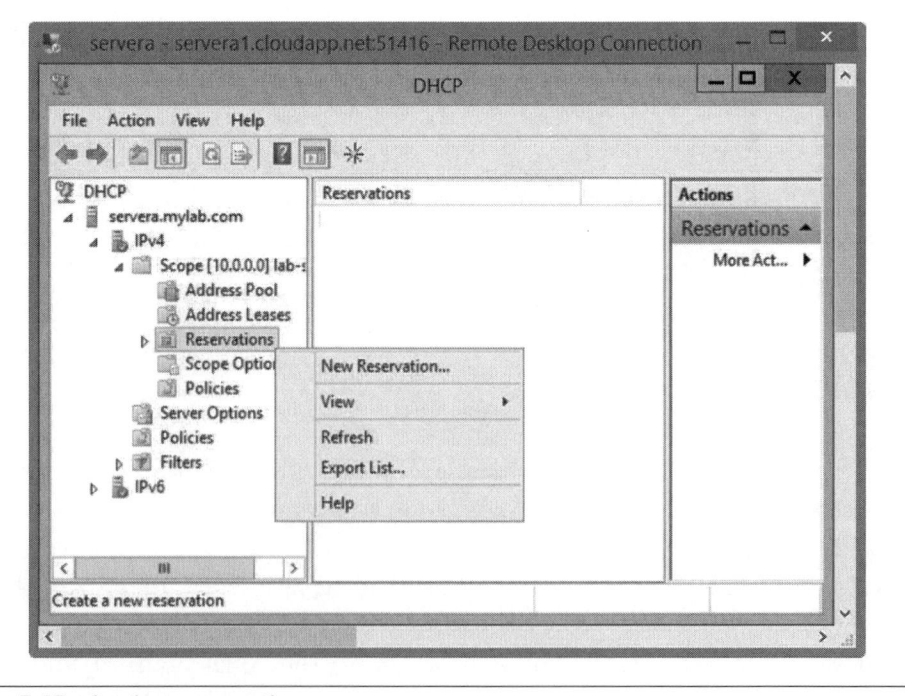

Figure 5.45   Creating new reservation.

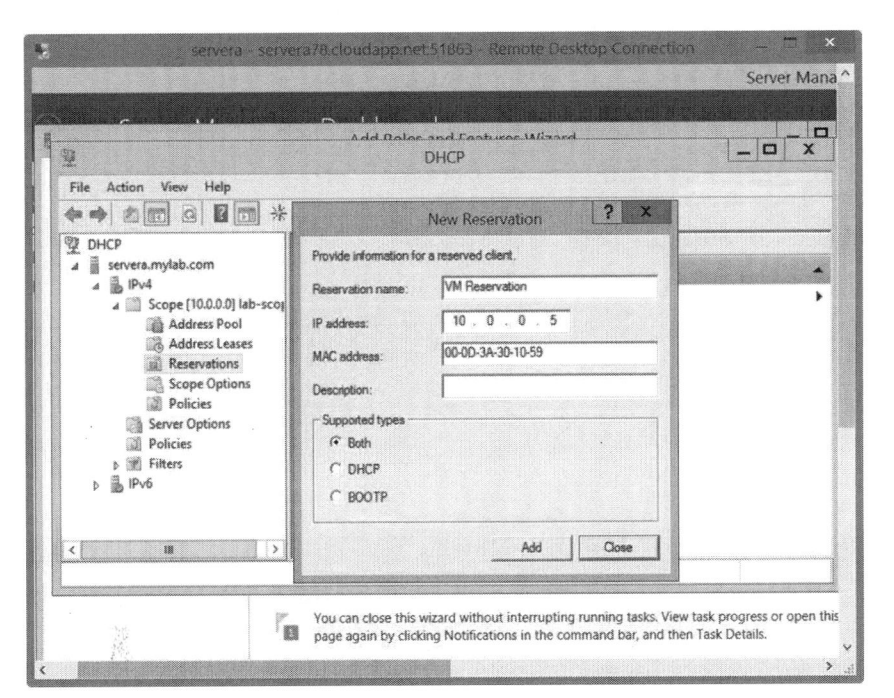

Figure 5.46 Reservation configuration.

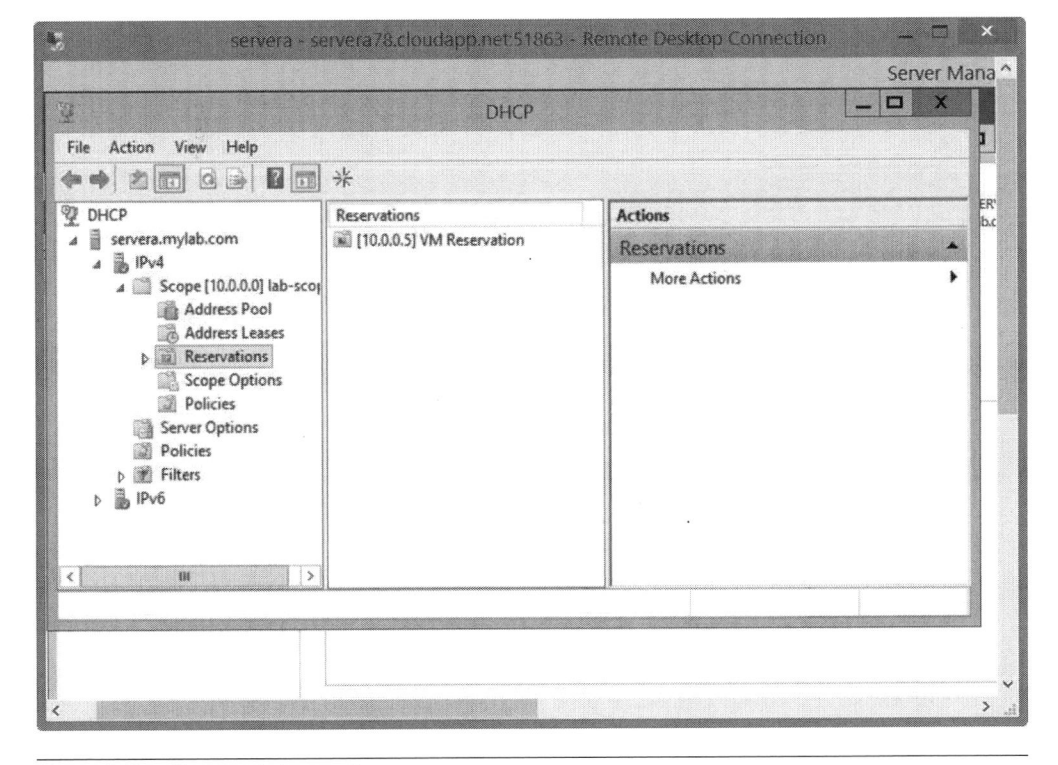

Figure 5.47 Newly created reservation.

Earlier, you have created a DNS server for hands-on practice. Note that a private IP address is assigned to the DNS server. Therefore, this DNS server cannot be used on the Internet. The DHCP server created here is also for hands-on practice only. A default DHCP server already exists on the existing virtual network.

The hands-on practice has covered the installation and configuration of DHCP and DNS services. It illustrates how to create a DHCP server and a DNS server. It shows how clients are able to access the DHCP and DNS servers. This hands-on practice also covered some topics in DNS management such as aging and scavenging. At the end of the activities, instructions are given to show you how to test the DNS service tool NSLOOKUP.

5.4 Summary

This chapter has examined some commonly used network services such as DHCP and DNS services. DHCP automatically assigns IP addresses to network hosts. This chapter explains how DHCP can accomplish that task. With the DHCP service, when a network host joins a network, it is automatically assigned an IP address. In the hands-on practice, the DHCP service is implemented with Windows Server 2012.

The DNS service is essential for the Internet computing environment. A network host on the Internet has an IP address associated with a human-friendly name. For a given host name, the DNS service is able to find the associated IP address or vice versa. This chapter explains the DNS hierarchy and how to look up an IP address recursively in the hierarchical DNS server system. The hands-on practice in this chapter illustrates how to create and manage DNS services.

Review Questions

1. What are the reasons to use DHCP?
2. Describe how a DHCP client can get its IP address from a DHCP server.
3. When the DHCP server is not reachable, what type of IP address will the DHCP client get?
4. What is the value of the default lease time?
5. How can a DHCP server renew a dynamic IP address?
6. Why do you need a permanent IP address?
7. How to assign a permanent IP address to a network host?
8. How does a DHCP relay work?
9. List the DHCP specifications that should be worked out before installing a DHCP service.
10. What properties should be specified for a DHCP scope?
11. Why do we need the DNS service?
12. List at least five category-based top-level domains.

13. What is the maximum number of layers that can be added to the name hierarchy?
14. What is a root server?
15. What is a forward lookup process?
16. What is a reverse lookup process?
17. Before forwarding the name resolution request to the root server, what does the operating system need to check first?
18. What is a DNS zone?
19. What is an NS DNS record?
20. What is an SOA DNS record?

6

NETWORKING WITH WINDOWS POWERSHELL

Objectives

- Understand Windows PowerShell.
- Understand Microsoft Azure PowerShell.
- Learn networking with Windows PowerShell.
- Manage Microsoft Azure with Microsoft Azure PowerShell.

6.1 Introduction

In an operating system, a shell is a computer program that provides a user interface. The user interface translates human readable commands into the code that can be processed by the operating system. For system management, each shell accepts a set of shell-specific commands that can be entered by users. Windows PowerShell is such a user interface provided by the Windows operating system. In the early days, PowerShell was designed mainly for server administrators. It was a separate package from the Windows operating system. Recently, PowerShell has been included in the Windows operating system to make it available to all users.

PowerShell is a task-based command-line shell. Built on the .NET Framework, PowerShell provides greater control and flexibility for system administration. Compared with the regular command prompt tool, PowerShell is a more sophisticated command prompt tool, which provides a wide range of functionalities. With PowerShell, network/system administrators can manage both local and remote networks. PowerShell provides a scripting language designed for system administration. PowerShell is easy to be adopted for different versions of Windows operating systems. It runs on Windows XP, Windows Server 2003, the later versions of Windows desktop operating systems, and the Windows server operating system. It is also included in application servers such as Exchange Server, System Center Operations Manager, Virtual Machine Manager, and so on.

PowerShell is also included in Microsoft Azure for deploying and managing cloud services. Most of the tasks accomplished by the Microsoft Azure Management Portal can be accomplished by Microsoft Azure PowerShell.

6.2 Windows PowerShell

To perform administrative tasks, PowerShell provides hundreds of standard commands called cmdlets pronounced as command-lets. The cmdlets are developed by Microsoft or a third party. A cmdlet is a single-function command-line tool. Windows PowerShell includes four types of commands: Cmdlets, PowerShell functions, PowerShell scripts, and native Windows commands. Multiple cmdlets can be combined together to form a script to handle a complicated task.

6.2.1 Cmdlets

When installing a Windows Server operating system, Windows PowerShell modules are included. The cmdlets in the Windows PowerShell modules are.NET classes designed to accomplish specialized administrative tasks such as managing services, monitoring processes, or navigating the registry. Cmdlets differ from commands in many ways. Cmdlets are not stand-alone executable commands. They are instances of.NET Framework classes. Implemented in.NET Framework classes, cmdlets often accomplish a task with a few dozen lines of code. In general, cmdlets depends on the Windows PowerShell runtime to handle tasks such as parsing, error presentation, and output formatting. It is easier to run scripting language code in PowerShell for tasks that need to be executed repeatedly and automatically. PowerShell provides an Application Programming Interface (API), which allows software vendors and application developers to create custom tools by embedding PowerShell functionalities. For high efficiency, cmdlets process input and output objects through a pipeline, which works like a manufacture production line.

These cmdlets can also be used for data management. Different cmdlets can share the same set of data. The data output from one cmdlet can be input to other cmdlets. The cmdlets can also be used to manage database objects. A script contains a set of cmdlets to accomplish a more complex task. A script can be used to run repeated jobs, access data centers, or instantiate other cmdlets.

A cmdlet is designed to use a consistent usage rubric and to accomplish a single task. To make it easy to use and to be intuitive, a cmdlet is structured with a verb–noun compound phrase separated by a hyphen. For example, the Get-Help cmdlet phase has Get as the verb and Help as the noun. The name of a cmdlet is not case sensitive. The capital letters, G and H, used in the cmdlet Get-Help is merely for clarity. Figure 6.1 illustrates the Get-Help cmdlet.

The PowerShell approved verbs used in the cmdlets can be categorized into groups such as Common, Communication, Data, Diagnostic, Lifecycle, and Security. As an illustration, we briefly introduce some of the verbs in each group. For the entire list of verbs, readers can refer to books specialized in Windows PowerShell. Figure 6.2 shows the PowerShell verbs that start with the letter r.

Common: The verbs in the Common group are generic and can be applied to almost any types of cmdlets. The Common verbs usually used by cmdlets are listed in Table 6.1.

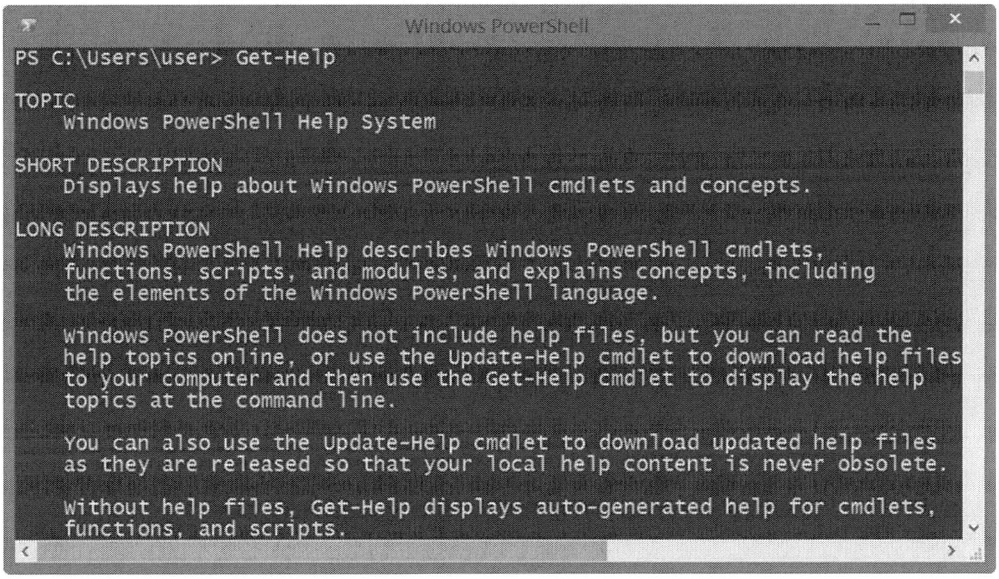

Figure 6.1 Get-Help Cmdlet.

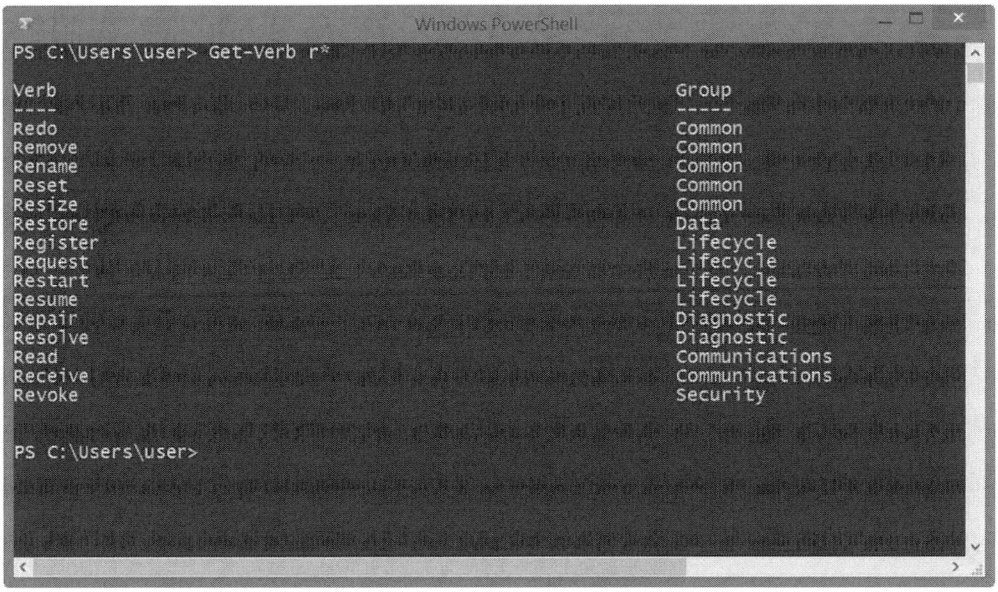

Figure 6.2 PowerShell Verbs Starting with Letter r.

Communication: The verbs in the Communication group are used to define communication actions. The Communication verbs commonly used by cmdlets are listed in Table 6.2.

Data: The verbs in the Data group are used for data management. The Data verbs commonly used by cmdlets are listed in Table 6.3.

Table 6.1 Common Verbs Used in Cmdlets

VERB	TYPE	USAGE
Add	Common	It adds a resource to a container or attaches an item to another item. For example, the Add-WindowsFeature cmdlet installs specified roles, role services, and features to a computer.
Remove	Common	This verb is paired with Add. It removes the specified resource from a container. For example, the cmdlet Remove-NetRoute removes all the IP routes on the computer, including default routes.
Clear	Common	It removes all the resources from a container without deleting the container. For example, the Clear-Content c:\mytest.txt cmdlet removes the content in the file mytest.txt without deleting the file.
Get	Common	It retrieves a resource and displays the resource information on the screen. For example, the Get-NetRoute cmdlet gets all the routes for the computer.
New	Common	It creates a new resource. For example, the cmdlet New-NetIPAddress –InterfaceIndex 1 –IPAddress 192.168.1.1 creates a new IP address for the network interface with the index 1.
Set	Common	It modifies an existing resource. For example, the cmdlet Set-NetIPAddress –InterfaceIndex 1 –IPAddress 192.168.1.2 changes the network adapter's IP address to 192.168.1.2
Reset	Common	It sets a resource back to its original state. For example, the cmdlet Reset-NetAdapterAdvancedProperty -Name MyAdapter -DisplayName "Private" resets the advanced property interrupt moderation to Private, which is the default value.
Select	Common	It locates a resource in a container. For example, the Select-String "Route" cmdlet finds the word Route in a file.
Rename	Common	It changes the name of a resource. For example, the Rename-Item -path c:\Myfile.txt -newname Hisfile.txt cmdlet changes the name of the text file Myfile.txt to Hisfile.txt.
Move	Common	It moves a resource from one location to another. For example, the move-item -path Myfile.txt -destination d:\Myfile_old.txt cmdlet moves the file Myfile.txt from current location to the D drive.

Table 6.2 Communication Verbs Used in Cmdlets

VERB	TYPE	USAGE
Connect	Communication	It links a source to a destination. For example, the cmdlet Connect-VirtualDisk connects a disconnected virtual disk to a specified computer.
Disconnect	Communication	This verb is paired with Connect. It breaks the link between a source and a destination. For example, the cmdlet Disconnect-VirtualDisk disconnects a virtual disk from the specified computer.
Read	Communication	It reads the information from a source, such as a file. For example, the cmdlet Read-S3Object -BucketName Mybackup -Key Mykey -File c:\Myfile reads the backup file Myfile.
Receive	Communication	It receives information sent from a source. For example, the cmdlet Receive-job gets the result of the Windows PowerShell background jobs in the current session.
Send	Communication	This verb is paired with Receive. It delivers information to a destination. For example, the cmdlet Send-MailMessage sends an email message.
Write	Communication	This verb is paired with Read. It adds information to a target. For example, the cmdlet Write-Error "Access denied." writes an "Access denied" error message.

Table 6.3 Data Verbs Used in Cmdlets

VERB	TYPE	USAGE
Back up	Data	It stores data by replicating it. For example, the cmdlet Backup-SPSite performs a backup of a site collection.
Compress	Data	It compresses the data of a resource. For example, the cmdlet Compress-SCVirtualDiskDrive dynamically compresses the data stored in a virtual hard disk.
Convert	Data	It converts the data from one representation to another. For example, the cmdlet Convert-Byte converts unit types.
Edit	Data	It modifies existing data. For example, the cmdlet Edit-Cmdlet -Cmdlet Get-MyData edits the cmdlet Get-MyData.
Expand	Data	This verb is paired with Compress. It expands the compressed data of a resource to its original state. For example, the cmdlet Expand-Archive -path my.zip expands the my.zip file.
Export	Data	It exports a resource to a persistent data store. For example, the cmdlet Export-Mailbox moves the contents of a mailbox to a specified mailbox folder.
Import	Data	This verb is paired with Export. It imports data from a persistent data store. For example, the cmdlet Import-Module imports one or more modules to the current session.
Initialize	Data	It initializes a resource for use. For example, the cmdlet Initialize-Disk initializes a RAW disk for the first time use by formatting the disk to get ready for data storage.
Merge	Data	It merges multiple resources into a single resource. For example, the cmdlet Merge-VHD merges virtual hard disks.
Publish	Data	It makes a resource available to others. For example, the cmdlet Publish-CsLisConfiguration publishes the Location Information Server configuration to the Central Management store.
Restore	Data	It sets a resource to a previous state. For example, the cmdlet Restore-Computer -RestorePoint 101 restores the local computer to the restore point 101.
Save	Data	It preserves data to avoid loss. For example, the cmdlet Save-Help downloads the newest Windows PowerShell help files and saves them to a specified directory.
Update	Data	It brings a resource up-to-date. For example, the cmdlet Update-List cmdlet updates a property value of an object.

Diagnostic: The verbs in the Diagnostic group are used to define diagnostic actions. The Diagnostic verbs commonly used by cmdlets are listed in Table 6.4.

Lifecycle: The verbs in the Lifecycle group are used to define the lifecycle of a resource. The Lifecycle verbs commonly used by cmdlets are listed in Table 6.5.

Security: The verbs in the Security group are used to define security. The Security verbs commonly used by cmdlets are listed in Table 6.6.

6.2.2 PowerShell Functions

Like a scripting language, Windows PowerShell allows users to create a function that has an input parameter and returns a value to a calling script. A function can be used to call another script unit repeatedly so that one does not need to write the same script multiple times. By using a function, a long and complicated script can be organized into clear and easily readable code.

Table 6.4 Diagnostic Verbs Used in Cmdlets

VERB	TYPE	USAGE
Debug	Diagnostic	It diagnoses operational problems. For example, the cmdlet Debug-Process diagnoses the processes running on a local computer.
Measure	Diagnostic	It measures the properties or retrieves the statistics about a resource. For example, the cmdlet Measure-Command measures the time it takes to run script blocks and cmdlets.
Repair	Diagnostic	It restores a resource to a normal condition. For example, the cmdlet Repair-VM repairs one or more virtual machines.
Resolve	Diagnostic	It performs a name resolution for a specified resource. For example, the cmdlet Resolve-DnsName performs a DNS name resolution for a specified name.
Test	Diagnostic	It checks the operation or consistency of a resource. For example, the cmdlet Test-VHD tests a virtual hard disk for any problems that can shut it down.
Trace	Diagnostic	It tracks the activities of a resource. For example, the cmdlet Trace-Command configures and starts a trace of a specified expression or command.

Table 6.5 Lifecycle Verbs Used in Cmdlets

VERB	TYPE	USAGE
Complete	Lifecycle	It acknowledges, verifies, or validates the state of a resource or process. For example, the cmdlet Complete-Migration finalizes the migration process.
Disable	Lifecycle	It makes a resource unavailable or inactive. For example, the cmdlet Disable-VMMigration disables the migration on one or more virtual machine hosts.
Enable	Lifecycle	This verb is paired with Disable. It makes a resource available or active. For example, the cmdlet Enable-VMMigration enables migration on one or more virtual machine hosts.
Invoke	Lifecycle	It performs an action, such as running a command or method. For example, the cmdlet Invoke-Expression runs commands or expressions on a local computer.
Resume	Lifecycle	It resumes an operation. For example, the cmdlet Resume-VM resumes a suspended virtual machine.
Register	Lifecycle	It creates an entry for a resource in a repository such as a database. For example, the cmdlet Register-ObjectEvent subscribes to the events that are generated by a Microsoft. NET Framework object.
Start	Lifecycle	It initiates an operation. For example, the cmdlet Start-VM starts a virtual machine.
Stop	Lifecycle	This verb is paired with Start. It discontinues an activity. For example, the cmdlet Stop-VM shuts down and saves a virtual machine.
Suspend	Lifecycle	This verb is paired with Resume. It pauses an activity. For example, the cmdlet Suspend-VM pauses a virtual machine.
Unregister	Lifecycle	This verb is paired with Register. It cancels the registration for a resource. For example, the cmdlet Unregister-Event cancels an event subscription.
Wait	Lifecycle	It makes an operation wait for a specified event to occur. For example, the cmdlet Wait-Event waits until a particular event is raised before continuing to run.

In PowerShell, a function has the following format:

```
function function_name($parameter1, $parameter2)
{
  code body
  return $parameter2
}
```

Table 6.6 Security Verbs Used in Cmdlets

VERB	TYPE	USAGE
Block	Security	It restricts access to a resource. For example, the cmdlet Block-Smb Share Access sets a deny access control entry (ACE).
Grant	Security	It permits access to a resource. For example, the cmdlet Grant-SmbShareAccess sets an allow access control entry (ACE).
Protect	Security	It defends a resource from attack or loss. For example, the cmdlet Protect-ScalingStore encrypts a store file using the private key in a certificate.
Revoke	Security	This verb is paired with Grant. It reverses a permission for accessing a resource. For example, the cmdlet Revoke-SmbShareAccess removes all the allow access control entries (ACEs).
Unblock	Security	This verb is paired with Block. It removes restrictions to a resource. For example, the cmdlet Unblock-SmbShareAccess removes all the deny access control entries (ACEs).
Unprotect	Security	This verb is paired with Protect. It removes the protection from a resource. For example, the cmdlet Unprotect-Scaling Store decrypts a store file using the private key in a certificate.

A function consists of four parts:

1. Function name
2. Input parameters
3. Code body
4. Return value

The function name is required. Within a PowerShell script, a function is called by its name. The input parameters are optional. The function can have no parameters if it does not use input values. The $ sign used in front of the name of a parameter indicates that the parameter is used as a variable. As input values, the values of parameters can be assigned in a script or be read from a command line. The function's code body is a list of Windows PowerShell cmdlets and statements that are used to accomplish a specific task. Functions can return values that are assigned to variables. The return values can be displayed on a monitor screen or passed to other functions or cmdlets. The keyword return is optional. For example, the following two functions with or without the keyword return will return the same value.

The first function returns the value assigned in the variable with the return keyword.

```
function multiplication ($value1, $value2)
{
    "Processing Multiplication"
    $product = $value1 * $value2
    return $product
}
```

To run the function in Windows PowerShell, use the following command:

```
C:\PS> $p = multiplication 10 2
C:\PS> $p
```

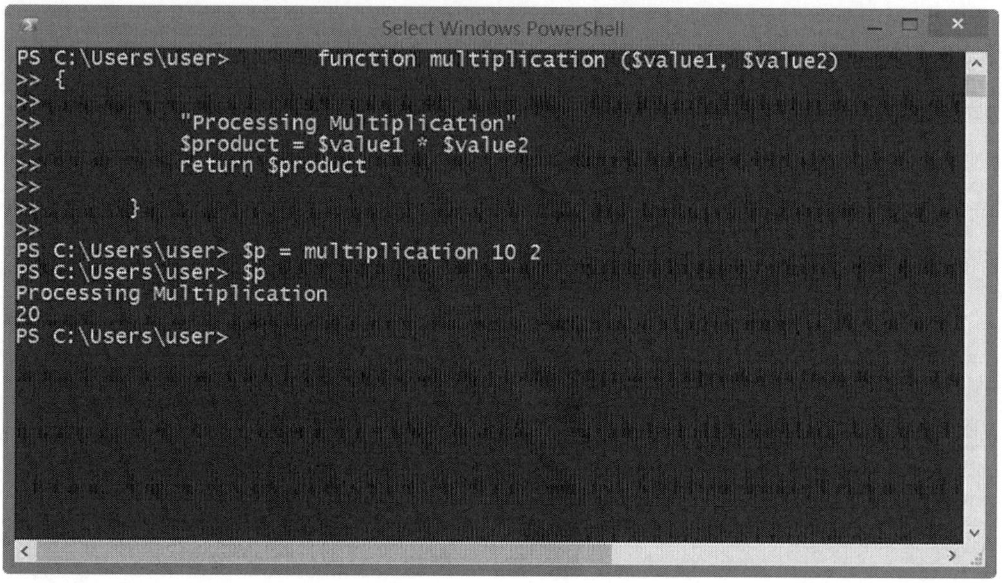

Figure 6.3 Output with return keyword.

As shown in Figure 6.3, the output is

```
Processing Multiplication
20
```

The next function returns the value assigned in the variable without the return keyword.

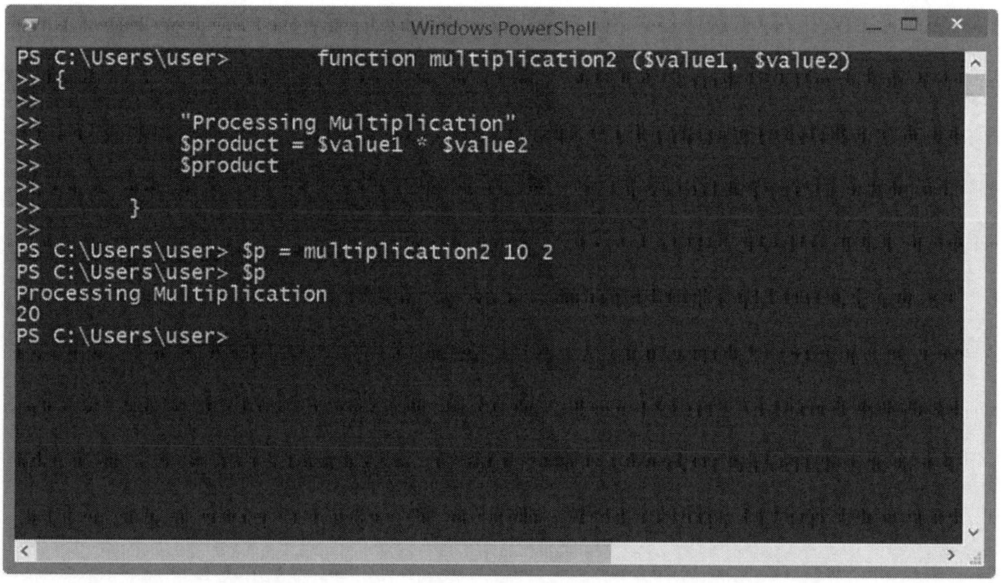

Figure 6.4 Output without return keyword.

```
function multiplication2 ($value1, $value2)
  {
    "Processing Multiplication"
    $product = $value1 * $value2
    $product
  }
```

To run the function in Windows PowerShell, use the following command:

```
C:\PS> $p = multiplication2 10 2
C:\PS> $p
```

As shown in Figure 6.4, the output is also

```
Processing Multiplication
20
```

6.2.3 Windows PowerShell Scripts

A Windows PowerShell script is a file that contains the PowerShell source code and has the.ps1 file extension. Similar to a scripting language such as Perl, Python, or VBScript, the PowerShell script is flexible and portable. The PowerShell script code is not compiled at runtime but is rather interpreted. To support scripting, a PowerShell package provides two components, PowerShell runtime environment and PowerShell Integrated Scripting Environment (ISE).

The runtime environment is a set of instructions that manage the processor stack, create space for local variables, and copy function-call parameters onto the top of the stack. During the execution of scripting code, these instructions are inserted into the executable code by the compiler to instruct the system how to load the executable code into memory, how to call system software routines, how to make function calls, and where to store the data. The PowerShell ISE is a graphic interface for Windows PowerShell. Figure 6.5 illustrates the PowerShell ISE.

As shown in Figure 6.5, the ISE window has three panes: Script Pane, Console Pane, and Add-on Tools Pane. The brief descriptions of the three panes are given as follows:

1. *Script Pane*: This pane is the code editor. In this pane, one can write, edit, run, and debug PowerShell scripts. This pane also allows the user to open and save the PowerShell script files.
2. *Console Pane*: This pane can be used to test the PowerShell script. Like the PowerShell command console, in this pane, one can view the script and examine the result of a PowerShell script.
3. *Add-on Tools Pane*: From this pane, one can add some add-on tools. The menu on the top part of Figure 6.5 provides the options on how to arrange add-ons.

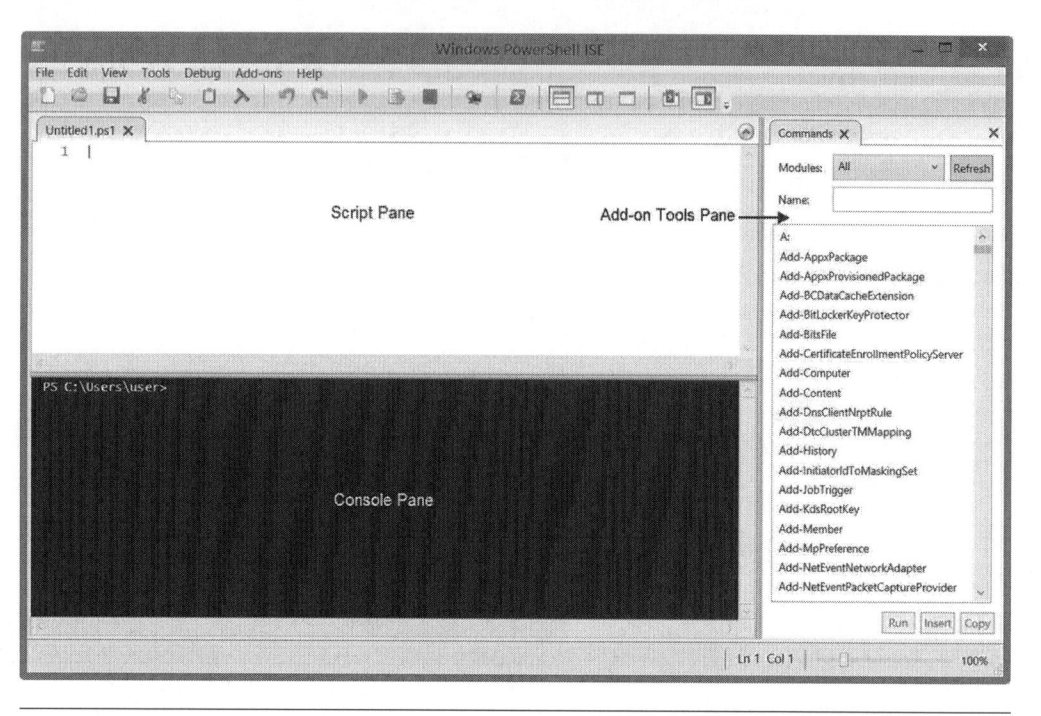

Figure 6.5   PowerShell ISE.

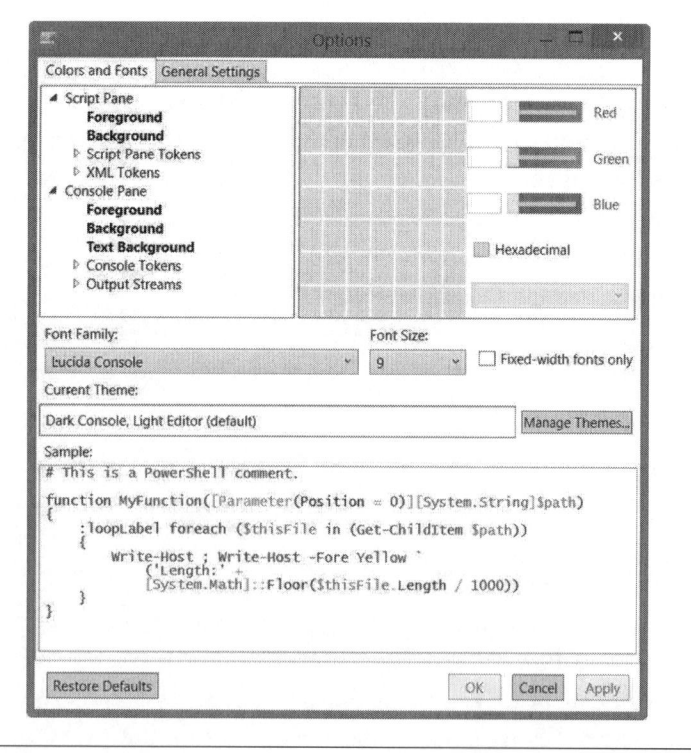

Figure 6.6   PowerShell ISE options.

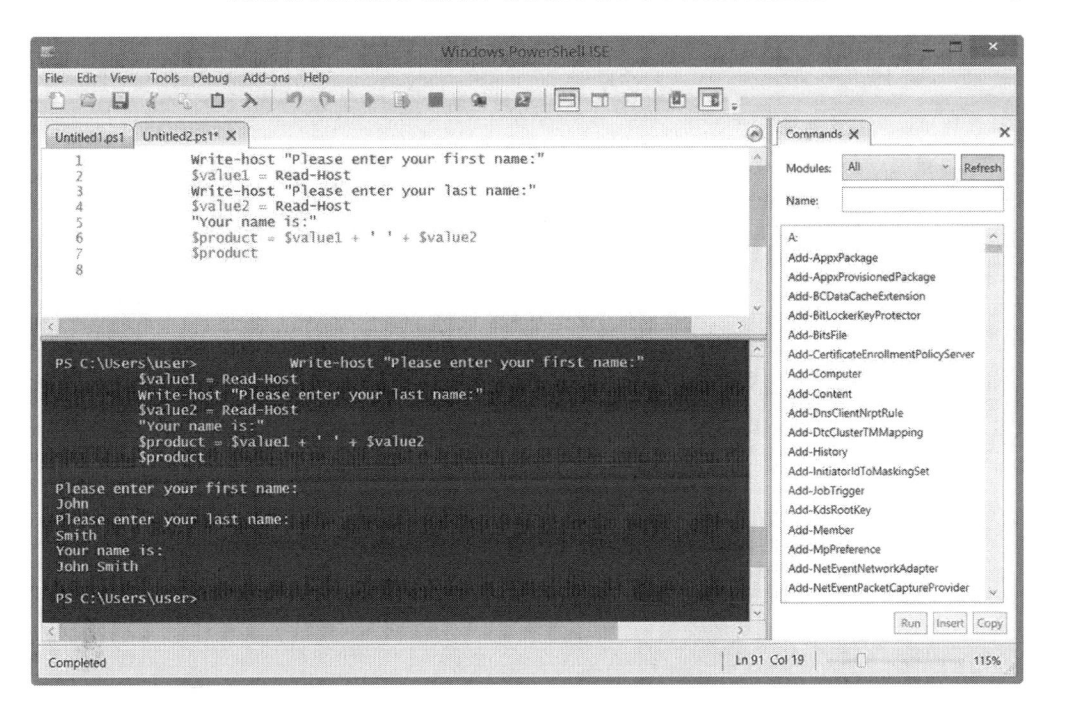

Figure 6.7 Script and output.

These three panes can be dragged to different locations to fit an individual's preference. Under the Tools/Option menu, there are more options for customizing the PowerShell ISE. The Tools/Option menu allows users to specify the colors, fonts, and themes. Users can also configure options shown in Figure 6.6. The settings can also be customized with a script.

The PowerShell ISE includes numerous tools for debugging and helping with coding. With the PowerShell ISE, one can read, write, edit, and run PowerShell scripts. One can also use the PowerShell ISE for debugging and getting help information. Figure 6.7 illustrates a simple example of a script in the script pane and the execution result in the console pane.

The PowerShell ISE saves the script with the extension.ps1. Once the script is saved, one can use it as a command in Windows PowerShell as shown in Figure 6.8 where the script Names.ps1 is executed.

6.2.4 Native Commands

Native commands are commands directly run by an operating system. For example, commands such as dir and copy are Windows native commands. Running a native command in PowerShell requires the creation of a new process. Therefore, it is less effective than running a cmdlet in the PowerShell environment. In addition, a native command may have its own input and output parameters that usually have different formats from those used by PowerShell. Running a native command in PowerShell is

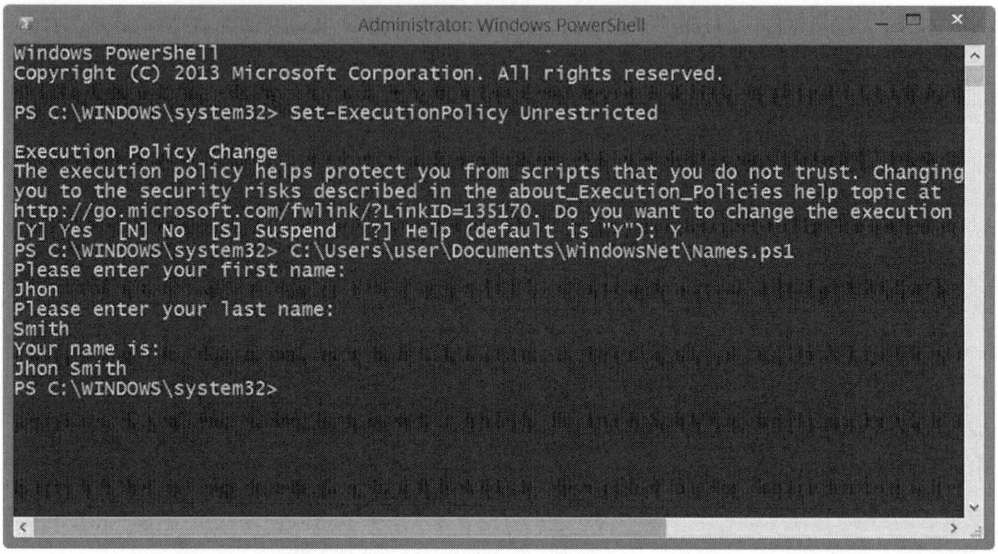

Figure 6.8   Running script in windows PowerShell.

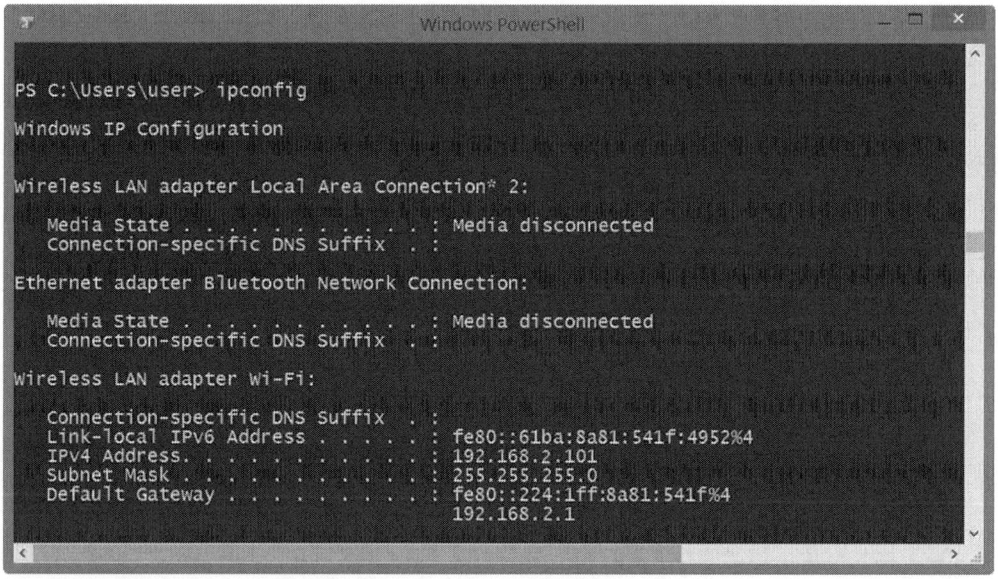

Figure 6.9   Native command in PowerShell.

very much like running it in the command prompt windows. Figure 6.9 illustrates the running of a native command in PowerShell.

6.3 Networking with PowerShell

Most of the network administration tasks can be done with PowerShell by running Windows PowerShell scripts or by using PowerShell cmdlets. This section discusses some of the network administration tasks that can be done through PowerShell cmdlets and scripts. For network administration, the following are some of the basic networking tasks that can be accomplished with PowerShell cmdlets:

- Cmdlets can be used to retrieve all IP addresses assigned to a network host.
- Cmdlets can be used to display the information about the current IP configuration for a network interface card. They can also be used to retrieve information such as MAC addresses and adapter types of a network interface card.
- To test network connection, cmdlets can be used to ping a remote network host. Information such as ResponseTime and StatusCode will be displayed. The cmdlets can also be used to get response from all the network hosts in a local network.
- With cmdlets, the network administrator can assign a DNS domain for a network interface card on a local network.
- Cmdlets can be used to configure DHCP settings. They can be used to specify DHCP properties and enable a set of network adapters to use dynamic IP addresses. They are used to identify DHCP-enabled network interface cards and retrieve DHCP properties. With cmdlets, the network administrator is able to configure the releasing and renewing of DHCP leases for all network hosts.
- Cmdlets can be used to create and remove a network share.
- By using cmdlets, the network administrator can access a network device such as a network accessible storage device. They can also be used to create a networked drive.
- PowerShell provides some cmdlets that are useful for diagnostics and troubleshooting of network connections.

For each of the aforementioned networking tasks, there is a set of cmdlets that can be used to accomplish the task. The command Get-Command can be used to display the related cmdlets for a specific networking task. For IP address management tasks, one can find related cmdlets, functions, and applications such as the ones shown in Figure 6.10.

In Figure 6.10, the column ModuleName lists the names of the cmdlets related to specific tasks. For example, the NetTCPIP module contains the cmdlets and functions for configuring a network protocol. Figure 6.11 shows the cmdlets and functions listed in NetTCPIP module.

Cmdlets can be used to display information about the current IP configuration for a network interface card. They can also be used to retrieve information such as MAC addresses and adapter types about a network interface card.

For tracing network connections, the related cmdlets, functions, and applications are shown in Figure 6.12. As applications, the .exe files contain the network commands used in the command prompt (Figure 6.12).

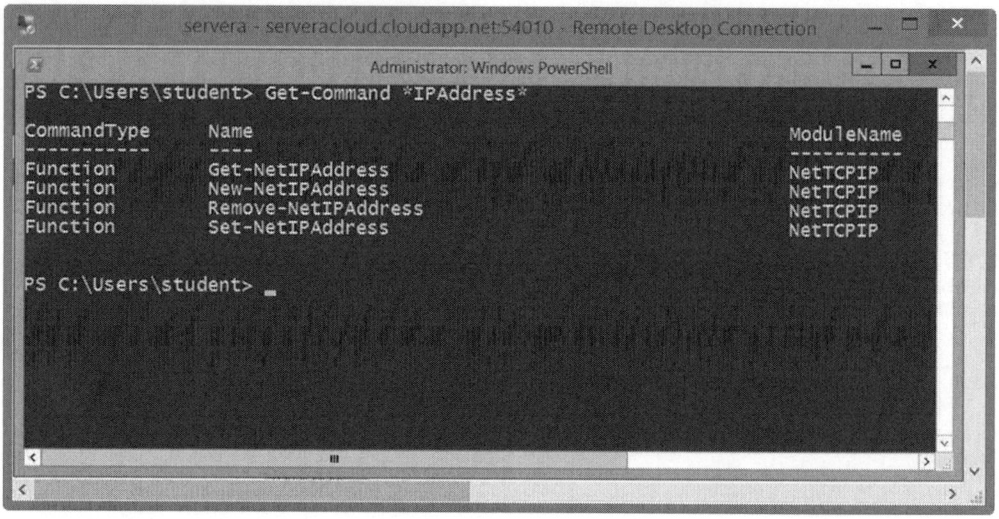

Figure 6.10 IP address-related functions.

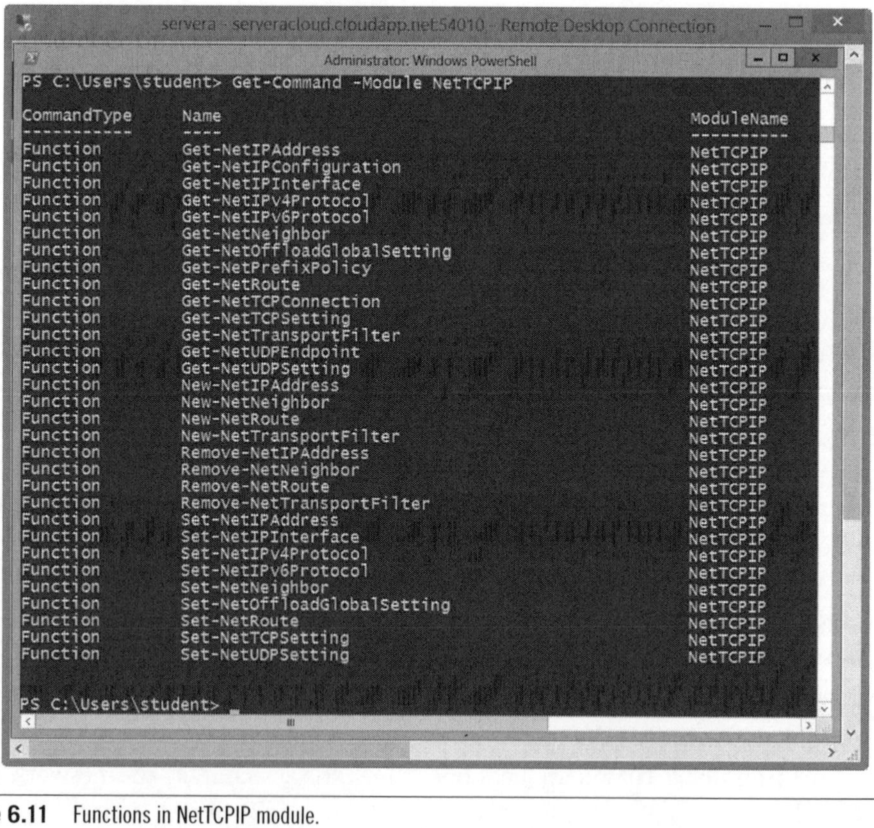

Figure 6.11 Functions in NetTCPIP module.

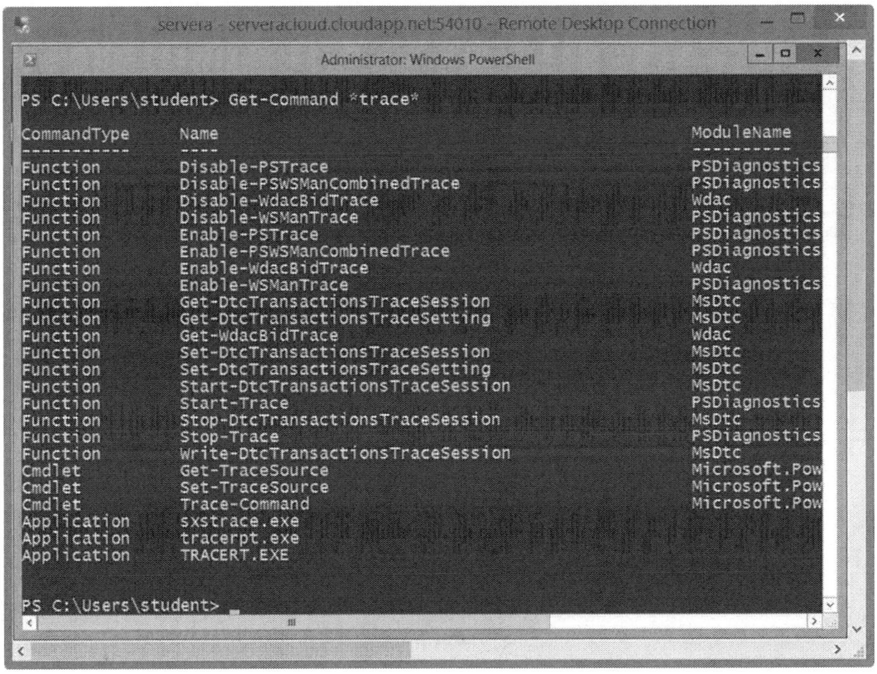

Figure 6.12   Trace-related Cmdlets, functions, and applications.

There are many cmdlets, functions, applications that are used by the network administrator to set up the DNS service. Figure 6.13 illustrate some of those cmdlets, functions, and applications.

For the configuration of the DHCP service, one can find some of the related cmdlets, functions, and applications shown in Figure 6.14.

Cmdlets can be used to create and remove a network share. Figure 6.15 shows some of the cmdlets, functions, and applications for sharing a network.

A set of cmdlets, functions, and applications are available for managing network devices. Figure 6.16 lists some of them.

A set of cmdlets, functions, and applications are also available for testing and troubleshooting of network services. Some of them are listed in Figure 6.17.

One can use the cmdlet Get-Help to find information on how to use the cmdlets, functions, and applications. For example, to get information about Set-Dnsclient, enter the following cmdlet in PowerShell as shown in Figure 6.18.

Figure 6.18 provides the SYNTAX information for Set-Dnsclient. For more information on how to use Set-Dnsclient, one can use the parameters -Details, -Full, or -Examples (Figure 6.19).

The example in Figure 6.19 illustrates how to use the cmdlet Set-Dnsclient, which has the parameters -InterfaceIndex and -ConnectionSpecificSuffix. In fact, PowerShell also provides the GUI tool Show-Command to help the user to select parameters. Figure 6.20 shows how to specify the cmdlet Set-Dnsclient in the Show-Command GUI.

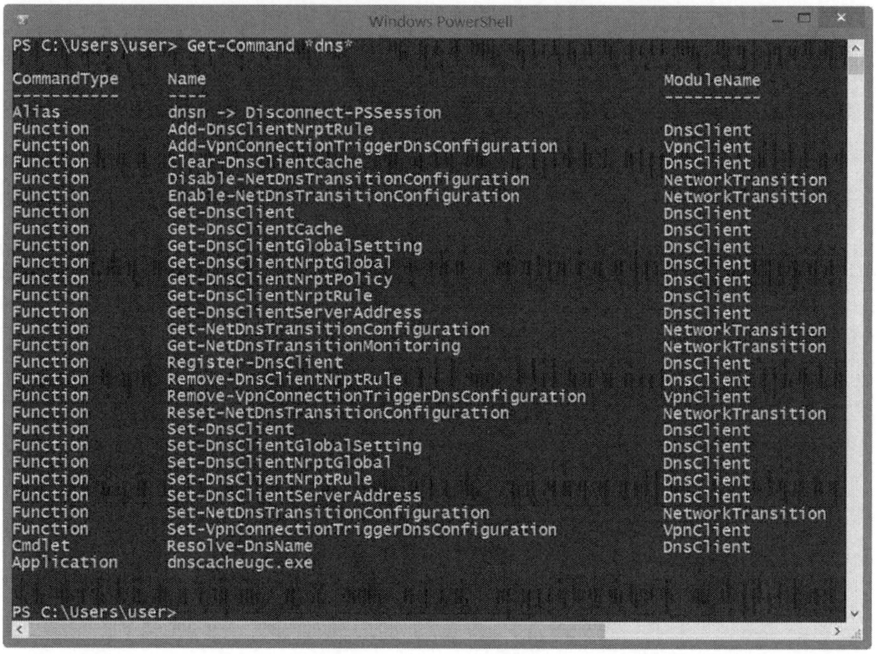

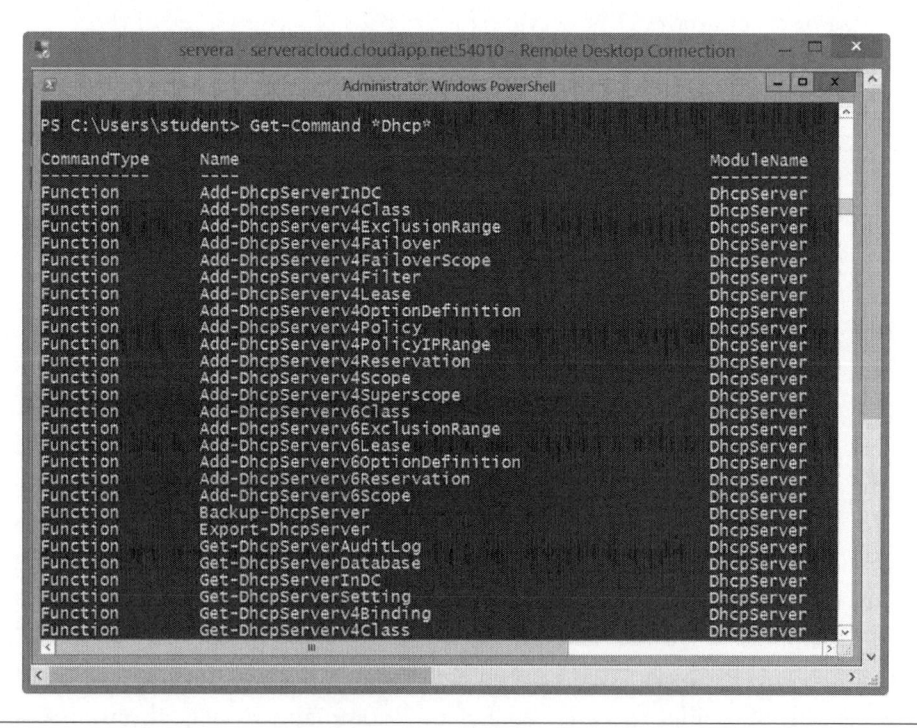

Figure 6.13   Cmdlets, functions, and applications related to DNS.

Figure 6.14   Cmdlets, functions, and applications related to DHCP.

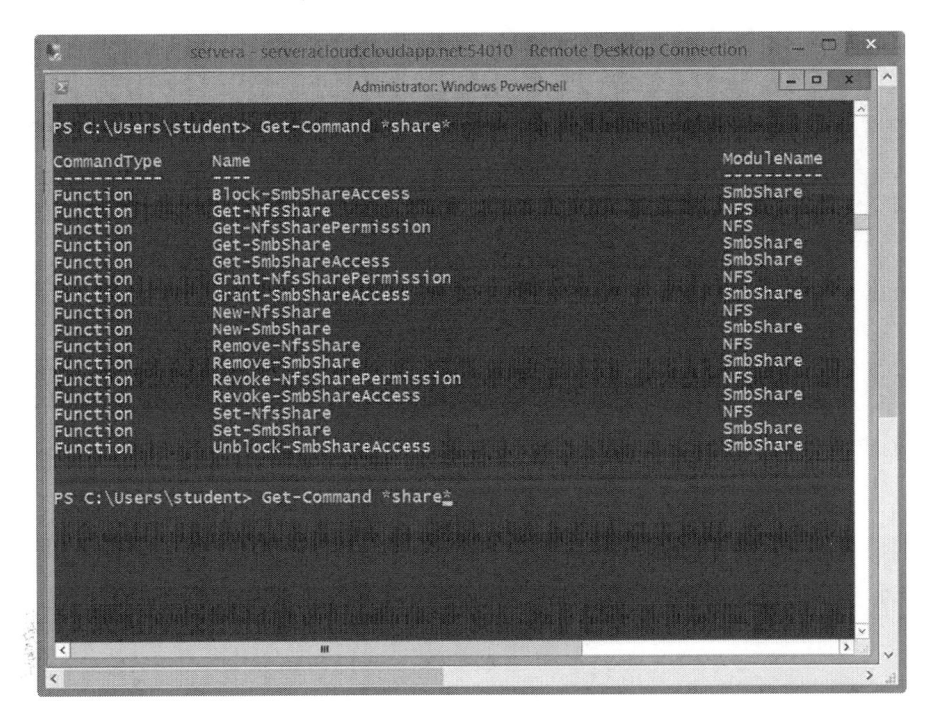

Figure 6.15   Cmdlets, functions, and applications related to network sharing.

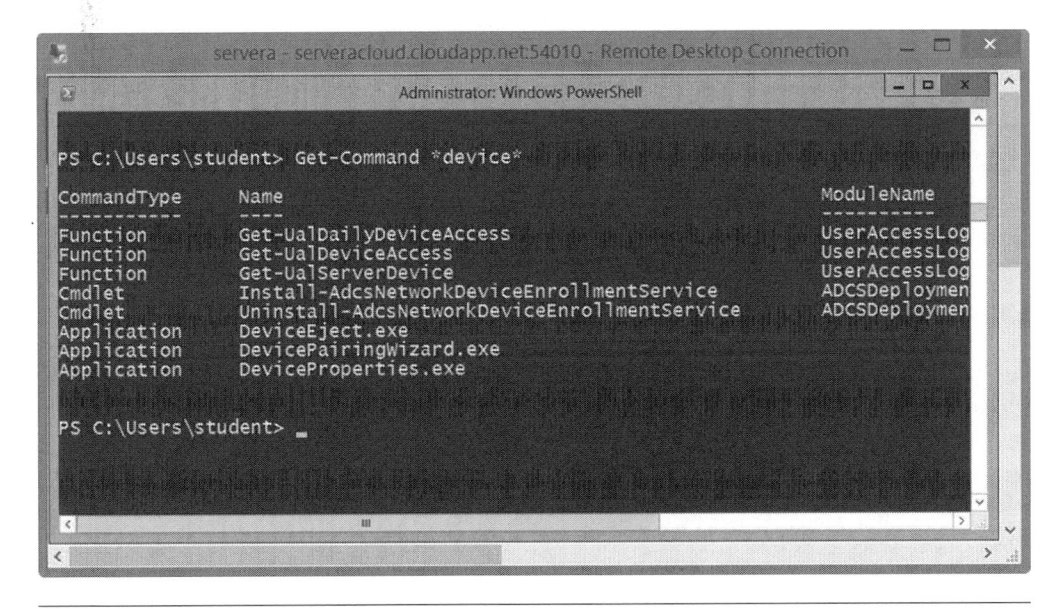

Figure 6.16   Cmdlets, functions, and applications related to device management.

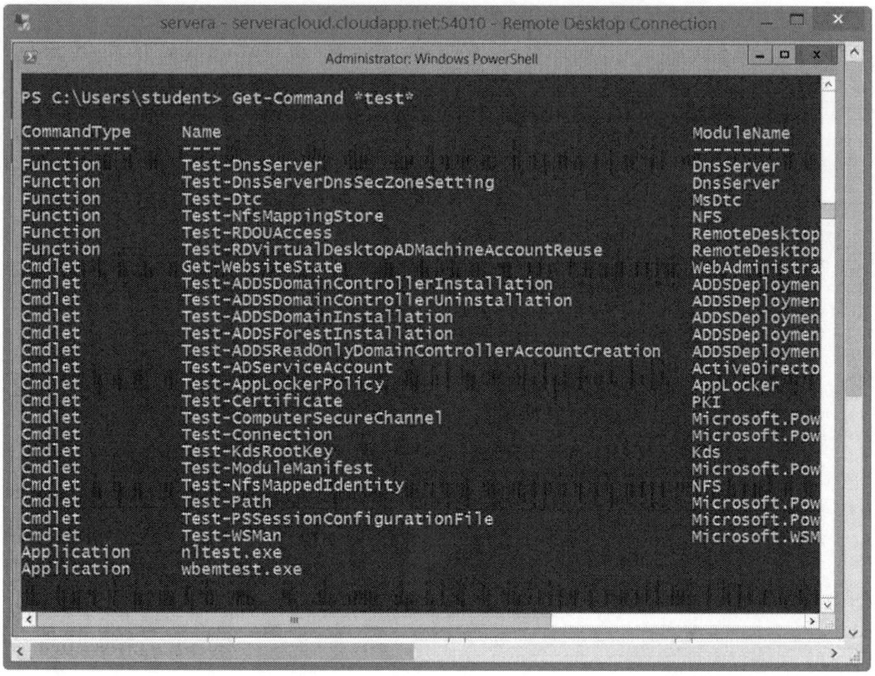

Figure 6.17   Cmdlets, functions, and applications for network testing.

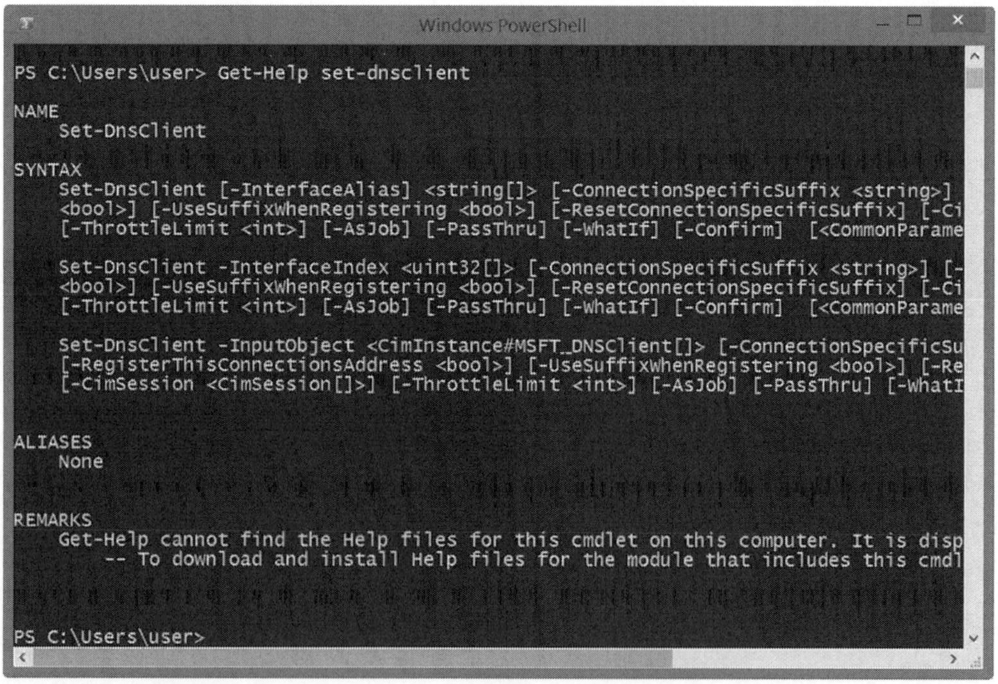

Figure 6.18   Help on Cmdlet Set-Dnsclient.

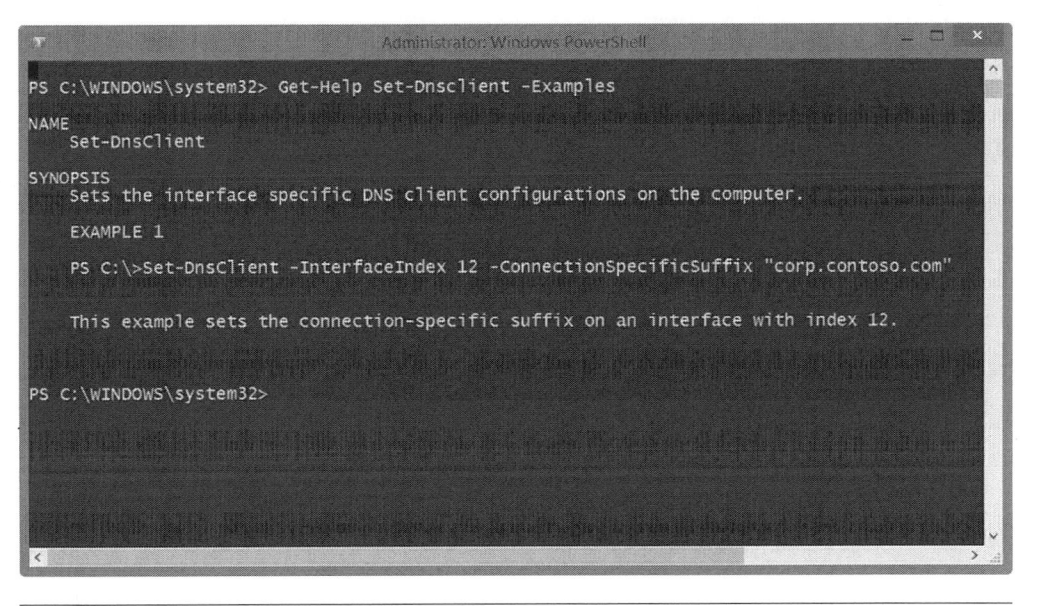

Figure 6.19 Get-Help with -examples parameter.

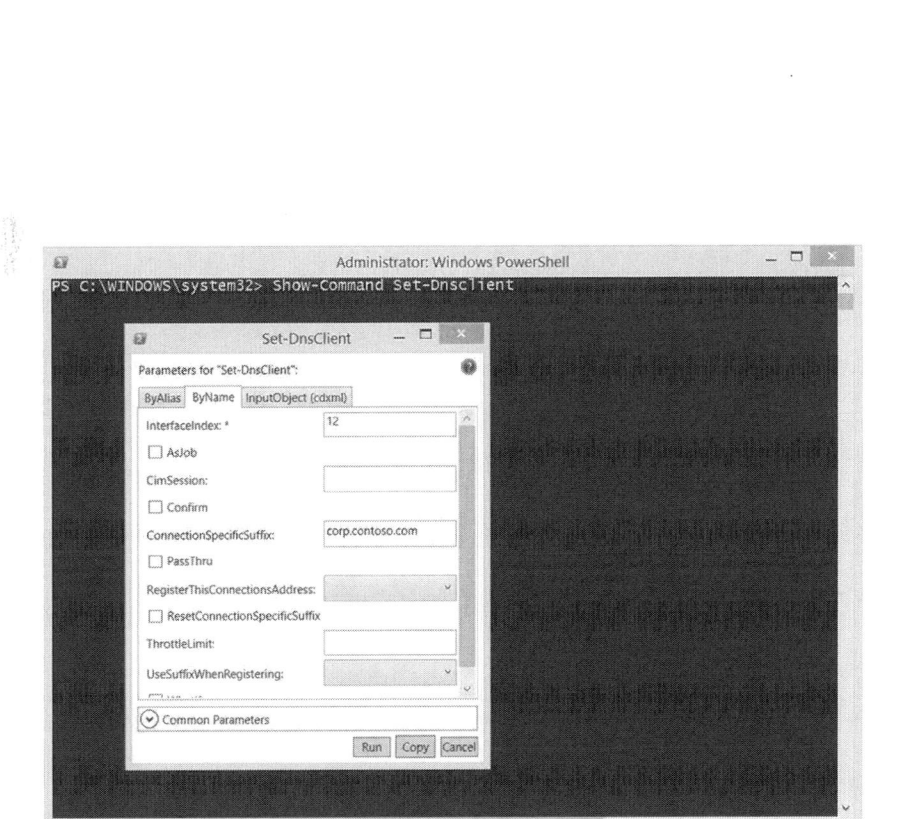

Figure 6.20 Show-Command GUI.

There are hundreds of cmdlets, functions, and applications used in networking. The coverage of these cmdlets, functions, and applications are beyond the scope of this book. To learn more about them, users can refer to books specialized in PowerShell.

Activity 6.1: Networking with Windows PowerShell

As stated earlier, PowerShell can be used for a wide range of network management tasks. For illustration purposes, in this activity, you will do hands-on practice for the following tasks:

Task 1: Basic Networking with PowerShell
Task 2: DNS Management with PowerShell
Task 3: Managing Active Directory with PowerShell

Task 1: Basic Networking with PowerShell

1. Log on to the Microsoft Azure Management Portal with your user name and password.
2. Select your virtual machine **servera** and click **CONNECT**.
3. Log on to your **servera** server with your username and password.
4. After you have logged on to servera, right click the **PowerShell** icon at the bottom of your screen and select **Run as Administrator**.
5. In the Windows PowerShell window, run the following PowerShell cmdlet to update the help on servera.

```
Update-Help
```

6. The basic networking starts to list all the NIC cards installed on servera. Enter the following cmdlet to view the information about the NICs.

```
Get-NetAdapter -Name *
```

7. As shown in Figure 6.21, the NIC with the name Ethernet 5 is running on the virtual machine servera.
8. To get the IP addresses, run the following cmdlet.

```
Get-NetIPConfiguration *
```

9. Figure 6.22 shows the IP address–related information for servera.
10. With PowerShell, you are able to ping a list of servers at the same time. For example, there are three IP addresses 10.0.0.4, 10.0.0.1, and 10.0.0.5. (Your server IPs should be different.) You can ping them through a simple PowerShell script as follows:

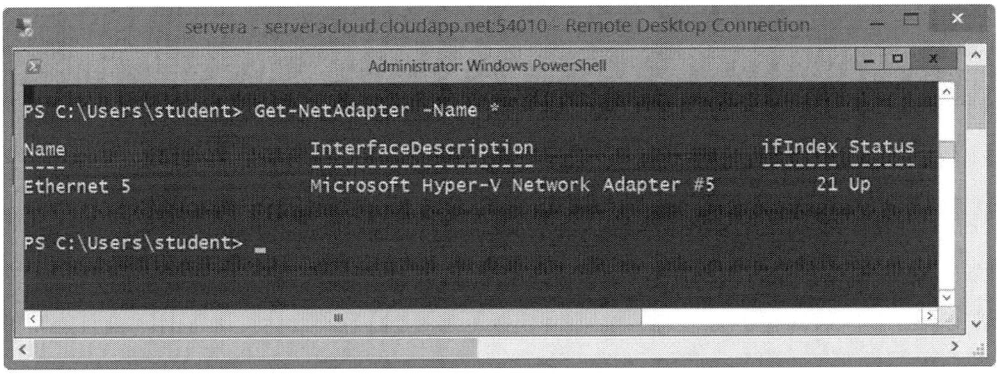

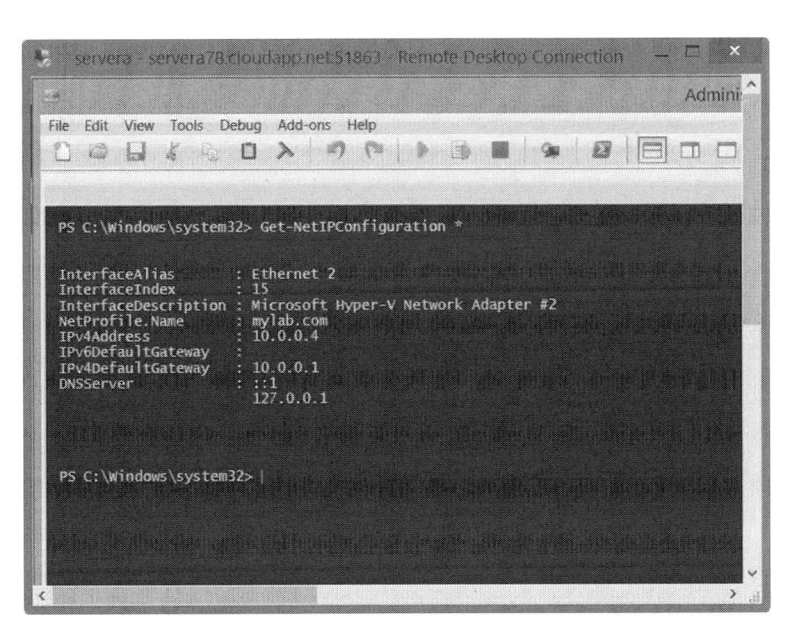

Figure 6.21 NIC information.

Figure 6.22 IP address-related information.

```
# Ping the IPs listed in the $ServerIPs
$ServerIPs = "10.0.0.4", "10.0.0.1", "10.0.0.5"
foreach ($ip in $ServerIPs) {
  if (test-Connection -ComputerName $ip -Quiet)
  {
    write-Host "$ip is up and Pinging "
  } else
  {
    write-Host "$ip is down and not pinging"
  }
}
```

11. To create a script, press the **Windows logo** key. Type the keyword **PowerShell**. Click **PowerShell ISE** to open the PowerShell ISE.

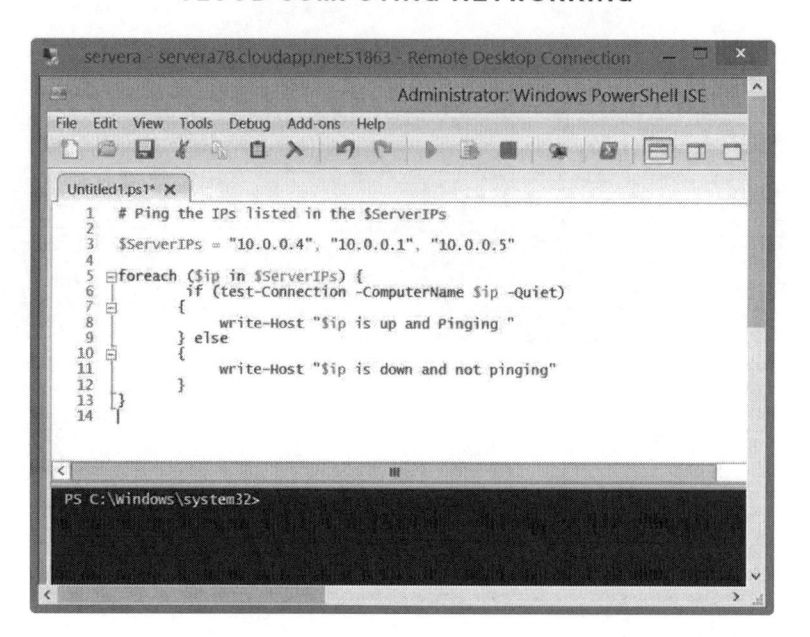

Figure 6.23   Ping script.

12. After the PowerShell ISE is opened, click **File | New**. Then, copy and paste the code in Step 10 as shown in Figure 6.23.

13. Press F5 to test the script. The result should be similar to the one in Figure 6.24.

    If one needs to ping a large number of servers at the same time, the variable ServerIPs can also take the list of IPs or server names from an external text file.

14. Save the script in the C drive with the name **myping.ps1**. Then, exit the PowerShell ISE.

15. To run the script, open PowerShell. Change to the **C** drive and run the script with the following two commands.

```
Set-ExecutionPolicy Unrestricted
./myping
```

16. The results should be similar to the one in Figure 6.25.

Task 2: DNS Management with PowerShell

After logging on to **servera**, right click the **PowerShell** icon and select **Run as Administrator**.

1. To view the list of zones on the DNS server, run the following cmdlet:

```
Get-DnsServerZone
```

Among the listed DNS zones, the one created by you earlier such as mylab. com should be there.

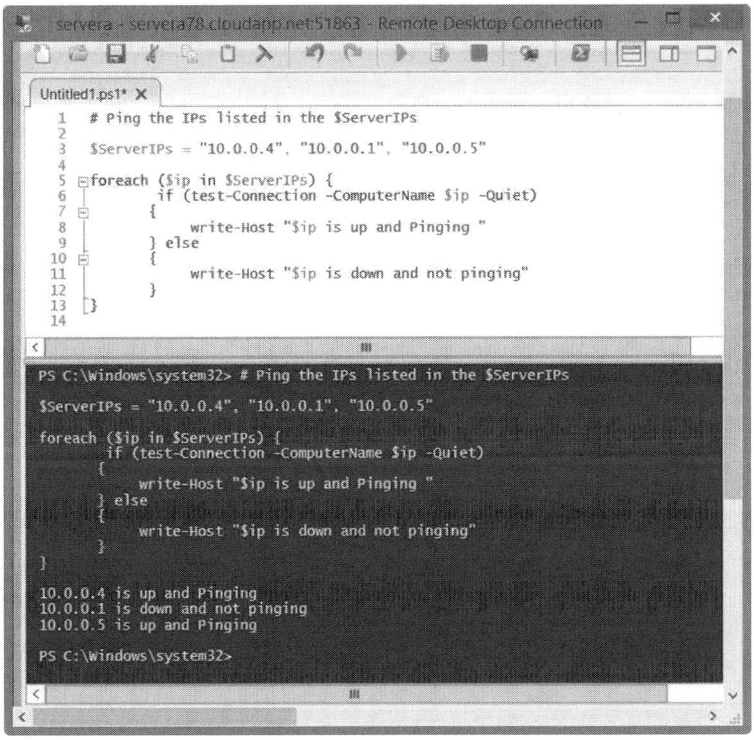

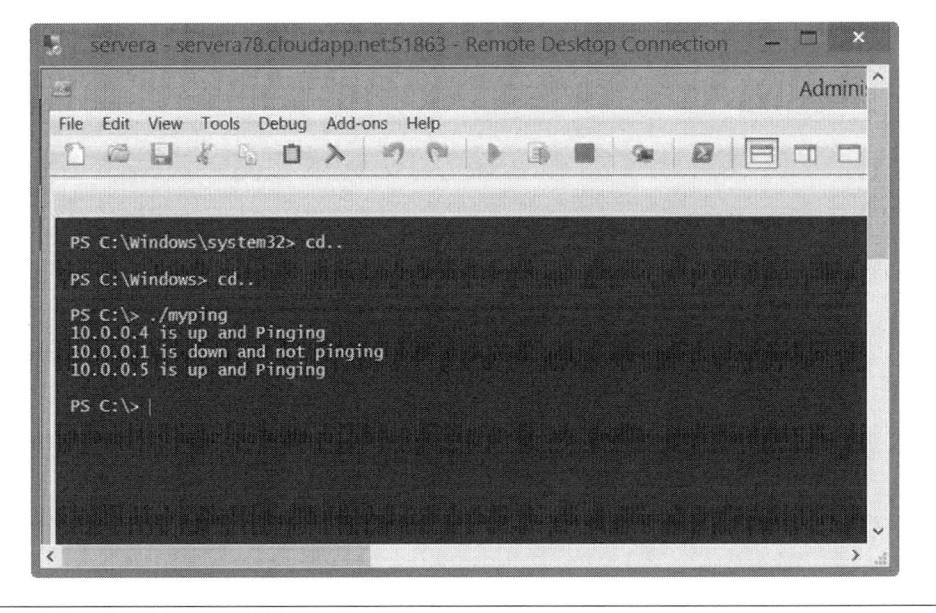

Figure 6.24   Script to Ping multiple IP addresses.

Figure 6.25   Running myping script.

2. To view the list of records stored on the DNS server, run the following cmdlet:

```
Get-DnsServerResourceRecord -ZoneName mylab.com
```

3. Among the records, the Type A records describe the IP addresses in the mylab.com zone. The Type SRV records are for specific services. The SOA records define the global parameters for the zone. To display only the Type A records, run the following cmdlets:

```
Get-DnsServerResourceRecord -ZoneName mylab.com | Where-Object
   {$_.RecordType -eq "A"}
```

The first cmdlet returns all the DNS records while the second cmdlet only writes out the Type A DNS records. Figure 6.26 shows the Type A records stored in the zone mylab.com.

4. Suppose that you need to create an alias www for servera. Run the following cmdlet to accomplish the task:

```
Add-DnsServerResourceRecordCName -Name "www" -HostNameAlias
   "servera.mylab.com" -ZoneName "mylab.com"
```

5. To view the result, run the following cmdlet:

```
Get-DnsServerResourceRecord -ZoneName mylab.com | where-object
   {$_.RecordType -eq "CNAME"}
```

Figure 6.27 shows that servera.mylab.com has the alias www.

6. To back up the DNS zones, run the following cmdlet:

```
Get-DnsServer | Export-Clixml -Path C:\DNSZoneBk.xml
```

The.xml file will be used for restoring the DNS zones.

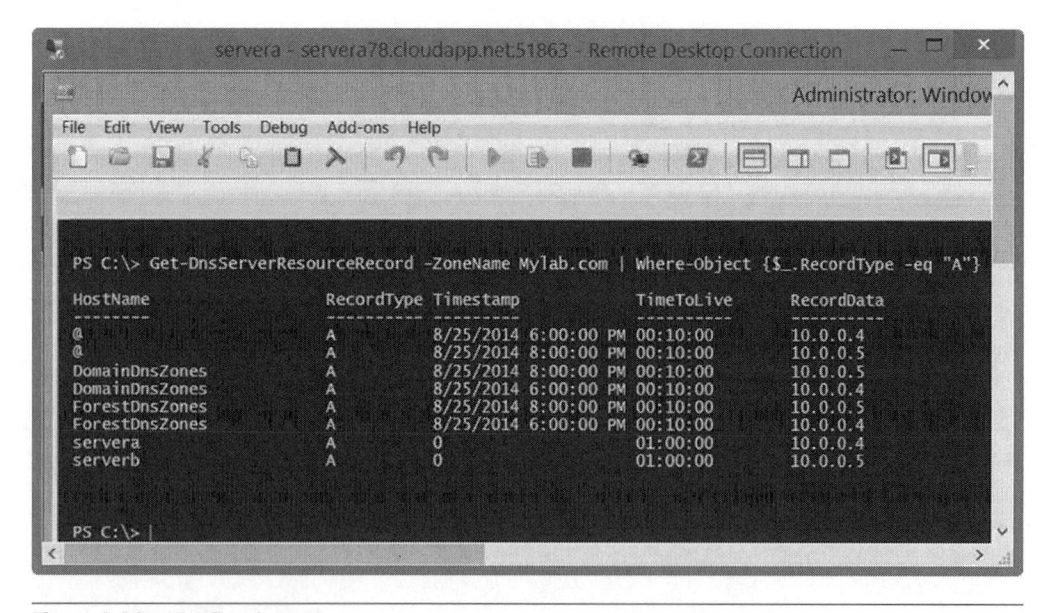

Figure 6.26   View Type A records.

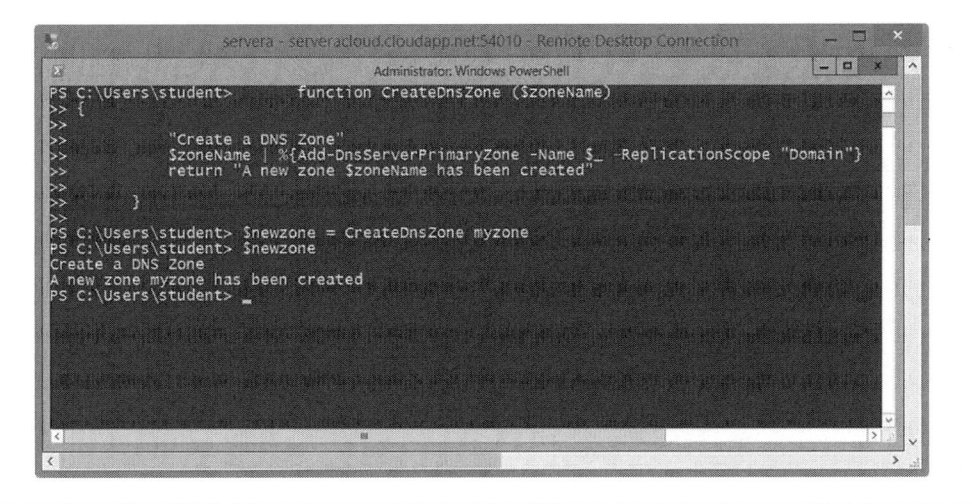

Figure 6.27 Alias for servera.

7. In this step, you will use a function to create a new DNS zone with the following code:

```
function CreateDnsZone ($zoneName)
{
  "Create a DNS Zone"
  $zoneName |%{Add-DnsServerPrimaryZone -Name $_
    -ReplicationScope "Domain"}
  return "A new zone $zoneName has been created"
}
```

Copy and paste this code in PowerShell as shown in Figure 6.28. Then, press the **Enter** key.

8. To run the function, enter the following code shown in Figure 6.28 and then press the **Enter** key:

```
$newzone = CreateDnsZone myzone
```

9. To view the result, enter the variable $newzone shown in Figure 6.28 and then press the **Enter** key.

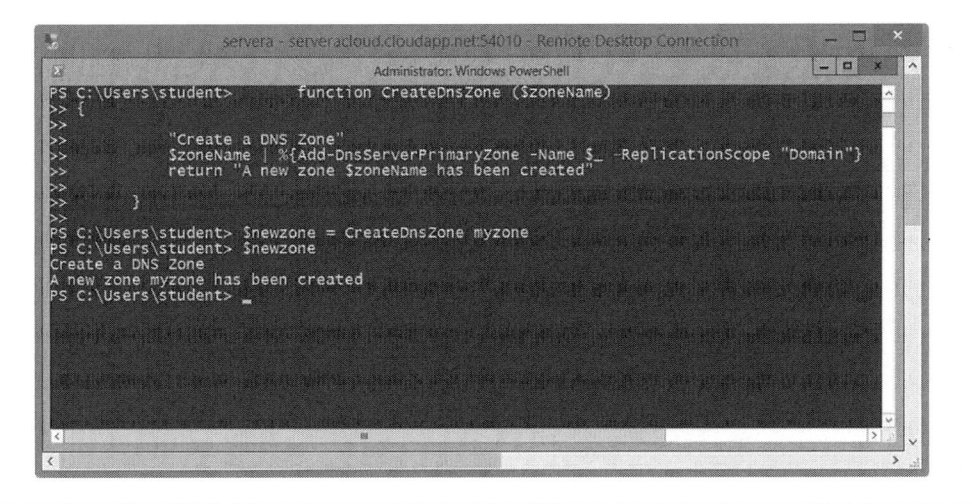

Figure 6.28 Create new DNS zone.

10. In this step, you will copy the NS records from the zone mylab.com to the newly created zone myzone with the following script:

```
#Read the input for the names of source and destination zones.
$source = Read-Host "Enter a source zone"
$destination = Read-Host "Enter a destination zone"
#Select type A records from the source zone and add the
#type A records to the destination zone.
Get-DnsServerResourceRecord -ZoneName $source -RRType A |
   Add-DnsServerResourceRecord -ZoneName $destination
#Display the copied records
Get-DnsServerResourceRecord -ZoneName $destination |
   Where-Object {$_.RecordType -eq "A"}
```

11. Copy and paste this code to the PowerShell ISE. Press **F5** to execute the script. In the console pane, enter the source as **mylab.com** and the destination as **myzone**. Then, press **Enter**. The result should be similar to the one in Figure 6.29. Then, save it with the file name **zonecopy.ps1** in the C drive.

12. To run the script, you need to clean up the Type A records previously copied into the zone myzone with the following cmdlets:

```
Get-DnsServerResourceRecord -ZoneName mylab.com -RRType A |
   Remove-DnsServerResourceRecord -Force -ZoneName myzone
```

Figure 6.29   Script testing.

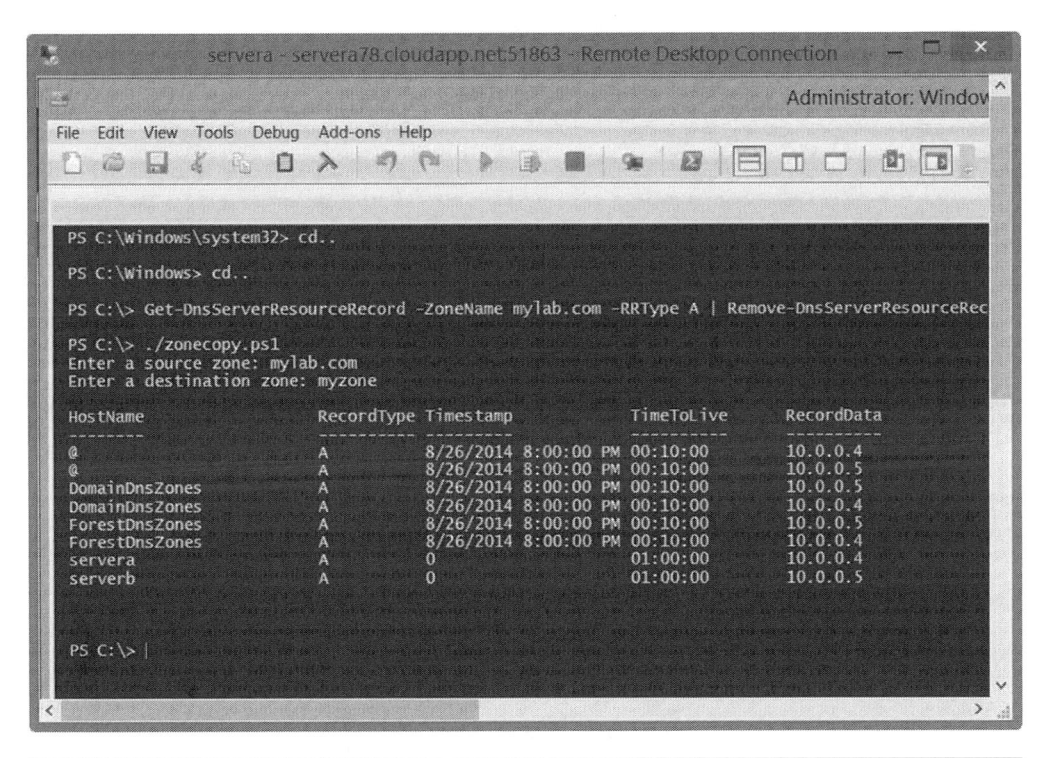

Figure 6.30   Running script zonecopy.

13. Change the directory to the C drive and enter the following command in PowerShell window. The execution result is shown in Figure 6.30. Enter the source as **mylab.com** and the destination as **myzone**.

```
./zonecopy.ps1
```

Task 3: Managing Active Directory with PowerShell

1. Assume that you are still logged on to **servera**. In Server Manager, click the **Tools** menu, and then select **Active Directory Module for Windows PowerShell**.

2. To update users' description, run the following cmdlets to describe all the users as the members of the CS department:

```
Get-ADUser -Filter 'Name -like "*"' -SearchBase " DC = mylab,DC
    = com" | Set-ADUser -Description "Member of the CS Department"
```

3. To view the change, run the following cmdlet. Figure 6.31 shows the result.

```
Get-ADUser student -Properties description
```

4. To view a user's membership, run the following cmdlet:

```
Get-ADPrincipalGroupMembership -Identity student
```

You will see the result similar to the one in Figure 6.32.

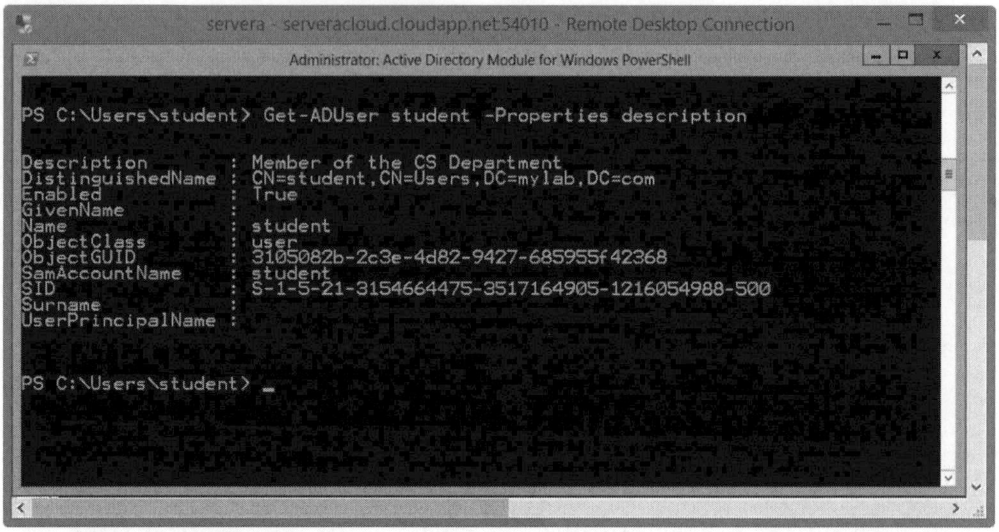

Figure 6.31 User description.

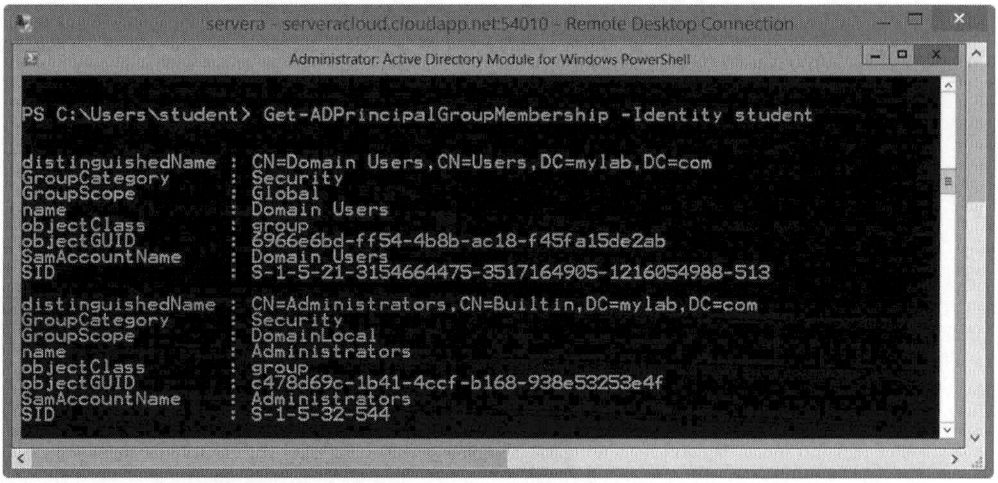

Figure 6.32 User's group membership.

5. To prevent the student user's password from expiring, run the following cmdlet:

```
Set-ADAccountControl -Identity student -PasswordNeverExpires
   $true
```

6. The next cmdlets will show the users who have not logged on for 30 days:

```
Search-ADAccount -AccountInactive -TimeSpan 30.00:00:00 |
   where {$_.ObjectClass -eq 'user'} | FT Name,ObjectClass -A
```

The result is shown in Figure 6.33.

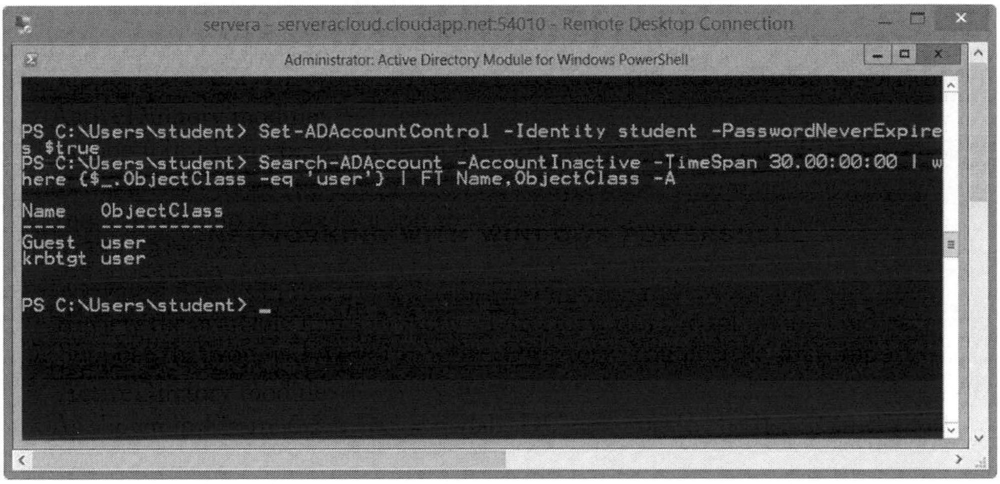

Figure 6.33   Inactive users.

7. Suppose that you will work in Active Directory. You need to first import the ActiveDirctory module:

```
Import-Module ActiveDirectory
```

You now need to set the location to AD:

```
Set-Location AD:
```

To view the available items in Active Directory, run the following cmdlet:

```
Get-ChildItem
```

As shown in Figure 6.34, DC = mylab, DC = com is in the list. Run the following cmdlet to set the location to DC = mylab, DC = com.

```
Set-Location "dc = mylab,dc = com"
```

8. To create a new user, run the following cmdlet:

```
New-ADUser -Name "Student Mary" -SamAccountName "studentm" `
-Path "DC = mylab,DC = com"
```

Run the following cmdlet to view the user account. Figure 6.35 shows the new user information:

```
Get-ADUser studentm
```

9. To set a password for the new user account, run the following cmdlet:

```
Set-ADAccountPassword -Identity studentm
```

10. When prompted to enter the current password, press the **Enter** key. When prompted for the desired password, enter a password for studentm and confirm it. Figure 6.36 shows the process.

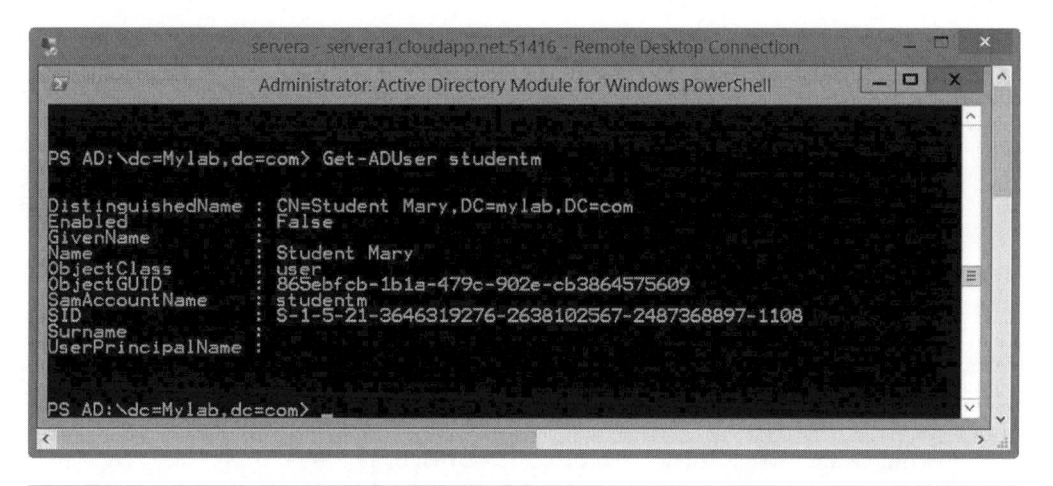

Figure 6.34　Setting location.

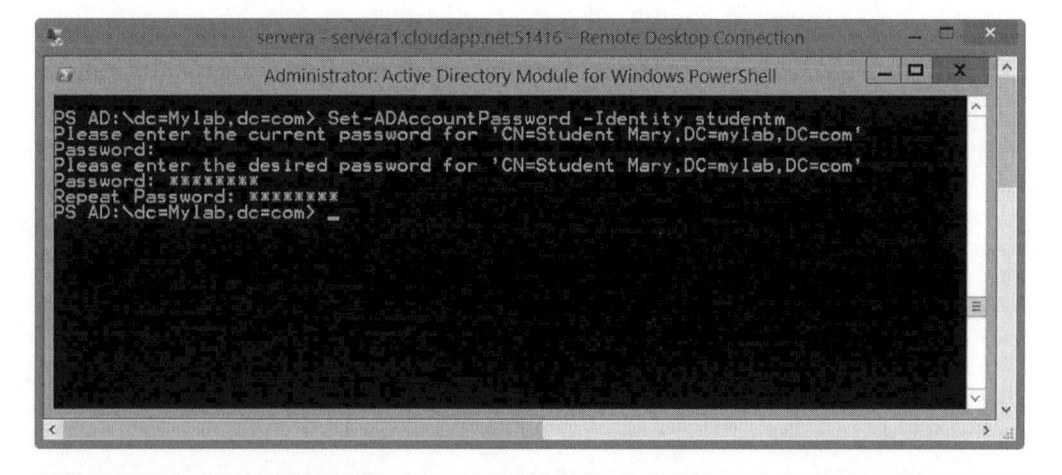

Figure 6.35　New user information.

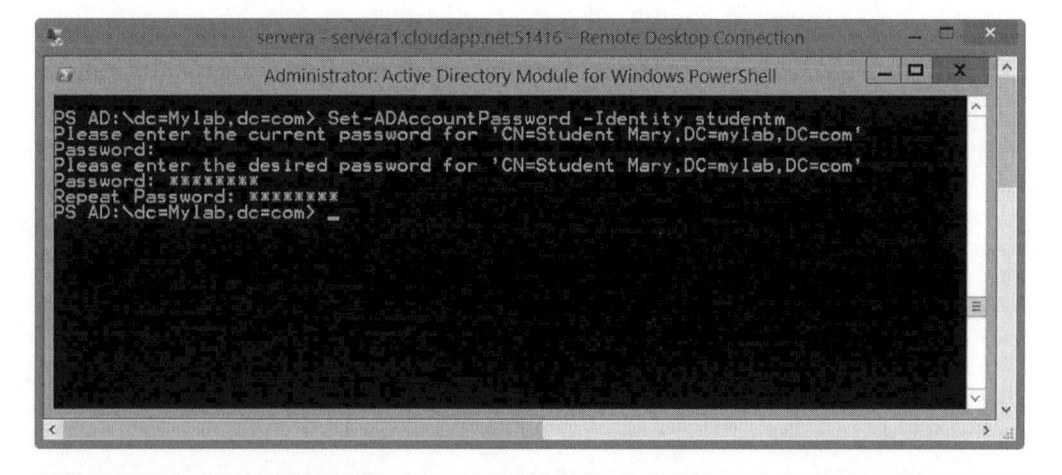

Figure 6.36　Setting password.

11. In the following, you are going to generate multiple user accounts with a script. First, open the PowerShell ISE by pressing the **Windows logo** key and type **PowerShell ISE**. Click the **PowerShell ISE** tile to open it. After the PowerShell ISE is opened, click **File** and **New**. Then, enter the following script:

```
Import-Module ActiveDirectory
foreach($i in 1..10) {
$AccountName = "student{0}" -f $i
$Password = Convertto-secureString -string "P@ssw0rd$i"
  -force -AsPlainText
New-ADUser -Name $AccountName -AccountPassword $Password
  -Path "DC = mylab,DC = com" -Enabled:$true
}
```

12. Press the **F5** key to run the script. The result is shown in Figure 6.37.
13. Save the script as **c:\users\student\User-Creation.ps1**. To verify the created users, in the PowerShell window, run the script by using the following command:

```
Get-ADUser -Filter 'Name -like "student*"'
```

Figure 6.38 partially displays the created users by the User-Creation script.

As mentioned earlier, PowerShell is much more powerful than what has been illustrated here. For more information about PowerShell, please refer to books specializing in PowerShell.

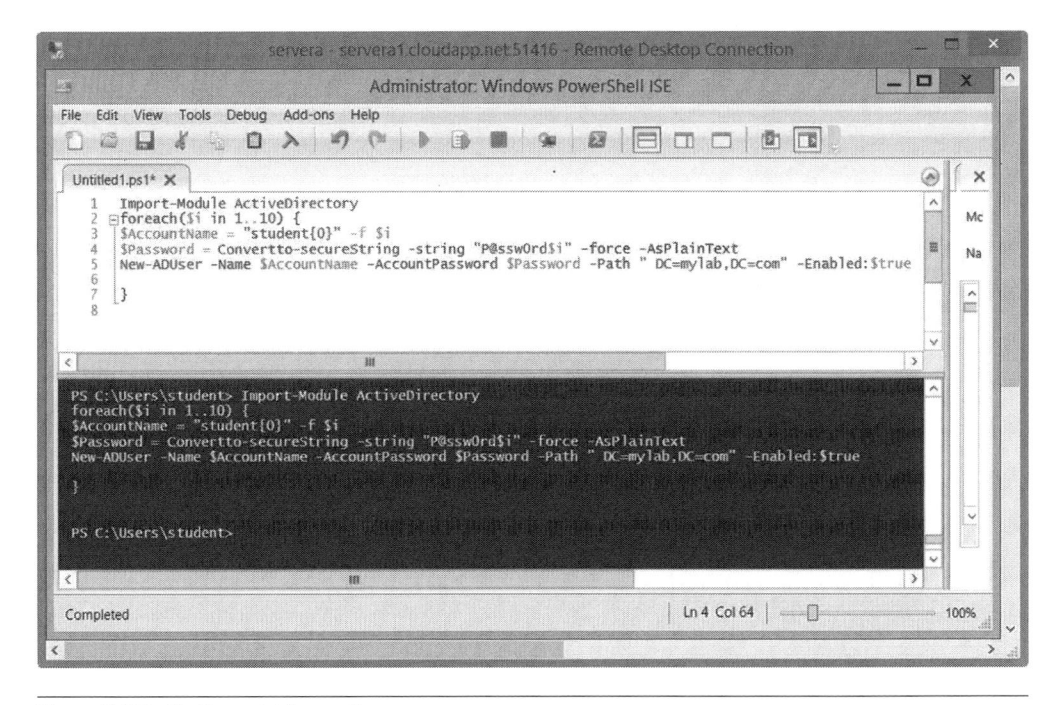

Figure 6.37   Testing script for creating users.

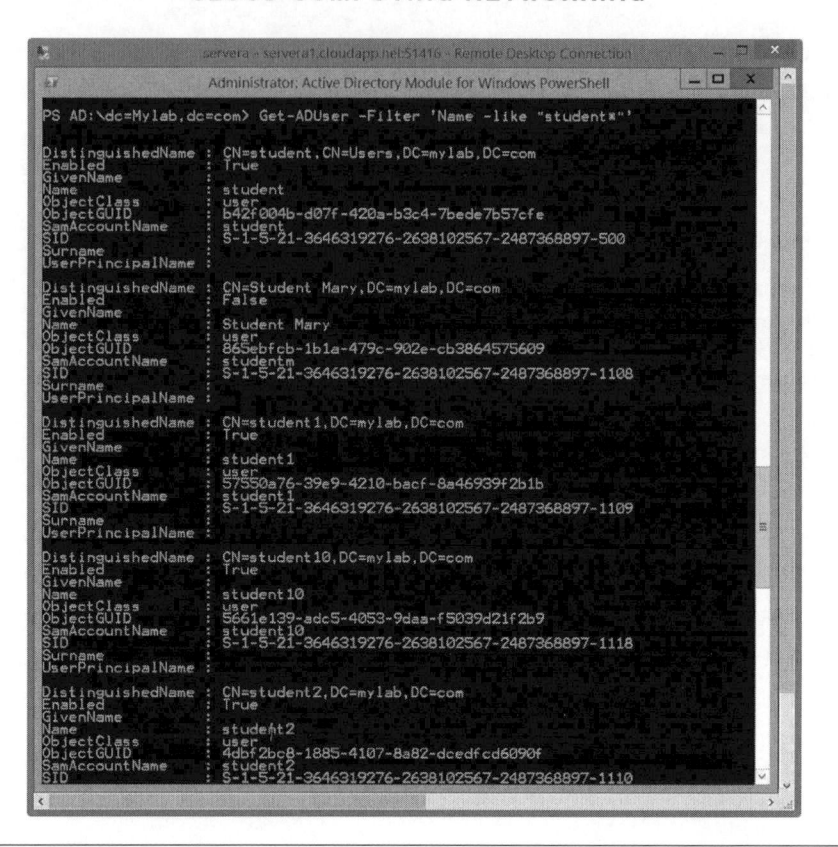

Figure 6.38   Displaying created users.

6.4 Microsoft Azure PowerShell

For the management of Microsoft Azure, one can use Microsoft Azure management cmdlets. Microsoft Azure management cmdlets can be used to accomplish the following management tasks:

- Managing subscriptions
- Deploying and managing virtual machines
- Managing virtual networks
- Managing storage accounts
- Deploying and managing cloud services
- Balancing workload
- Developing virtual websites
- Managing cross-premises networks

Microsoft Azure PowerShell cmdlets can be used to control and automate the service deployment process. These management tasks can either be done interactively by executing the cmdlets or automatically by running scripts. In Chapter 3, you used Azure PowerShell to retain the IP address for your virtual machine. Activity 6.2 will carry out more activities with Azure PowerShell.

Activity 6.2: Using Microsoft Azure PowerShell

Microsoft Azure PowerShell is explained in Chapter 3. After Microsoft Azure PowerShell is installed, you can conduct some cloud management tasks.

Task 1: Preparing Microsoft Azure PowerShell

For this task, you need to download and install the Microsoft Azure PowerShell module. Then, you will configure Microsoft Azure PowerShell for managing the Microsoft Azure platform.

1. Log on to the Microsoft Azure Management Portal with your user name and password.
2. Select your virtual machine **serverb** and click **CONNECT**.
3. Log on to **serverb** with your username and password.
4. To view Microsoft Azure PowerShell, press the **Windows logo** key and type **Power**. You should be able to see the Microsoft Azure PowerShell tile as shown in Figure 6.39.
5. Click the Microsoft Azure PowerShell tile to open it. After the command prompt is opened, type **Help Azure**. You will see a similar result as one displayed in Figure 6.40.

Task 2: Managing Microsoft Azure with Microsoft Azure PowerShell

Microsoft Azure PowerShell cmdlets are used to manage subscriptions, storage accounts, storage Blobs, tables, and queues; they are also used to deploy and manage virtual

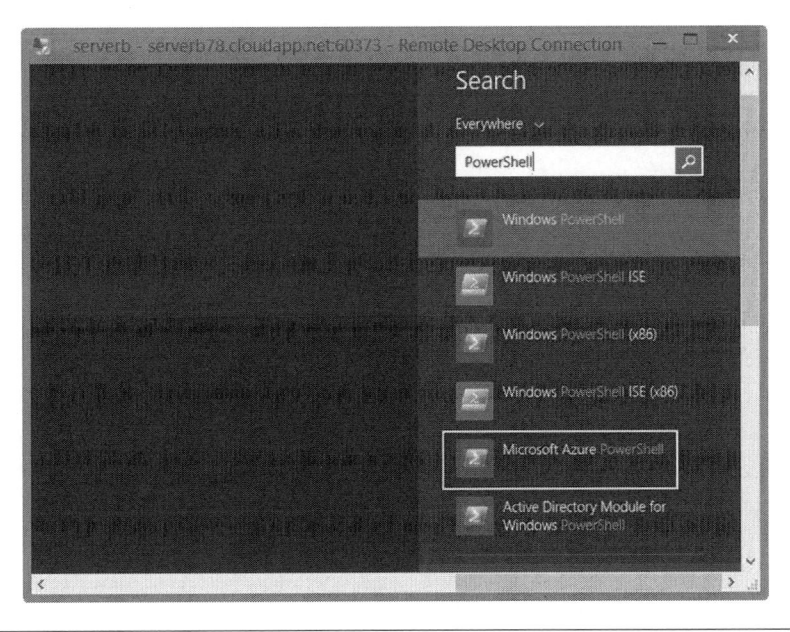

Figure 6.39　Microsoft Azure PowerShell.

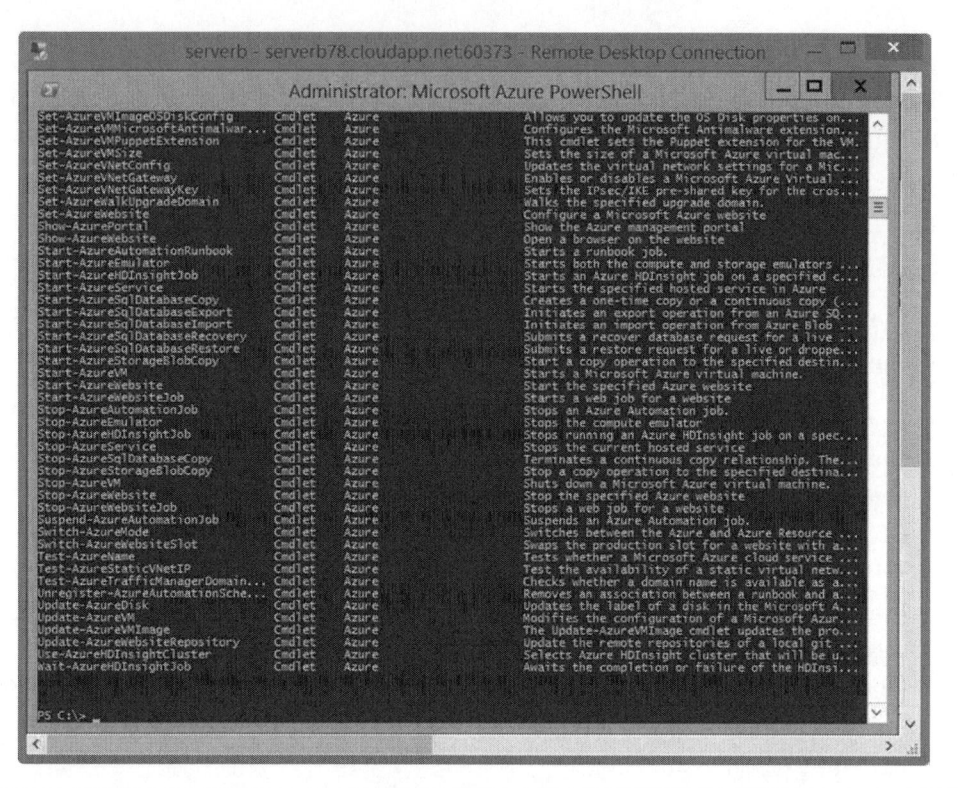

Figure 6.40   Help Azure Command in Window Azure PowerShell.

machines, manage virtual networks, deploy and manage cloud services, deploy and manage websites, and so on. You can find detailed information about Microsoft Azure management cmdlets from the following website (Microsoft, Windows Azure Management Cmdlets, May, 2015): http://msdn.microsoft.com/en-us/library/jj152841.aspx

To illustrate the usage of Microsoft Azure PowerShell, we will run a few cmdlets to carry out some of the management tasks in Microsoft Azure.

1. Assume that you are still connected to the virtual machine **serverb**. Press the **Windows logo** key and click the **Microsoft Azure PowerShell** tile.
2. To add the Microsoft Azure account information, enter the cmdlet

```
Add-AzureAccount
```

as shown in Figure 6.41. Then, press the **Enter** key.
3. Enter your email address and password to sign in to your Microsoft Azure account.
4. Once you have signed in, you can get your account information. To do so, run the cmdlet

```
Get-AzureSubscription
```

to view the subscription information.

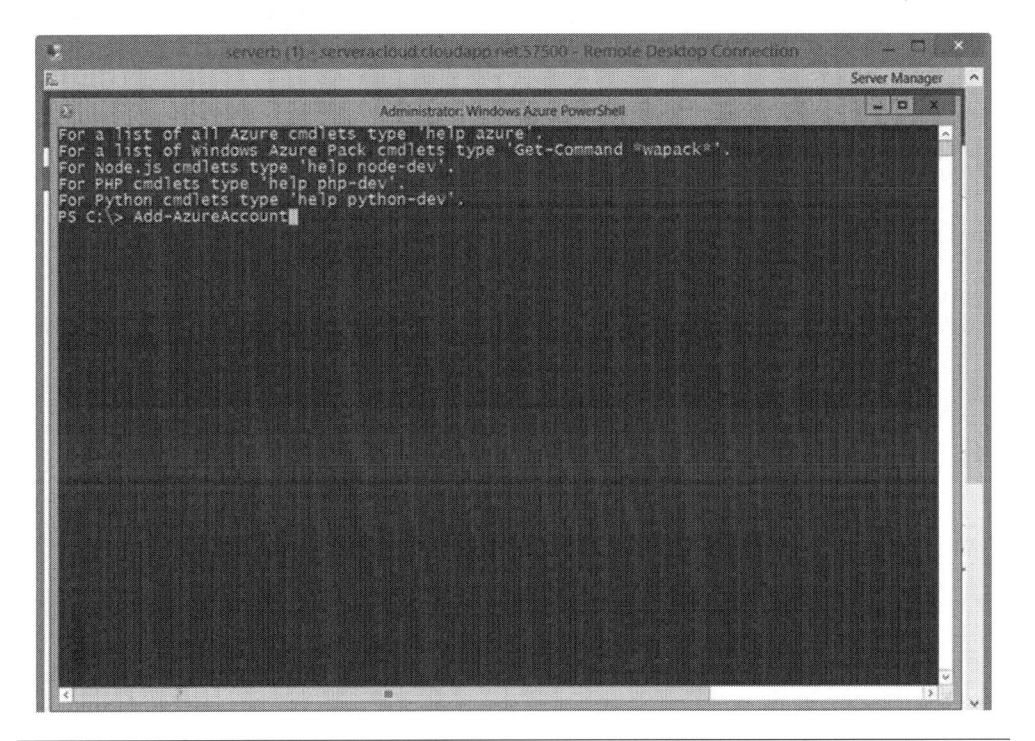

Figure 6.41   Add-AzureAccount Cmdlet.

5. Many cmdlets are used to manage virtual machines. As an illustration, the next task is to get the information about your virtual machines by entering the cmdlet

```
Get-AzureVM
```

as shown in Figure 6.42. The information about the virtual machines, servera and serverb, is displayed in Figure 6.42.

6. With cmdlets, you can start and stop a virtual machine as shown in Figure 6.43. For example, to stop the virtual machine servera, use the following cmdlet (note: your service name may be different):

```
Stop-AzureVM -ServiceName servera78 -Name servera
  -StayProvisioned
```

To start the virtual machine servera, use the following cmdlet:

```
Start-AzureVM -ServiceName servera78 -Name servera
```

7. You can also get the information about the disks used to host servera and serverb. To do so, enter the cmdlet

```
Get-AzureDisk
```

as shown in Figure 6.44.

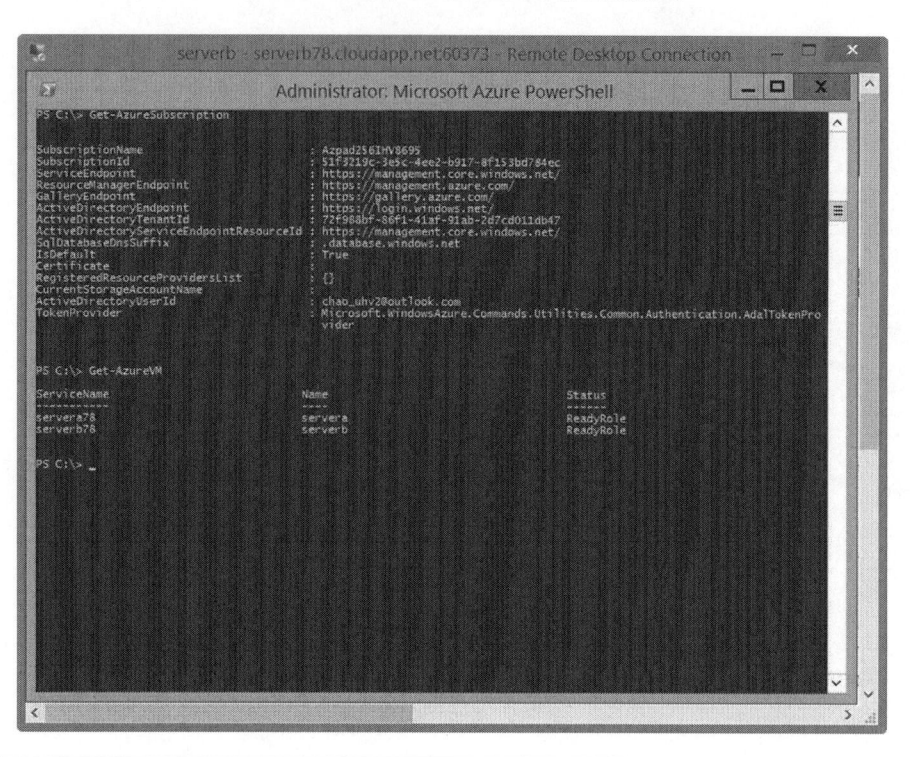

Figure 6.42 Get-AzureVM Cmdlet.

Figure 6.43 Stopping and starting virtual machine.

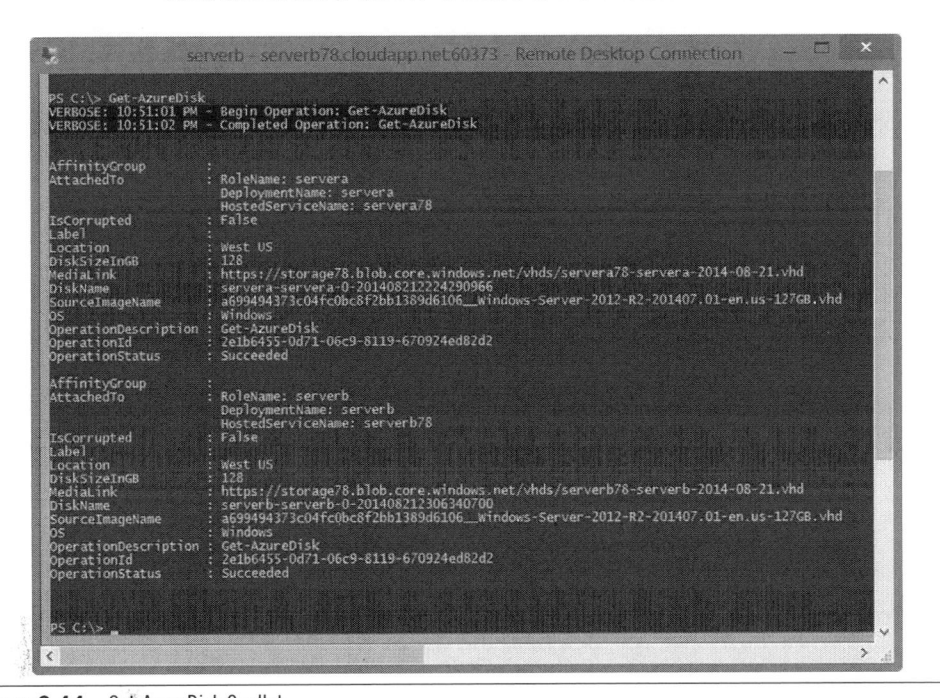

Figure 6.44   Get-AzureDisk Cmdlet.

8. To illustrate the management of virtual networks, let us create a subnet while creating a new virtual machine called serverc. To begin, you need to get your subscription name and storage account name by using the following two cmdlets:

```
Get-AzureSubscription
Get-AzureStorageAccount
```

9. You can now set the subscription with the following cmdlet (Figure 6.45):

```
Set-AzureSubscription -SubscriptionName yoursubscription
 -CurrentStorageAccount yourstorageaccount
```

Once the subscription is set, use the following cmdlets to create a virtual machine serverc meanwhile creating a virtual network mysubnet to host the virtual machine. To create a new virtual machine you need to specify the Name, InstanceSize, ImageName. You also need to add AzureProvisioningConfig and set the password. You can create a subnet with the cmdlet Set-AzureSubnet only when creating a new virtual machine with the cmdlet New-AzureVM. Note that the name of the subnet is case sensitive. The cmdlets to accomplish these tasks are listed as follows:

```
New-AzureVMConfig -Name serverc -InstanceSize ExtraSmall
 -ImageName MSFT__Win2K8R2SP1-Datacenter-201208.01-en.
 us-30GB.vhd | Add-AzureProvisioningConfig -Windows -Password
 P@ssw0rd | Set-AzureSubnet -Subnetname mysubnet
```

The result of the execution is shown in Figure 6.45.

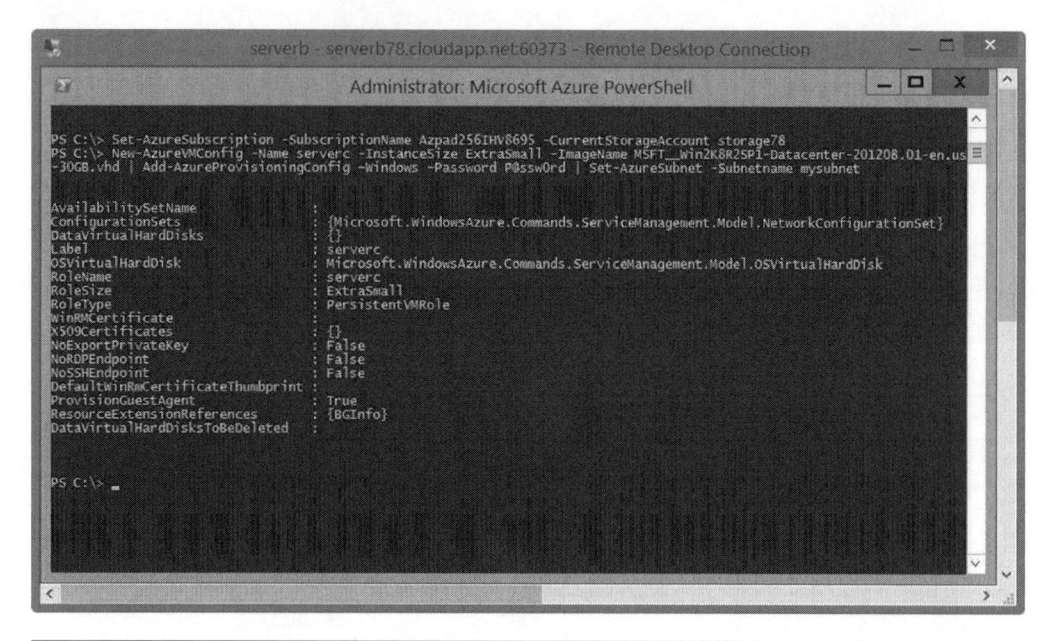

Figure 6.45 Creating virtual machine and virtual subnet.

10. In the Microsoft Azure Management Portal, delete serverc and shutdown both servera and serverb before exiting the Microsoft Azure Management Portal.

There are many other operations that can be done through Microsoft Azure PowerShell. Detailed coverage of Microsoft Azure PowerShell is beyond the scope of this book. Readers can look for books that are specialized in Microsoft Azure PowerShell for more information.

6.5 Summary

PowerShell is a powerful tool for networking. This chapter discusses Windows PowerShell and Microsoft Azure PowerShell. It explains why PowerShell is needed in a networking process. It describes all four types of PowerShell commands, cmdlets, PowerShell functions, PowerShell scripts, and native Windows commands. For cmdlets, this chapter introduces the commonly used verbs in the cmdlet naming structure. This chapter also demonstrates how to create PowerShell functions and PowerShell scripts. The native Windows commands are briefly covered in this chapter.

Microsoft Azure PowerShell can be used to carry out most of the tasks accomplished by the Microsoft Azure Management Portal. A list of networking-related cmdlets are described in this chapter. For hands-on practice, this chapter demonstrates how to conduct basic networking with PowerShell, how to manage DNS with PowerShell, and how to manage Active Directory with PowerShell. It also demonstrates how to create virtual machine and virtual subnet with Microsoft Azure PowerShell.

Review Questions

1. What is a shell in an operating system?
2. Why PowerShell is important for system administration and networking?
3. What can be accomplished by Microsoft Azure PowerShell?
4. What are the four types of Windows PowerShell commands?
5. What are the differences between cmdlets and regular commands?
6. What is a PowerShell script and what do you do with it?
7. How is a cmdlet structured?
8. What are the approved cmdlet verb groups?
9. What do you do with a PowerShell function?
10. What are the components of a PowerShell function?
11. What are the components provided by PowerShell to support scripting?
12. What is runtime and how is it used in the scripting process?
13. What do you do with the PowerShell ISE?
14. What networking tasks can be done with PowerShell cmdlets?
15. What tasks can be accomplished by Microsoft Azure management cmdlets?
16. Use a cmdlet to view the information of your Ethernet 2 NIC.
17. Write a script to ping your host IP, DNS server IP, and gateway IP. Run your script in PowerShell.
18. Use a cmdlet to display only the SRV type of DNS records.
19. Use a function to create a new DNS zone StudentZone. Run your function in PowerShell.
20. Create a user account for student studentEd with P@ssw0rd! as the password.

7

INTERNET DATA
TRANSACTION PROTECTION

Objectives

- Understand and implement SSL services.
- Understand and implement certificate services.

7.1 Introduction

Microsoft Azure provides a platform for developers to develop and deploy Internet-based applications such as websites and mobile services. Supported by Microsoft Azure, these Internet applications are scalable, flexible, and are easily integrated with Microsoft Azure SQL Database and Microsoft Azure Storage services. To make the Internet-based applications secure to use, Microsoft Azure provides various services to enhance security.

Running a successful website or web-based business needs the trust from customers. Customers expect their personal and financial information to be well protected. The Secure Sockets Layer (SSL) protocol and certificates are the commonly used security measures to protect web-based services. SSL provides the encryption and authentication mechanisms to protect customer information during online transactions. The SSL protocol uses a third party's certificate that brings trust to the customers by ensuring the customers that they are dealing with a certified web service.

SSL and certificates are vital technologies to keep web-based services secure. This chapter covers these technologies in detail.

7.2 Secure Sockets Layer

By design, SSL can provide security with any application layer protocols such as IMAP, FTP, and Telnet. SSL is particularly optimized for the protocol HTTP. Therefore, Hyper Text Transfer Protocol Secure (HTTPS) is commonly known as HTTP over SSL. The port 443 is used by HTTPS to provide secure data transactions between web browsers and web servers. Before data are transmitted across a network, a web service client will authenticate the server and negotiate an encryption key with the server. Then the data to be transferred are encrypted with the encryption key. The following illustrates how SSL and certificates are used to protect customers' information.

1. For a secure online data transaction, a customer issues an SSL connection request by entering the protocol https in a web browser.
2. After the web server receives the https request from the web browser, the web server will send its public key with its certificate back to the web browser.
3. When the web browser receives the certificate, it will contact a third party, such as Thawte or VeriSign, to verify if the certificate is valid.
4. Once the certificate is approved by the third party, the web browser encrypts the information such as the user name and password with the public key.
5. With the same public key, the web browser also encrypts a symmetric key that can be used by both the web browser and web server. The use of the symmetric key can make the encryption faster and simpler.
6. Then, the encrypted information will be sent to the web server.
7. When the encrypted information arrives at the web server, the web server will decrypt the information with its private key. From here on, both the web browser and the web server will use the symmetric key to encrypt and decrypt the data transmitted across the network.
8. Based on the requests from the web browser, the web service collects the needed documents. Then, it encrypts the documents with the symmetric key.
9. The web server sends the encrypted information to the web browser.
10. Once the web browser receives the encrypted information, it will decrypt it with the symmetric key. Then, the decrypted information will be displayed on the computer screen.

During the process, SSL uses the public and private keys, the symmetric key, encryption, and certification technologies. The following section will describe these technologies in detail.

Cryptography is the science for securing information. It includes the processes of encrypting and decrypting. The use of cryptography is to meet the requirements of data confidentiality, integrity, nonrepudiation, and authentication.

7.2.1 *Confidentiality*

Confidentiality prevents information from being seen by unauthorized individuals. Confidentiality can be achieved by clearly defining who can access to what information. A properly defined authentication system should be in place to prevent unauthorized individuals from accessing confidential data. During the data transaction process in a public network, it is possible that unauthorized individuals can capture the data. To prevent the unauthorized individuals from understanding the data content, encryption processes are used to encode the data to a form that cannot be understood. Encryption can be carried out in different ways. There are three basic encryption methods: symmetric encryption, asymmetric encryption, and hash encryption.

7.2.1.1 Symmetric Encryption   Symmetric encryption uses a single key to encrypt and decrypt data. By using the same key, encryption and decryption can be done very fast. Consequently, this type of encryption is suitable when a large amount of data need to be transmitted. On the other hand, symmetric encryption can be potentially unsafe. If hackers steal the key, they can decrypt the encrypted information. Thus, no secret can hide from the hackers. It is critical to prevent the hackers from getting the symmetric key, especially when transmitting the symmetric key across the Internet. We need to make sure that the symmetric key is encrypted before sending it across the Internet. The encryption of the symmetric key can be done by another type of encryption method called asymmetric encryption.

7.2.1.2 Asymmetric Encryption   Asymmetric encryption uses two keys for encryption and decryption. A public key is used for encryption and a private key for decryption. When a client contacts a server for a data transaction, the server generates a public/private key pair. The server sends the public key to the client so that the client can encrypt the data with this public key. It is possible for anyone to capture the public key when it is sent over the Internet; this means that whoever captures the public key can encrypt the data and send the encrypted data back to the server. Once encrypted, the data will not be readable without the private key. Only the server has the private key for decryption although anyone can send the encrypted information. The benefit of asymmetric encryption is that the private key is never transmitted across the Internet. That is why asymmetric encryption is safer. On the other hand, asymmetric encryption takes more process power. For the encryption of a large amount of data, symmetric encryption is about 1000 times faster than asymmetric encryption. Therefore, for a large data transaction on the Internet, asymmetric encryption is used to encrypt and deliver the symmetric key through the Internet. Once the symmetric key is delivered, the client and server use the symmetric key to encrypt, deliver, and decrypt the data. Figure 7.1 illustrates the asymmetric encryption process.

For encryption, the server chooses the strongest encryption method supported by both the client and the server. If there is no encryption method supported by both parties, the encryption process ends with a failure alert. Windows Server supports SSL 3.0 Cipher Suites or later. The encryption methods included in SSL 3.0 Cipher Suites are RC4 128, 3DES EDE CBC, and several other weaker encryption methods. RC4 stands for Rivest Cipher 4. RC4 128 means that the encryption is at the 128-bit level that uses an encryption key with 1024 bits. RC4 is widely used for data encryption.

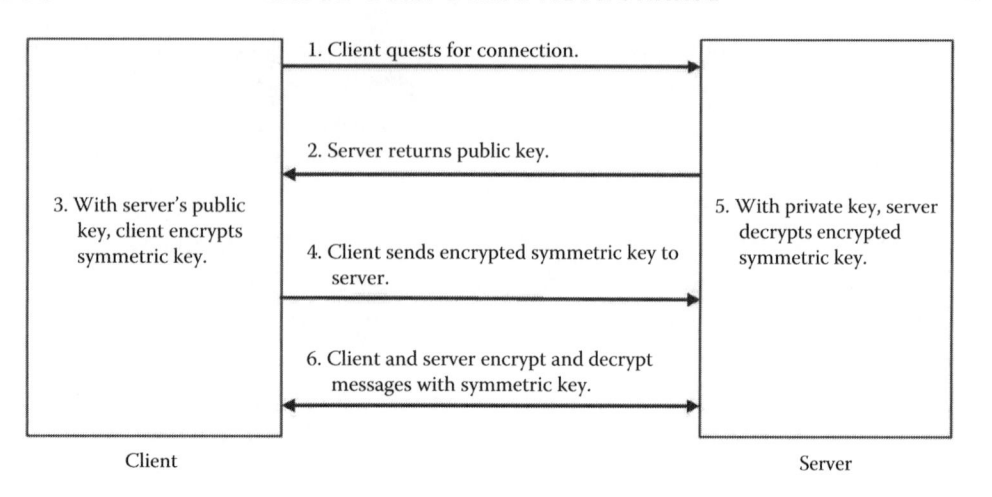

Figure 7.1 Asymmetric encryption.

It is a simple and efficient encryption method. RC4 has weaknesses; for example, information about the key can be revealed in the first few bytes of output. On the other hand, if used properly, RC4 is still a safe encryption method. 3DES stands for Triple Data Encryption Standard; EDE stands for Encrypt Decrypt Encrypt; and CBC stands for Cipher Block Chaining. The original DES encryption method is at the 56-bit level, which is relatively insecure. 3DES triples the encryption level to improve security without redesigning the encryption method completely. The more bits are used in a key, the more secure the encryption. The encryption at the 128-bit level is commonly used to secure personal and financial information.

7.2.2 Integrity

In addition to preventing unauthorized users from understanding data content, we need to prevent data from being altered intentionally or unintentionally by unauthorized individuals. The violation of integrity can also be caused by the equipment and environment such as temperature. In addition to preventing the intentional modification of data content, measures taken to ensure integrity also include controlling the physical environment of networked terminals and electrical surges. The hashing technology is often used to protect integrity.

7.2.2.1 Hash Encryption   Hashing is used to detect if data content has been altered during a data transaction. Based on the original document or message, a hashing function generates a fixed-length hash value. It is almost impossible for two different messages to generate the same hash value. A change made to the original message during a transit will result in a different hash value. By comparing with the original hash value, the difference will be detected. Microsoft Azure provides hashing functions such as Message Digest 5 (MD5) and Secure Hash Algorithm (SHA) to carry out hashing tasks.

- MD5: The MD5 hash function can generate a 128-bit (16-byte) hash value. An MD5 hash value is typically a hexadecimal number.
- SHA: SHA is a family of five hash functions, SHA-1, SHA-224, SHA-256, SHA-384, and SHA-512, published by the National Institute of Standards and Technology (NIST). SHA-1 is a widely used hashing function that typically generates a 160-bit hash value.

A hash value can never be decrypted. Therefore, hashing is also called one-way encryption. This feature makes the hashing technology suitable for verifying integrity. Hashing can also be used to verify passwords, identify duplicated data values, and so on.

7.2.3 Nonrepudiation

Previously, you have learned that hashing makes sure data content is not altered by unauthorized individuals. However, even with the hashing technology, a hacker may still tamper the integrity of data. The hacker can intercept the original public key during the public key exchange process. Then, the hacker can replace the original public key with his own public key. After the encrypted data are returned to the hacker, the hacker can use his own private key to decrypt the message encrypted by the sender. The hacker may also modify the message, make hash ciphertext and re-encrypt the ciphertext with the receiver's public key. Then, the modified message and its hash ciphertext are retransmitted to the receiver. In such a way, the receiver is not able to detect the flaw. This type of attack is called a man-in-the-middle attack.

To repudiate means to deny. The term nonrepudiation means that someone cannot deny that he/she has not done something. For example, after a person signs a registered letter, he cannot say that he has not received the letter. Similarly, on the Internet, the digital signature is used to sign a document. The digital signature ensures that the sender of the document should sign the document before transmitting it across the Internet. By doing so, the hacker cannot deny that the fake document is from him. Therefore, the digital signature ensures that one knows who created the document and ensure that the document has not been altered since its creation.

In practice, the digital signature can be formed by using an asymmetric encryption. To sign a message, the sender first creates a hash value by running the hashing function. Then, the sender encrypts the hash value with the sender's private key. By doing so, the sender signs the message with his/her digital signature. Meanwhile, the sender also creates a symmetric key and uses the symmetric key to encrypt the original message. Once the message is encrypted with the symmetric key, the symmetric key is then encrypted with the receiver's public key. Now, the sender has three items:

1. The digital signature, which is the hash value encrypted with the sender's private key
2. The encrypted original message, which is encrypted with the symmetric key
3. The encrypted symmetric key, which is encrypted with the receiver's public key

Now, the sender transfers all the three items to the receiver. On the receiver side, the receiver decrypts the symmetric key with his/her own private key. The decrypted symmetric key is then used to decrypt the encrypted message. Meanwhile, the receiver decrypted the hash value with the sender's public key. If the hash value is sent by a hacker, the receiver is not able to decrypt the hash value by using the sender's public key. That is how the digital signature works here. At this point, the receiver has three items, too:

1. The original message
2. The hash value
3. The symmetric key

Now, the receiver can hash the original message and use it to compare the hash value sent by the sender to detect the difference. If the document has been altered during the transaction, the two copies of hash values will not match. In such a way, we can prevent hackers from altering sensitive information. Figure 7.2 illustrates the process.

The digitally signed message including the public key and certificate can then be transmitted to all the recipients.

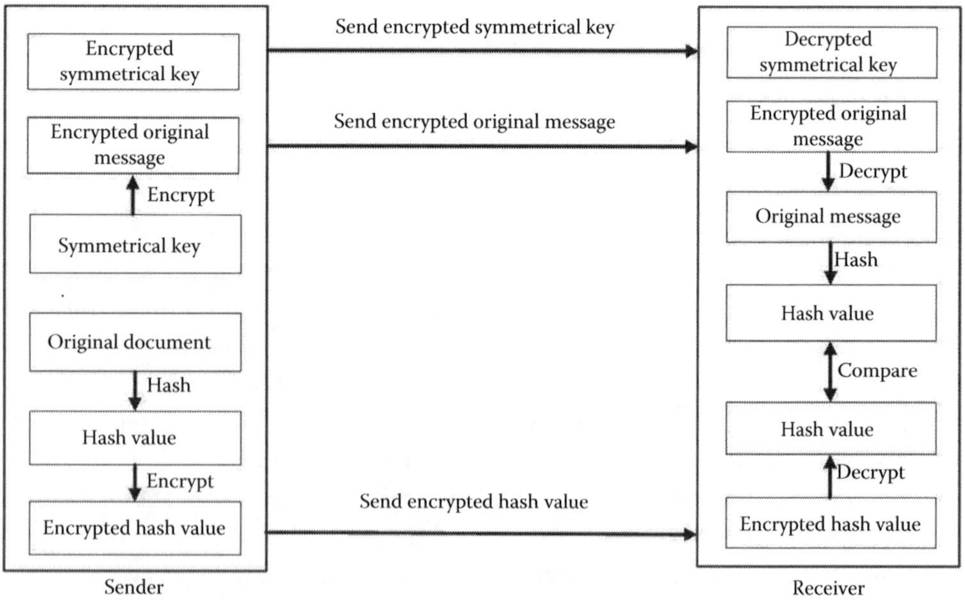

Figure 7.2   Digital signature process.

7.2.4 Authentication

Authentication is a mechanism used to verify the identity of a user or a computer. With authentication, the sender and the receiver can confirm each other's identity. In SSL, the client needs to make sure that the server is authenticated by a trusted third-party organization. On the other hand, for some applications, the server may not need to authenticate the client. Server authentication is commonly done through a certificate service, which will be described in next section.

7.3 Certificate Services

In Windows Server, Certificate Services is the Microsoft implementation of Public Key Infrastructure (PKI). In general, PKI certificate management software is designed to accomplish tasks such as signing certificates, storing a list of revoked certificates, distributing public keys, and so on. Several standards can be used for PKI components. The standard used by Windows Server is X.509, which defines how a certificate should be structured. An X.509 certificate can accomplish the following tasks:

- It identifies a server to make sure that the server is verified by a trusted agent.
- It distributes the public key to clients for encryption and verification of the digital signature.
- It sends encrypted data to the server, which can decrypt the data.

There are two types of X.509 certificates:

1. *Client certificate*: It is used to identify a client such as a computer or application.
2. *Server certificate*: It is used to identify a server.

For the management of certificates, users can access a certificate service through a website or via Active Directory. As part of the PKI, a certificate authority (CA) is the component that issues and manages certificates and public keys for message encryption. The CA examines the request for a certificate. If approved, the CA can then issue a certificate.

A certificate works like a passport or driver's license. Many web-based applications such as email, remote desktop, smart card, and web browser can be configured to use the certificate service. As a form of identification, a certificate contains the information about a server, a public key, a digital signature of the issuer, a validity period, and a serial number. A CA is equivalent to a government agency such as the driver's license office. The CA can issue both client certificates and server certificates. To issue a client certificate, the CA needs the client to provide the information about the client identification, the client's organization, and the application used by the client. To issue a server certificate, the CA requires the server to provide the information about the server identification, organization identification, as well as the information about the server itself.

Normally, a CA is a third-party organization that is trusted by both the client and the server. VeriSign and DigiCert are two well-known certificate authority organizations. An enterprise can also serve as a CA for its internal server identification. For the management of certificates, a CA can accomplish the following tasks:

- Renewing and revoking certificates.
- Maintaining certificate revocation lists (CRLs), which contain certificates that are no longer valid.
- Backing up and restoring certificate services.
- Maintaining certificate service websites, which can be used to request certificates. The websites also allow users to retrieve CRLs and to check on pending certificates.
- Importing and exporting certificates, and so on.

To get a certificate, one can register to a third-party CA organization. An enterprise can create a CA service on Windows Server so that the enterprise's clients can get certificates from this enterprise CA. Windows Server provides four types of CAs.

1. *Enterprise root CA*: This CA is the starting point of a certificate hierarchy. It is the most trusted CA. A client computer or application accepts a certificate issued by a subordinate CA only if the root CA is trusted. This CA integrates with Active Directory. Therefore, it is able to use the certificate template that automates the certificate creation process.
2. *Enterprise subordinate CA*: This CA is certified by its root CA. After being certified by the root CA, this CA can issue certificates to computers and applications. The enterprise subordinate CA is able to use the certificate template.
3. *Stand-alone root CA*: A stand-alone root CA does not integrate with Active Directory. As a result, it is not able to use the certificate template. The administrator must manually approve each certificate to be issued. The stand-alone root CA is the most trusted CA in a nonenterprise hierarchy.
4. *Stand-alone subordinate CA*: This CA is a member of an existing nonenterprise hierarchy. Before it can issue certificates to computers and applications, it needs to certify the stand-alone root CA. Again, it is not able to use the certificate template and the administrator must manually approve a certificate to be issued.

If an organization needs to issue certificates internally in an Active Directory–enabled environment, an enterprise CA is a wise choice. On the other hand, if certificates are issued to computers and applications outside the Active Directory–enabled environment, a stand-alone CA is a good choice.

7.4 Enabling SSL

With the available CA service, SSL can now be implemented on web-based services. Depending on where the certificate is issued, SSL can be enabled differently. Suppose an organization offers a web-based service such as the Internet email and it wants the users to trust the website. If the certificate is issued by a third-party organization, which is trusted by the public, enabling SSL on a website is relatively easy. The following steps show how to enable SSL for a website when using a third-party issued certificate.

1. In a web browser, open the certificate configuration dialog on the Internet Options menu.
2. Select a trusted CA such as VeriSign and provide the certificate information to the CA.
3. The selected CA will process a certificate request and generate a server certificate for the server used in the web service.
4. Install the certificate in the browser's authorities store.
5. Once the certificate is installed, enable the SSL service.
6. Since the client's browser has already loaded the certificates issued by the third-party organization, the client can now access the website by using the protocol https.

When a certificate is issued by the internal CA, warnings will be issued for potential damage. A hacker can create a CA service to collect customer information. The following steps illustrate how to enable the SSL service for a website:

1. Make sure that the enterprise or stand-alone CA is created and is ready to issue certificates.
2. Provide certificate information about the organization's website to the CA.
3. Based on the website information, the CA generates a server certificate for the website used in the web service.
4. Install the certificate on the website. Then, enable SSL on the website.
5. When a client access the SSL-enabled website, the client will get a warning if the certificate is provided by an enterprise root CA. The client's web browser does not trust the enterprise root CA that is not certified by the third-party organization.
6. To make the browser trust the enterprise root CA, ignore the warning and go ahead to add the certificate in the browser's authorities store.
7. Now, the client can use the protocol https to access the website such as the Internet email or remote desktop.

Once SSL is enabled, the data transaction across the Internet will be much safer. In fact, it is required by the Payment Card Industry (PCI) that the SSL service must be enabled for collecting credit card information. It is advised that all websites dealing with private personal information should implement SSL services.

7.5 Certificates on Microsoft Azure

The applications on Microsoft Azure can also be protected with SSL and certificates. Microsoft Azure supports three types of certificates, such as management certificate (.CER), service certificate (.PFX), and SSH keys.

7.5.1 Management Certificate (.CER)

With a management certificate, a client can access the resources available in the Microsoft Azure subscription. The management certificate provides authentication for application deployment on Microsoft Azure. The following are some usages of the management certificate:

- The management certificate is used to authenticate a client application during the application deployment process on Microsoft Azure.
- It can be used to authenticate application developers during the application deployment process.
- The management certificate can also be used to authenticate requests made by the tool Microsoft Azure Service Management REST API.

The management certificate is an x.509 v3 certificate, which has only a public key. When a client application is deployed, the management certificate is uploaded to Microsoft Azure and is saved as a .CER file. Microsoft Azure can store up to 100 management certificates.

7.5.2 Service Certificate (.PFX)

A service certificate is saved as a .PFX file. This type of certificate is designed for securing the communication between a client and a deployed service. The main usages of a service certificate are summarized as follows:

- It can be used for Windows to access a Microsoft Azure instance through remote desktop. As an example, the SSL certificate used to secure endpoint communication can be considered as a service certificate.
- As described earlier, the SSL certificate is commonly used to protect the data transaction between a browser and a website.
- It can be used for client authentication for a Windows Communication Foundation (WCF) service, which is a framework for building service-oriented applications.

To make a web-based application a trusted application, the certificate needs to be signed by a third party like VeriSign or DigiCert. This type of certificate can also be uploaded to Microsoft Azure and stored in the service that uses the certificate. Once it is uploaded, the network administrator can update and renew the certificate on Microsoft Azure. The network administrator can also assign the certificate to a newly developed service.

7.5.3 SSH Keys

SSH keys are used by Linux virtual machines for the authentication of remote access. The Microsoft Azure Management Portal can work with the 2048-bit SSH public key included in an x509 certificate.

A certificate contains a private or a public key. A .CER file does not contain a private key. The key contained in a management certificate should have the length of at least 2048 bits. When stored on the client computer, the certificate should contain a private key. The certificate should also contain a thumbprint that is generated by using the SHA1 algorithm and that is unique. Due to its uniqueness, the thumbprint is used to search for a particular certificate in a certificate store.

In order to protect web applications on Microsoft Azure, certificates need to be uploaded to Microsoft Azure through the Microsoft Azure Management Portal or by using the programmatic tool Windows Azure Service Management REST API. To upload a certificate to the Microsoft Azure Management Portal, the certificate needs to be exported as a .CER file.

The certificates on Microsoft Azure can be signed by the trusted third-party certificate organizations. These certificates can also be self-signed; that is, they can be signed by the developers of the applications. When connected to an application with a self-signed certificate, a web browser will display an alert to warn the user. Therefore, self-signed certificates are usually used for testing.

Activity 7.1: Certificate Services

In this activity, you are going to develop certificate services for web applications. The activity is to accomplish the following tasks:

> Task 1: Installing and Configuring CA
> Task 2: Certificate Management with CA
> Task 3: Creating SSL Certificate for Web Server
> Task 4: Repairing Certificate

To carry out these tasks, assume that you have two virtual machines created on Microsoft Azure. Each of them has Windows Server 2012 as the operating system. Also, assume that Active Directory has been installed and configured on both of the virtual machines. Now, you are ready for Task 1.

Task 1: Installing and Configuring CA

1. Log on to the Microsoft Azure Management Portal. Log on to the virtual machine **servera** as **student**. Make sure that the student account is a member of both the Enterprise Admin group and the Domain Admin group.

2. In Server Manager, click **Add Roles and Features** to open the Add Roles and Features Wizard.

3. On the Before you begin page, click **Next**.

4. On the Select installation type page, make sure that **Role-based or feature-based installation** is selected, and then click **Next**.

5. On the Select destination server page, make ensure that **studenta.mylab.com** is selected. Click **Next**.

6. On the Select server roles page, in **Roles**, select **Active Directory Certificate Services**. When you are prompted to add required features, click **Add Features** as shown in Figure 7.3, and then click **Next**.

7. On the Select features page, click **Next**.

8. On the Active Directory Certificate Services page, click **Next**.

9. On the Select role services page, check **Certification Authority** as shown in Figure 7.4 and then click **Next**.

10. On the Confirm installation selections page, click **Install**. After the installation is complete, click the link **Configure Active Directory Certificate Services on the destination server** as shown in Figure 7.5.

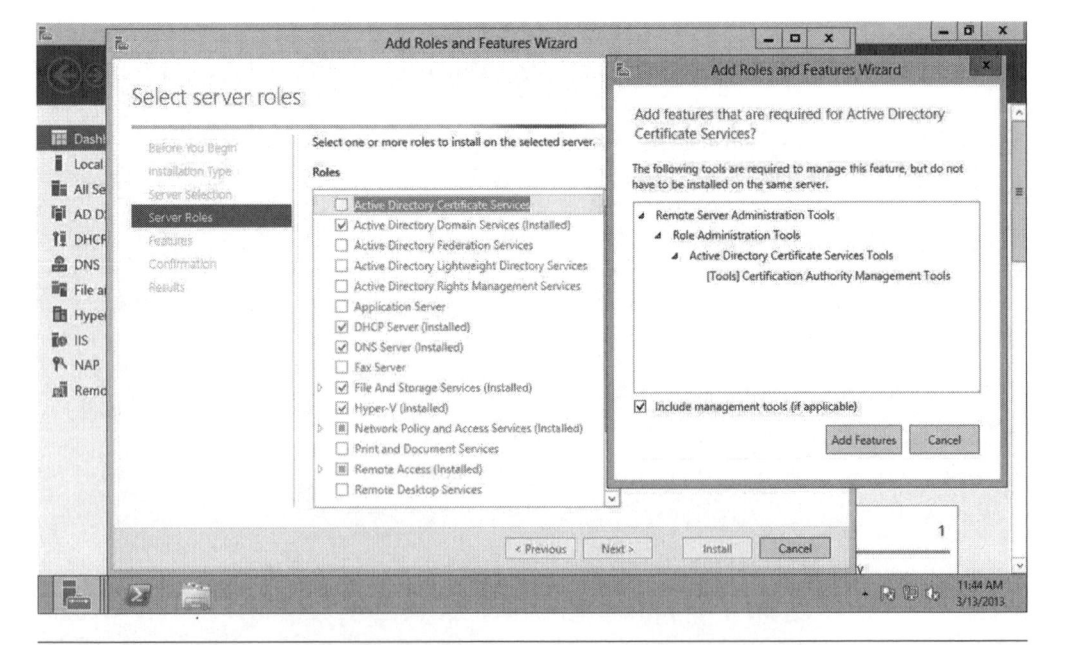

Figure 7.3   Adding active directory certificate services.

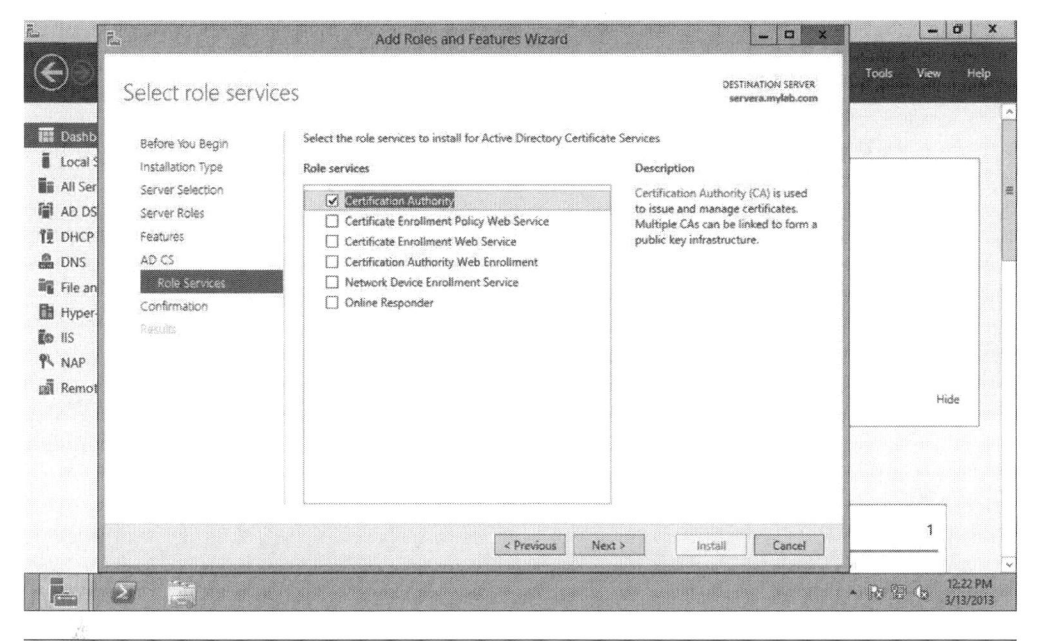

Figure 7.4   Selecting certificate authority.

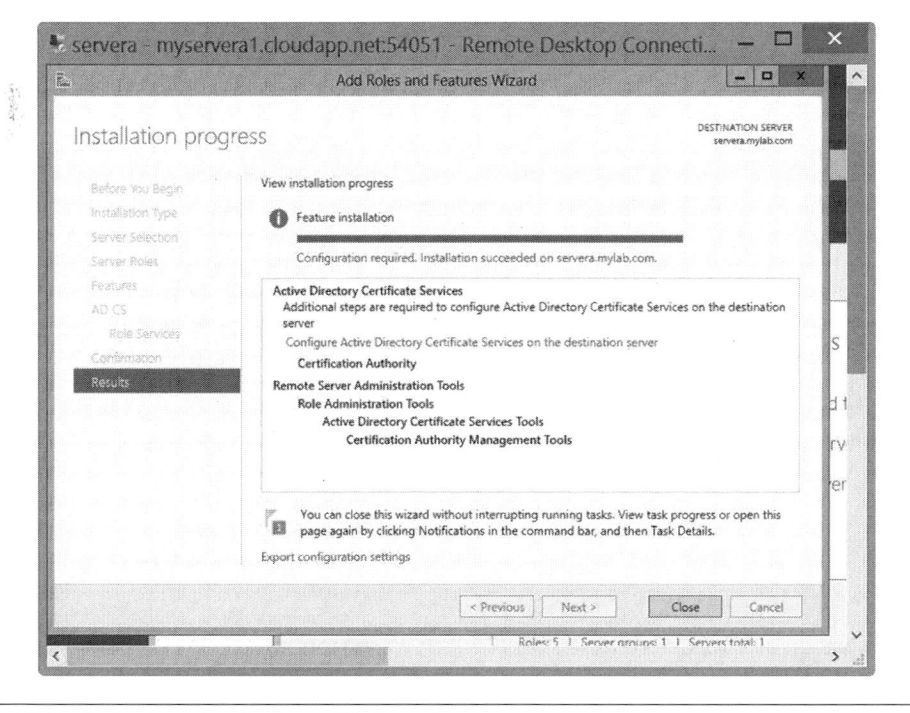

Figure 7.5   Configuring active directory certificate services.

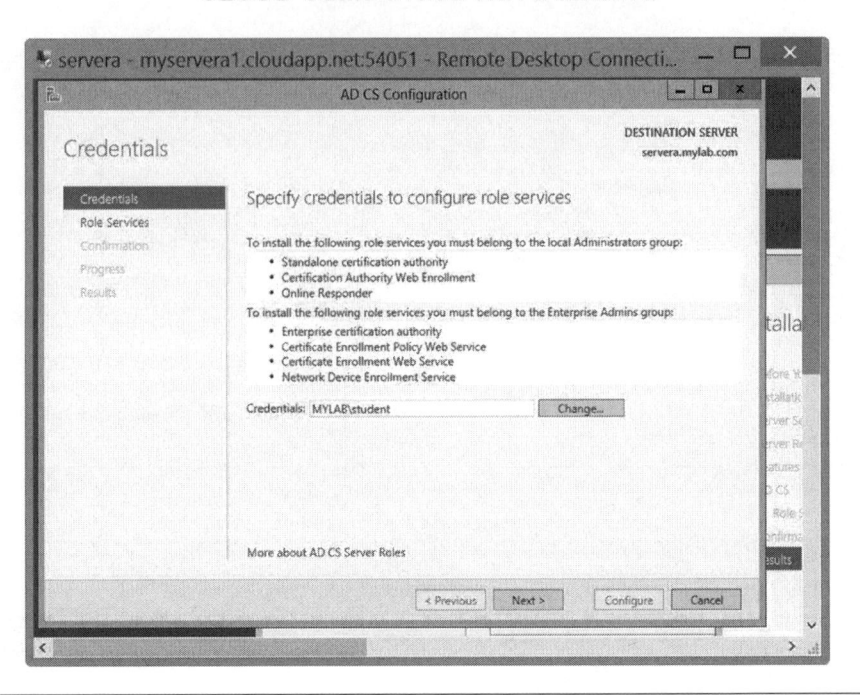

Figure 7.6   Specifying credentials.

11. The AD CS Configuration wizard opens. Specify your user account as shown in Figure 7.6 and assume that you are a member of the Enterprise Admin group. Then, click **Next**.
12. On the Role Services page, verify that **Certification Authority** is selected as shown in Figure 7.7, and then click **Next**.
13. On the Setup Type page, verify that **Enterprise CA** is selected as shown in Figure 7.8, and then click **Next**.
14. On the CA Type page, verify that **Root CA** is selected as shown in Figure 7.9, and then click **Next**.
15. On the Private Key page, verify that **Create a new private key** is selected as shown in Figure 7.10, and then click **Next**.
16. On the Cryptography for CA page, keep the default settings for CSP (**RSA#Microsoft Software Key Storage Provider**) and hash algorithm (**SHA1**). Also, keep the default setting for the key length as 2048 (Figure 7.11). Click **Next**.
17. On the CA Name page, keep the suggested common name for the CA as shown in Figure 7.12. Click **Next**.
18. On the Validity Period page, take the default setting of 5 years as shown in Figure 7.13 and click **Next**.
19. On the CA database page, take the default location as shown in Figure 7.14 and click **Next**.
20. On the Confirmation page, click **Configure** to apply your selections as shown in Figure 7.15, and then click **Close**.

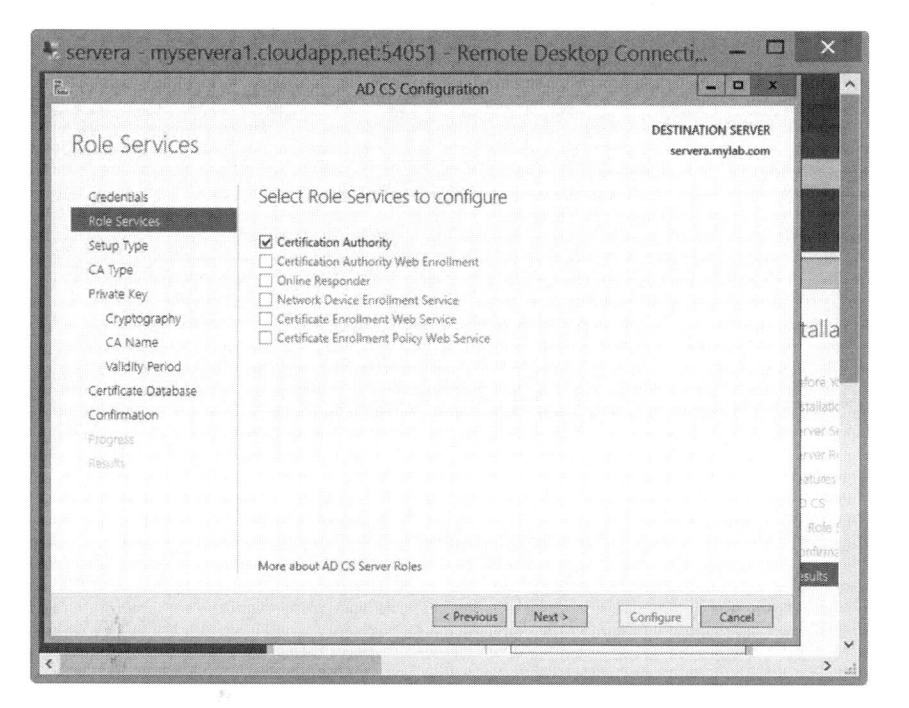

Figure 7.7 Selecting certificate authority to configure.

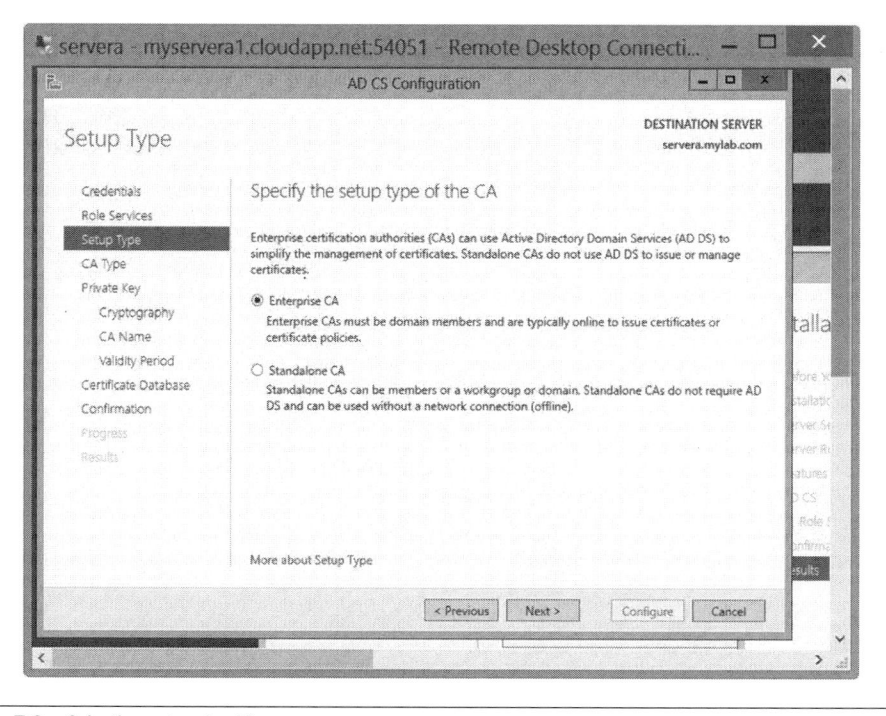

Figure 7.8 Selecting enterprise CA.

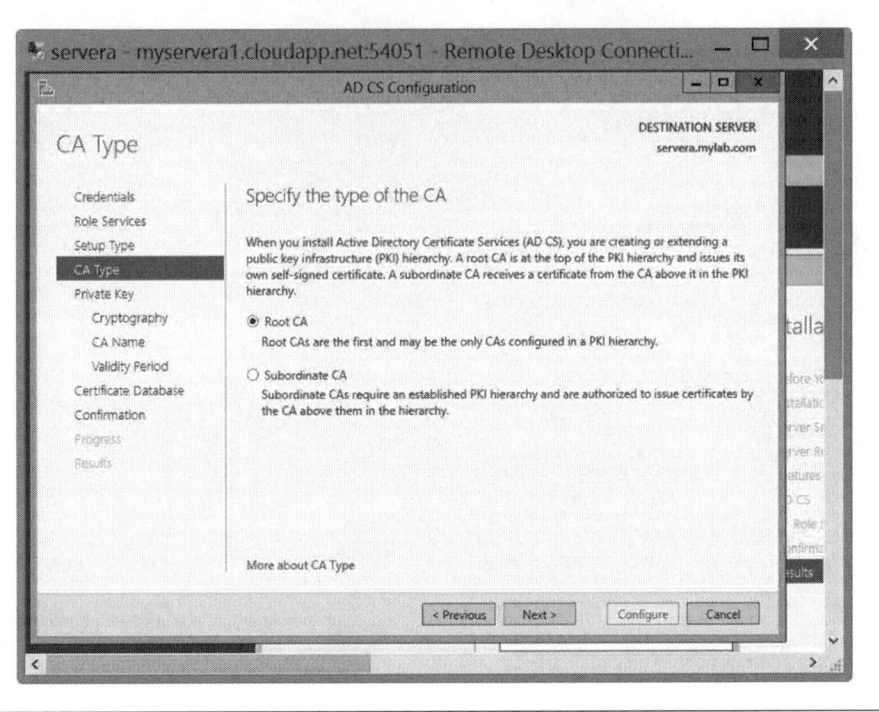

Figure 7.9   Selecting root CA.

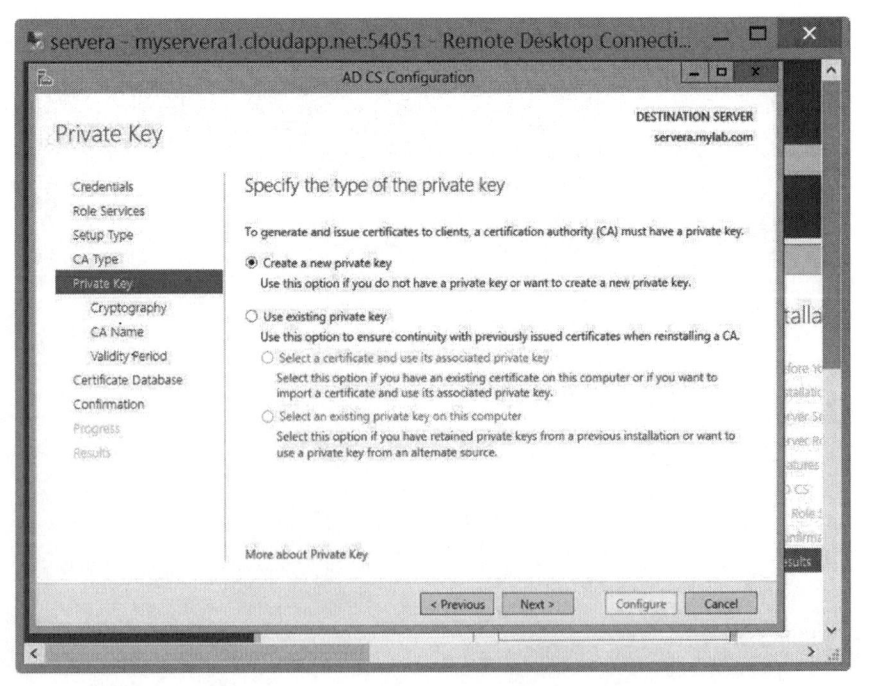

Figure 7.10   Creating new private key.

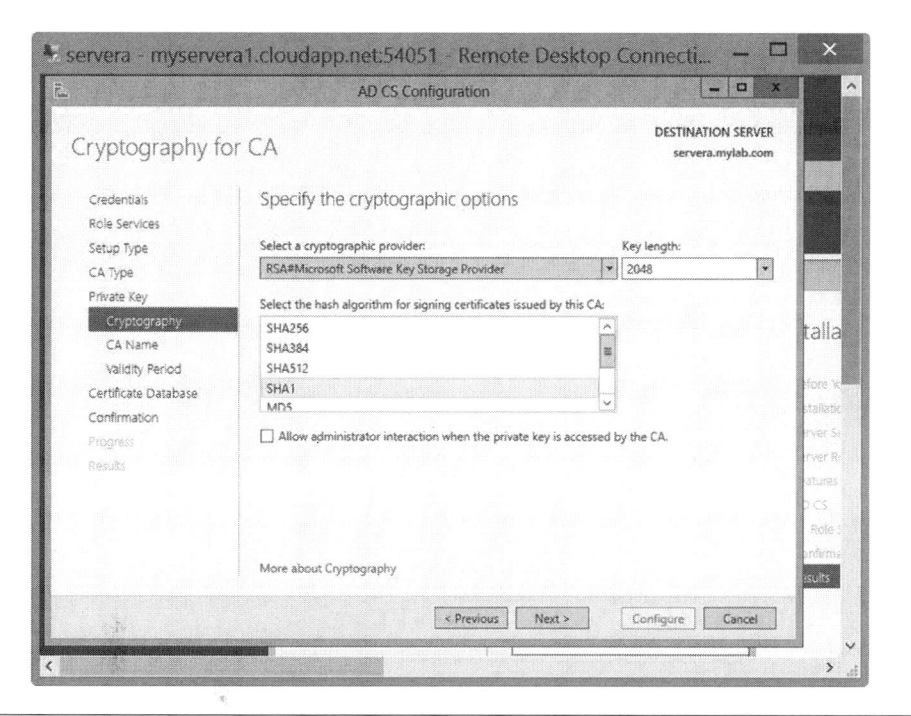

Figure 7.11 Specifying cryptographic options.

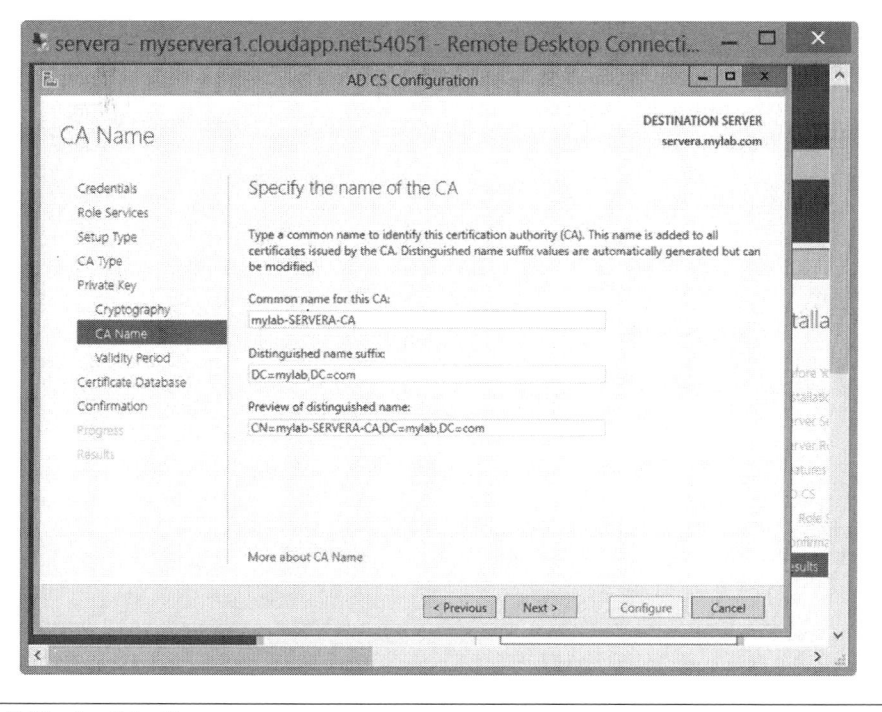

Figure 7.12 Specifying CA name.

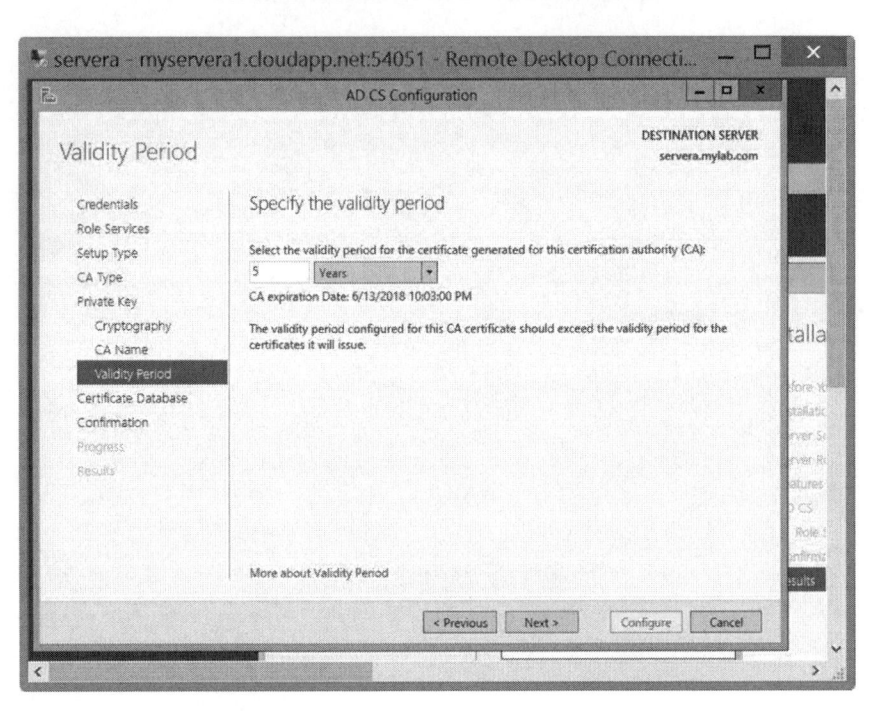

Figure 7.13 Specifying validity period.

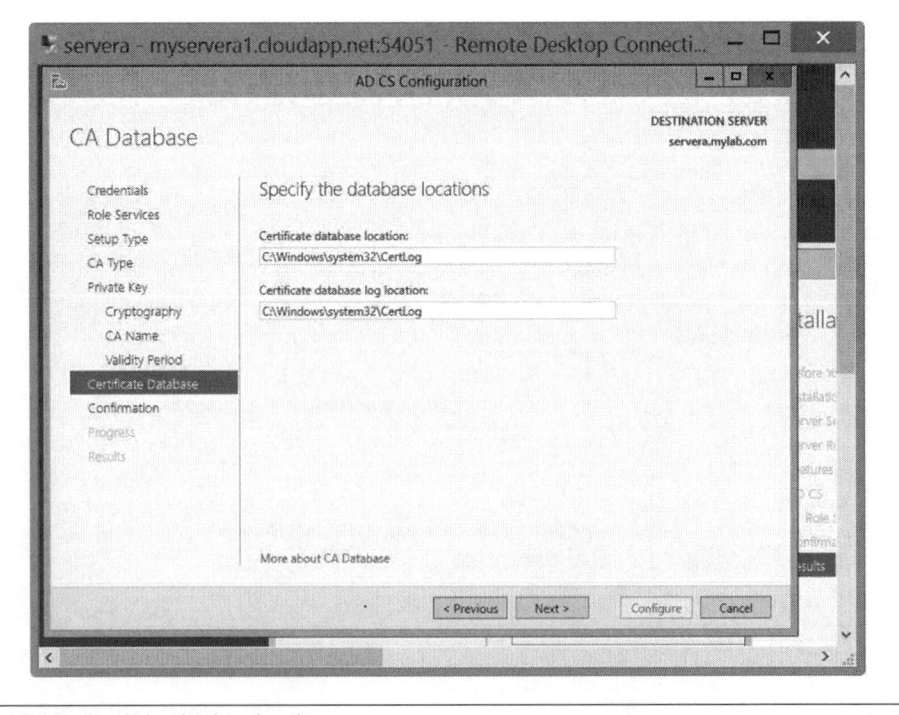

Figure 7.14 Specifying database location.

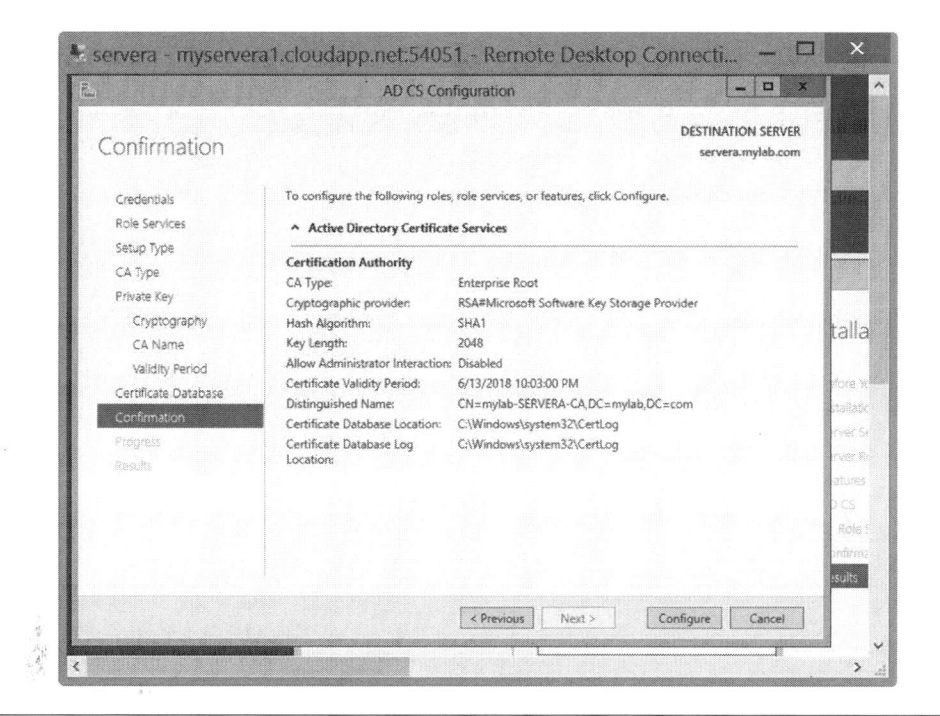

Figure 7.15   Configuring certificate services.

Task 2: Certificate Management with CA

In this part of the activity, you will perform some certificate management tasks.

Backing up certificate services: In this part of the activity, you will learn how to back up a CA to a file.

1. In System Manager, click the **Tools** menu and click **Certificate Authority** (Figure 7.16).
2. In the Certification Authority dialog, right click the certificate, for example, **mylab-SERVERA-CA** as shown in Figure 7.17. Then, select **All Tasks** and **Back up CA**.
3. On the Welcome page of the Certification Authority Backup Wizard, click **Next**.
4. Check **Private and CA certificate** and **Certificate database and certificate database log**. Enter the location to save the backup as **C:\CertBack** as shown in Figure 7.18. Then, click **Next** and **OK** to allow the creation of the CertBack folder.
5. For the password, enter **P@ssw0rd** and confirm it as shown in Figure 7.19. Click **Next**.
6. Click **Finish**.

Restoring certificate services database: In this part of the activity, you will learn how to restore the CA with the backup created in the previous step.

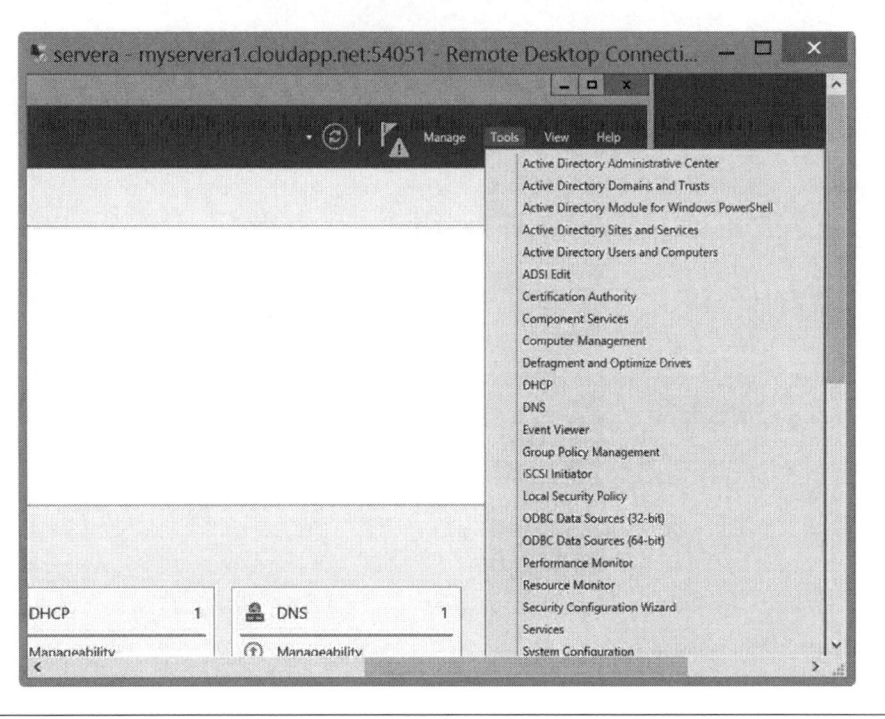

Figure 7.16 Opening certificate authority.

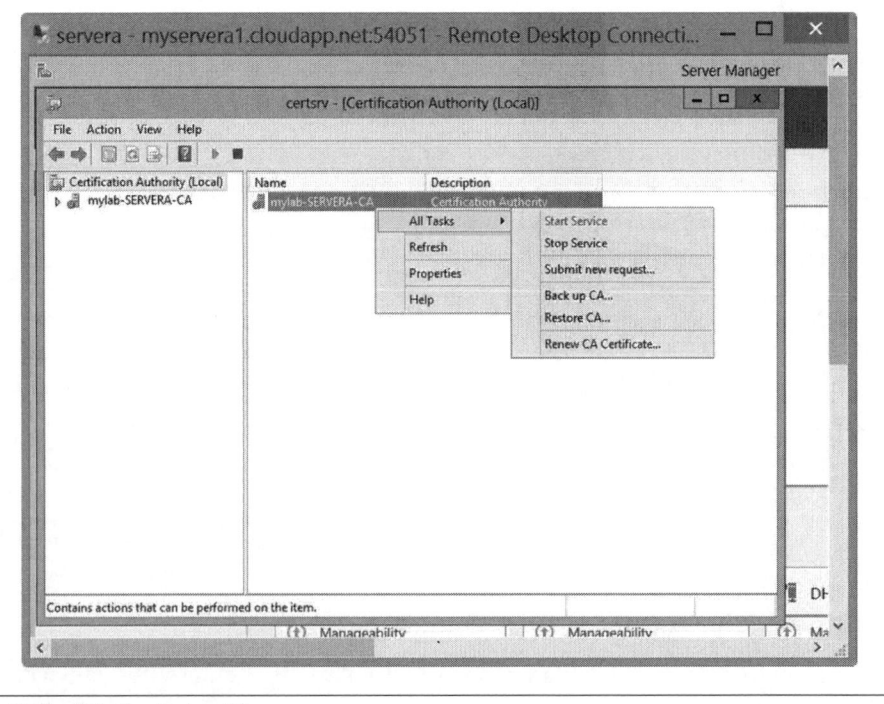

Figure 7.17 Selecting back up CA.

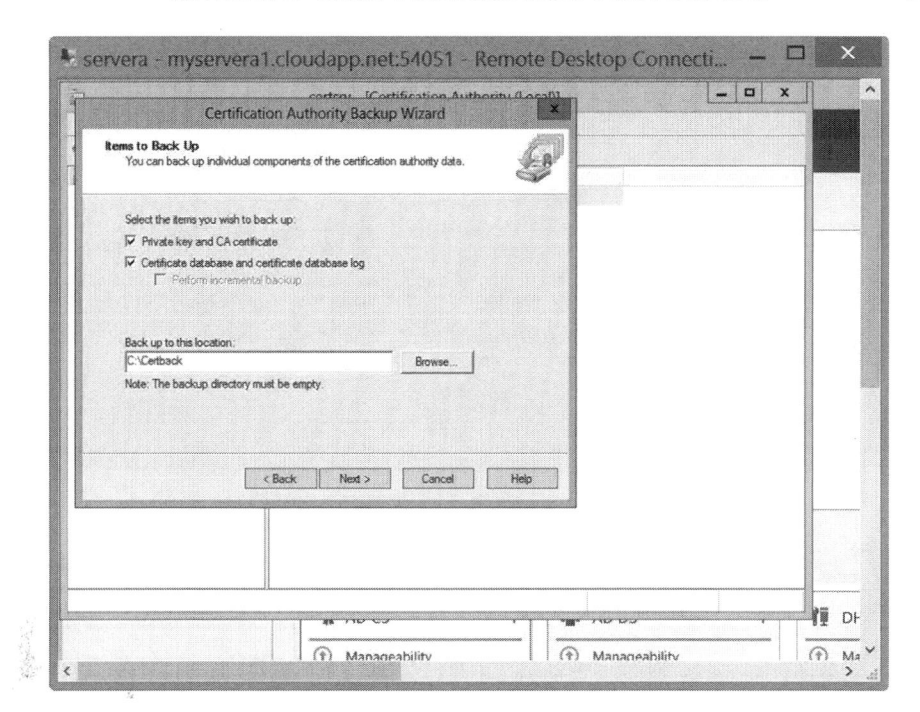

Figure 7.18 Backup configuration.

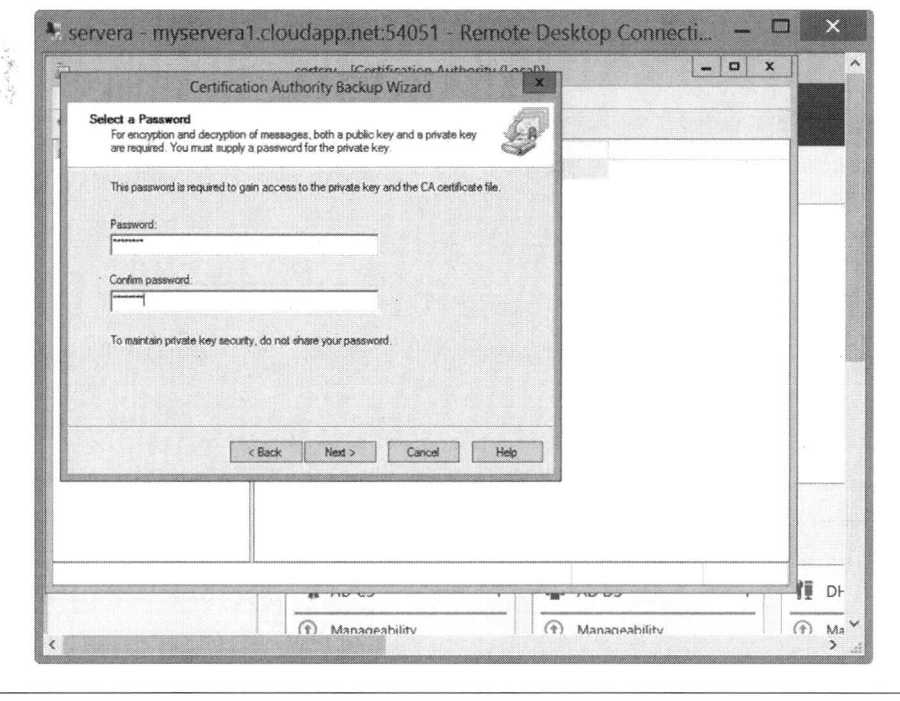

Figure 7.19 Entering password.

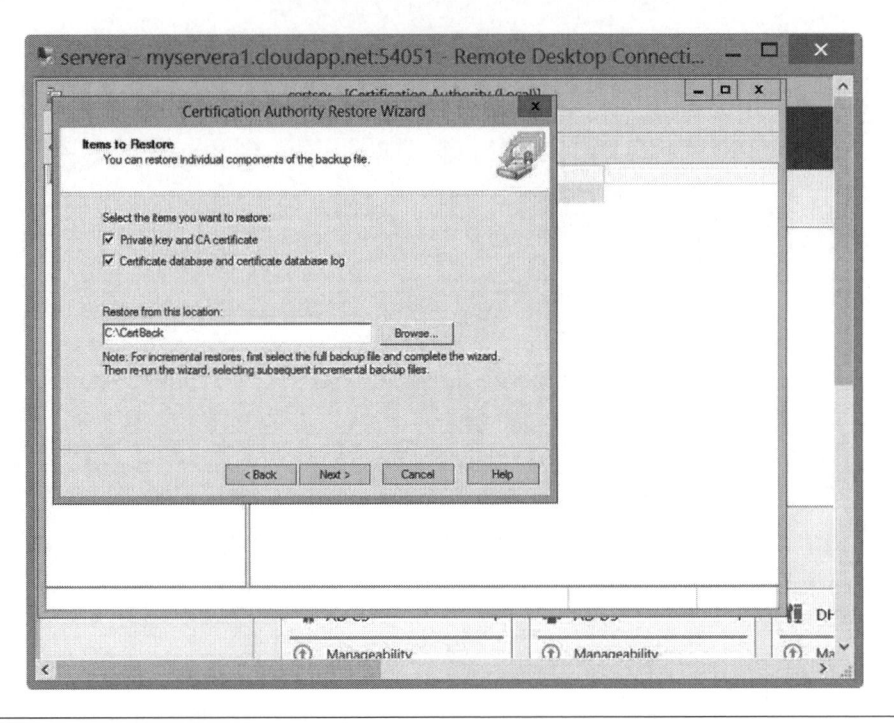

Figure 7.20 Configuring restore.

1. Assume that the Certification Authority dialog is still open, right click the server **mylab-SERVERA-CA**, select **All Tasks** and **Restore CA**. Click **OK** to stop the service.
2. In the Certification Authority Restore Wizard, click **Next**.
3. Check **Private and CA certificate** and **Certificate database and certificate database log**. Enter the location to save the backup as **C:\CertBack** (Figure 7.20). Then, click **Next**.
4. Enter the password **P@ssw0rd** and click **Next**.
5. Click **Finish** and click **Yes** to restart the service.

Requesting certificate: In this part of activity, you will learn how to request a certificate for your application.

1. Press the **Windows logo** key. Type **mmc** and click the **mmc** icon (Figure 7.21).
2. Click **File** and click **Add/Remove Snap-in** as shown in Figure 7.22.
3. Double click **Certificates** on the left pane and click **OK** to select **My user account** (Figure 7.23). Then, click **Finish**.
4. Click **OK** to add the snap-in.
5. In the left pane, double click **Certificates—Current User** to expand the folder as shown in Figure 7.24.
6. Right click **Personal** and select **All Tasks** and **Request New Certificate** as shown in Figure 7.25.

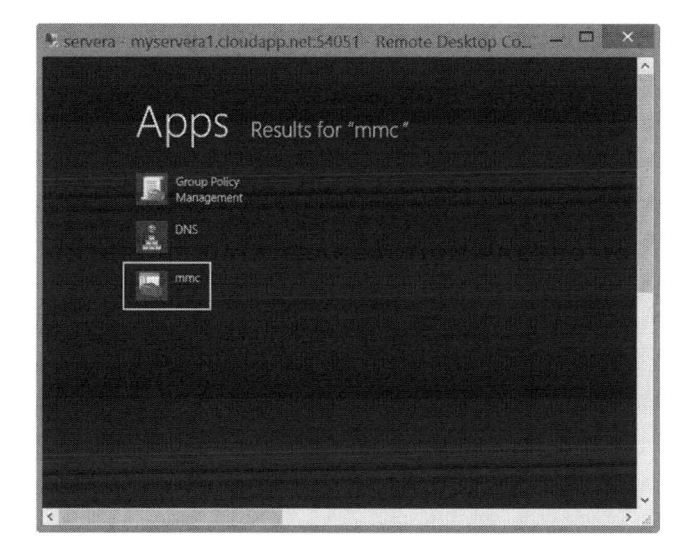

Figure 7.21   Opening mmc.

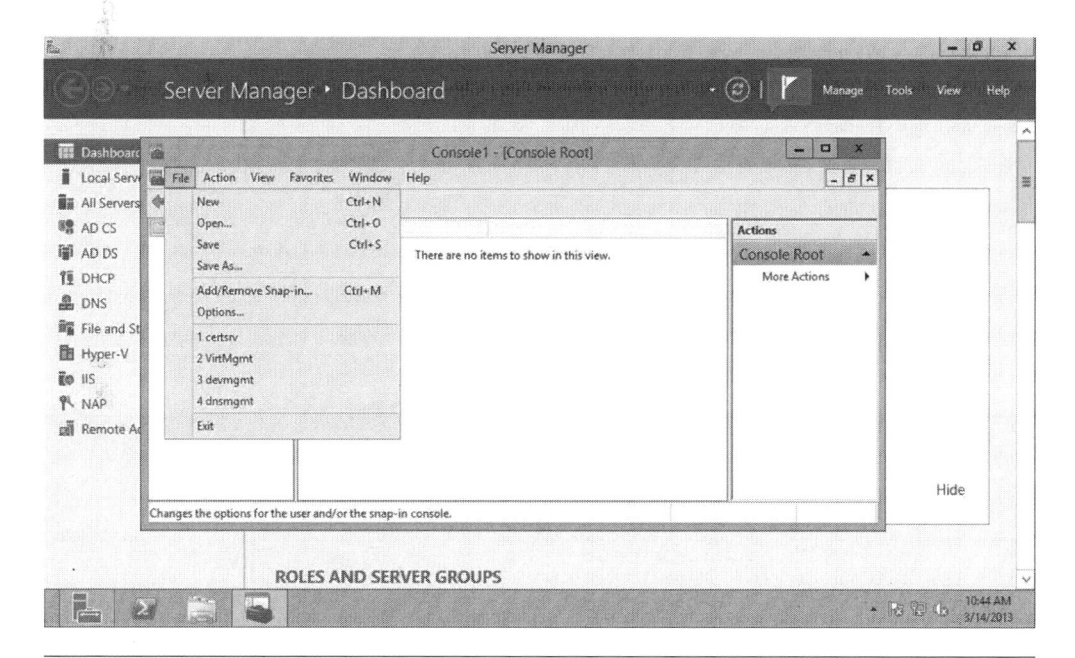

Figure 7.22   Add/Remove snap-in.

7. On the Before You Begin page, click **Next**.

8. On the Select Enrollment Policy page, click **Next**.

9. On the Request Certificates page, check the **User** checkbox as shown in Figure 7.26 and click **Enroll**.

10. After enrolled as shown in Figure 7.27, click **Finish**.

11. Double click the **Personal** node and double click **Certificates** in the middle pane. You should be able to see the certificate issued to the user **student** (Figure 7.28).

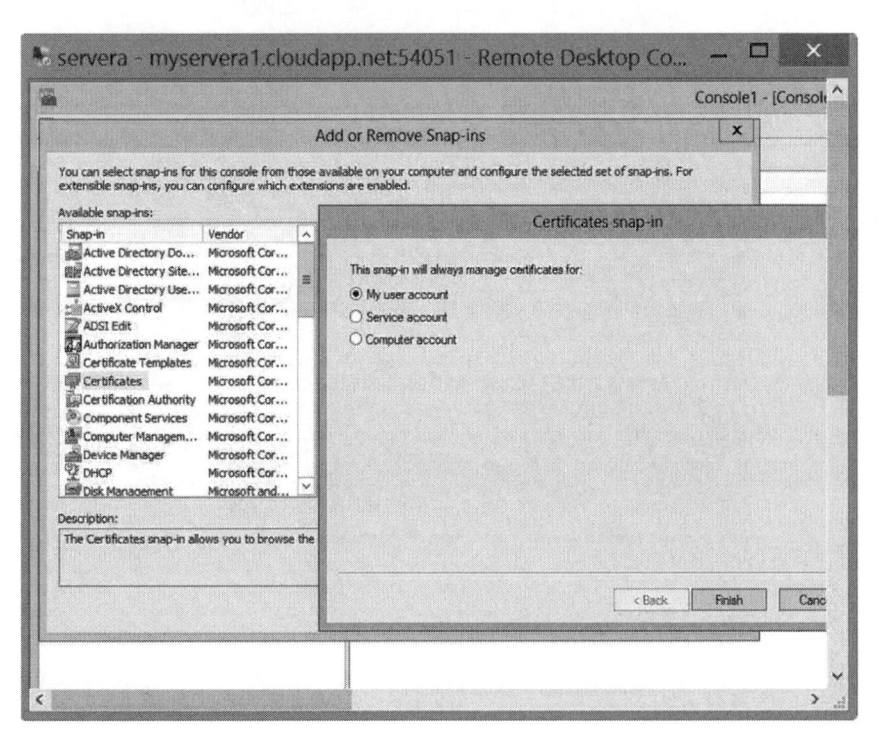

Figure 7.23   Adding certificate snap-in.

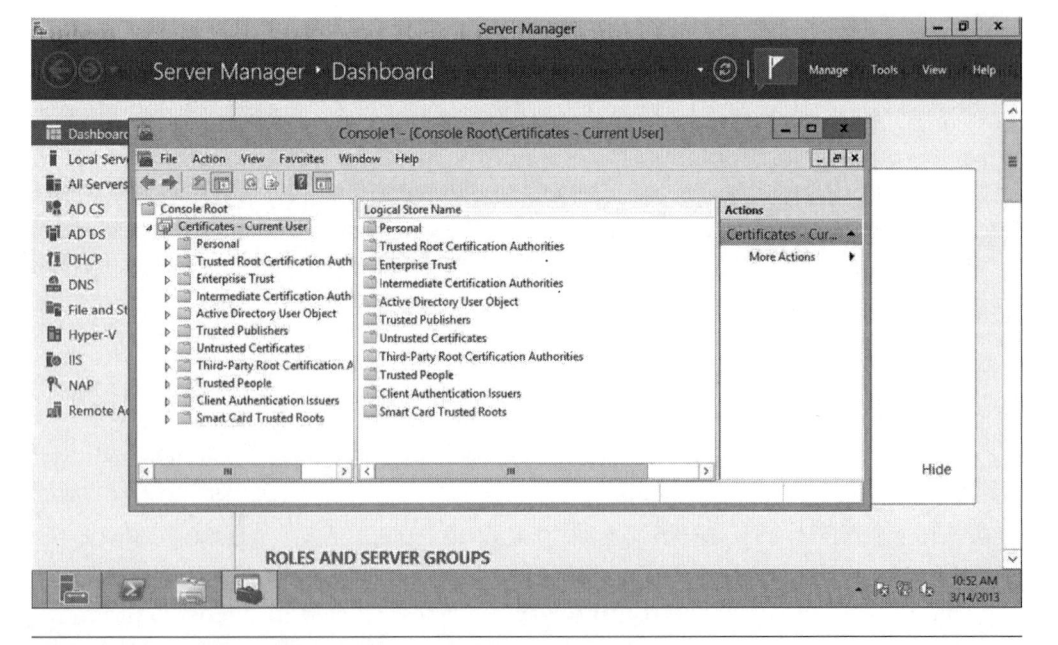

Figure 7.24   Expanding certificate—Current user folder.

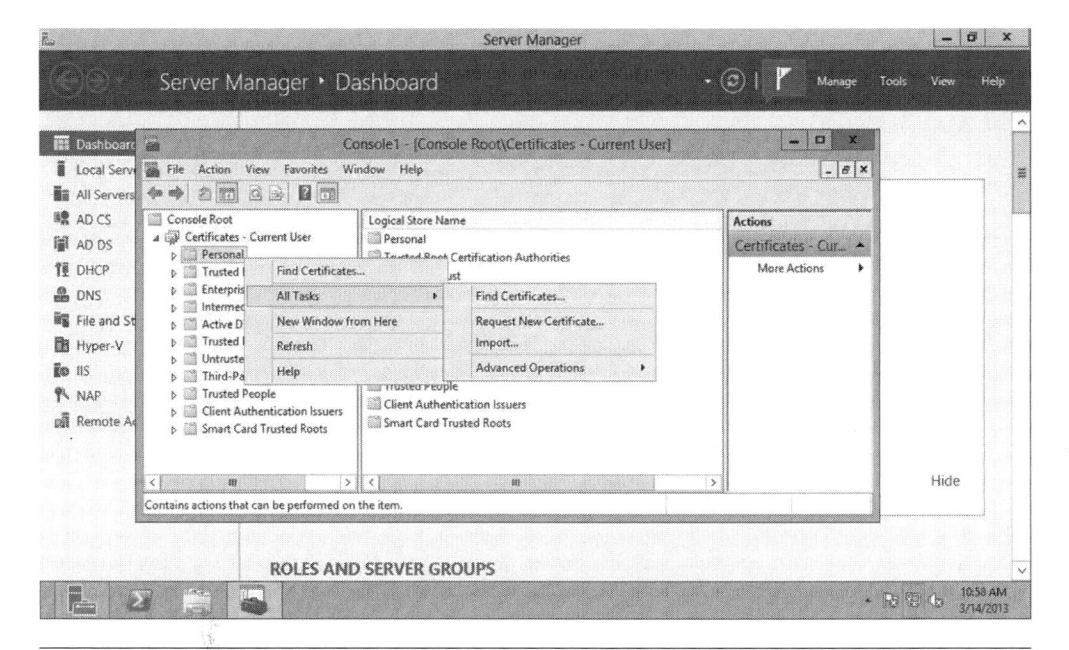

Figure 7.25 Requesting new certificate.

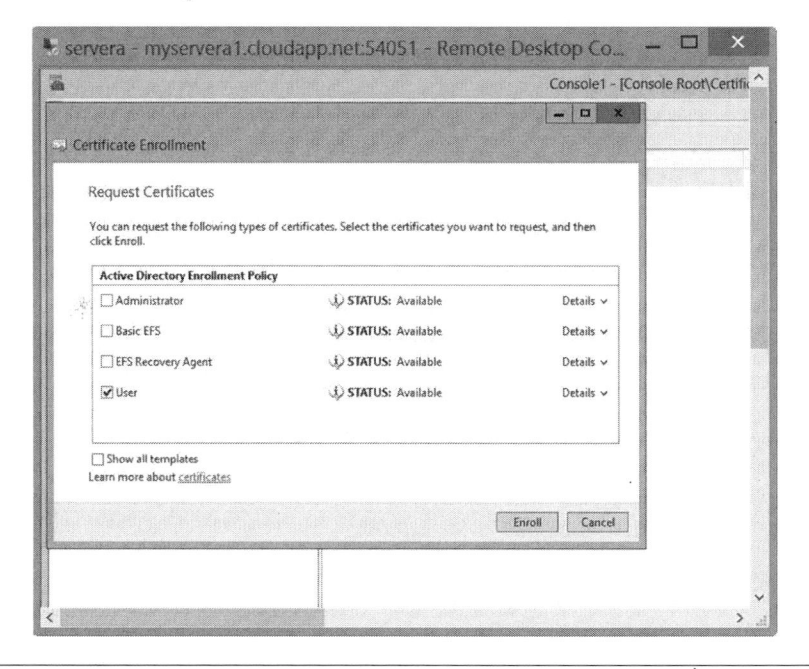

Figure 7.26 Requesting user certificate.

Exporting and importing certificates: In this part of the activity, you will learn how to export and import a certificate.

1. Right click the new certificate **student** and select **All Tasks** and **Export** (Figure 7.29).
2. On the Welcome page, click **Next**.

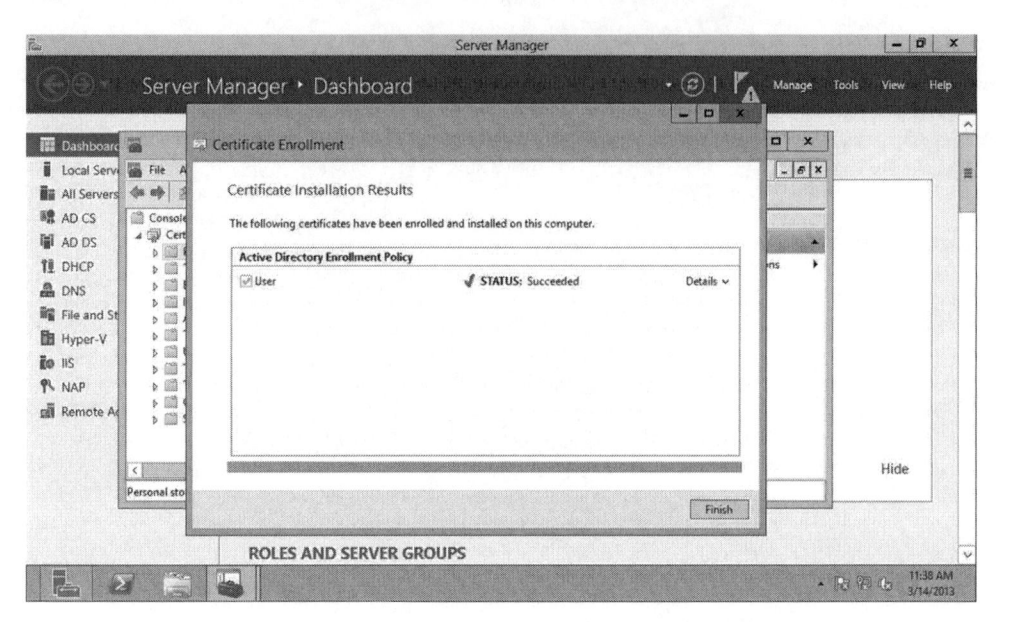

Figure 7.27 Certificate installed successfully.

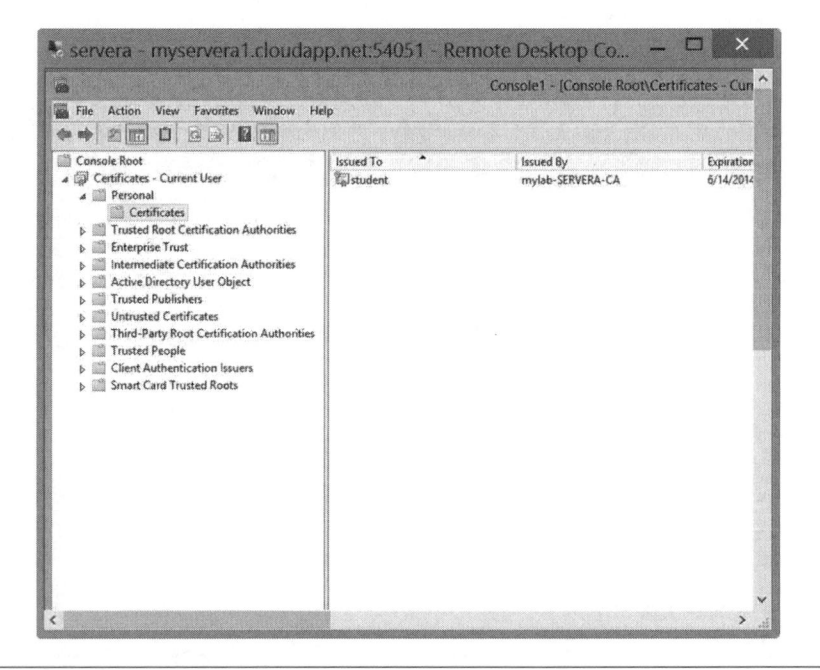

Figure 7.28 User certificate.

3. On the Export Private Key page, click **Yes, export the private key** as shown in Figure 7.30 Then, click **Next**.

4. On the Export File Format page, accept the default export file format and click **Next**.

5. On the Security page, check the **Password** checkbox. Enter the password, **Passw0rd!**, confirm it as shown in Figure 7.31, and click **Next**.

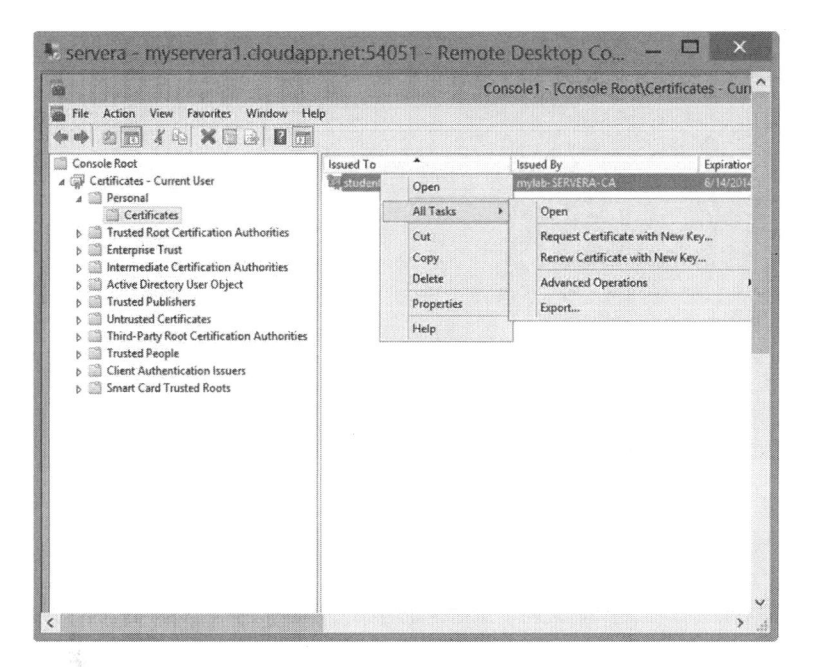

Figure 7.29 Exporting certificate.

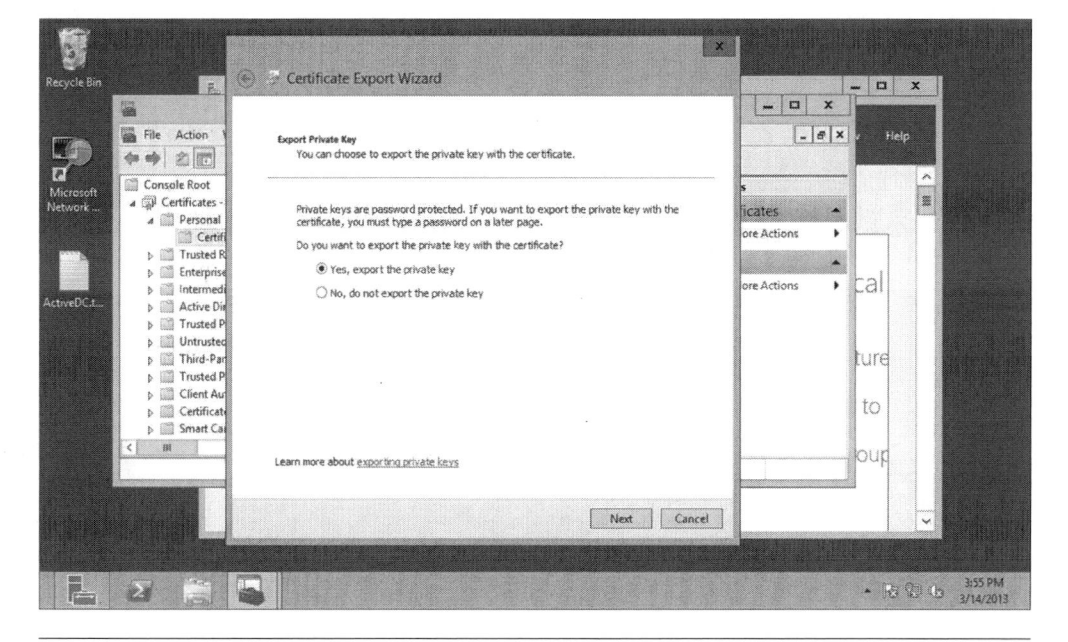

Figure 7.30 Exporting private key.

6. Browse to the **Documents** folder, type the file name **mycertificate** as shown in Figure 7.32, and click **Save**. Then, click **Next**.
7. Click **Finish** and **OK**.
8. To demonstrate the import process, right click the current **student** certificate and select **Delete** as shown in Figure 7.33. Then, click **Yes** to confirm it.

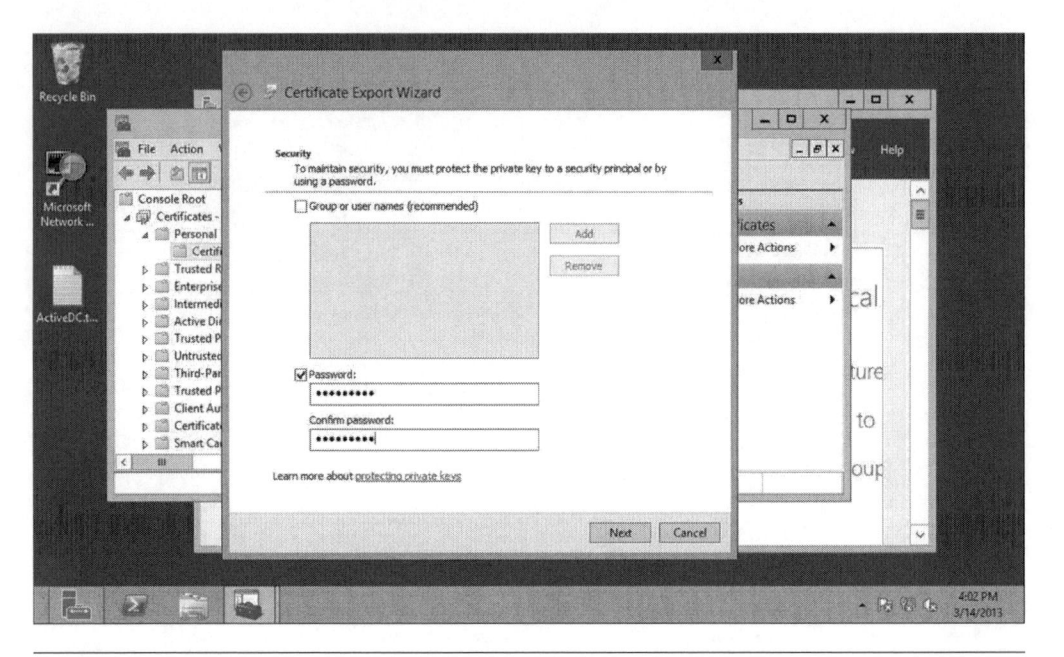

Figure 7.31 Protecting private key with password.

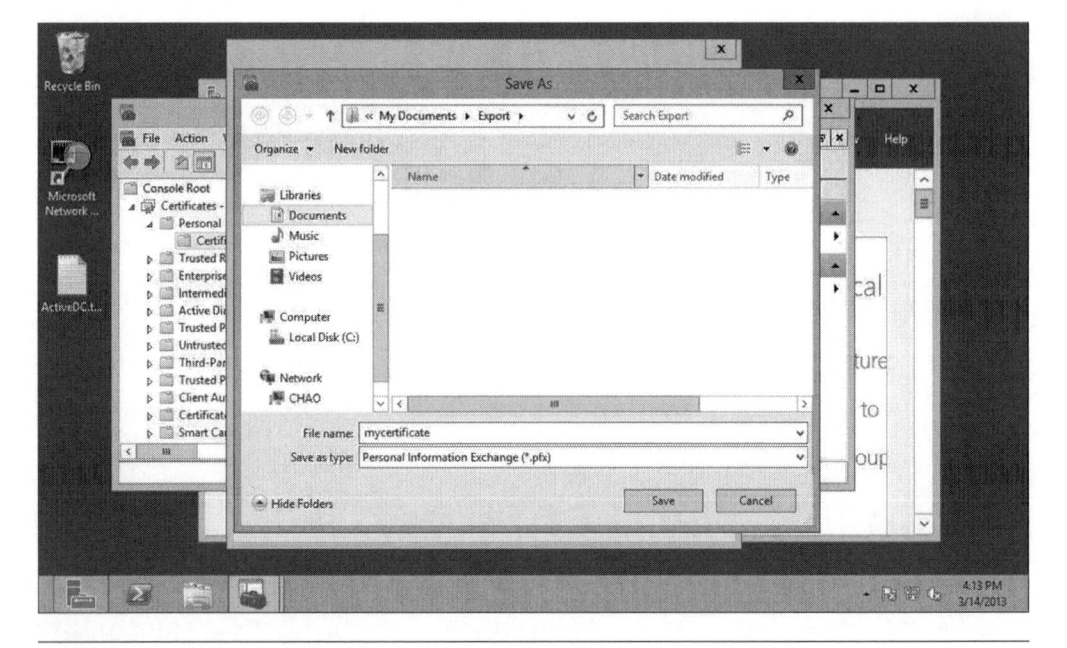

Figure 7.32 Saving certificate.

9. Right click **Certificates** in the left pane. Select **All Tasks** and **Import** as shown in Figure 7.34.

10. Click **Next** on the Welcome page.

11. Browse to **Documents**. In the file type drop-down list, select **Personal Information Exchange**; click **mycertificate** and **Open** as shown in Figure 7.35. Then click **Next**.

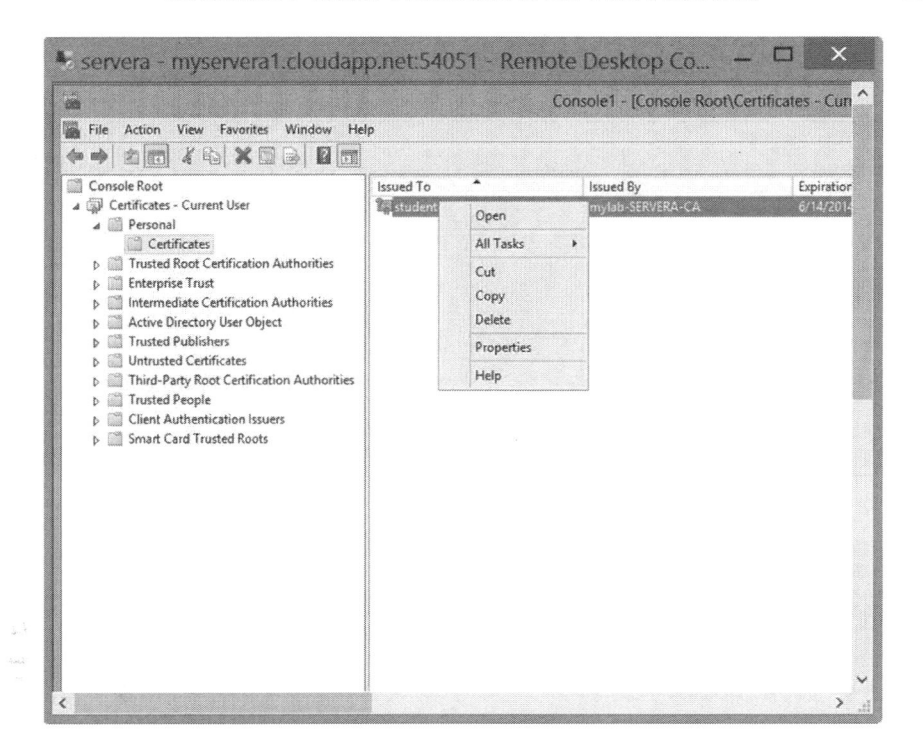

Figure 7.33 Deleting existing certificate.

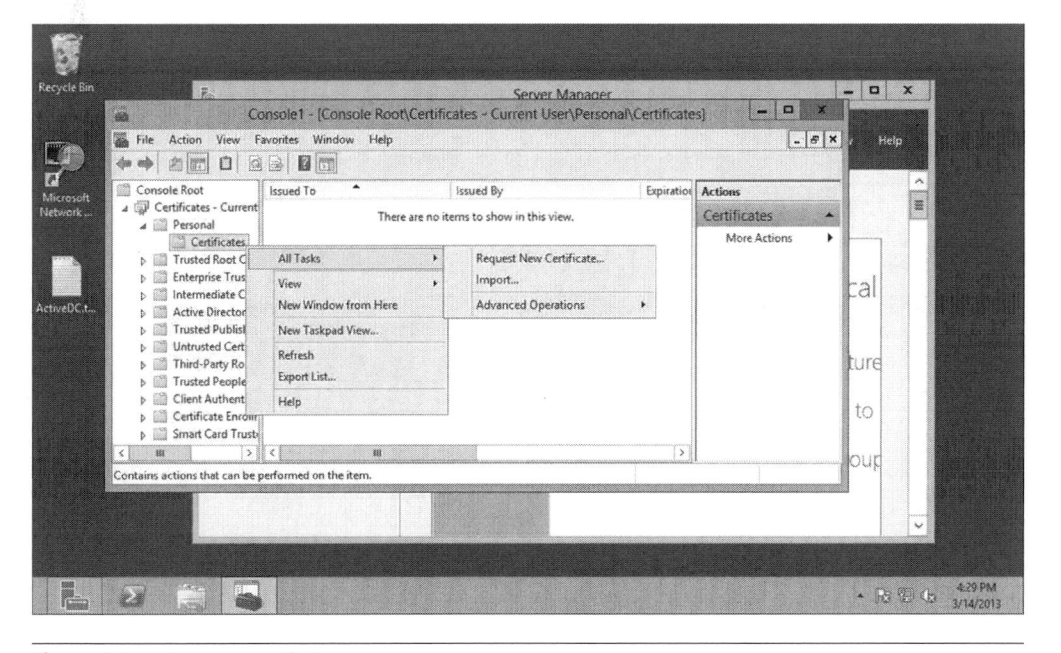

Figure 7.34 Importing certificate.

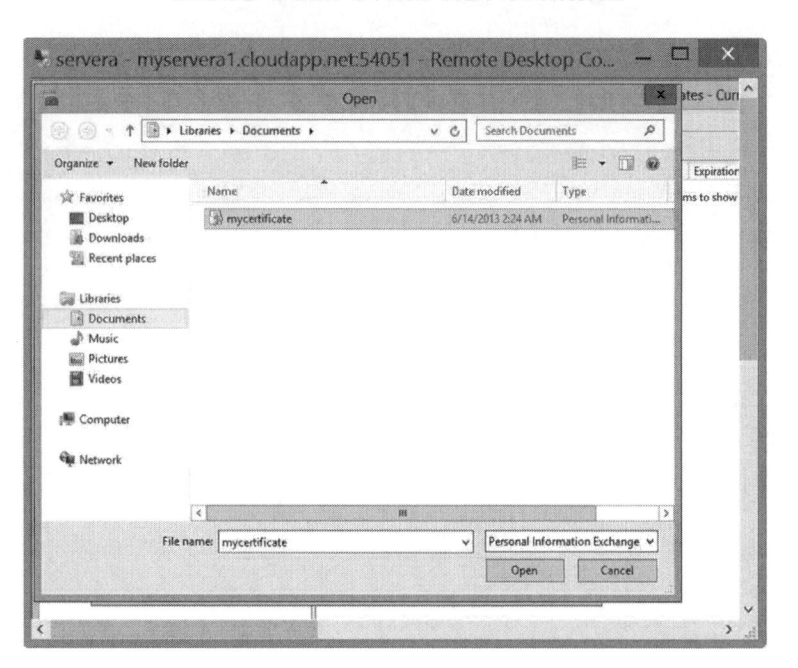

Figure 7.35   Opening certificate.

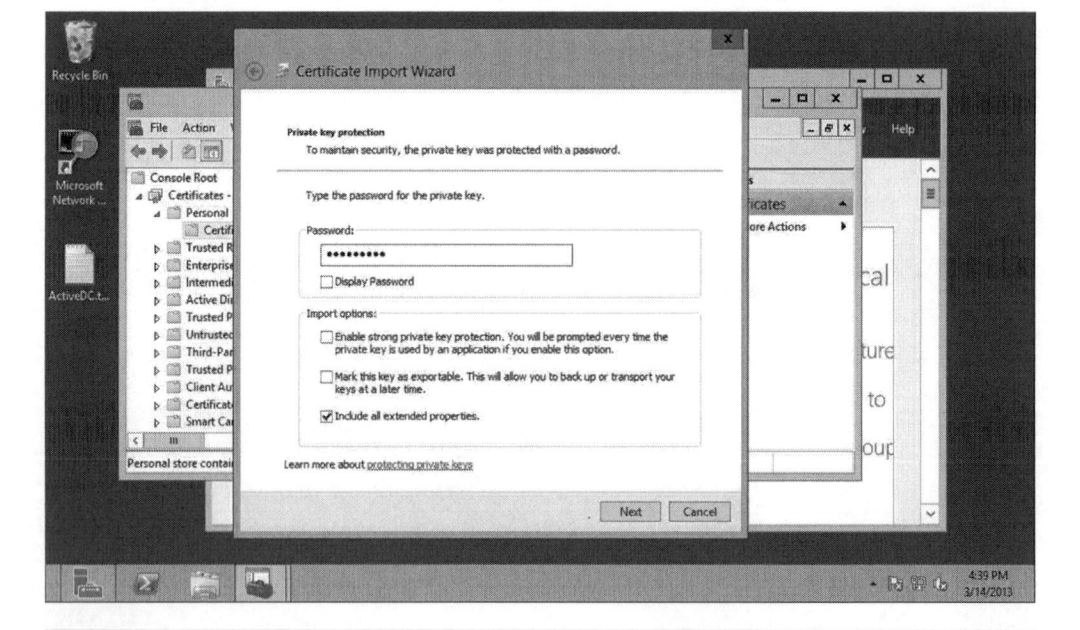

Figure 7.36   Entering password.

12. Type the password **Passw0rd!** and click **Next** (Figure 7.36).
13. Make sure that the option **Place all certificates in the following store** is selected as shown in Figure 7.37 and click **Next**.
14. On the completing page, click **Finish**. As you can see, the user certificate has been imported as shown in Figure 7.38.

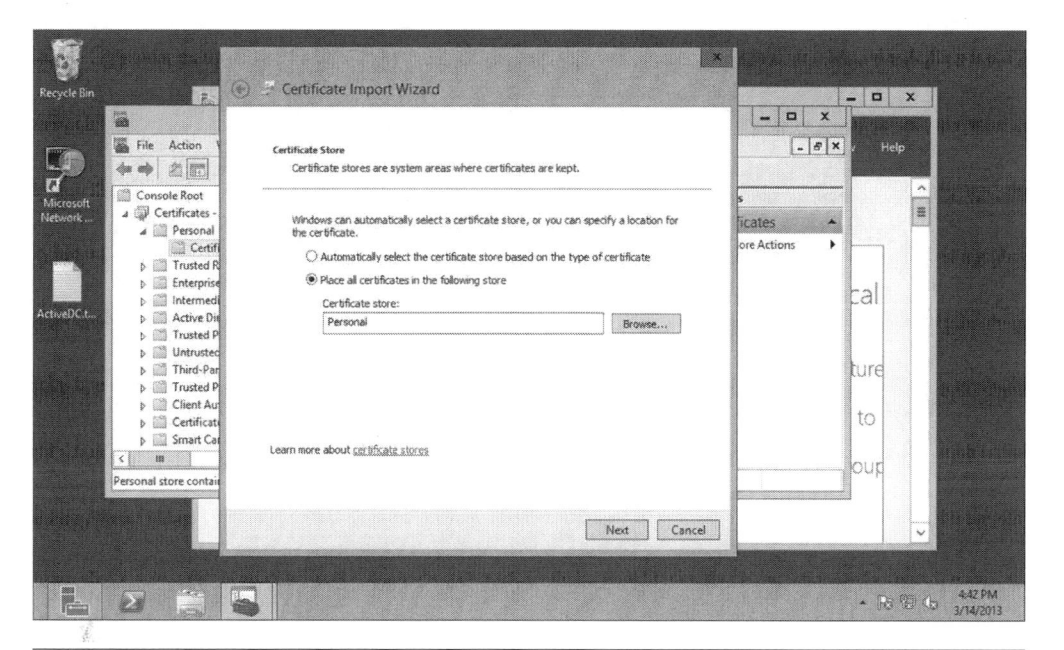

Figure 7.37 Specifying certificate store.

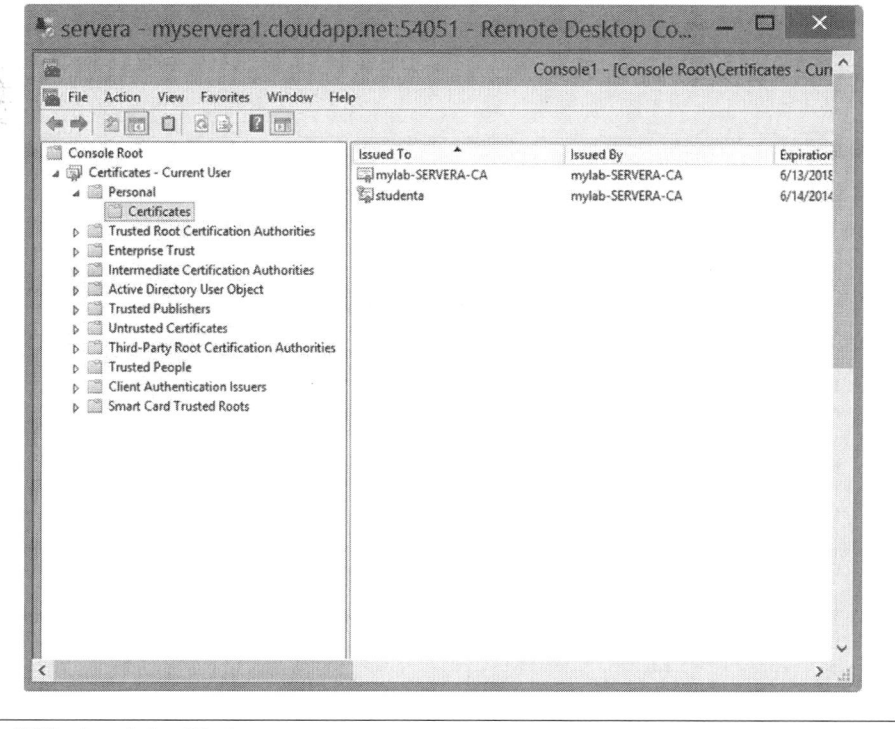

Figure 7.38 Imported certificate.

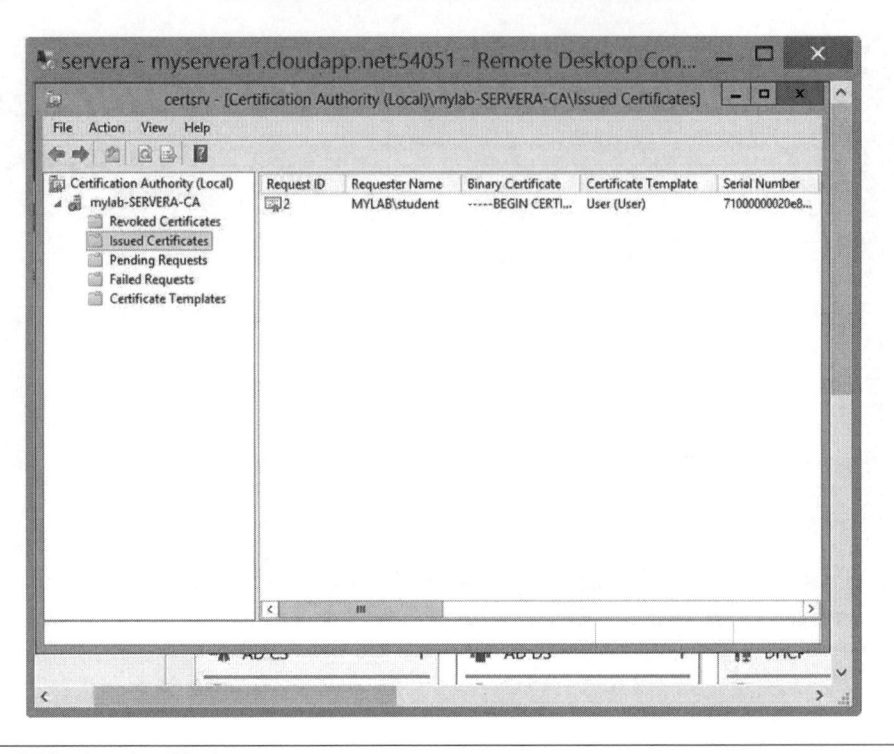

Figure 7.39   Issued certificate.

Revoking certificate: In this part of the activity, you will learn how to revoke a certificate.

1. On Server Manager, click **Tools** and **Certification Authority**.
2. Expand the node **mylab-SERVERA-CA** and click **Issued Certificates** as shown in Figure 7.39.
3. Right click **MYLAB\student**, select **All Tasks** and **Revoke Certificate** as shown in Figure 7.40.
4. Select the reason code **Change of Affiliation** as shown in Figure 7.41 and click **Yes**.
5. Click the **Revoked Certificates** node in the left pane as shown in Figure 7.42.
6. Click **Action**, select **All Tasks** and **Publish** as shown in Figure 7.43.
7. While **NEW CRL** is selected as shown in Figure 7.44, click **OK**. ·
8. You can now close the snap-ins.

Task 3: Creating SSL Certificate for Web Server

In this task, you will first install the web server, Internet Information Services (IIS). Then, you will create an SSL certificate for the web server. You will start with the installation of the web server using the following steps.

1. Assume you are logged on **servera**. In Server Manager, click **Add Roles and Features**. The Add Roles and Features Wizard will open.
2. On the Before You Begin page, click **Next**.

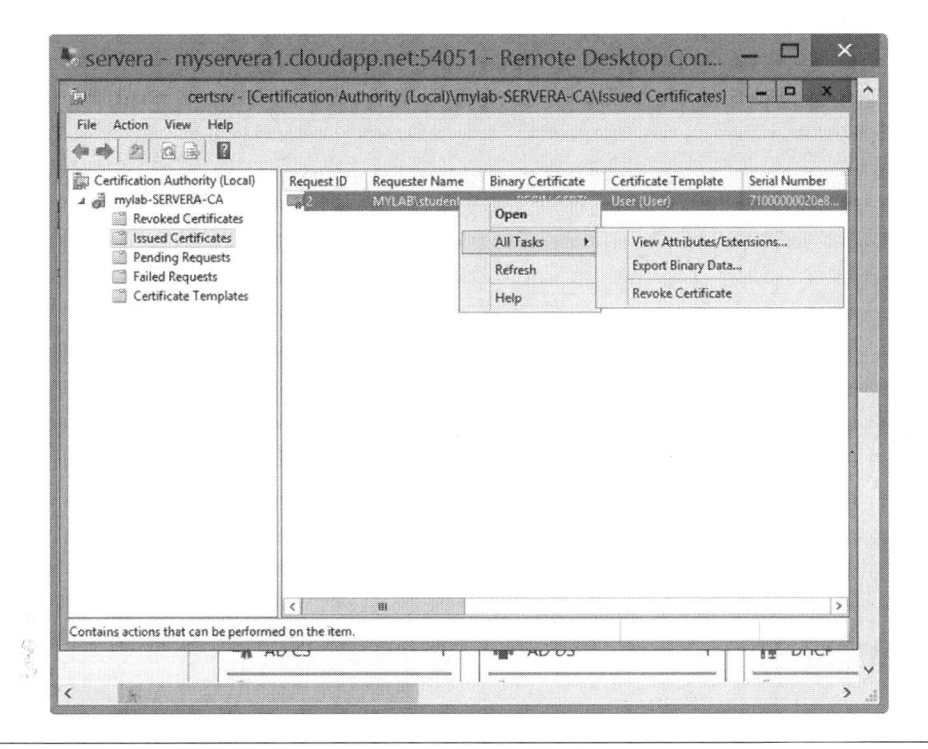

Figure 7.40   Revoking certificate.

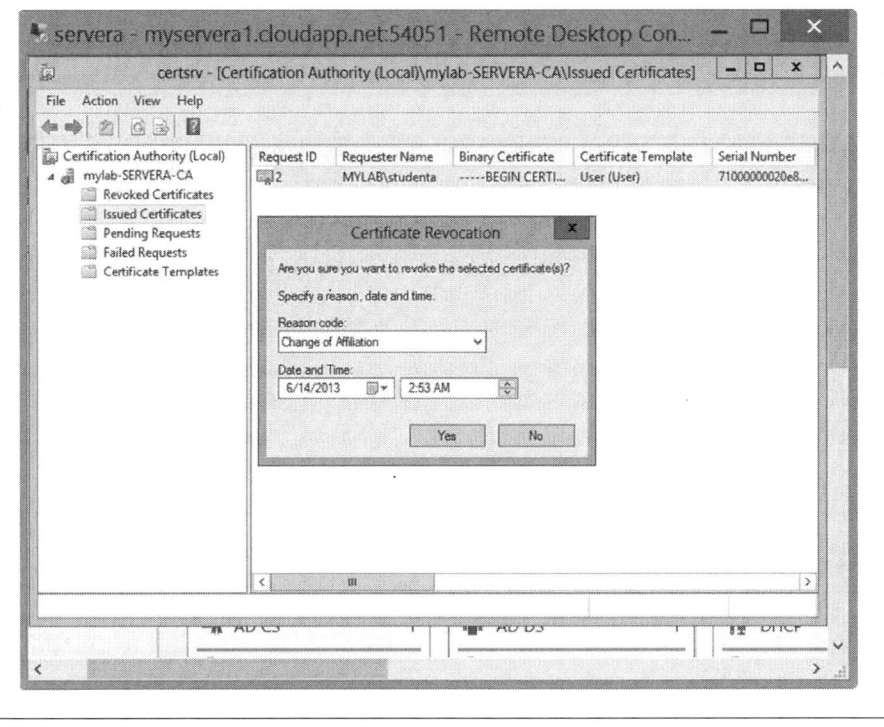

Figure 7.41   Specifying reason for revoking certificate.

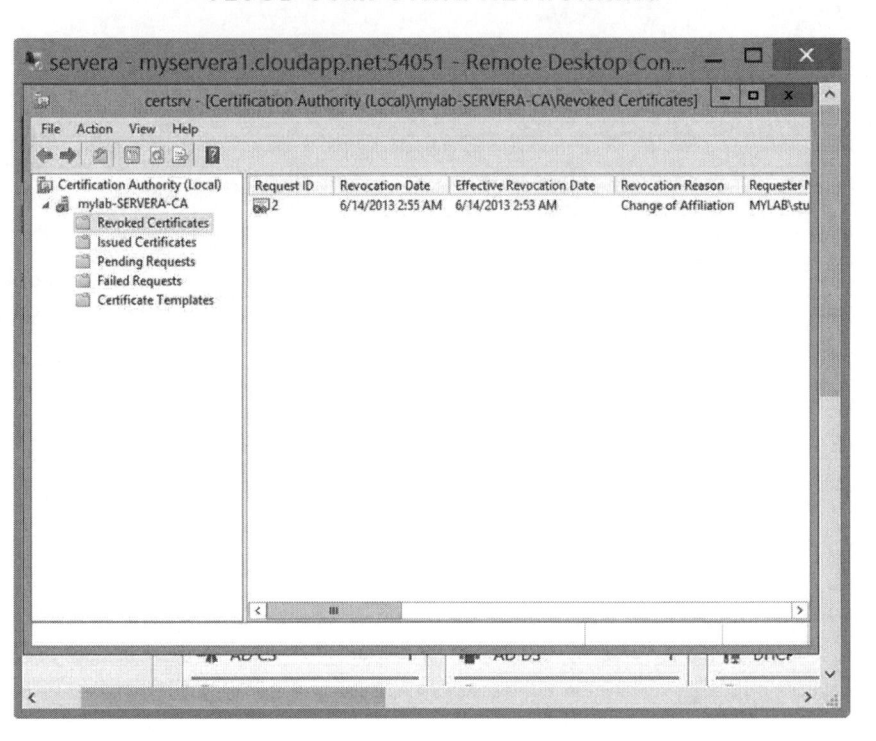

Figure 7.42   Revoked certificate.

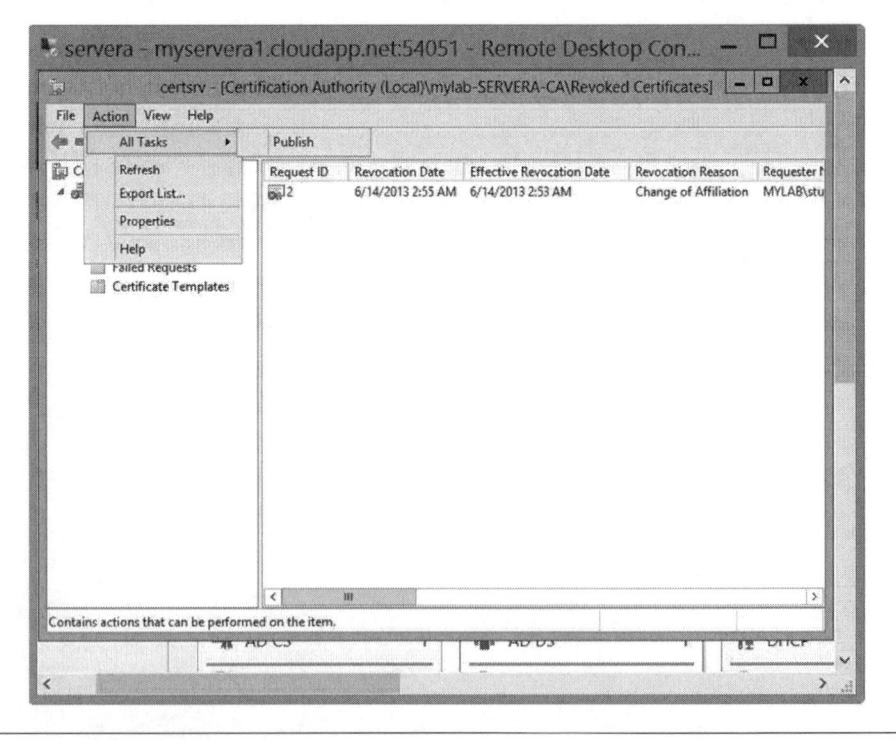

Figure 7.43   Publishing CRL.

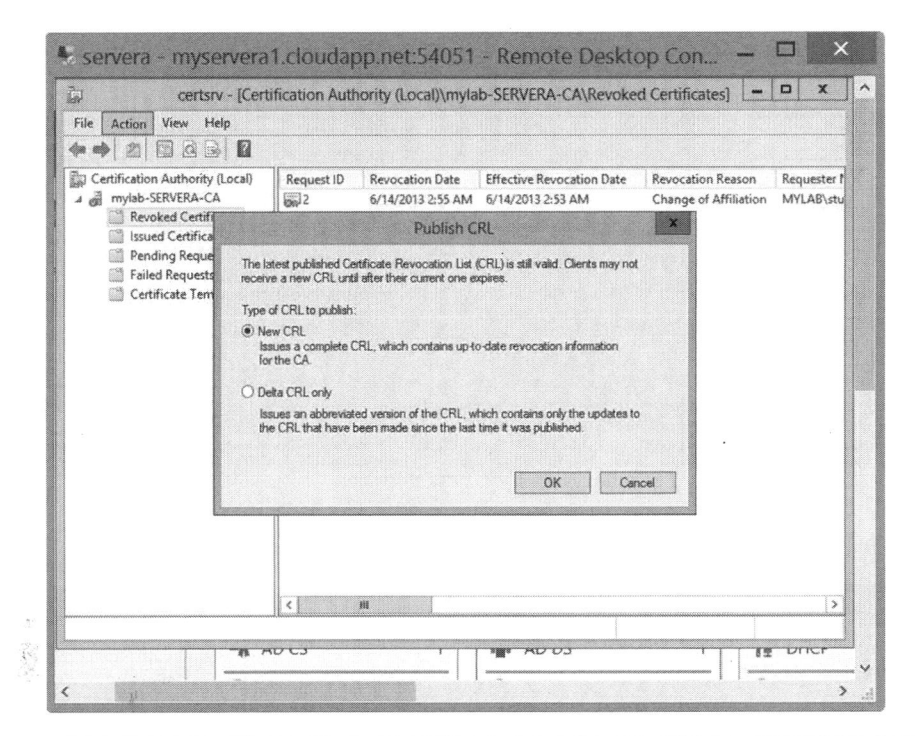

Figure 7.44 New version of CRL.

3. On the Installation Type page, click **Next**.

4. On the Server Selection page, click **Next**.

5. On the Select server roles page, select **Web Server (IIS)**, and click **Add Features** as shown in Figure 7.45. Then, click **Next**.

6. Click **Next** until you have accepted all of the default web server settings, and click **Restart the destination server automatically if required**. Then, click **Install**.

7. Verify that all installations are successful, and then click **Close**.

8. Press the **Windows icon** key to open the Start menu. Click the **Administrative Tools** tile.

9. Double click IIS Manager as shown in Figure 7.46.

10. Click the **SERVERA** node in the left pane. Double click the **Server Certificates** icon (Figure 7.47).

11. In the Actions pane, click **Create Certificate Request** shown in Figure 7.48.

12. On the Distinguished Name Properties page of the Request Certificate Wizard, type the information for **Common name**, **Organization**, **Organizational unit**, **City**, **State**, and **Country** (Figure 7.49), and then click **Next**.

13. On the Cryptographic Service Provider Properties page, select **Microsoft RSA SChannel Cryptographic Provider** from the Cryptographic service provider drop-down list.

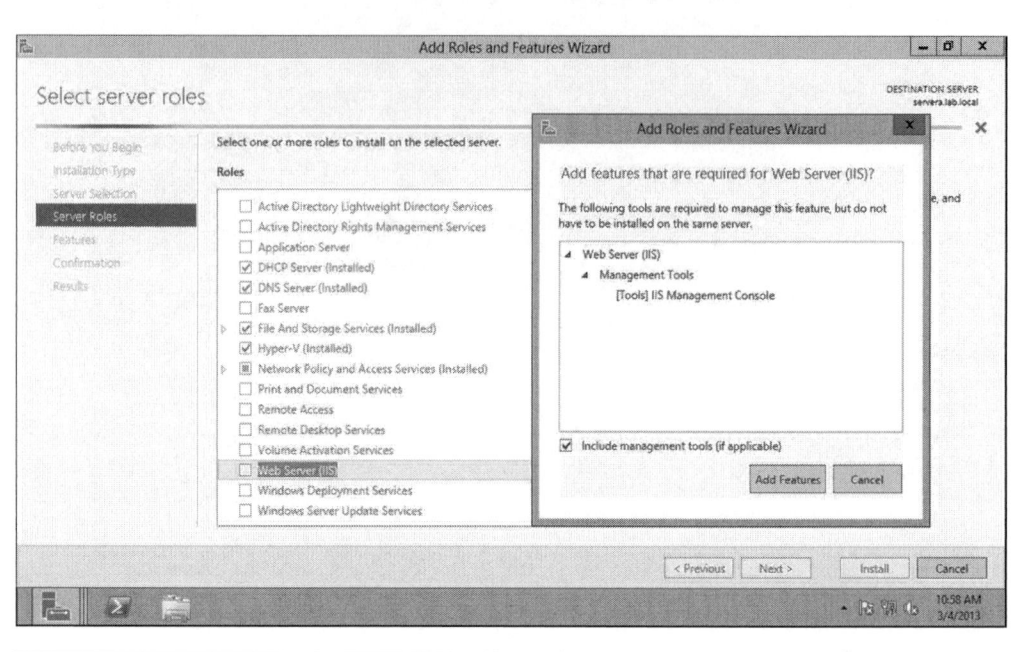

Figure 7.45   Adding web server (IIS) role.

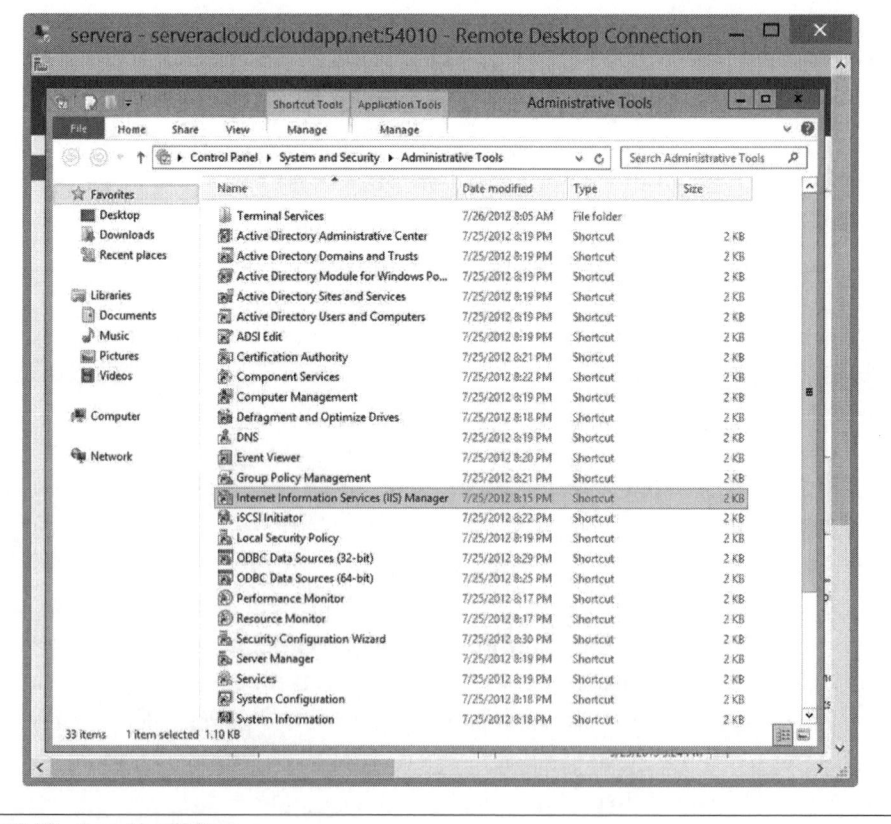

Figure 7.46   Launching IIS Manager.

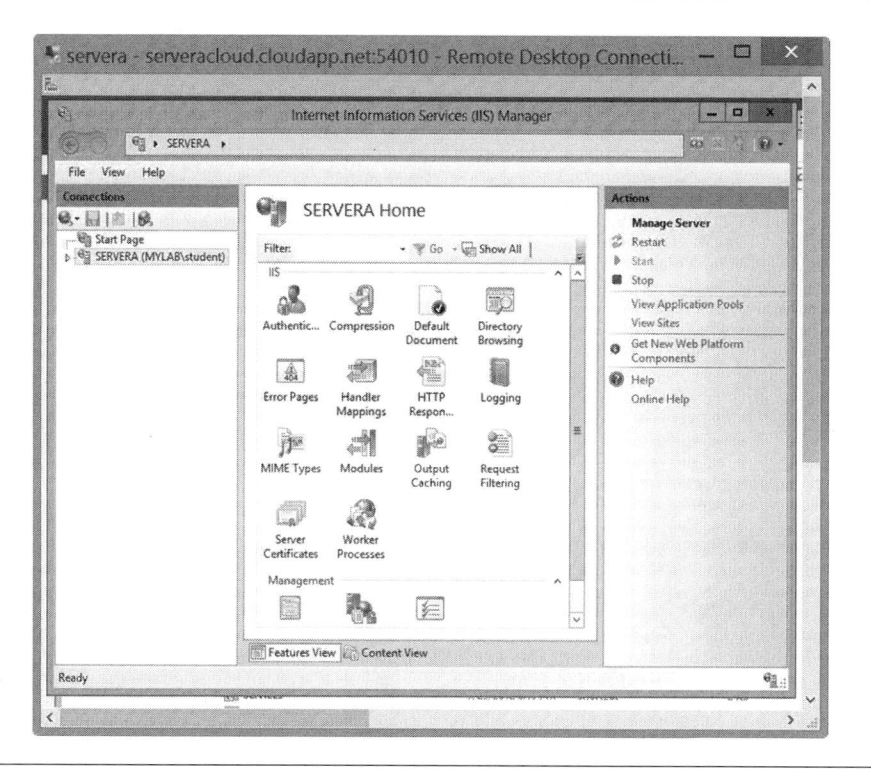

Figure 7.47 Opening server certificates for configuration.

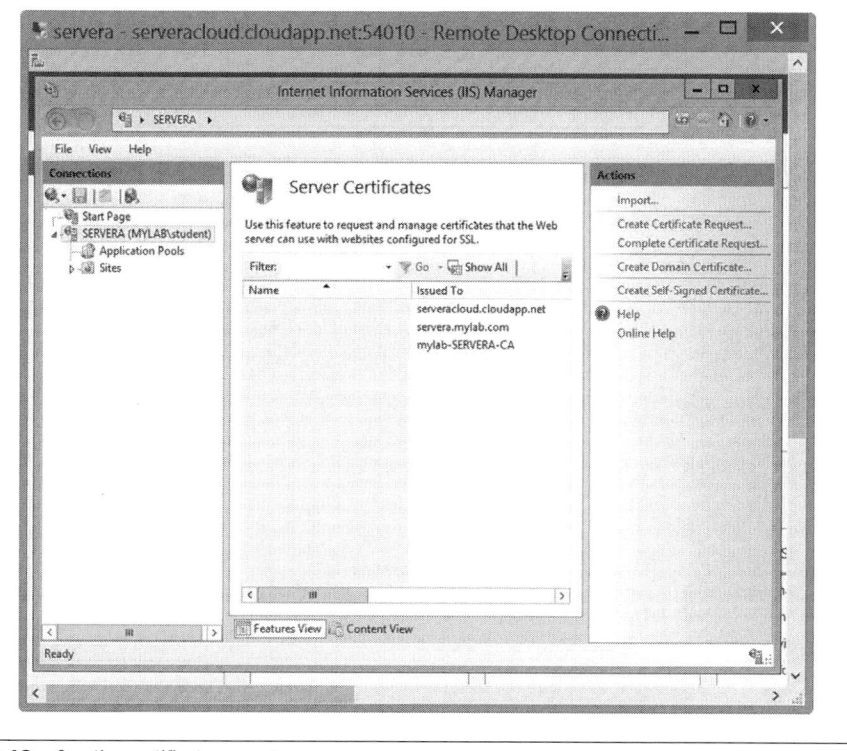

Figure 7.48 Creating certificate request.

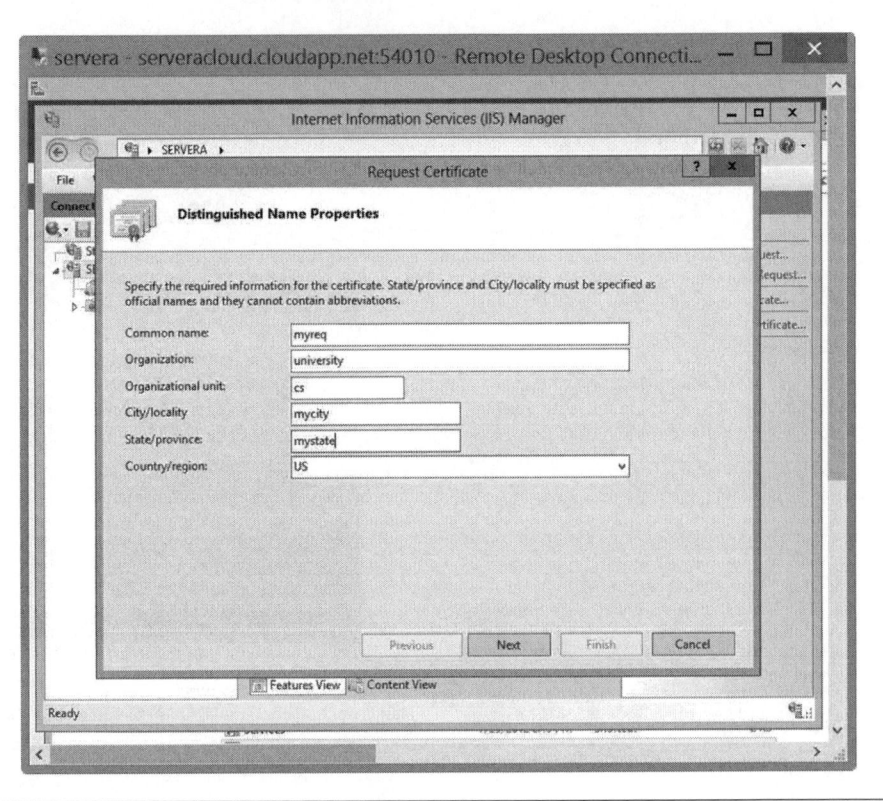

Figure 7.49   Specifying required information for new certificate.

14. In the Bit length drop-down list, select the bit length **2048** as shown in Figure 7.50. Then, click **Next**.

15. On the File Name page, in the Specify a file name for the certificate request textbox, type a certificate request file name, such as **c:\mycert.req** as shown in Figure 7.51, and then click **Finish**.

16. To submit the request to the root CA created on servera, you need to run the command certreq.exe. To do so, press the **Windows icon** key and type **cmd**. Right click the **cmd** icon and select **Run as Administrator**.

17. When the command window is open, enter the following command as shown in Figure 7.52.

```
certreq.exe -submit -attrib "CertificateTemplate:WebServer"
   c:\mycert.req mycert.cer
```

18. When the Certification Authority List dialog opens, select **mylab-SER-VERA-CA** as shown in Figure 7.52 and click **OK**.

19. If successful, you should get result as shown in Figure 7.53.

20. To see if the certificate has been issued by the CA, in the Server Manager dialog, click the **Tools** menu and select **Certification Authority**.

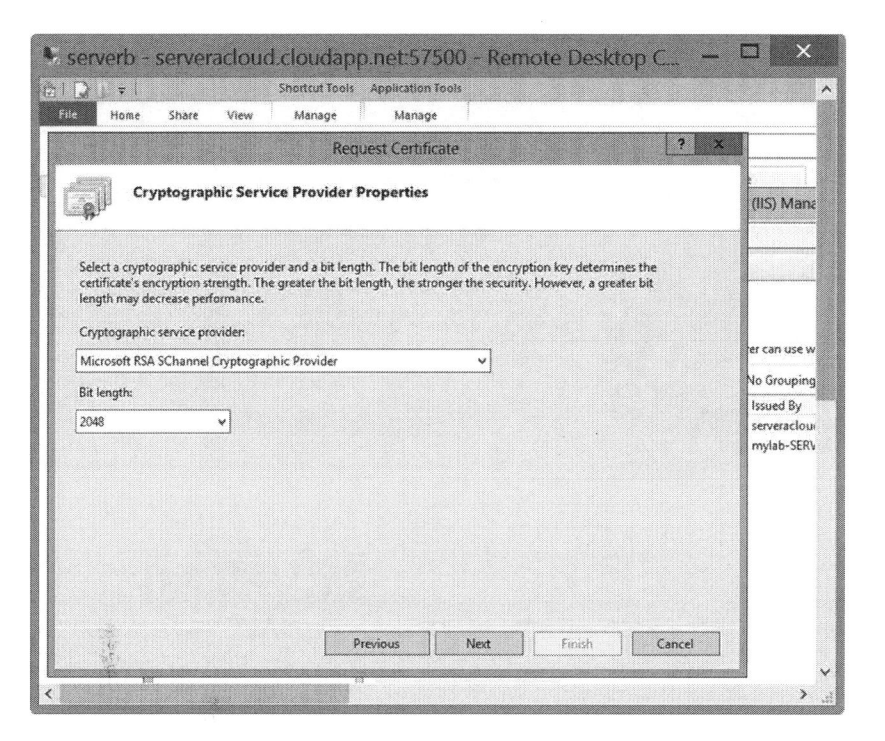

Figure 7.50 Configuring cryptographic service.

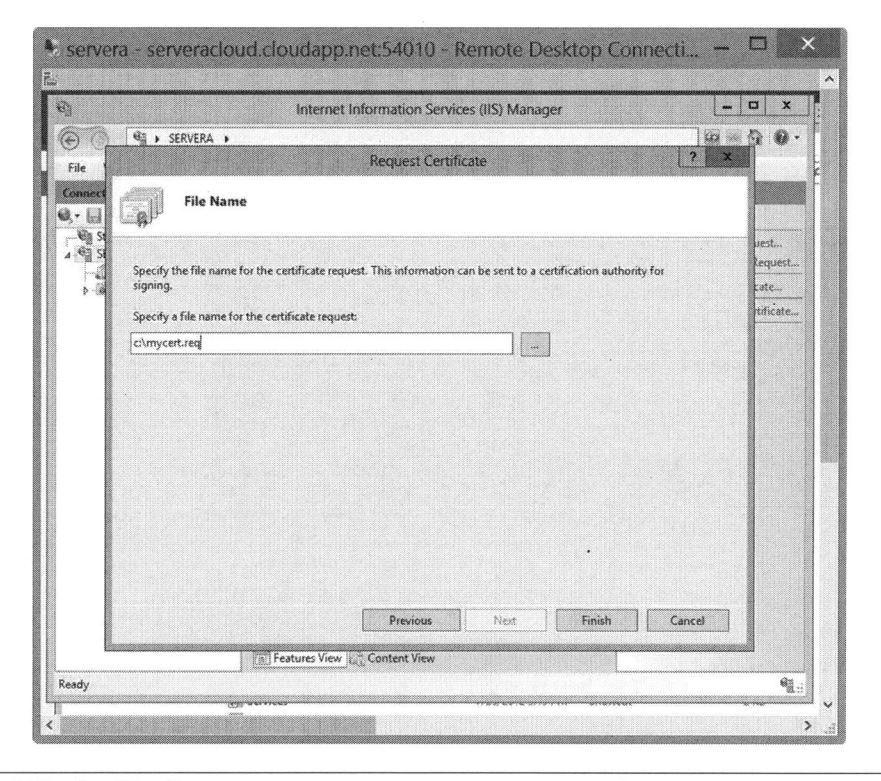

Figure 7.51 Specifying file name.

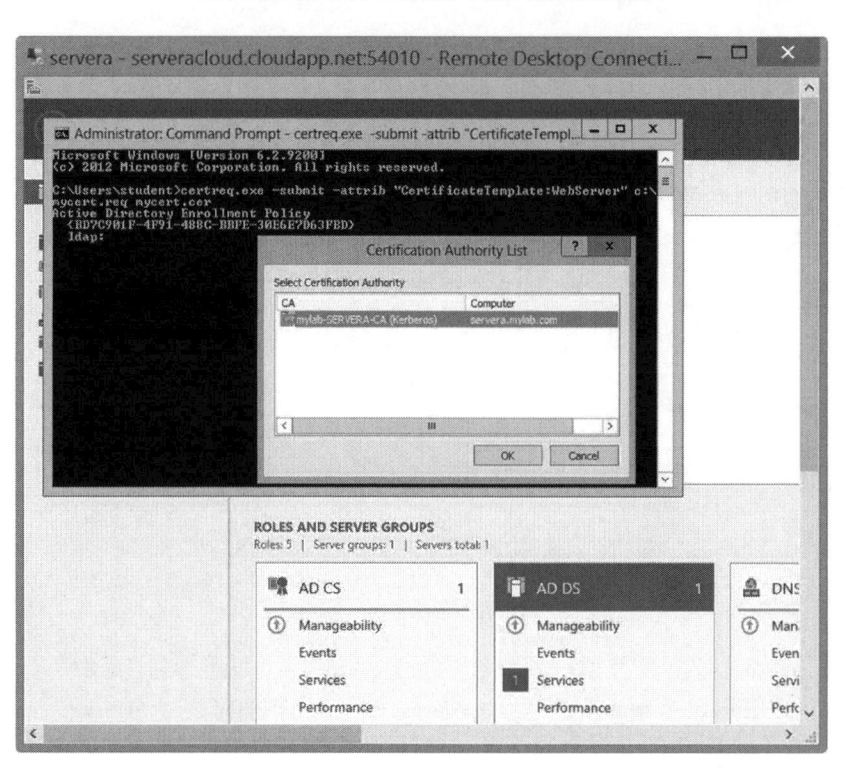

Figure 7.52   Running command certreq.exe.

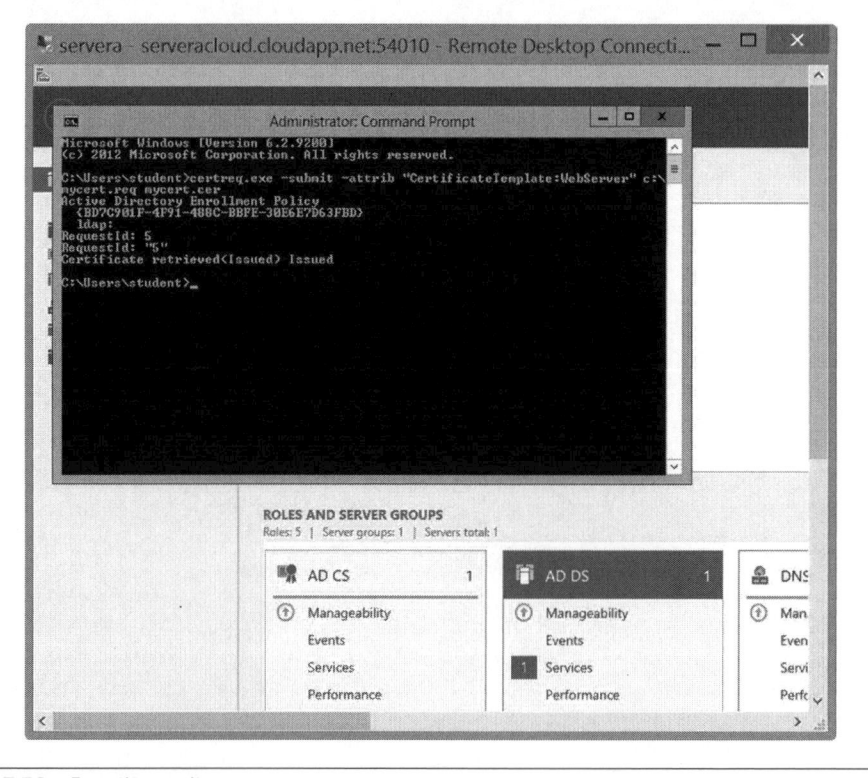

Figure 7.53   Execution result.

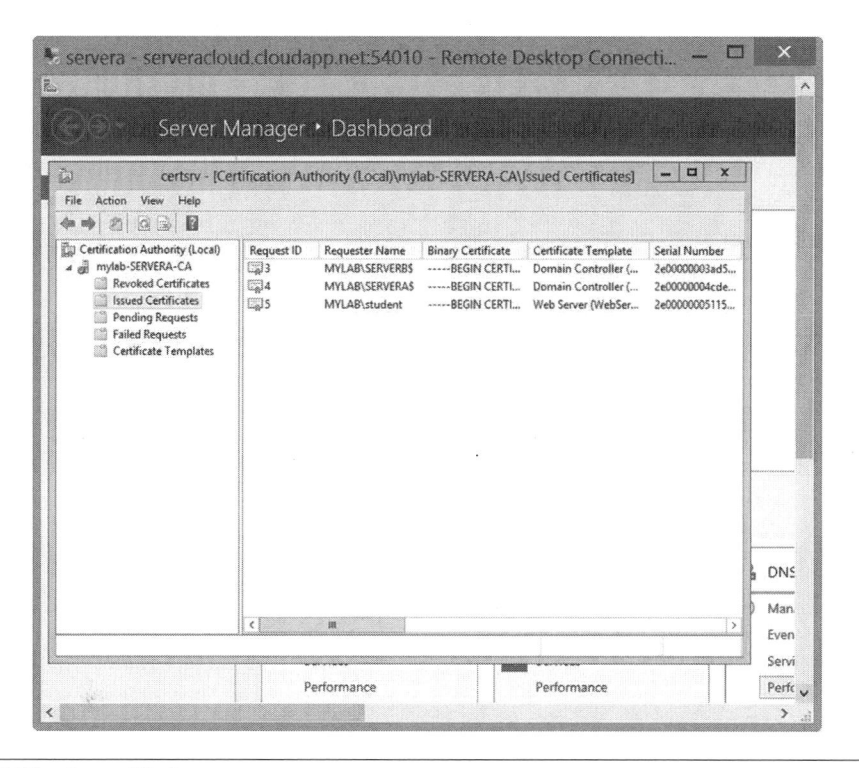

Figure 7.54 New certificate.

21. Expand the **mylab-SERVERA-CA** node and double click the **Issued Certificates** node. You should be able to see that Request ID 5 has been issued to the user student as shown in Figure 7.54.
22. To complete the certificate, in the IIS Manager dialog, click the **Complete Certificate Request** link as shown in Figure 7.55.
23. In the Specify Certification Authority Response window, browse for and select the certificate file **c:\users\student\mycert.cer** (or, where you saved your mycert.cer file) and provide a friendly name such as **mycert** for the certificate, then click **OK**. You may see the Error message "Failed to remove the certificate." In such a case, do the following to solve the problem.

Task 4: Repairing Certificate

When the "Failed to remove the certificate" error occurs, the private key may be missing. Without the private key, you will not be able to decrypt the message encrypted with the public key generated by the certificate. The following steps are used to recover the private key of an SSL certificate.

1. In the IIS Manager, delete the newly added certificate that causes the error message.
2. The first step to fix the problem is to add a certificate snap-in. To do so, press the **Windows icon** key and type **mmc**.

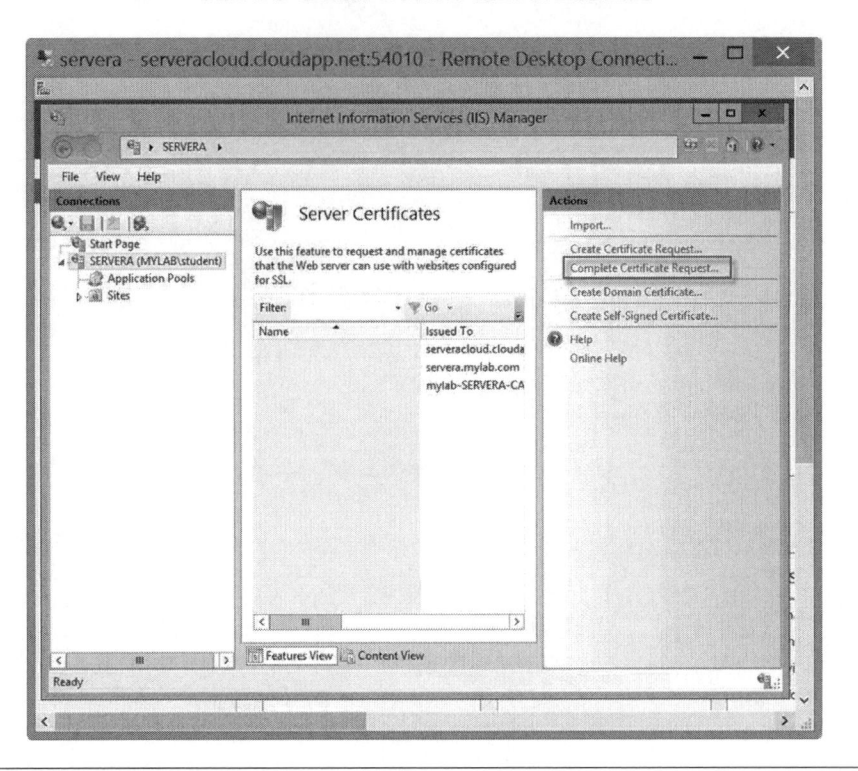

Figure 7.55   Completing certificate request.

3. From the **File** menu, choose **Add/Remove Snap-in**. Select **Certificates** and then click **Add** as shown in Figure 7.56.
4. Choose the **Computer account** option and click **Next**.
5. Select **Local Computer** and then click **Finish**.
6. Click **Close**, and then click **OK**. The snap-in for **Certificates (Local Computer)** appears in the console as shown in Figure 7.57.
7. The next step is to import your server certificate into the personal certificate store. Expand the **Certificates (Local Computer)** node in the left preview panel.
8. Right click the **Personal** node and select **All Tasks**, and then **Import** (Figure 7.58).
9. The Certificate Import Wizard appears. On the Welcome page, click **Next** to go to the File to Import page.
10. Browse and find the file **c:\Users\student\mycert.cer** and click **Next**.
11. Select the option **Place all certificates in the following store** as shown in Figure 7.59 and click **Next**. Then, click **Finish**.
12. You can now configure your certificate to include the private key. Locate the file **c:\Users\student\mycert.cer** and double click it.
13. Click the **Details** tab. Write down the serial number of the certificate shown in Figure 7.60.
14. Assume that the command prompt window is still open, enter the following command and press **Enter**.

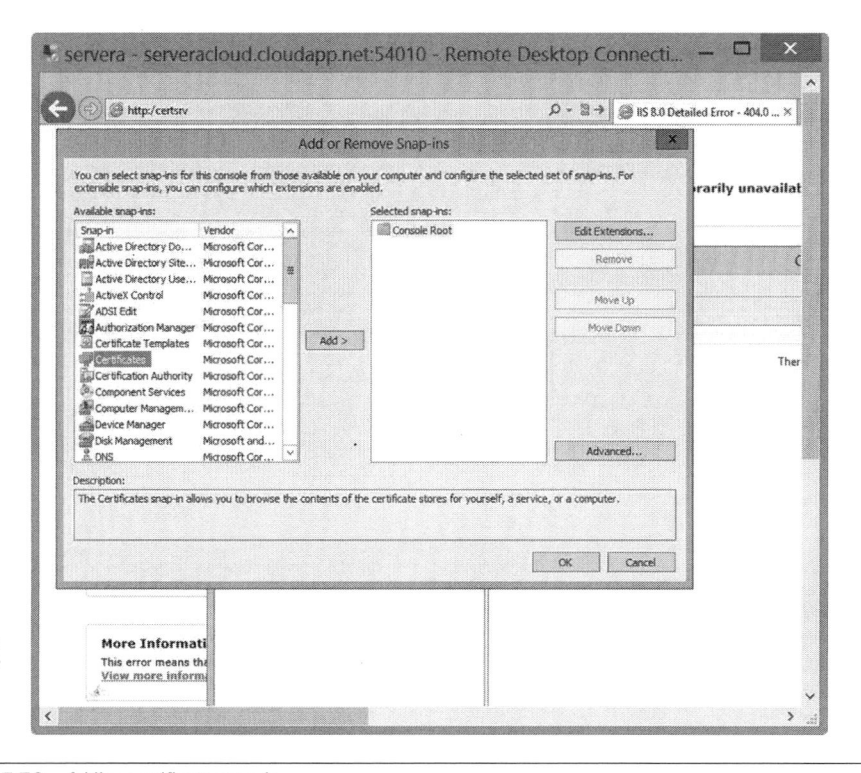

Figure 7.56 Adding certificate snap-in.

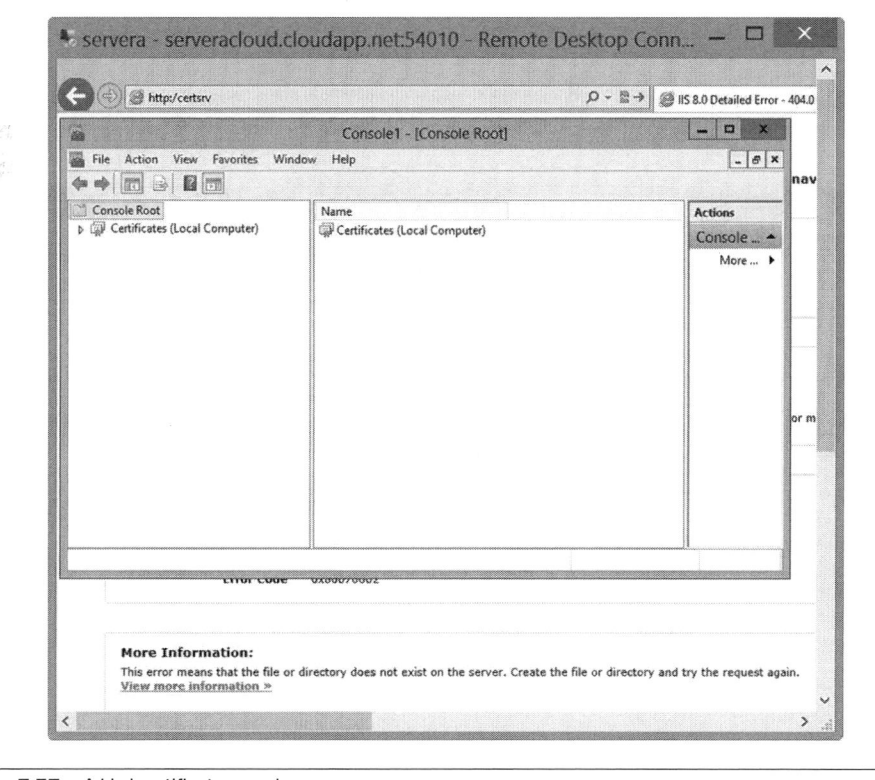

Figure 7.57 Added certificate snap-in.

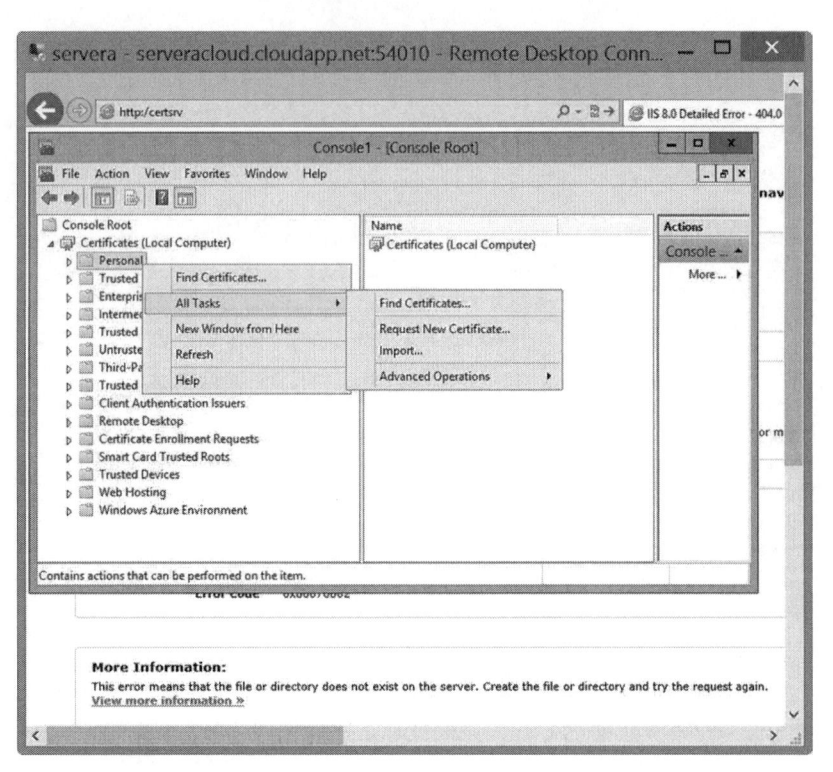

Figure 7.58   Importing certificate for repair.

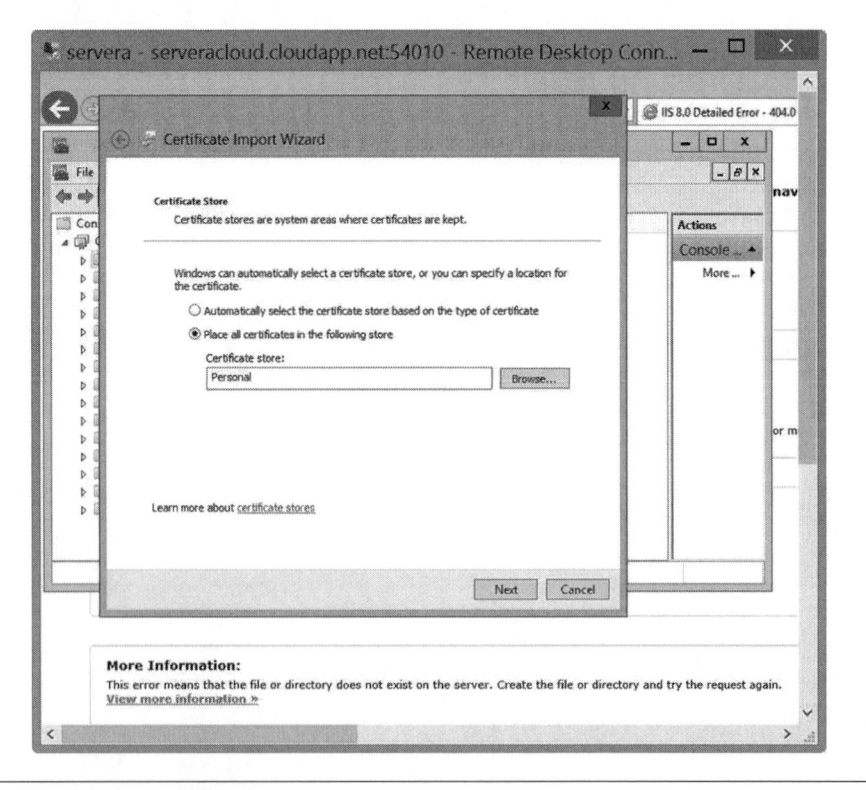

Figure 7.59   Selecting certificate store.

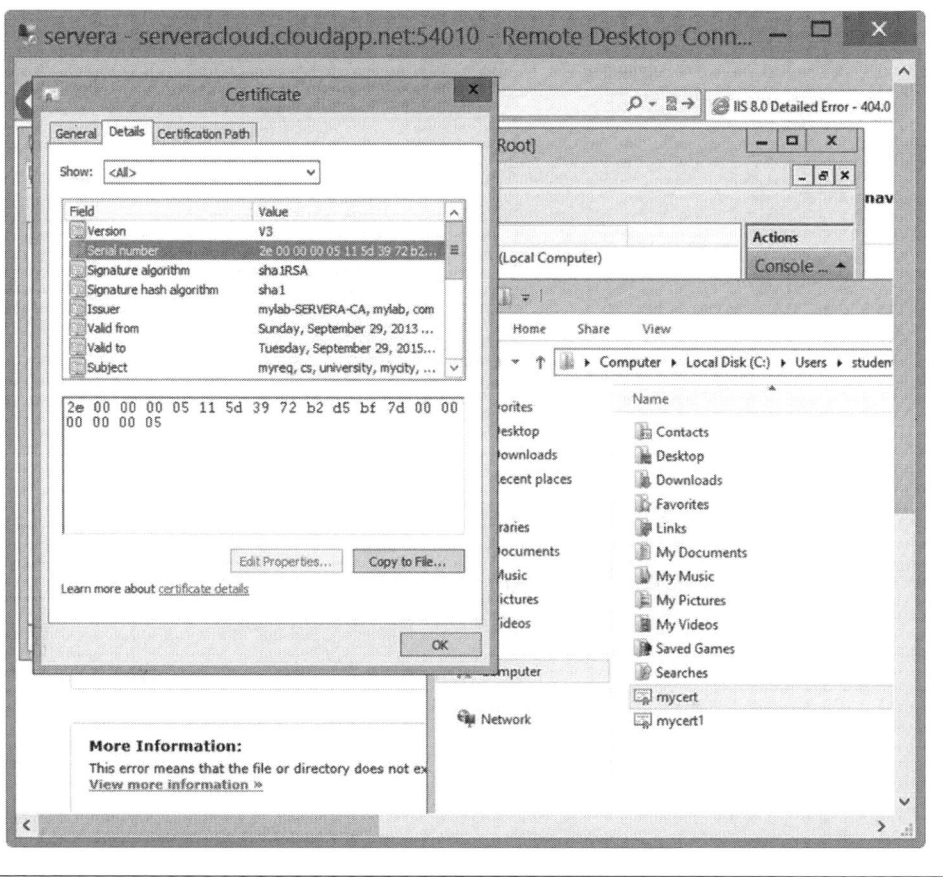

Figure 7.60 Serial number.

```
certutil -repairstore my
   2e00000005115d3972b2d5bf7d000000000005
```

Your serial number should be different from the one in Figure 7.61.

15. If successful, you should get the message "command completed successfully" (Figure 7.61).

16. Now, in the IIS dialog, click the **Complete Certificate Request** link as shown in Figure 7.55. In the Specify Certification Authority Response window, browse for and select the certificate file **c:\users\student\mycert.cer** and provide a friendly name for the certificate, then click **OK**. This time, you should have no error message. The newly completed certificate is shown in Figure 7.62.

17. To verify that the private key has been included, in the IIS dialog, select **mycert** and click **View**.

18. As seen in Figure 7.63, the private key is included in the certificate.

19. In the Microsoft Azure Management Portal, shutdown both servera and serverb before exiting the Microsoft Azure Management Portal.

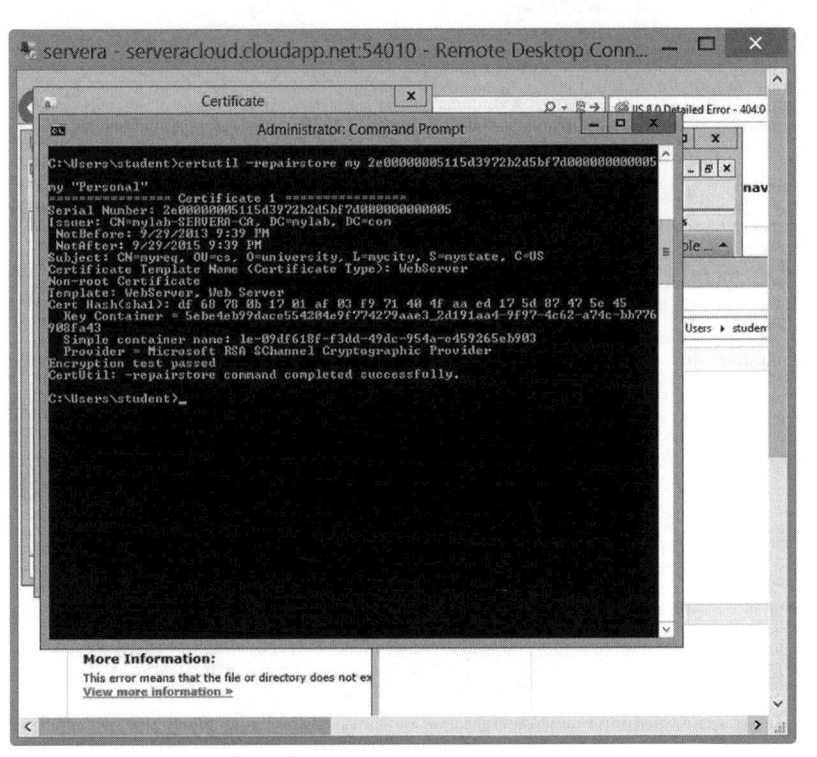

Figure 7.61   Running certutil command.

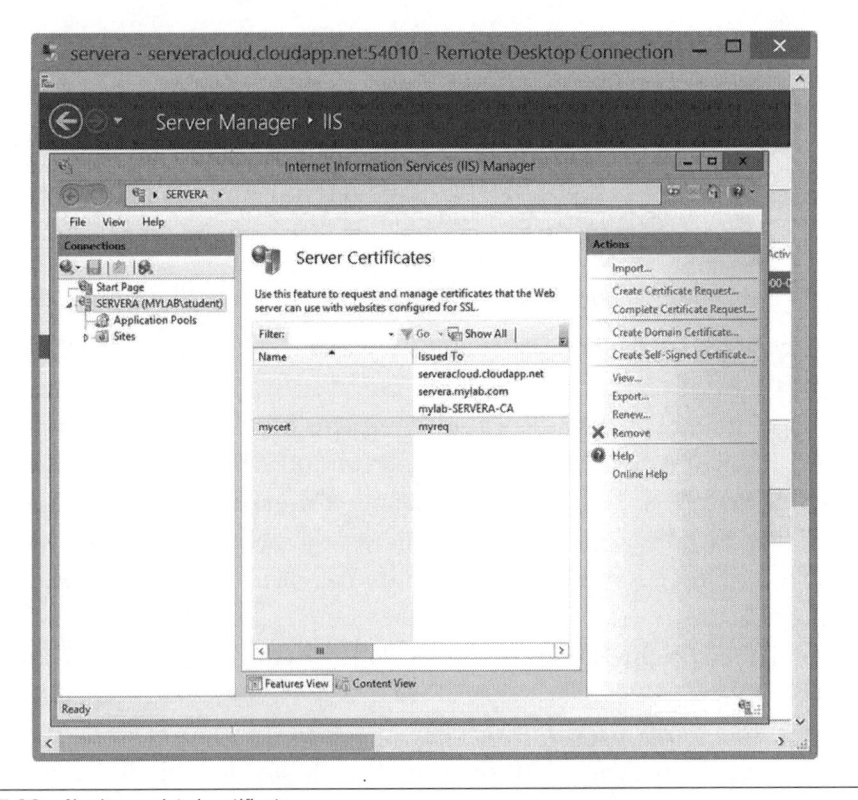

Figure 7.62   Newly completed certificate.

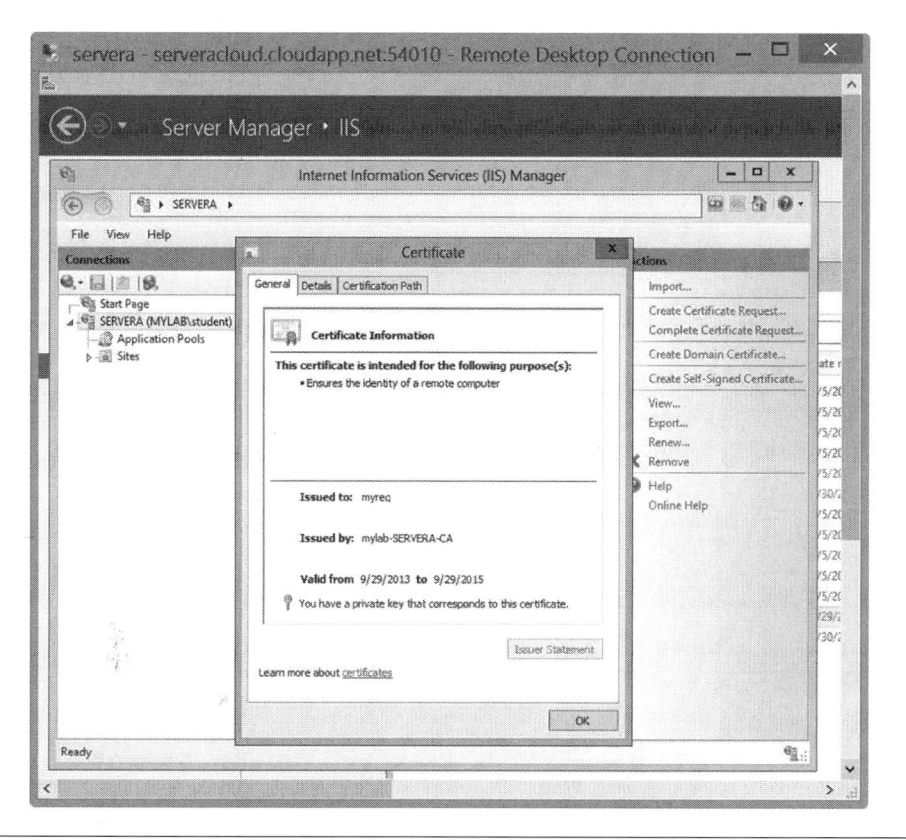

Figure 7.63 Private key included.

In this activity, you have developed a CA on Windows Server. The CA is used to create and manage certificates. This activity illustrates how to request an SSL certificate for a web server and how to repair a certificate to include the private key in the certificate.

7.6 Summary

This chapter discusses security issues related to authentication and encryption for data transferred over a network. In particular, it examines SSL certificates designed to secure private data transferred across the Internet. In today's ecommerce, SSL certificates are use by almost every online business to protect their customer information. This chapter introduces the authentication and encryption methods used by the SSL protocol. To enable SSL on a website, a certificate is issued to identify a web server and to provide the encryption key. The hands-on activities provided by this chapter demonstrate how to create and manage a CA. The hands-on practice also shows how to request and submit SSL certificates for web servers. Network security is the highest priority in network management. More network security–related topics will be covered in the next chapter.

Review Questions

1. How can SSL bring trust to customers?
2. Why HTTPS is also called HTTP over SSL?
3. Which port is used by HTTPS?
4. How are SSL and certificates used to protect customer information?
5. What is the objective of cryptography?
6. What is symmetric encryption?
7. Describe the advantage and disadvantage of symmetric encryption.
8. What is asymmetric encryption?
9. Describe the advantage and disadvantage of asymmetric encryption.
10. Explain how asymmetric encryption works.
11. Name two encryption methods in SSL 3.0 Cipher Suites.
12. How can integrity be violated?
13. What is hash encryption?
14. Describe how hash encryption works.
15. Name two hashing functions provided by Microsoft Azure.
16. What does nonrepudiation mean?
17. What is a digital signature?
18. What tasks can be accomplished by an X. 509 certificate?
19. What tasks can be accomplished by a CA?
20. What is the enterprise root CA?

INTERNET PROTOCOL SECURITY

Objectives

- Understand how IP Security (IPSec) protects Transmission Control Protocol/Internet Protocol (TCP/IP).
- Understand IPSec encryption and IPSec authentication.
- Implement IPSec.

8.1 Introduction

In the previous chapter, the Secure Sockets Layer (SSL) protocol and certificates are introduced for protecting the application layer protocols, especially HTTP during IP communication across the Internet. In this chapter, we are going to examine another security technology used to protect Transmission Control Protocol/Internet Protocol (TCP/IP) used for IP communication over the Internet.

As we know, it is the IP packet that carries data across the Internet. However, TCP/IP created in the early years of the computer industry lacks security measures. IP packets can be captured on the Internet by some free software. Hackers are able to read and alter the data content in a captured packet. The IP Security (IPSec) technology is designed to protect TCP/IP and all the protocols located above the Internet layer. IPSec has been widely used in the areas of virtual private networks (VPNs), routing, and client–server-based applications. The security measures provided by IPSec encrypt the data content carried by IP packets. In addition, IP packets can be digitally signed by IPSec to protect their integrity. In this chapter, you will learn more about IPSec and implement IPSec through hands-on activities.

8.2 TCP/IP-Related Security Issues

After a computer is connected to a network and starts to communicate with other computers through TCP/IP, data communication becomes vulnerable to hackers and computer viruses. During IP communication across the Internet, IP packets are the main target of hackers. The following are some of the common ways that hackers can corrupt and eavesdrop on IP communication:

- *Packet sniffing*: With older network protocols such as IP, which transmits data in clean text, data content is readable by anyone who can capture the packet.

There is a lot of free software available on the web that hackers can use to easily capture an IP packet. The software that can be used to capture IP packets is called a packet sniffer. The packet sniffer can be used to view data content stored in a packet. It is particularly harmful if the packet contains user names, passwords, and financial information.

- *IP spoofing*: IP spoofing is another way to intrude a network. From captured IP packets, hackers can obtain the source and destination IP addresses. Through these IP addresses, they are able to gain unauthorized access to computer systems. In an IP spoofing process, a hacker modifies the packet header so that the source address appears to be sent by a trusted host to gain the trust of the victim computer. Once the source address is changed to the hacker's IP address, all the receivers will respond to the hacker. In such a way, the hacker can cause great damage if all the information is returned to the hacker.

- *Denial-of-service*: The denial-of-service attack can be performed by sending a sequence of requests for a network service. When the server cannot handle so many requests, the server will shut down the service. Most of the time, the protocols such as Hypertext Transfer Protocol (HTTP) or File Transfer Protocol (FTP) are used to attack the web server or FTP server. Sometimes, protocols such as TCP/IP and ICMP can also be used by hackers to flood servers with junk network packets or false information.

- *Man-in-the-middle*: During the asymmetric encryption process, the public key is delivered to the sender for encrypting the data content. However, a hacker can intercept and replace the original public key with his own public key. As the sender encrypts the data with the hacker's public key, the hacker is able use his own private key to decrypt the message. Once the message is decrypted, the hacker can make some changes to the data content. Then, the hacker re-encrypts the modified message with the receiver's public key and retransmits the modified message to the receiver.

- *Data replay*: Data replay is a process that makes a stream of continuous snapshots of data. Originally, data replay is used to back up data for recovery. However, hackers can use the same process to cause some damage. Once an IP packet is captured by a hacker, the hacker can replay the packet repeatedly. If the packet is for withdrawing money from a bank, the data replay can continue to withdraw money repeatedly.

All these security issues are related to IP packets. During IP communication, the packets can be captured, viewed, altered, replaced, and duplicated. These hacked packets can cause some significant damage to an organization. IPSec is the technology designed to deal with these security problems. The next section describes how IPSec works to protect IP packets.

8.3 IP Security

IPSec is designed for securely exchanging IP packets at the Internet layer. As an Internet layer protocol, IPSec can secure protocols located in the layers above the Internet layer. It can protect protocols such as HTTP in the application layer. It also protects the TCP protocol in the transport layer as well as the IP protocol in the Internet layer. IPSec secures packet transmission in three different ways:

1. IPSec uses encryption to maintain confidentiality.
2. IPSec uses authentication to make sure that users and network hosts involved in data communication are trusted.
3. IPSec uses the digital signature to prevent data content from being altered in a packet.

IPSec encryption can run under two different modes: the tunnel mode and transport mode. With the tunnel mode, the IP communication between two networks is encrypted. With the transport mode, the IP communication between two network hosts is encrypted.

8.3.1 Tunnel Mode

The encryption or authentication run under the tunnel mode protects the communication between two routers. When a network host wants to deliver data to another host of a different network, the network host first sends the data to the router that is physically linked to another router. There is no encryption or authentication for IP communication between the network host and its gateway router. Before the router transfers the data to the other router, the encryption or authentication is applied to the IP packet. Then, the secured data are delivered to the other router. Once the data are received by the destination router, the destination router decrypts the data and delivers the data to the destination host. Behind the destination router, no encryption or authentication is applied to the data communication within the destination network. The tunnel mode is illustrated in Figure 8.1.

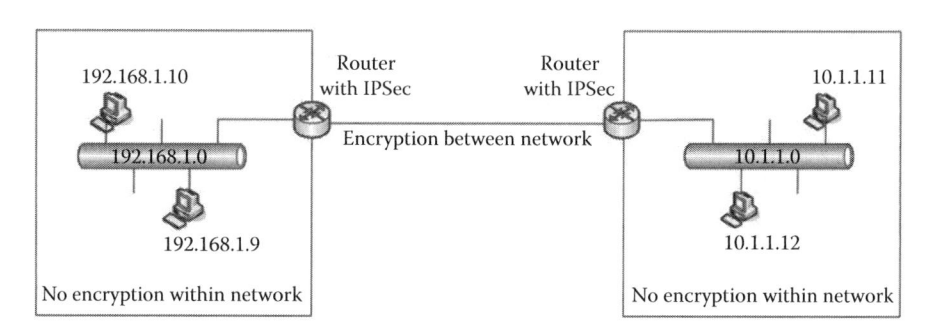

Figure 8.1 Tunnel Mode Encryption.

By providing encryption or authentication for the IP communication between two routers, the communication between the two networks is protected. Performance can also be improved by using the tunnel mode since it does not require each individual network host to support the IPSec technology. On the other hand, by not providing encryption or authentication within a network, the IP communication within the network is not protected.

8.3.2 Transport Mode

The encryption or authentication run under the transport mode protects the IP communication between two network hosts. Before the sender delivers data to the destination, the IP packet is secured by the sender. After the secured data reach the receiver, the receiver decrypted the data to get the original message. It is required that the hosts involved in the IP communication must support IPSec. Servers and routers can be configured to support IPSec. However, some other network hosts such as network printers are not capable of supporting IPSec. Therefore, the transport mode encryption cannot run on every network host. Figure 8.2 illustrates the transport mode encryption.

While implementing IPSec, one can use either the tunnel mode or transport mode. Depending on the way the authentication and encryption are implemented, the tunnel mode or the transport mode can also be combined with two algorithms, Authentication Header (AH) and Encapsulation Security Payload (ESP). During the configuration of IPSec, a network administrator can specify whether to use the AH algorithm or the ESP algorithm (Figure 8.3).

If authentication, not encryption, is the required security measure, the tunnel mode or the transport mode can team up with the AH algorithm to secure IP communication. The combination is called AH tunnel mode or AH transport mode. In addition, to make sure that the content carried by a packet is not altered during transmission, the AH algorithm adds the digital signature and the checksum. When the AH algorithm is used, the IP packet is encapsulated with AH and the IP header. The original

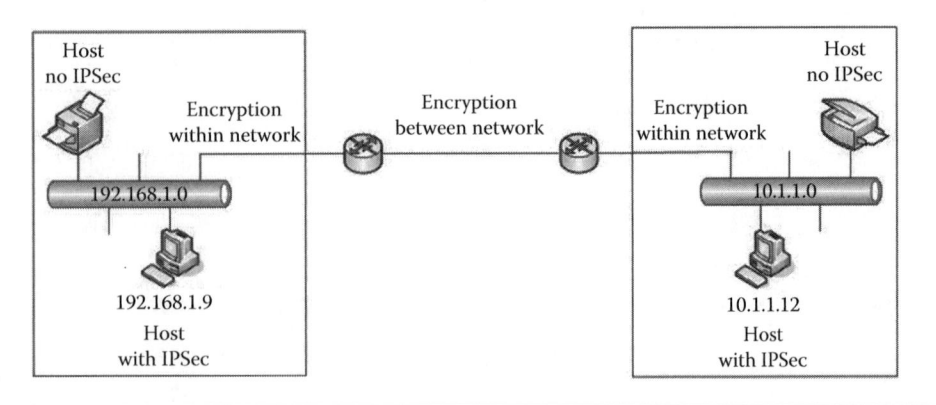

Figure 8.2   Transport Mode Encryption.

Custom Security Method Settings   X

Specify the settings for this custom security method.

☐ Data and address integrity without encryption (AH) :
  Integrity algorithm:

  | SHA1 | ⌄ |

☑ Data integrity and encryption (ESP):
  Integrity algorithm:

  | SHA1 | ⌄ |

  Encryption algorithm:

  | 3DES | ⌄ |

Session key settings:

  ☐ Generate a new key every: ☐ Generate a new key every:

  | 100000 | Kbytes | 3600 | seconds

                                        OK   Cancel

Figure 8.3   Selecting Algorithm.

IP packet and the additional AH and IP header are digitally signed for integrity and authentication. AH is used to make sure that both ends of the communication are trusted. When AH is used with the transport port mode, it is added to the original IP packet as shown in Figure 8.4.

When AH is used with the tunnel mode, AH and an additional IP header are added to the original IP packet. The additional IP header contains IP addresses of the source and destination routers, which serve as the tunnel end points. AH digitally signs the original IP packet, the AH header as well as the additional IP header. The illustration of the AH tunnel mode is given in Figure 8.5.

If both authentication and encryption are required as the security measure, the tunnel mode or the transport mode can team up the ESP algorithm to secure

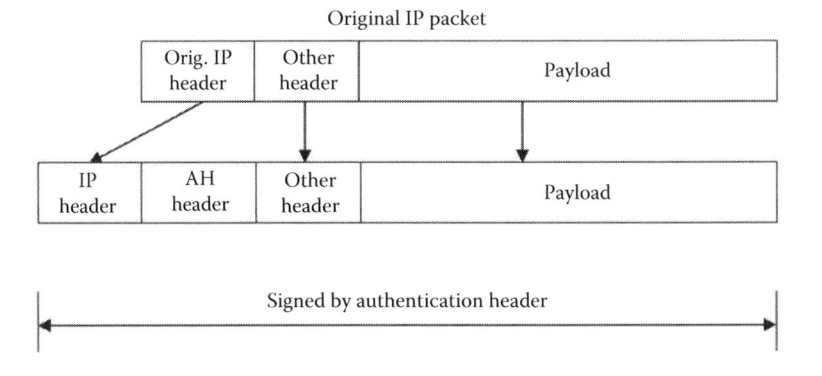

Figure 8.4   AH Transport Mode.

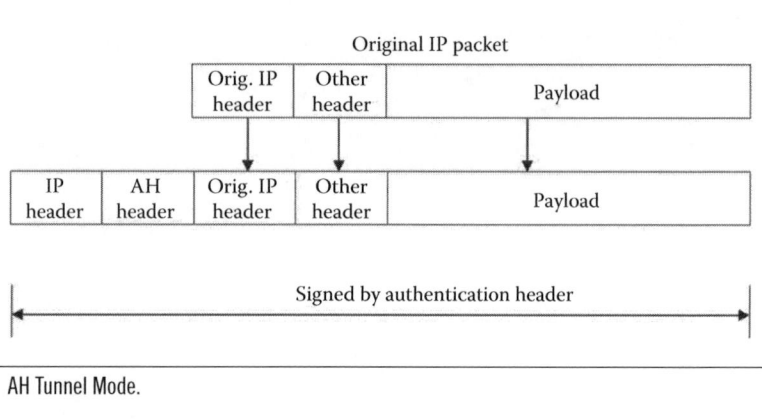

Figure 8.5   AH Tunnel Mode.

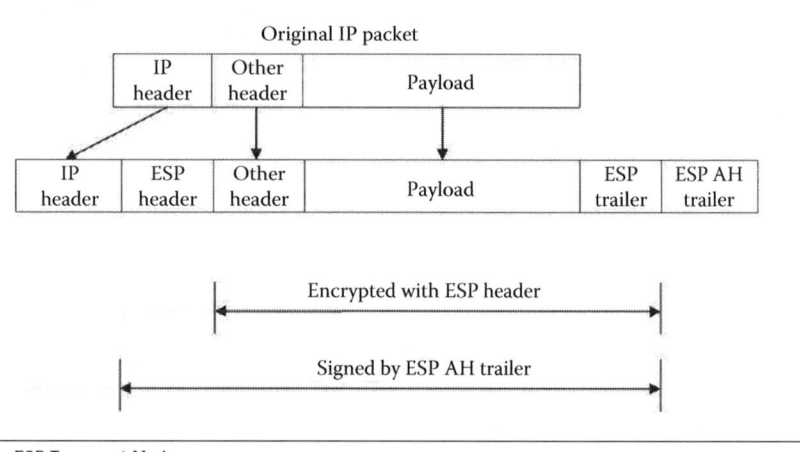

Figure 8.6   ESP Transport Mode.

IP communication. When ESP is used with the transport mode, three sections, the ESP header, ESP trailer, and ESP AH trailer, are added to the original IP packet. In the ESP transport mode, the payload section and the ESP trailer are encrypted with the ESP header to protect confidentiality. The ESP header, IP header, and ESP AH trailer are unencrypted. The ESP AH trailer digitally signs the ESP header, ESP trailer, and the payload section to make sure that the content carried by a packet is not altered during transmission. Figure 8.6 illustrates the ESP transport mode.

When ESP is used with the tunnel mode, the sections of the ESP header, ESP trailer, additional IP header, and ESP AH trailer are added to the original IP packet. The additional IP header is used for the IP communication between two routers. The tunnel mode encrypts the payload as well as the original header. The encryption by the tunnel mode is more secure by hiding the original IP header. In addition, the ESP AH trailer digitally signs the original IP packet as well as the ESP header and the ESP trailer. The ESP tunnel mode is illustrated in Figure 8.7.

With the encryption and authentication mechanisms provided by IPSec, all protocols located on layer higher than the Internet layer are automatically protected. In addition, with the tunnel mode, the network hosts that are not IPSec enabled can also

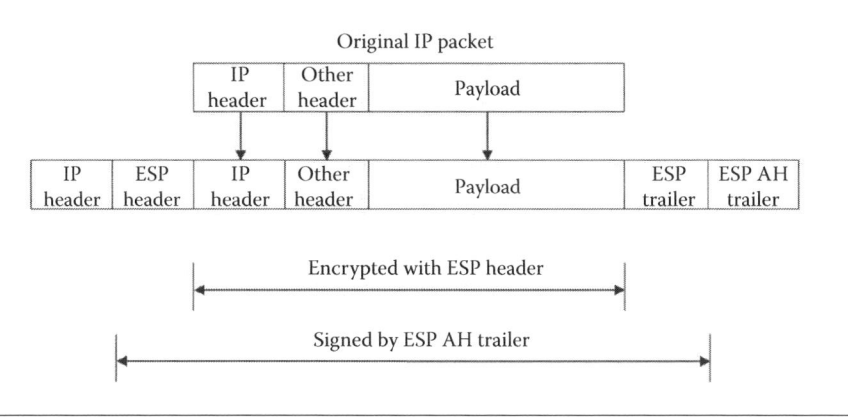

Figure 8.7   ESP Tunnel Mode.

be protected by IPSec. With these advantages, the IPSec technology has been widely used by VPNs to secure IP communication on the public Internet.

On the other hand, IPSec has a few disadvantages. It consumes more computing resources due to the computation of encryption/decryption and authentication. It consumes more network bandwidth and has lower performance than that of a regular IP packet. When the tunnel mode is implemented, the local network is not protected by IPSec. This may open the door for network viruses such as worms, which can easily spread across the entire local network. When the transport mode is implemented, not all the network hosts can be protected by IPSec. IPSec has difficulty in dealing with the restrictions set on firewalls. It requires more experience to configure IPSec. IPSec may not be a good choice for the communication between your home network and a virtual network in the cloud. IPSec traffic is often blocked by the Internet Service Providers (ISPs) since ISPs consider IPSec traffic as business traffic, and therefore, a higher rate will be charged.

8.4 Creating and Using IP Security (IPSec)

By examining the pros and cons of IPSec, we see IPSec is not for every IP communication. It is only for IP communication that really needs to be secure. An IPSec policy is a way to direct how the operating system uses IPSec. It decides which IP communication needs to be protected by IPSec. It also specifies which authentication or encryption algorithm to use.

When creating IPSec to secure IP traffic, there are two tools available that can accomplish the task. The network administrator can use either IP Security Policy or Windows Firewall with Advanced Security. With the IP Security Policy MMC snap-in, one can configure IPSec policies that can be applied to older network hosts such as computers running on earlier Windows operating systems such as Windows Server 2003. This MMC snap-in is the tool to use if a network includes both new and old Windows operating systems. Although the IP Security Policy MMC snap-in can be used to create IPSec rules for newer version Windows operating systems, it does not have the new features provided by the tool Windows Firewall with Advanced Security. The following briefly describes the tools IP Security Policy and Windows Firewall with Advanced Security.

8.4.1 IP Security Policy

With the IP Security Policy tool, network administrators can specify the encryption to be applied only to a specific application instead of all the applications on the network. Network administrators can configure IPSec policies based on the security requirements of the IP communication. The IPSec policies can be applied to a local computer, a domain member, or a remote computer. An IPSec policy consists of a set of rules including the elements such as the IP filter list, IPSec filter action, authentication method, tunnel endpoint, and connection type. These elements are described in the following.

IP filter list: An IP filter identifies a certain type of IP packets that need to be secured. It can specify an IP address, a network host name, a port, a subnet, a protocol, or a network service such as DHCP or DNS for IPSec protection. For example, if a server is hosting two applications, one is the website for promoting the company and the other one is the database server, SQL Server, for processing the company's information. The company may consider protecting the database server with IPSec. In such a case, the IP communication through the port 1433 should be protected by IPSec. An IP filter list is a collection of IP filters. Figure 8.8 shows the existing IPSec filter lists in Windows Server.

IP filter action: An IP filter action specifies the security action to be used on an IP filter list. The IP filter list and IP filter action together can be used to determine which

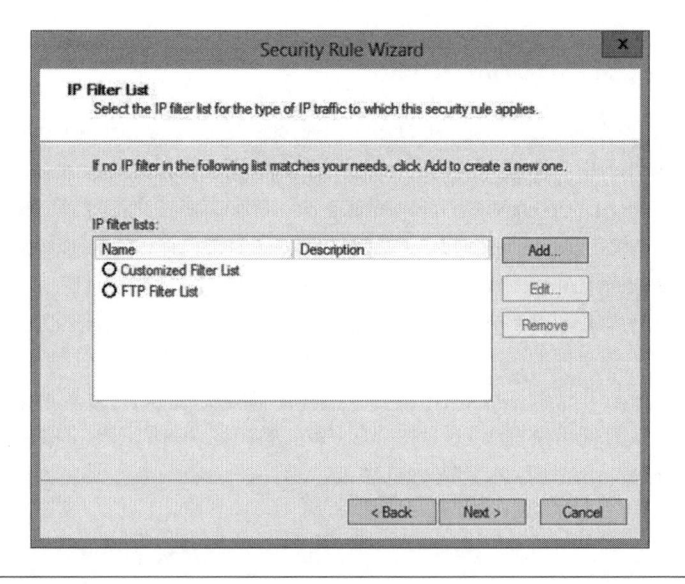

Figure 8.8 IP Filter Lists.

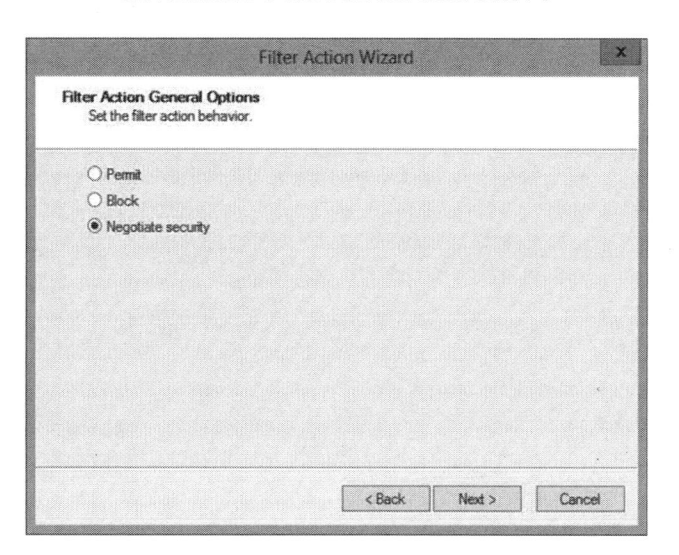

Figure 8.9 Selecting Filter Action.

IP communication should be secured by IPSec and how the IP communication is secured. One can choose the default action shown in Figure 8.9 or create a customized action. The **Permit** option lets the IP communication not be affected by IPSec. The **Block** option stops the IP communication that is specified on the IPSec filter list. The **Negotiate security** option allows the network administrator to specify the encryption method to be used for the IP communication. The IP filter action can also be configured to specify which IPSec mode to use. The network administrator can also decide whether to allow unencrypted IP communication of network hosts that do not support IPSec.

Authentication method: The security policy dictates which security method to use during the authentication process. It also specifies which method to use for the key exchange as shown in Figure 8.10. Kerberos Version 5 is the default authentication method. Kerberos is used for the client and server to verify each other's identity for safe IP communication. Kerberos uses the domain's Active Directory to store its security account information.

Connection type: A connection type specifies which type of connection to use such as remote access connection, LAN connection, or all network connections shown in Figure 8.11.

Tunnel endpoint: When the tunnel mode is implemented, the tunnel endpoint is specified for the IP process (Figure 8.12).

A rule is a collection of these IPSec elements. One or more rules form an IPSec policy. In Windows Server, after an IP policy is created, the default rule is Default Response as shown in Figure 8.13.

By properly configuring the properties and options of IPSec, IP communication can be securely protected without costing a lot of bandwidth and network resources.

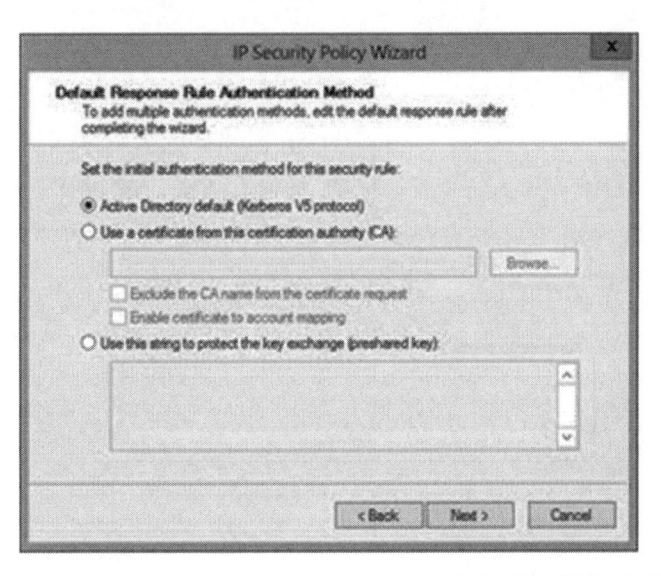

Figure 8.10   Selecting Authentication Method.

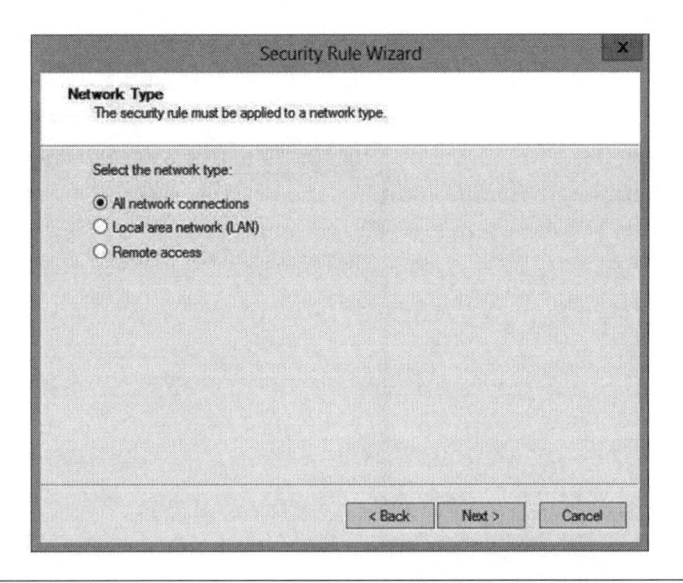

Figure 8.11   Selecting Connection Type.

8.4.2 Windows Firewall with Advanced Security

With IP Security Policy, one can specify a tunnel by providing the IP addresses explicitly for the two endpoints. If one needs to create tunnels from multiple clients to a server, the rules have to be specified for each client. The tool Windows Firewall with Advanced Security has an option **Any** which takes the client computer's IP address (Figure 8.14). This feature allows one rule to be used by multiple clients.

By integrating with the firewall, IPSec policies can be integrated with other technologies. IPSec can be implemented with the Network Access Protection (NAP) technology. NAP is used to prevent unhealthy network hosts from accessing

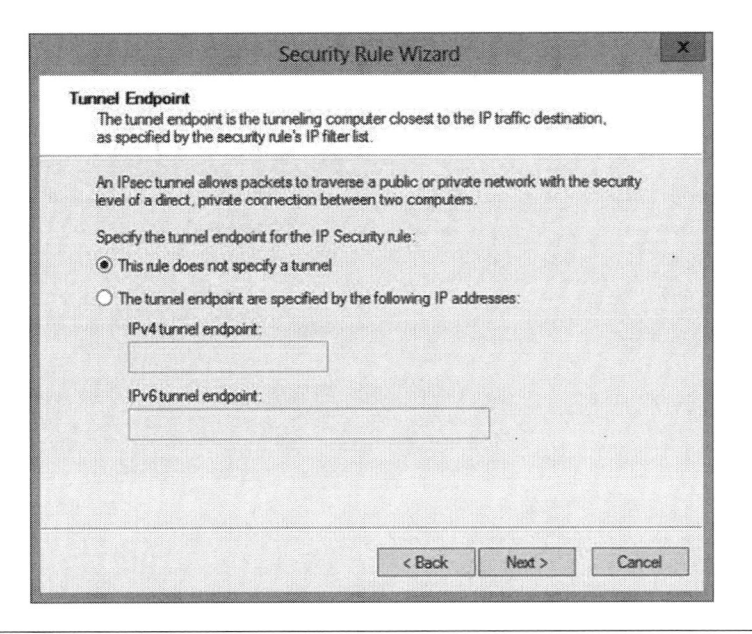

Figure 8.12 Configuration of Endpoint.

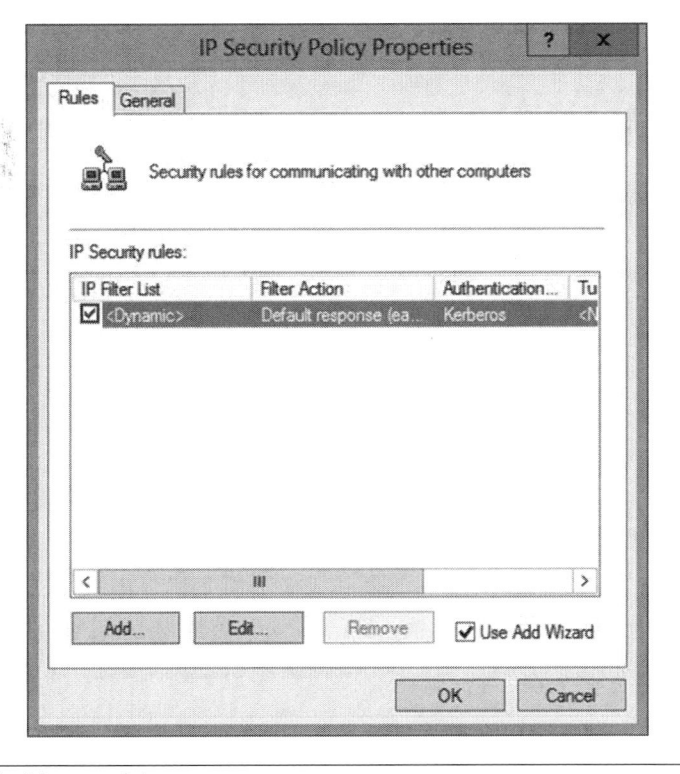

Figure 8.13 Default Response Rule.

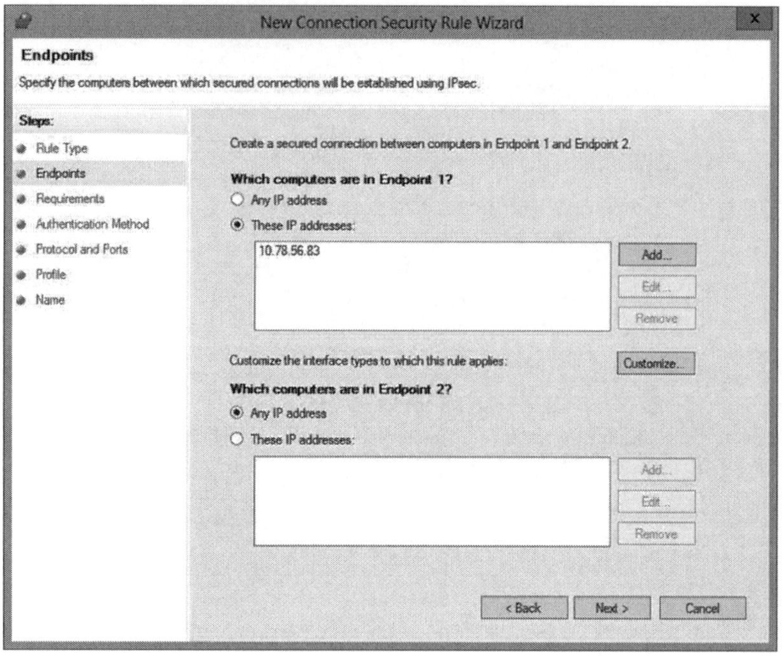

Figure 8.14   Any IP Address.

network resources. The health policy addresses issues related to virus protection, spyware protection, firewall protection, and Windows updates. It is used to evaluate clients that initiate access to network resources. By doing so, noncompliant clients are restricted from accessing the IPSec protected network resources.

The authentication mechanism can be easily enforced before the IP communication gets started. Authentication can be implemented with the following options (Figure 8.15).

- For the option **Request authentication for inbound and outbound connections**, authentication is requested for all IP communication. However, this option allows IP communication that is not authenticated.
- For the option **Require authentication for inbound connections and request authentication for outbound connections**, only the authenticated inbound IP data are accepted.
- For the option **Require authentication for inbound and outbound connections**, only the authenticated IP communication is accepted.
- For the option **Do not authenticate**, no IP communication is authenticated.

Figure 8.16 shows the available authentication methods for secure connections.

IPSec can be configured to shield a network host from those unauthorized network hosts. With the tool Windows Firewall with Advanced Security, the network administrator can define the isolation policy. Isolation can be applied to a tunnel, or a server, server to server, a domain, or an entire network level (Figure 8.17).

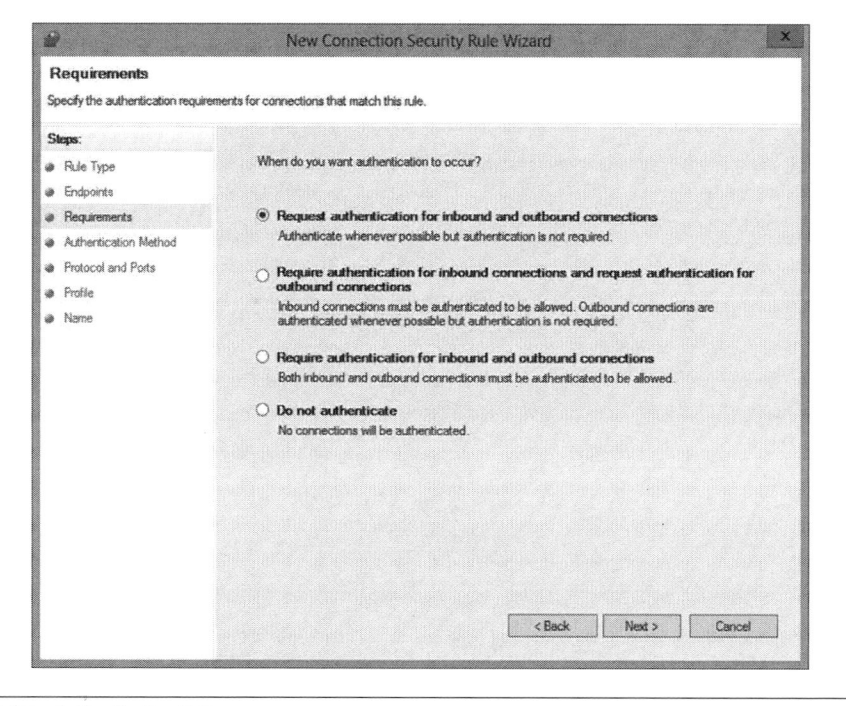

Figure 8.15 Authentication Options.

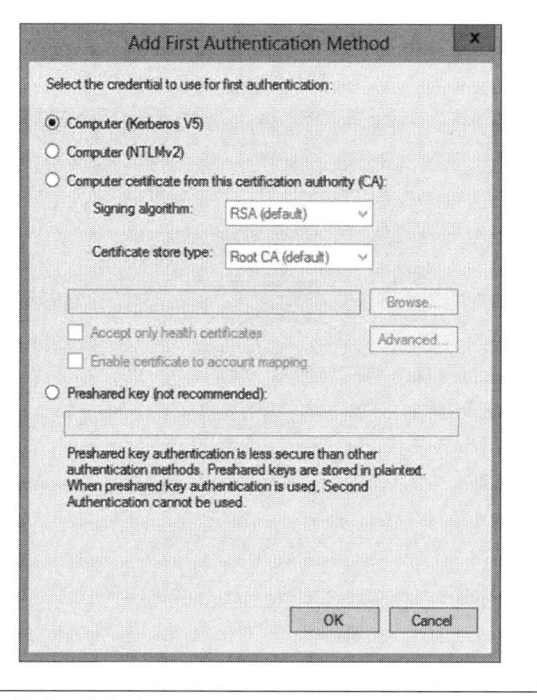

Figure 8.16 Adding Authentication Method.

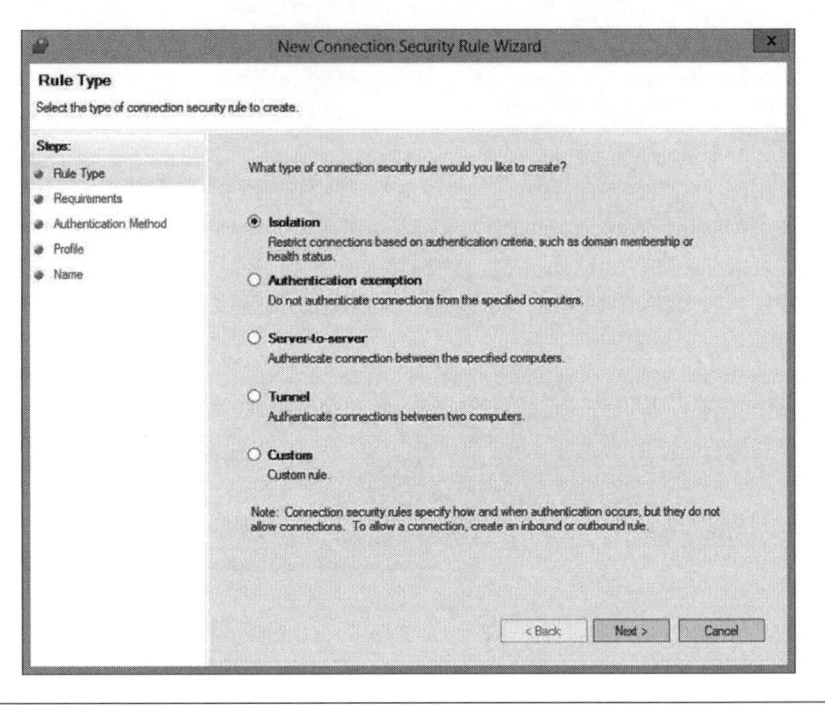

Figure 8.17   Selecting Isolation.

In the following, we will implement IPSec with both IP Security Policy and Windows Firewall with Advanced Security tools. Activity 8.1 covers the IP Security Policy and Activity 8.2 covers Windows Firewall with Advanced Security.

Activity 8.1: IPSec Implementation with IP Security Policy

In this activity, you will use the tool IP Security Policy MMC snap-in to implement an IP security policy, IPSec filter rule, IPSec filter list, and IPSec filter action.

1. Log on to the Microsoft Azure Management Portal.
2. Connect to the virtual machine **servera** and log on as **student**.
3. In Server Manager, click **Tools** and select **Local Security Policy** (Figure 8.18).
4. Right click IP Security Policies on Local Computer and select Create IP Security Policy (Figure 8.19).
5. On the Welcome page, click **Next**.
6. On the IP Security Name page, enter the name **IP Security Policy** and the description **Secure ICMP Traffic**. Then, click **Next** (Figure 8.20).
7. In the Requests for Secure Communication page, check the checkbox **Activate the default response rule**, and click **Next** (Figure 8.21).
8. Make sure that the option **Active Directory default** is selected, and click **Next**.

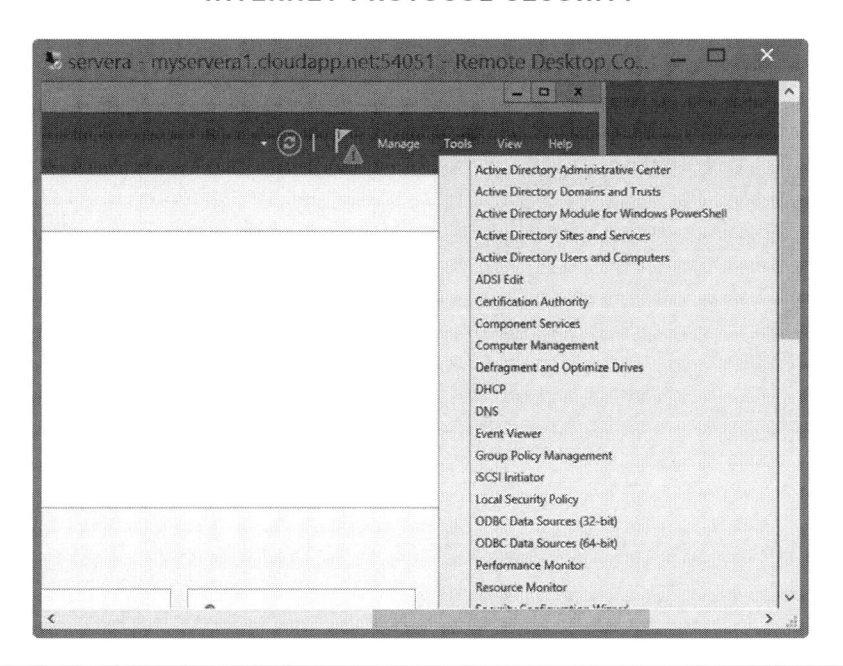

Figure 8.18 Opening Local Security Policy Dialog.

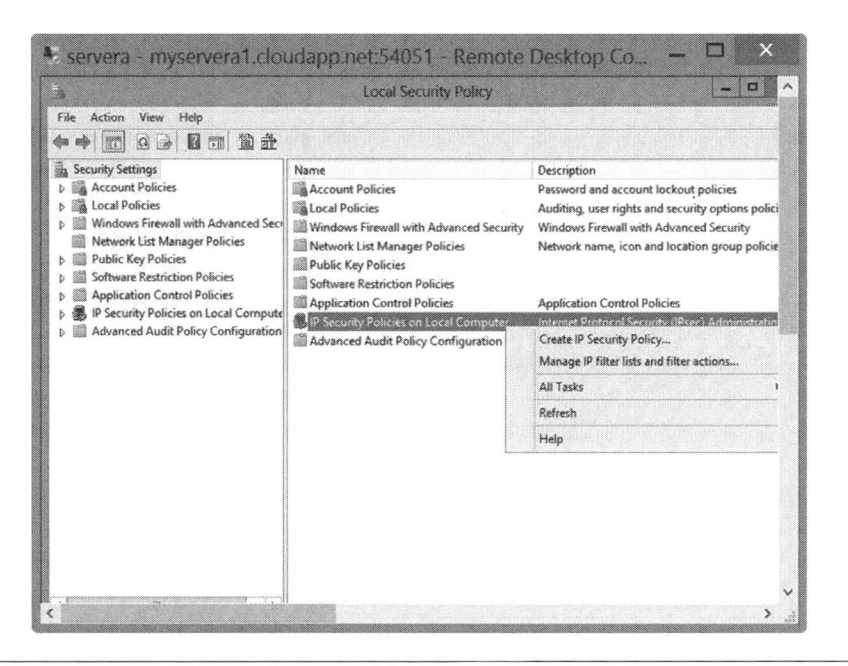

Figure 8.19 Creating IP Security Policy.

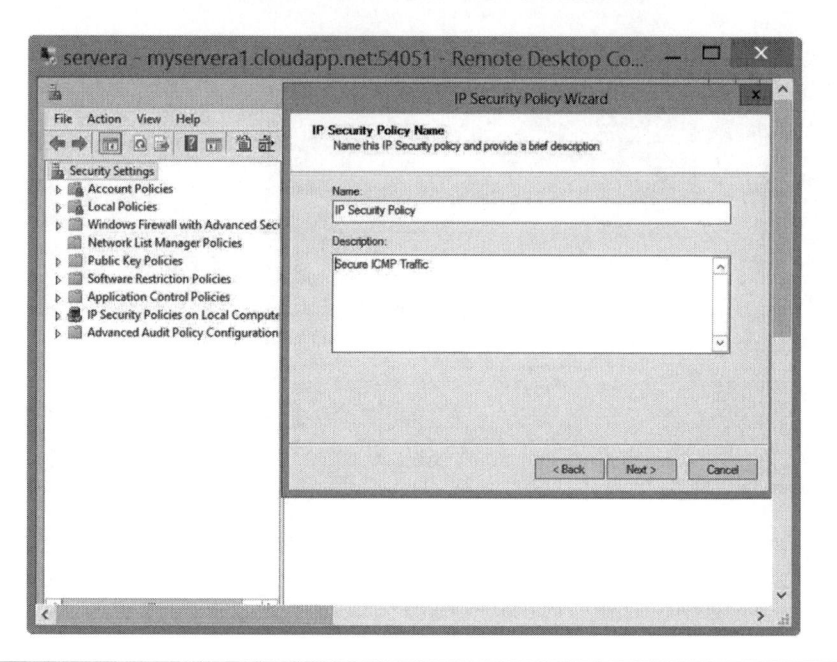

Figure 8.20   IP Security Policy Name.

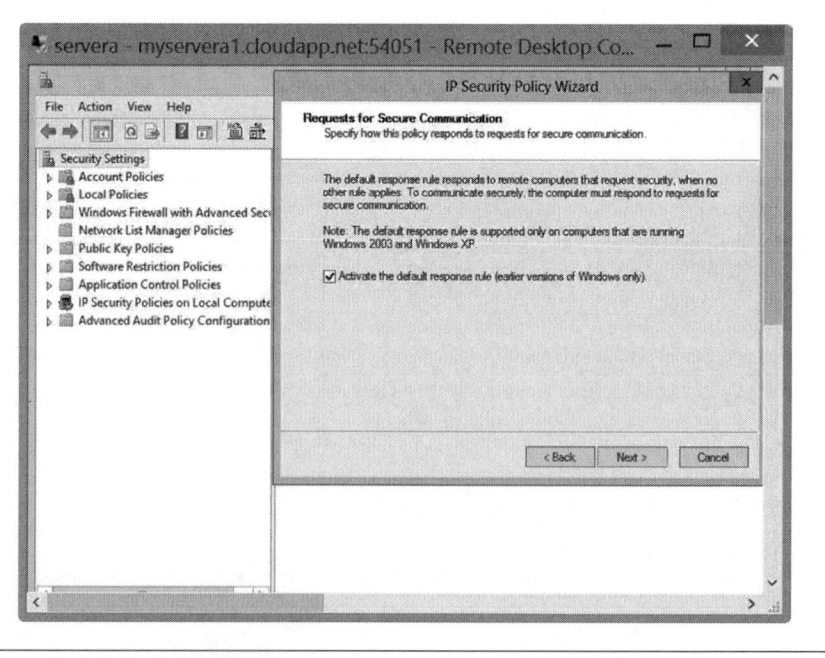

Figure 8.21   Requests for Secure Communication.

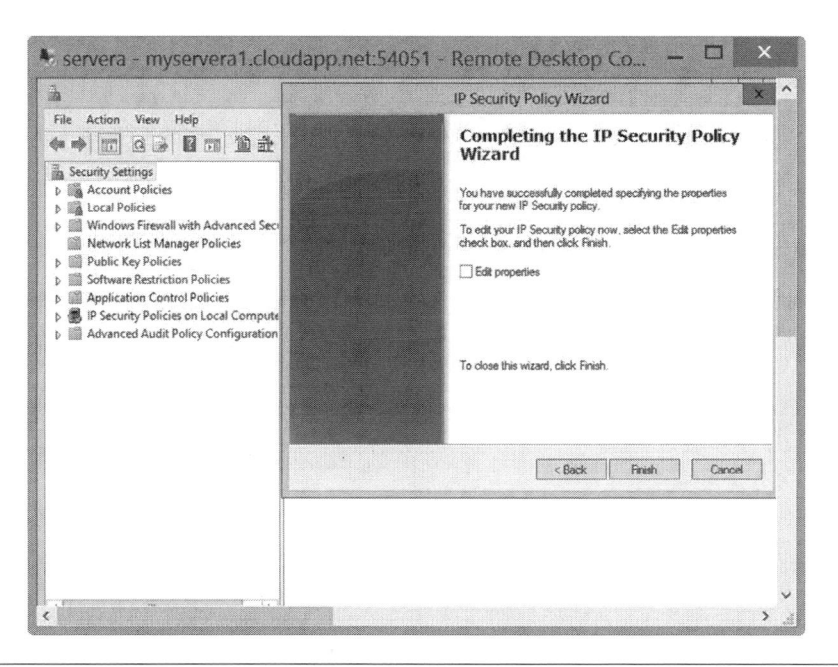

Figure 8.22 Deselecting Edit Properties.

9. Deselect **Edit properties** (Figure 8.22), and click **Finish**.
10. Double click **IP Security Policies on Local Computer** in the left pane; you will see that **IP Security Policy** has been created (Figure 8.23).

Creating new IPSec filter rule: Follow the steps below to create a new IPSec filter rule.

1. Right click **IP Security Policy** and select **Properties** (Figure 8.24).
2. Click **Add** to open the Security Rule Wizard. Click **Next** on the Welcome page.
3. On the Tunnel Endpoint page, make sure that the option **This rule does not specify a tunnel** is checked (Figure 8.25), and click **Next**.
4. On the Network Type page, make sure that the **All network connections** option is selected (Figure 8.26), and click **Next**.
5. On the IP Filter List page, click **Add**.
6. In the IP Filter List dialog, change the name to **ICMP Filter List** (Figure 8.27), and click **Add**.
7. On the Welcome page, click **Next** four times to go to the IP Protocol Type page. From the Select a protocol type dropdown list, select **ICMP** (Figure 8.28). Then, click **Next**.
8. Click **Finish**. In the IP Filter List dialog, click **OK** (Figure 8.29).
9. On the IP Filter List page, select **ICMP Filter List** (Figure 8.30), and click **Next**.
10. On the Filter Action page, click **Add**. Click **Next** on the Welcome page.

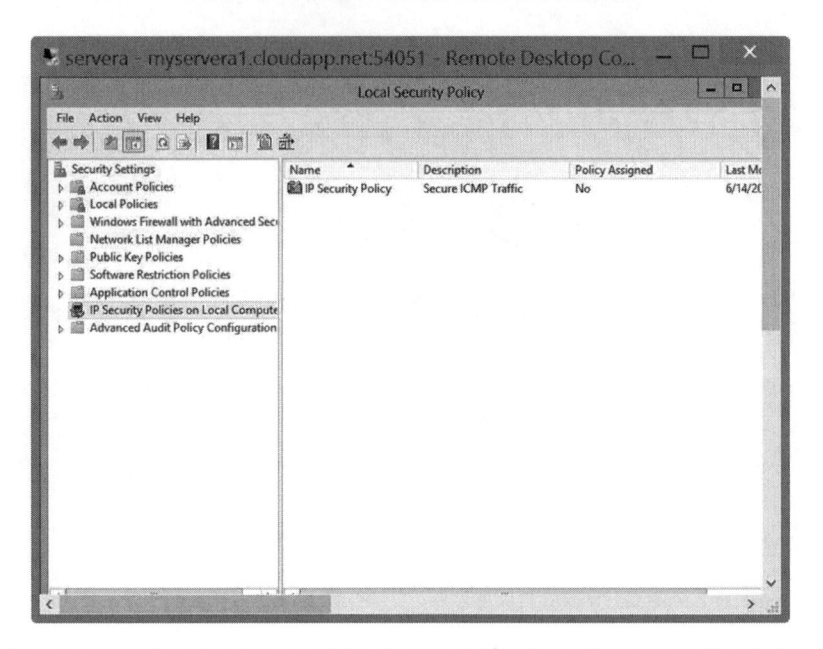

Figure 8.23   IP Security Policy.

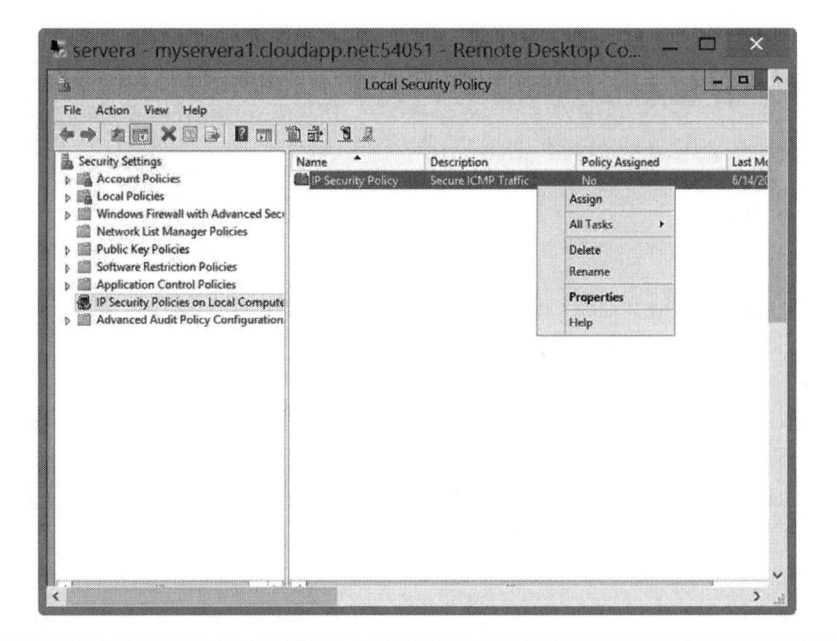

Figure 8.24   Creating New IPSec Filter Rule.

11. Change the name to **ICMP Filter Action** (Figure 8.31), and click **Next**.
12. Check the **Permit** option (Figure 8.32), and click **Next**.
13. Click **Finish**.
14. On the Filter Action page, select the **ICMP Filter Action** option (Figure 8.33), and click **Next**.
15. Click **Finish**. Then, click **OK** on the IP Security Policy Properties page.

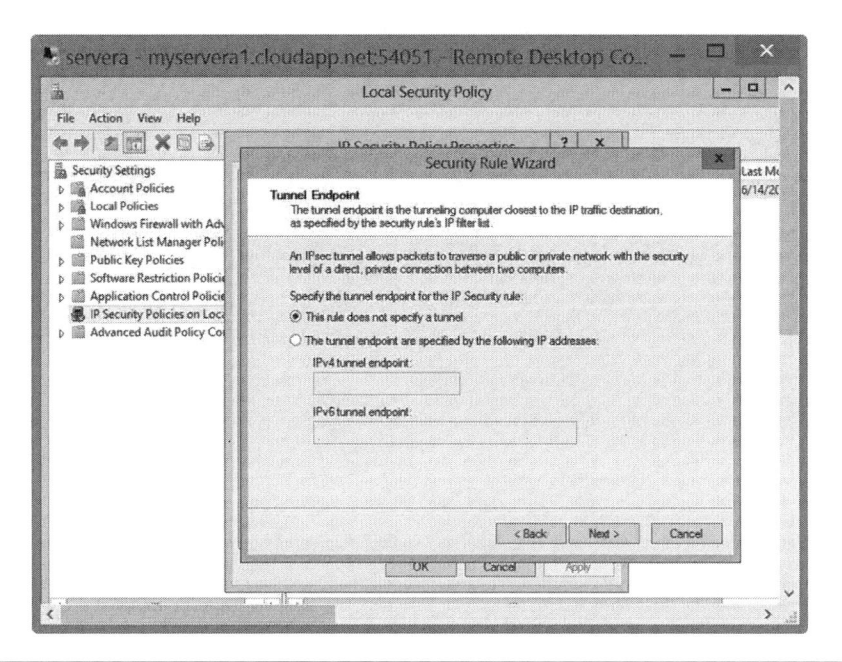

Figure 8.25 Specifying Tunnel Endpoint.

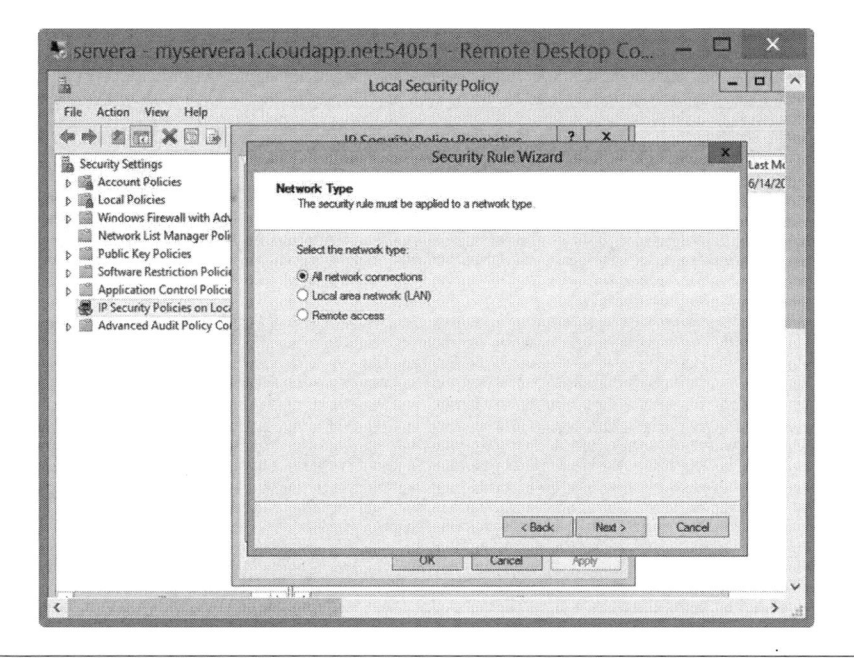

Figure 8.26 Selecting Network Type.

Creating customized IPSec filter list: In this part of the activity, you will learn how to create a customized IPSec filter list.

1. Right click IP Security Policies on Local Computer and select Manage IP filter lists and filter actions (Figure 8.34).
2. In the **Manage IP filter lists and filter actions** dialog, click **Add**.

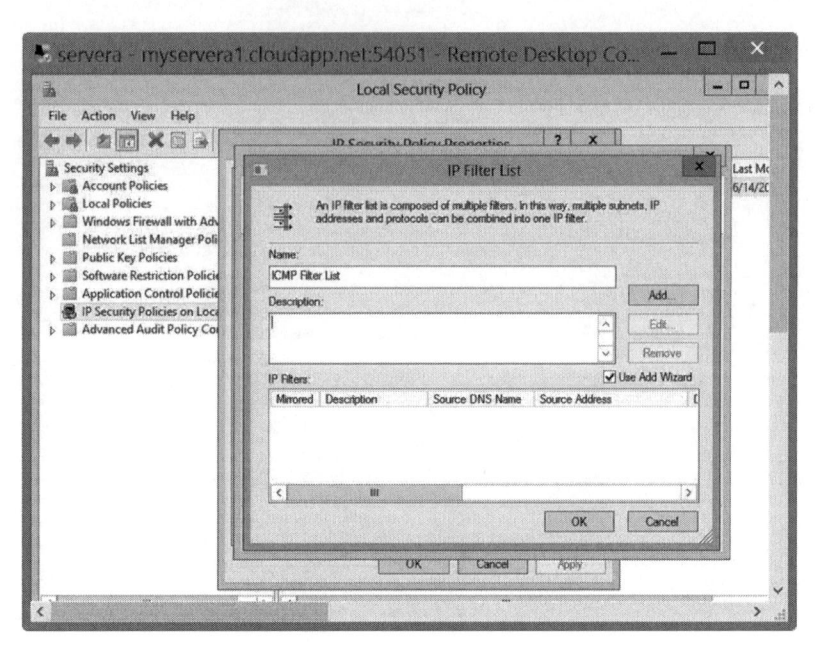

Figure 8.27   IP Filter List Configuration.

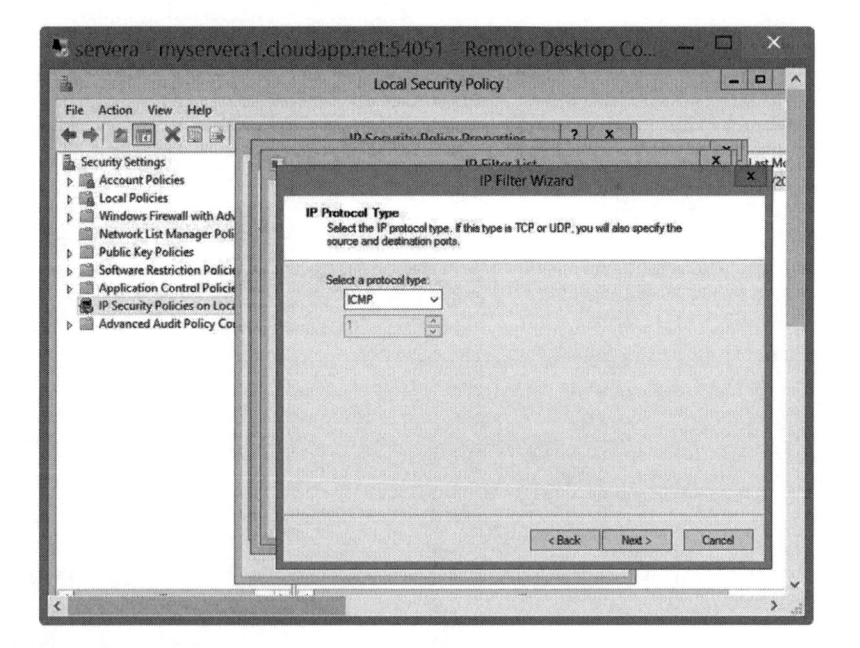

Figure 8.28   Selecting IP Protocol Type.

3. Change the name to **Customized Filter List** (Figure 8.35), and click **Add**.
4. Click **Next** on the Welcome page.
5. Click **Next** on the IP Filter Description and Mirrored Properties page.
6. From the Source address dropdown list, select **My IP Address** (Figure 8.36), and click **Next**.

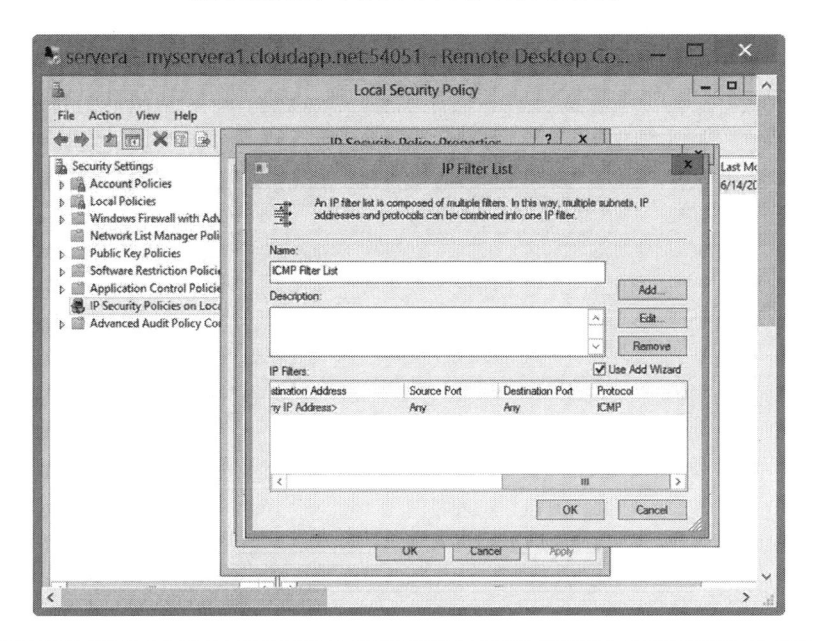

Figure 8.29 Completing IP Filter List Configuration.

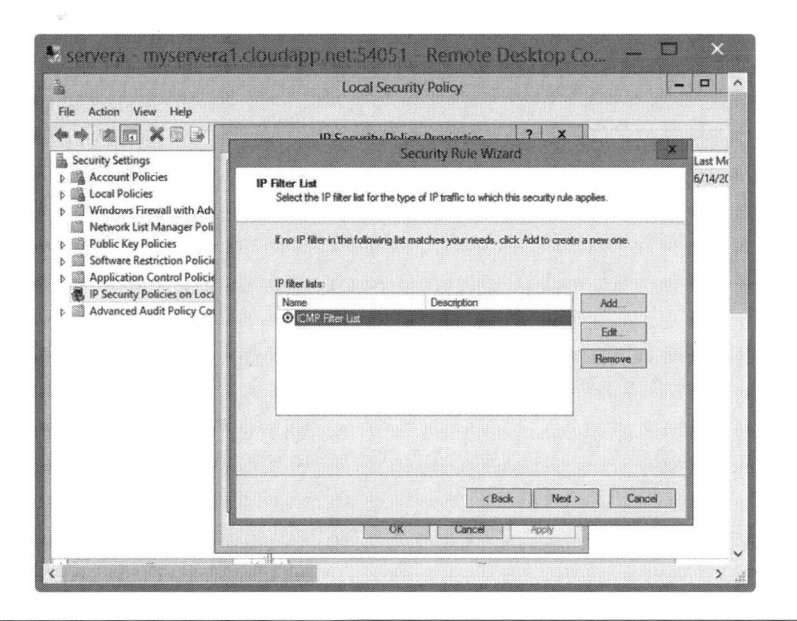

Figure 8.30 Selecting IP Filter List.

7. From the Destination address dropdown list, select **Any IP Address** (Figure 8.37) and click **Next**.

8. From the Select a protocol type dropdown list, select **TCP** (Figure 8.38) and click **Next**.

9. Select the option **From this port** and type the port number **23** to secure the Telnet protocol (Figure 8.39). Then, click **Next**.

10. Click **Finish**. Then, click **OK** in the IP Filter List dialog.

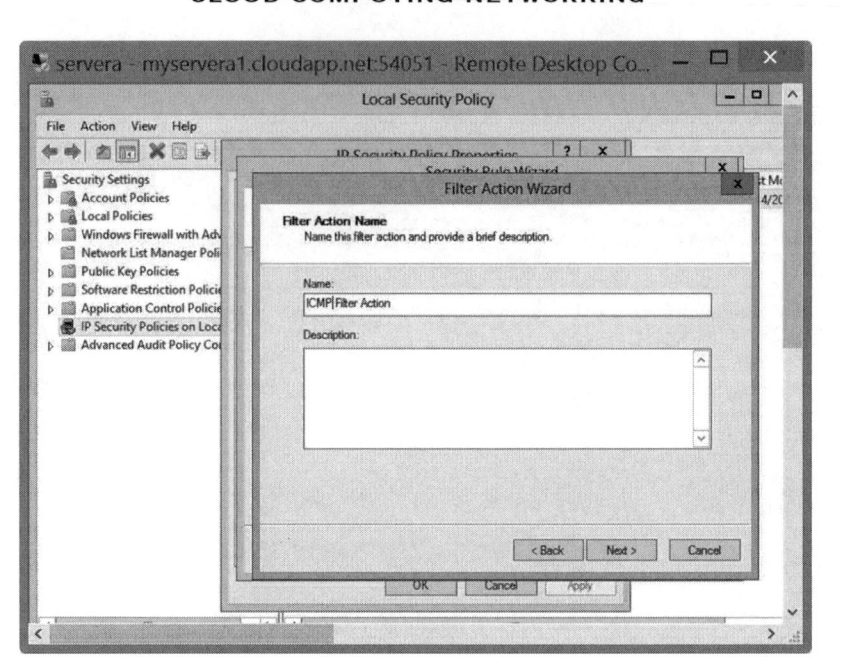

Figure 8.31   Configuring IP Filter Action.

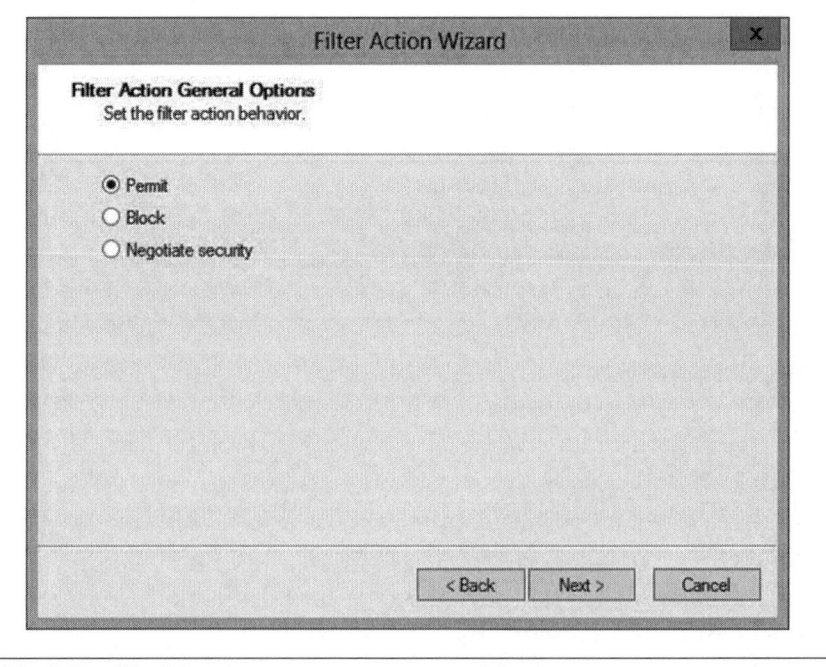

Figure 8.32   Setting Filter Action.

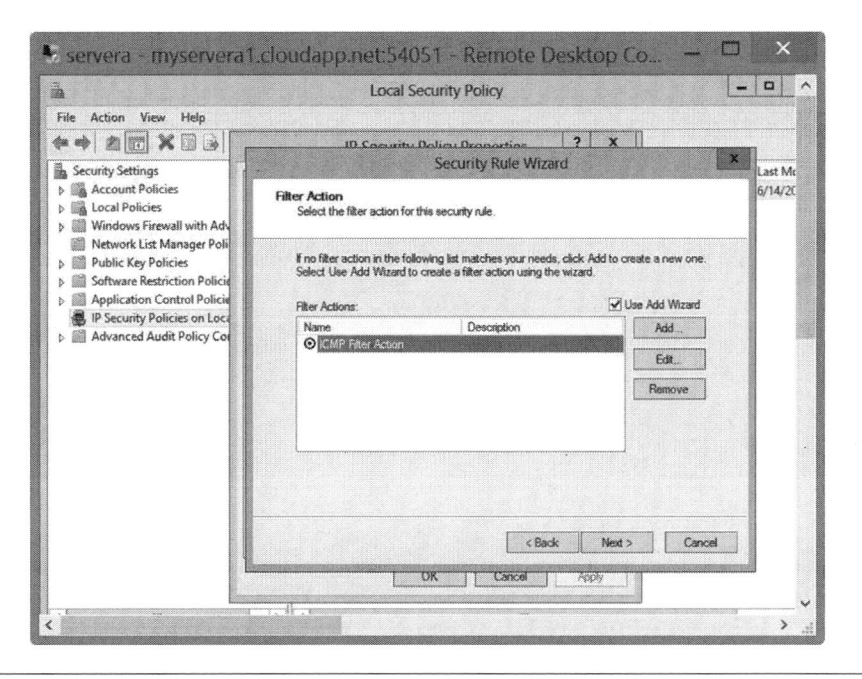

Figure 8.33   Selecting Filter Action for Security Rule.

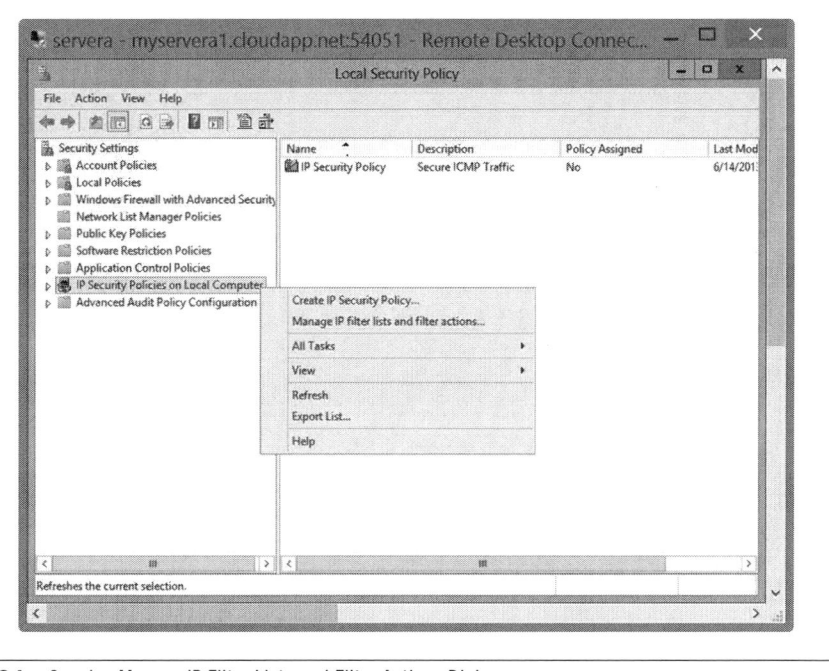

Figure 8.34   Opening Manage IP Filter Lists and Filter Actions Dialog.

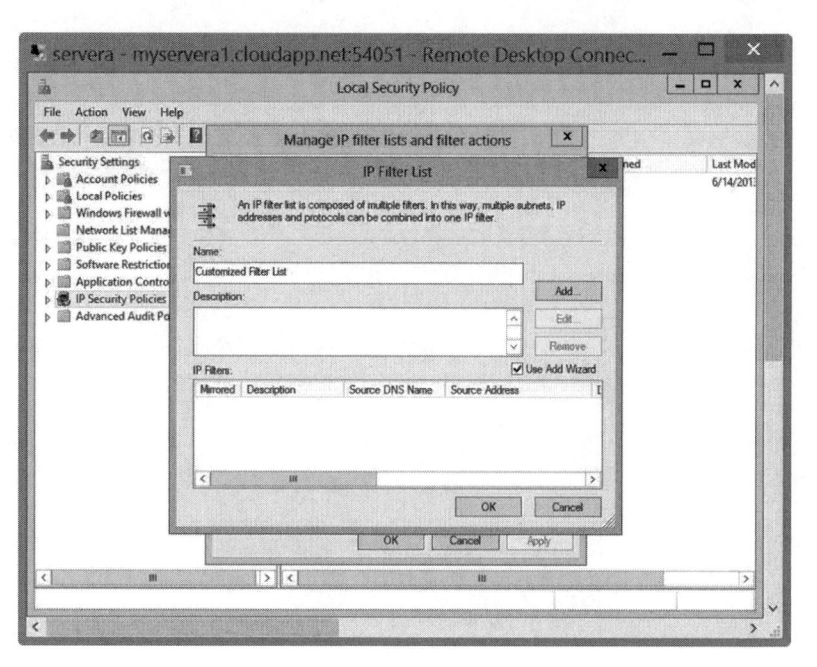

Figure 8.35 Naming Customized Filter List.

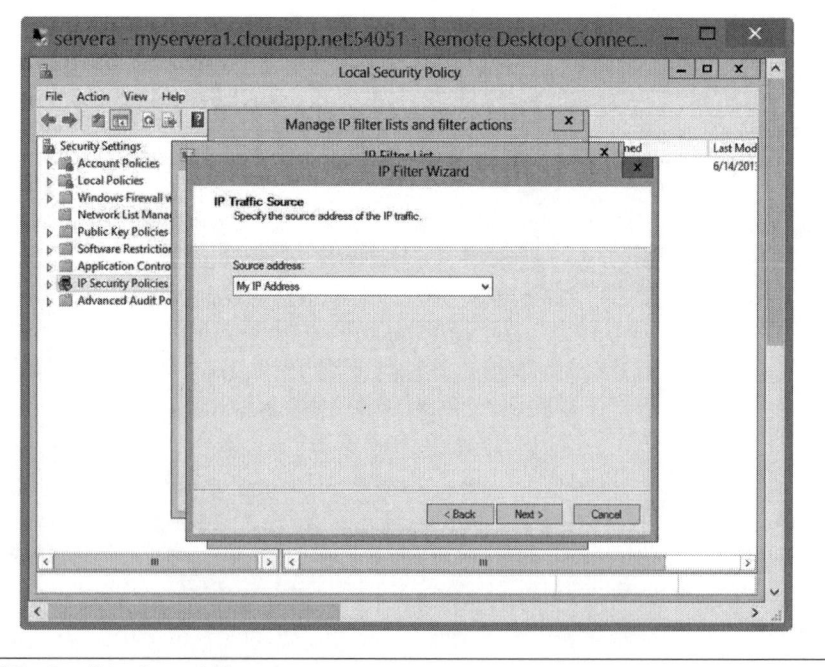

Figure 8.36 Specifying Source Address.

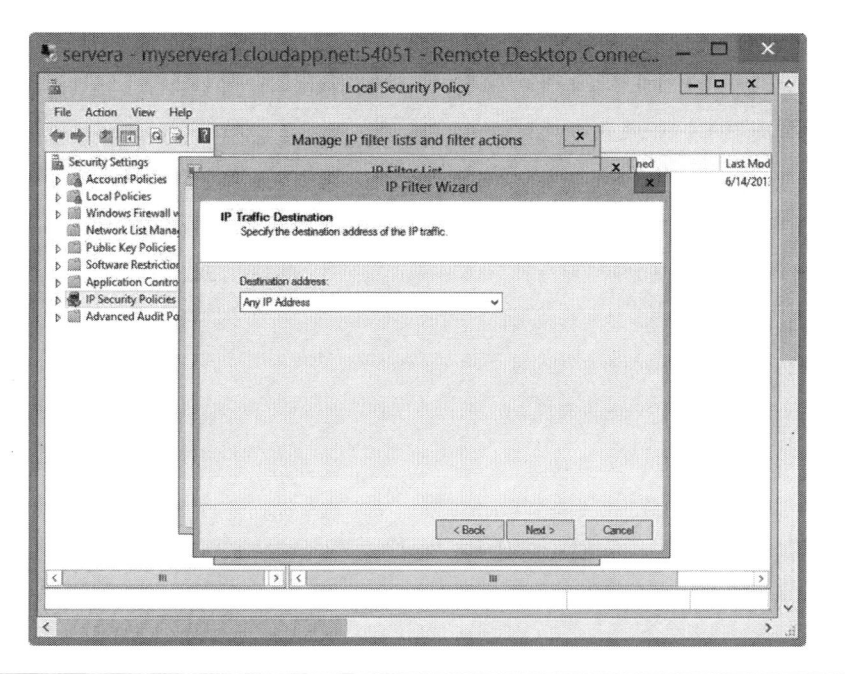

Figure 8.37   Specifying Destination Address.

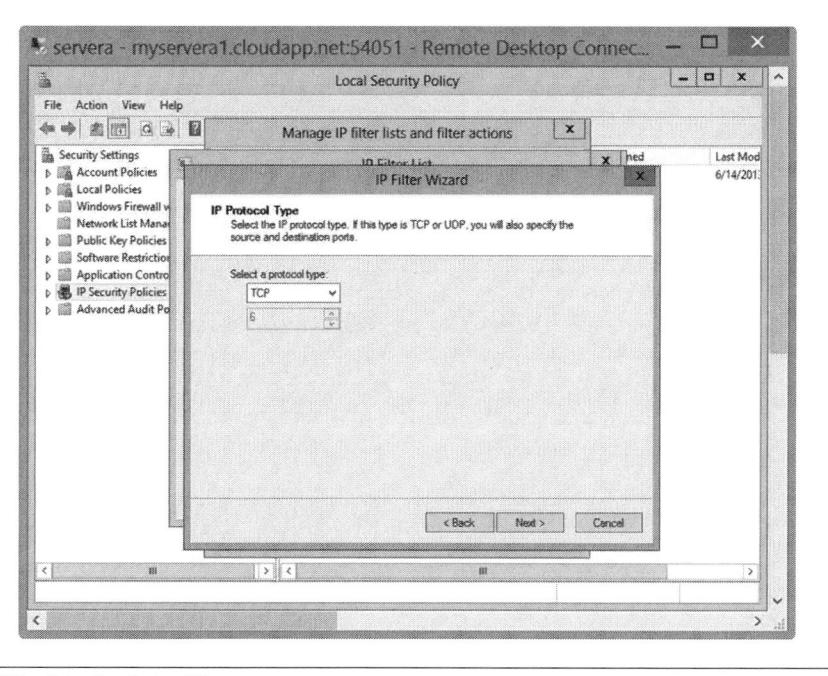

Figure 8.38   Selecting Protocol Type.

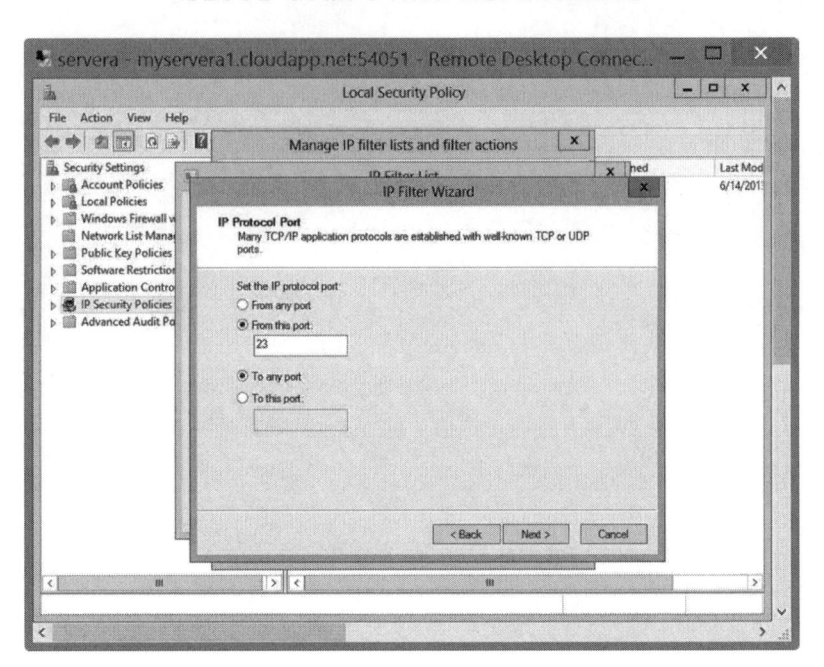

Figure 8.39 Specifying Communication Port.

Creating customized filter action: In this part of the activity, you will create a customized filter action for the IP filter list created above.

1. In the Manage IP filter lists and filter actions dialog, click the tab **Manage Filter Actions** (Figure 8.40).
2. Click **Add**. On the Welcome page, click **Next**.
3. Change the name to **Customized Filter Action** (Figure 8.41), and click **Next**.
4. Make sure that the option **Negotiate security** is selected (Figure 8.42), and click **Next**.
5. Make sure that the option **Do not allow unsecured communication** is selected, and click **Next**.
6. Click **Custom** and click **Settings**. Make sure that **Data integrity and encryption (ESP)** is checked (Figure 8.43). Then, click **OK**.
7. Click **Next**. Then, click **Finish** and **Close**.

Adding customized filter list and filter action to IP Security Policy: In this part of the activity, you will add a customized filter list and filter action to the IP security policy created earlier.

1. Right click **IP Security Policy** (Figure 8.44), and select **Properties**.
2. Click **Add**. Then, click **Next** on the Welcome page.
3. Make sure the option **This rule does not specify a tunnel** is selected, and click **Next**.
4. Make sure the option **All network connections** is selected, and click **Next**.

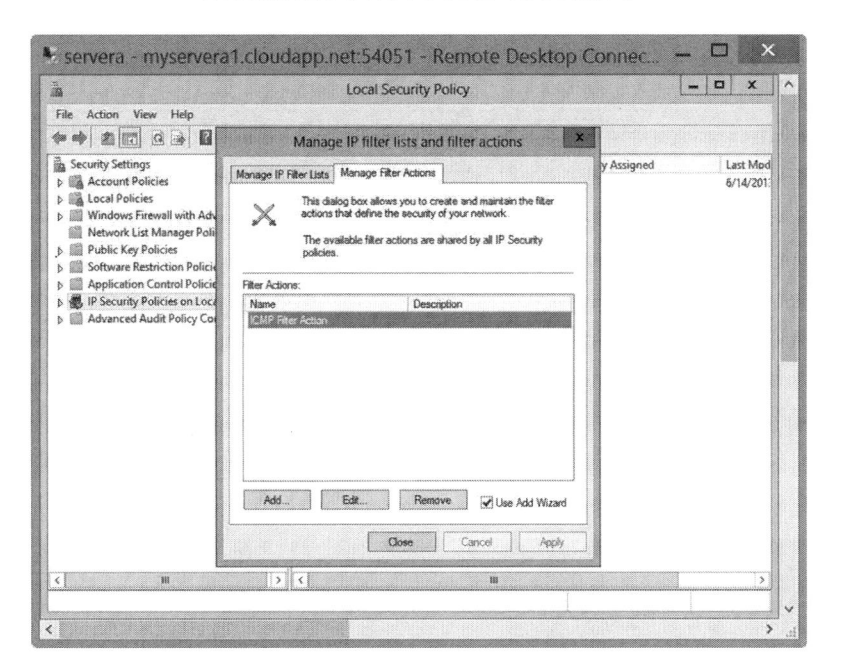

Figure 8.40 Adding Filter Action.

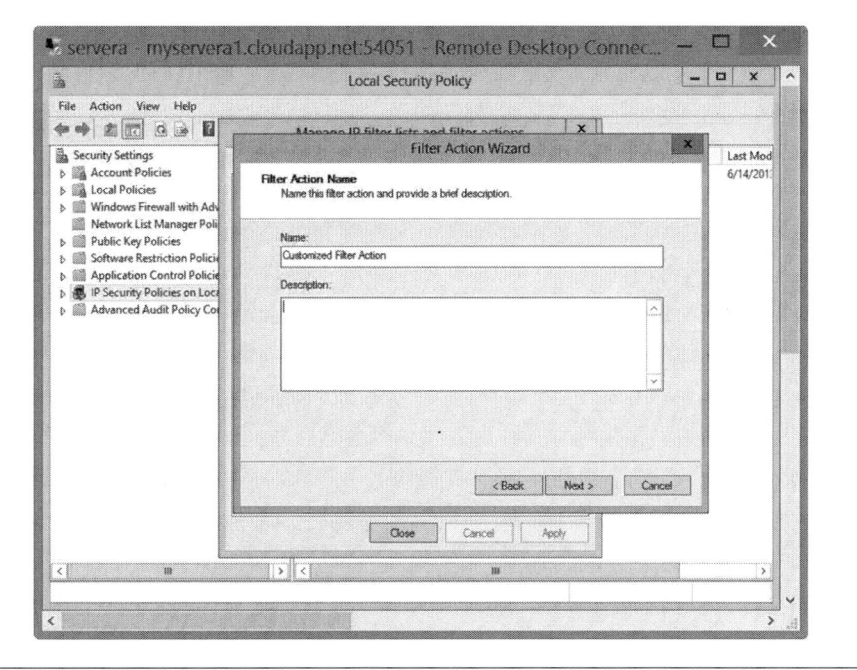

Figure 8.41 Filter Action Name.

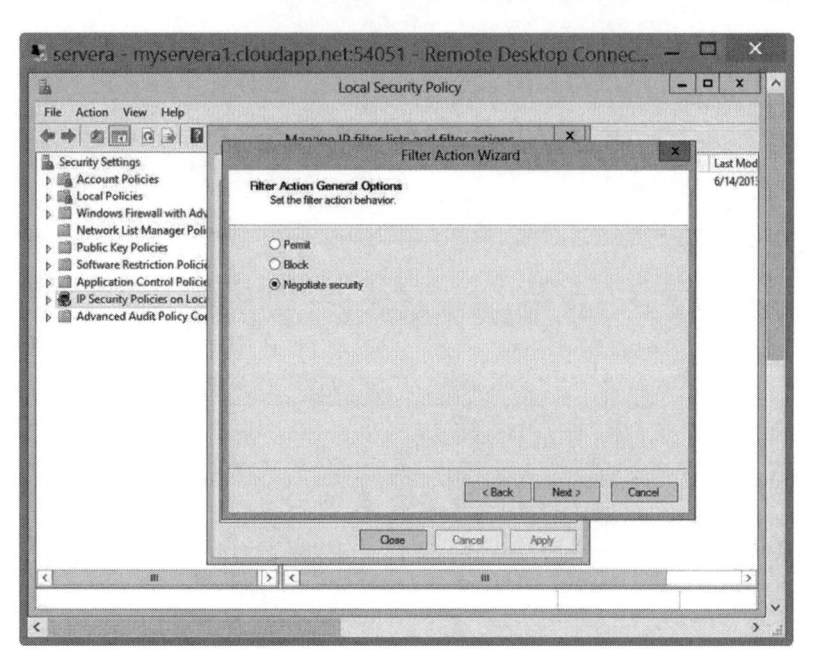

Figure 8.42   Setting Filter Action Behavior.

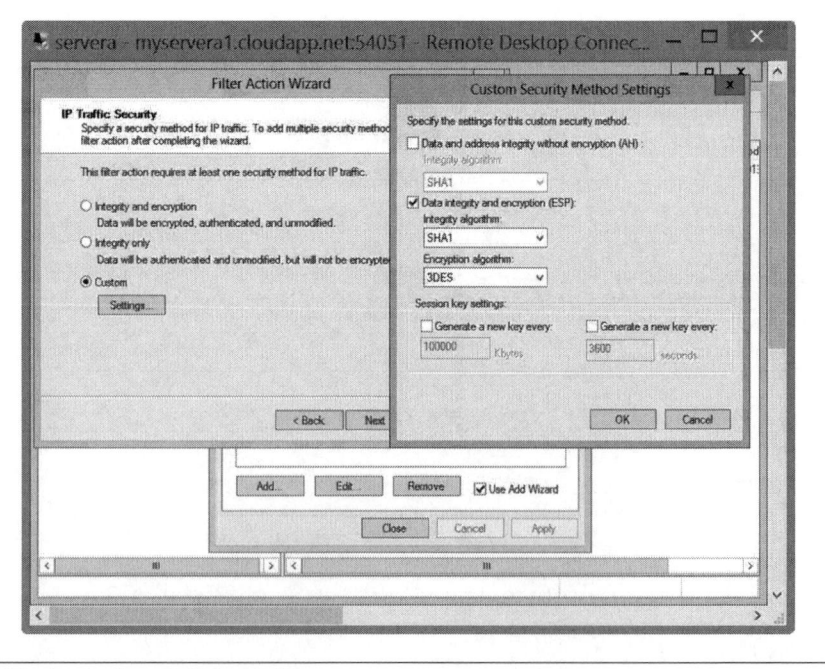

Figure 8.43   Custom Security Method Settings.

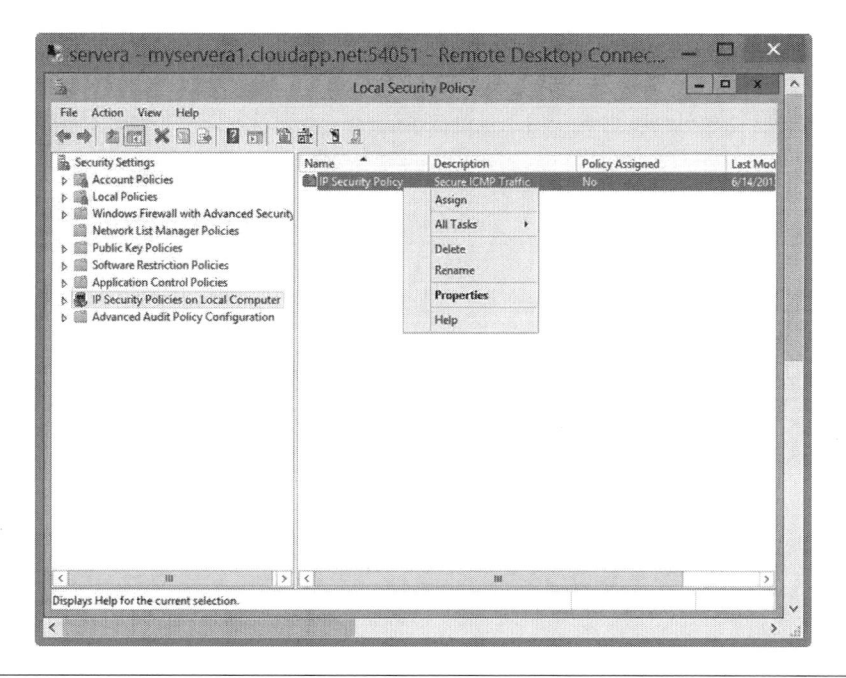

Figure 8.44   Opening IP Security Policy Properties Dialog.

5. Select the option **Customized Filter List** (Figure 8.45), and click **Next**.
6. Select the option **Customized Filter Action** (Figure 8.46) and click **Next**.
7. Make sure that the option **Active Directory default (Kerberos V5 protocol)** is selected and click **Next**.
8. Click **Finish** and click **OK** in the IP Security Policy Properties dialog.
9. Right click **IP Security Policy** and select **Assign** to assign the security policy to the local computer (Figure 8.47).

The next activity will use the IPSec management tool Windows Firewall with Advanced Security to implement IPSec.

Activity 8.2: IPSec Implementation with Windows Firewall with Advanced Security

In this activity, you will implement a customized IPSec rule for the protocol TCP at the port 445 commonly used for network resource sharing.

   Linking group policy object: To accomplish this task, you will first link a Group Policy Object (GPO) to the organizational unit (OU) CS created in Chapter 4.

1. Log on to the Microsoft Azure Management Portal.
2. Connect to the virtual machine **servera** and log on as **student**.
3. Press the **Windows logo** key and type **Group**. Click the **Group Policy Management** tile to open the Group Policy Management console.

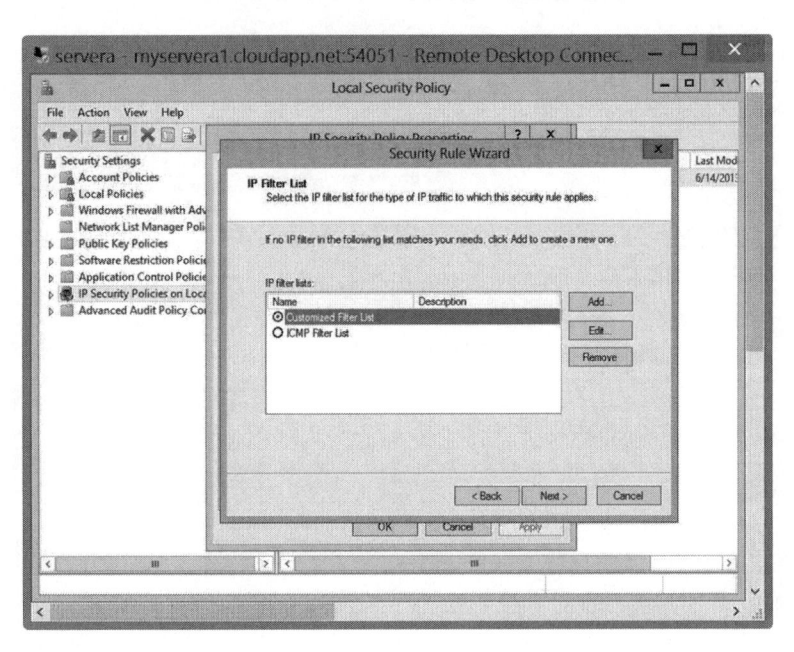

Figure 8.45   Selecting Customized Filter List.

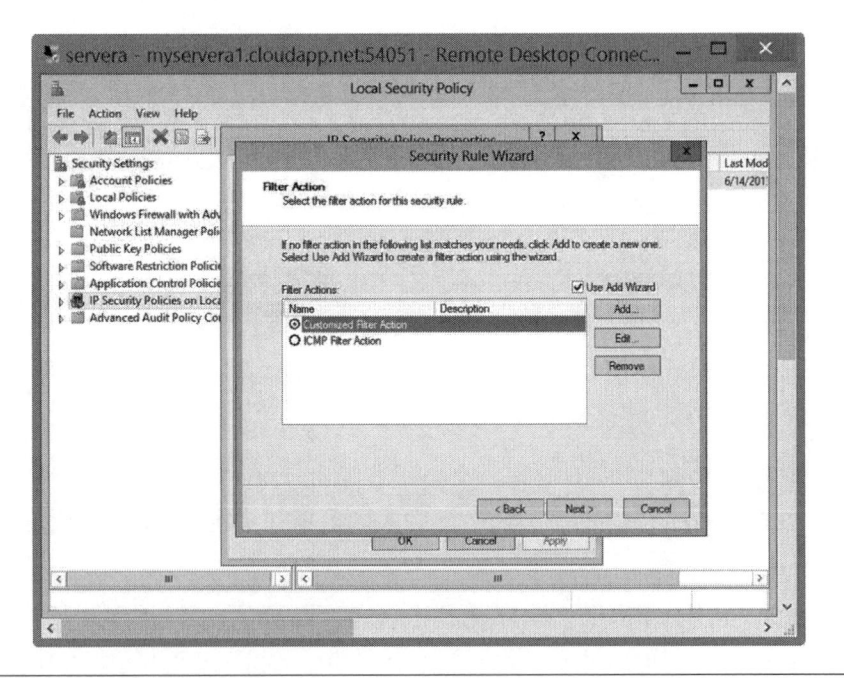

Figure 8.46   Selecting Customized Filter Action.

4. IPSec rules can be applied to a specific domain or OU. To do so, right click the node CS_OU in the left pane and then click **Link an Existing GPO** (Figure 8.48).
5. In the **Select GPO** dialog, click **Default Domain Controller's Policy** (Figure 8.49) and then click **OK**.

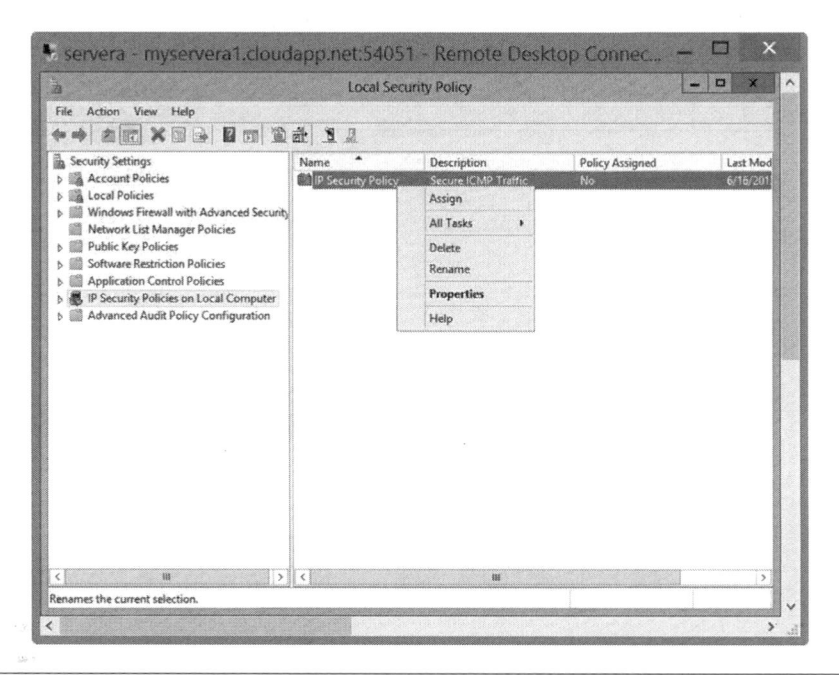

Figure 8.47 Assigning Security Policy to Local Computer.

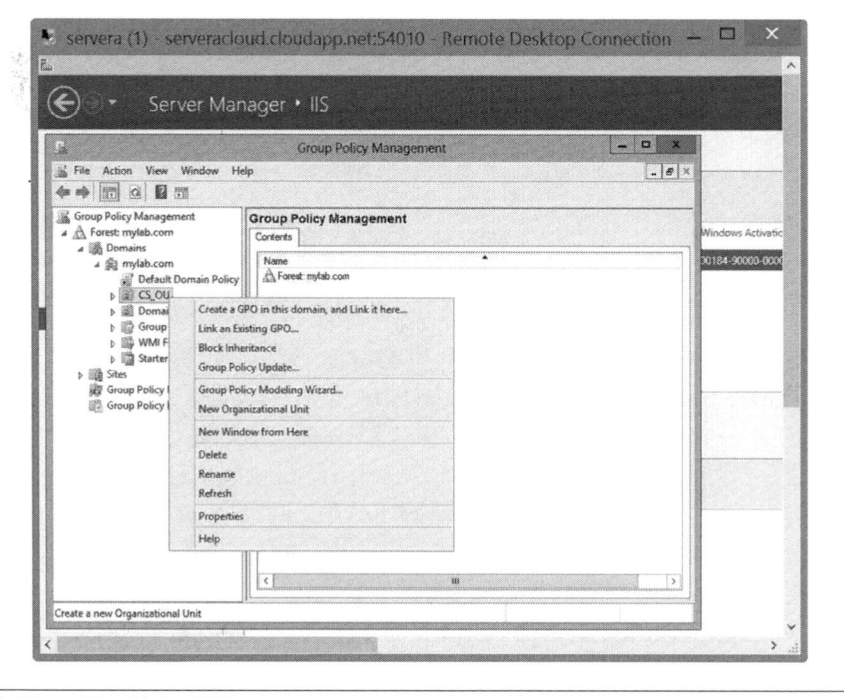

Figure 8.48 Linking Existing GPO.

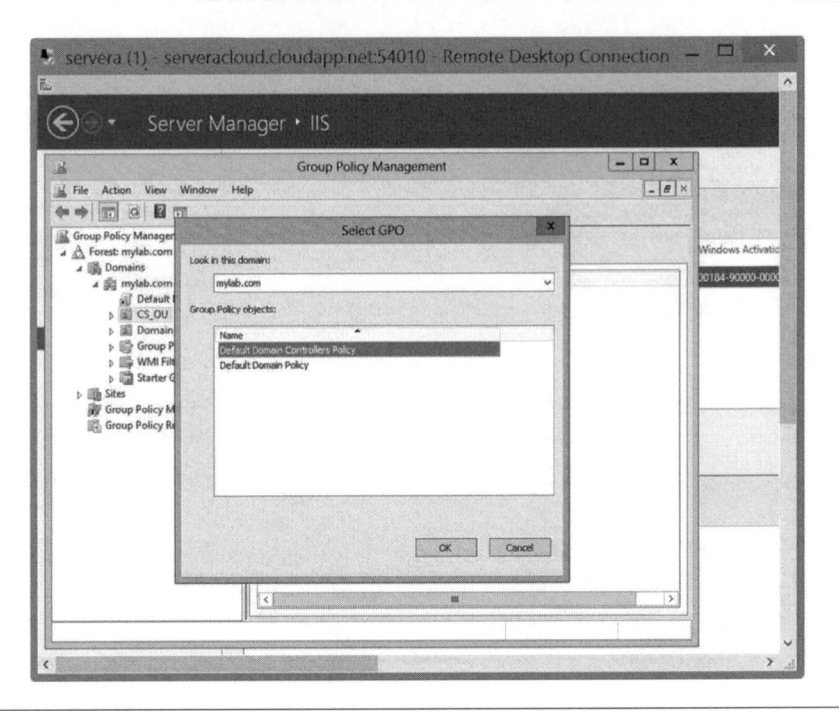

Figure 8.49   Selecting Default Domain Controller's Policy.

Server side connection security rule configuration for servera: In this part of the activity, you will create a connection security rule on the server **servera** which is used as Endpoint 1 in a secure connection. The secure connection in this part of the activity protects the TCP traffic through the port 445.

1. To open the Windows Firewall with Advanced Security tool, click **Tools** and click **Windows Firewall with Advanced Security**.
2. In the left pane, right click **Connection Security Rules** and then click **New Rule** (Figure 8.50).
3. After the New Connection Security Rule Wizard is opened, on the Rule Type page, select **Custom** (Figure 8.51), and then click **Next**.
4. On the Endpoints page, for Endpoint 1, check the option **These IP addresses** and click **Add**. After the IP Address dialog is opened, check the option **Predefine set of computers** and select **Default gateway** from the Predefined set of computers dropdown list (Figure 8.52). Then, click **OK**.
5. For Endpoint 2, check the option **These IP addresses** and click **Add**. After the IP Address dialog is opened, check the option **This IP address or subnet** and select the IP address for the default gateway, such as 10.0.0.1 shown in Figure 8.53. (Your IP address for the default gateway should be different.) Then, click **OK** and click **Next**.
6. On the Requirements page, check the option **Request authentication for inbound and outbound connections** (Figure 8.54), and click **Next** twice.

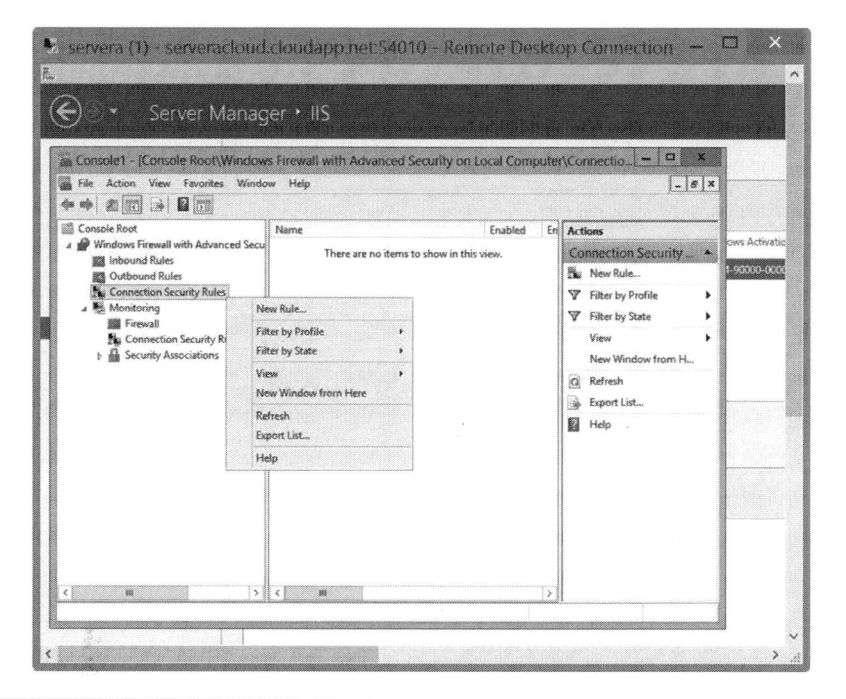

Figure 8.50 Creating New Rule.

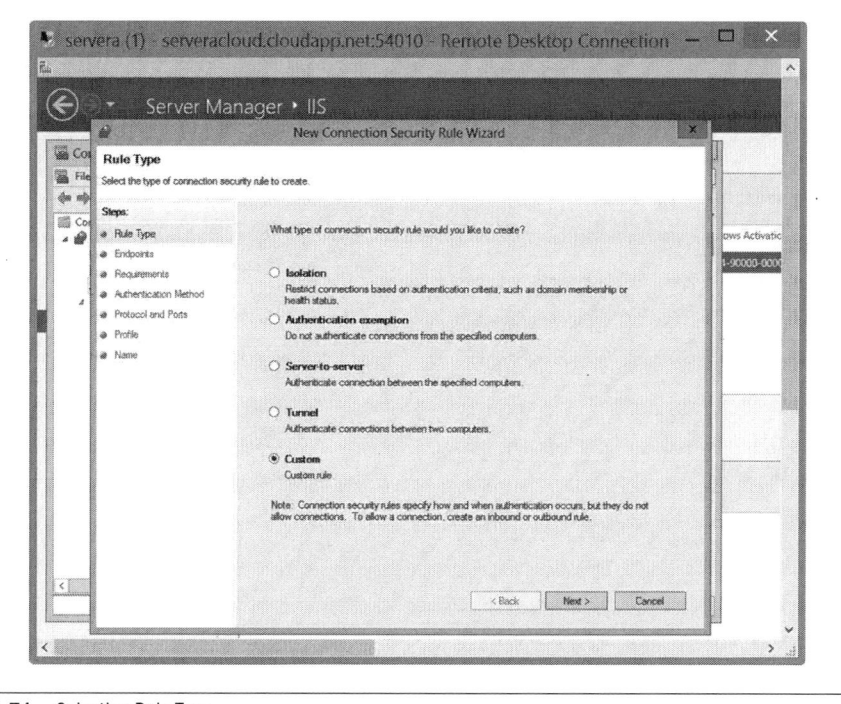

Figure 8.51 Selecting Rule Type.

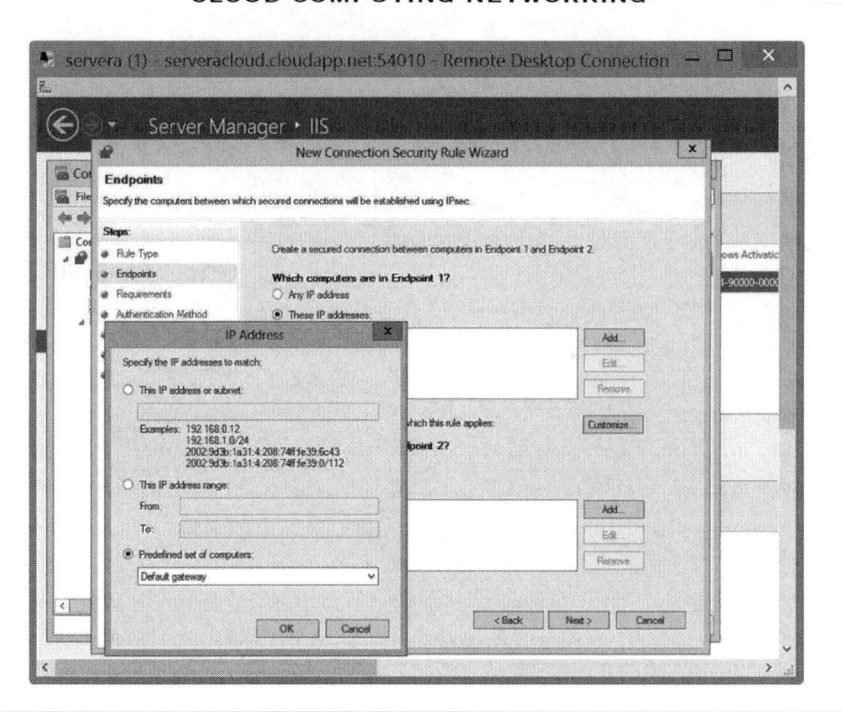

Figure 8.52   Configuring IP Address for Endpoint 1.

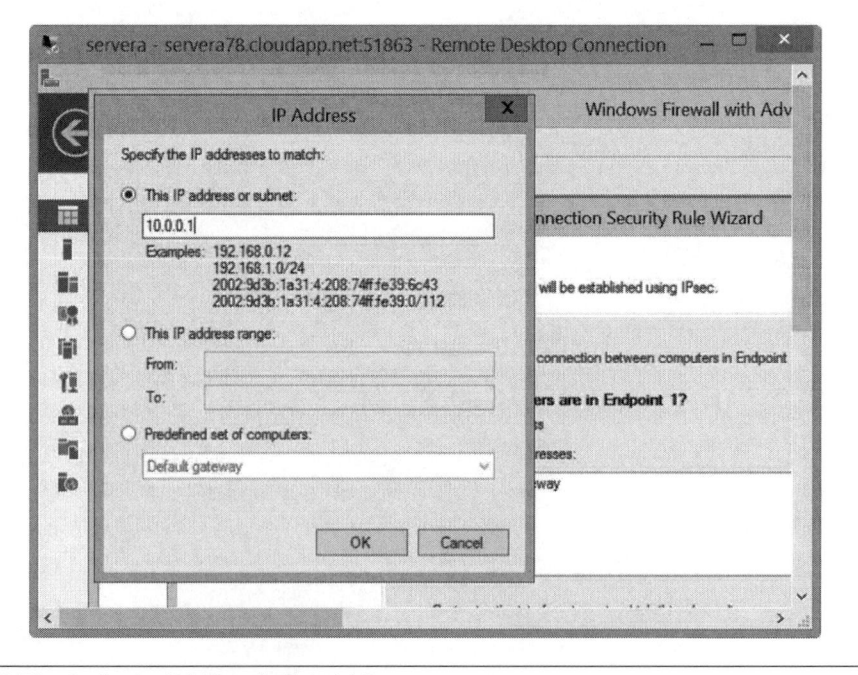

Figure 8.53   Configuring IP Address for Endpoint 2.

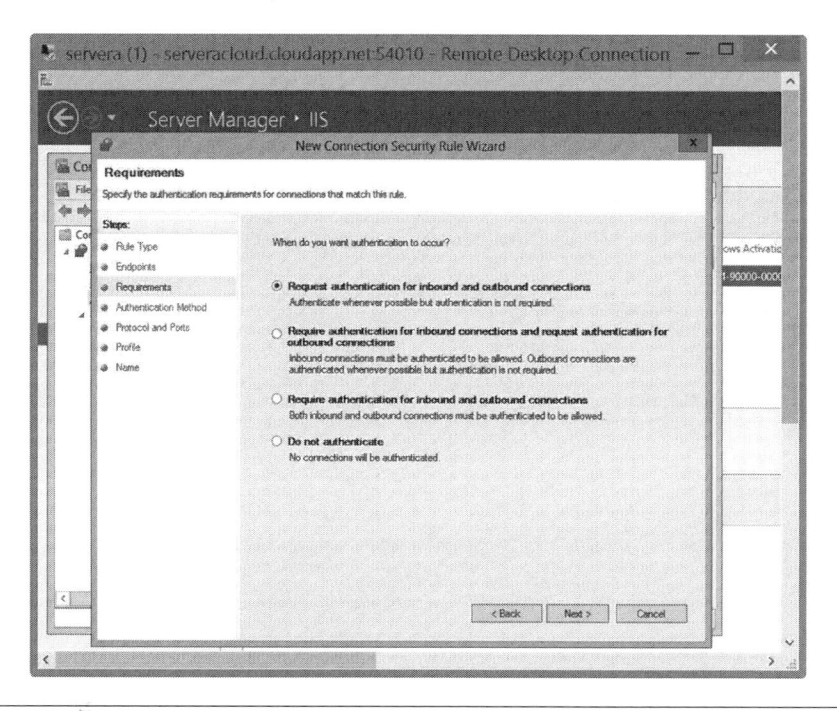

Figure 8.54 Configuring Requirement.

7. On the Protocol and Ports page, select **TCP** as the protocol type. For Endpoint 1, specify the port by typing **445**. For Endpoint 2, use **All ports** (Figure 8.55). Then, click **Next**.

8. On the Profile page, you can keep the default to apply the rule to Domain, Private, and Public (Figure 8.56), and then click **Next**.

9. Name your rule as **Myrule** (Figure 8.57) and then click **Finish**.

Server side connection security rule configuration for serverb: In this part of the activity, you will use serverb as Endpoint 2 in a secure connection.

1. Connect to the virtual machine **serverb** and log on as **student**.

2. Click **Tools** and click **Windows Firewall with Advanced Security**.

3. In the left pane, double click **Connection Security Rules**. Then, right click **Connection Security Rules** and select **New Rule**.

4. After the New Connection Security Rule Wizard is opened, on the Rule Type page, select **Custom**, and then click **Next**.

5. In the Endpoints page, for Endpoint 1, configure the IP address for both endpoints (Figure 8.58). The IP address for Endpoint 1 is the IP address of the default gateway for servera and the IP address for Endpoint 2 is **Any IP address**. Then, click **OK**.

6. In the Requirements page, you can keep the default and click **Next** twice.

7. On the Protocol and Ports page, select **TCP** as the protocol type. For Endpoint 1, specify the port by typing **445**. For Endpoint 2, use **All ports** (Figure 8.59). Then, click **Next** twice.

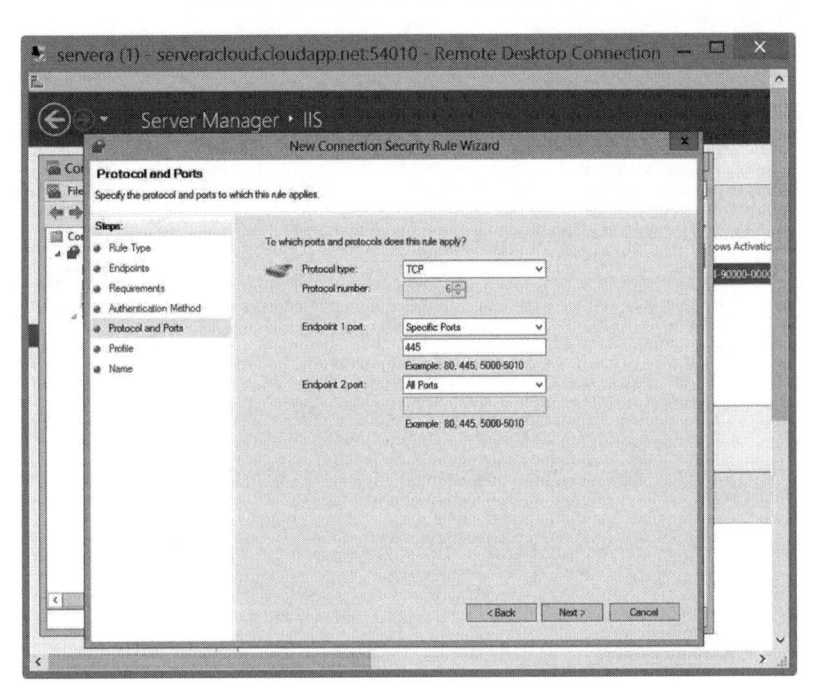

Figure 8.55 Specifying Protocol and Ports.

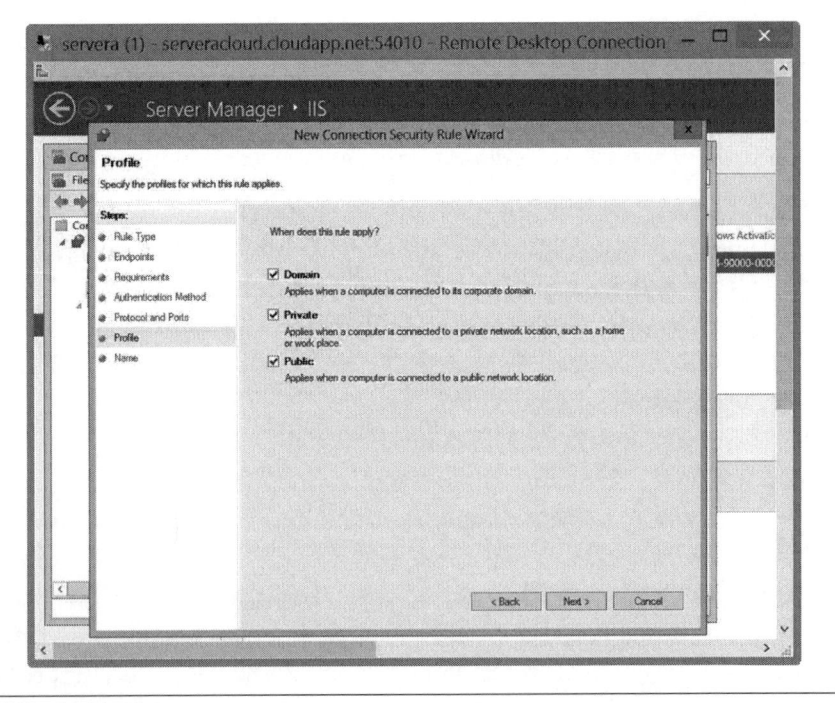

Figure 8.56 Applying Rule.

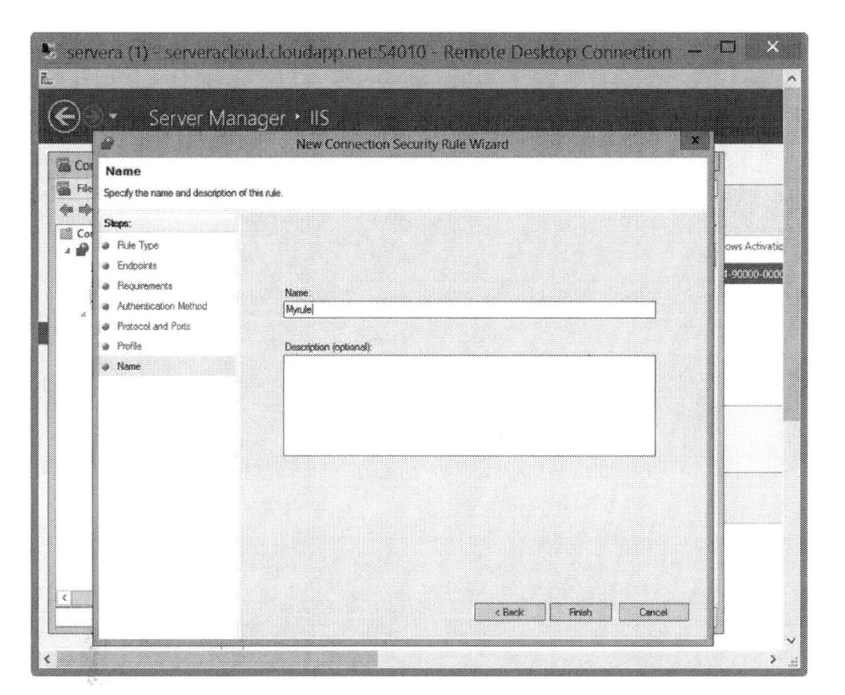

Figure 8.57 Rule Name.

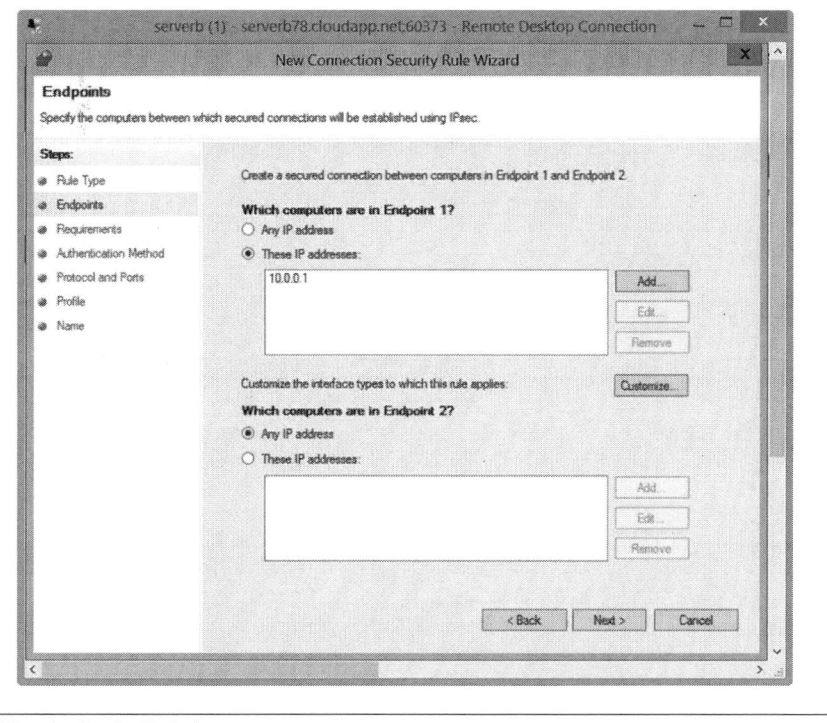

Figure 8.58 Configuring Endpoints.

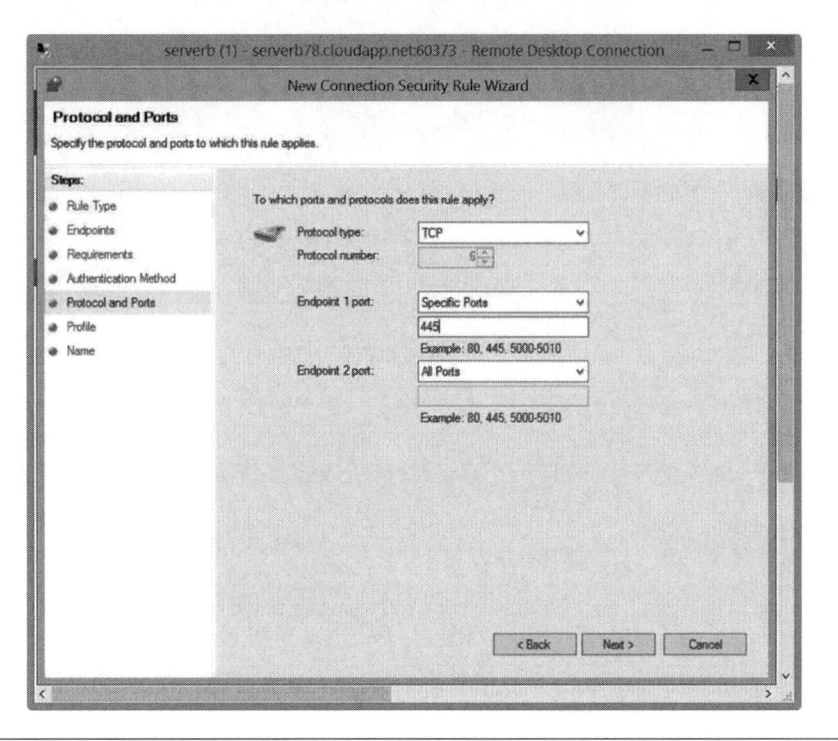

Figure 8.59   Protocol and Port Specification.

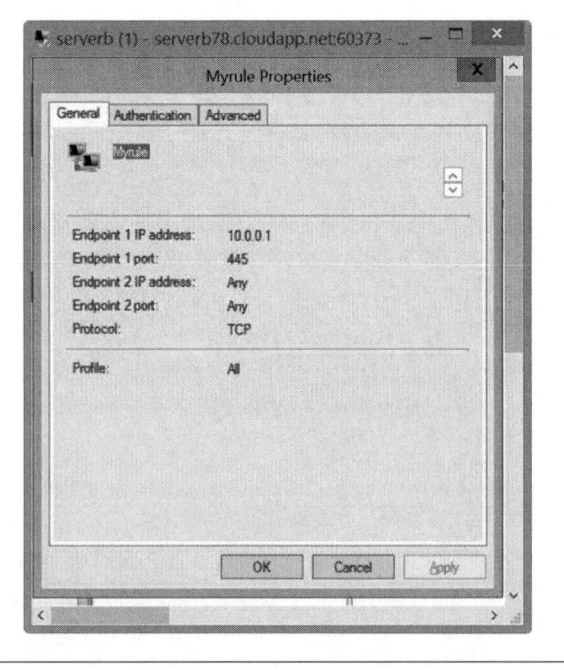

Figure 8.60   Myrule Properties.

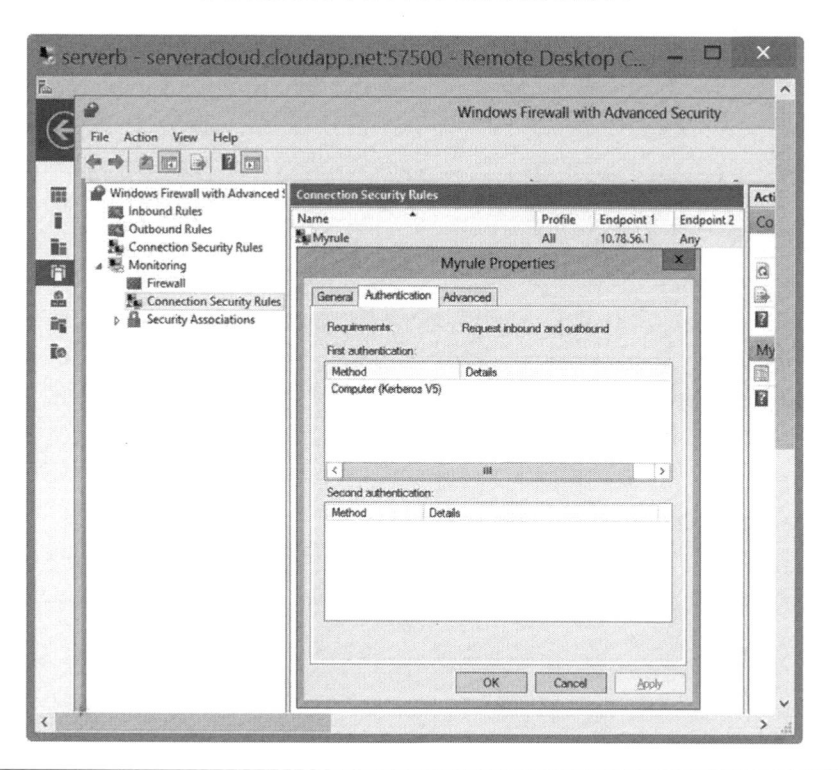

Figure 8.61   Default Authentication Method.

8. Name your rule as **Myrule**, and then click **Finish**.
9. To view the just created secure connection, in the Windows Firewall with Advanced Security window, expand the **Monitoring** node.
10. Click on **Connection Security Rules** and right click **Myrule** and select **Properties**. Under the General tab, you can see the rule configuration shown in Figure 8.60.
11. Click the **Authentication tab**; you should be able to see the default authentication method Computer (Kerberos V5) as shown in Figure 8.61.
12. In the Microsoft Azure Management Portal, shutdown both servera and serverb before exiting the Microsoft Azure Management Portal.

When using Windows Firewall with Advanced Security to configure IPSec, you can also implement IPSec with an Enterprise CA, which is covered in the last chapter. The Enterprise CA can be used for issuing and managing digital certificates. It can also be used for automatic certificate approval and automatic computer certificate enrollment.

8.5 Summary

This chapter discusses some IPSec-related issues. IP communication security has the highest priority in the data transaction between two networks. In order to effectively protect IP communication, IPSec needs to be implemented on the data sender and the data receiver. This chapter provides information about how to design IPSec policies. To be able to do so, network administrators need to know what authentication and encryption to be implemented in IPSec. They also need to know the IP addresses of the endpoints. They should decide what to protect with IPSec. IPSec can be used to protect a domain and a network, or isolate a network host from the public network.

This chapter introduces two ways to implement IPSec. Network administrators can use the tool IP Security Policy to implement IPSec for a network that is mixed with new and old network technologies. On the other hand, the tool Windows Firewall with Advanced Security can work with the newly developed features that can implement IPSec between two network hosts.

The IPSec, SSL, and certificate technologies have been widely used with the VPN technology to protect the IP communication over the public network. Later, you will learn about the VPN technology and use it for the data transaction between a network host on Microsoft Azure and a network host on your home network.

Review Questions

1. Why is IPSec needed?
2. What is packet sniffing?
3. What is IP spoofing?
4. What is denial-of-service?
5. What is man-in-the-middle?
6. What is data replay?
7. How does IPSec secure packet transmission?
8. Explain how the tunnel mode works.
9. Describe the advantage and disadvantage of the tunnel mode.
10. Explain how the transport mode works.
11. What is the disadvantage of the transport mode?
12. Describe how the AH algorithm is used with the transport mode.
13. Describe how the AH algorithm is used with the tunnel mode.
14. Describe how the ESP algorithm is used with the transport mode.
15. Describe how ESP algorithm is used with the tunnel mode.
16. What are the advantages of IPSec?
17. What are the disadvantages of IPSec?
18. What are the two tools used to implement IPSec?
19. Describe the tool IP Security Policy.
20. Describe the tool Windows Firewall with Advanced Security.

9

ROUTING AND REMOTE
ACCESS SERVICE

Objectives

- Understand Routing.
- Understand Network Address Translation (NAT).
- Gain Knowledge of Routing and Remote Access Service (RRAS).
- Configure an RRAS router.

9.1 Introduction

As mentioned earlier, TCP/IP and routers are two key technologies for today's Internet. With routers, various types of networks can be linked together to form the Internet. During a routing process, a router can find the shortest path to a destination network. The router can identify a network host with a destination IP address and knows where to find the destination network host. It can also deliver data packets from one network to another network where the data packets may be framed differently. Therefore, the router is considered by many as a complicated network device.

Windows Server provides Routing and Remote Access Service (RRAS), which is a service that manages routing and remote access. With RRAS, Windows Server can be configured as a software router for connecting two networks. A routing service passes and manages data traffic between two local area networks (LANs), between a LAN and a wide area network (WAN), between two WANs, and between a LAN and the Internet. The RRAS routing service also provides the Network Address Translation (NAT) service. NAT is a service that allows network hosts on a private network to share a single Internet connection. The remote access service provides services such as dial-up connections and virtual private network (VPN) connections. The VPN can connect a home computer to a computer on an organization's network, or it can even make a site-to-site connection between two routers located on two different networks. A dial-up connection connects two network hosts through a regular phone line. In this chapter, we are going to examine the routing service in detail. Remote access through VPN will be covered in the next chapter.

9.2 Routing

The configuration of routing protocols used by a router is often complicated and requires more training. To understand how a router works, this section will start with the explanation on how a router is used to link two networks.

9.2.1 Connecting Network Segments to Router

To surf the Internet, a student's home network needs to be linked to the Internet. The home network and the Internet use different technologies. A data packet framed on the home network is different from the packet framed on the Internet. Also, the home network is a private network and the Internet is a public network. The DNS server, DHCP server, and subnet mask used by the home network are also different from those by the public network. In general, an enterprise-level network may include the Internet, WAN, and LAN; this makes the transmission of packets from one type of network to another type of network a challenging task. Even two network segments with the same type of network technology, such as Ethernet, are still difficult to directly transmit data between them if the two network segments have different network configurations. To pass data packets from one network segment to another, we need to use a network device called a router, which can perform the following tasks:

- A router should have at least two or more network interface cards (NICs) to physically connect to two or more network segments.
- A router can convert data packets from one type of frame to another type of frame.
- A router should have a storage device to store information about networks and routes from one network segment to another network segment.
- A router should be able to update the stored information about changes made to the network structure or configuration.
- By using the stored information, a router can calculate the shortest path from the source network segment to the destination network segment.
- When delivering data packets across multiple network segments, a router can dynamically redefine their transmission to comply with the constraints imposed by different network segments.

To be able to calculate the shortest path and store routing information, a router has to have a CPU and memory just like a computer. To be able to communicate with the network hosts in a network segment, the router's NIC must be configured to have the same network ID as the network hosts in the same network segment. Figure 9.1 illustrates how a router's NICs are configured.

As shown in Figure 9.1, the left-hand side of the router is connected to the network segment with the network ID 192.168.2.0. Therefore, the NIC on the left-hand side of the router is configured to have an IP address 192.168.2.1 so that the router can communicate with the network hosts in the network 192.168.2.0. Similarly, the router's

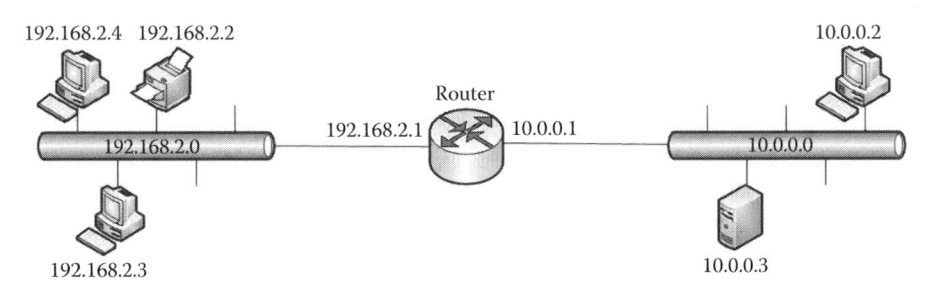

Figure 9.1 Router connection.

right-hand side NIC is configured connected to have the IP address 10.0.0.1 so that it can communicate with the network hosts in the network with the ID 10.0.0.0. In fact, a NIC on the router can be configured to have any IP address that is valid for the subnet of the connected network segment. For example, the NIC on the right-hand side of the router can be assigned the IP address 10.0.0.135. However, the IP address 10.0.0.1 is easy to remember.

A packet framed with one network technology will not work in another network segment where packets are framed differently. To forward an IP packet from one network segment to another network segment, the sender first encapsulates the IP packet with the frame used by the sender's network segment. When the frame reaches the router, the router moves the IP packet out of the frame and then encapsulates the IP packet with the frame used by the destination network segment. In such a way, the IP packet can be delivered to the network host in the destination network segment.

A router can have more than two NICs to connect to more than two network segments. The router in Figure 9.2 connects three network segments. Although connecting multiple network segments to one router may reduce the cost on routers, it may not be a good idea to connect too many network segments to a router due to security, reliability, and performance reasons. It can cause a bottleneck due to busy network

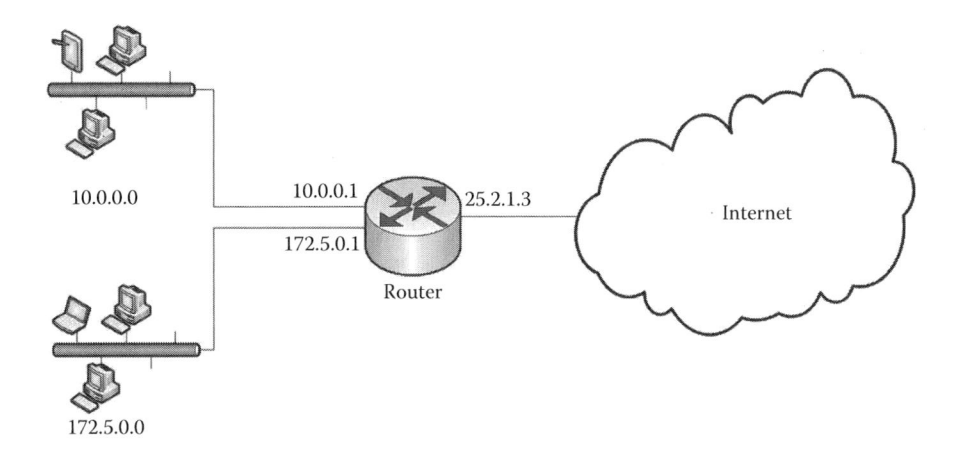

Figure 9.2 Multiple network connections.

traffic if multiple network segments are connected to one router. It can also result in malfunction of the router and jams multiple network segments' traffic. Also, a network virus can pass from one network segment to multiple network segments through the router. Therefore, the network administrator should come up with a good design by carefully balancing the cost, reliability, performance, and security.

A router uses a routing table to store and manage network segment information. The next section will talk about the routing table.

9.2.2 Routing Table

In a routing table, each row contains information about a network segment. The information about a network segment includes the destination network ID, subnet mask, default gateway, NIC, and so on (Table 9.1).

The routing table content is related to the router illustrated in Figure 9.1. The definitions for the columns in the routing table are given as follows:

- *Destination*: This column defines the IP address of a destination network.
- *Gateway*: This column defines the IP address of a gateway which leads to another network segment. The value 0.0.0.0 or "*" means that the destination network is directly connected.
- *Genmask*: This column defines the subnet mask for the destination network.
- *Flags*: This column defines the routing status. The commonly used flags are listed as follows:
  - U: The route is up.
  - G: The route uses an external gateway.
  - R: The route is a reinstated route for dynamic routing.
  - D: The route is dynamically installed.
  - M: The route is modified.
  - !: The route is rejected.
- *Metric*: This column defines the distance to the destination network. Depending on the routing protocols, the distance can be measured in many ways. It can be the number of networks crossed, or other measures.
- *Ref*: This column defines the number of references to this route.
- *Use*: This column defines the count of packets transmitted via this route.
- *Iface*: This column defines the name of the NIC to which this route sends a packet.

Table 9.1 Routing Table

DESTINATION	GATEWAY	GENMASK	FLAGS	METRIC	REF	USE	IFACE
192.168.2.0	*	255.255.255.0	U	0	0	0	eth0
127.0.0.0	0.0.0.0	255.0.0.0	U	0	0	0	lo
10.0.0.0	192.168.2.1	255.0.0.0	UG	100	0	0	eth1

By using the information stored in the routing table, the router can calculate the shortest path between two network segments. After the router receives a packet sent by a network host, the router compares the destination address of the packet with the entries stored in the routing table. If there is a match, the packet will be forwarded to the next router along the path to the destination network. Jumping from one router to another is called hopping.

9.2.3 Routing across Networks

In this section, you are going to find out how a router is able to decide to which router it can forward a packet. Each network has its own data transmission capacity. While transmitting data packets through multiple network segments, a router should be able to dynamically adjust the payload size acceptable by the network segments along the path to the destination. This section will discuss two topics that can accomplish the tasks:

1. Identifying the next hop router for a given designation IP address.
2. Dynamically adjusting the payload size.

9.2.3.1 Identifying Next Hop Router The network segment where the sender is located may not be directly linked to destination network segment. Therefore, the router needs to deliver the packet to the next router, which is on the path to the destination network segment. As shown in Figure 9.3, there are four network segments. To deliver the packet to the network 192.168.1.0, the router R3 needs to decide whether to forward the packet to the router R1 or to R2.

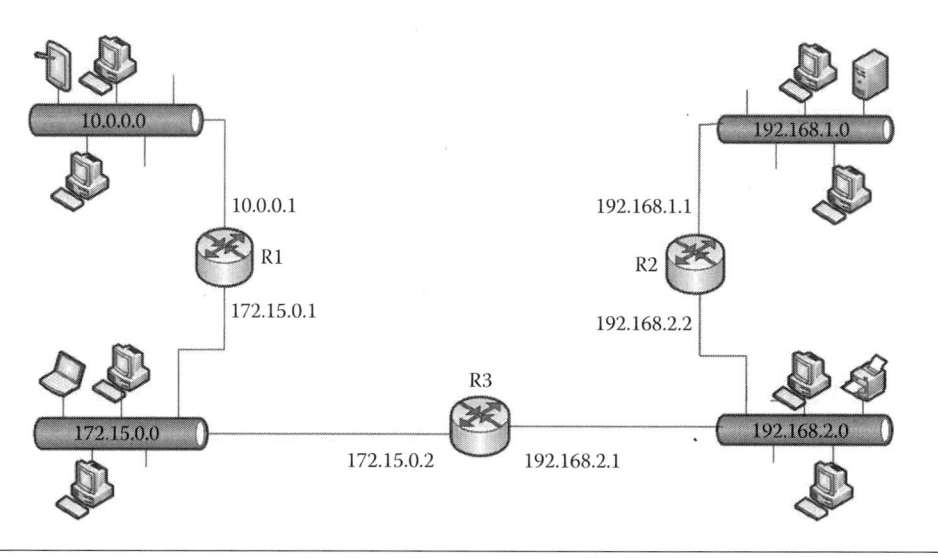

Figure 9.3 Network with four segments.

If a network consists of multiple network segments, there will be multiple rows in the routing table; each row represents a network segment. Corresponding to Figure 9.3, the routing table should contain four rows. There are three routers in Figure 9.3 and there should be three routing tables as partially displayed from Tables 9.2 through 9.4.

Suppose that one needs to send a packet with the destination IP address 192.168.1.2. The network host assigned the destination IP address is located in the network segment with the network ID 192.168.1.0. When the packet arrives at the router R3, the router R3 performs the AND operation on the destination IP address carried by the packet with the entries in the Genmask column. The result of the AND operation is shown in Table 9.5.

In Table 9.5, the AND operation is performed on the equivalent binary form of the IP address and subnet mask. The result of the AND operation is represented by the decimal form. The AND result in Table 9.5 indicates that 192.168.1.0 is the matching destination network ID. From Table 9.4, the next hop for 192.168.1.0 in R3 is R2's IP address 192.168.2.2. Therefore, the packet should be delivered to the corresponding next hop 192.168.2.2.

Table 9.2 Routing Table for Router R1

ROUTING TABLE ON ROUTER R1		
DESTINATION	GENMASK	NEXT HOP
10.0.0.0	255.0.0.0	Direct
172.15.0.0	255.255.0.0	Direct
192.168.2.0	255.255.255.0	172.15.0.2
192.168.1.0	255.255.255.0	172.15.0.2

Table 9.3 Routing Table for Router R2

ROUTING TABLE ON ROUTER R2		
DESTINATION	GENMASK	NEXT HOP
10.0.0.0	255.0.0.0	192.168.2.1
172.15.0.0	255.255.0.0	192.168.2.1
192.168.2.0	255.255.255.0	Direct
192.168.1.0	255.255.255.0	Direct

Table 9.4 Routing Table for Router R3

ROUTING TABLE ON ROUTER R3		
DESTINATION	GENMASK	NEXT HOP
10.0.0.0	255.0.0.0	172.15.0.1
172.15.0.0	255.255.0.0	Direct
192.168.1.0	255.255.255.0	192.168.2.2
192.168.2.0	255.255.255.0	Direct

Table 9.5 Result of AND Operation

INDEX	OPERATION	RESULT	EXPLANATION
1	192.168.1.2 AND 255.0.0.0	192.0.0.0	No match to the destination 10.0.0.0
2	192.168.1.2 AND 255.255.0.0	192.168.0.0	No match to the destination 172.15.0.0
3	192.168.1.2 AND 255.255.255.0	192.168.1.0	Match to the destination 192.168.1.0
4	192.168.1.2 AND 255.255.255.0	192.168.1.0	No match to the destination 192.168.2.0

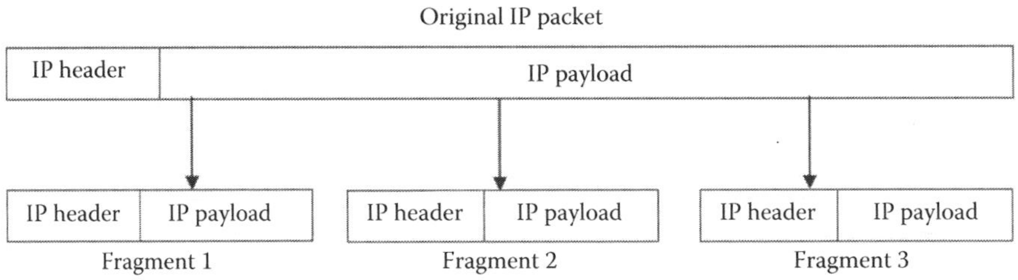

Figure 9.4 Fragmentation.

9.2.3.2 Dynamically Adjusting Payload Size Frames used by different network technologies may have different size limits for payload sections. That is, there is a chance that the payload size used by the sender is much larger than the payload size of the frame used by another network segment. In this case, during the data transmission process, the original payload needs to be sliced into multiple smaller IP payloads shown in Figure 9.4. Slicing a payload into multiple smaller payloads is called fragmentation.

In Figure 9.4, the original IP packet is sliced into three smaller IP packets to comply with the restriction imposed by a network segment along the routing path.

The maximum size of a payload is defined by a network parameter called the maximum transmission unit (MTU). The MTU specifies the maximum amount of data a frame can carry. The MTU is used to determine how to slice a packet. During the journey to the destination, it is possible that a packet will be fragmented multiple times. The fragments will not be reassembled until they reach the ultimate destination.

9.2.4 Updating Routing Table

After a network is added, dropped, or changed, the routing table needs to be updated accordingly. The routing table can be dynamically updated by a routing protocol. It can also be updated manually. To dynamically update routing tables, the routing protocol exchanges the routing information with the other routers in the neighborhood. Once a change is made in one of the routing tables in the neighborhood, the routing protocol recalculates the optimal route to each destination network. Then, the routing table will be updated according to the new calculation. For a manually updated routing table, the routing table's content remains unchanged unless it is changed manually by the network administrator.

For static routing, as the routing can be updated manually, there is no need for the router to calculate routes. Therefore, the static router does not support a CPU and there is no need to support a routing protocol. In such a case, the static router does not consume a lot of network bandwidth. Without a CPU, a static router is easy to build and costs less. The disadvantage of static routing is that it cannot keep up with the changes occurring in a network's structure. Static routing is not fault tolerant. It is not able to find a new route to the destination if the static route is blocked due to network equipment failure. Also, it does not scale well to a large network with many routers. The network of a large organization may include many routers which can generate a large number of entries in the routing table; it is impossible for the network adminis-trator to handle such a large number of routing tables manually.

The features of static routing make it suitable for a small network with a few rout-ers and the routes remain unchanged most of the time. For example, students' home networks use static routing. As shown in Figure 9.5, the router for a home network only connects a local network and the Internet.

During a long journey to a destination on the Internet, a packet will first be sent to the router that directly connects the home network and the Internet. At that router, the packet is encapsulated with the frame used by the Internet. Through the modem, the packet will be delivered to the Internet. On the Internet, the packet will be sent to the ISP. From the ISP, other routers will take care of the rest of the journey. What the router at the home network does is to deliver packets from the home network to the ISP. Therefore, there is no change in the routing table. For this type of routing task, static routing is a good choice.

Since the router at home connects one local network and the Internet, the routing table should only have two entries as shown in Table 9.6.

As shown in Table 9.6, the first row contains the information about the local network at home. The home network has the network ID 192.168.1.0. Since the home network is connected to the router directly, the sign * is used for the gateway.

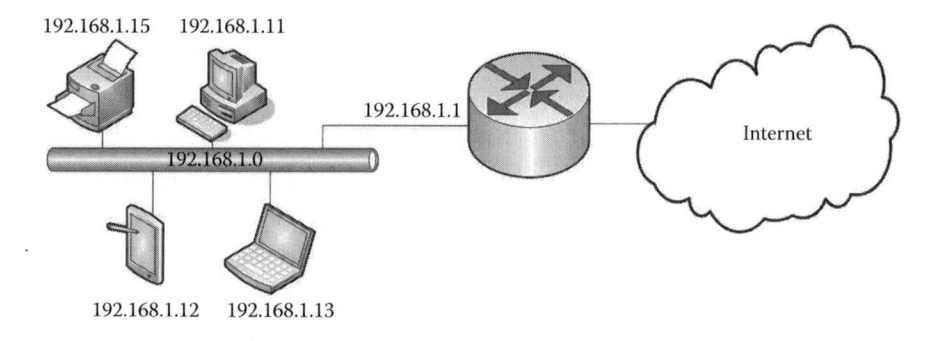

Figure 9.5 Home network.

Table 9.6 Static Routing Table

DESTINATION	GATEWAY	GENMASK
192.168.1.0	*	255.255.255.0
Default	192.168.1.1	0.0.0.0

As the home network is a Class C private network, the column Genmask has the value 255.255.255.0. The second row contains the information about the default route to the ISP. Therefore, the value for the Destination column is the keyword default. Sometimes, the value 0.0.0.0 may also be used to represent the default route. Each routing table can have one default route. As a default route, the value for the Genmask is 0.0.0.0. If the destination is not listed in the routing table, the packet will be sent to the gateway specified by the IP address in the default gateway cell. Since the gateway is 192.168.1.1, all the packets sent by a network host in the network 192.168.1.0 are sent to the NIC configured with the IP address 192.168.1.1, no matter what the destination IP address is.

To configure a router with static routing, the user can use a user interface provided by the router. Through the user interface, the user can enter the information about each route manually. After the routing information is entered, the router updates the routing table based on the route information entered by the user. After the static routing table is updated, it will remain the same until the user changes the configuration manually.

Although, for home networks like the one mentioned earlier, static routing is adequate, it is not suitable for a large network with many routers. Static routing is also not appropriate for networks that need to change their topologies frequently. Once a network segment is added or removed, it is required that the routing table be updated immediately. It is impossible for a network administrator to manually update a routing table that fast. Routing table updates have to be done automatically by routing protocols. To support dynamic routing, a router should include a CPU and memory to perform calculations.

9.2.5 Routing Calculation

During a dynamic routing process, the routing table recalculates the optimal routes according to changes made to the network. Once the routing table is updated, the updated routing information will be forwarded to the routers in the neighborhood for them to update their own routing tables.

The calculation of an optimal route is done by computer algorithms. The criteria of the optimal route can be defined as the minimum time delay, the least amount of network traffic, the minimum number of hops to get to the destination, and other costs. The computer algorithms used to perform routing calculations are differentiated by the method used to calculate the optimal route and the method used to exchange routing information. There are two major algorithms for calculating the optimal route; they are the link state (LS) routing algorithm and the distance vector (DV) routing algorithm.

9.2.5.1 Link State Routing Algorithm The LS routing algorithm calculates a list of optimal routes to each destination in the network. To do so, it requires information about each router in the network and every cost to go from one router to another router in the network. When the LS routing algorithm is used, a routing protocol such as Open Shortest Path First (OSPF) performs the following tasks:

- Sending messages to other routers in the network to get their IP addresses.
- Measuring the costs of delivering packets to other routers. For example, you can use an echo packet to measure the time delay for transmitting a packet between two routers.
- Calculating the optimal route to the destination router based on the measures of the costs. The commonly used computer algorithm to accomplish this task is Dijkstra's shortest path algorithm.
- Exchanging routing information with other routers for them to update their routing tables.

The routers in a network can be represented logically in a mathematical structure called a weighted graph. Each router is considered a node in the graph. The connection between two routers is termed an edge in the graph. The cost is the weight of an edge. Figure 9.6 shows a simple example of a weighted graph.

In Figure 9.6, there are six routers marked as R1, R2, R3, R4, R5, and R6, which are the nodes of the graph. The connections that link these routers are represented by the edges. Every edge is weighted with a number which is the cost to go from one router to another router.

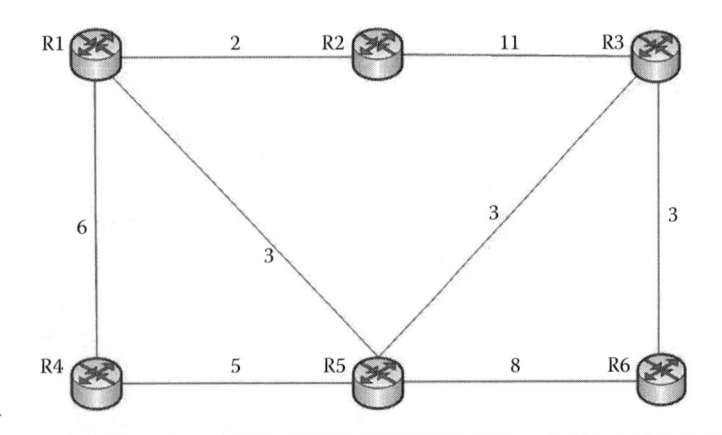

Figure 9.6   Network graph representation.

To calculate the shortest path with Dijkstra's shortest path algorithm, it is required to input the values such as the weights, number of nodes, the edges, as well as the router ID which is a unique number assigned to a router. With the input information, Dijkstra's shortest path algorithm calculates the global shortest path from a router to each other router in the network.

To understand how Dijkstra's shortest path algorithm calculates the shortest path, let us examine it with a set of tables called status record array. Suppose that one needs to find the shortest path from R1 to R6 on the network shown in Figure 9.6. R1 is considered the source node and R6 is considered the sink node.

1. The table to be used has four columns which define Node IDs, Sum of Weights, Status, and Previous. The status of a node can be either permanent or tentative. Initially, all nodes are tentative except the source node as shown in Table 9.7. Once a node is marked as permanent, it will not be used again in the process. At the end of the process, linking all the previous nodes will form the shortest path.

2. In this step, check to see if there are nodes marked as tentative that are directly linked to the nodes that are marked as permanent. If there are, compare the weights of the links that directly connect the tentative nodes to the permanent nodes. For the tentative node on the link that has the least weight, update the value in the Status column to permanent. In our example, the node R1 is marked as permanent as shown in Table 9.7. According to Figure 9.6, R2, R4, and R5 are directly linked to R1 and are marked as tentative in Table 9.7. The weight for the link from R2 to R1 is 2. The weight for the link from R4 to R1 is 6. The weight for the link from R5 to R1 is 3. The link from R2 to R1 has the minimum weight. Therefore, we update the status of R2 to permanent as shown in Table 9.8. Since R1 is the permanent node previously linked to R2, we add the node R1 in the column Previous. We also update sum of weights to 2 for R2.

3. In this step, check if the status of the sink node (destination node) is marked as permanent. If not, repeat Step 2. In our example, the tentative nodes R4, R5, and R3 are directly linked to the permanent nodes R1 and R2. Among these links, the link from R5 to R1 has the least weight. Therefore, update

Table 9.7　Initial Status Record Array

NODE	SUM OF WEIGHTS	STATUS	PREVIOUS
R1	0	Permanent	
R2		Tentative	
R3		Tentative	
R4		Tentative	
R5		Tentative	
R6		Tentative	

Table 9.8   Updating R2 in Status Record Array

NODE	SUM OF WEIGHTS	STATUS	PREVIOUS
R1	0	Permanent	
R2	2	Permanent	R1
R3		Tentative	
R4		Tentative	
R5		Tentative	
R6		Tentative	

Table 9.9   Updating R5 in Status Record Array

NODE	SUM OF WEIGHTS	STATUS	PREVIOUS
R1	0	Permanent	
R2	2	Permanent	R1
R3		Tentative	
R4		Tentative	
R5	3	Permanent	R1
R6		Tentative	

Table 9.10   Updating R3 and R4 in Status Record Array

NODE	SUM OF WEIGHTS	STATUS	PREVIOUS
R1	0	Permanent	
R2	2	Permanent	R1
R3	$3+3=6$	Permanent	R5
R4	6	Permanent	R1
R5	3	Permanent	R1
R6		Tentative	

the status for R5 as permanent; the sum of weights is 3 for R5. In the column Previous, add R1 for R5 as shown in Table 9.9.

4. Repeat Step 3. This time, we have the tentative nodes R3, R4, and R6 linked to the permanent nodes R1, R2, and R5. Among these links, the link from R3 to R5 has the smallest weight sum which is $3+3=6$. The weight sum is the accumulative weight from the source to the current tentative node. Also, the link from R4 to R1 has the weight sum as 6. In such a case, we need to update the values in the column Sum of Weights, Status, and Previous for both R3 and R4 as shown in Table 9.10.

5. Since the status of the sink node is not permanent yet, repeat Step 3. This time, only one tentative node, R6, is left. It is directly linked to the permanent nodes R5 and R3. Among the links, the weight sum for the link from R6 to R5 is $3+8=11$. The weight sum for the link from R6 to R3 is $3+3+3=9$. Since the link from R6 to R3 has a smaller weight sum, we update the values in the columns Sum of Weights, Status, and Previous as shown in Table 9.11.

Table 9.11 Updating R6 in Status Record Array

NODE	SUM OF WEIGHTS	STATUS	PREVIOUS
R1	0	Permanent	
R2	2	Permanent	R1
R3	$3+3=6$	Permanent	R5
R4	6	Permanent	R1
R5	3	Permanent	R1
R6	$3+3+3=9$	Permanent	R3

6. Once the sink node is marked permanent, the process can be stopped. As shown in Table 9.11, the status of the sink node R6 is now permanent. The process of finding the shorted path from R1 to R6 can stop. The shortest path can be identified by looking at the nodes in the column Previous. Starting from R6, its previous node is R3, the previous node for R3 is R5, and the previous node for R5 is R1 which is the source node. We now have the following optimal route from the source node R1 to the sink node R6:

$$R1 \rightarrow R5 \rightarrow R3 \rightarrow R6$$

The weight sum for this route is $3+3+3=9$. In fact, many routes can go from R1 to R6. For example, the route $R1 \rightarrow R2 \rightarrow R3 \rightarrow R6$ has the weight sum $2+11+3=16$. However, among all these routes, the one selected by Dijkstra's shortest path algorithm has the optimal value.

Earlier, Dijkstra's shortest path algorithm is used on a very simple network. For today's Internet environment, a large network frequently changes its topologies and it requires a routing table to be updated as soon as a change occurs. Dijkstra's shortest path algorithm included in many routing protocols is used to update the optimal route immediately whenever a change is made to the network topology.

As shown in the preceding example, Dijkstra's shortest path algorithm can be used to find the shortest path for each pair of nodes in the network. For large networks with many routers, it may take a long time to run Dijkstra's shortest path algorithm. Therefore, Dijkstra's shortest path algorithm works well for small or medium-sized networks. Moreover, this algorithm is very sensitive to the inaccuracy of values input into it. If the weight of each edge is measured incorrectly, the decision on the optimal route will vary significantly. There are some alternative routing algorithms that are easier to process and less sensitive to the inaccuracy of the input values. The DV routing algorithm is this type of algorithm which will be described in the next section.

9.2.5.2 Distance Vector Routing Algorithm Unlike the LS routing algorithm (such as Dijkstra's shortest path algorithm), which requires the information about each router in the network, the DV routing algorithm only needs to know the information about the routers in its neighborhood. The DV algorithm uses the number of hops crossed to reach the destination router as the measure of distance. Among all the routers reaching the destination router, the one that crosses the minimum number of hops is considered an optimal route. The well-known Routing Information Protocol (RIP) is the protocol that uses the DV algorithm.

By using the DV routing algorithm, a router can perform the following tasks:

- A router in the network stores information of the distances to the other routers in the neighborhood that are directly connected to it.
- Each router periodically sends its routing table to the other routers in its neighborhood.
- When a router receives routing tables from other routers in the neighborhood, it examines the routing information to see if there are distances that are shorter than those that are currently in use.
- If there are shorter distances used by the neighboring routers, the router updates its own routing table accordingly.

For a router to use the DV algorithm, the routing table includes the information about the destination and the distance from the route to the destination. As an example, let us consider the network displayed in Figure 9.6. To understand how a router updates its routing table, let us consider the router R1 and the routers in its neighborhood. The routing table for the node R1 is given in Table 9.12.

R1 is directly linked to the routers R2, R4, and R5. For its neighbors to update their routing tables, R1 sends its current routing information to them. After R1's neighbors get the routing information from R1, they will update their own routing tables based on R1's routing information. Then, each of the neighboring routers sends the updated routing information to other neighbors for further update until all the routers in the neighborhood are updated with the latest routing information.

The following set of tables illustrates the process of finding the shortest path from one router to other routers in the neighborhood. To show how the routing table is updated at each router, let us use the network in Figure 9.6 again. Initially, each router only knows the direct neighboring routers. The routing information at each router is shown in Table 9.13.

Initially, since no information is exchanged yet, each router only knows the weights from their directly linked neighboring routers. As shown in Table 9.13,

Table 9.12 Routing Table on Node R1

DESTINATION	WEIGHT	NEXT HOP
R1	0	R1
R2	2	R2
R3	6	R5
R4	6	R4
R5	3	R5
R6	9	R5

Table 9.13 Initial Routing Information at Each Router

FROM R1	TO R1	TO R2	TO R3	TO R4	TO R5	TO R6
via R1	0	**2**		**6**	**3**	
via R2						
via R3						
via R4						
via R5						
via R6						

FROM R2	TO R1	TO R2	TO R3	TO R4	TO R5	TO R6
via R1						
via R2	**2**	0	**11**			
via R3						
via R4						
via R5						
via R6						

FROM R3	TO R1	TO R2	TO R3	TO R4	TO R5	TO R6
via R1						
via R2						
via R3		**11**	0		**3**	**3**
via R4						
via R5						
via R6						

FROM R4	TO R1	TO R2	TO R3	TO R4	TO R5	TO R6
via R1						
via R2						
via R3						
via R4	**6**			0	**5**	
via R5						
via R6						

FROM R5	TO R1	TO R2	TO R3	TO R4	TO R5	TO R6
via R1						
via R2						
via R3						
via R4						
via R5	**3**		**3**	**5**	0	**8**
via R6						

FROM R6	TO R1	TO R2	TO R3	TO R4	TO R5	TO R6
via R1						
via R2						
via R3						
via R4						
via R5						
via R6			**3**		**8**	0

the number in a cell is the weight and the numbers in bold indicates the optimal route to another router.

As the routers start to exchange routing information with their neighboring routers, each router will get more routing information from its neighboring routers. For instance, R1 gets the routing information from R2, R4, and R5. R2 gets the routing information from R1 and R3, and so on. Once R1 receives the routing information from R2, it knows how to get to R3 through R2. Similarly, once R1 gets the routing information from R5, it knows how to get to R3 and R6 through R5. Based on the new information, each router updates the routing information as shown in Table 9.14.

Before the information exchange, R1 only knows it can reach R2, R4, and R5. After the information exchange, R1 now knows how to reach R3 though R2 and reach R6 through R5. Through R2, R1 can get to R3 with the accumulative weight $2 + 11 = 13$. Through R5, R1 can get to R4 with the accumulative weight $3 + 5 = 8$. Through R5, R1 can get to R3 with the accumulative weight $3 + 3 = 6$. Through R5, R1 can also get to R6 with the accumulative weight $3 + 8 = 11$. Similarly, the weigh sums for other routes can be updated accordingly. Table 9.14 shows the routes from R1, R2, R3, R4, R5,

Table 9.14   Updated Routing Information after First Routing Information Exchange

FROM R1	TO R1	TO R2	TO R3	TO R4	TO R5	TO R6
via R1	0	2		6	3	
via R2			13			
via R3						
via R4					11	
via R5			6	8		11
via R6						

FROM R2	TO R1	TO R2	TO R3	TO R4	TO R5	TO R6
via R1				8	5	
via R2	2	0	11			
via R3					14	14
via R4						
via R5						
via R6						

FROM R3	TO R1	TO R2	TO R3	TO R4	TO R5	TO R6
via R1						
via R2	13					
via R3		11	0		3	3
via R4						
via R5	6			8		11
via R6						

FROM R4	TO R1	TO R2	TO R3	TO R4	TO R5	TO R6
via R1		8			9	
via R2						
via R3						
via R4	6			0	5	
via R5	8		8			13
via R6						

FROM R5	TO R1	TO R2	TO R3	TO R4	TO R5	TO R6
via R1		5		9		
via R2						
via R3		14				6
via R4						
via R5	3		3	5	0	8
via R6						

FROM R6	TO R1	TO R2	TO R3	TO R4	TO R5	TO R6
via R1						
via R2						
via R3		14			6	
via R4						
via R5	11		11	13		
via R6			3		8	0

and R6 to other routers. When multiple routes are available between a pair of routers, select the routes with the smallest weight sum.

As the routers continue to exchange routing information with their neighboring routers, each router will get more routing information from its neighboring routers. For instance, R1 gets the routing information from R2, R4, and R5. This time, R5 has a better route to R6. Hence, R1 updates its routing table with a better route to R6 as shown in Table 9.15.

After each router updates its routing table, the routers will exchange routing information again. For instance, R1 gets the routing information from R2, R4, and R5. This time, the weight sum from R1 to R3 via R2 can be updated to $2 + 8 = 10$ where 8 is the weight sum from R2 to R3 as shown in Table 9.15. Similarly, the weight sum from R2 to R4 is 8 in Table 9.15. Therefore, the weight sum from R1 to R4 via R2 is $2 + 8 = 10$. With the same rules, the routing table at each router is updated as shown in Table 9.16.

As long as the content of the routing table gets updated, the routers continue to exchange routing information. Since some of the routing tables still update their

Table 9.15 Updated Routing Information after Second Routing Information Exchange

FROM R1	TO R1	TO R2	TO R3	TO R4	TO R5	TO R6
via R1	0	2		6	3	
via R2			13	10	7	16
via R3						
via R4		14	14		11	19
via R5		8	6	8		9
via R6						

FROM R2	TO R1	TO R2	TO R3	TO R4	TO R5	TO R6
via R1			8	8	5	13
via R2	2	0	11			
via R3	17			19	14	14
via R4						
via R5						
via R6						

FROM R3	TO R1	TO R2	TO R3	TO R4	TO R5	TO R6
via R1						
via R2	13			19	16	24
via R3		11	0		3	3
via R4						
via R5	6	8		8		9
via R6						

FROM R4	TO R1	TO R2	TO R3	TO R4	TO R5	TO R6
via R1		8	12		9	17
via R2						
via R3						
via R4	6			0	5	
via R5	8	10	8			11
via R6						

FROM R5	TO R1	TO R2	TO R3	TO R4	TO R5	TO R6
via R1		5	9	9		14
via R2						
via R3	9	14		11		6
via R4						
via R5	3		3	5	0	8
via R6						

FROM R6	TO R1	TO R2	TO R3	TO R4	TO R5	TO R6
via R1						
via R2						
via R3	9	11		11	6	
via R4						
via R5	11	13	11	13		
via R6			3		8	0

information in Table 9.16, we need to make another update, and you will have the result shown in Table 9.17.

Since the content in Table 9.17 has been changed, we need to exchange the routing information one more time. The result is shown in Table 9.18.

This time, there is no new update in the content as shown in Table 9.18. The exchange of routing information can be stopped. Each router has the optimal routes to other routers in the network. For instance, the optimal route from R1 to R6 needs to pass R5. The optimal route from R5 to R6 needs to pass R3. Therefore, the optimal route is as follows:

$$R1 \rightarrow R5 \rightarrow R3 \rightarrow R6$$

The optimal route is exactly the same as the one found by Dijkstra's shortest path algorithm. The features of the DV algorithm make it suitable for a large network with many routers.

Another way to deal with a large network is to divide it into regions. In a region, a routing table contains the routing information to other routers in the same region as usual. In addition, the routing table also includes the information of the other routers'

Table 9.16 Updated Routing Information after Third Routing Information Exchange

FROM R1	TO R1	TO R2	TO R3	TO R4	TO R5	TO R6
via R1	0	2		6	3	
via R2			10	10	7	15
via R3						
via R4		14	14		11	17
via R5		8	6	8		9
via R6						

FROM R2	TO R1	TO R2	TO R3	TO R4	TO R5	TO R6
via R1			8	8	5	11
via R2	2	0	11			
via R3	17			19	14	14
via R4						
via R5						
via R6						

FROM R3	TO R1	TO R2	TO R3	TO R4	TO R5	TO R6
via R1						
via R2	13			19	16	24
via R3		11	0		3	3
via R4						
via R5	6	8		8		9
via R6						

FROM R4	TO R1	TO R2	TO R3	TO R4	TO R5	TO R6
via R1		8	12		9	15
via R2						
via R3						
via R4	6			0	5	
via R5	8	10	8			11
via R6						

FROM R5	TO R1	TO R2	TO R3	TO R4	TO R5	TO R6
via R1		5	9	9		12
via R2						
via R3	9	11		11		6
via R4						
via R5	3		3	5	0	8
via R6						

FROM R6	TO R1	TO R2	TO R3	TO R4	TO R5	TO R6
via R1						
via R2						
via R3	9	11		11	6	
via R4						
via R5	11	13	11	13		
via R6			3		8	0

routes, one router from each of the other regions. As an example, let us consider the network in Figure 9.7.

According to the networking theory, routing in a network with regions is called hierarchical routing, which can significantly reduce a router's workload. Without dividing the network into regions, each router will have a routing table, which contains 18 entries, one for each router in the network. The calculation of optimal routes will take significant computing resources. To simplify the routing tables, the network can be divided into regions shown in Table 9.19.

After the large network is divided into regions, instead of 18 entries, the routing table for the router R7 in Region 2 has only 7 entries as shown in Table 9.20. Since R7 belongs to Region 2 which includes four routers R7, R8, R13, and R14, the routing table includes four rows for four routers. The routing table also includes three additional rows, for the three other regions as shown in Table 9.20. For the routers in the other regions, the routing table uses the region IDs as destinations and only sends updated routing information to one of the routers in each region. To simplify the discussion, let us assume that the weight for each edge is 1. Then, the routing table for the router R7 looks like the one in Table 9.20.

Table 9.17 Updated Routing Information after Fourth Routing Information Exchange

FROM R1	TO R1	TO R2	TO R3	TO R4	TO R5	TO R6
via R1	0	2		6	3	
via R2			10	10	7	13
via R3						
via R4		14	14		11	17
via R5		8	6	8		9
via R6						

FROM R2	TO R1	TO R2	TO R3	TO R4	TO R5	TO R6
via R1			8	8	5	11
via R2	2	0	11			
via R3	17			19	14	14
via R4						
via R5						
via R6						

FROM R3	TO R1	TO R2	TO R3	TO R4	TO R5	TO R6
via R1						
via R2	13			19	16	22
via R3		11	0		3	3
via R4						
via R5	6	8		8		9
via R6						

FROM R4	TO R1	TO R2	TO R3	TO R4	TO R5	TO R6
via R1		8	12		9	15
via R2						
via R3						
via R4	6			0	5	
via R5	8	10	8			11
via R6						

FROM R5	TO R1	TO R2	TO R3	TO R4	TO R5	TO R6
via R1		5	9	9		12
via R2						
via R3	9	11		11		6
via R4						
via R5	3		3	5	0	8
via R6						

FROM R6	TO R1	TO R2	TO R3	TO R4	TO R5	TO R6
via R1						
via R2						
via R3	9	11		11	6	
via R4						
via R5	11	13	11	13		
via R6			3		8	0

The hierarchical routing method here is a two-level hierarchical system. In general, hierarchical routing can be more than two levels of regions for a large complicated enterprise-level network.

So far, we have discussed how a router works. The routing protocol is the key to carry out the routing functionality. In the next section, we are going to examine another RRAS service, NAT, which allows network hosts on a private network to share a single Internet connection.

9.3 Network Address Translation

As we know, private IP addresses cannot be recognized on the Internet. For a computer with a private IP address to access the Internet, its IP address has to be translated into a public IP address before it can communicate with other computers on the Internet. NAT is this kind of service that does the translation. NAT can be implemented with a hardware device or software. Operating systems such as Windows Server or Linux often provide the NAT software. NAT is also often built in a router or a firewall.

Table 9.18 Updated Routing Information after Fifth Routing Information Exchange

FROM R1	TO R1	TO R2	TO R3	TO R4	TO R5	TO R6	FROM R2	TO R1	TO R2	TO R3	TO R4	TO R5	TO R6
via R1	0	2		6	3		via R1			8	8	5	11
via R2			10	10	7	13	via R2	2	0	11			
via R3							via R3	17			19	14	14
via R4		14	14		11	17	via R4						
via R5		8	6	8		9	via R5						
via R6							via R6						

FROM R3	TO R1	TO R2	TO R3	TO R4	TO R5	TO R6	FROM R4	TO R1	TO R2	TO R3	TO R4	TO R5	TO R6
via R1							via R1		8	12		9	15
via R2	13			19	16	22	via R2						
via R3		11	0		3	3	via R3						
via R4							via R4	6				0	5
via R5	6	8		8		9	via R5	8	10	8			11
via R6							via R6						

FROM R5	TO R1	TO R2	TO R3	TO R4	TO R5	TO R6	FROM R6	TO R1	TO R2	TO R3	TO R4	TO R5	TO R6
via R1		5	9	9		12	via R1						
via R2							via R2						
via R3	9	11		11		6	via R3	9	11		11	6	
via R4							via R4						
via R5	3		3	5	0	8	via R5	11	13	11	13		
via R6							via R6			3		8	0

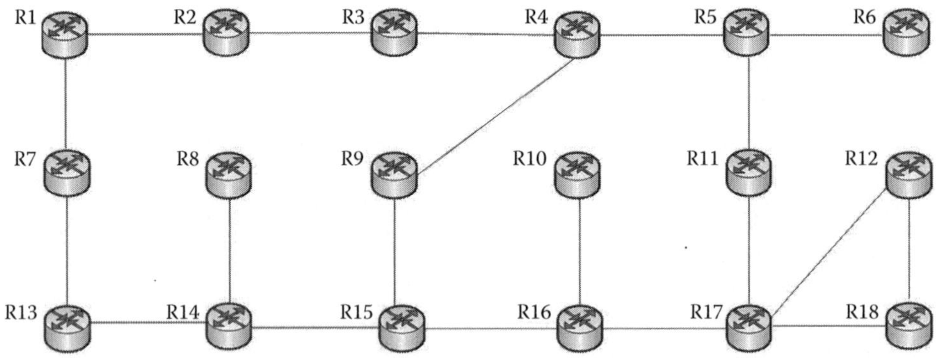

Figure 9.7 Network with 18 routers.

9.3.1 NAT Technology

When transmitting an IP packet from a computer on the private network to a computer on the public network, the IP packet contains the private source IP address and the public destination IP address. As the packet moves across the router that connects the private network and the Internet, NAT replaces the private source IP address

Table 9.19 Regions and Routers in Them

REGION	ROUTER
Region 1	R1, R2, R3, R4, R5, R6
Region 2	R7, R8, R13, R14
Region 3	R9, R10, R15, R16
Region 4	R11, R12, R17, R18

Table 9.20 Routing Table for R7 with Regions

DESTINATION	WEIGHT	ROUTER TO CONTACT	NEXT HOP
R7	0	R7	R7
R8	3	R8	R13
R13	1	R13	R13
R14	2	R14	R13
Region 1	1	R1	R1
Region 3	3	R15	R13
Region 4	5	R17	R13

with the router's public IP address used to connect to the Internet. Once the source IP address of the packet becomes the public IP address, it can be delivered to the destination computer across the Internet. NAT records the original private IP address in a table to remember which computer on the private network has sent the IP packet. When the destination computer sends the response IP packet back to the router, NAT replaces the destination IP address with the recorded private IP address of the computer on the private network. Then, the response IP packet can be delivered to that computer across the private network. Figure 9.8 shows how NAT does the translation for outbound traffic and inbound traffic.

In Figure 9.8, the computer with the private IP address 192.168.1.10 is the sender. When the IP packet reaches the NAT router, the NAT router replaces the source address 191.168.1.10 with the router's external (public) IP address 20.0.0.1.

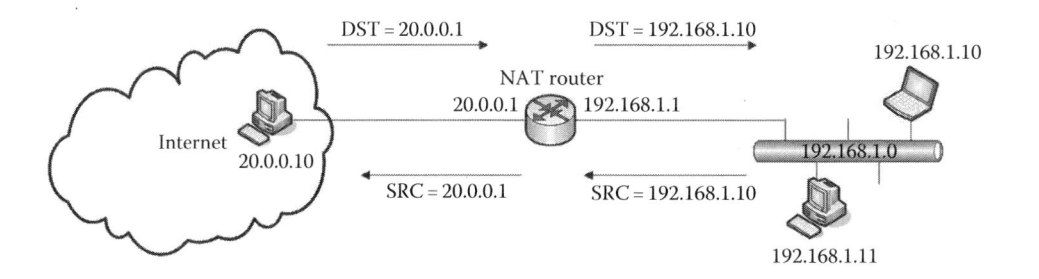

Figure 9.8 NAT service.

The IP address 20.0.0.1 is an Internet recognizable IP address so that it can be used to communicate with the computer that has the IP address 20.0.0.10. After the NAT router receives the response from the Internet computer, it replaces the destination IP address 20.0.0.1 with the recorded private IP address 192.168.1.10 so the response can be sent to the sender across the private network.

In case that two computers on the same private network communicate with the same public computer, both private source IP addresses will be replaced with the same public IP address. When the public computer sends response back to the NAT router, the NAT router needs to find a way to replace the public IP address with one of private IP addresses. However, this time, NAT has a difficult time figuring out which private IP address to be used to replace the public IP address since there are two private IP addresses corresponding to the same public IP address. The sophisticated NAT solves the problem by using port numbers provided by the protocol TCP or UDP. As shown in Figure 9.9, when replacing the private IP addresses with the public IP address, NAT records the private IP addresses with different port numbers.

In Figure 9.9, two computers with the IP addresses 192.168.1.10 and 192.168.1.11 on the private network are communicating with the same public computer on the Internet. When the computer with the IP address 192.168.1.10 sends an IP packet to the NAT router, the NAT router replaces the private source IP address with the public IP address 20.0.0.1:1110. When the computer with the IP address 192.168.1.11 sends an IP packet to the NAT router, the NAT router replaces the private source IP address with the public IP address 20.0.0.1:1111. NAT records the pair 192.168.1.10 and 20.0.0.1:1110 and the pair 192.168.1.11 and 20.0.0.1:1111 in the NAT table. Later, to respond to the request carried by the packet with the source IP address 20.0.0.1:1110, the IP address 20.0.0.1:1110 will be used as the destination address.

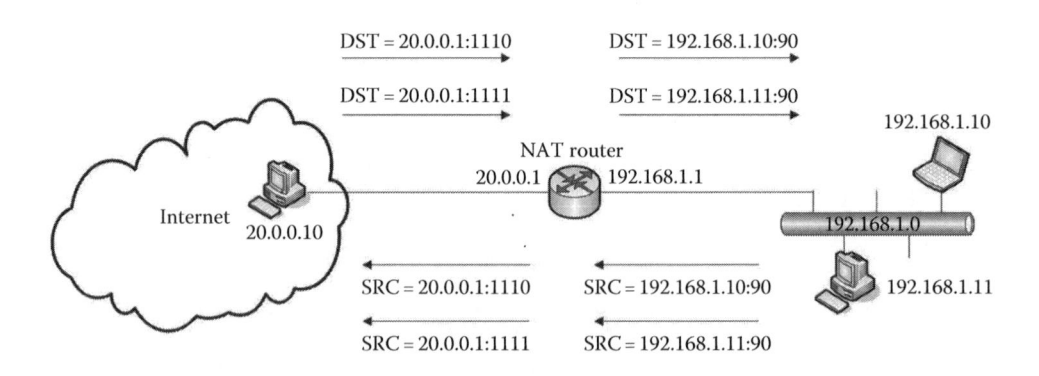

Direction	Old IP	New IP
Out	192.168.1.10:90	21.1.1.1:1110
Out	192.168.1.11:90	21.1.1.1:1111
In	21.1.1.1:1110	192.168.1.10:90
In	21.1.1.1:1111	192.168.1.11:90

Figure 9.9 NAPT service.

Similarly, to respond to the request carried by the packet with the source IP address 20.0.0.1:1111, the IP address 20.0.0.1:1111 will be used as the destination address. When the responding packets are delivered to the NAT router, the NAT router checks the destination addresses. If the destination address is 20.0.0.1:1110, NAT will translate it back to 192.168.1.10. Similarly, NAT will translate the destination address 20.0.0.1:1111 to 192.168.1.11. With the distinguished private destination addresses, the responding packets can now be sent to the right senders.

When NAT uses port numbers to identify senders' source IP addresses, it is called Network Address Port Translation (NAPT).

Now that NAT has been briefly explained, the next section will provide some information on its usage.

9.3.2 NAT Applications

By allowing private networks to access the Internet, the NAT service has a wide range of applications. The following are some of the common usages of NAT:

- The most common usage of NAT is to allow the network hosts on a private network to access the Internet. The network function that allows many network hosts to share a single public IP address is called IP Masquerade or MASQ.
- With NAT, a network host on the Internet can communicate with the e-mail server or web server placed behind a NAT router on a private network.
- NAT can also be used to redirect packets to a different destination.

The NAT table can be updated dynamically or statically. With the dynamic update, translations are dynamically added to the NAT table whenever they are available. If many network hosts on a private network need to access the Internet, it is necessary to use the dynamic update. With the static update, translations are manually added to the table and stay that way until they are manually modified. To allow the network hosts on a public network to communicate with the web server or e-mail server on a private network, the static NAT table update may be used to link the computers on the public network to the dedicated servers on the private network. For example, you can configure all the traffic with the port number 80 to be sent to the web server on the private network. When the web server communicates through a specific port such as the port 8080, NAT can be configured to translate the default port number 80 used by the web server to the port number 8080 or vice versa. By doing so, NAT is used to redirect the http traffic to the port 8080.

9.4 Routing and Remote Access Service

A router can be implemented with a dedicated hardware router or with a piece of software. The software-based router is less expensive and is suitable for light routing tasks.

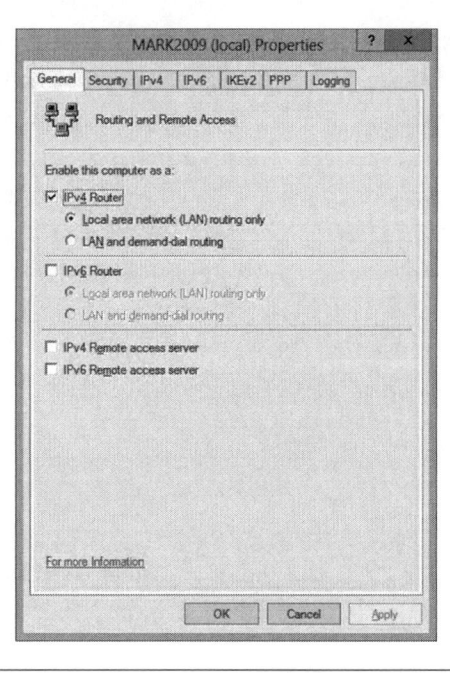

Figure 9.10   Router configuration.

RRAS provided by Microsoft can be used to create a software-based router. RRAS can also be configured to be a VPN server, a firewall, and a NAT router.

The configuration of RRAS can be done through the Route and Remote Access snap-in as shown in Figure 9.10.

We can see in Figure 9.10 that the option IPv4 Router is checked in the properties of the RRAS server. Therefore, the RRAS server can be used as a router.

The Route and Remote Access snap-in allows users to view the routing table. Figure 9.11 shows a routing table with two NICs, Ethernet and Ethernet 2, connected to a router.

In Figure 9.11, there is also a loopback interface which is used for testing.

Destination	Network mask	Gateway	Interface	Metric	Protocol	
127.0.0.0	255.0.0.0	127.0.0.1	Loopback	51	Local	
127.0.0.1	255.255.255.255	127.0.0.1	Loopback	306	Local	
169.254.0.0	255.255.0.0	0.0.0.0	Ethernet	286	Local	
169.254.219.40	255.255.255.255	0.0.0.0	Ethernet	286	Local	
169.254.255.255	255.255.255.255	0.0.0.0	Ethernet	286	Local	
192.168.1.0	255.255.255.0	0.0.0.0	Ethernet 2	276	Local	
192.168.1.2	255.255.255.255	0.0.0.0	Ethernet 2	276	Local	
192.168.1.255	255.255.255.255	0.0.0.0	Ethernet 2	276	Local	
224.0.0.0	240.0.0.0	0.0.0.0	Ethernet	286	Local	
255.255.255.255	255.255.255.255	0.0.0.0	Ethernet	286	Local	

MARK2009 - IP Routing Table

Figure 9.11   Routing table.

Windows Server provides the routing protocol RIP which is easy to configure and manage. RIP measures a packet's traveling distance by counting the number of hops. The measure may not be accurate since a hop across a network connected with the copper wire takes much more time than a hop across a network connected with the optical fiber. Also, RIP is less efficient in updating the routing information with other routers in the neighborhood. By using the Route and Remote Access snap-in, one can configure the following properties of RIP:

- Type of event to be logged (Figure 9.12).
- Accepting routing updates from which routers: A router may accept the routing updates from all routers in the neighborhood, or from a list of dedicated routers, or ignore the routing updates (Figure 9.13).
- The routing table update can be set as the Periodic update mode which removes the entries related to a neighborhood router which is unreachable, or the Auto static update mode which never automatically removes an entry in the routing table (Figure 9.14).
- Specifying an outgoing protocol as the RIP Version 1 broadcast, or RIP Version 2 broadcast, or RIP Version 2 multicast, or Silent RIP which disables outgoing announcements to other routers (Figure 9.14).
- Specifying an incoming protocol as Ignore incoming packets, RIP Versions 1 and 2, RIP Version 1 only, or RIP Version 2 only (Figure 9.14).
- Specifying the weight for a hop in a route (Figure 9.14).
- Forcing authentication between routers when updating routing tables (Figure 9.14).

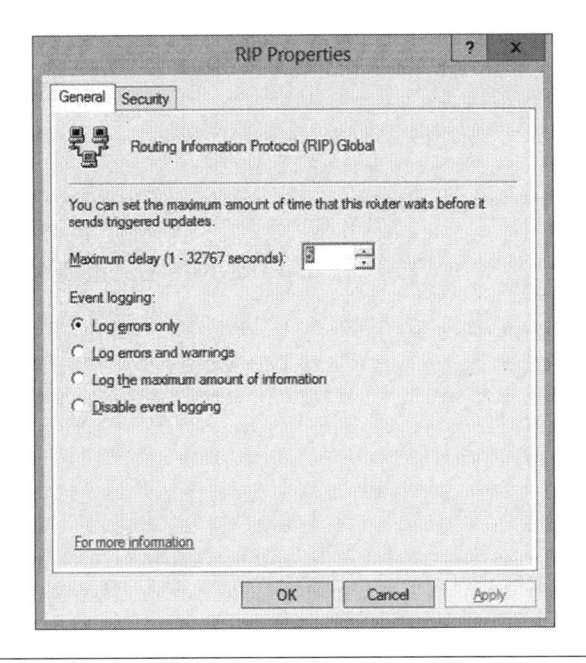

Figure 9.12 Log options.

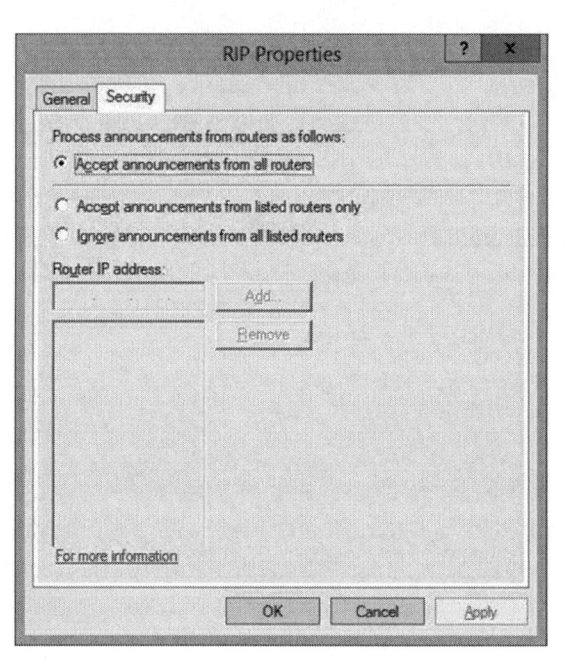

Figure 9.13   Security options.

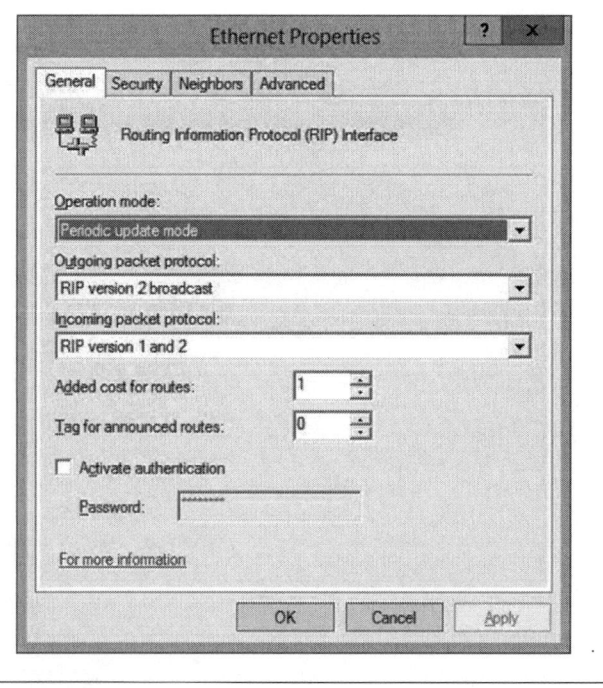

Figure 9.14   RIP general properties.

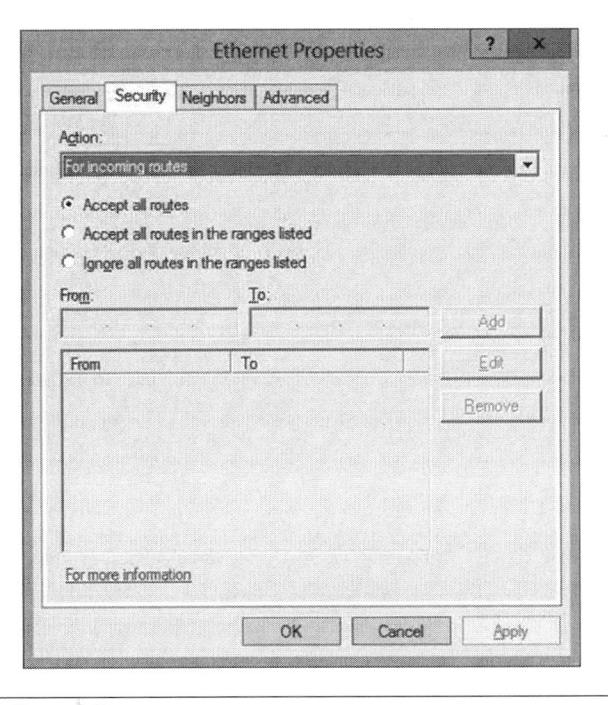

Figure 9.15   RIP security properties.

- Specify which incoming and outgoing routes are accepted on a NIC. One can choose to accept all routes, accept certain routes, or ignore certain routes (Figure 9.15).
- Specifying how a route interacts with the neighborhood routers. The options are use broadcast or multicast only, use neighbors in addition to broadcast and multicast, and use neighbors instead of broadcast or multicast (Figure 9.16).
- Specifying how often routing table announcements are sent, how long the entries in the routing table are kept, when the entries are removed from the routing table after they have been expired (Figure 9.17).
- Using split-horizon processing and poison-reverse processing to prevent routing loops in case of a router failure (Figure 9.17).
- Specifying if to send a triggered update when a change is made to the routing table (Figure 9.17).
- Specifying if to send a cleanup update when a router is shut down (Figure 9.17).
- Specifying if host routes or default routes should be processed or included in the received or sent announcements (Figure 9.17).
- Specifying if the router should stop aggregating multiple routes as a single router entry (Figure 9.17).

In Activity 9.1, you are going to configure some of these properties.

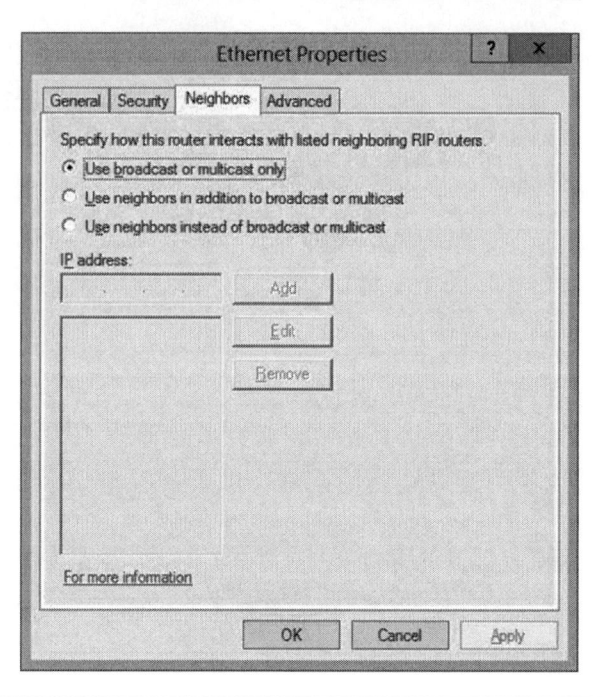

Figure 9.16   RIP neighbor properties.

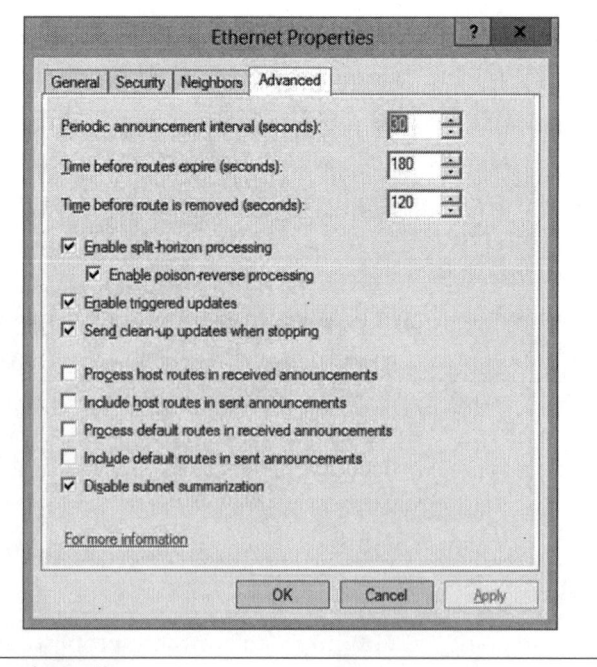

Figure 9.17   RIP advanced properties.

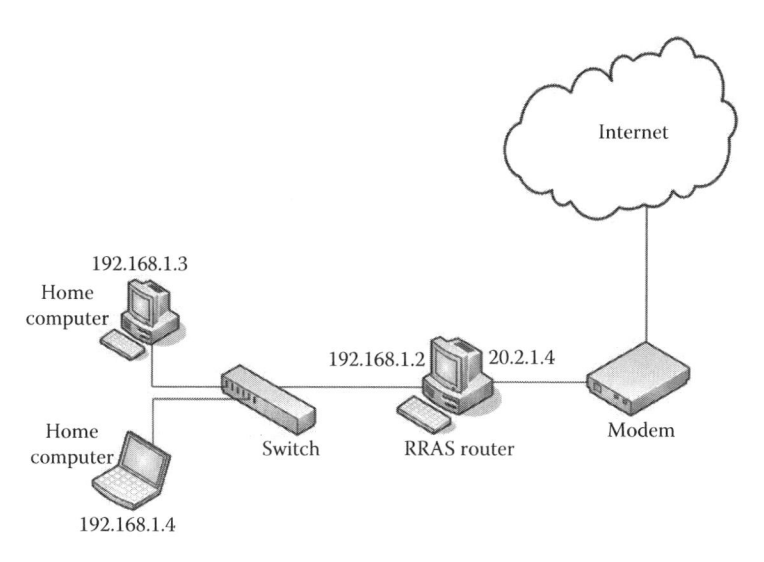

Figure 9.18   Home network.

Activity 9.1: Routing

In this activity, you will configure Windows Server 2012 so that it can route IP traffic. A home network can be set up as shown in Figure 9.18.

The RRAS server needs to be installed with two NICs. One NIC is connected to the switch which is linked to other home computers. The other NIC is connected to the Internet through the modem provided by your ISP. The computer used as the RRAS server should have the Windows Server 2012 or later installed. As a student, you can download Windows Server 2012 R2 or later from the Dreamspark website. The RRAS server does not need to be a powerful computer. A computer with 2 GB RAM and 60 GB hard drive space should be enough. Such a configured router will be used to communicate with the virtual network on Microsoft Azure. If a laptop computer is used as the RRAS server for the project, a USB to Fast Ethernet adapter can be used as the second NIC. The Internet side of the IP address should be different from the one in Figure 9.18. It depends on the IP address assigned by your ISP. Although Figure 9.18 shows two home computers, you only need one home computer for this activity. Note that not all modems assign a public IP address to the RRAS router. Some of the sophisticated modems actually include a built-in router. In such a case, your RRAS router may not get a public IP address. To allow the host on your home network to access the Internet, the key is that you need a public IP address to complete this activity. If there is no public IP address, you can only complete this activity on two private networks.

The activity can be done through the following tasks:

Task 1: Checking on Network Interface Cards
Task 2: Installing RRAS
Task 3: Installing and Using RIP

Task 1: Checking on Network Interface Cards

In this task, you will configure and test the IP addresses for both of the NICs installed on your RRAS server:

1. Assume that you have a computer used as the RRAS server which has the Windows Server 2012 installed. The RRAS server should have two NICs installed and you should have the administrator privilege on your RRAS server.
2. If you work at home, connect one of the NICs of the RRAS server directly to your Internet modem and connect the other NIC to the switch as shown in Figure 9.18. One NIC is used as the internal NIC and the other one is used as the external link. For example, you can use the Ethernet NIC as the external NIC and the Ethernet 2 NIC as the internal NIC.
3. Configure the internal NIC to have a fixed IP address as shown in Figure 9.19.
4. Configure the external NIC to have a dynamic IP address (Figure 9.20) which will be assigned by your ISP.
5. Reset the power of your Internet modem and reboot your RRAS server.
6. After logging on to your computer, press the **Windows logo** key and type **cmd**. Right click the **cmd** tile and select **Run as Administrator** to open the command window.
7. To find out which NIC is able to connect to the Internet, run the command `ipconfig`
8. Your RRAS server should have the public IP address on one of your NICs where the Ethernet NIC has the public IP address (Figure 9.21).

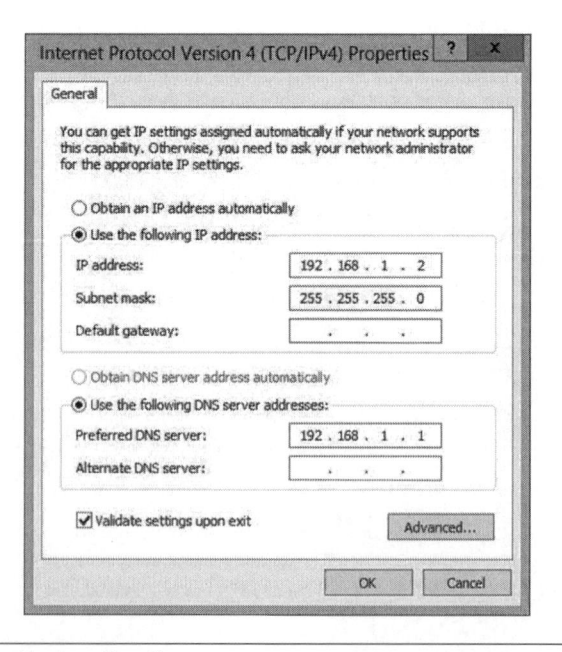

Figure 9.19   Internal IP address configuration.

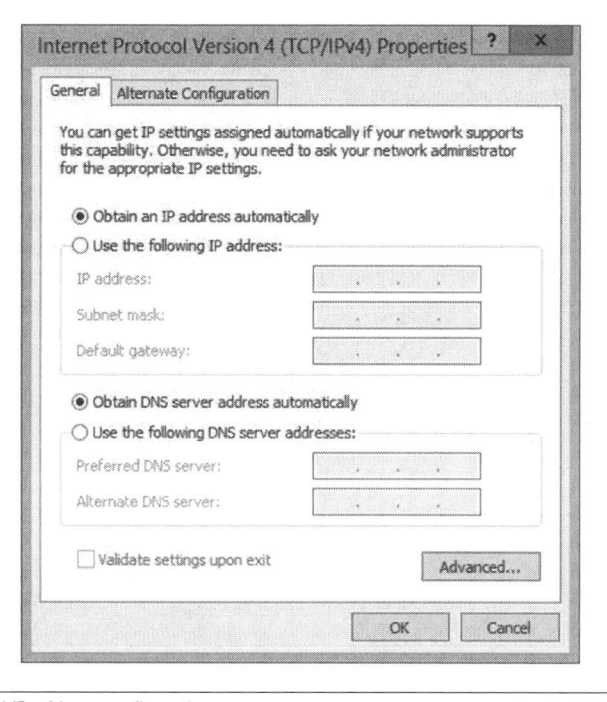

Figure 9.20 External IP address configuration.

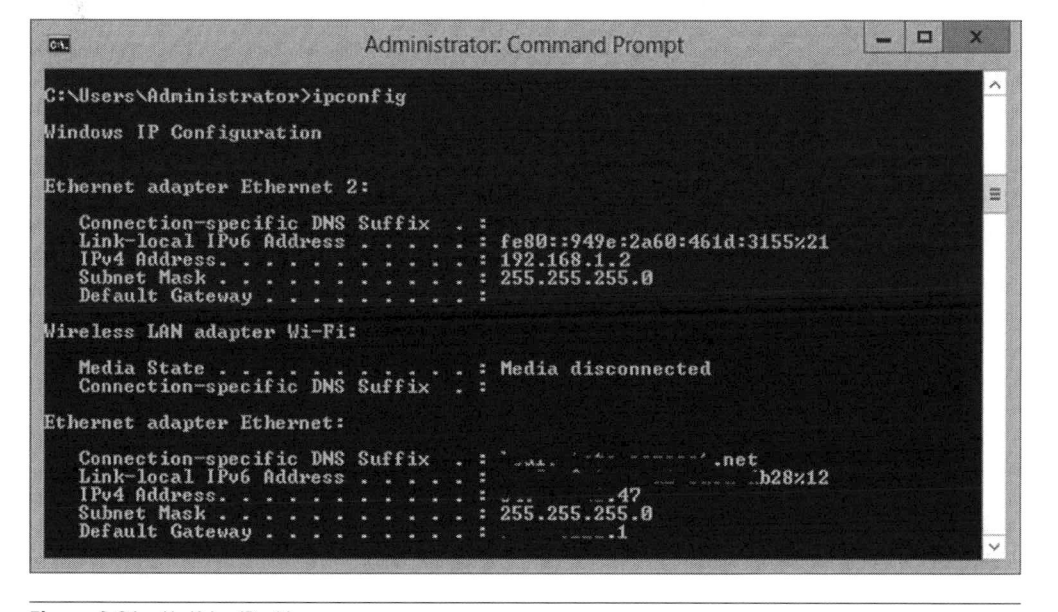

Figure 9.21 Verifying IP addresses.

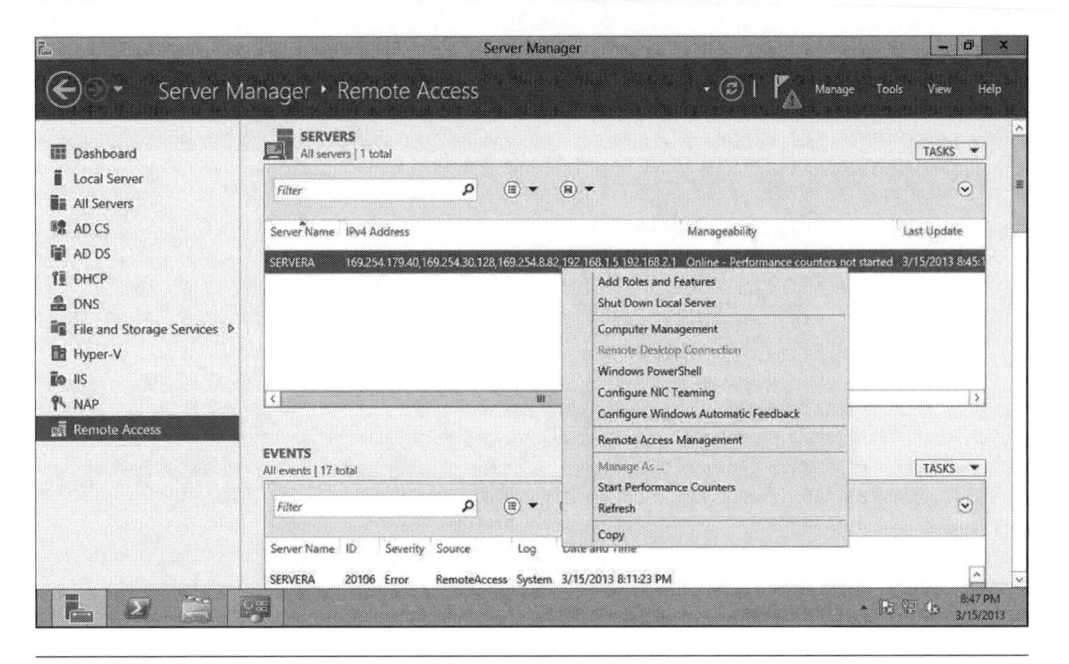

Figure 9.22　Adding roles and features.

Task 2: Installing RRAS

In this task, you will install and configure RRAS on your RRAS server:

1. Log on to your RRAS server as an administrator. To install routing protocols, in Server Manager, click **Remote Access** on the left-hand side of your screen. Right click your server in the middle and select **Add Roles and Features** (Figure 9.22).
2. Click **Next** three times to go to the Select server roles page. Expand the **Remote Access** node and check the **Routing** checkbox as shown in Figure 9.23.
3. Click **Next** twice to go to the Confirm installation selections page. Then, and click **Install** (Figure 9.24).
4. After the installation process is completed, press the **Windows logo** key to display the Start menu. Then, click **Administrative Tools**.
5. Double click **Routing and Remote Access** as shown in Figure 9.25.
6. If your server is already started, right click the name of your server in the left pane and select **Disable Routing and Remote Access** to disable the currently running service as shown in Figure 9.26. Click **Yes** to confirm it.
7. Right click the name of your server in the left pane and select **Configure and Enable Routing and Remote Access** as shown in Figure 9.27.
8. Click **Next** on the Welcome page.
9. On the Configuration page, click the option **Custom configuration** and click **Next** as shown in Figure 9.28.

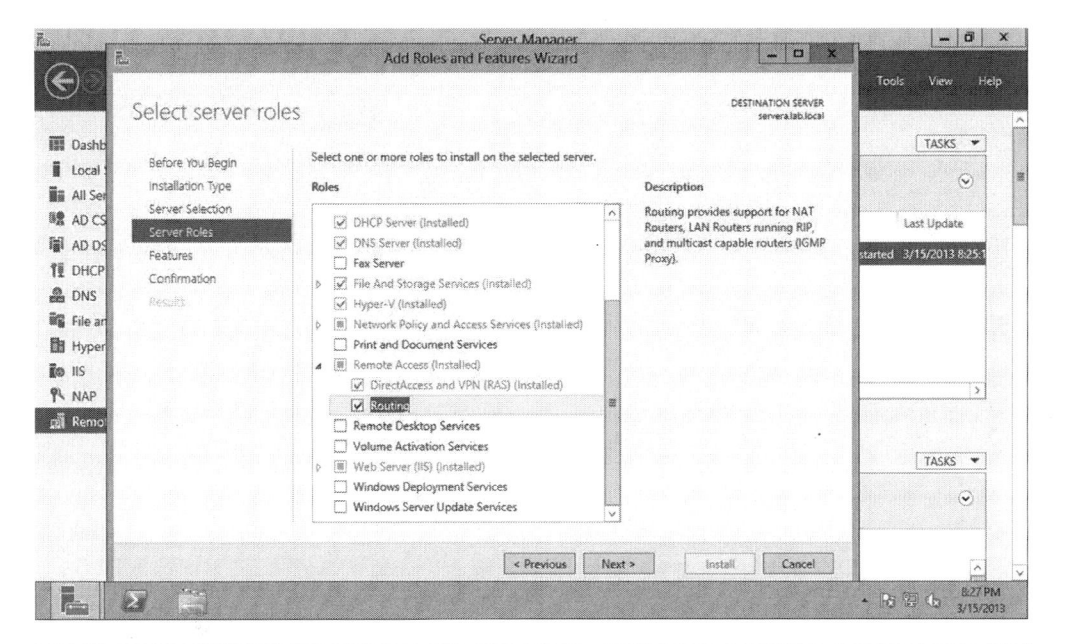

Figure 9.23   Selecting server role.

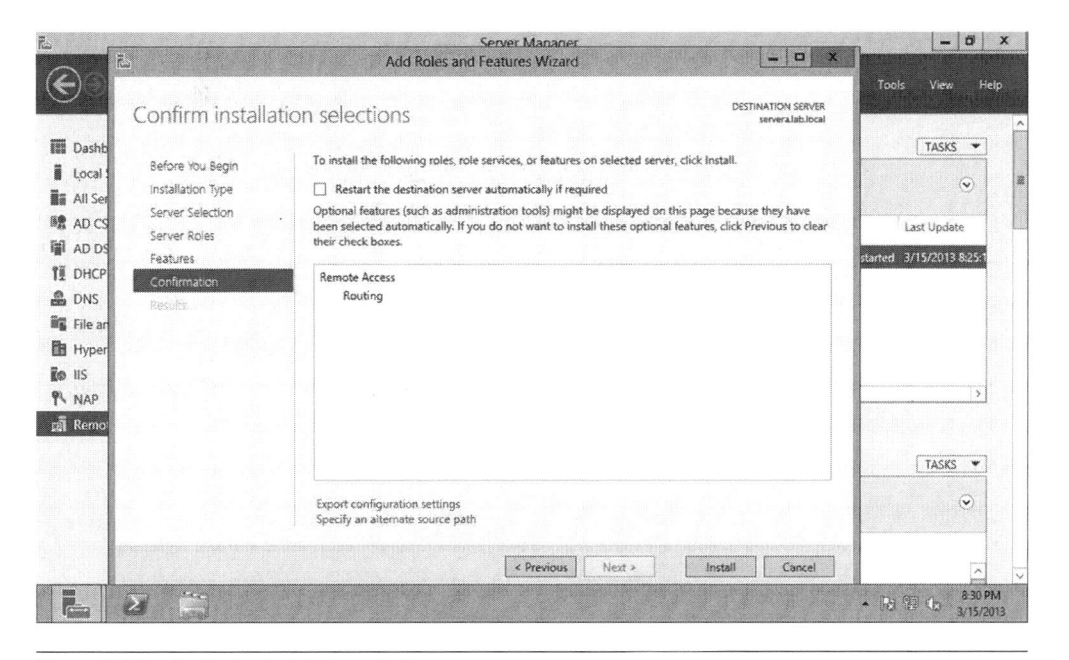

Figure 9.24   Confirming installation selections.

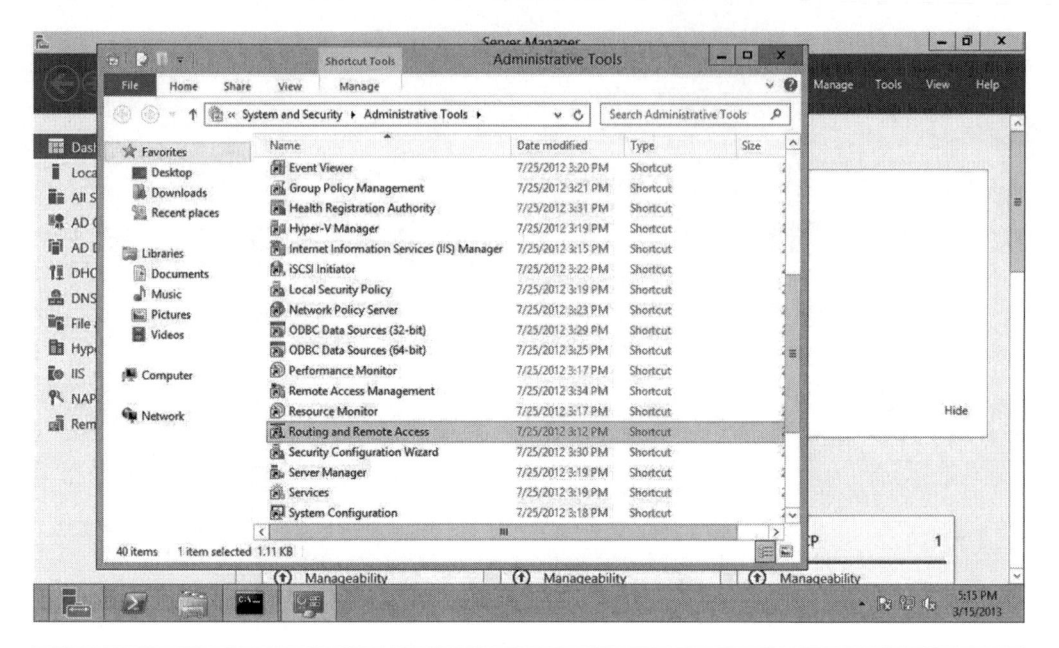

Figure 9.25 Opening routing and remote access.

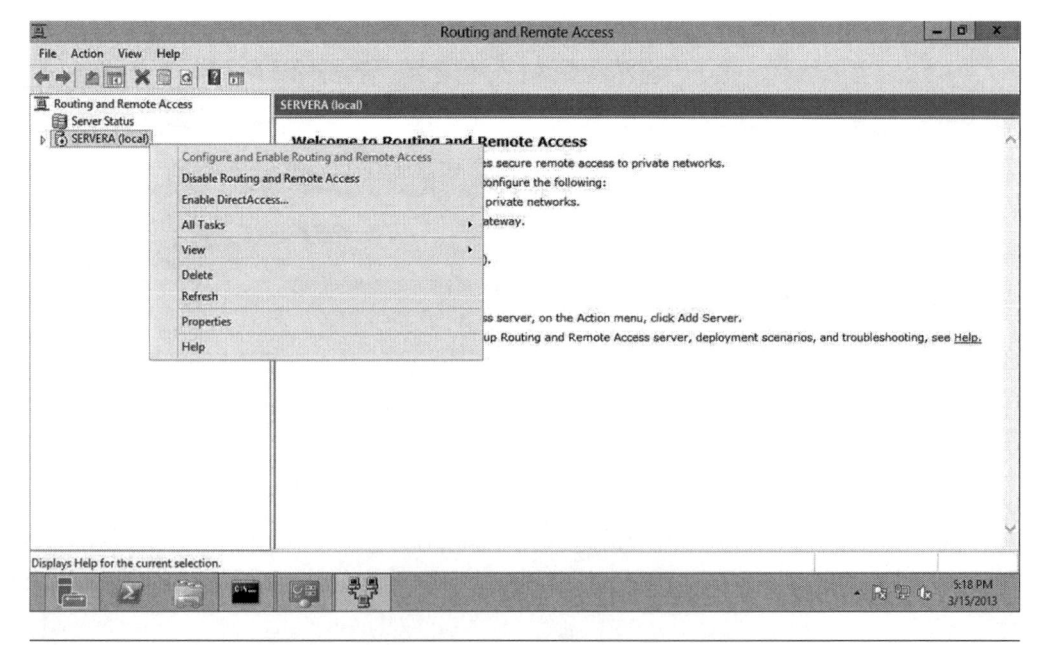

Figure 9.26 Disabling routing and remote access.

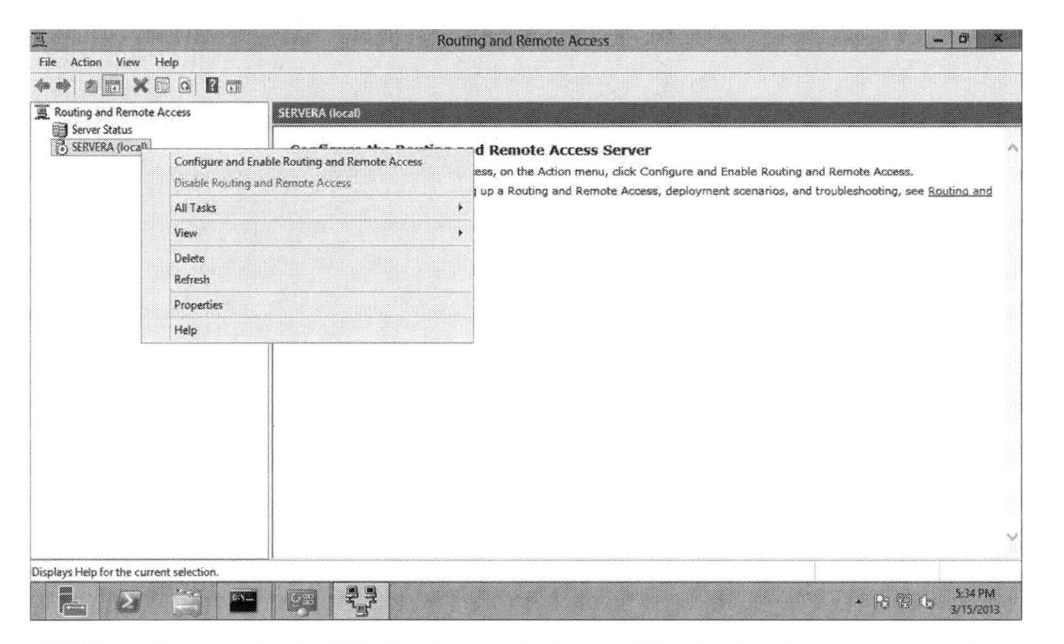

Figure 9.27   Configuring and enabling routing and remote access.

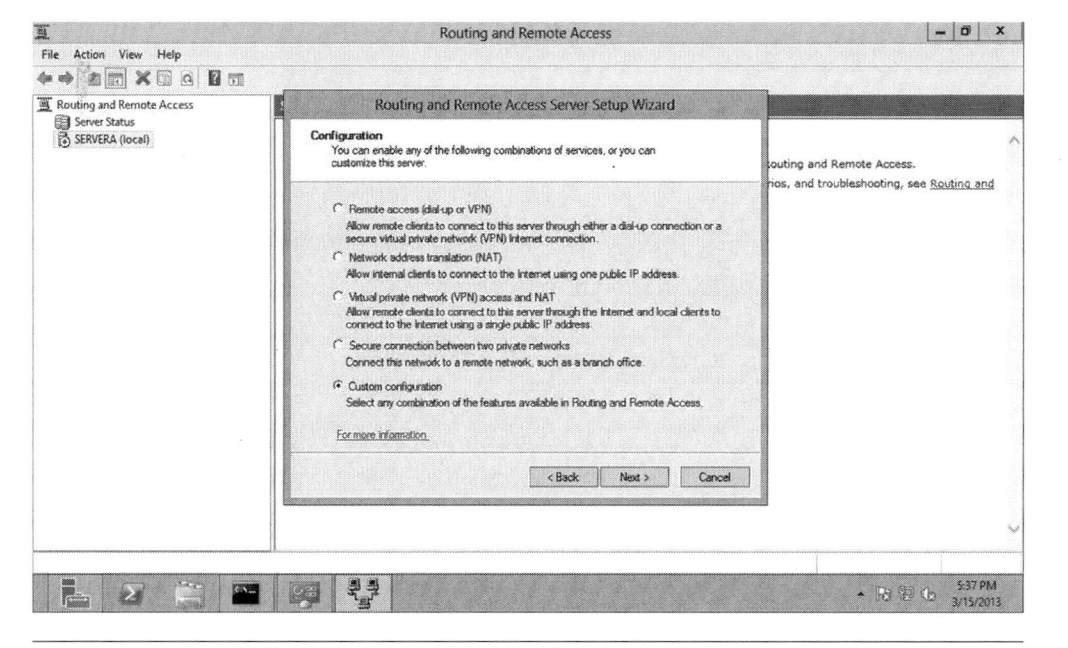

Figure 9.28   Service configuration.

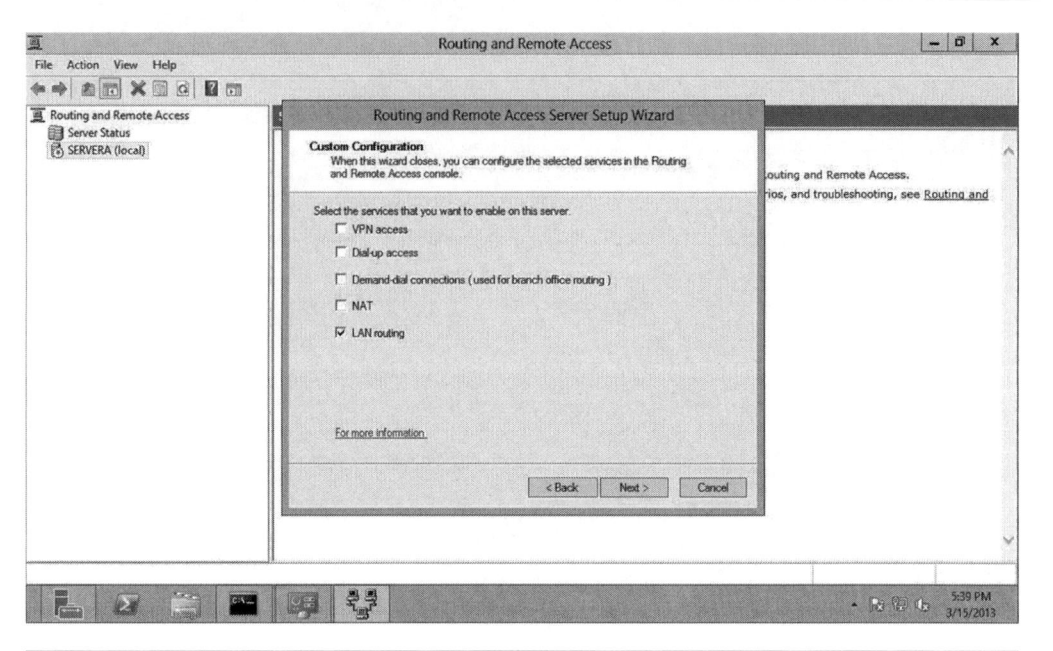

Figure 9.29   Custom configuration.

10. On the Custom Configuration page, check the checkbox **LAN routing** as shown in Figure 9.29, and click **Next**.
11. Click **Finish** and click **Yes** to confirm it. When prompted to start the service, click **Yes**.

Task 3: Installing and Using RIP

For this task, you install and apply the routing protocol RIP for dynamic routing:

1. Double click **IPv4** in the left pane. Right click **General** and select **New Routing Protocol** (Figure 9.30).
2. In the New Routing Protocol dialog, select **RIP Version 2 for Internet Protocol** and click **OK** as shown in Figure 9.31.
3. Right click **RIP** and select **New Interface** as shown in Figure 9.32.
4. Select the network interface adapter **Ethernet** (External NIC) and click **OK** as shown in Figure 9.33.
5. Click **OK** to accept the default configuration for RIP properties.
6. Right click **RIP** and select **New Interface**. Select the network interface adapter **Ethernet 2** and click **OK** as shown in Figure 9.34.
7. Click **OK** to accept the default RIP configuration.
8. To view the routing table, right click **Static Routes** and click **Show IP Routing Table** as shown in Figure 9.35.
9. The routing table includes the routes through both the Ethernet and Ethernet 2 NICs as shown in Figure 9.36.

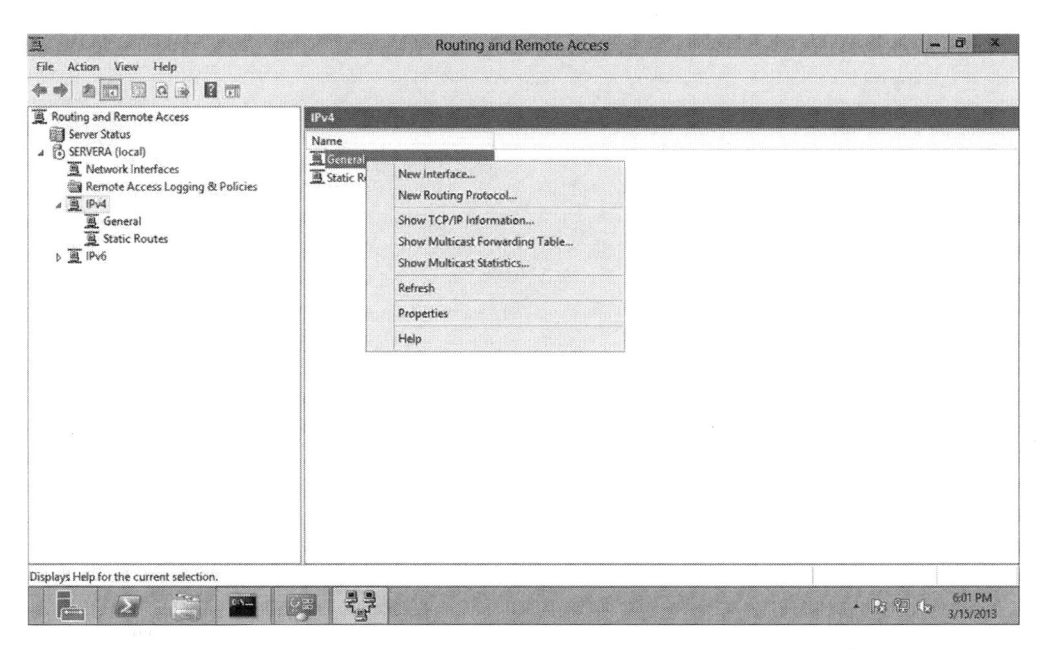

Figure 9.30   New routing protocol.

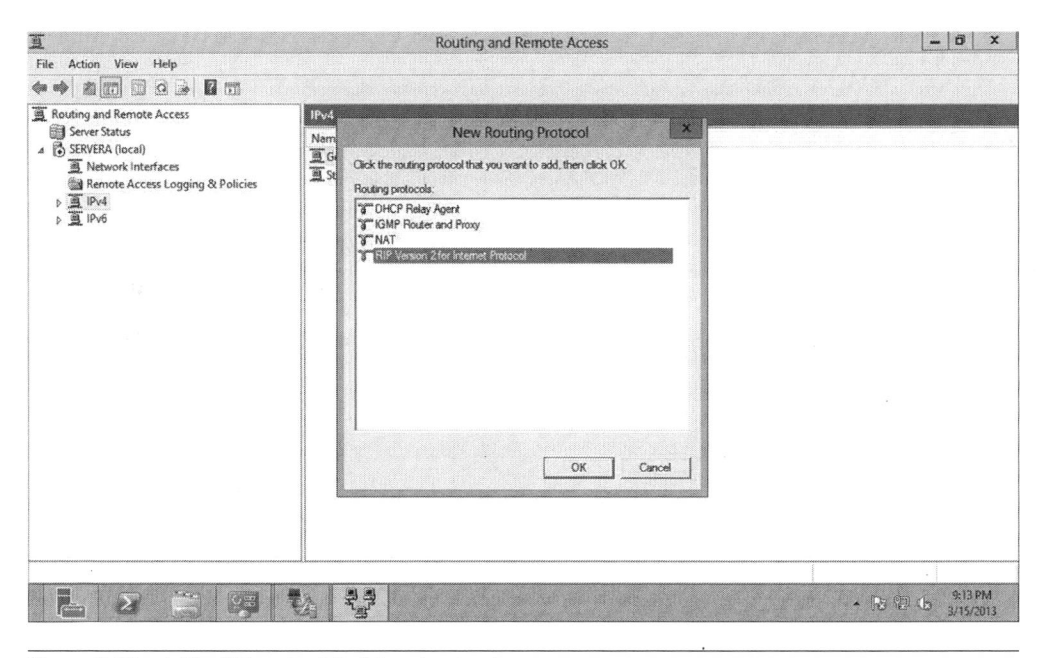

Figure 9.31   Adding RIP version 2 for Internet protocol.

10. Click **General** under the IPv4 node in the left pane. Right click **Ethernet** and select **Properties**. After the Ethernet Properties dialog is opened, check the option **Enable IP router manager** as shown in Figure 9.37. Then, click **OK**. Similarly, enable **IP router manager** for Ethernet 2.

11. To be able to test the communication between the RRAS server and a computer on the home network, you need to enable ICMP for both inbound and

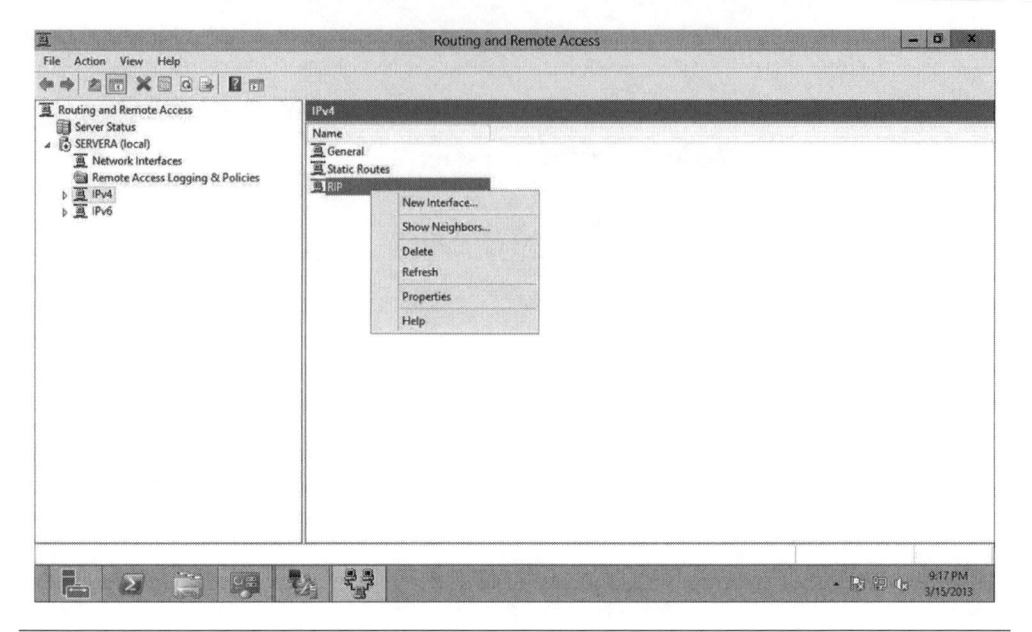

Figure 9.32   Adding NIC to routing service.

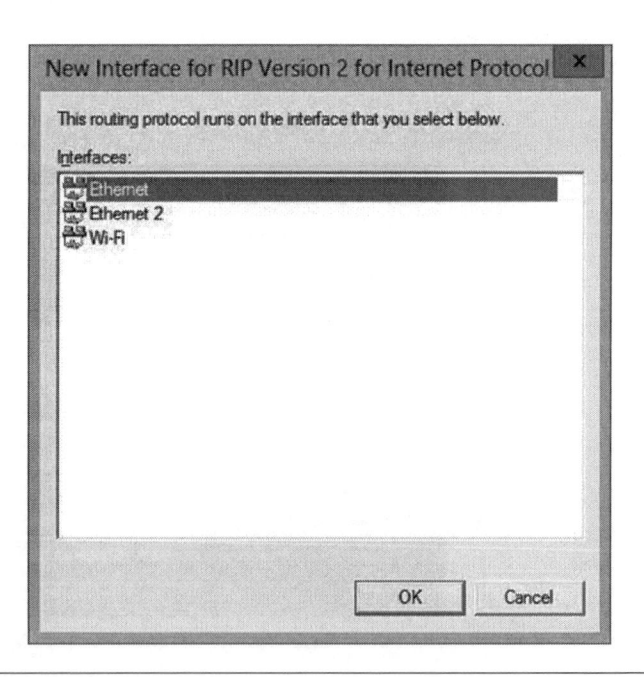

Figure 9.33   Selecting external NIC.

outbound traffic. To do so, click the **Tools** menu and select **Windows Firewall with Advanced Security**. Once the dialog is opened, click **Inbound Rules** and enable both **File and Printer Sharing (Echo Request - ICMPv4-In)** and **File and Printer Sharing (Echo Request - ICMPv6-In)** as shown in Figure 9.38. Similarly, enable these two protocols for **Outbound Rules**. Do the same for your home computer to be used to communicate with the RRAS server.

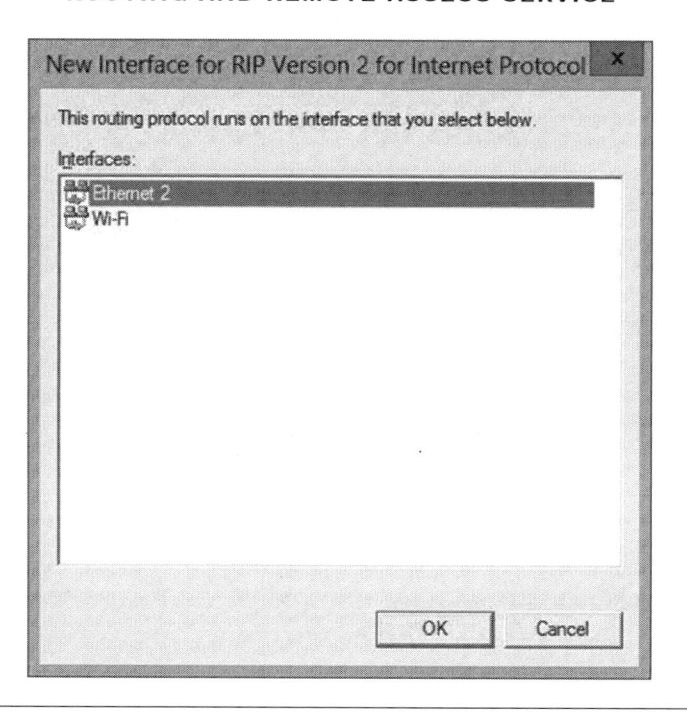

Figure 9.34   Selecting internal NIC.

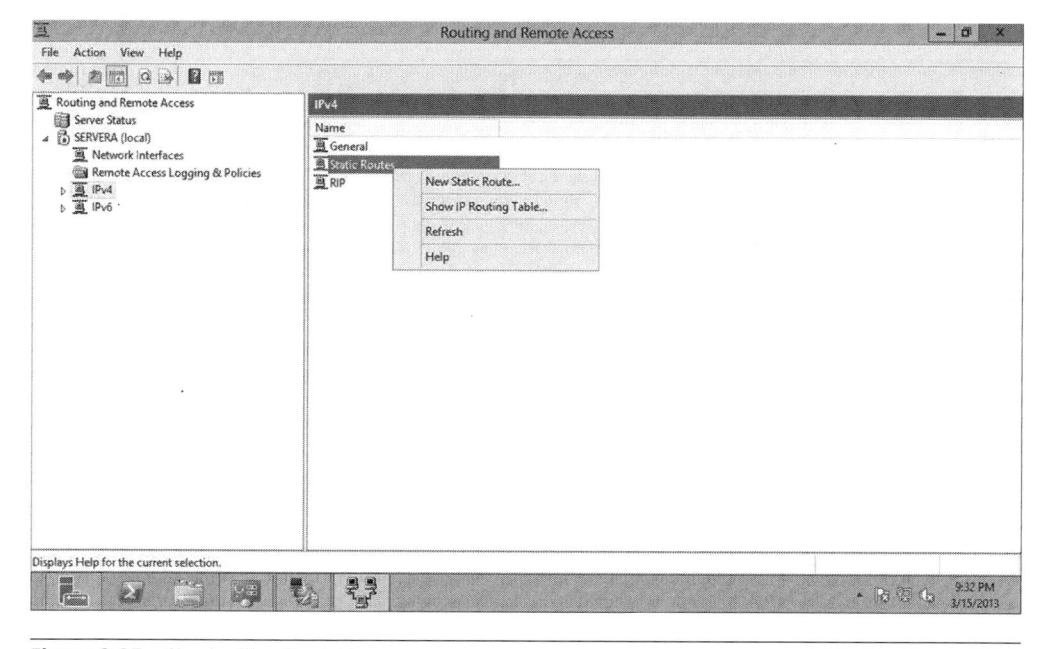

Figure 9.35   Showing IP routing table.

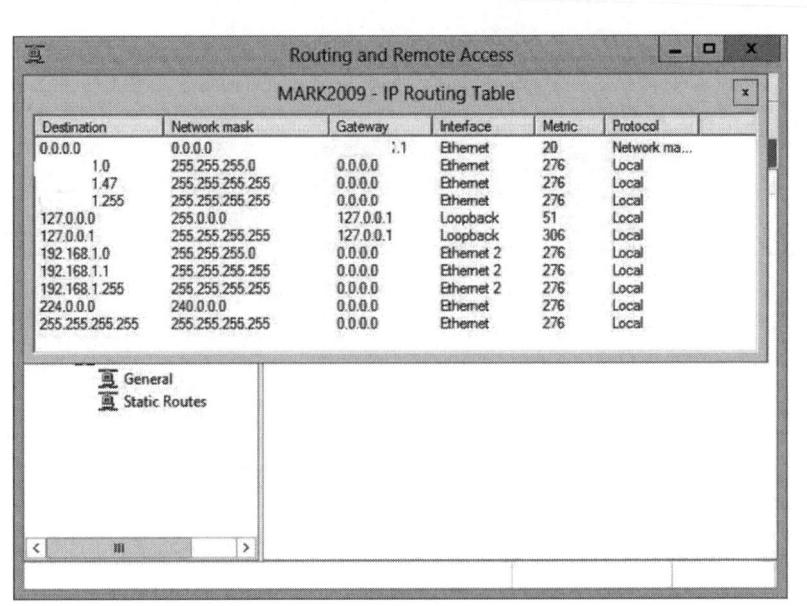

Figure 9.36   Routing table.

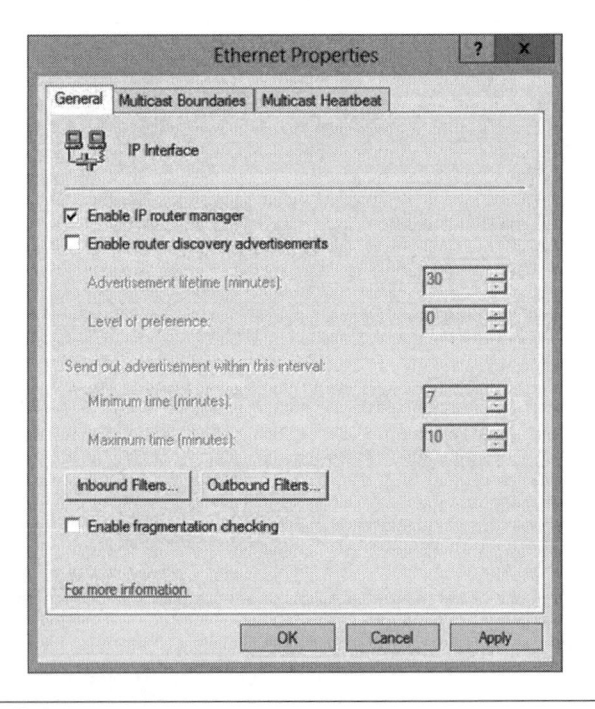

Figure 9.37   Enabling IP router manager.

12. You can now ping from your computer on your home network to the RRAS server and vice versa to make sure that the communication is established. To ping the external NIC on the RRAS server from the home computer, open the command prompt window and use the ping command to ping the IP address of the external NIC as shown in Figure 9.39.

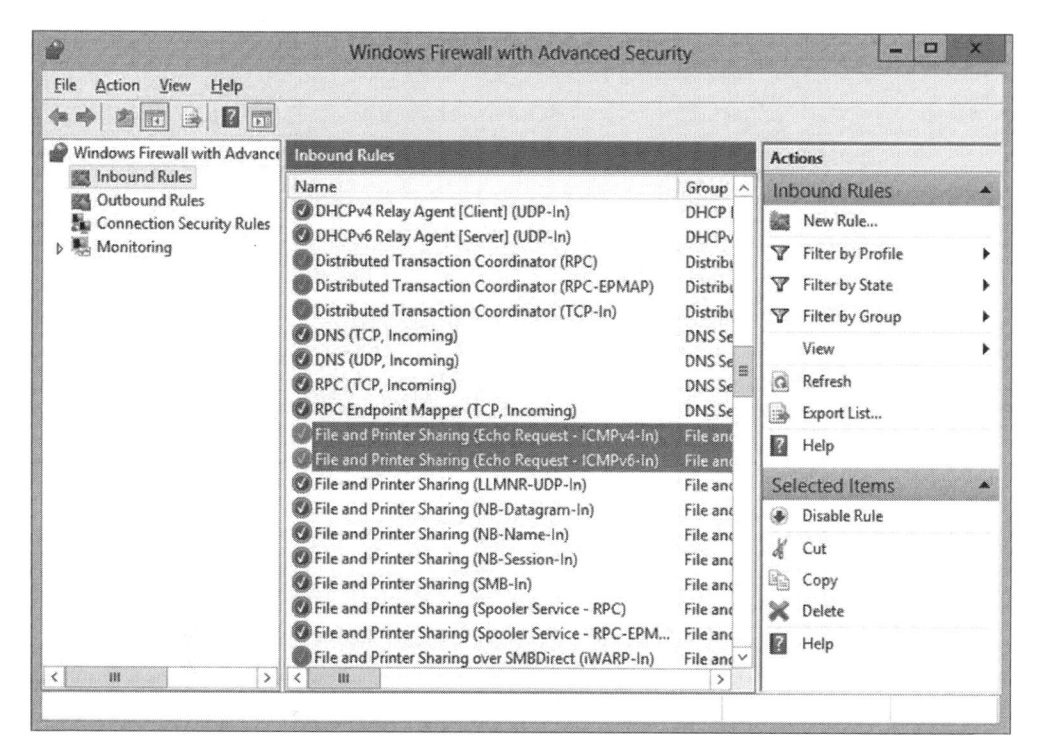

Figure 9.38 Enabling ICMP.

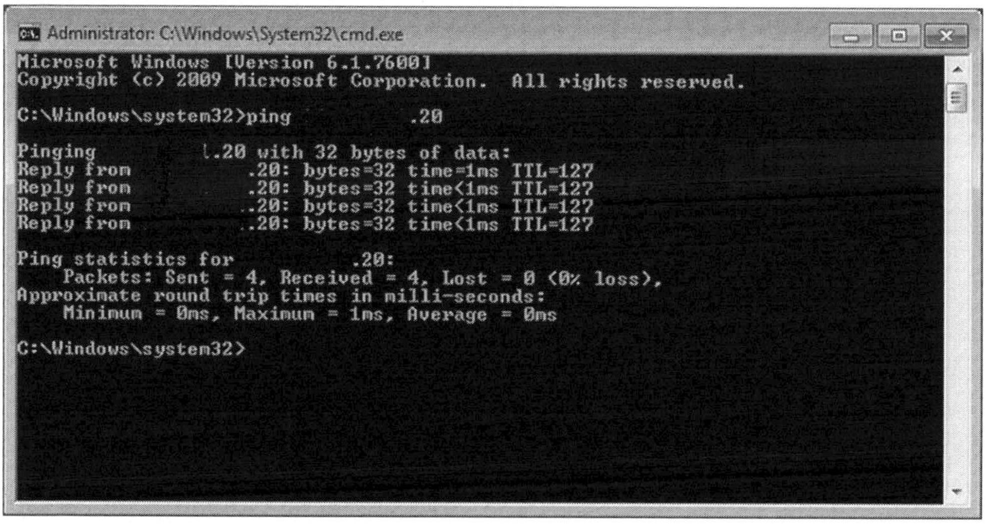

Figure 9.39 Pinging external NIC from home computer.

Earlier, a computer installed with Windows Server 2012 has been used to implement the RRAS router. As described in the activity, two NICs are used to connect your home network and the Internet. Although the computer is configured as a router, it does not have network services such as DNS and DHCP on it. Therefore, it is not a fully functioning router yet. Later, the RRAS router developed here will be used to illustrate a site-to-site connection to the virtual network on the cloud. For now, you should temporarily disconnect it from your home network. It is only used for illustration.

Activity 9.2: NAT

In this activity, you will configure the RRAS server as a NAT router so that your home computers can share the Internet. Assume that your home network is set up as shown in Figure 9.18:

1. On your computer installed with RRAS, in Server Manager, click **Tools** and **Routing and Remote Access**.
2. To install NAT, expand the **IPv4** node, right click **General**, and then click **New Routing Protocol** (Figure 9.40).
3. In the **New Routing Protocol** dialog, select **NAT**, and then click **OK**.
4. Right click **NAT**, and then click **Properties** as shown in Figure 9.41.
5. In order for the RRAS server to be able to respond to DHCP address requests, click the **Address Assignment** tab, select the **Automatically assign IP addresses by using the DHCP allocator** check box as shown in Figure 9.42.
6. To have a private subnet for your home network, enter **192.168.1.0** and a subnet mask of 255.255.255.0. Your NAT server can now respond to DHCP requests with address assignments from 192.168.1.1 through 192.168.1.254. Then, click **OK**.

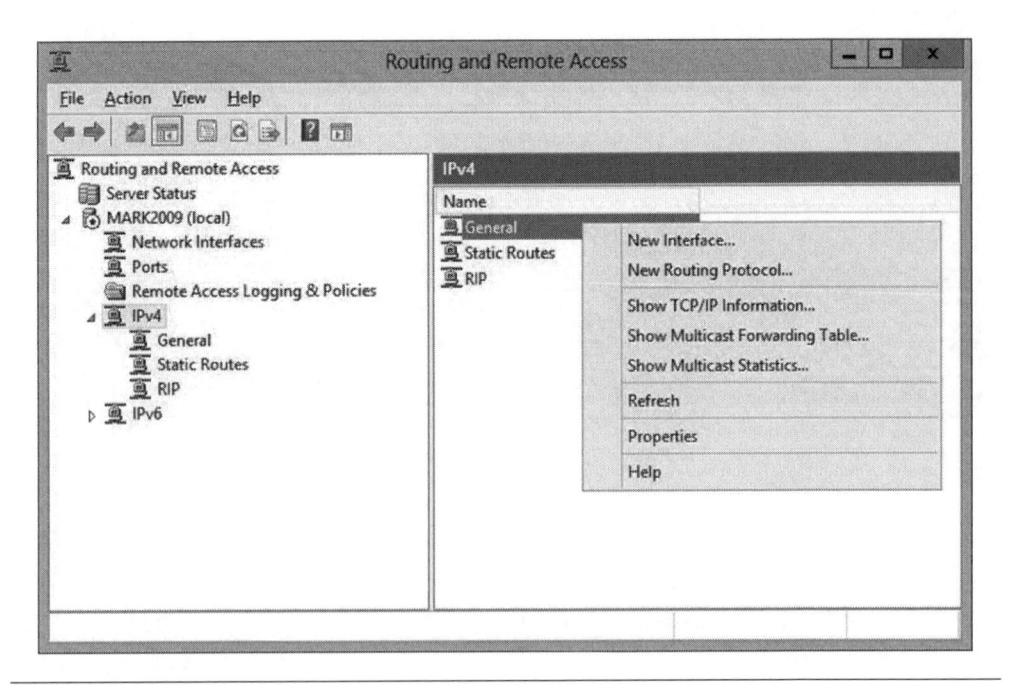

Figure 9.40   Installing NAT.

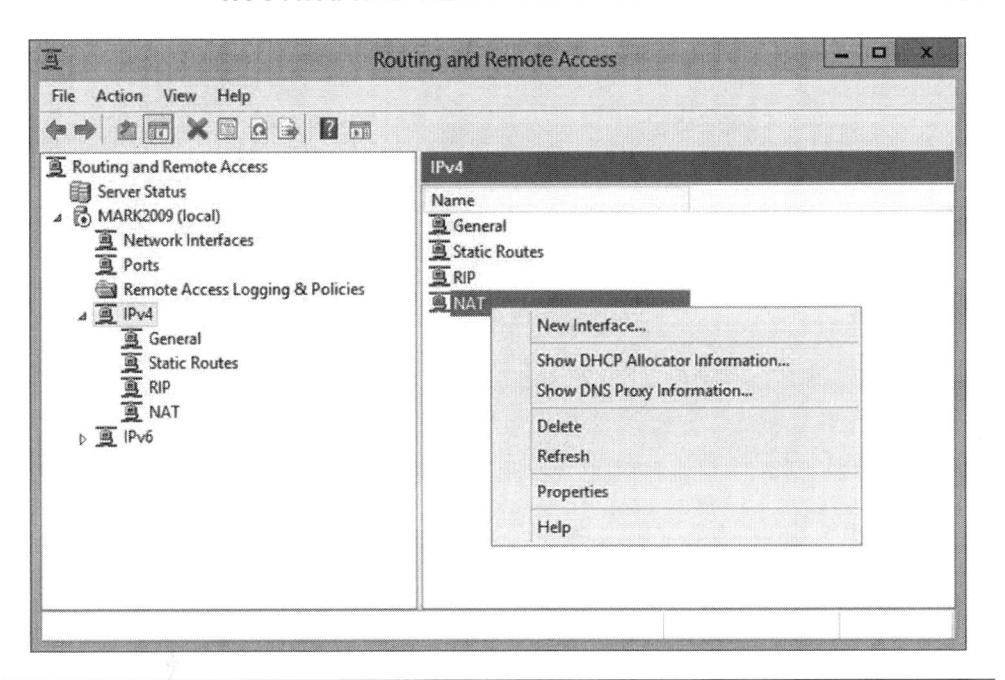

Figure 9.41 Configuring NAT.

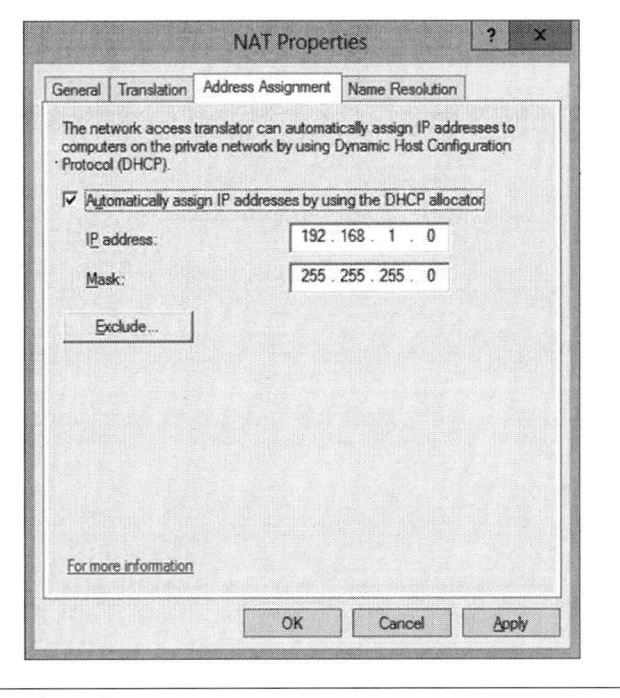

Figure 9.42 Address assignment.

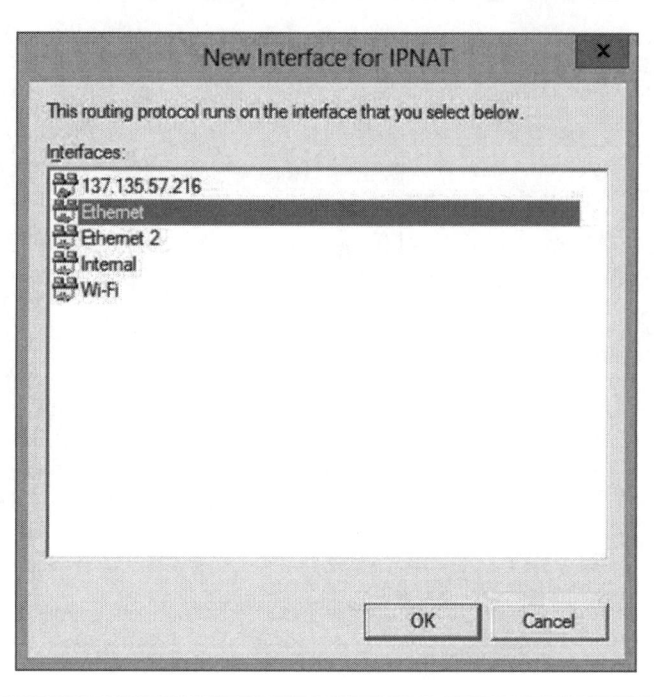

Figure 9.43 Selecting public NIC.

7. To specify your external NIC as the public interface of NAT, right click **NAT,** and then click **New Interface**. Select the interface **Ethernet,** and then click **OK** (Figure 9.43).
8. Click the **NAT** tab, select **Public interface connected to the Internet** and **Enable NAT on this interface,** and then click **OK** (Figure 9.44).
9. To add the private interface to NAT, right click **NAT,** and then click **New Interface**. Select the interface **Ethernet 2,** and then click **OK** as shown in Figure 9.45.
10. Under the **NAT** tab, select **Private interface connected to private network,** and then click **OK** as shown in Figure 9.46.
11. To test the connection, log on to one of the computers on your private home network. Open the command prompt and enter the following command:
    ```
    ipconfig
    ```
12. You will see that your home computer is assigned an IP address with the network ID 192.168.1.0 (Figure 9.47).
13. Now, the computers on your home private network can access the Internet as shown in Figure 9.48.

Earlier, a NAT service has been developed. With the NAT service, a number of computers on a private network can share one public IP address. Most of the DSL routers also include the NAT service. That is why home computers on a private network can all access the Internet though a DSL router.

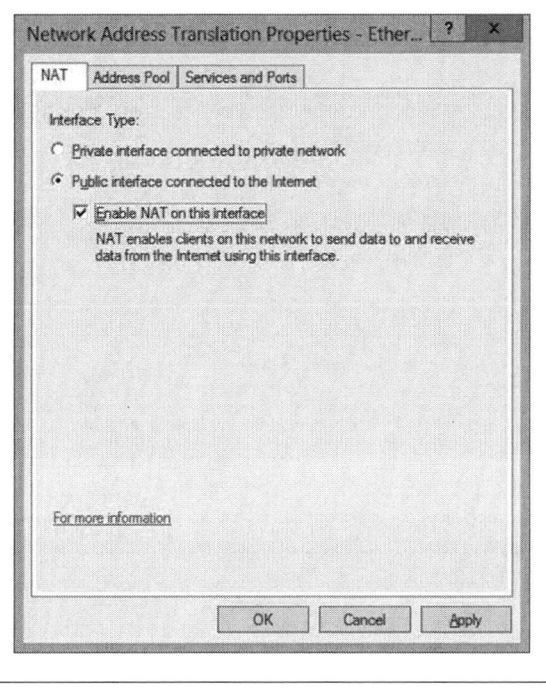

Figure 9.44   Specifying public interface.

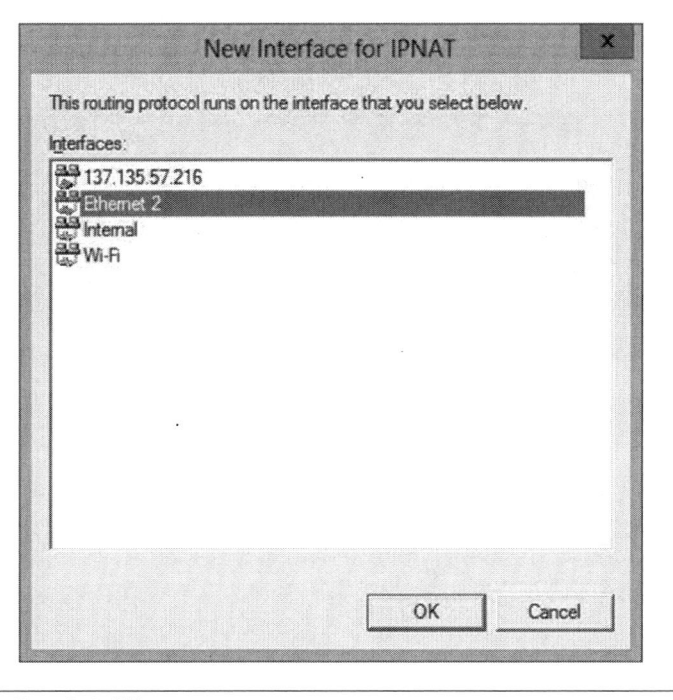

Figure 9.45   Selecting private NIC.

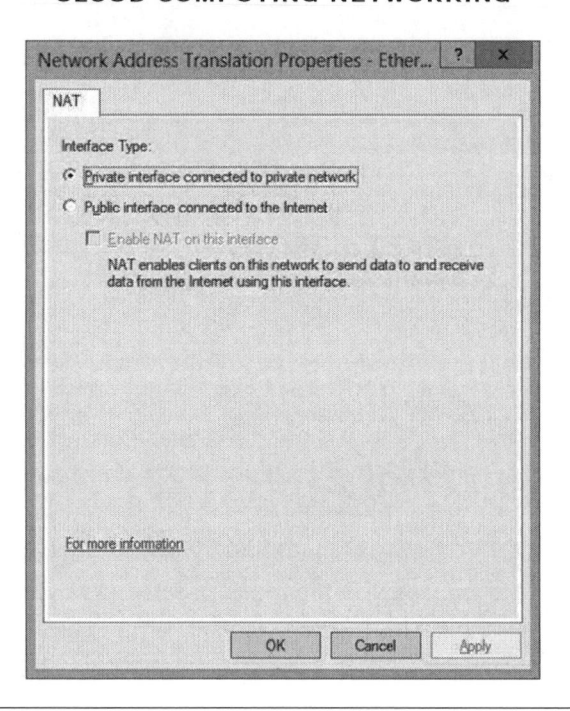

Figure 9.46   Specifying private interface.

```
C:\Windows\system32\cmd.exe

Wireless LAN adapter Wireless Network Connection:

   Media State . . . . . . . . . . . : Media disconnected
   Connection-specific DNS Suffix  . :

Ethernet adapter Local Area Connection:

   Connection-specific DNS Suffix  . :
   Link-local IPv6 Address . . . . . : fe80::e069:94d4:a5f5:fca0%11
   IPv4 Address. . . . . . . . . . . : 192.168.1.4
   Subnet Mask . . . . . . . . . . . : 255.255.255.0
   Default Gateway . . . . . . . . . : 192.168.1.2

Tunnel adapter Reusable Microsoft 6To4 Adapter:

   Media State . . . . . . . . . . . : Media disconnected
   Connection-specific DNS Suffix  . :

Tunnel adapter Teredo Tunneling Pseudo-Interface:

   Media State . . . . . . . . . . . : Media disconnected
   Connection-specific DNS Suffix  . :

Tunnel adapter 6TO4 Adapter:
```

Figure 9.47   Private IP address assigned by NAT.

9.5 Summary

This chapter introduces routing which passes network traffic from one network to another network. A routing protocol can be used to automatically update the routing table and to find the shortest path from a source network to a destination network. This chapter explains how a router can accomplish these tasks. It introduces the NAT service which allows computers with private IP addresses to share a single public IP

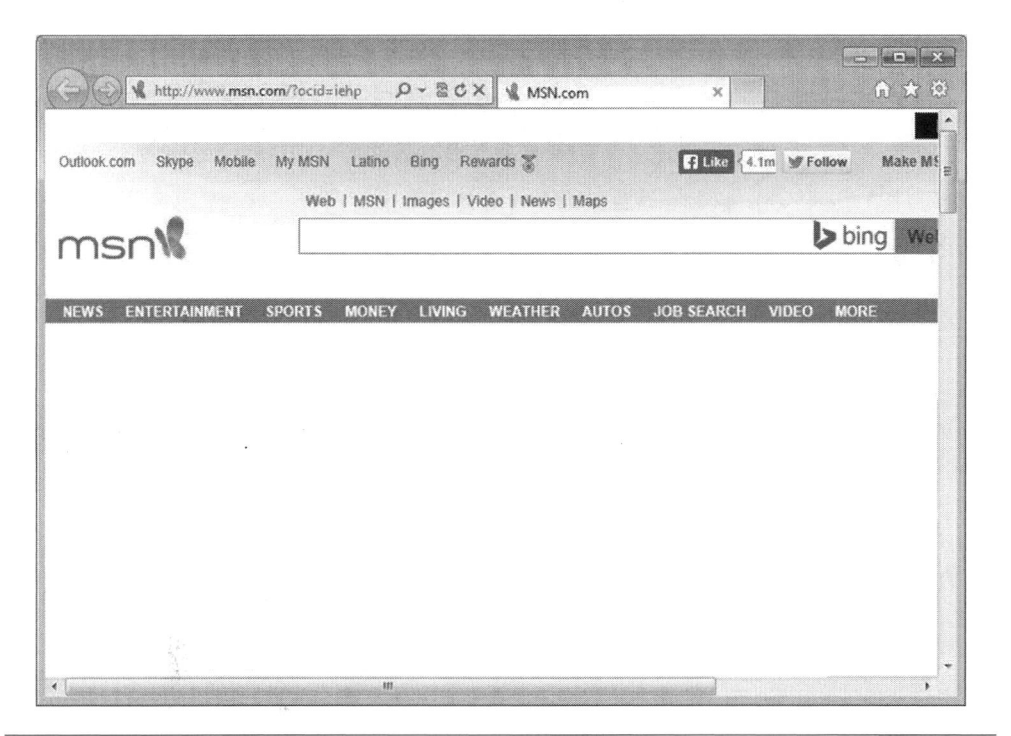

Figure 9.48   Accessing Internet from private network.

address. With NAT, the computers on the private network at home or in a small office are able to access the Internet. This chapter discusses some of the RRAS configuration options and carries out the configuration tasks in the hands-on practice. The RRAS router developed here will play a key role in linking the home network to the virtual network on the cloud.

Review Questions

1. What do you do with a router?
2. What is Routing and Remote Access Service (RRAS)?
3. What is Network Address Translation (NAT)?
4. What tasks can a router perform?
5. What are the disadvantages for a router to link too many networks?
6. How are the columns defined in a routing table?
7. What is the maximum transmission unit (MTU)?
8. When will fragments be reassembled?
9. What are the advantages and disadvantages of static routing?
10. What criteria can be possibly used to measure an optimal route?
11. What are the two major algorithms for calculating an optimal route?
12. What routing tasks can be performed by the routing protocol OSPF?
13. Compared with the distance vector (DV) routing algorithm, what are the disadvantages of Dijkstra's shortest path algorithm?

14. What routing tasks can be performed by a router with the DV routing algorithm?
15. What is hierarchical routing?
16. How does NAT work?
17. What are the usages of NAT?
18. What are the advantages and disadvantages of RIP?
19. What are the options provided by RRAS for the incoming protocol?
20. What are the options provided by RRAS for the outgoing protocol?

10

VIRTUAL PRIVATE NETWORK

Objectives

- Gain knowledge of the virtual private network (VPN) architecture.
- Understand VPN tunneling.
- Understand VPN security.
- Remotely access Microsoft Azure through a VPN.
- Set up point-to-site and site-to-site connections.

10.1 Introduction

Previously, we have discussed network security measures such as Secure Sockets Layer (SSL) certificates and Internet Protocol Security (IPSec). By using SSL certificates or IPSec, a virtual private network (VPN) allows users to remotely access network resources through the Internet. In this chapter, we are going to take a look at how these security measures are used in the VPN technology. A VPN allows a computer on the home network to access virtual machines created on Microsoft Azure. The VPN technology allows the virtual machines created on Microsoft Azure to share the network resources available on the home network and vice versa. With a VPN, an organization can deliver private messages through the public network such as the Internet. While a data transaction is carried out through the Internet, the VPN technology provides the authentication and encryption mechanisms to protect the data transaction. This chapter examines how the VPN service works. VPN-related concepts and technologies are introduced. This chapter also describes the configuration of VPN servers and VPN clients and VPN service management.

10.2 Virtual Private Network Architecture

The VPN architecture consists of VPN servers, VPN clients, and the public network connecting the VPN servers and clients. Usually, the public network is the Internet. When using the Internet to deliver messages, the IP packets can be easily intercepted by hackers. Various encryption mechanisms are used for confidentiality. To be able to connect to a VPN server, the client computer must have the VPN client software installed and must be configured so that it is able to communicate with the VPN server. When the client requests a connection to the VPN server, the VPN server checks the client's authentication information. If the user is authenticated, the VPN server will establish a secure connection to link the VPN client to the VPN server. The secure connection is established with the tunneling protocol that is provided by the VPN server software. Before a data transaction begins, the data need to be encrypted and then transmitted to the receiver over the public network. Once the data are delivered to the receiver, they will be decrypted. This is how the VPN delivers private data over the public network.

The VPN can protect data transactions through various types of network connections. The most common usage of the VPN is to access a server through the Internet. Once a client logs on to a VPN server remotely, the client is able to access the network where the VPN server is located. For example, by using the VPN, a student can remotely access a lab server located on campus through the Internet. After having logged on to the VPN server, the student can access the network resources such as a specific computer in the lab or the network printer. Figure 10.1 illustrates the remote access to an on-campus network with the VPN technology.

A VPN can also be used to protect data transactions over a site-to-site connection in an organization's network. The site-to-site connection links two private networks. For example, a university system may include multiple campuses. Each campus has its own private network. The VPN can be used to protect data transactions between campuses. Data transactions among business partners can also be protected by the VPN. Figure 10.2 illustrates a site-to-site VPN connection.

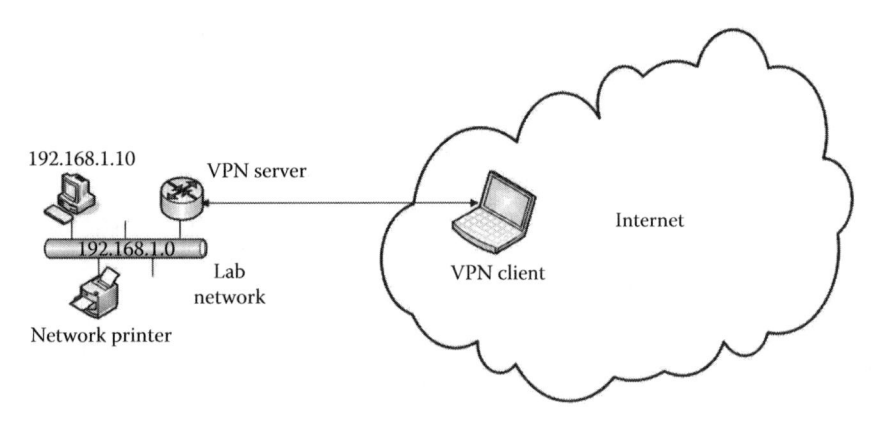

Figure 10.1 Remote access through VPN.

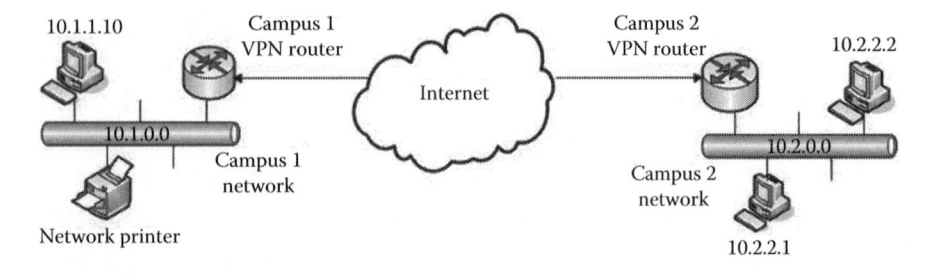

Figure 10.2 Site-to-site VPN connection.

In Figure 10.2, the routers are configured as the endpoints of the VPN connection. The VPN routers connect the Internet to the local area networks. Through the VPN routers, the data on the Internet can be forwarded to the local area networks.

By using a VPN on the Internet, there is no need to develop a WAN to connect multiple sites. The operation cost can be significantly reduced. The Internet also provides worldwide connections. With a site-to-site connection, a private cloud can be integrated into Microsoft Azure to form a hybrid cloud. The hybrid cloud can leverage the best of both worlds.

Before a secure connection can be established between two endpoints, the endpoints need to agree on a contract of how they will protect their data transaction and how they will securely exchange information. Such a contract is called a security association (SA). Internet Key Exchange (IKE) is a protocol that manages SAs. IKE is designed to centralize SA management. With IKE, information exchange between two endpoints is protected. It is also used to protect information exchange between a network host and an IKE-enabled network.

It takes two phases for IKE to establish a secure communication. During the first phase, IKE establishes an authenticated and secure channel that is named Phase 1 SA. IKE makes both endpoints agree on the authentication and encryption algorithms. At Phase II, corresponding to a Phase 1 SA, two SAs are generated by IKE, one for the inbound communication and the other for the outbound communication. IPSec policies are used to determine the maximum number of Phase II SA negotiations.

10.3 VPN Tunneling

In the VPN, the tunneling technology uses a secure protocol such as IPSec to encapsulate an unsecure protocol such as the TCP/IP protocol suite. The tunneling protocol establishes a secure connection between the VPN client and the VPN server. The tunneling protocol carries out security-related tasks such as encryption and authentication. To establish a tunnel that is a secure connection between the VPN server and the VPN client, both of the tunnel endpoints must be configured to agree on parameters such as IP address assignments and encryption. Once the tunnel is created, the tunnel client encapsulates the IP packet with a tunneling protocol and then transfers the packet to the tunnel server. The tunnel server takes the IP packet out of the encapsulation and forwards the IP packet to the destination network host.

The commonly used encapsulating protocols are IPSec, Point-to-Point Tunneling Protocol (PPTP), and SSL. The following sections briefly describe VPNs using these three protocols.

10.3.1 Internet Protocol Security VPN

When used in the VPN technology, IPSec can be used as a tunneling VPN protocol or used as an encryption utility with other protocols. For example, L2TP is a tunneling protocol. However, it is not sufficient for the VPN since it does not provide encryption for data transaction. Often, IPSec is used to provide encryption for L2TP. IPSec can also be used to enhance authentication for L2TP. When L2TP/IPSec is used, an IP packet is first encapsulated in an L2TP packet. Then, the L2TP packet is encapsulated into an IPSec packet as shown in Figure 10.3. The use of L2TP/IPSec can authenticate both the VPN server and the VPN client, which makes L2TP/IPSec more secure. The disadvantage of the L2TP/IPSec VPN is that the configuration of L2TP/IPSec is more complex than other types of VPN connections.

As a well-established tunneling protocol, IPSec has been implemented in various routers and network operating systems. As mentioned previously in this book, IPSec can provide a wide range of protection against the following:

- Address spoofing
- Attack from an untrusted network device
- Data alteration
- Data corruption
- Data replay
- Denial-of-service attack
- Identity theft
- Packet sniffing

Although IPSec has a wide range of protection for the IP communication between two subnets and between a host and a subnet, it has a disadvantage for not working well with network address translation (NAT). NAT is a network service usually used by a home network for multiple home computers to share a single Internet connection. Therefore, it is difficult to use the IPSec VPN for the home network. It is possible that L2TP/IPSec can operate over NAT if L2TP/IPSec is properly configured. Another IPSec disadvantage is that it slows down network traffic.

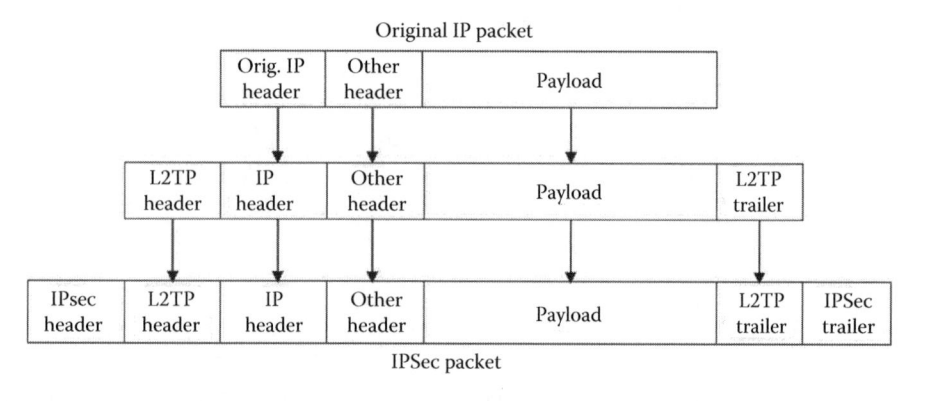

Figure 10.3 L2TP/IPSec encapsulation.

10.3.2 Secure Sockets Layer VPN

Unlike the IPSec VPN that creates a tunnel between a client and a server, the SSL-based VPN creates a tunnel from a client to a specific network resource through a proxy server. Once the client's request arrives at the proxy server, the proxy server authenticates the client. It then forwards the request to the network resource such as a server on a private network. In such a way, the SSL-based VPN can avoid a direct connection between the client and the network resource. By not directly connecting the client and the server, SSL is considered safer than IPSec. The SSL-based VPN uses the split tunneling approach, which allows the client to access multiple servers such as file servers, database servers, mail servers, and other servers on an organization's network through the VPN connection.

The configuration of the SSL-based VPN is flexible. It provides a better control on remote access and more configuration options. By using the SSL-based VPN, network administrators can assign different privileges to different clients. The SSL-based VPN requires only a single TCP or UDP port to establish a tunnel. With this feature, the SSL-based VPN can easily deal with firewalls. It is supported by a wide range of operating systems including Windows and different versions of UNIX operating systems. Since the SSL certification is implemented through a Web browser, the SSL-based VPN does not require the client computer to install VPN client software. This feature simplifies the client-side VPN configuration and reduces the cost of purchasing client software.

On the other hand, since no client software is required, the SSL-based VPN needs a browser on the client computer to allow active content so that the VPN can work properly. By doing so, it makes the Web browser a target of malicious applets. Additional security enforcement is necessary to block unsigned activities and plug-ins. Also, through the Web browser, anyone can attempt to remotely access the VPN server. Therefore, strong user authentication is the key to prevent unqualified users from accessing the VPN server. Another disadvantage is that the server side configuration is more complicated than that of IPSec.

10.3.3 Point-to-Point Tunneling Protocol VPN

Jointly developed by Microsoft, 3COM, and some other companies, PPTP is another popular tunneling protocol. It is widely accepted and supported by Windows and Linux operating systems. PPTP is designed to work with the NAT service. Being able to work with NAT is very important for students whose computers are linked to private networks behind the NAT service. It is also important for small businesses where multiple computers share a single Internet connection through the NAT service. Another advantage of PPTP is that setting up the PPTP VPN is relatively easy. PPTP VPN devices are often less expensive. PPTP only uses a small portion of the bandwidth for its operation.

On the other hand, PPTP has some weaknesses. First, PPTP does not encrypt the control message used in establishing a connection between a VPN server and a client. The VPN connection established by PPTP may be vulnerable to hackers' attacks. Second, PPTP only authenticates the user who requests a VPN connection; it does not authenticate the network hosts involved in the VPN process. By not authenticating the network hosts, a hacker can re-direct the VPN traffic from the real VPN server to the fake VPN server. From the fake VPN server, the hacker can collect client information without the clients' knowledge. This can cause a serious security concern. Therefore, PPTP may not be secure enough for some data transaction that requires high-level protection. Third, PPTP may have some difficulty working with firewalls.

PPTP encapsulates Point-to-Point Protocol (PPP) frames into IP packets for data transaction on the Internet. For security enhancement, the encapsulated PPP frames can be encrypted. The PPP frames can also be compressed to reduce network traffic. In PPTP, PPTP control packets are used to control a connection by performing tasks such as creating, maintaining, and terminating a tunnel. Figure 10.4 illustrates a PPTP control packet that consists of an Ethernet header, an IP header, a TCP header, a PPTP control message, and an Ethernet trailer.

There are many types of PPTP control messages that are used to accomplish various tasks. Table 10.1 displays some of the PPTP control messages.

One can find more PPTP control messages from the standard RFC 2637 in the Internet Engineering Task Force (IETF) RFC (Request for Comments) Database.

The encapsulation of the PPP payload can be carried out in multiple layers. Initially, the PPP payload is encrypted. Then, a PPP frame is created by including the encrypted payload and a PPP header. To encapsulate the PPP frame, PPTP uses a modified version of Generic Routing Encapsulation (GRE), which is a tunneling protocol used to encapsulate a wide variety of protocols in the Internet layer. Then, the encapsulated GRE and PPP payload are encapsulated with an IP header for the IP communication on the network. To pass the network interface, the encapsulated IP packet is encapsulated again with the Ethernet header and trailer. PPTP inherits the encryption, compression, or authentication algorithms from PPP. Figure 10.5 illustrates a tunneled PPTP data packet that is encapsulated on multiple levels.

Once the receiver receives the PPTP tunneling data, it removes the Ethernet header and trailer, the IP header, the GRE header, and the PPP header. Then, it decrypts and processes the PPP payload.

PPTP connections use the same authentication mechanisms as PPP connections such as Microsoft Challenge-Handshake Authentication Protocol version 2

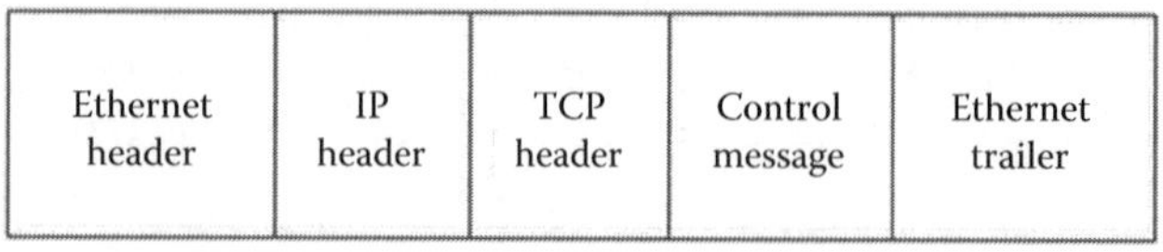

Ethernet header	IP header	TCP header	Control message	Ethernet trailer

Figure 10.4 PPTP control packet.

Table 10.1 PPTP Control Messages

MESSAGE TYPE	USAGE
Start-Control-Connection-Request	Before other PPTP messages can be delivered, a PPTP client sends this request first.
Start-Control-Connection-Reply	Once it receives a request from the PPTP client, the PPTP server replies to the Start-Control-Connection-Request message.
Outgoing-Call-Request	To create a PPTP tunnel, the PPTP client sends this message to create a PPTP tunnel. The Call ID included in this message is used to identify the tunneled traffic.
Outgoing-Call-Reply	The PPTP server sends this message to respond to the Outgoing-Call-Request message sent by the PPTP client.
Echo-Request	This message is sent by the PPTP client or server to keep a tunnel alive. Without this message, the PPTP tunnel is eventually terminated.
Echo-Reply	This message is sent by the PPTP client or server to reply to the Echo-Request message.
WAN-Error-Notify	The PPTP server sends this message to notify VPN clients about the error conditions on the PPP interface of the PPTP server.
Set-Link-Info	The PPTP client and PPTP server use this message to set PPP-negotiated options.
Call-Clear-Request	The PPTP client sends this message to indicate that a tunnel is to be terminated.
Call-Disconnect-Notify	The PPTP server sends this message to respond to the Call-Clear-Request message sent by the PPTP client.
Stop-Control-Connection-Request	The PPTP client or the PPTP server sends this message to inform the others that the control connection is being terminated.
Stop-Control-Connection-Reply	The PPTP client or the PPTP server sends this message to reply to the Stop-Control-Connection-Request message.

Tunneled PPTP data

Ethernet header	IP header	GRE header	PPP header	PPP payload	Ethernet trailer

Figure 10.5 PPTP data tunneling.

(MS-CHAP v2) and encryption mechanisms such as Microsoft Point-to-Point Encryption (MPPE). PPTP supports a wide range of security measures for authentication, packet filtering, and encryption.

10.3.4 VPN Tunneling Type

Depending on how the VPN technology is used in establishing a secure connection between a VPN server and a VPN client, there are two types of tunneling, voluntary tunneling and compulsory tunneling. In voluntary tunneling, VPN clients handle their connections to the VPN server. They make connections and create the tunnels. In compulsory tunneling, the Internet Service Provider (ISP) handles connections to the VPN server. Based on a client's request, the ISP creates a tunnel between the VPN client and the VPN server. Table 10.2 summarizes these two types of tunneling methods.

Table 10.2 Tunneling Types

TUNNELING TYPE	FUNCTION	USAGE
Voluntary tunneling	The client computer initiates a VPN connection and then creates a tunnel to the VPN server. VPN client software and protocols need to be installed on the client computer. The client computer is a tunneling end point.	Voluntary tunneling is used if VPN clients need to choose their own tunneling destinations.
Compulsory tunneling	The ISP handles VPN connections. When a VPN client makes a request to the ISP, the ISP establishes a tunnel to the VPN server. The ISP server is then a VPN client and must have the VPN client software and tunneling protocol installed.	When a company outsources its VPN service to an ISP which deploys tunnels to serve the VPN clients in a local region, compulsory tunneling is used by the ISP. Multiple clients can share the same tunnel.

10.4 VPN Security

For security, a VPN provides various authentication and encryption methods to protect private data being transmitted over a public network. This section first introduces the methods commonly used in VPN authentication. Then, it examines a few commonly used VPN encryption methods.

10.4.1 VPN Authentication

Before the data transaction through a VPN tunnel can get started, the connection between the VPN server and VPN client needs to be authenticated. VPN authentication is the mechanism that validates the legitimacy of users or computers that access the VPN server. When a VPN client requests a connection to the VPN server, the VPN client sends the user credentials to the VPN server for authentication. The VPN server can authenticate the VPN client in one of the two ways, Windows authentication or Remote Authentication Dial-In User Service (RADIUS).

10.4.1.1 Windows Authentication   Active Directory can be used to implement Windows authentication. The VPN client needs to have an account in Active Directory or on the VPN server, which allows the user or the VPN client to access the VPN server. The user account properties and remote access policies are used to determine what type of permission can be assigned to the connection. The authentication can be done at the user level or at the computer level.

The user-level authentication can be done by using any of the PPP authentication methods. There are several PPP authentication protocols that can be used to identify VPN users and grant or deny user access to network resources based on the users' credentials. The following describe some of the strong PPP authentication protocols.

MS-CHAP: Microsoft Challenge Handshake Authentication Protocol (MS-CHAP) is the Microsoft version of the CHAP protocol. The protocol has two versions, MS-CHAP v1 and MS-CHAP v2. MS-CHAP v1 is no longer supported by the later versions of the Windows operating system. MS-CHAP v2 is a password-based authentication protocol. With MS-CHAP v2, the VPN server uses either an Active Directory user account or a local user account to authenticate a VPN client. When Active Directory is used, network administrators can use Group Policy settings to enforce the use of strong passwords and the expiration time period. It is also possible to use MS-CHAP v2 without Active Directory. In such a case, the VPN client does not have to be the member of Active Directory. However, the VPN client needs to have an account on a local computer, which may cause some concerns of the network administrator. As one of the authentication protocols used by PPTP, MS-CHAP v2 is an encrypted authentication mechanism which provides strong protection for the exchange of user credentials and encryption keys. It is an often used authentication protocol when a certificate is not used.

Extensible Authentication Protocol (EAP): EAP is another commonly used PPP authentication protocol. EAP can be used for point-to-point connections as well as wireless networks. The wireless standard IEEE 802.11 (Wi-Fi) has adopted EAP as its authentication mechanism to ensure that laptop computers join wireless networks legally. During the authentication process, the VPN client initiates a request to access the VPN server. Actually, EAP is an authentication framework, not a specific authentication mechanism. Therefore, the VPN server does not perform authentication. It collects the user's credentials and then validates the user's credentials through an authentication server such as a Windows domain controller or a RADIUS server. The authentication server then decides whether to allow or disallow the VPN client to access the VPN server. If the VPN client is allowed, the VPN server will take the request from the VPN client. As EAP is designed to be used by wireless networks, it allows the client and server to dynamically take in additional authentication plug-in modules. This feature makes EAP a highly flexible authentication protocol.

As an authentication framework, EAP can work with various authentication methods called EAP methods. Although there are about 40 different methods available, the following five are commonly used.

- *EAP-MD5 Challenge*: This EAP method is the simplest EAP method and is the least secure one among all EAP methods.
- *Lightweight EAP (or LEAP)*: Developed by Cisco, this EAP method is a modified version of MS-CHAP. When using this EAP method, sufficiently complex passwords are required.
- *Transport Layer Security (TLS)*: This EAP method is a very secure EAP method. Both the VPN client and the VPN server are strongly authenticated. It is used in certificate-based security environments. Only when the VPN server is the member of Activate Directory, the TLS method is supported. When the VPN server is configured as a stand-alone VPN server, the TLS method is not supported. For certificate-based authentication, a VPN client first submits a user certificate to the VPN server to prove that the VPN client

is trustable. On the other hand, the VPN server presents a server certificate to the VPN client to assure that the VPN client is dealing with a trusted VPN server. The server certificate is authorized by the third-party certification authority (CA). The certificate also includes an encrypted public key for the encryption of data content.

- *Protected EAP (PEAP)*: While providing authentication as strong as the TLS method, this EAP method encrypts the authentication process.
- *EAP-Fast*: This EAP method is an enhanced version of LEAP method. It offers the level of security equal to that of PEAP.

When compared with MS-CHAP v2, EAP-TLS is a more secure authentication protocol for user-level authentication since it is a certificate-based method. On the other hand, MS-CHAP v2 is a password-based authentication method. MS-CHAP v2 uses either an Active Directory user account or a local user account to authenticate a VPN client. When the certificate service is not available, MS-CHAP v2 should be the choice for authentication. With MS-CHAP v2, the VPN server does not need to join the Active Directory domain. In such a case, network administrators need to make sure that strong passwords be used with MS-CHAP v2.

Computer-level authentication is provided for a L2TP/IPSec VPN connection. It is performed through the exchange of computer certificates or through a pre-shared key. Exchanging certificates is more secure but is also a more complicated authentication method. It requires the deployment of the public key infrastructure. The configuration of a pre-shared key is relatively simple for both the VPN server and the VPN client. The disadvantage of the pre-shared key is that the VPN server can only use one pre-shared key. When VPN clients need to access the same VPN server, these VPN clients have to use the same pre-shared key for authentication. This authentication method may cause some concerns on security and maintenance. The newer versions of the Windows Server operating system after Windows Server 2008 make the certificate service enrollment easier than using pre-shared keys over the long term. Therefore, the computer certificate authentication method is preferred over the pre-shared key method.

10.4.1.2 Remote Authentication Dial-In User Service   In a situation where an organization has multiple sites, each site may need a VPN server for remote access. A user may end up with multiple accounts, one for each site. In such a case, it is difficult to update the user's accounts on multiple VPN servers.

The centralization of authentication provided by RADIUS is the solution. With RADIUS, a local VPN server can forward a connection request to the central server for authentication. The update of a user's account can be done on the central RADIUS server.

As a centralized authentication mechanism, RADIUS can be used to implement authentication for a VPN connection. In addition to authenticating VPN connections,

RADIUS can also be used for connections to wireless access points and network switches. It can be used to authenticate any request for connecting to a network. The VPN server forwards user credentials to the RADIUS server for authentication. Once the user credentials are authenticated, the RADIUS server permits the connection and set the connection parameters such as authorizing the connection attempt. In addition to a yes or no response to an authentication request, RADIUS can inform the VPN server of other applicable connection parameters for the user such as maximum session time, and so on.

As described earlier, two components, the RADIUS client and RADIUS server, are involved in a RADIUS process. In general, RADIUS client is a network host that receives authentication requests from other network hosts and forwards authentication requests to the RADIUS server.

A RADIUS client can be a VPN server, a wireless access point, a switch, or a remote access dial-up server. The RADIUS server is another server that does the centralized authentication. By examining a user's credentials, the RADIUS server makes a decision to authorize or deny the connection request. When multiple RADIUS servers are used, the optional component, RADIUS proxy, is used to pass a connection request forwarded by a RADIUS client to the appropriate RADIUS server.

10.4.2 VPN Encryption

To ensure confidentiality, the VPN encrypts the data to be transmitted over a public network. When L2TP/IPSec is used as the tunneling protocol, data encryption can be done between a client application and the server hosting the network resources. When PPTP is used as the tunneling protocol, data encryption is supported if MS-CHAP v2 or EAP-TLS is used as the authentication protocol. PPTP provides the encryption algorithm MPPE for data encryption. During an encryption process, the sender creates data encryption with an encryption key. The encrypted data are then delivered to the receiver. The receiver decrypts the encrypted data with a key, which may or may not be the same as the encryption key used by the sender. The length of the key size determines the strength of the encryption. The larger the key size, the more secure the encryption is. On the other hand, the longer key size requires more computing power and computation time for processing the encryption.

MPPE is a type of data encryption used by Microsoft for encrypting data across PPP and VPN connections. MPPE keys have three settings, 40-bit (basic setting), 56-bit (stronger setting), or 128-bit (strongest setting). The 40-bit setting refers to a VPN connection that is secured with a 40-bit encryption key. Similarly, the 128-bit setting refers to a VPN connection that is secured with a 128-bit encryption key. The 40-bit setting is suitable for a connection that involves an older computer that does not support the 56-bit setting or the 128-bit setting. On the other hand, the 128-bit setting is recommended if it is supported. The 56-bit setting is used with 56-bit DES or 168-bit 3DES encryption by the L2TP/IPSec protocol. It is required that both the VPN client and the VPN server use the same setting to establish a connection. The exact setting of the encryption key is negotiated by the VPN client and the VPN server when establishing the connection.

10.5 Remote Accessing on Microsoft Azure

From an on-premises network, a local network or a local computer can be connected to virtual networks on Microsoft Azure. Network administrators can accomplish this in two ways, the site-to-site connection and the point-to-site connection.

Site-to-Site Connection: With a site-to-site VPN, the network administrator can create a secure connection between a virtual network on Microsoft Azure and an on-premises network. Microsoft Azure provides the VPN endpoint called Windows Azure Virtual Network Gateway. The other VPN endpoint is the VPN device located on the on-premises network. The VPN connection between these two endpoints is a secure site-to-site connection. The supported VPN device on the on-premises network can be a compatible Cisco router, a compatible Juniper router, Microsoft Routing and Remote Access Service, or a device from WatchGuard, F5, or Citrix. Once the VPN connection is established, the network hosts on the virtual network are able to communicate with the network hosts on the on-premises network. Also, the network hosts on the on-premises network can share network resources on Microsoft Azure and vice versa. IPSec is the tunneling protocol used for site-to-site connections. IPSec provides the authentication and encryption for the data transaction. Figure 10.6 illustrates a site-to-site connection that links the on-premises network and the virtual network created on Microsoft Azure.

Point-to-Site Connection: With a point-to-site VPN, the network administrator can create a secure connection between a network host located on the on-premises network and a virtual network on Microsoft Azure. Unlike the site-to-site connection,

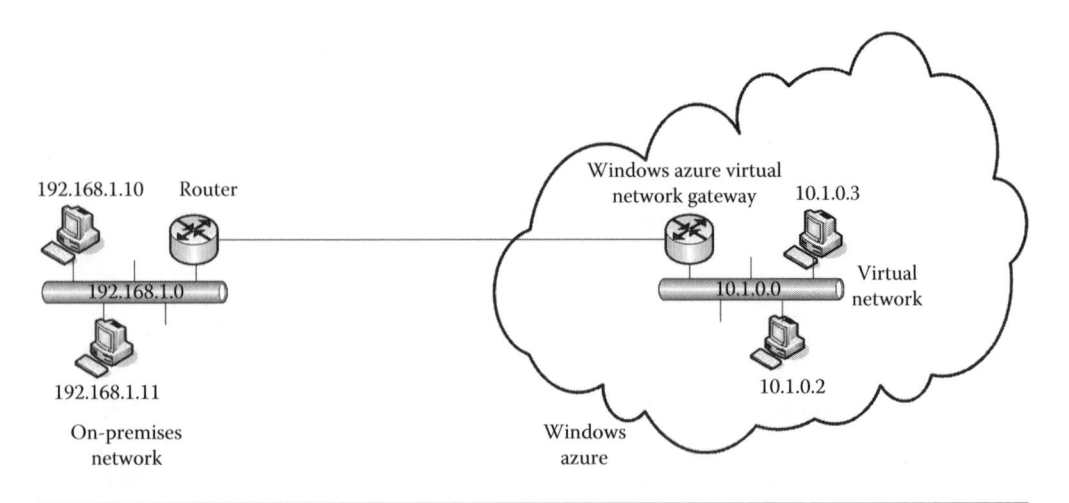

Figure 10.6   Site-to-site connection.

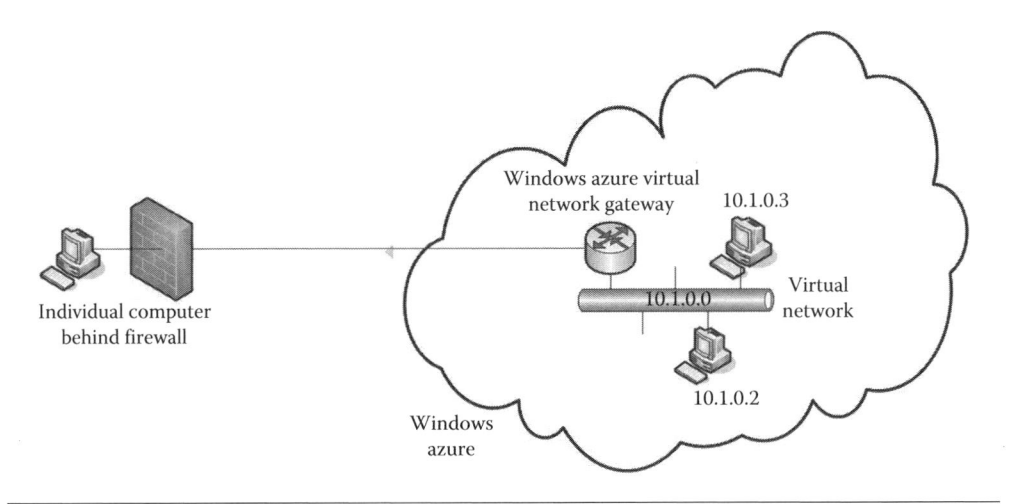

Figure 10.7 Point-to-site connection.

the point-to-site connection does not require a VPN device. This greatly simplifies the configuration of the VPN connection to Microsoft Azure. This feature makes it possible to connect a home computer to a virtual network on Microsoft Azure. Students can configure their home computers as VPN clients. By doing so, their home computers can share the network resources available on Microsoft Azure. For the point-to-site connection, the Secure Sockets Tunneling Protocol (SSTP) is used as the tunneling protocol. SSTP is an SSL-based VPN protocol. It provides a mechanism to transport PPP and L2TP traffic via an SSL 3.0 channel. SSL provides the key negotiation, traffic integrity checking, and encryption. The SSTP protocol allows a VPN connection to bypass a firewall or other Web proxies and still keep the data transaction secure. Therefore, SSTP is the choice for individual computers to connect to a Microsoft Azure virtual network, which is a highly protected network. Figure 10.7 illustrates a point-to-site connection, which links an individual computer to a virtual network on Microsoft Azure.

In this section, we have looked at how the VPN technology is used to establish a secure connection between an on-premises network and a virtual network on Microsoft Azure. By doing so, an organization's network can extend its internal network to Microsoft Azure. Reversely, the VPN technology can extend a virtual network on Microsoft Azure to an organization's local network. This makes the network resources on Microsoft Azure available to the network hosts located in the on-premises network and vice versa. The implementation of the site-to-site connection and point-to-site connection will be shown in the following hands-on activities.

Activity 10.1: Point-to-Site Connection between Local Computer and Microsoft Azure

The point-to-site VPN allows you to establish a connection from individual computers on your home network to the virtual network on Microsoft Azure. Since the

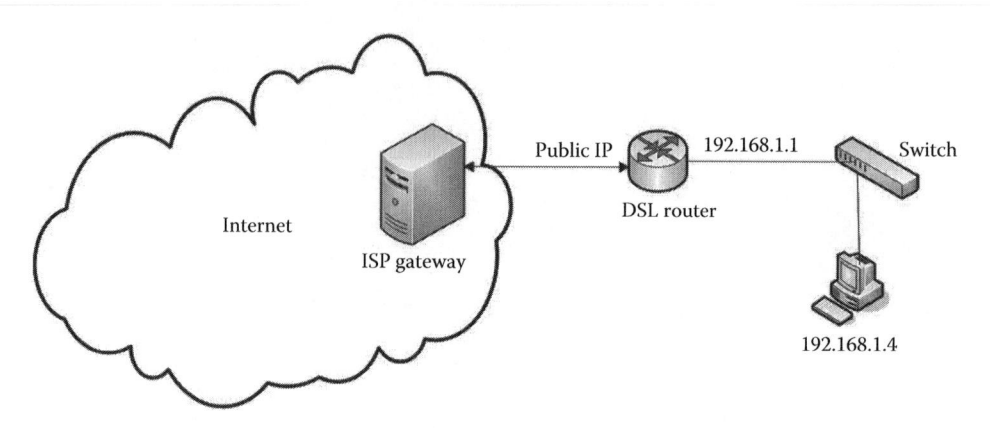

Figure 10.8 Home network setup.

computers on a home network are often located behind a NAT device, SSTP will be used to secure the point-to-site connection so that it is able to work through firewalls and NAT devices. Suppose that the structure of your home network is similar to the one in Figure 10.8.

Usually, the DSL router and the switch shown in Figure 10.8 are integrated as one unit. The home computer's IP address can be different from the one in Figure 10.8. The DSL router's internal IP address can be configured differently.

To create a point-to-site connection, you need to have the information about the IP address space of the virtual network on Microsoft Azure, the IP address space of your home network, and the IP address of the DNS server used to resolve the host names of the virtual machines. Assume that you are going to use the IP address space 10.0.0.0/11 for your virtual network on Microsoft Azure and the IP address space 192.168.1.0/24 for your home network. When specifying the home network IP address space, be sure not to make it overlap with the IP address space of the virtual network on Azure. Suppose that the DNS server for the virtual network is 10.0.0.4. You may also create some subnets on your virtual network. For example, you can create a subnet 10.0.0.0/27. You will also be prompted to create a subnet for the VPN gateway. The VPN gateway is a virtual machine configured as a VPN server. For reliability, the VPN server is replicated to another server on Microsoft Azure. These servers are placed to the same subnet called the VPN gateway subnet. The VPN gateway can be created by Microsoft Azure after clicking the Add Getaway Subnet button.

To resolve the virtual machine names on the virtual network, you can dedicate a server as the DNS server. When creating the virtual network on Microsoft Azure, you can dedicate an IP address to the DNS server which may not even exist at the time when you create the virtual network. The DNS server's IP address in our example is 10.0.0.4.

The process to establish the point-to-site connection can be done through the following tasks.

Task 1: Creating Virtual Network
Task 2: Preparing VPN Gateway
Task 3: Creating and Uploading Certificates
Task 4: Downloading and Installing VPN package

Task 1: Creating Virtual Network

1. Log on to the Microsoft Azure Management Portal. Click the virtual network **mynet** and click the **DASHBOARD**.
2. Click Configure. Under DNS servers, specify the DNS server name as **mydns** and the DNS IP address as **10.0.0.4** (Figure 10.9). Click the **SAVE** button to save the configuration.
3. Check the checkbox **Configure point-to-site connectivity** (Figure 10.10). In the drop-down list, under STARTING IP, select 192.168.0.0. The address space that you want to assign to the network hosts on your home network after the VPN connection is established. If your original home network ID is 192.168.0.0, you may consider using 172.16.0.0.
4. You will be prompted to create the Gateway subnet, click **add gateway subnet**. Click the **SAVE** button to save the configuration.

Task 2: Preparing VPN Gateway

1. After the point-to-site connectivity is configured, click the link **DASHBOARD** of the virtual network shown in Figure 10.11.

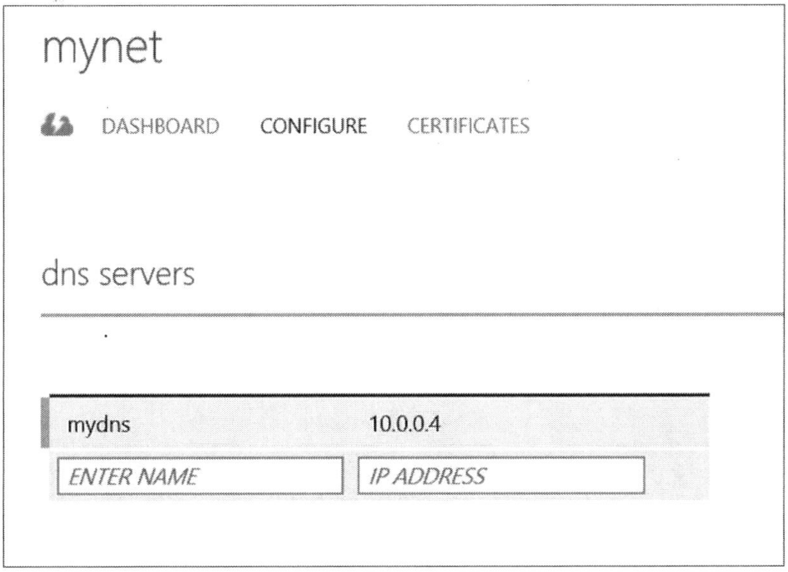

Figure 10.9 Virtual network configuration.

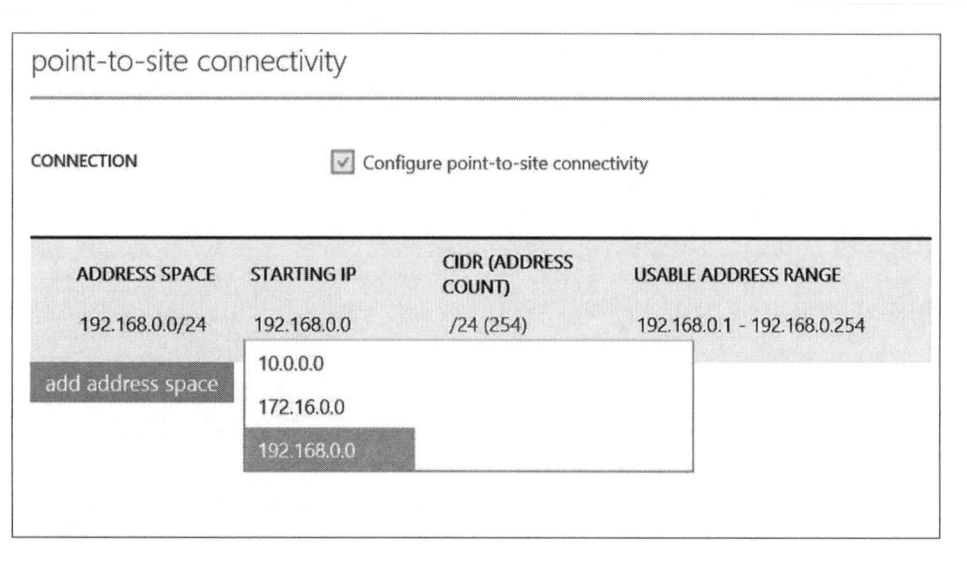

Figure 10.10   Specifying point-to-site connectivity.

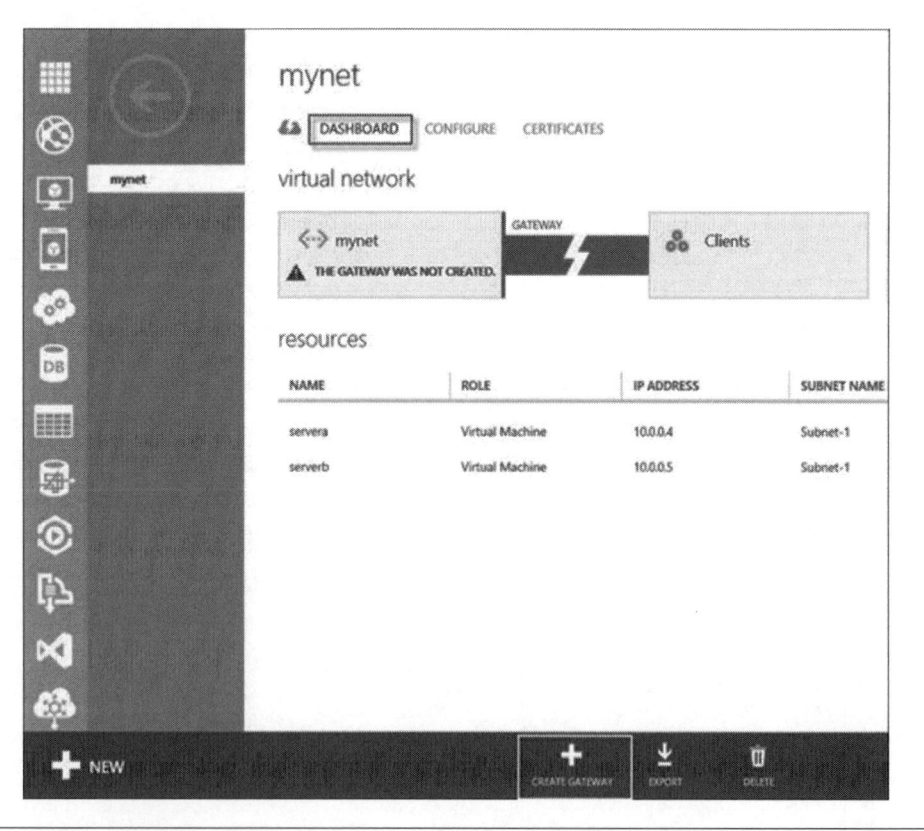

Figure 10.11   Virtual network dashboard.

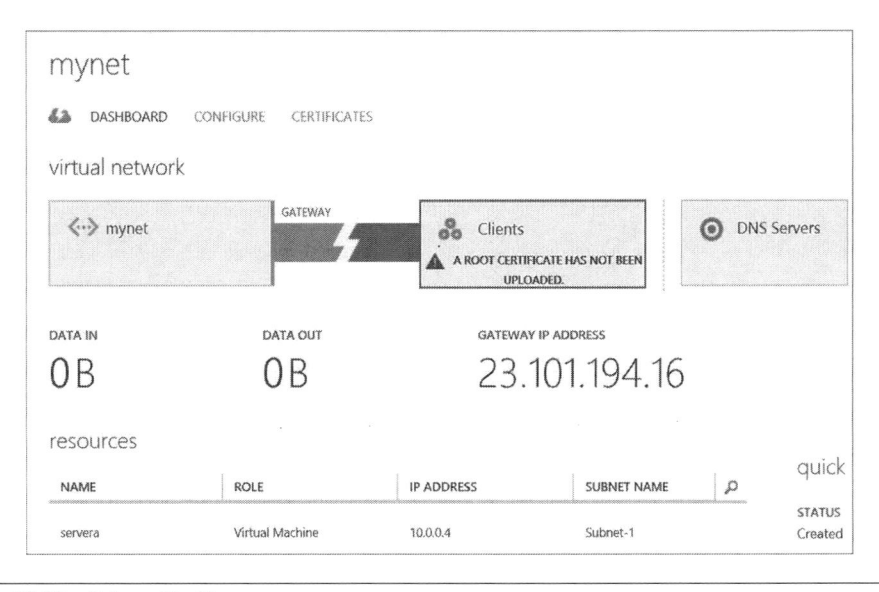

Figure 10.12 Gateway IP address.

2. At the bottom of your screen (Figure 10.11), click **CREATE GATEWAY** to start provisioning the gateway for the virtual network.

3. Once the gateway is created, the gateway IP address will be displayed on the dashboard as shown in Figure 10.12.

Task 3: Creating and Uploading Certificates

For a VPN client to securely connect to the VPN, the VPN client needs to be authenticated by the VPN server. Certificates are used to carry out the authentication task. A certificate can be created by using the makecert utility, which is included in the Windows SDK package. With the makecert utility, one can generate a root certificate used for client authentication.

1. On your local server, download the Windows SDK from the website in the following. Then, install only the utility component. (Microsoft, Windows Software Development Kit (SDK) for Windows 8, May, 2015).
   http://msdn.microsoft.com/en-us/library/windows/desktop/hh852363.aspx

2. After the installation is complete, open the command prompt window by pressing the **Windows Logo** key. Type **cmd** and right click the CMD tile. Click **Run as Administrator**.

3. After the command prompt window is open, change the directory to C:\Program Files (x86)\Windows Kits\8.1\bin\x86\

4. In the command prompt window, run the following command to create a certificate called MyCloudCert (Figure 10.13).

```
makecert -sky exchange -r -n "CN = MyCloudCert" -pe -a
   sha1 -len 2048 -ss My "MyCloudCert.cer"
```

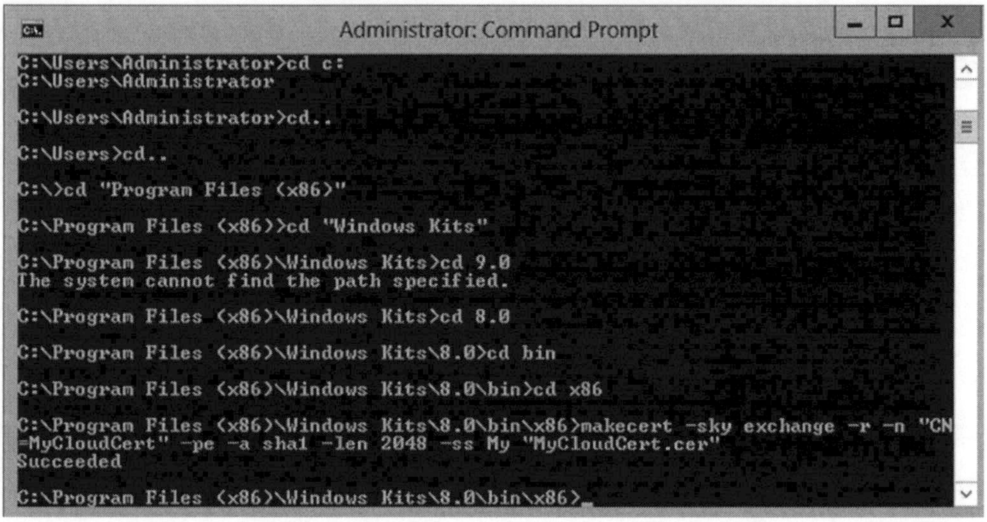

Figure 10.13   Creating certificate.

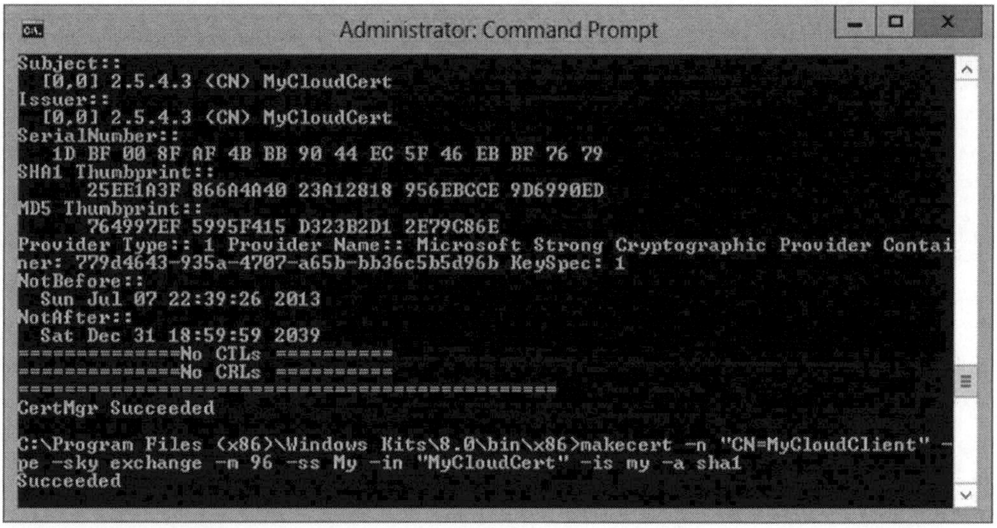

Figure 10.14   Client certificate.

5. On your local server, you need to create a client certificate for authentication. To do so, run the following command in the command prompt window (Figure 10.14).

```
makecert -n "CN = MyCloudClient" -pe -sky exchange -m 96 -ss
  My -in "MyCloudCert" -is my -a sha1
```

6. To export the root certificate, enter the following command to open certmgr.msc.

```
certmgr
```

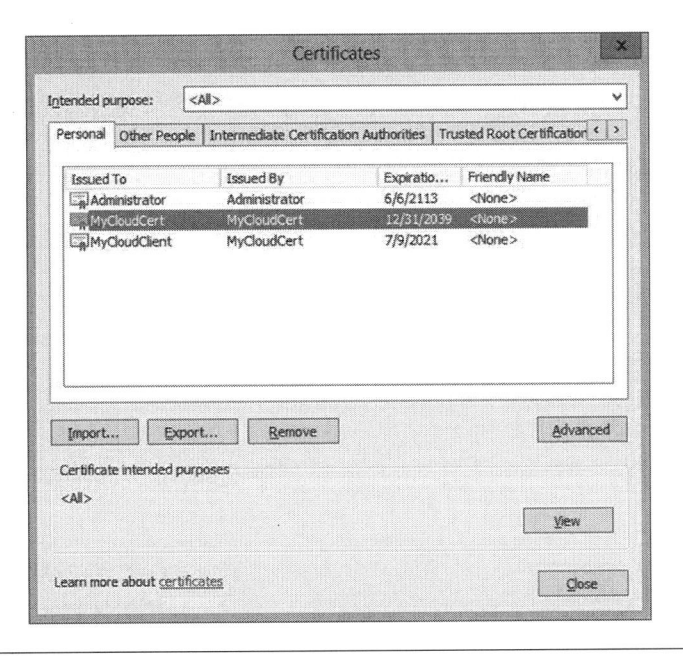

Figure 10.15   Exporting root certificate.

7. Once the Certificates dialog is open, click the root certificate **MyCloudCert** and click the **Export** button as shown in Figure 10.15.
8. Once the Certificate Export Wizard is open, on the Welcome page, click **Next**.
9. Check the option **No, do not export the private key**. Then, click **Next**.
10. Make sure that the option **DER encoded binary X.509 (CER)** is checked (Figure 10.16) and click **Next**.
11. Save the root certificate as **MyCloudCert** (Figure 10.17). Click **Next**, and then click **Finish**.
12. In the Certificate dialog, click the root certificate **MyCloudClient** and click the **Export** button as shown in Figure 10.18.
13. Once the Certificate Export Wizard is open, on the Welcome page, click **Next**.
14. Check the option **Yes, export the private key** (Figure 10.19). Then, click **Next**.
15. On the Export File Format page, take the default and click **Next**.
16. Enter your password such as **Passw0rd!** and confirm it. Then click **Next**.
17. Save the file as **mycloudclient**. Then, click **Next** and **Finish**.
18. The certificate MyCloudCert.cer file needs to be uploaded to the virtual network hosted by Microsoft Azure. Assume that the Microsoft Azure Management Portal is still open. Click the virtual network **mynet** and click **CERTIFICATES** as shown in Figure 10.20. Then, click **UPLOAD A ROOT CERTIFICATE**.

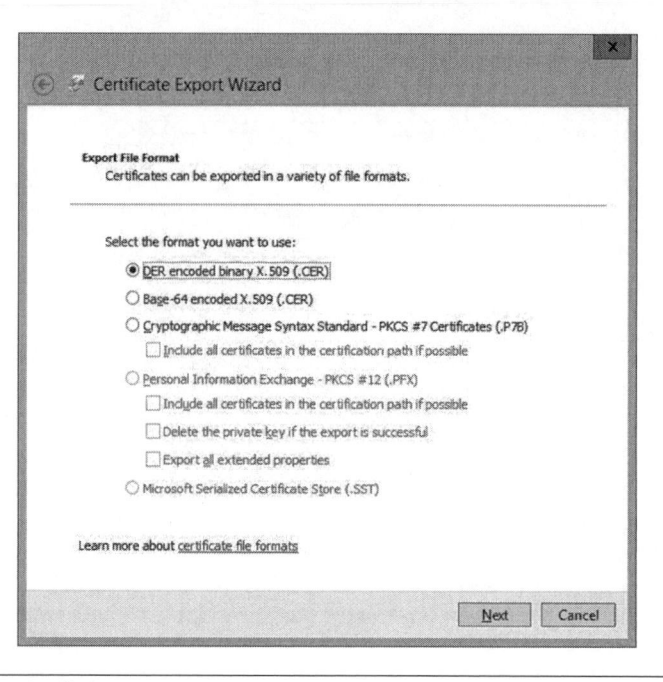

Figure 10.16   Exporting file format.

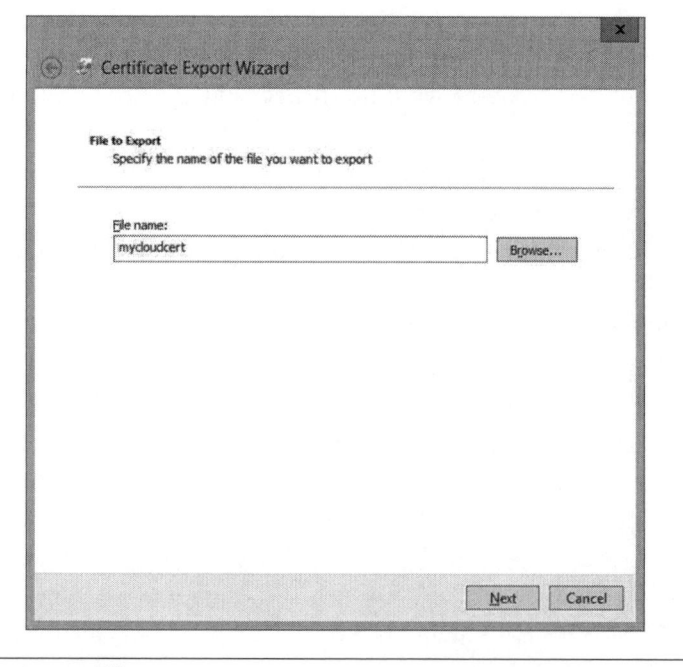

Figure 10.17   Naming export file.

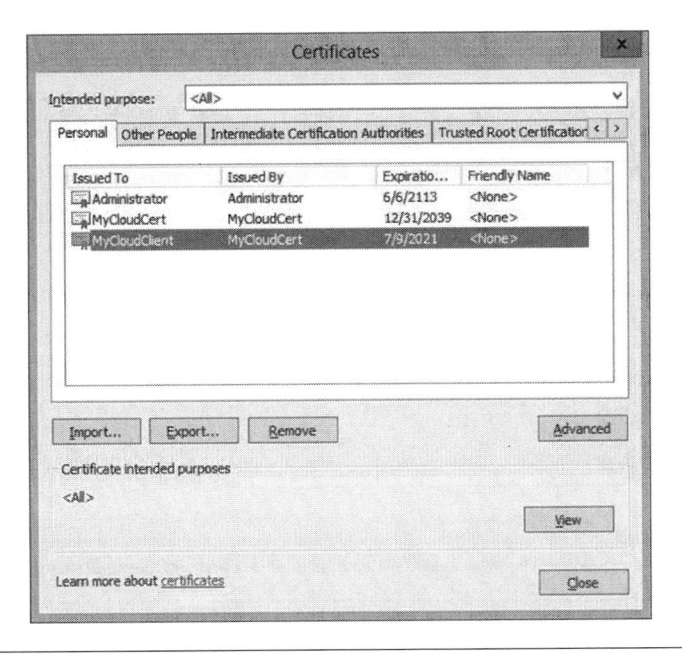

Figure 10.18 Exporting client certificate.

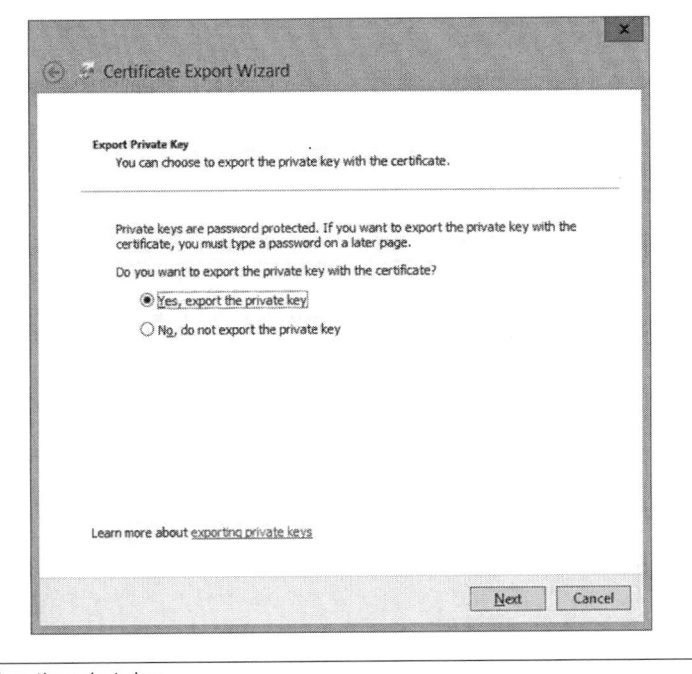

Figure 10.19 Exporting private key.

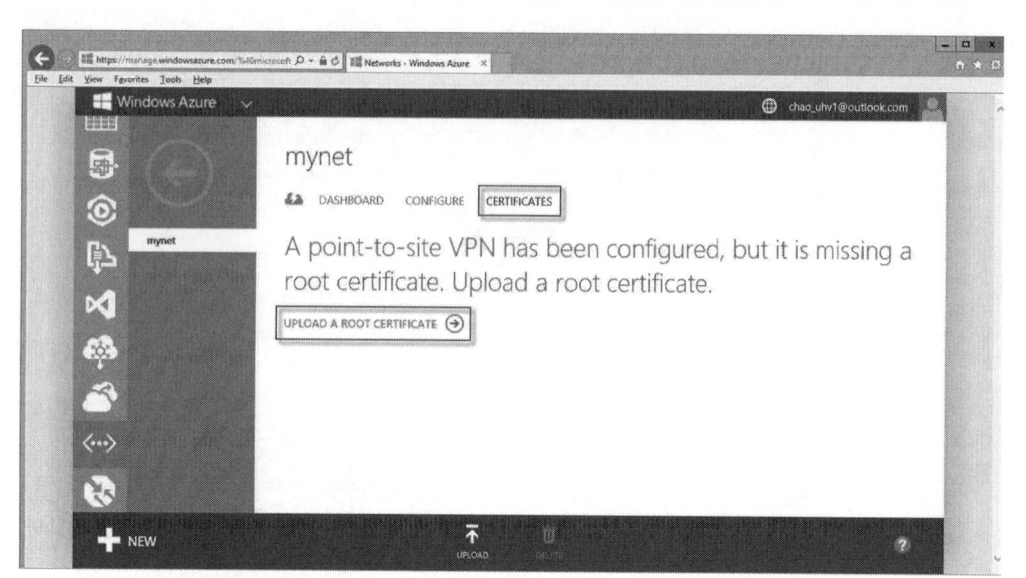

Figure 10.20 Uploading client certificate.

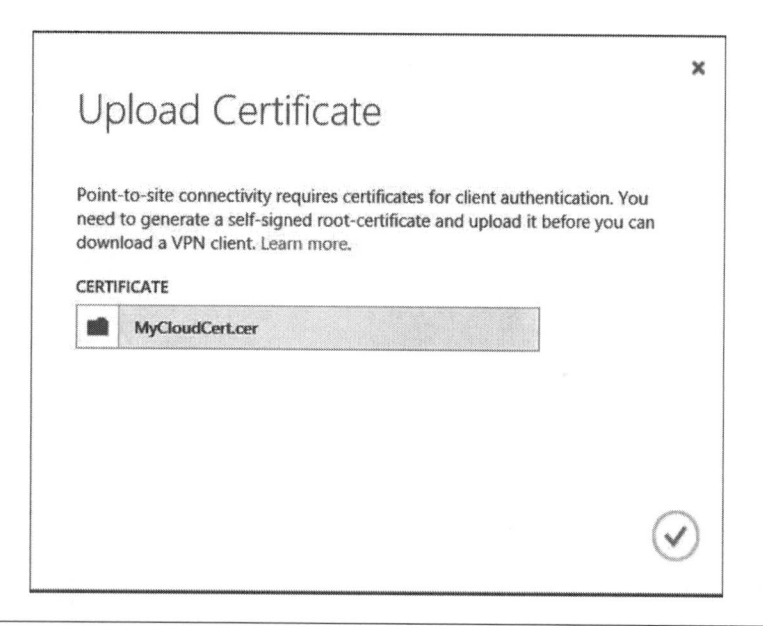

Figure 10.21 Uploading certificate.

19. Find the certificate MyCloudCert.cer in the folder C:\Program Files (x86)\ Windows Kits\8.0\bin\x86\. Click the checkmark icon to upload the file (Figure 10.21).

20. Once the root certificate is uploaded, click **DASHBOARD**. You should be able to see the link **Download the 64-bit Client VPN Package** on your screen. Depending on the operating system of your local server, you may download the 64-bit client VPN package or the 32-bit client VPN package.

Task 4: Downloading and Installing VPN Package

The downloaded client VPN package is used to configure the VPN settings on the local server. It configures the Routing and Remote Access Service (RRAS) on the local server to create a VPN session. Through the VPN session, your local server is able to connect to the virtual network on Microsoft Azure.

1. Once the package is downloaded, you will be prompted to run the package. You may see a warning message, click **Actions**, **More option**, and **Run anyway** (Figure 10.22), and **Yes**.
2. After the package is successfully executed, click the **network icon** at the right-bottom corner of your local server. You will see that the VPN session mynetlab is created (Figure 10.23).
3. Click **mynet** and click **Connect**. In the Windows Azure Virtual Network dialog, click **Connect** again (Figure 10.24).
4. If the connection is successfully established, click the **network icon** on the taskbar, you should be able to see **Connected** for the mynet VPN session (Figure 10.25).
5. To verify that the VPN connection is working, open the command prompt window and run the command

   ```
   ipconfig/all
   ```

   You will see that the local server gets the IP address 192.168.0.2 from the VPN server (Figure 10.26).

   The point-to-site connection is now working as expected.

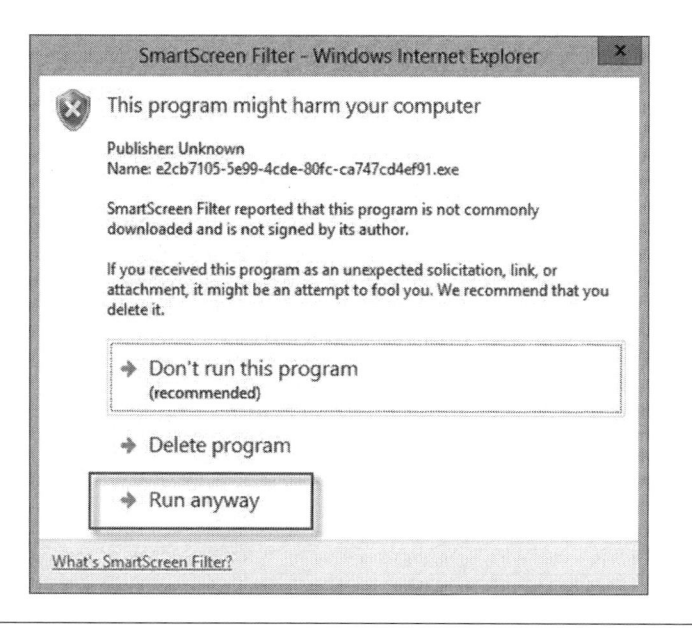

Figure 10.22 Warning message.

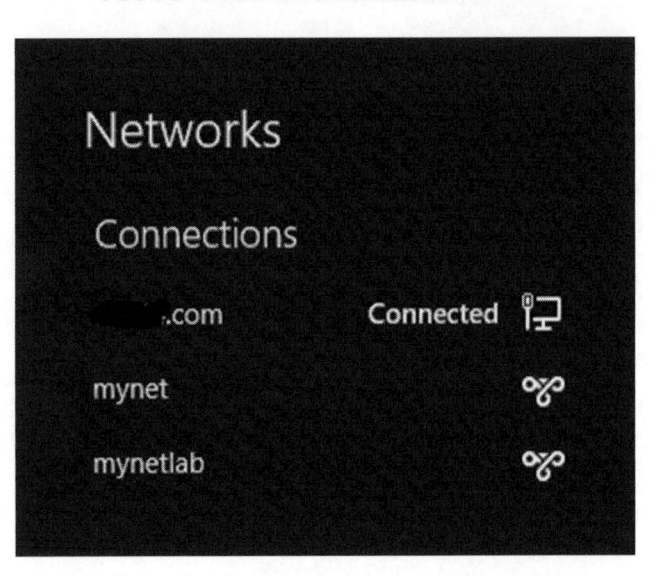

Figure 10.23   VPN connection to virtual network.

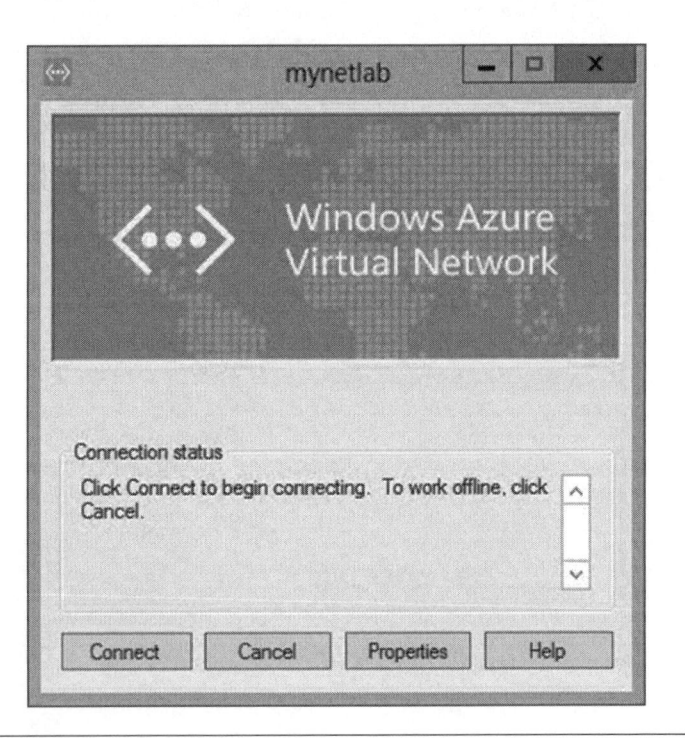

Figure 10.24   Connecting to virtual network.

6. You can now communicate with the virtual machine created on the cloud. For example, you can now ping the virtual machine 10.0.0.4 created earlier in Chapter 1 as shown in Figure 10.27 (You may need to start **servera** on Microsoft Azure first).

7. Once the point-to-site VPN connection is established, you can even remotely log on to the virtual machine with the IP address 10.0.0.4 on the cloud.

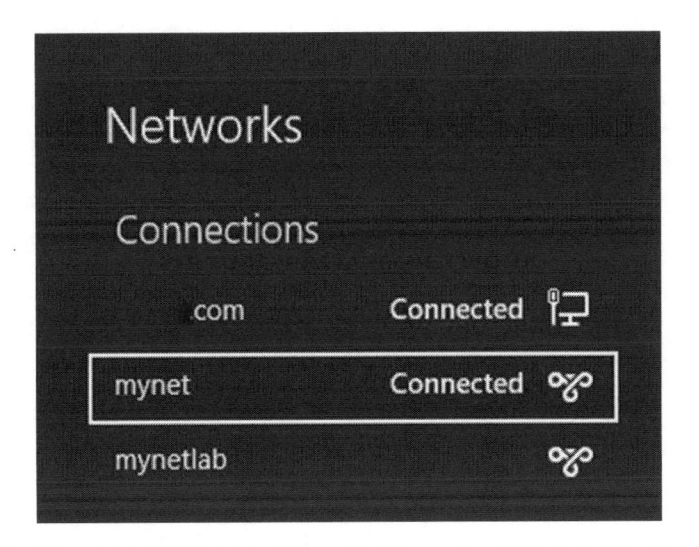

Figure 10.25   Successfully connected to virtual network.

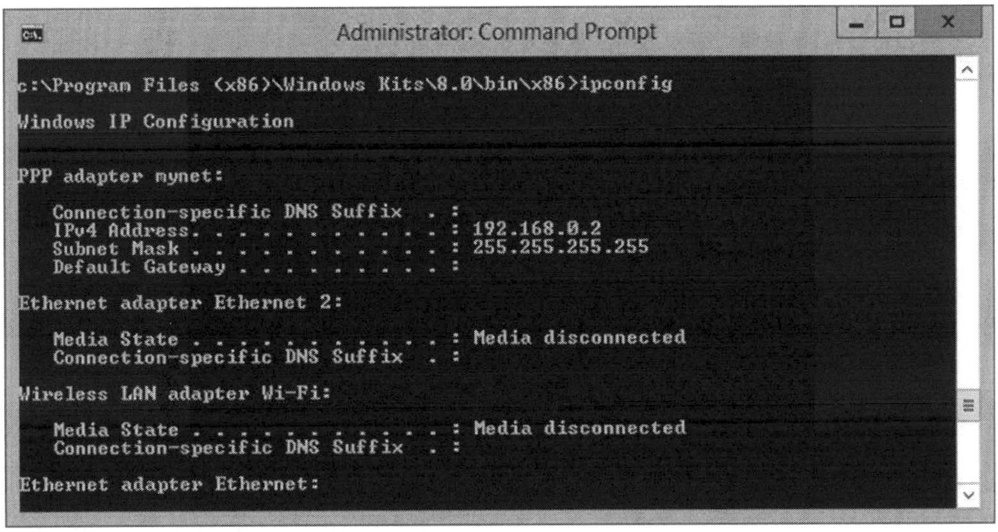

Figure 10.26   Local server IP address.

To do so, press the **Windows logo** key and type **Remote Desktop**. Click the **Remote Desktop Connection** tile to open the remote desktop connection dialog as shown in Figure 10.28.

8. Enter the virtual machine IP **10.0.0.4** and click **Connect**. You will be prompted to enter the user name and password of the virtual machine as shown in Figure 10.29.

9. Once connected, you should be able to see the virtual machine desktop as shown in Figure 10.30. You have now a way to connect to the virtual machine directly from a home computer without going through the Microsoft Azure Management Portal.

Figure 10.27   Pinging virtual machine on cloud.

Figure 10.28   Remote desktop connection.

The activity mentioned earlier has illustrated how to connect a home computer to the virtual network on Microsoft Azure. You can in fact connect your entire home network to the virtual network on Microsoft Azure. The next activity will cover the site-to-site VPN connection.

Activity 10.2: Site-to-Site Connection between Microsoft Azure and On-Premises Network

A site-to-site connection allows an on-premises network to be extended to a virtual network on Microsoft Azure. In production, the VPN server should not be behind the Network Address Translation (NAT) device. For demonstration purposes, in the home network environment, you may use the router created in Chapter 9. It has two NICs and Windows Server 2012 installed. The external NIC is directly connected to the

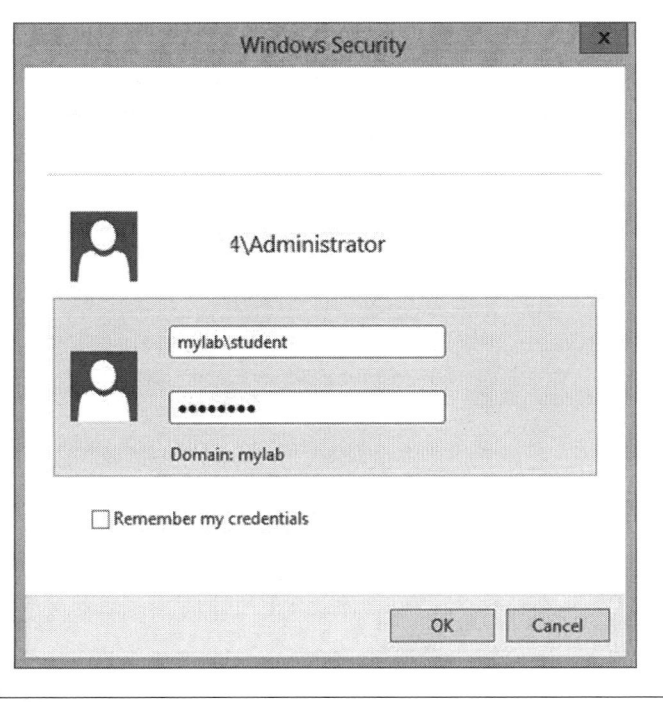

Figure 10.29 Logging on to virtual machine.

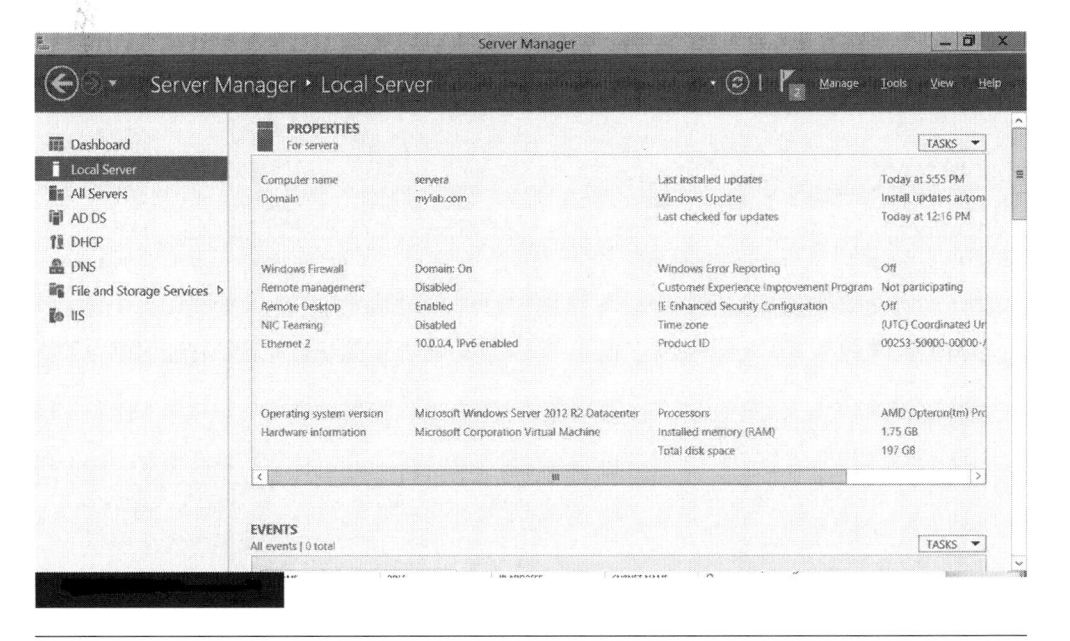

Figure 10.30 Virtual machine desktop.

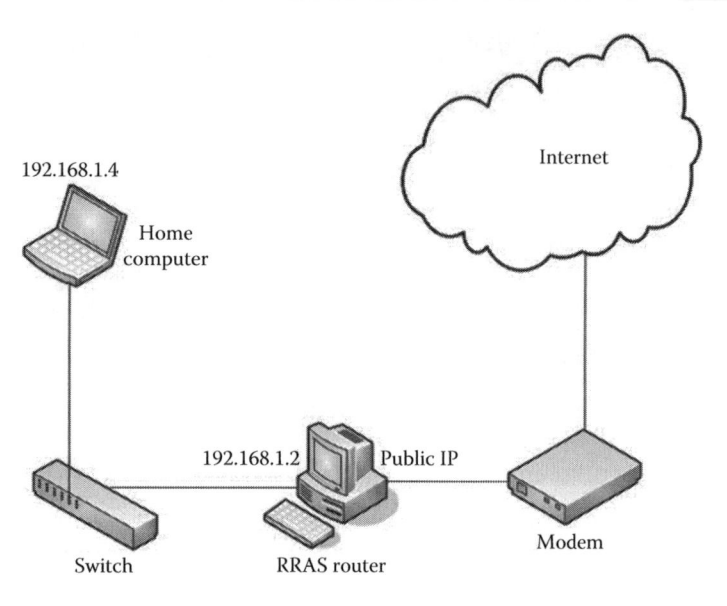

Figure 10.31   Network setup for site-to-site connection.

ISP modem and the internal NIC links the home network as shown in Figure 10.31. The following demonstrates the site-to-site connection.

If you have completed Activity 10.1 in this chapter, you can continue to create a site-to-site connection. This activity requires some of the configurations in Activity 10.1. Your first task is to create a new virtual network on Microsoft Azure through the following steps.

1. Log in to the Microsoft Azure Management Portal.
2. To illustrate the site-to-site connection, let us first create a new virtual network on Microsoft Azure. In the lower left-hand corner of your screen, click **New**. In the navigation pane, click **NETWORK SERVICES**, and then click **VIRTUAL NETWORK**. Click **CUSTOM CREATE** to begin the configuration wizard (Figure 10.32).
3. On the Site-to-Site Connectivity page, specify your network name to be used by your on-premises network and the IP address of the VPN server on your on-premises network. On the Virtual Network Details page, specify the network name as **mynetlab**. In the LOCATION drop-down list, select **West US** as shown in Figure 10.33.
4. Click the **Next** arrow. On the DNS Servers and VPN Connectivity page, specify the DNS server name and IP address. For DNS, depending on where the DNS server is located, you may use the default DNS server **mydns** (Figure 10.34) or you may enter the IP address of the DNS server on your on-premises network, or the IP address of an outside DNS server that is able to resolve the names of the virtual machines on your on-premises network. If you do not have a DNS server yet, you can leave it empty. A default

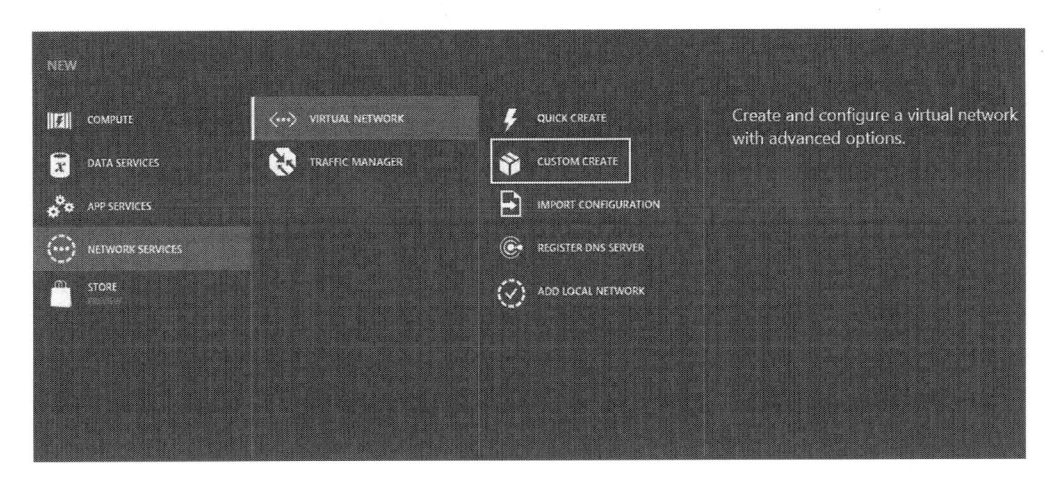

Figure 10.32   Creating virtual network on Microsoft Azure.

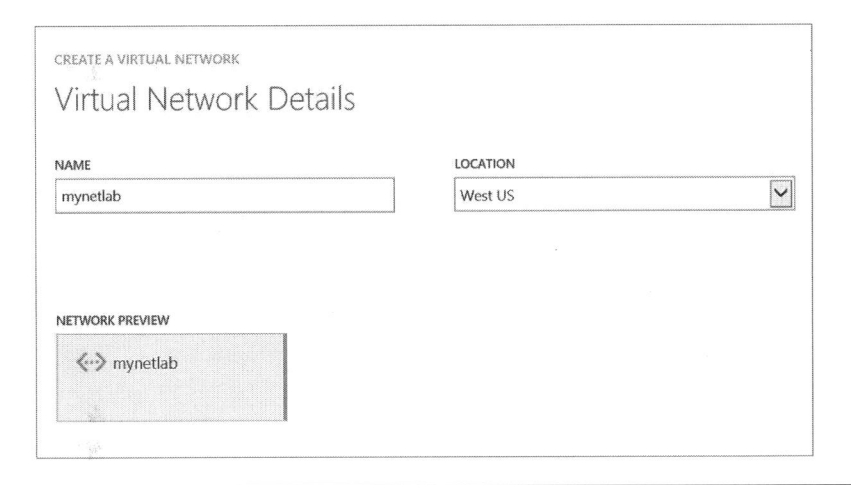

Figure 10.33   Specifying virtual network details.

DNS server will be assigned to you. However, the default DNS server will not resolve the names of the virtual machines on your on-premises network. Check the option **Configure site-to-site VPN**. Then, click the **Next** arrow.

5. The IP address of the **external NIC** can be used for VPN DEVICE IP ADDRESS. Specify the network that will be used as your home network. In this example, 10.1.1.0/24 is used for the home network (Figure 10.35). Then, click the **Next** arrow.

6. On the Virtual Network Address Spaces page, click **add gateway subnet**.

7. Then, review the settings (Figure 10.36) and click the **check** mark.

8. After the virtual network is created, on the DASHBOARD of the virtual network mynetlab, click **CREATE GATEWAY** at the bottom of your screen and select **Dynamic Routing** as shown in Figure 10.37.

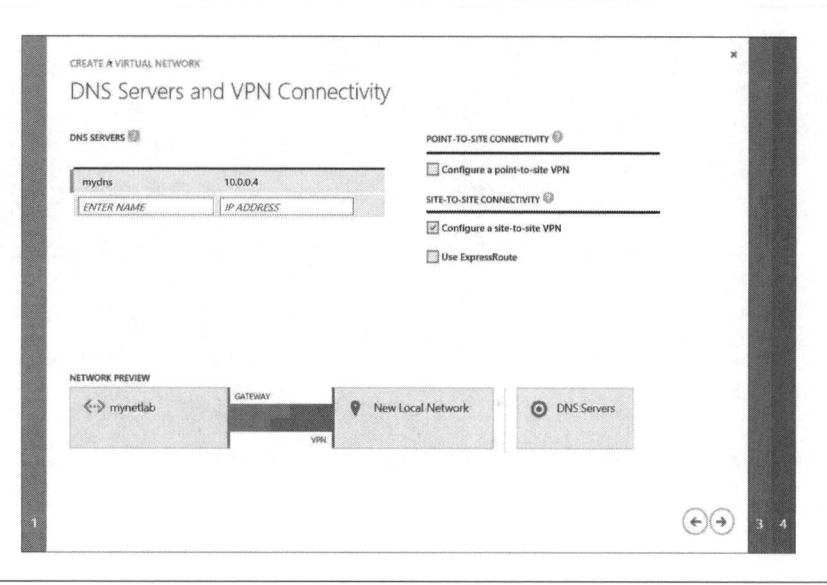

Figure 10.34 Configuring DNS server and VPN connectivity.

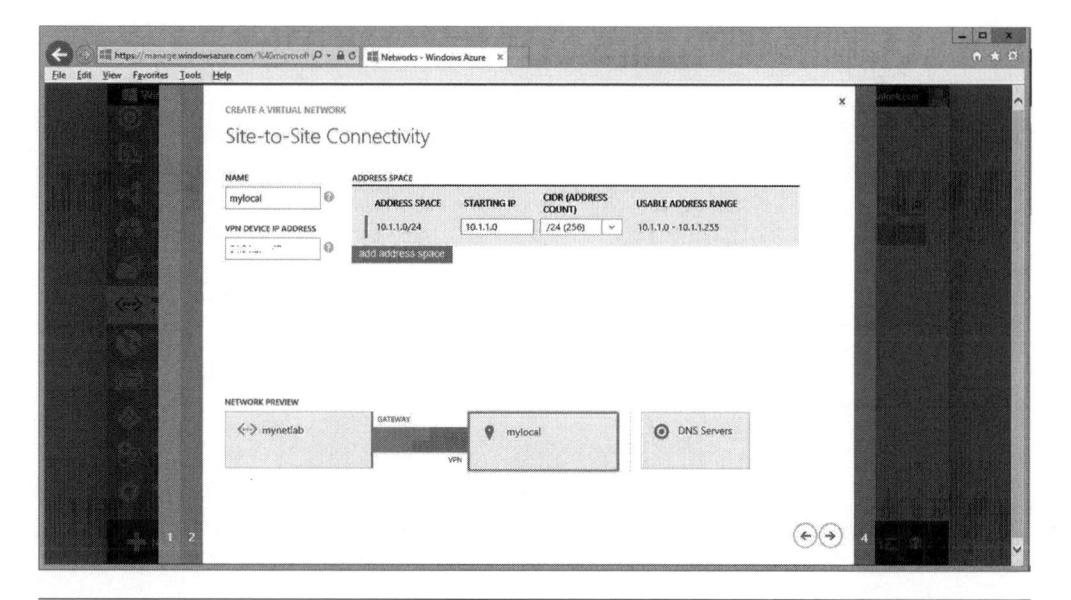

Figure 10.35 Site-to-site connectivity.

9. Wait a few minutes. Once the dynamic routing is set, on the mynetlab dashboard, click the link **Download the VPN Device Script** to your local server. When prompted, select **Microsoft Corporation** as the vendor (Figure 10.38). Then, click the **check mark**.

10. Open the downloaded file **vpnDeviceScript.cfg** with Notepad and save the file as a PowerShell script **vpnDeviceScript.ps1**.

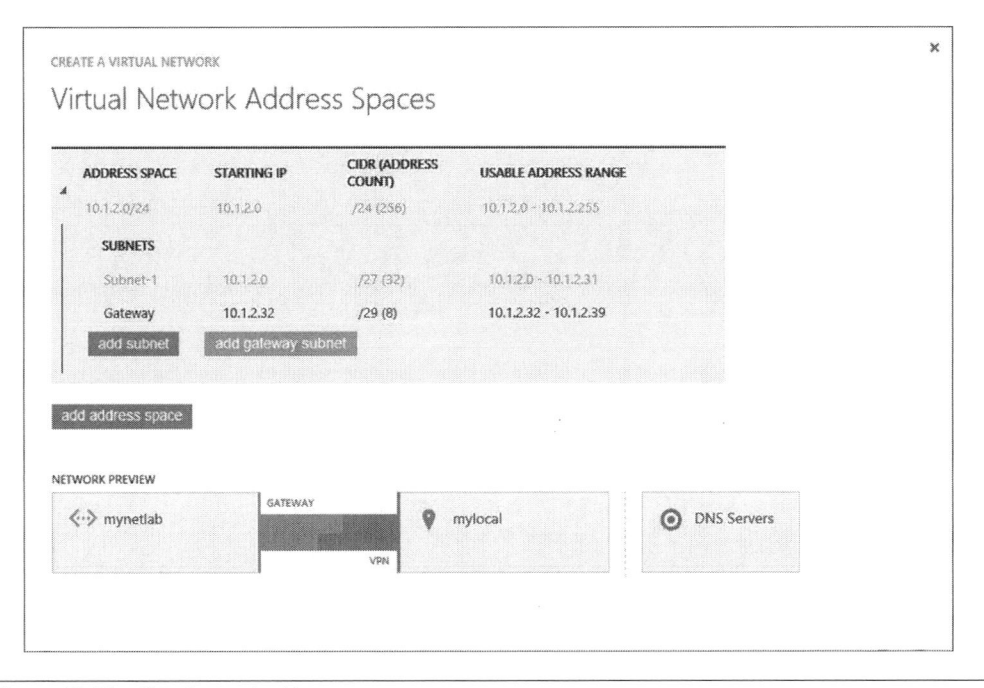

Figure 10.36 Virtual network address spaces.

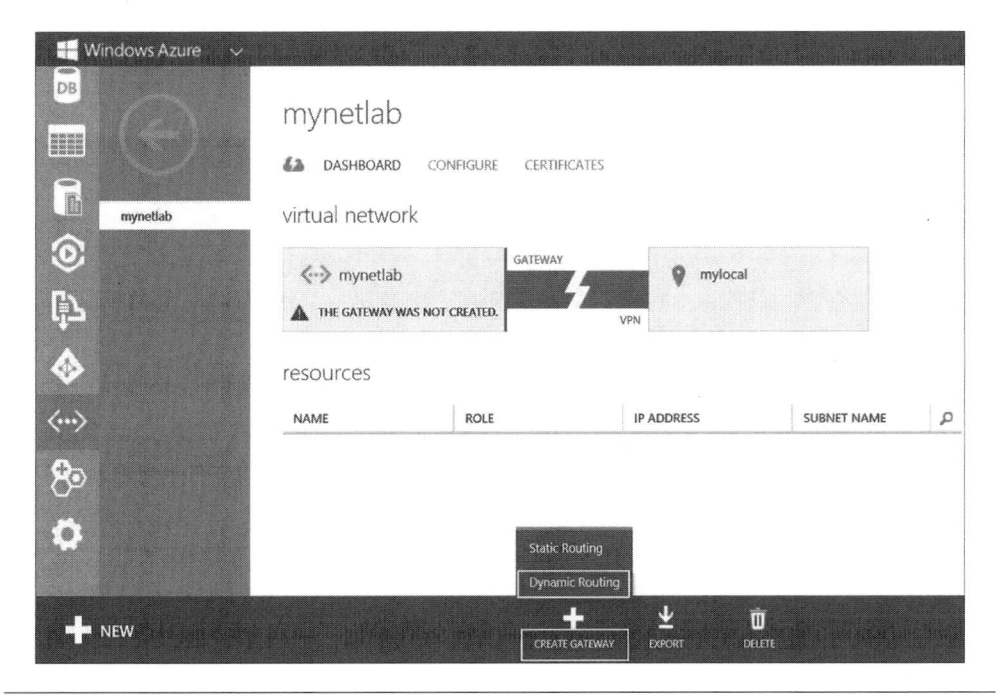

Figure 10.37 Creating gateway.

Figure 10.38   Downloading VPN service configuration script.

11. To prepare the connection between the virtual network on Microsoft Azure and the on-premises network, we need to open the following ports in the firewall.
    - UDP Port Number 500 for IKEv2
    - UDP Port Number 4500 for IKEv2
    - UDP Port Number 1701 for L2TP control
    - IP Protocol Type 50 for Encapsulating Security Payload (ESP) useful to enhance authentication and connectionless integrity

    To do so, log on to the local server. Click **Tools** and select **Windows Firewall with Advanced Security**.

12. In the Windows Firewall with Advanced Security, click **Inbound Rules**. Then, click **New Rule** in the Action pane.

13. On the Rule Type page, select the option **Port**. Then, click **Next** (Figure 10.39).

14. On the Protocol and Ports page, click the option **UDP** and enter the port number **500** for the option **Specific local ports** (Figure 10.40). Then, click **Next**.

15. On the Action page, click the option **Allow the connection**. Then, click **Next** twice.

16. On the Name page, enter the name **UDP500** and click **Finish** (Figure 10.41).

17. Similarly, you can create new rules for UDP4500 and UDP1701.

18. To create a rule for the ESP protocol, click **New Rule** in the Action pane.

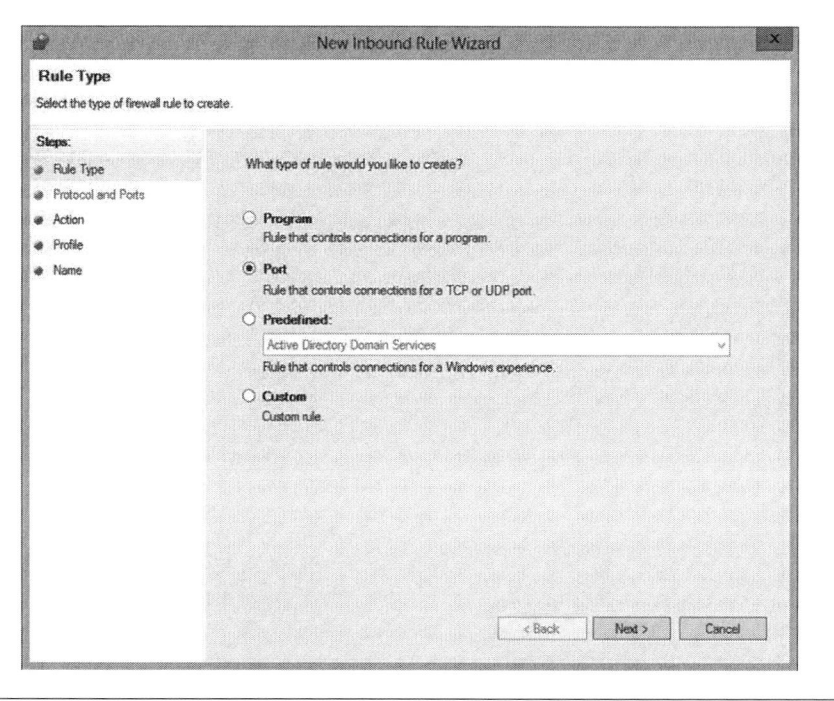

Figure 10.39 Rule type configuration.

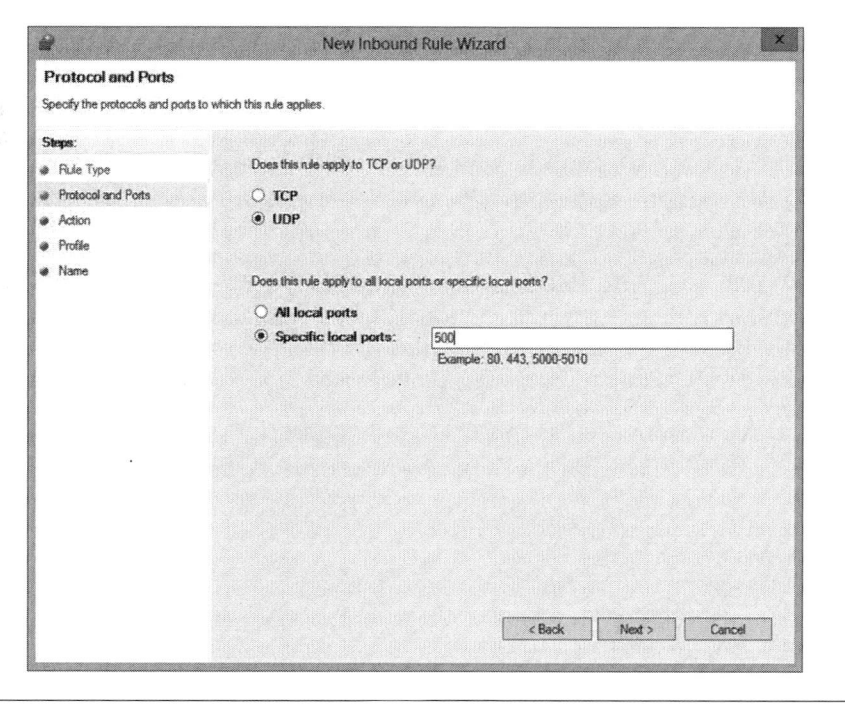

Figure 10.40 Protocol and port configuration.

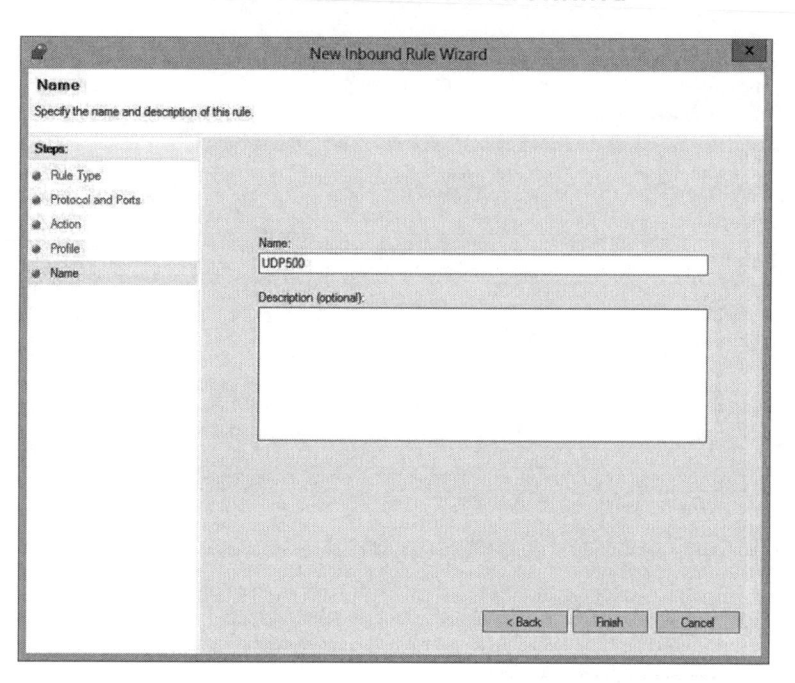

Figure 10.41   Specifying rule name.

19. On the Rule Type page, click the option **Custom** and click **Next** (Figure 10.42).
20. On the Program page, select the option **All programs** and click **Next** (Figure 10.43).
21. On the Protocol and Ports page, select **Custom** in the Protocol Type drop-down list. Enter **50** as the protocol number (Figure 10.44).
22. Click **Next** four times to go to the Name page. Enter the name **ESP50** and click **Finish** (Figure 10.45).
23. The newly created firewall inbound rules are shown in Figure 10.46.
24. Similarly, you can create outbound rules as shown in Figure 10.47.
25. To run the script **vpnDeviceScript.ps1**, click the **PowerShell** icon at the bottom of your screen. In the PowerShell window, change the directory to where the vpnDeviceScript.ps1 file is located and run the script by executing the following command as shown in Figure 10.48.
26. Once the file is successfully executed, RRAS should be installed. To view RRAS, in System Manager, click **Tools** and select **Routing and Remote Access**. To see the result, click the **Network Interfaces** node (Figure 10.49). The demand-dial interface 137.135.56.113 is created. (*Note*: Your demand-dial interface name should be different.)
27. Now, log on to the Microsoft Azure Management Portal. You will see that the mynetlab virtual network is connected to the mylocal on-premises network as shown in Figure 10.50.
28. In the Microsoft Azure Management Portal, shutdown both servera and serverb before exiting the Microsoft Azure Management Portal.

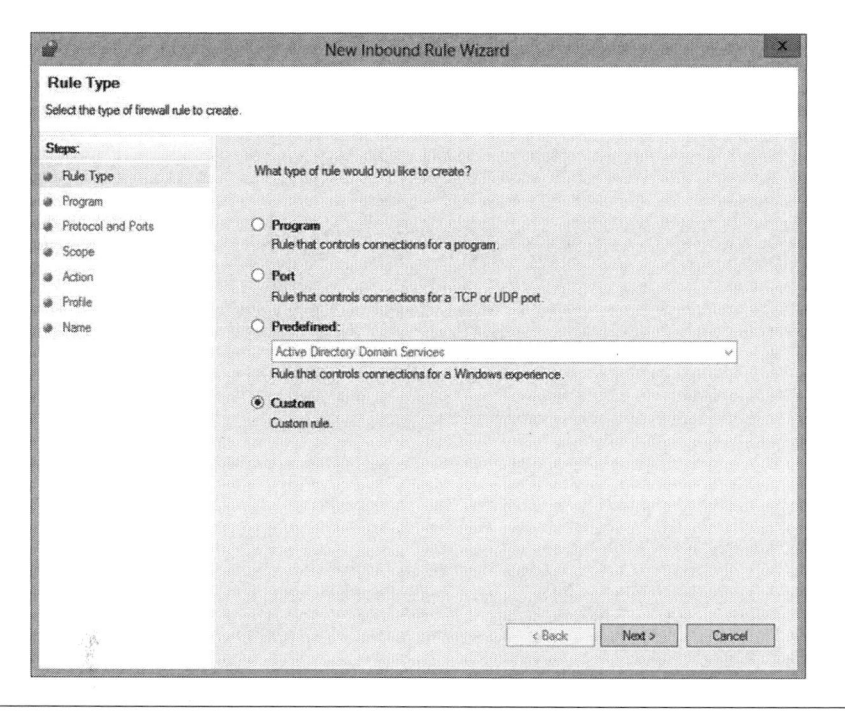

Figure 10.42 Specifying rule type.

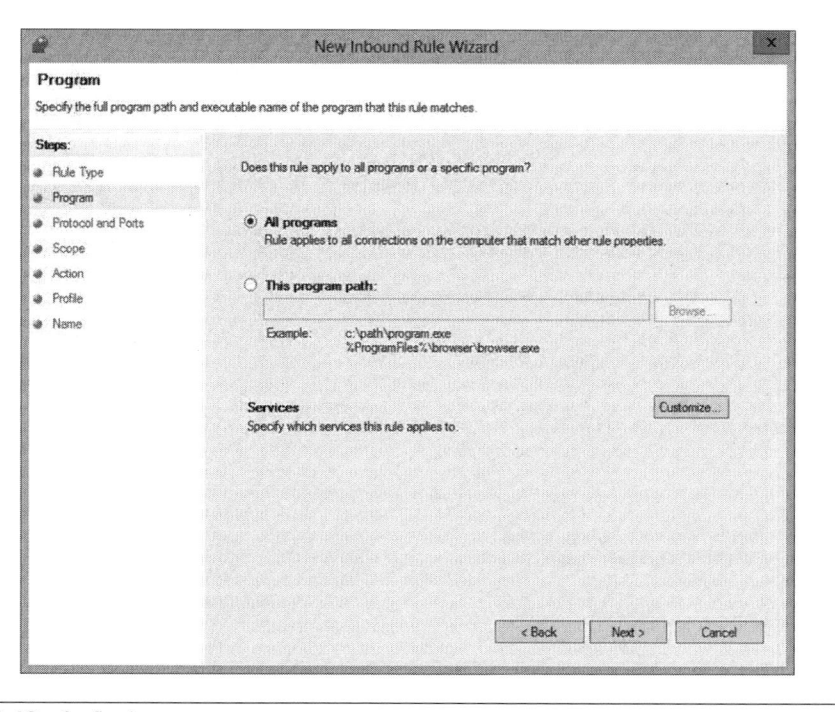

Figure 10.43 Configuring program.

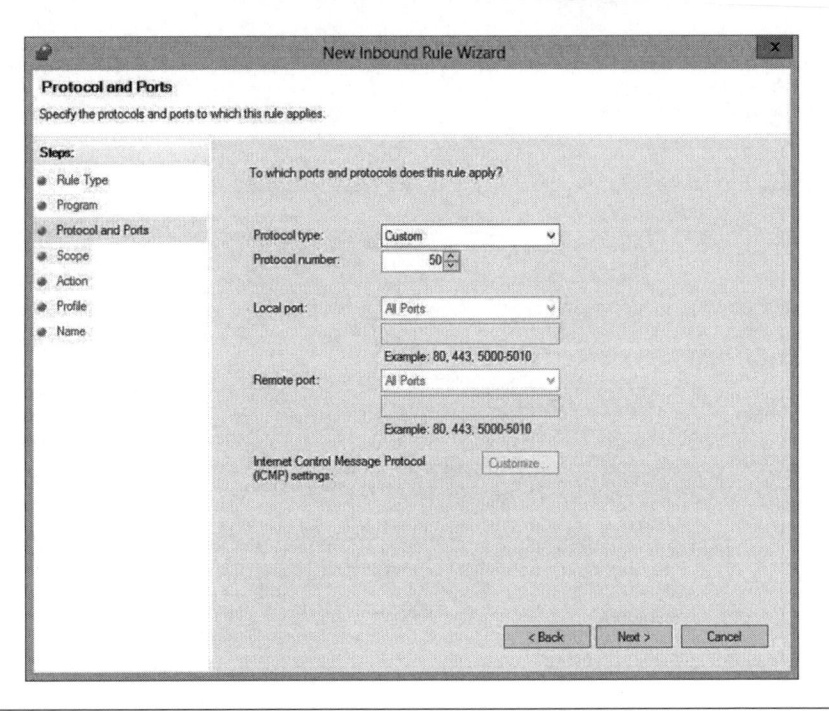

Figure 10.44   Specifying protocol and port.

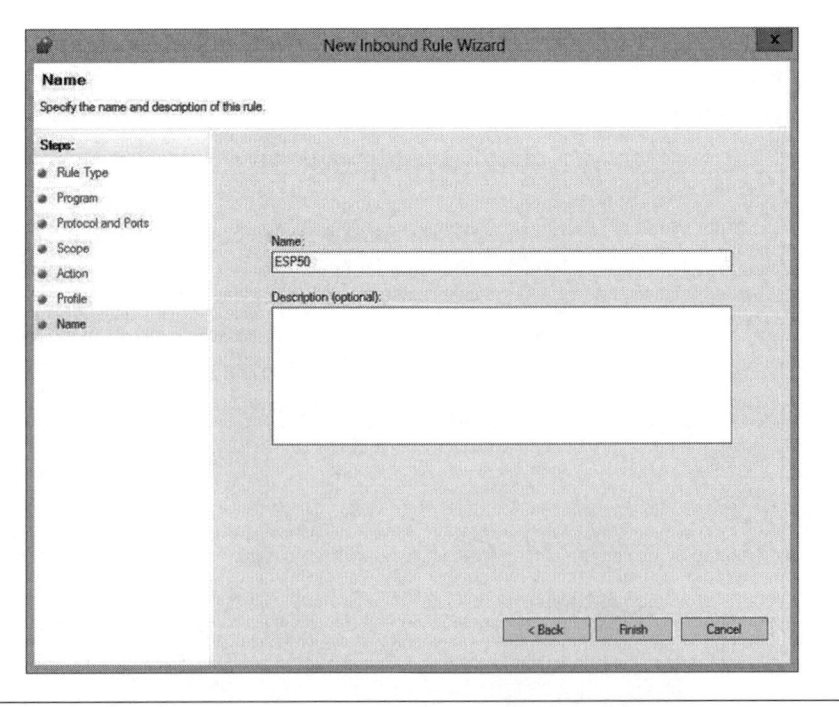

Figure 10.45   Specifying rule name.

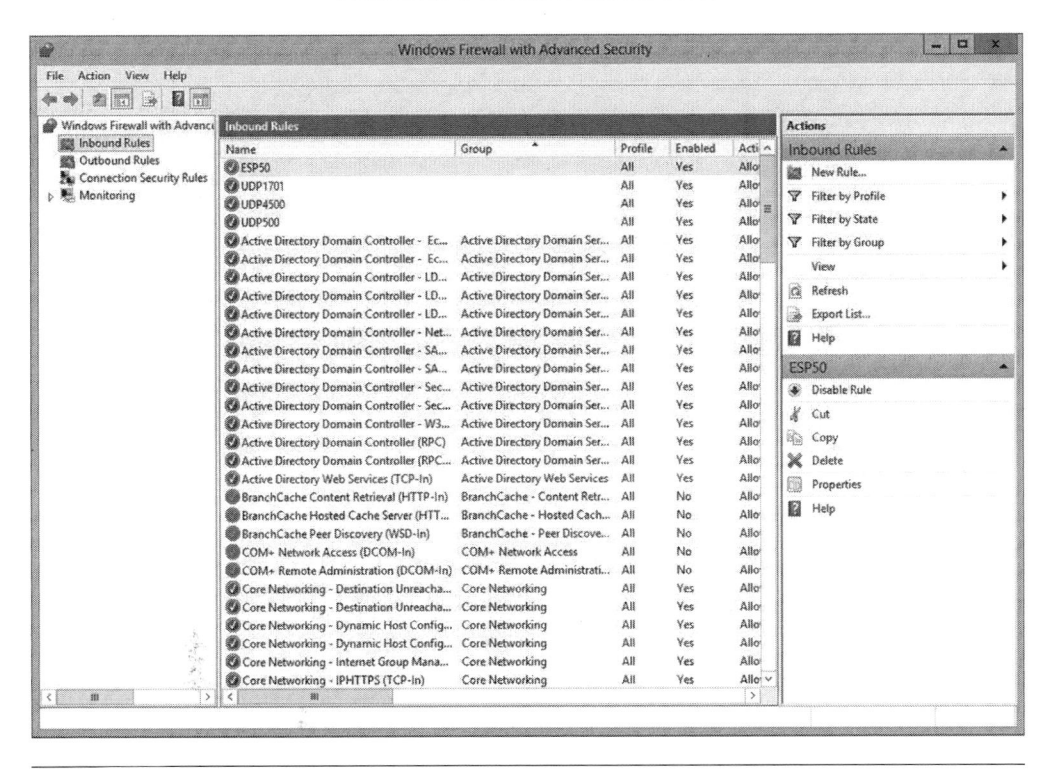

Figure 10.46 Firewall inbound rules.

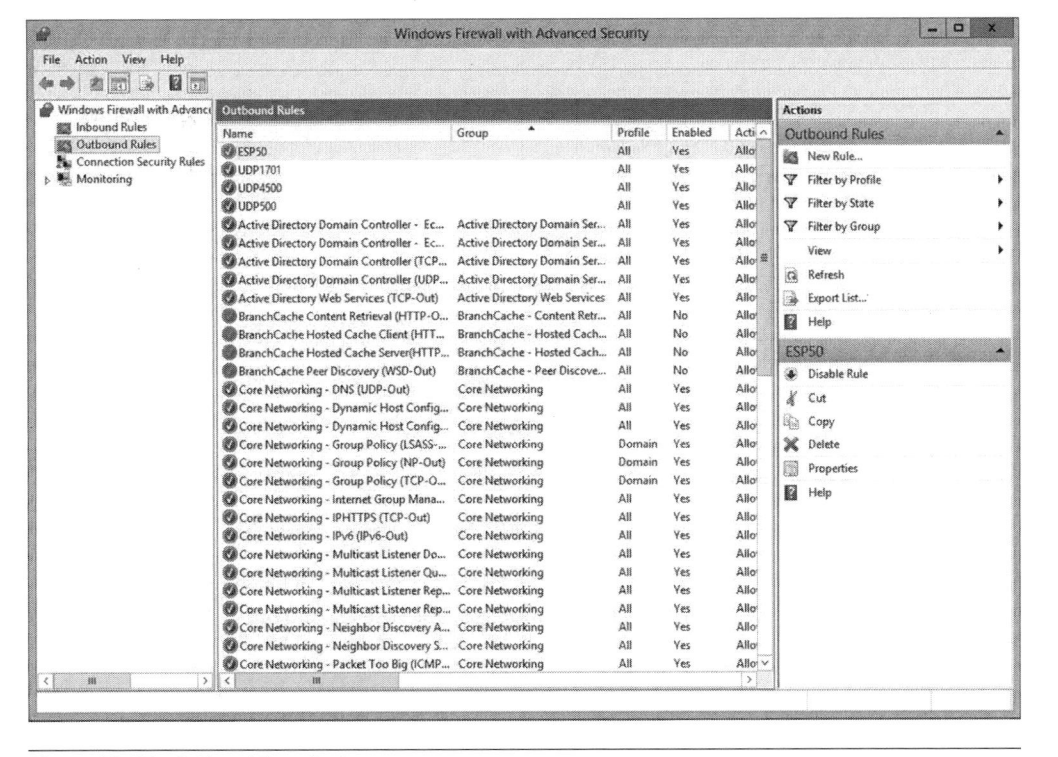

Figure 10.47 Outbound firewall rules.

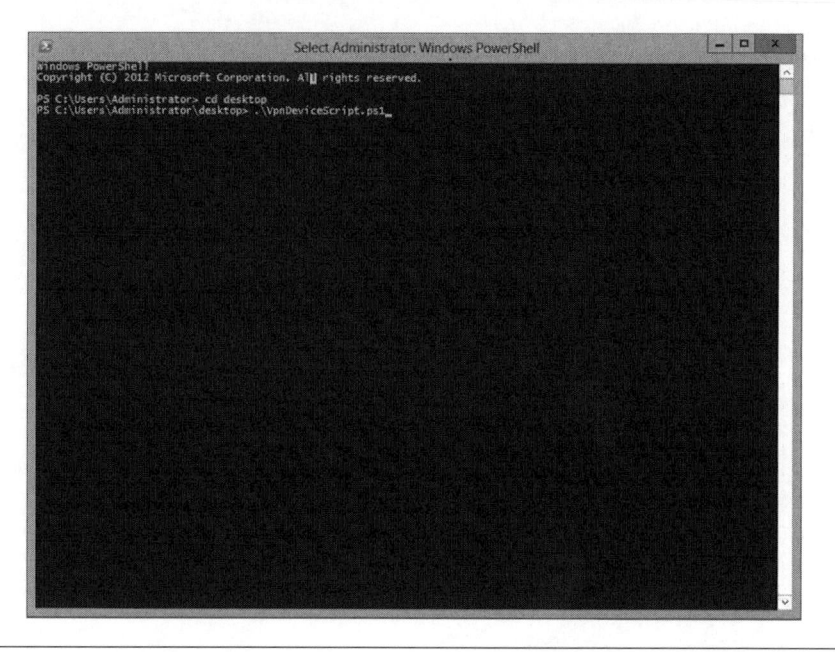

Figure 10.48   Running vpnDeviceScript.ps1 Script.

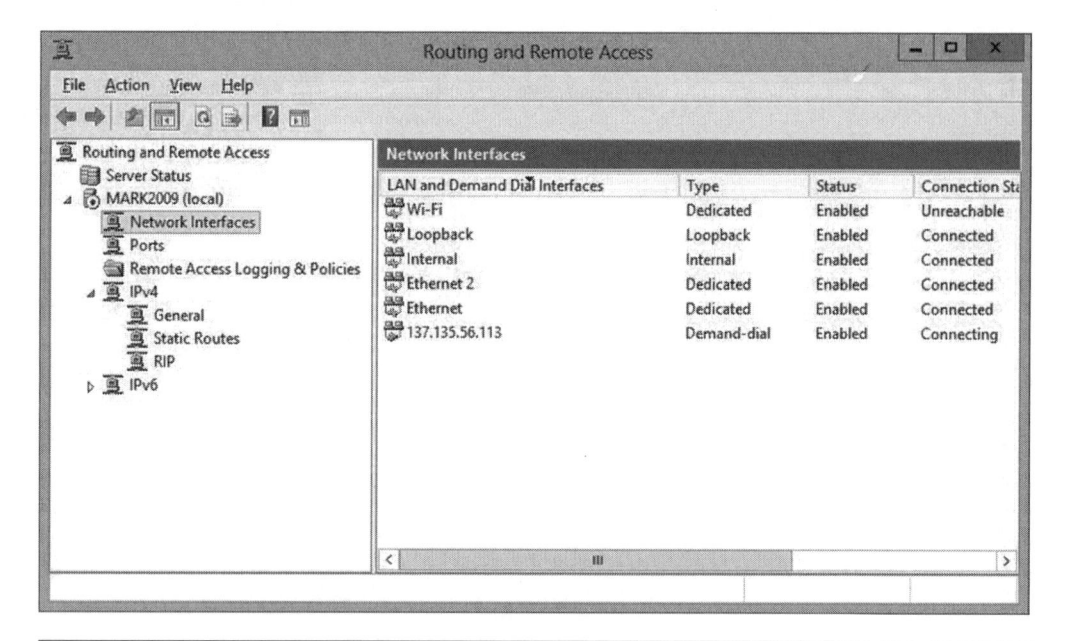

Figure 10.49   Routing and remote access.

Due to the limitation of the subscription, we are not able to create new virtual machines on the virtual network mynetlab. If you have the full subscription of Microsoft Azure, you will be able to create virtual machines and develop network services such as Active Directory, DNS, DHCP, and so on. Then, your on-premises computers can join the domain hosted by the virtual machines. Or, you can have your virtual machines on Microsoft Azure to join the domain hosted by the on-premises server.

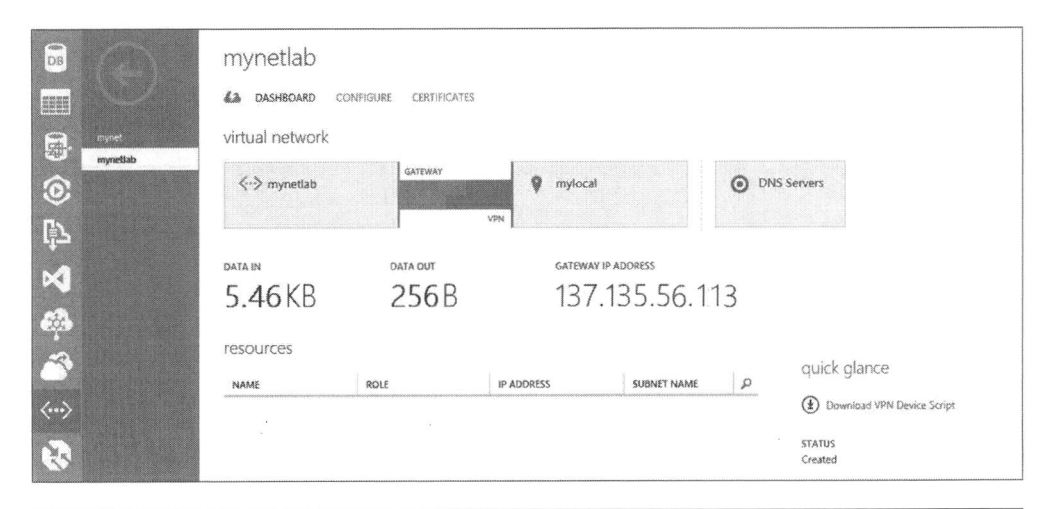

Figure 10.50 Established site-to-site connection.

10.6 Summary

This chapter discusses the VPN that can be used to share network resources. VPN is a service that allows client computers to remotely access another network securely. With the VPN technology, a local computer can share network resources stored on another network. Through the public Internet, users at home can log on to an organization's private network or to a virtual network on Microsoft Azure. To protect the confidentiality and integrity of data, various data encryption and authentication methods are used by the VPN technology. This chapter introduces VPN tunneling protocols. It also describes some of the strongest VPN authentication and encryption methods of the current VPN technology. The hands-on activities demonstrate point-to-site and site-to-site connections. Through these connections, an individual host or an on-premises network can be extended to a virtual network created on Microsoft Azure. These hands-on activities help to enhance the understanding of the VPN technology.

Review Questions

1. What do you do with VPN?
2. Describe the VPN architecture.
3. Describe the process of connecting to a VPN server.
4. Explain the site-to-site connection through an example.
5. What is SA?
6. What is Internet Key Exchange (IKE)?
7. How does IKE establish a secure communication?
8. What is tunneling?
9. Explain the tunneling process.
10. What are the three commonly used protocols for tunneling?

11. Describe how L2TP/IPSec works.
12. What are the advantages and disadvantages of IPSec when used as a tunneling protocol?
13. When used as a tunneling protocol, what are the advantages of SSL?
14. When used as a tunneling protocol, what are the disadvantages of SSL?
15. Why an SSL-based VPN is considered safer than an IPSec-based VPN?
16. When used as a tunneling protocol, what are the advantages and disadvantages of the PPTP?
17. Describe encapsulating the PPP payload with PPTP.
18. What is MS-CHAP v2 and how is it used in authentication?
19. What is EAP and how is it used in authentication?
20. What is MPPE and how is it used in encryption?

11

HYBRID CLOUD

Objectives

- Understand hybrid cloud.
- Develop private cloud.
- Develop hybrid cloud.

11.1 Introduction

More and more organizations have included cloud computing in their IT infrastructures. They can either subscribe cloud services from a public cloud provider such as Amazon Web Service or Microsoft Azure or may construct their own private clouds with a virtualization technology such as VMware or Hyper-V. Many organizations have both the public cloud and the private cloud. It may not be easy for the organizations to deal with both the public cloud and the private cloud. They need to use two different cloud access mechanisms, one for the public cloud and one for the private cloud. As the public cloud and the private cloud are constructed on different types of networks, there is no easy way to transmit data between the public cloud and the private cloud. It is also difficult for the public cloud to share the services with the private cloud.

A hybrid cloud is formed by integrating the private cloud with the public cloud. The hybrid cloud deploys software, application development platforms, and services on the public cloud and transfers the data back to the data center created on the private cloud. The virtual machines created on the public cloud can be configured so that they can join the domain created for an on-premises network. Figure 11.1 illustrates a hybrid cloud environment.

The hybrid cloud allows an organization to take advantage of both the private cloud and the public cloud. With the public cloud, the hybrid cloud has the following benefits:

- It meets the needs of various types of businesses with great scalability.
- It is cost-effective. The hybrid cloud can reduce the cost on the hardware and software expenditure as well as the cost on the management of the infrastructure.

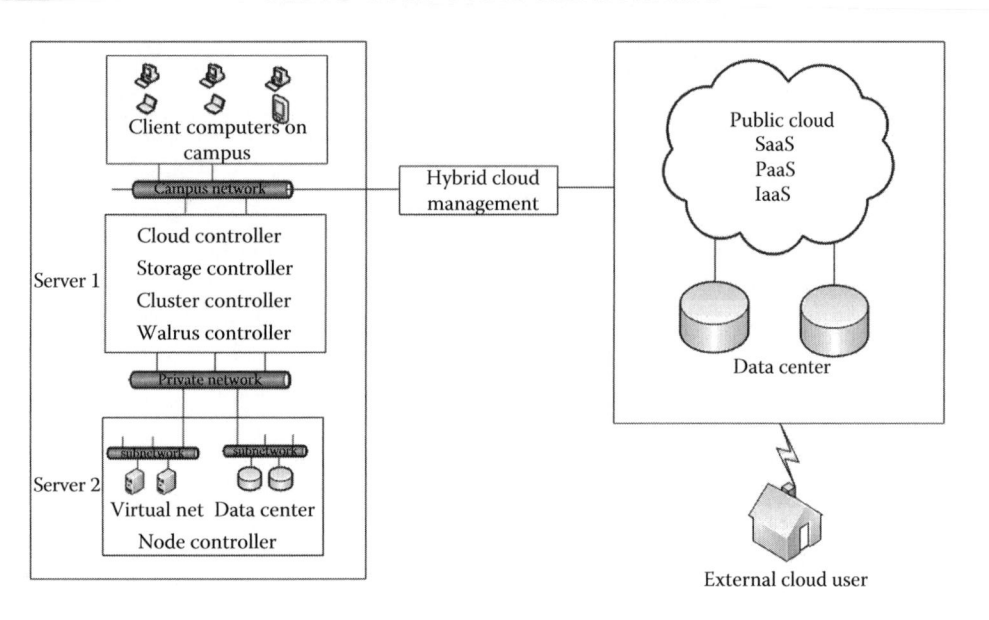

Figure 11.1 Hybrid cloud.

- It allows the user to pay for only the computing resources that are actually used.
- As the public cloud provider takes care of the system maintenance, the hybrid cloud can reduce the effort on system management.
- It extends the on-premises data centers to the public cloud for better availability.
- It is able to deliver capacity on demand.

The hybrid cloud can take advantage of the private cloud so that the hybrid cloud can have the following benefits:

- With the hybrid cloud, one does not have to store the mission-critical data to the third-party storage devices on the public cloud.
- Network administrators can have better control on enforcing security rules and user management.
- With the hybrid cloud, there is a better control on allocating computing resources.
- The hybrid cloud allows one to continue to use the existing on-premises IT infrastructure without paying the subscription fees to public cloud providers.

As described earlier, the hybrid cloud gives us the best of both worlds. Therefore, in today's enterprise computing environment, the hybrid cloud can be a game changer. It makes sense to use the hybrid cloud to support an organization's business activities.

11.2 Hybrid Cloud Solution

An organization often has multiple computing resources and services. To deal with the multiple computing resources and services, a hybrid cloud does a better job. The following are some of the scenarios where the hybrid cloud is a better choice.

Data protection: With a hybrid cloud, a university can place its web-based applications on a public cloud meanwhile keep the students' data on a private cloud on its campus so that the university has the total control of the students' data. The computer lab–based activities can also be carried out in a public cloud environment. In general, the hybrid cloud is ideal for the data center–based enterprise level computing.

File backup: To avoid data loss, files need to be backed up in a storage facility. Some valuable data may need to be stored in multiple locations. In this case, storing the data to a public cloud can be an ideal solution. In case that the data on the private cloud get lost, through the hybrid cloud, the data can be restored in no time.

Data center outsourcing: As an organization grows larger, its internal data center may eventually run out of room. One of the logical solutions is to use the data center outsourcing service provided by a reputable data center company. A public cloud is able to serve as a reputable data center company for storing a large amount of data. For data center outsourcing, a hybrid cloud plays a critical role in implementing an outsourced data center. The hybrid cloud provides an environment for the ease of secure data migration. It has the ability to manage data transactions between the public cloud and the private cloud. It can also ease the management of the existing applications and operating systems.

Application hosting: Hosting applications such as the e-mail server Microsoft Exchange requires servers, networks, and a database. It is a mountainous job and it requires high scalability. Instead of implementing and maintaining the IT infrastructure for hosting the application package, we may offload the email server to a public cloud service. By doing so, the IT service department can focus their effort on services that need more controls from the administrators.

Web hosting: An international enterprise may deploy its web services across the world. For better performance, it requires multiple web servers to be deployed geographically across multiple locations. It needs multiple IT infrastructures to support these web servers. It is also a challenging task to keep these web services consistent. In such a case, it can offload the web servers to a public cloud and keep the data centers on a private cloud so that they can be managed in a single hybrid environment. By connecting a web server locally to a data center can reduce the latency and improve the end user experience.

Experimenting and testing: A hybrid cloud provides an ideal environment for experimenting and testing. Its scalability and flexibility allow it to generate various types of IT infrastructures to experiment with a new solution and to test the portability of the solution in various environments. With no need to construct new physical IT infrastructures, the experiments and tests can be done in a short time with minimum cost.

11.3 Hybrid Cloud Technology

For a hybrid cloud to be beneficial, the hybrid cloud should be designed to have the following features:

- The hybrid cloud should provide a portal to allow users to provision their own computing resources.
- The hybrid cloud should support a multiple-tenant computing architecture. That is, each of the organizations can subscribe an instance of software. Each organization can configure its instance of the software according to its needs without causing a problem on other software instances. The hybrid cloud should allow the users to specify the location at a higher level such as country although the users may not be able to specify where to store the data at a low level.
- The hybrid cloud should provide a broad range of network access. It should allow multiple users to access the hybrid cloud from multiple locations and with various remote accessing mechanisms. The public cloud should be able to communicate with the private cloud directly.
- The hybrid cloud should have adequate scalability depending on the users' subscriptions. The users should be able to scale their usage of computing resources up and down automatically. The reaction to a scale-up demand should be fast enough so that the users will not experience a slow down.
- The hybrid cloud should provide usage reports and operating statistics.
- The hybrid cloud should provide all the three types of cloud services: Infrastructure as a Service (IaaS), Platform as a Service (PaaS), and Software as a Service (SaaS).
- The hybrid cloud should provide on-premises data center for storing mission-critical data.

Some of these features are from the public cloud. Others are from the private cloud. This requires the hybrid cloud to bind the public cloud and the private cloud. The hybrid component that can be used to bind the public cloud and the private cloud is called the cloud management platform.

11.3.1 Hybrid Cloud Management Strategies

To manage a hybrid cloud in a multi-domain environment, it is necessary to draft a management policy. The management policy may include the following guidelines.

The first thing involved in cloud management is to find out what to manage. The common cloud management tasks may include performance monitoring, security enforcement, disaster recovery, load balancing, and dealing with emergency events. Hybrid cloud administrators may also be involved in problem solving for issues related to networking and storage in multiple clouds. The hybrid cloud manager also needs to identify the best way to carry out the management tasks.

Once the management tasks are identified, a management policy should be established on making changes on a hybrid cloud. It needs to make it clear on who has the permission of installation and making changes in the hybrid cloud. It needs rules to enforce security measures. For user management, the policy needs to categorize users so that each group of users has proper permissions. The rule on the intellectual property should also be considered in the policy.

Based on restriction of availability, the policy needs to specify the cloud technology to use and the cloud services to subscribe. For the cross-platform cloud management tools used for managing the hybrid cloud, the management policy may include a section which identifies a list of trusted vendors providing the management tools, the budget for purchasing these tools, the tasks to be accomplished with these tools, and the limitations of these tools. The policy needs to clarify whether to use a single tool which is like a Swiss army knife that performs multiple tasks or to use a set of tools, each of them accomplishing a certain task.

In the policy, the responsibility of the IT service personnel should be addressed. A dedicated person should be appointed as the hybrid cloud administrator responsible for the overall success. The IT service personnel should also be identified for networking, storage device, operating system, data center, and security management.

When the management job is too complicated or too specific, it may require custom coding to get the job done. The hybrid cloud should be able to run code scripts across multiple clouds.

11.3.2 Hybrid Cloud Management Platform

Managing hybrid clouds can be challenging. Cloud management platform software is designed to ease the complexity. The cloud management platform software usually provides the following functionalities:

- View and manage multiple clouds in the same environment.
- Create and manage virtual machines in an integrated environment. It is able to provide templates to develop virtual machines fast.
- Offer services across multiple clouds.
- Have the ability to leverage the existing IT infrastructure.
- Supply portable cloud developing and managing tools.
- Provide unified reporting and analysis for the usage of the clouds.
- Support cross-environment application deployment.

There are many such types of software available. To name a few, consider the following commonly used cloud management software:

- vCloud Director is a cloud management suite developed by VMware. It can be used to build hybrid clouds by integrating a public cloud with a private cloud built with VMware products. vCloud Connector can also be used to migrate virtual machines between private and public clouds.
- Microsoft System Center 2012—App Controller is capable of helping users easily configure, deploy, and manage virtual machines and services across private and public clouds. It is designed to integrate Microsoft Azure and a private cloud hosted by System Center Virtual Machine Manager (SCVMM).
- Cloud Lifecycle Management (CLM) provided by EMC is a cloud management platform which can be deployed to a customer's on-premises data center. It allows users to manage public clouds through an organization's firewall.
- RightScale is also a popular choice for the management of clouds. It is deployed as a public SaaS service meanwhile managing private clouds through an organization's firewall. With RightScale, users are able to manage budgets across multiple public cloud providers. It also allows the users to access virtual images running in multiple clouds.
- Another popular cloud management platform is Eucalyptus. As the Eucalyptus API is fully compatible with the Amazon API, the applications and tools created for the Amazon public cloud can be easily applied to a private cloud. Eucalyptus lets users manage multiple cloud providers by using a single console.
- OpenStack is an open-source cloud management platform for deploying clouds. OpenStack is popular among Linux distributions such as Red Hat and Ubuntu Linux. OpenStack supports commonly used hypervisors such as KVM and Xen for developing the virtualized IT infrastructure. OpenStack is also built to support various public clouds such as Amazon Web Services and Microsoft Azure. OpenStack includes a set of open-source tools dedicated to carry out a wide range of cloud management tasks such as creating and monitoring virtual images as well as virtual image management.

The choice of a cloud management platform depends on the features provided by the software and the experience of using the software. Some of the software is designed for a specific hypervisor and others may be designed for various hypervisors. Some of them are easy to use and others may require more hands-on experience. The choice of a cloud management platform deeply depends on the types of tasks to accomplish, the budget constraints, the support by the software vendors, and compatibility with the cloud technologies used in a hybrid cloud.

11.3.3 Virtualization Technology

The key technology for constructing a scalable hybrid cloud is virtualization. The virtualization technology is used to build a pool of computing resources for the hybrid cloud. For example, it can be used to create virtual networks, virtual machines, virtual switches, virtual storage, and virtual images or templates. These virtualized computing resources are used to build the cloud infrastructure. The virtualized computing resources are critical for data management, network communication, and running application. The virtualization technology is capable of providing resource sharing, virtual machine isolation, and load balancing. Cloud computing relies on virtualization for providing the features such as high scalability, use of pooled resources, and rapid provisioning.

Virtualization is realized with the hypervisor which is the software used to create, host, and manage virtualized computing resources. Once instructed by the host operating system, the hypervisor allocates the CPU, memory, disk space, and communication bandwidth resources, and then loads the virtual machines. With the hypervisor, multiple virtual machines and virtual networks can be created on one or a group of physical servers. In addition, the hypervisor can also be used to create and manage file replication and desktop computer virtualization. Figure 11.2 illustrates a virtualized computing environment.

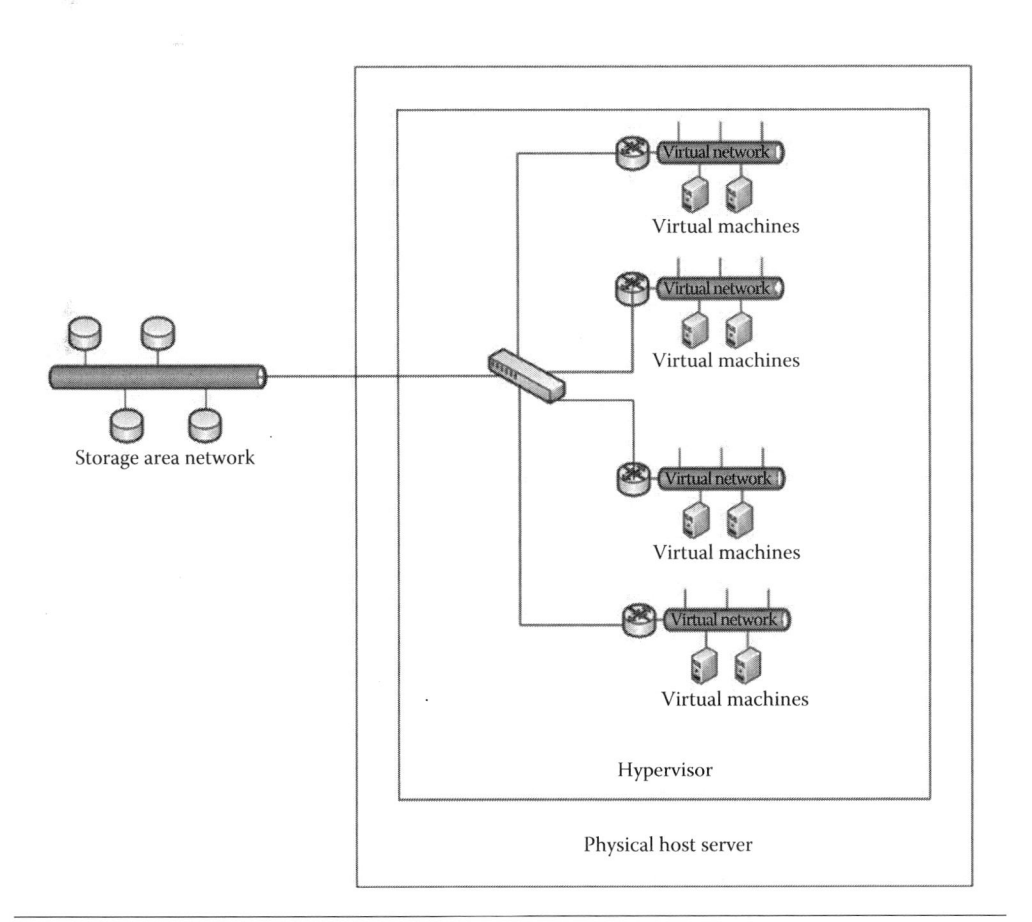

Figure 11.2 Virtualized computing environment.

There are two types of hypervisors, bare metal hypervisor and embedded hypervisor. The bare metal hypervisor is also called the native hypervisor or Type 1 hypervisor. The bare metal hypervisor runs directly on the hardware of a host computer. By directly running on the hardware, the bare metal hypervisors has better performance and better security. Microsoft Hyper-V, VMware ESX/ESXi, KVM, and Citrix XenServer belong to this type of hypervisor. On the other hand, the embedded hypervisor, also called the hosted hypervisor or Type II hypervisor, runs like a piece of software on an operating system such as Windows or Linux. Although this type of hypervisor has lower performance, it is easier to install and does not need much configuration. The well-known VMware Workstation is this type of hypervisor. Each of these hypervisors has its pros and cons. The choice of a hypervisor depends on the tasks to be performed and features provided by the hypervisor to meet the requirements.

Virtualization and cloud computing software provided by VMware is designed to run on x86-compatible computers. VMware offers vSphere as the virtualization operating system, VMware Workstation for desktop development and management of virtual machines, vSphere Client as the client application used for the management of vSphere, vCenter as the centralized management tool for the vSphere suite, vCloud Director for cloud computing management, and many other tools. VMware provides many advanced features and scalability for its hypervisor. On the other hand, the implementation of vSphere may require powerful hardware and the licensing cost may be too high for small businesses. Therefore, VMware offers a low-cost package for small businesses and the VMware Academic Program (VMAP) package which includes all the aforementioned software and more for an annual subscription fee of $250 for education institutions to learn about the cutting-edge virtualization technology.

Included in Windows Server 2008 or later, Hyper-V is a Windows Server virtualization platform. Windows 8 Pro or later also bundles Hyper-V. Hyper-V can be used to host, create, and manage virtual machines and virtual networks. With Hyper-V, a single physical server is able to host multiple virtual networks and virtual machines which can be configured to provide a broad range of network services. Although Hyper-V does not include as many advanced features as VMware does, it is relatively easy to use and can be installed on a laptop computer.

Originally developed by the University of Cambridge, Xen is an open-source virtualization product. Xen is also designed to operate on x86-compatible computers. It is the primary open-source competitor to commercial virtualization products such as VMware and Microsoft Hyper-V. As an open-source product, Xen is included by many Linux distributions. Red Hat, Inc. includes Xen in its server software Red Hat Enterprise Linux (RHEL). Other Linux distributions such as Debian and SuSE also include Xen in their enterprise server software. Xen has been used by cloud providers such as Amazon Web Service and Rackspace Cloud to provide cloud services, including SaaS, PaaS, and IaaS. In 2007, Citrix Systems acquired XenSource.

The full version of Xen is not free. The free Xen version supports only up to four virtual machines and 4 GB of RAM.

As our hands-on activity is carried out on Windows Server, Hyper-V is our choice for virtualization in the hands-on practice.

11.4 System Center Virtual Machine Manager

In the hybrid cloud development process, the first step is to make sure that our organization's private cloud is up and running. If you do not have a private cloud, you need to create one. SCVMM is a tool used to create a private cloud; it can be downloaded for a free 3-month evaluation.

SCVMM is a package for developing the virtual infrastructure. At first, SCVMM is virtual machine management software. Today, SCVMM has been developed as the package for managing the entire virtualized data center. In addition to supporting Hyper-V, SCVMM can also be used to manage other types of hypervisors such as VMware and Citrix XenServer. For private cloud development, SCVMM is able to integrate network segments, network hosts, and storage devices into a unified pool of computing resources. Multiple virtual machines can be provisioned together to form a unit. It is able to perform bare metal installation, that is, installing a virtual machine directly to a hard disk that has no operating system installed. It can turn off host computers when they are idle and turn them back on when needed. It is able to communicate with network storage directly and perform load balancing by moving the virtual machines among host computers. Through SCVMM, users can also deploy a database server and database applications.

11.4.1 SCVMM Installation Consideration

As software, SCVMM runs on a server which has Windows Server 2012 as the operating system. Before SCVMM can be installed, the server needs to be configured to meet the following prerequisites:

- Before the installation, the operating system should be backed up.
- The hosting server needs to have at least 4 GB RAM.
- The users of SCVMM need to have domain accounts.
- PowerShell and .NET Framework should be installed.
- SQL Server 2012 should be installed. Ideally, SQL Server and SCVMM should be installed on two separate servers. If possible, the SCVMM's library should also be installed on a separate server. In the production environment, consider installing SCVMM on a small server cluster.
- A list of roles including ASP.NET, Active Directory Domain Service, Web Server (IIS), and Hyper-V should be installed.

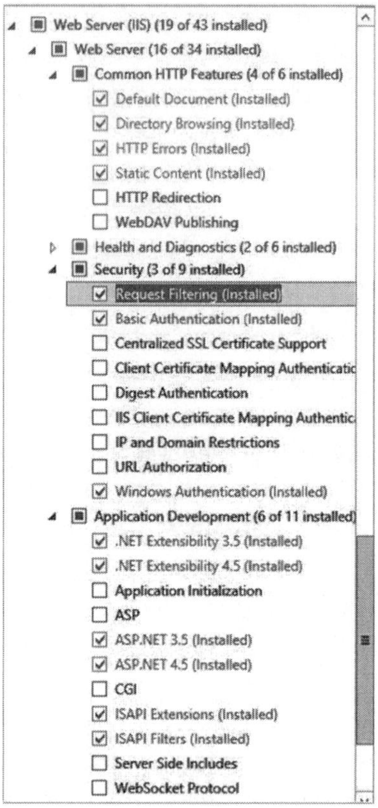

Figure 11.3 Web Server (IIS) configuration.

- Web Server (IIS) should be configured to include items such as NET Extensibility, ISAPI Extensions, ISAPI filters, request filtering, and so on. Figure 11.3 shows the Web Server (IIS) configuration.
- The encryption key used by SCVMM should be stored in Active Directory so that the key will be available for all the SCVMM components.

Once the prerequisites are taken care of, download the SCVMM package and then start the installation process. After SCVMM is successfully installed, the next task is to create a private cloud which is the necessary component for a hybrid cloud.

11.4.2 Creating Private Cloud

After SCVMM is installed, it can now be used to create a private cloud. Before the private cloud can be built, the network administrator needs to prepare a fabric for the private cloud. The fabric is an infrastructure needed for host server management. It is also used for creating and deploying virtual machines and services to the private cloud. The fabric consists of hosts, host groups, the library, networks, and storage.

The configuration of a host group allows the network administrator to group a set of servers together for the private cloud. The host group can have a mixture of

Hyper-V, VMware ESX, and Citrix XenServer hosts. The configuration of the hosts allows the network administrator to specify placement weights, dynamic optimization, power optimization, networks, storage resources, and so on.

Host groups can also be configured to have a hierarchical structure so that child host groups can inherit the settings from the parent host group. Through the hierarchical structure, the private cloud can allow the administrator to delegate the provisioning of VMs in the cloud. Figure 11.4 shows a host group created in a fabric.

For the development of the private cloud, the network administrator needs to configure the library which provides access to file-based resources such as virtual hard disks, virtual floppy disks, ISO images, scripts, driver files, and application packages. The library can also provide access to non-file-based resources such as virtual machines, service templates, and profiles that reside in the VMM database. Figure 11.5 illustrates the library contents.

Networks are a fabric component that needs to be configured by the network administrator. Through the configuration of network virtualization, one can deploy multiple virtual networks on the same physical network. The virtual networks can be named according to their functions so that it is easier to connect virtual machines to a virtual network that serves a particular function. The load balancers can be integrated with a logical network. In addition, the networking component can also be configured for monitoring network traffic, enhancing the network security, or controlling the usage of network bandwidth; Figure 11.6 illustrates the networking component in a fabric.

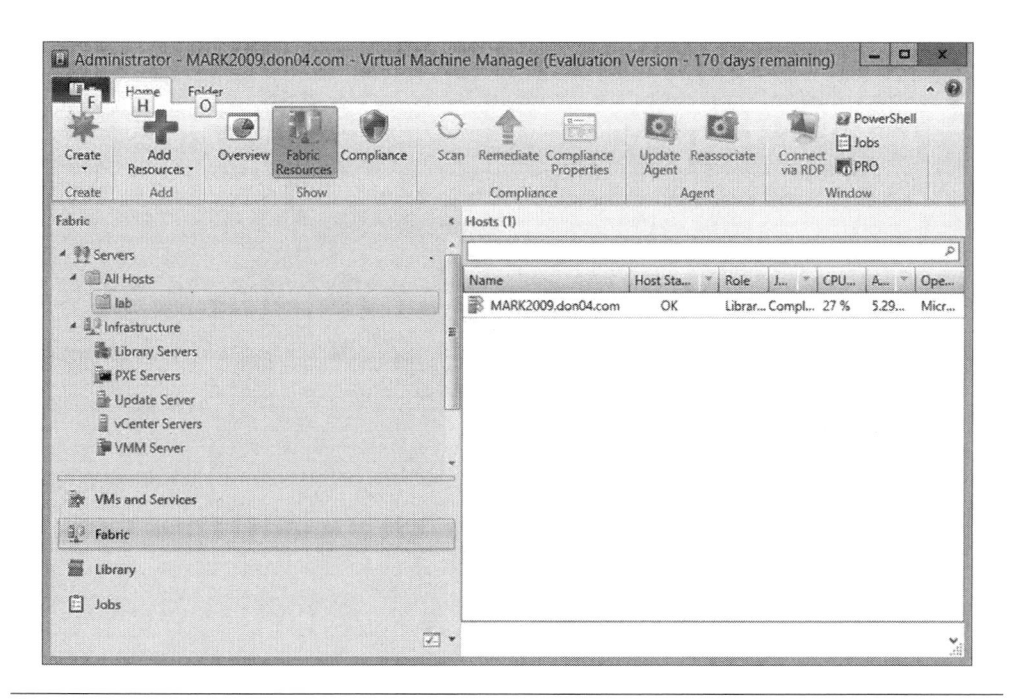

Figure 11.4 Host group in fabric.

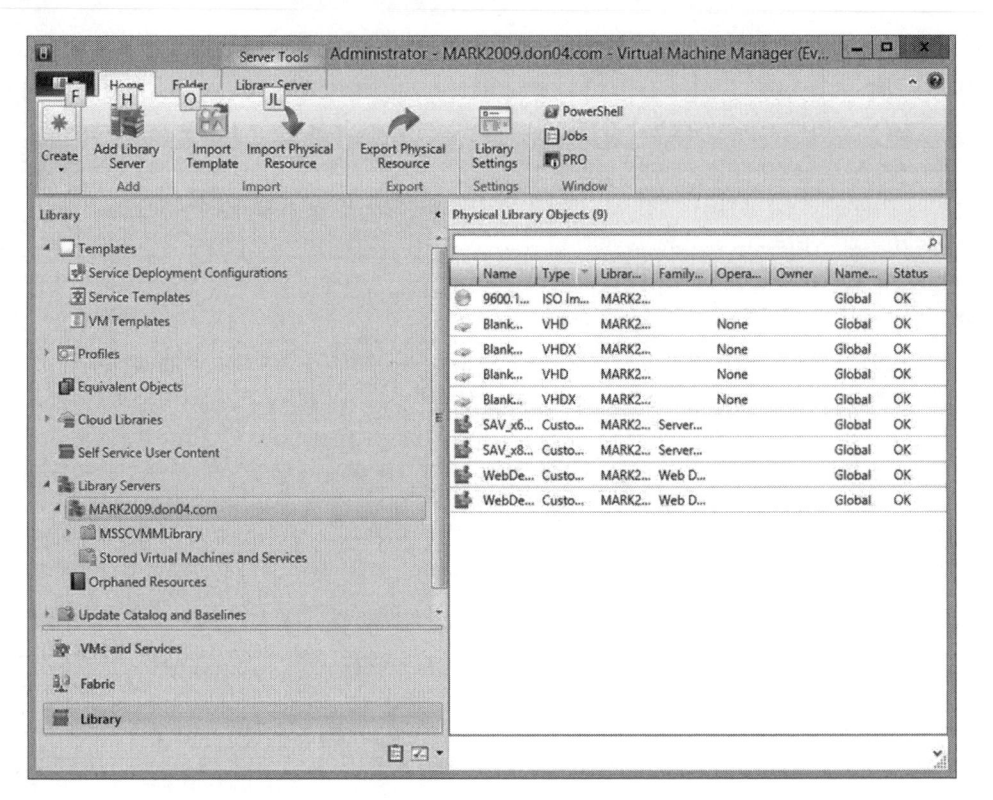

Figure 11.5 SCVMM library.

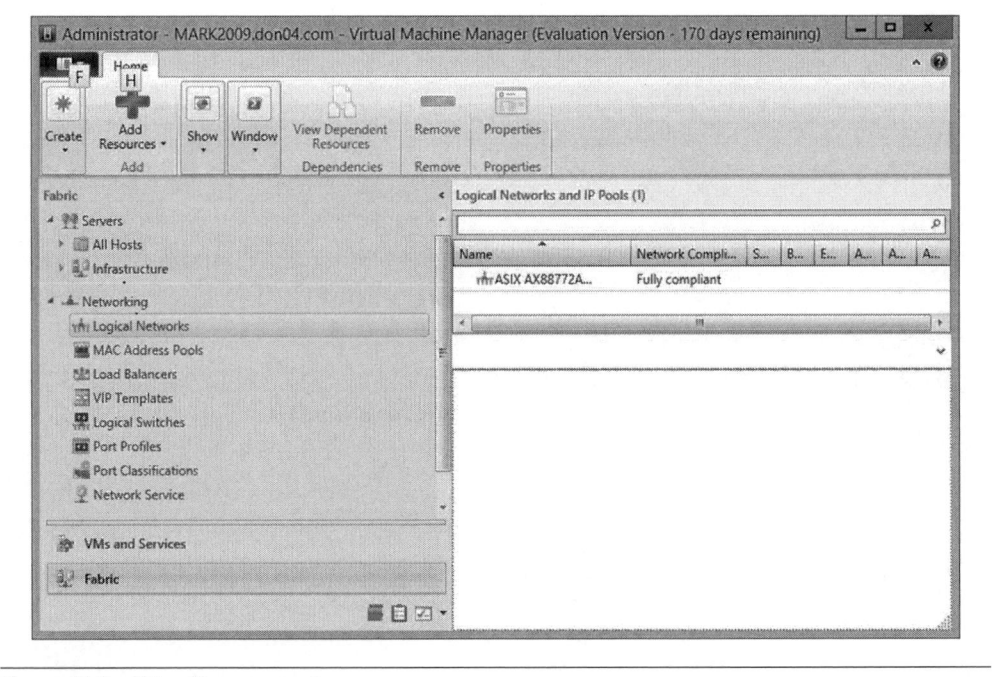

Figure 11.6 Networking component.

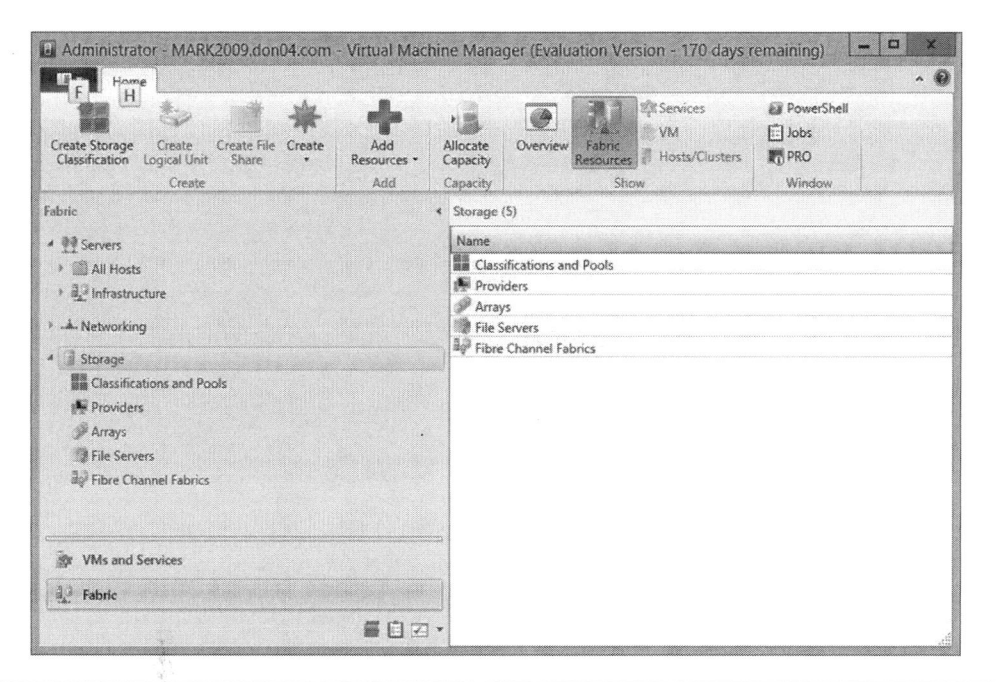

Figure 11.7 Storage component.

Another fabric component that needs to be configured is storage. Virtual Machine Manager (VMM) is able to use local storage as well as remote storage. The local storage is the storage space available on a server. The remote storage is an external storage device where the storage hardware, such as storage area network (SAN), is used to enhance scalability. Figure 11.7 illustrates the fabric storage component.

After the fabric is prepared, it is time to create a private cloud. To help with the development of the private cloud, SCVMM provides Create Cloud Wizard as shown in Figure 11.8.

As shown in Figure 11.8, the wizard allows the user to specify resources, logical networks, load balancers, VIP templates, port classifications, storage, capacity, and capacity profiles.

On the Resources page, you can specify a host or a host group where the private cloud will be created. If the host groups are created in the fabric, they will show up on this page. You can also choose to use VMware resources on this page. Figure 11.9 shows the Resources page.

The logical networks page allows the user to create and define logical networks by specifying the IP address, MAC pooling, and load balancer integration. The logical network is essential to the private cloud to be created. Figure 11.10 shows the Logical Networks page.

On the Load Balancers page, you can select the load balancer that you want to make available to the private cloud. The Microsoft Network Load Balancing (NLB) tool balances the workload among servers in a host group to make the Internet server applications more available and scalable. Figure 11.11 shows the Load Balancers page.

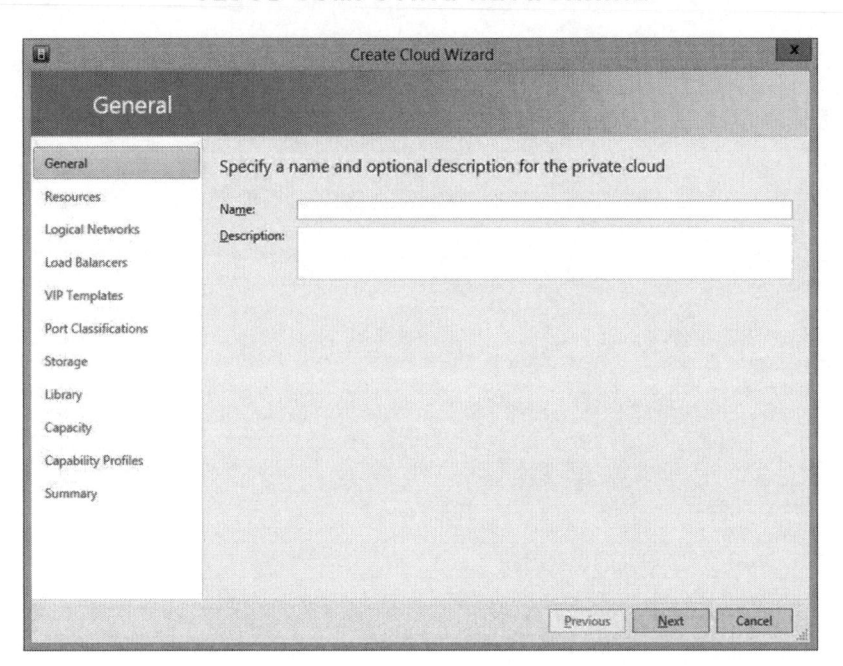

Figure 11.8 Create Cloud Wizard.

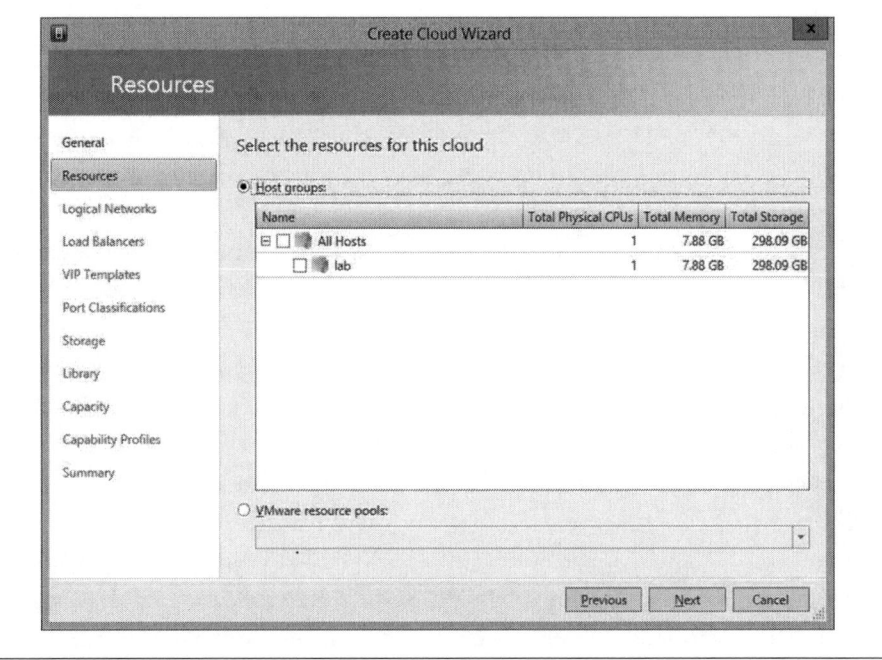

Figure 11.9 Resources page.

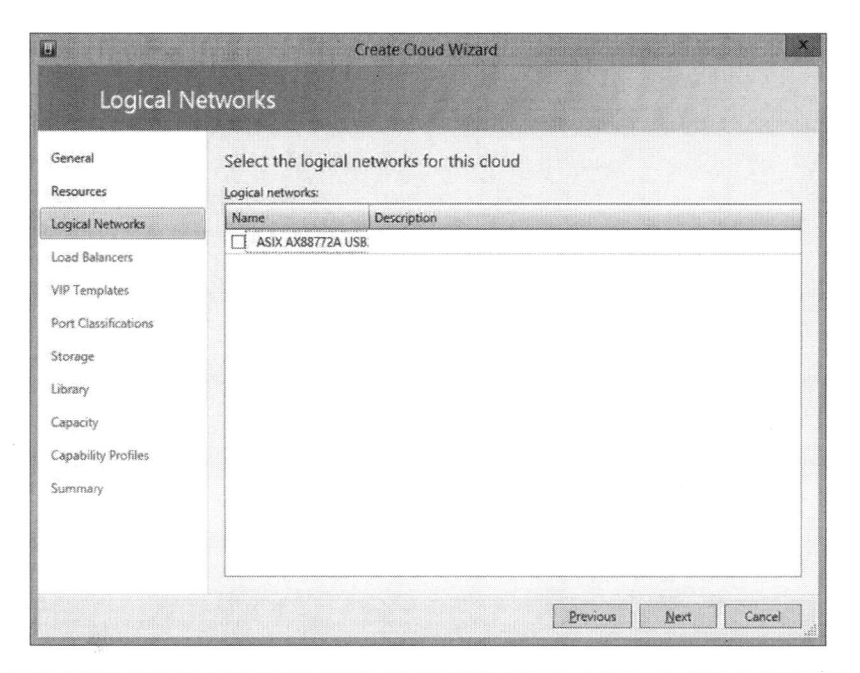

Figure 11.10 Logical networks page.

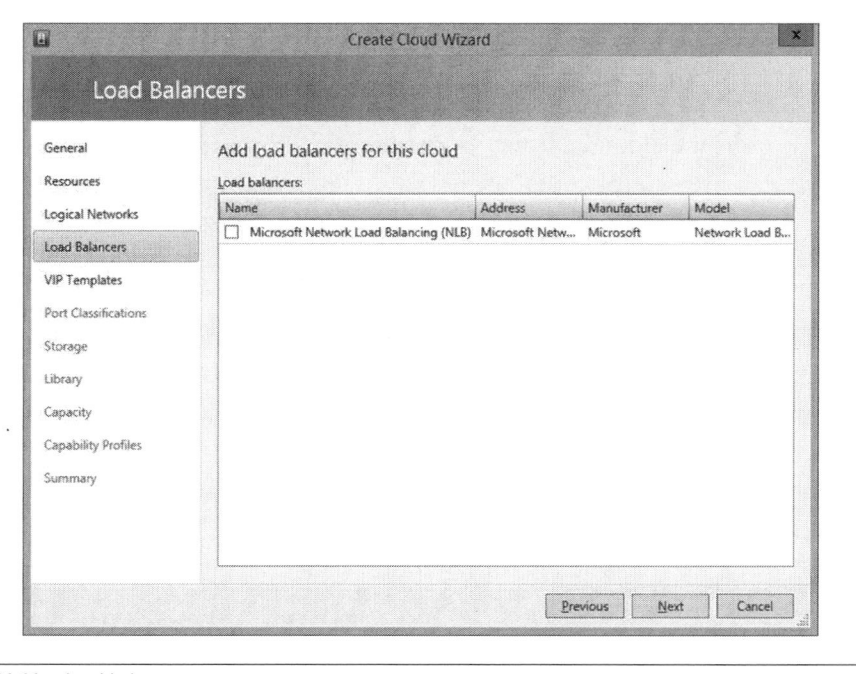

Figure 11.11 Load balancers page.

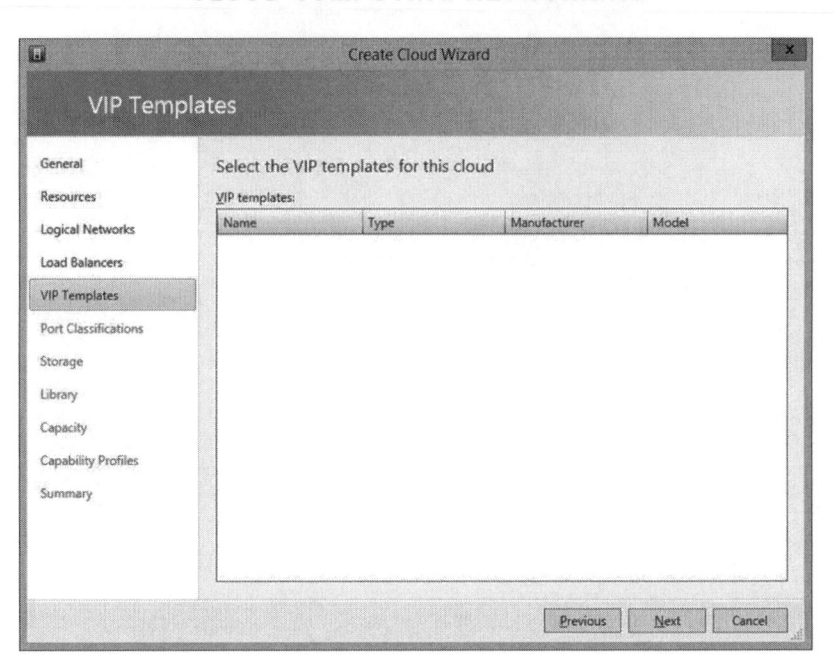

Figure 11.12   VIP templates page.

VIP stands for Virtual IP. A VIP template contains load balancer settings for a specific type of network traffic. A load balancer may have specific needs for a given network protocol. In such a case, the VIP template offers options specialized for that protocol based on the manufacturer and model. Figure 11.12 illustrates the VIP Templates page.

Port classification specifies a global name used to identify a type of virtual network adapter port profile. This global name can be used across multiple logical switches.

On the Storage page, you can specify whether to use local storage or remote storage. You can also add the storage created in the fabric. The page allows you to select the desired rating among multiple storage devices. Figure 11.13 shows the Storage page.

On the Library page, you can specify how the virtual machines will be hosted by the private cloud. Here, you can choose the templates and scripts. Figure 11.14 shows the folders in a library server.

The next page is about the configuration of capacity control for the private cloud. By default, the private cloud will use all the available resources, including the CPU, memory, and storage. You can also allow the private cloud to use only part of the available resources. Figure 11.15 shows the Capacity page.

On Capability Profiles page, you can specify the host server profile. A virtual machine can be created with three default profiles, Hyper-V (Windows), ESX Server (VMware), or XenServer (Citrix). More profiles can be added to the list. Figure 11.16 shows the Capability Profiles page.

Once the private cloud is created, it can be connected to Microsoft Azure through App Controller which is browser-based cloud management software. By connecting

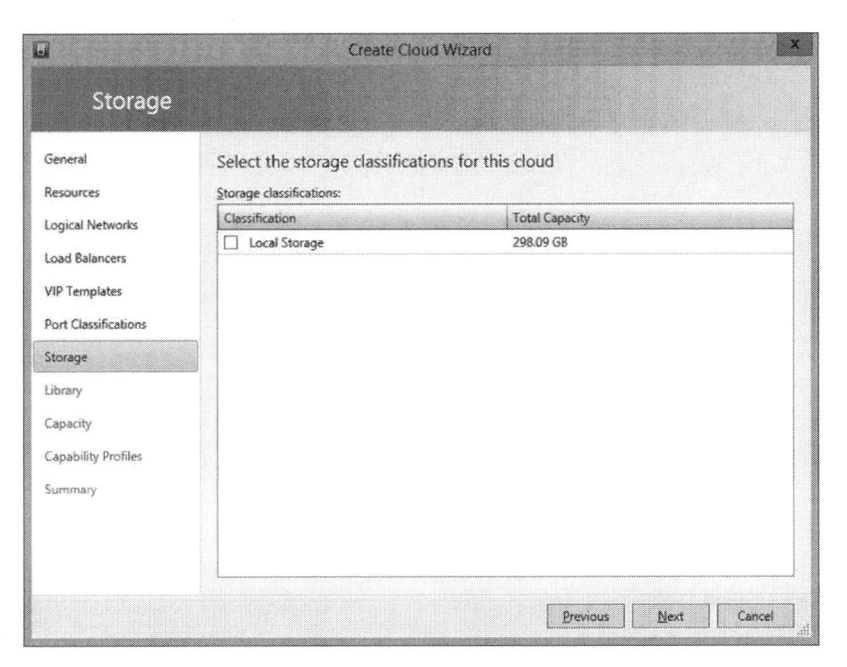

Figure 11.13 Storage page.

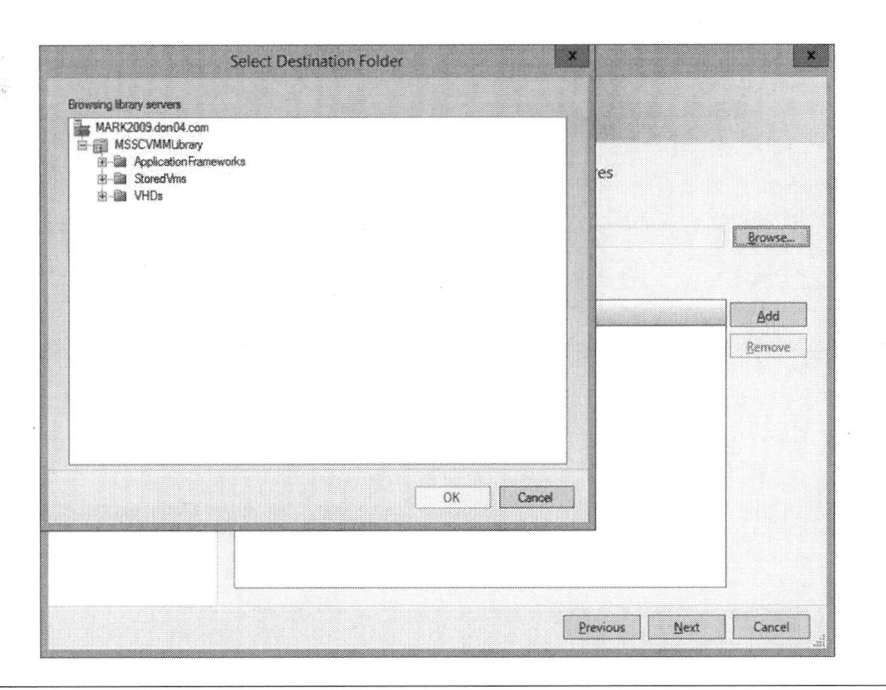

Figure 11.14 Folders in library server.

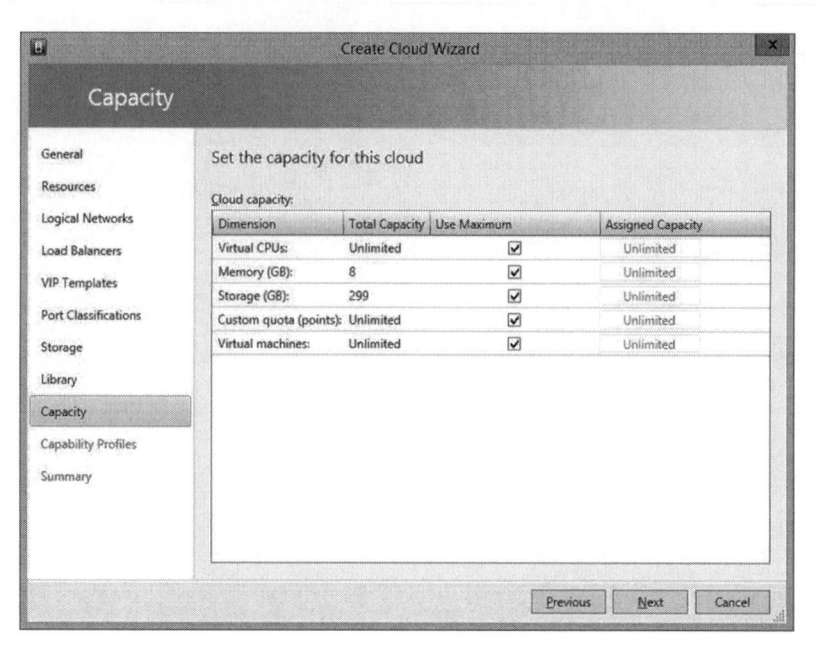

Figure 11.15 Capacity page.

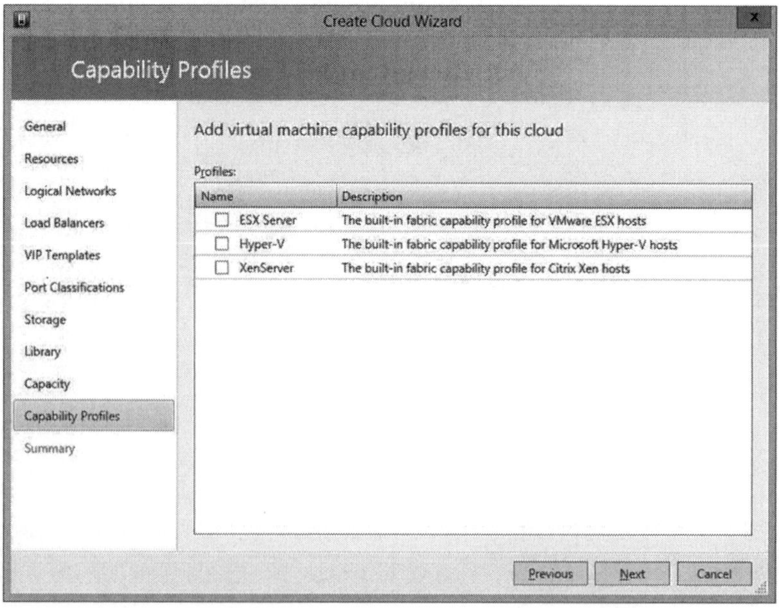

Figure 11.16 Capacity profiles page.

to the public cloud Microsoft Azure, we form a hybrid cloud which has the best of both the public cloud and private cloud. The hands-on activity will illustrate the use of App Controller for hybrid cloud management.

Activity 11.1: Developing Hybrid Cloud with System Center 2012 R2

In this activity, you will use System Center 2012 R2 to create and manage private cloud. The project is going to be accomplished with the following tasks:

Task1: Installing and configuring Windows Server 2012 R2
Task2: Installing and configuring server roles
Task 3: Installing and configuring software
Task 4: Private cloud development
Task 5: Hybrid cloud development

In this project, you need to install VMM in the lab with three virtual machines, including the operating system Windows Server 2012 R2. The lab consists of a domain controller with an isolated domain, SQL Server to host the database required for VMM, and a VMM management server.

Task 1: Installing and Configuring Windows Server 2012 R2

It is recommended that your computer should have 6 GB or more RAM and 250 GB free hard drive space. The minimum requirement is 4 GB RAM and 100 GB free hard drive space.

1. Download the Windows Server 2012 R2 ISO image file from the site (Microsoft, Microsoft DearmSpark, May, 2015) https://www.dreamspark.com.
2. After the ISO image file is downloaded, right click the ISO image file to see if the **Burn disk image** option listed. If not, you need to download and install Windows Media Player.
3. The installation of Windows Server 2012 R2 can be done in two ways, upgrade or custom. For the custom installation, a new copy of Windows Server 2012 R2 will be installed. This type of installation does not keep any existing files on the hard disk. To install Windows Server 2012 R2 with the custom option, insert the installation DVD and reboot the system. When prompted, press any key to continue the installation. The custom installation can avoid a lot of trouble which may occur later in this project.

    To install Windows Server 2012 R2 with the upgrade option, insert the installation DVD into the DVD drive. Change the directory to the DVD drive and click the setup file. You may get an error message which says that ADPREP needs to be run. In such a case, start the command prompt and change the directory to the DVD drive. From the DVD drive, run the following commands:

```
cd support\adprep
adprep/forrestprep
adprep/domianprep
```

Then, restart the installation process to upgrade your current operating system. You may also have an error message that says Online Data retrieval failures occurred. In that case, click the **Start** icon and type **run**. Enter the command **regedit** to open the registry editor. Delete the registry key:

```
HKEY_LOCAL_MACHINE\SOFTWARE\Microsoft\Windows\
   CurrentVersion\WINEVT\Channels\Microsoft-Windows-DxpTask
   Ringtone/Analytic
```

4. After Windows Server 2012 R2 is installed, make sure that you, as a user, have the permission as the Domain Admins or Enterprise Admins. As a server, your computer needs to have a fixed IP address. Configure one of the NICs on your computer with the fix IP address, such as 192.168.1.2. After Windows Server 2012 R2 is installed, through the local server link, you can change the server name to something like MARK2009.

Task 2: Installing and Configuring Server Roles

In this task, for developing the private cloud, the following server roles will be added:

- Active Directory Domain Service
- Web Server (IIS)
- Hyper-V

To do so, follow the steps:

1. To add the Active Directory Domain Service role, click the link **Add roles and features** on the Server Manager page as shown in Figure 11.17.
2. Click **Next** three times to go to the Select server roles page. Check the **Active Directory Domain Services** option. In the Add features that are required for Active Directory Domain Services dialog, click **Add Features**. Then, click **Next**.
3. On the Select features page, click **Next** several times to go to the Confirm installation selections page. Check the **Restart the destination server automatically if required** check box and click **Install**. The Installation progress page displays the status during the installation process.
4. When the process completes, in the message details, click **Promote this server to a domain controller** and the Active Directory Domain Services Configuration Wizard will open.
5. On the **Deployment Configuration** page, select **Add a new forest**. For the root domain name, type the fully qualified domain name (FQDN) for your

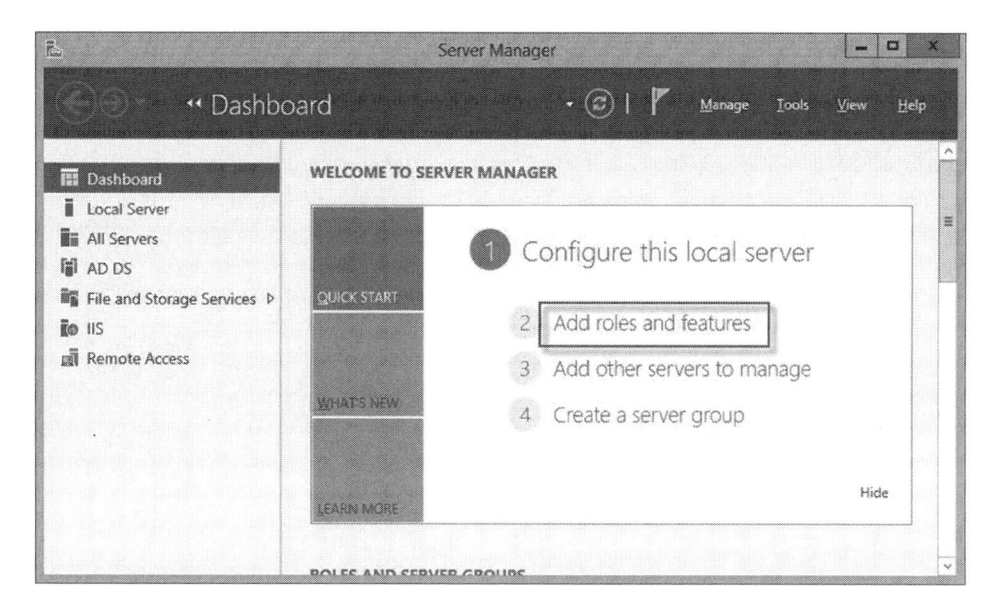

Figure 11.17 Adding roles and features.

domain. For example, if you like to have FQDN mark2009.dns04.com as the domain name, type **dns04.com**. Click **Next**.

6. On the **Domain Controller Options** page, type the password of your choice and confirm it; click **Next**.

7. On the **DNS Options** page, click **Next** several times until you get to the **Review Options** page.

8. On the **Review Options** page, review your selections. If you want to export the settings to a Windows PowerShell script, click **View script**. The script opens in Notepad, and you can save it to the folder location of your choice. Click **Next**.

9. On the **Prerequisites Check** page, make sure that your selections are validated. When the check completes, click **Install**.

10. Once the installation is complete, you will see that AD DS is added to the Dashboard list.

11. Next, you need to install the server role Web Server (IIS). Again, on the Server Manager page, click **Add roles and features** as shown in Figure 11.17.

12. Click **Next** three times to go to the **Select server roles** page, check the option **Web Server (IIS)** and click **Add Features**.

13. Click **Next** twice to the go to the **Role Services** page. Check the following services:

  a. Common HTTP Features

    i. Default Document

    ii. Directory Browsing

    iii. HTTP Errors

    iv. Static Content

  b. Health and Diagnostics
   i. HTTP Logging
   ii. Request Monitor
  c. Performance
   i. Static Content Compression
  d. Security
   i. Request Filtering
   ii. Basic Authentication
   iii. Windows Authentication
  e. Application Development
   i. NET Extensibility 3.5
   ii. NET Extensibility 4.5
   iii. ASP.NET 3.5
   iv. ASP.NET 4.5
   v. ISAPI Extensions
   vi. ISAPI Filters
  f. Management Tools
   i. IIS Management Console
   ii. IIS 6 Management Compatibility
   iii. IIS 6 Metabase Compatibility
   iv. IIS Management Scripts and Tools

14. After these services are checked, click **Next** to go to the **Confirm installation selections** page. You may see the warning "Do you need to specify an alternate source path? One or more installation selections are missing source files..." as shown in Figure 11.18.

  This is due to the service ASP.NET 3.5. You may uncheck the service ASP. NET 3.5 and.NET Extensibility 3.5 and install other services first. Then, use the same aforementioned procedure to add the features ASP.NET 3.5 and .NET Extensibility 3.5. This time, when you get to the Confirm installation selections page, insert the installation DVD into the DVD drive, say D drive. Click the link **Specify an alternative source path** as shown in Figure 11.18. On the Specify Alternate Source Path page, enter the path **d:\sources\sxs** as shown in Figure 11.19.

15. Next, you need to install the Hyper-V role. Again, on the Server Manager page, click **Add roles and features** as shown in Figure 11.17.

16. Click **Next** a few times to go to the **Select server roles** page. Check the option **Hyper-V** and click **Yes** on the Add Features prompt. After the Hyper-V role is checked as shown in Figure 11.20, click **Next** three times.

17. You need to create a virtual switch so that the virtual machines can communicate with other network hosts on an external network. To do so, select an external NIC, for example, **Ethernet 2** (Figure 11.21).

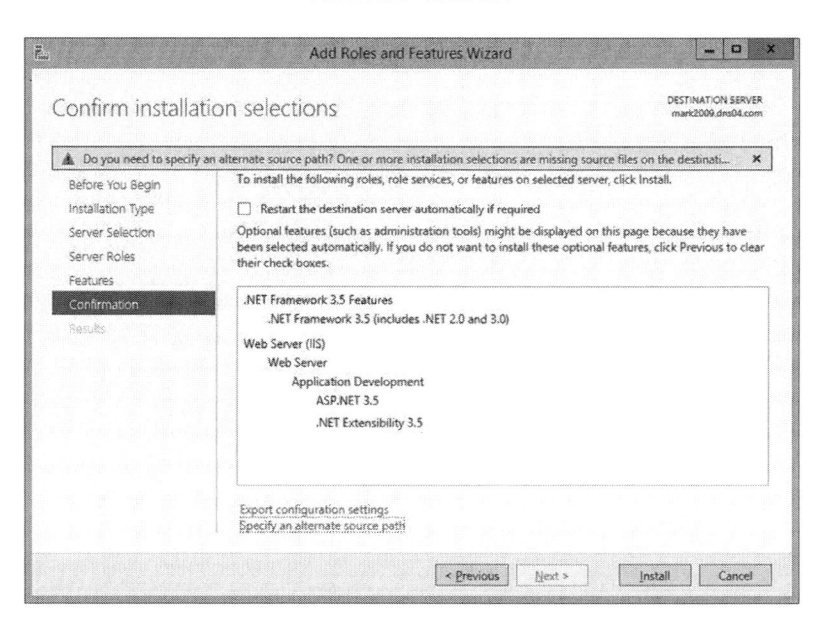

Figure 11.18 Warning message.

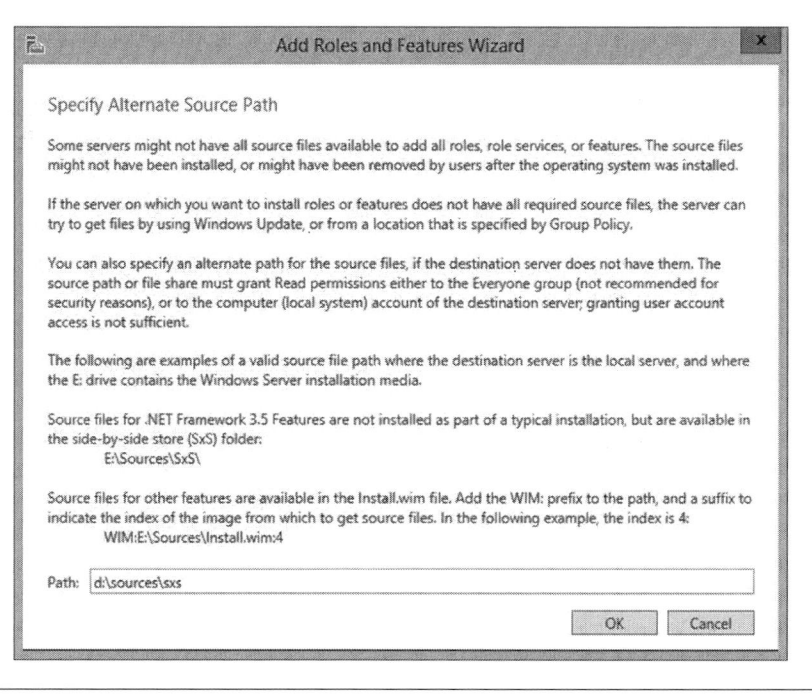

Figure 11.19 Alternate path.

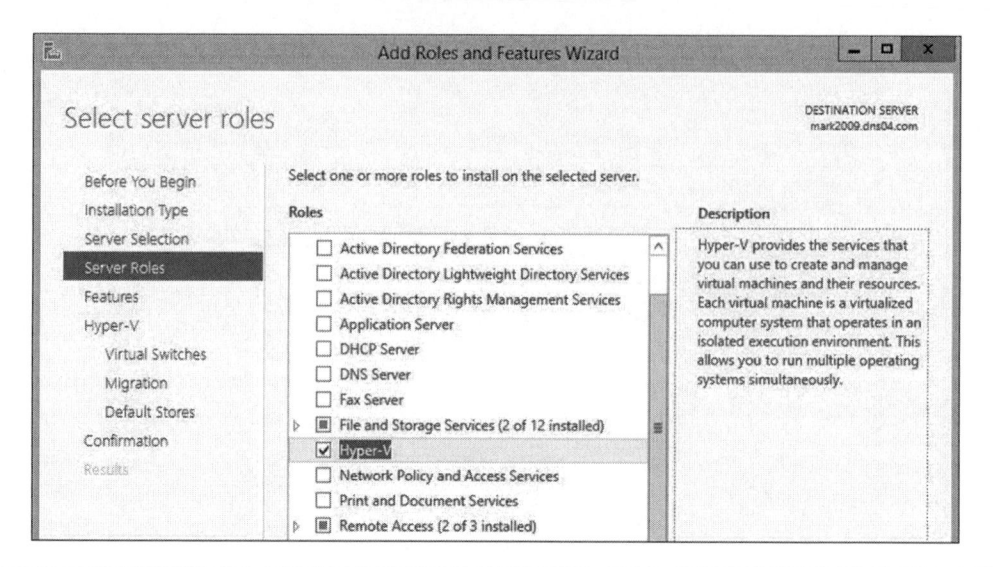

Figure 11.20   Selecting Hyper-V role.

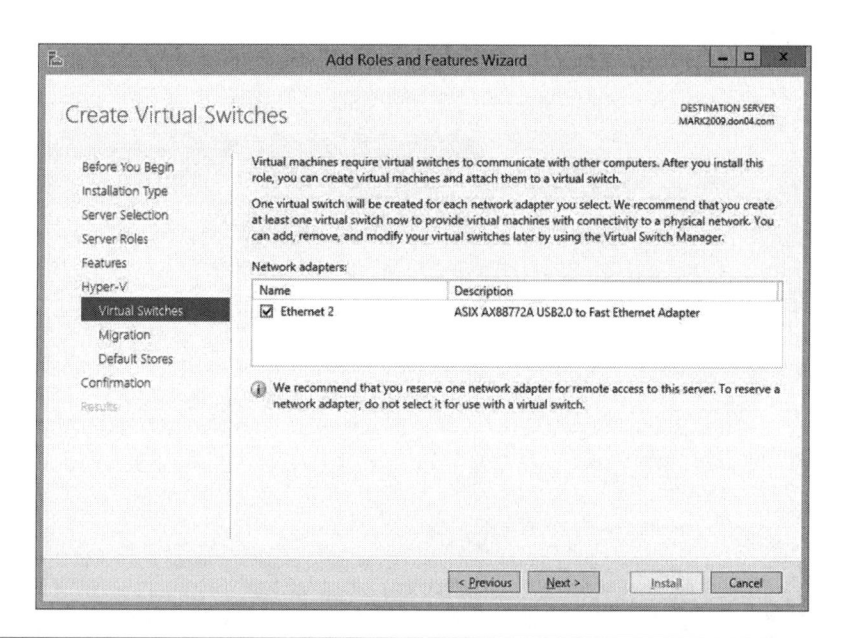

Figure 11.21   Creating virtual switch.

18. Click **Next** to go the Virtual Machine Migration page. Make sure the option **Allow this server to send and receive live migrations of virtual machines** is checked as shown in Figure 11.22.
19. Click **Next** twice and click **Install**.
20. After the server roles are added, you may need to create a student account with the administrator's permission for later use. To do so, click **Tools** in Server Manager and select **Active Directory Users and Computers**. Expand your domain node and right click at the **Users** node. Then, select **New** and **User**.

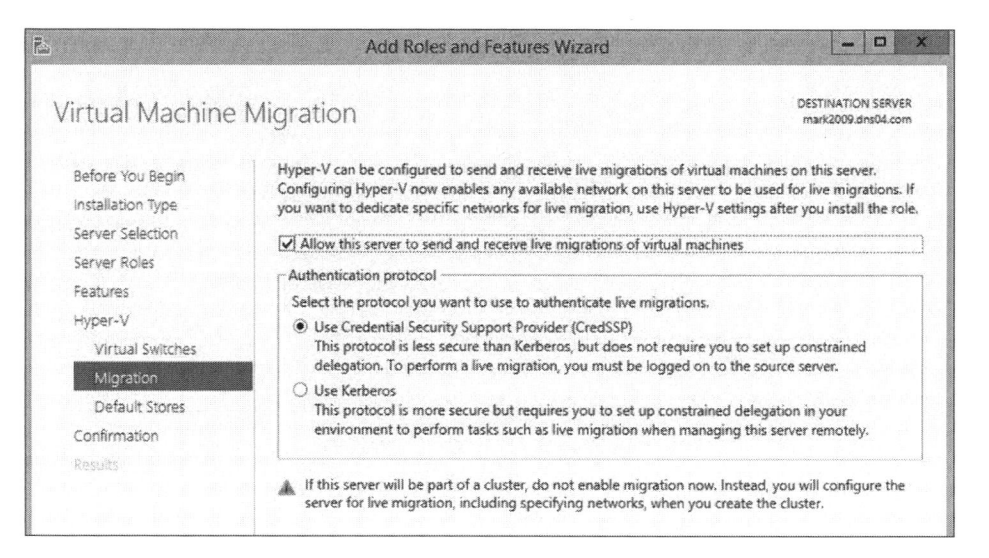

Figure 11.22   Virtual machine migration.

Create a **student** account, enter the password, and uncheck the option **User must change password at next logon**. Right click the newly created student account and select **Properties**. Under the tab **Member of**, click **Add**. Click the **Advanced** button and the click **Find Now** to make the student a member of Administrator, Domain Admin, and Enterprise Admin. Then, click **OK**.

Task 3: Installing and Configuring Software

In this task, you will install the following software:

- SQL Server 2012
- Windows Assessment and Deployment Kit (ADK)
- System Center R2 Virtual Machine Manager (SCVMM)
- System Center R2 App Controller (SCAC)

Part 1: Installing and Configuring SQL Server 2012   The following steps are used to illustrate the installation of SQL Server 2012.

1. To install SQL Server 2012, download the Enterprise 64-bit version of SQL Server 2012 from the DreamSpark website and burn the file to a DVD disk. (Note: the Developer version from DreamSpark may not work for this project.)
2. Insert the DVD disk to a DVD drive. When prompted, run the **SETUP. EXE** file.
3. On the SQL Server Installation Center page, click the link **Installation** in the left pane. In the right pane, click the link **New SQL Server stand-alone installation or add features to an existing installation** as shown in Figure 11.23.

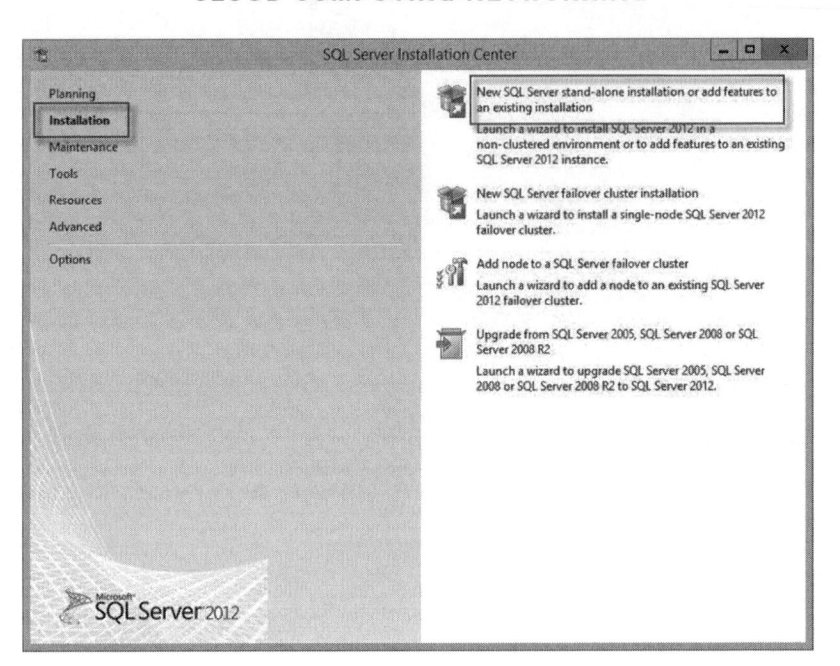

Figure 11.23   SQL server installation center.

4. On the Setup Support Rules page, if successful, click **OK**.
5. On the Product Key page, make sure that the product key has been added and click **Next**.
6. On the License terms page, accept the license terms and click **Next**.
7. On the Product Updates page, click **Next**.
8. On the Setup Support Rules page, if there are no failures even with a few warnings as shown in Figure 11.24, click **Next**.
9. On the Setup Role page, check the option **SQL Server Feature Installation** and click **Next**.
10. On the Feature Selection page, select the following features and click **Next**.
    a. Database Engine Service
        i. SQL Server Replication
        ii. Full Text and Semantic Extraction for Search
        iii. Data Quality Services
    b. Management Tools Basic
        i. Management Tools—Complete
11. On the Installation Rules page, if there is no failure, click **Next**.
12. On the Instance Configuration page, take the default and click **Next**.
13. On the Disk Space Requirements page, if you have enough disk space, click **Next**.
14. On the Server Configuration page, take the default, click **Next**.
15. On the Database Engine Configuration page, click the **Add Current User** button as shown in Figure 11.25. Then, click **Next**.
16. On Error Reporting page, click **Next**.

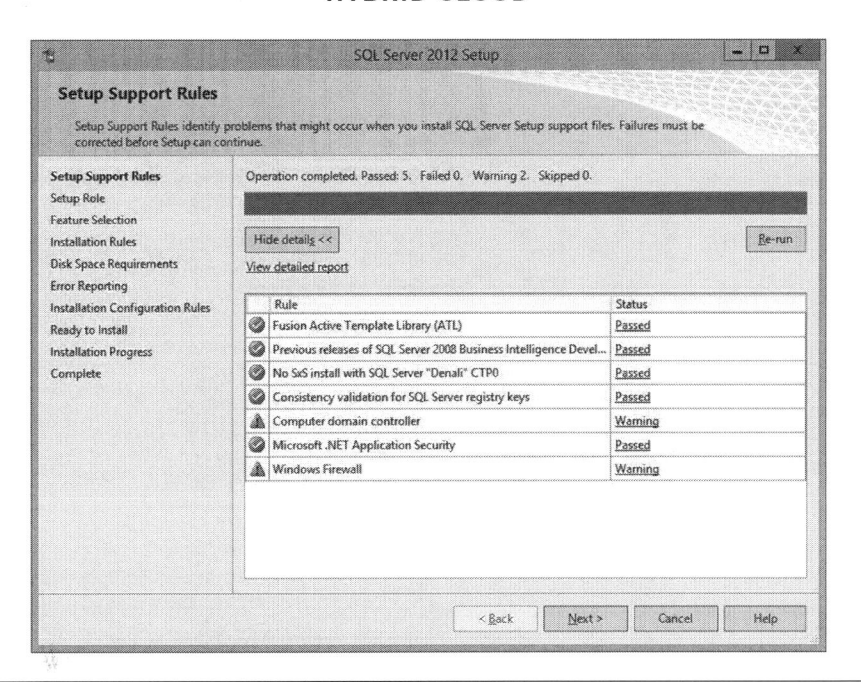

Figure 11.24 Setting up support rules.

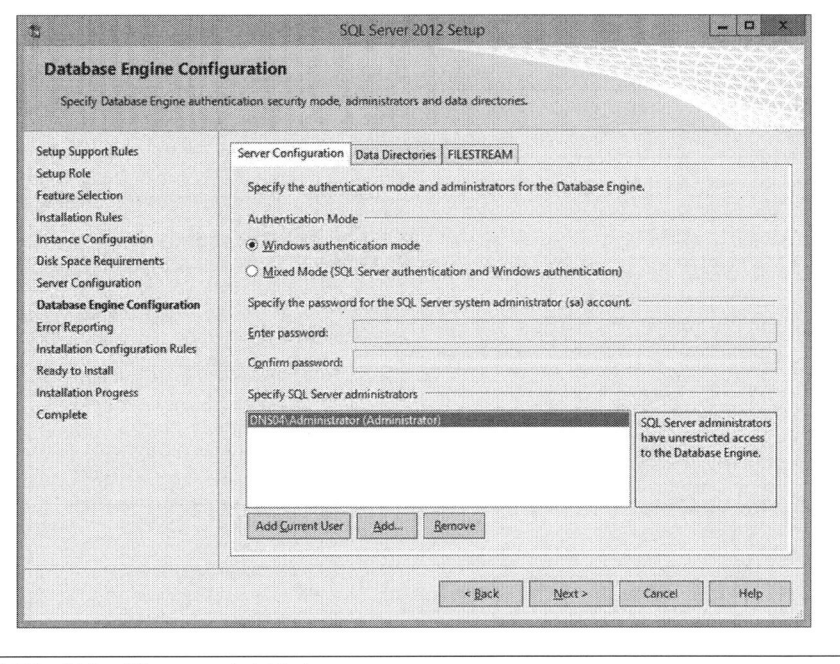

Figure 11.25 Adding SQL server administrator.

Figure 11.26   Installed SQL server components.

17. On the Installation Configuration Rules page, if there is no failure, click **Next**.
18. On the Ready to Install page, click the **Install** button.
19. On the Complete page, if the installation is successful, click **Close**.
20. To view the installed SQL Server, click **Start** and type **SQL**, You will see the installed SQL Server components as shown in Figure 11.26. Right click **SQL Server Management Studio** and select **Pin to Start**. You should be able to log on to SQL Server with the local admin account.

Part 2: Installing and Configuring Windows Assessment and Deployment Kit (Windows ADK) for Windows 8.1   The following steps are used to illustrate the installation of Windows Assessment and Deployment Kit.

1. Download the ADK package from the following website. You may need to configure the Internet options to allow file download (Microsoft, Download Center, May, 2015).

   http://www.microsoft.com/en-eg/download/details.aspx?id = 39982

2. Install the ADK package with the default setting.

Part 3: Installing and Configuring System Center R2 Virtual Machine Manager (SCVMM) for Windows 8.1 The following steps are used to illustrate the installation of System Center R2 Virtual Machine Manager (SCVMM).

1. You may download the entire System Center 2012 R2 package from the URL below, which includes SCVMM and SCAC. Extract the SCVMM package by right clicking the downloaded file and select **Run as Administrator**. During the extraction process, record the path to where the installation files are being placed (Microsoft, TechNet Evaluation Center, May, 2015).

   http://technet.microsoft.com/en-us/evalcenter/dn205295.aspx

2. Navigate to the directory SC2012 R2 SCVMM where the installation files are located. Double click the file **setup**. When prompted, click **Install** as shown in Figure 11.27.

3. On the Select features to install page, select the features shown in Figure 11.28. Click **Next**.

4. On the Product registration information page, enter the information shown in Figure 11.29. If you do not have the product key, you will have 90 days to use the software. Click **Next.**

5. On the License agreement page, agree to the license terms. Click **Next**.

6. On the Customer experience improvement program page, it is up to you. Click **Next**.

7. On the Microsoft update page, select **On**. Click **Next**.

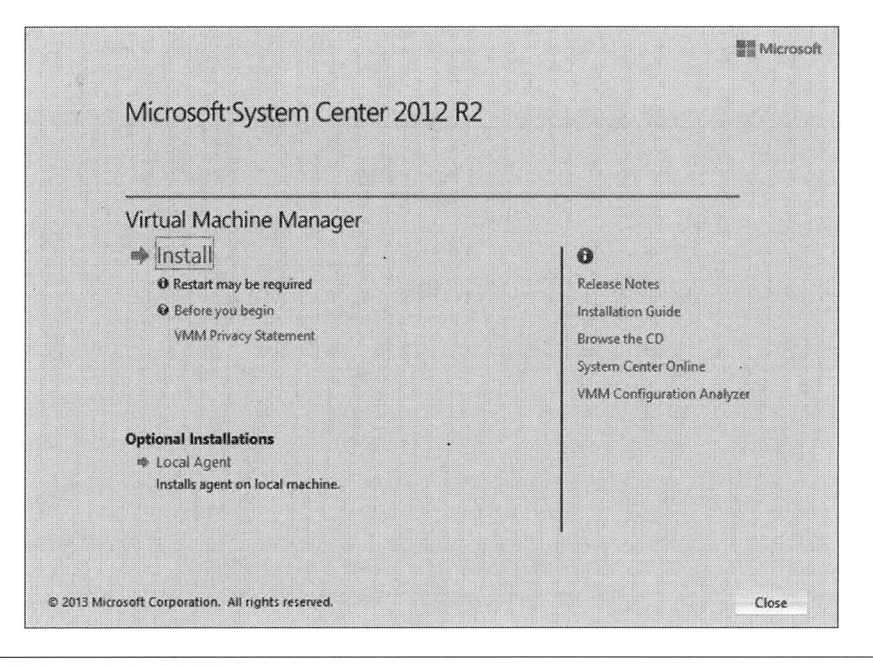

Figure 11.27   Installing SCVMM.

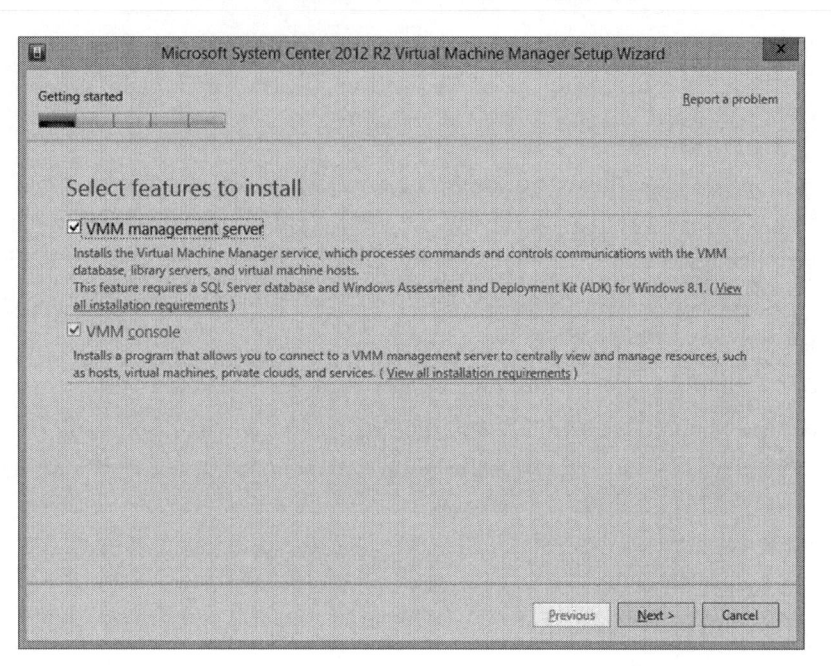

Figure 11.28 Selecting features.

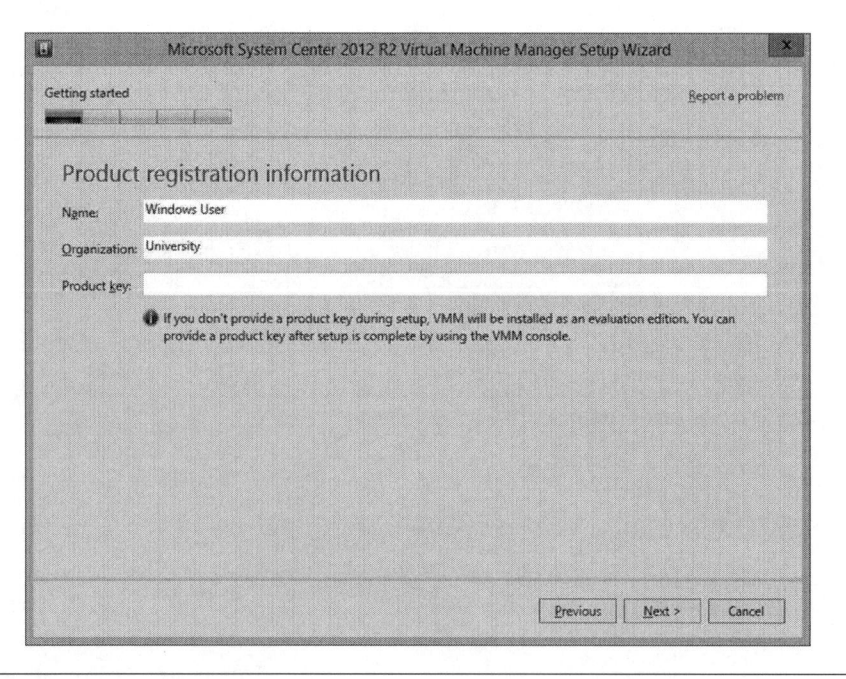

Figure 11.29 Product registration.

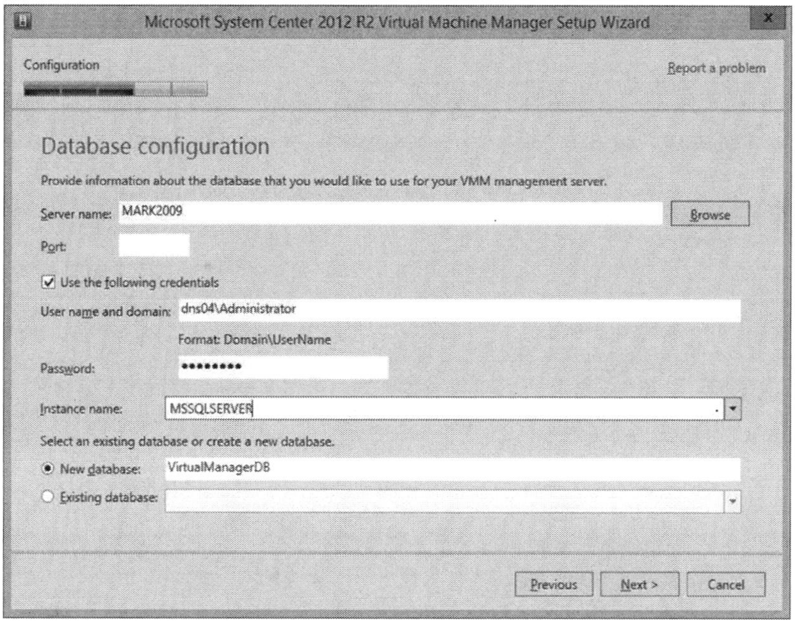

Figure 11.30 Database configuration.

8. On the Installation location page, keep the default. Click **Next**.
9. On the Database configuration page, configure the database as shown in Figure 11.30. (These settings should be exact or the login to the database will fail. Your server name may be different.)
   a. *Server name*: Take the default SQL Server name, or click browse and select another SQL Server name.
   b. *Port*: Keep the default or leave it blank if it is blank.
   c. Click the check box **Use the following credentials**.
   d. Enter the domain user name and password.
   e. *Instance name*: Select **MSSQLSERVER** or, if you renamed it, select that instance.
   f. Select an existing database or create a new database: Select **New database** and keep the default name **VirtualManagerDB**.
   g. Click **Next**.
10. On the Configure service account and distributed key management page, select **Domain account** and enter the domain account credentials (Figure 11.31). Click **Next**.
11. On the Port configuration page, keep the default. Click **Next**.
12. On the Library configuration page, check the option **Create a new library share** as shown in Figure 11.32.
    Take the default and click **Next**.
13. On the Installation summary page, make sure everything is correct. Click **Install**.

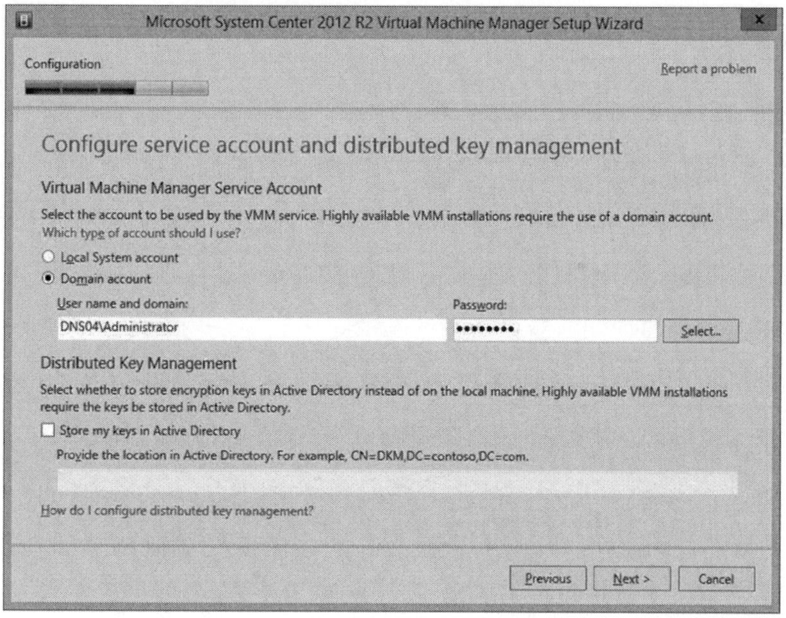

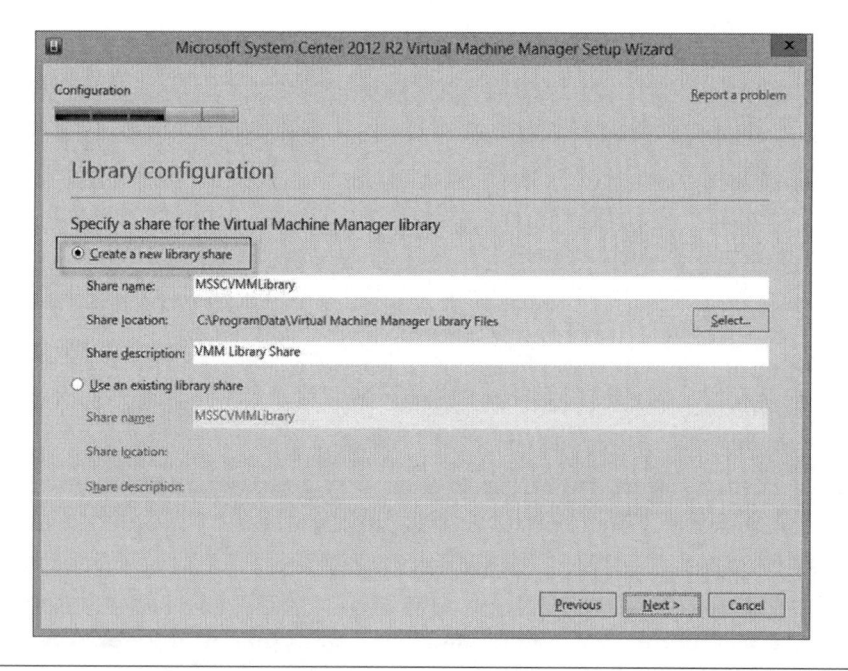

Figure 11.31 Domain account.

Figure 11.32 Library configuration.

14. If the installation of SCVMM is successful (Figure 11.33), click **Close**. SCVMM will launch automatically.

(If the installation fails, chances are that it cannot connect to the data base. To confirm this, log on to SQL Server and see if VirtalManagerDB is listed as a database. Unfortunately, you will need to uninstall SCVMM and

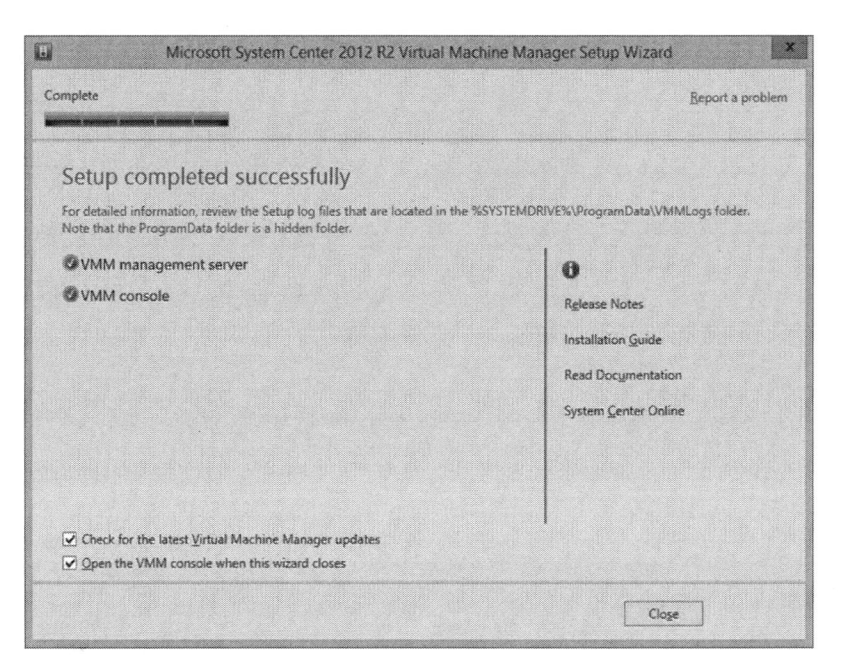

Figure 11.33 Virtual machine manager setup wizard.

reinstall it because there is no way to change the settings without reinstalling SCVMM.)

15. You should be able to see the Connect to Server dialog opened automatically. Click the **Connect** button to sign in with the local admin or domain account. Once logged in, you will see the GUI interface shown in Figure 11.34. If successful, close it and **restart** your computer. Also, there is an icon on your desktop to open the Virtual Machine Manager console.

Part 4: System Center R2 App Controller The following steps are used to illustrate the installation of App Controller.

1. Before the installation, make sure that the IIS role has been added as shown in Task 2. An error may occur if IIS is not enabled or IIS features are missing.
2. If you have not done so, download the SCAC file from the following website. Otherwise, extract the SC2012_R2_SCAC file in the folder where the file is downloaded. During the extraction process, record the path to where the installation files are placed. (Microsoft, System Center Evaluations, May, 2015). https://www.microsoft.com/en-us/evalcenter/evaluate-system-center-2012-r2.
3. Navigate to the directory where the installation files are located. Double click the file **Setup**. When prompted, click **Install** as shown in Figure 11.35.
4. On the Product registration page, click **Next**.
5. On the License terms page, agree with the license terms and click **Next**.
6. On the Install missing software page, if there is missing software, you will be prompted to install the software. Click **Install** if prompted (Figure 11.36).

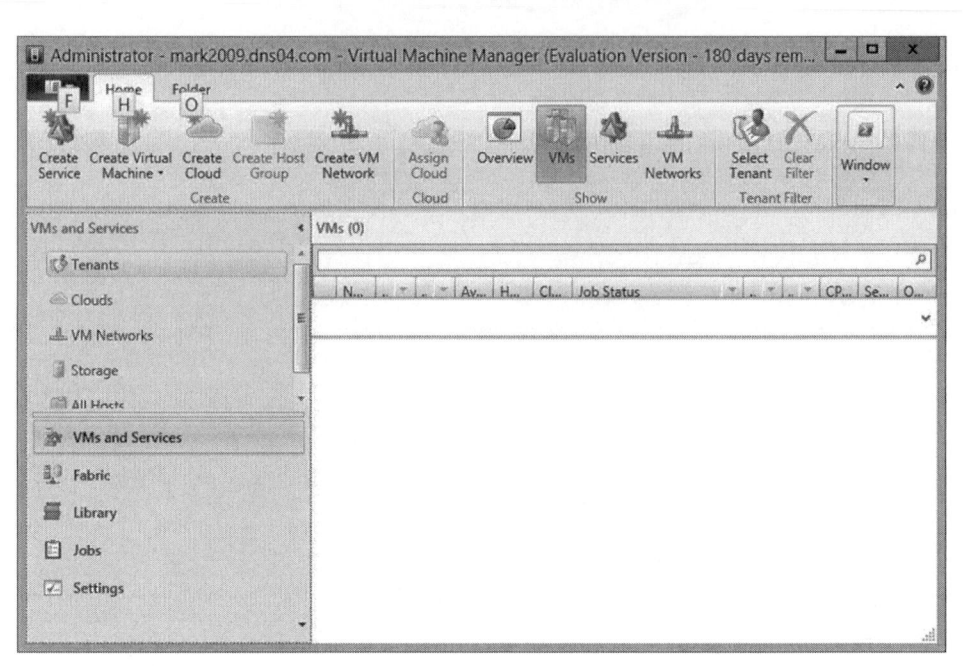

Figure 11.34 Virtual machine manager.

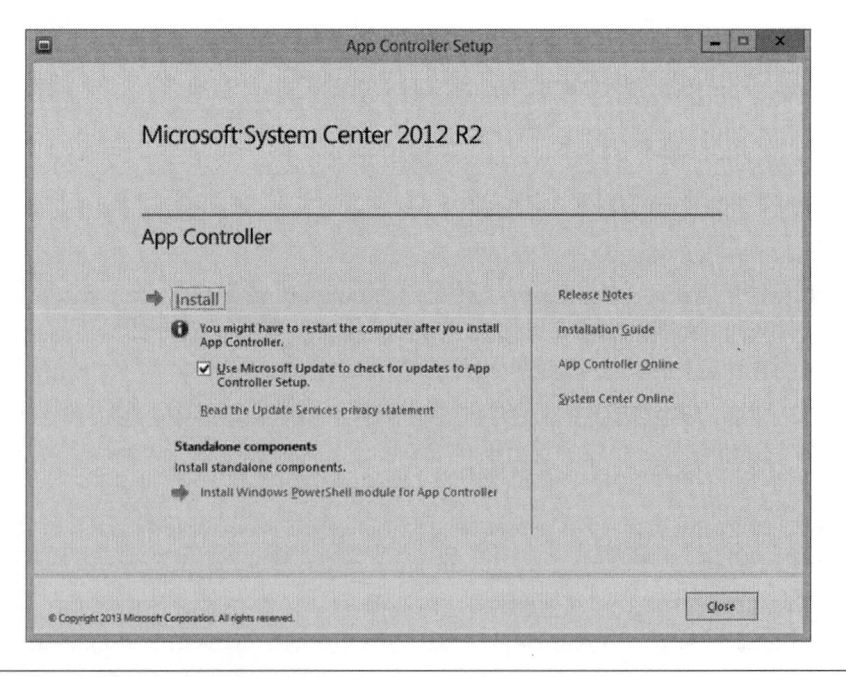

Figure 11.35 App controller installation dialog.

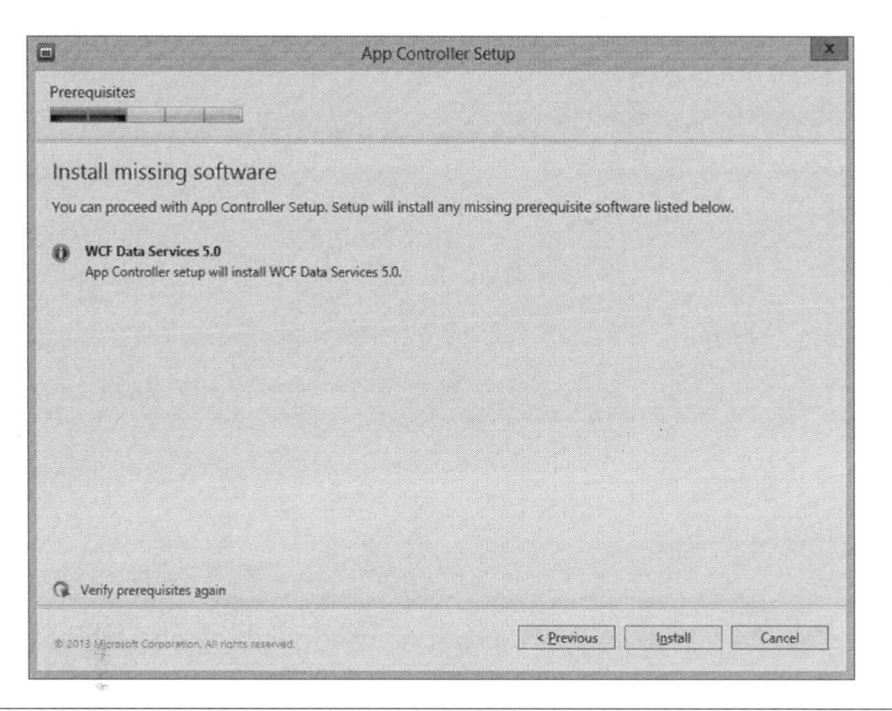

Figure 11.36 Installing missing software.

7. On the Select the installation path page, take the default and click **Next**.
8. On the Configure the services page, specify the domain user account and password you created before (Figure 11.37). Then, click **Next**.
9. On the Configure the website page, configure the website (Figure 11.38):
    a. IP address: Select the IP address of the server from the list.
    b. Port: Keep the default **443** for HTTPS.
    c. SSL certificate: Check Generate self-signed certificate.
       Click **Next**.
10. On the Configure the SQL Server database page, configure the SQL Server database as follows (Figure 11.39):
    a. Server name: Type the name of the server running SQL Server.
    b. Port: By default, it is blank, keep it blank.
    c. Database name: Enter the database name **AppController**.
       Click **Next**.
11. On the Help improve App Controller for System Center 2012 R2 page, the option is up to you. Also, check the option **Use Microsoft Update to receive updates for App Controller for System Center 2012 R2 and other Microsoft products** as shown in Figure 11.40. Then, click **Next**.
12. On Confirm the settings page, click **Install**.
13. On the Setup completed successfully page, select **Start the App Controller website when Setup closes** and click **Finish** as shown in Figure 11.41.

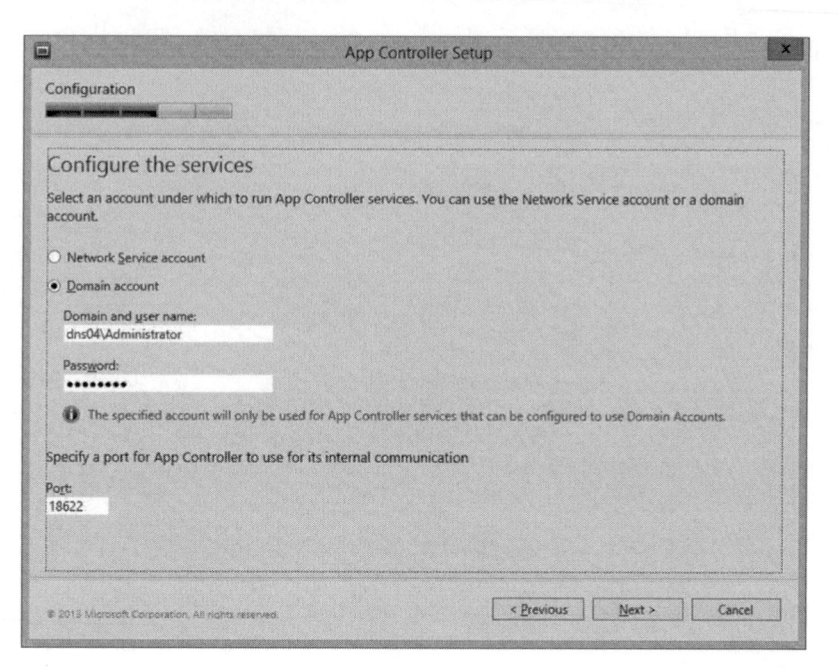

Figure 11.37   Configuring services.

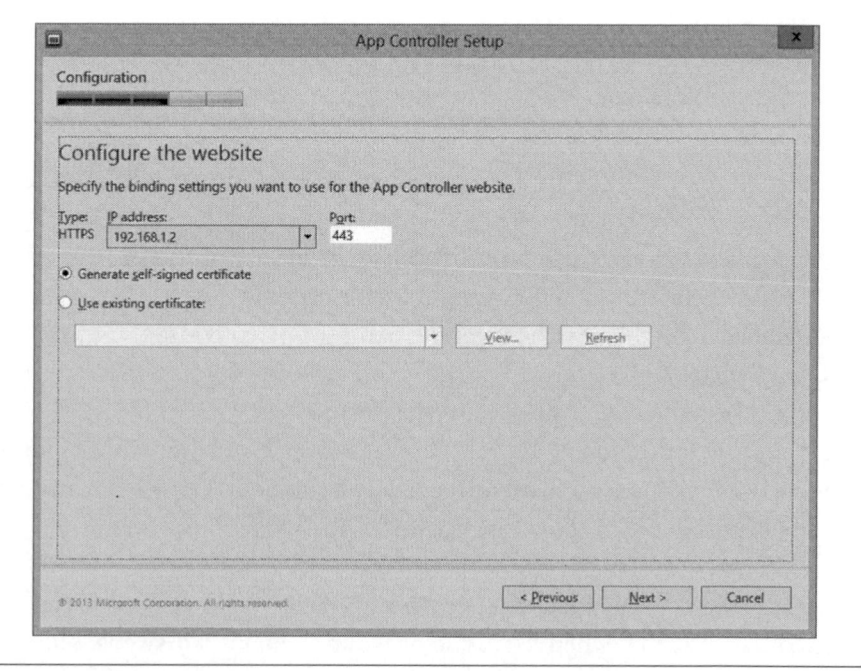

Figure 11.38   Configuring website.

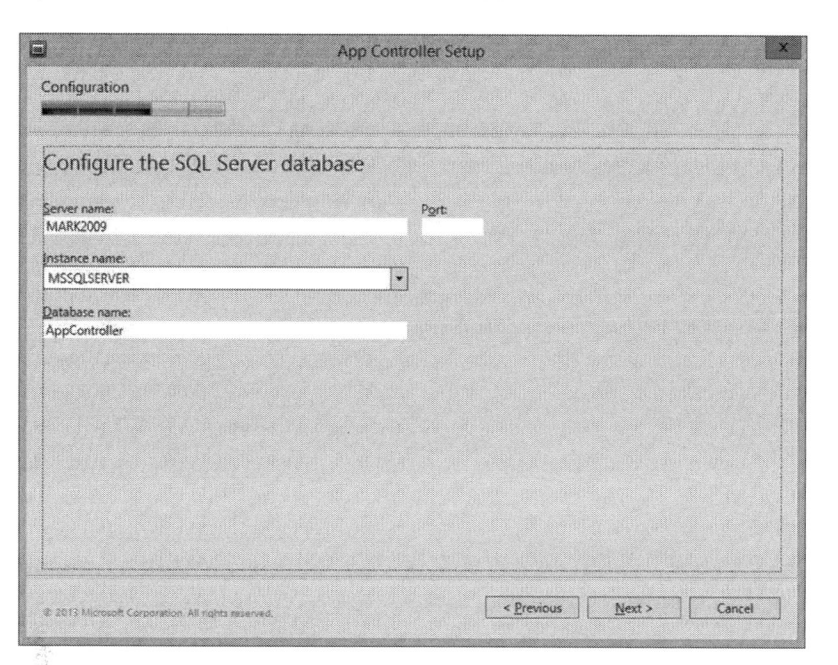

Figure 11.39 Configuring SQL server database.

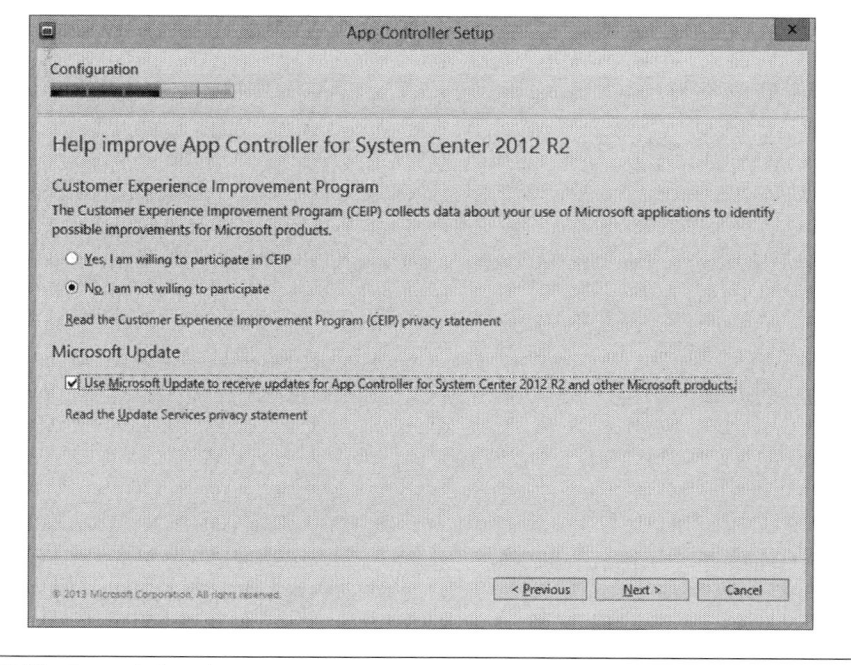

Figure 11.40 App controller setup.

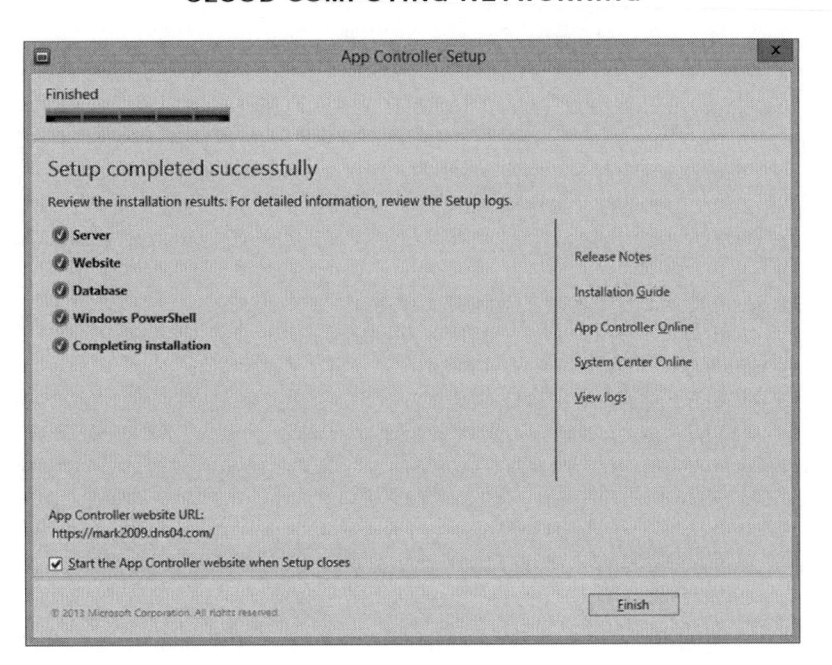

Figure 11.41   Completed setup.

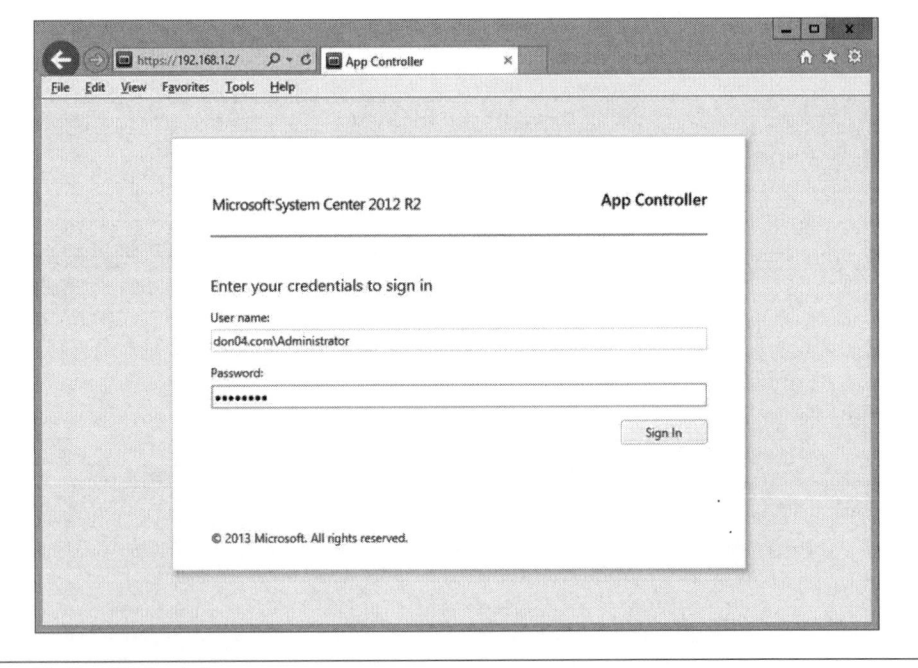

Figure 11.42   SCAC website.

14. Internet Explorer (IE) will launch and should be able to sign in. If the SCAC website cannot be opened due to the name resolution issue, you may use the IP address of the external NIC as the URL to open the SCAC website as shown in Figure 11.42. You may need to follow the instruction to install Silverlight first.

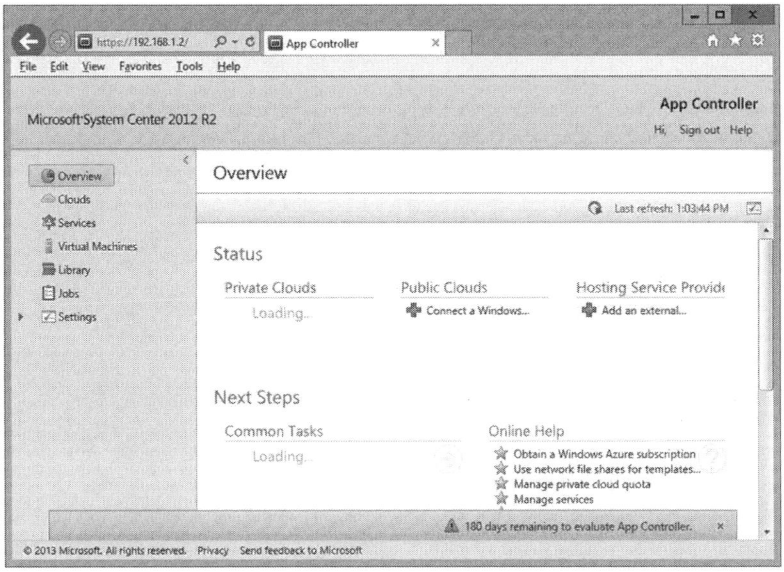

Figure 11.43   Management website.

15. After you have successfully logged in, you will see the website shown in Figure 11.43.
16. You can now close the website and restart your computer.

Task 4: Private Cloud Development

Part 1: Adding ISO File

1. Double click the **Virtual Machine Manager Console** icon on the desktop.
2. After the Virtual Machine Manager Connection dialog opens, click the **Connect** button. (Note: If you see the error message "Unable to connect to the VMM management server localhost…," on Sever Manager, click **Tools**, **Services**, and start the service **System Center Virtual Machine Manager**. Then, click **Connect** again.)
3. To add images to the Library Share, on the lower left side, click **Library** and click **Library Servers**, you should see your server name. Expand your server's node, you will see MSSCVMMLibrary (Figure 11.44).
4. Right click **MSSCVMMLibrary** and click **Explore**. Once the **MSSCVMMLibrary** folder is opened, search for the following file, which is a Windows 8 testing iso file.
   9200.16384.WIN8_RTM.120725–1247_X64FRE_SERVER_EVAL_EN-US-HRM_SSS_X64FREE_EN-US_DV5.

   Copy and paste this iso file to the MSSCVMMLibrary folder. Then, close the **MSSCVMMLibrary** folder.
5. Once done, right click **MSSCVMMLibrary** and click **Refresh**. In the Physical Library Objects window, you will see the ISO file shown in Figure 11.45.

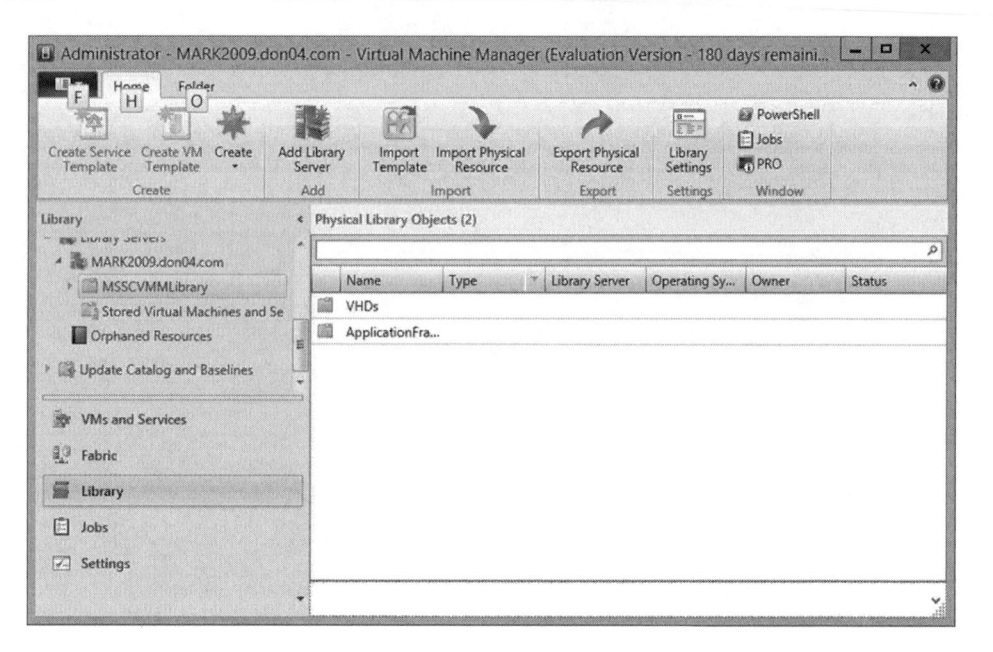

Figure 11.44   Library.

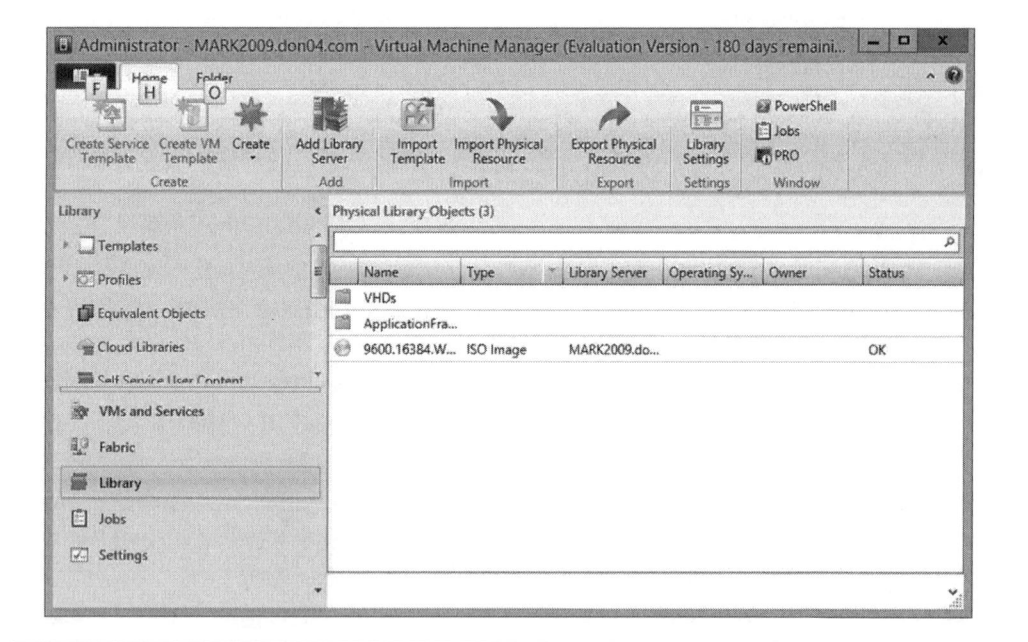

Figure 11.45   iso file in MSSCVMM library.

Part 2: Preparing Fabric

1. To create a host group structure, click the **Fabric** workspace.
2. In the Fabric pane, expand **Servers**, right click **All Hosts**, and then click **Create Host Group** as shown in Figure 11.46.
3. VMM creates a new host group that is named New host group. Rename the group **lab** and press **Enter**.

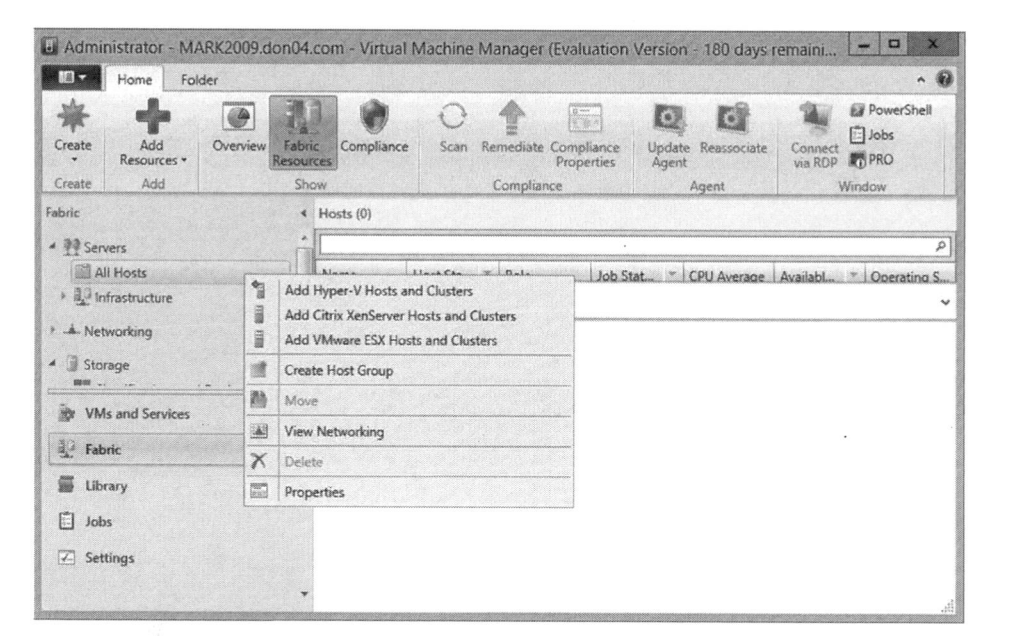

Figure 11.46   Creating host group.

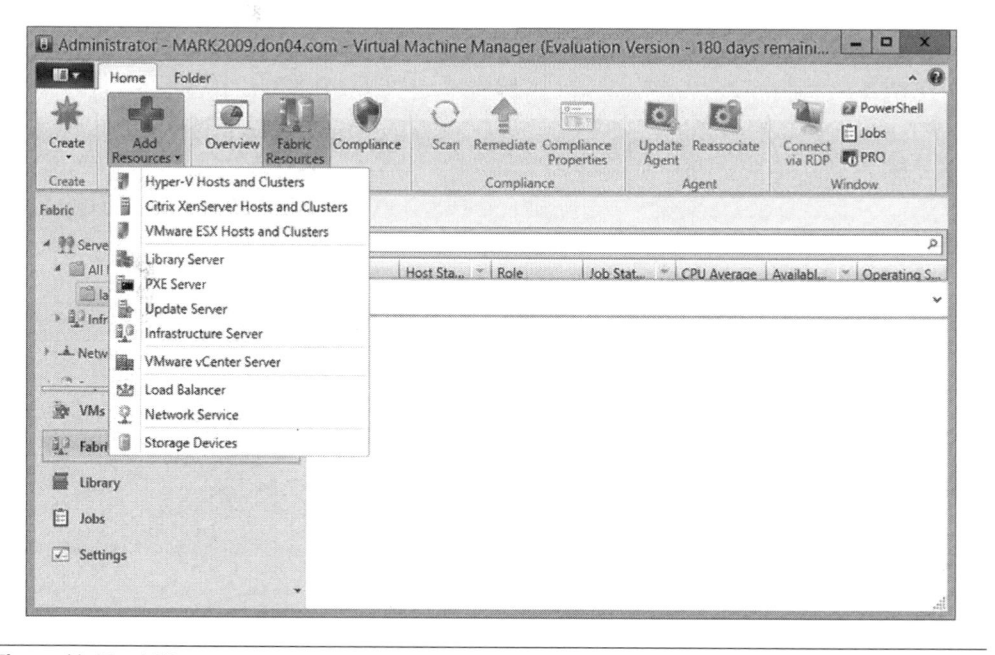

Figure 11.47   Adding resource.

4. Click the host group **lab**. On the upper part of the screen, click **Add Resources** and select **Hyper-V Hosts and Clusters** to open the Add Resource Wizard (Figure 11.47).

5. After the Add Resource Wizard is opened, click **Windows Server computers in a trusted Active Directory domain**, and then click **Next**.

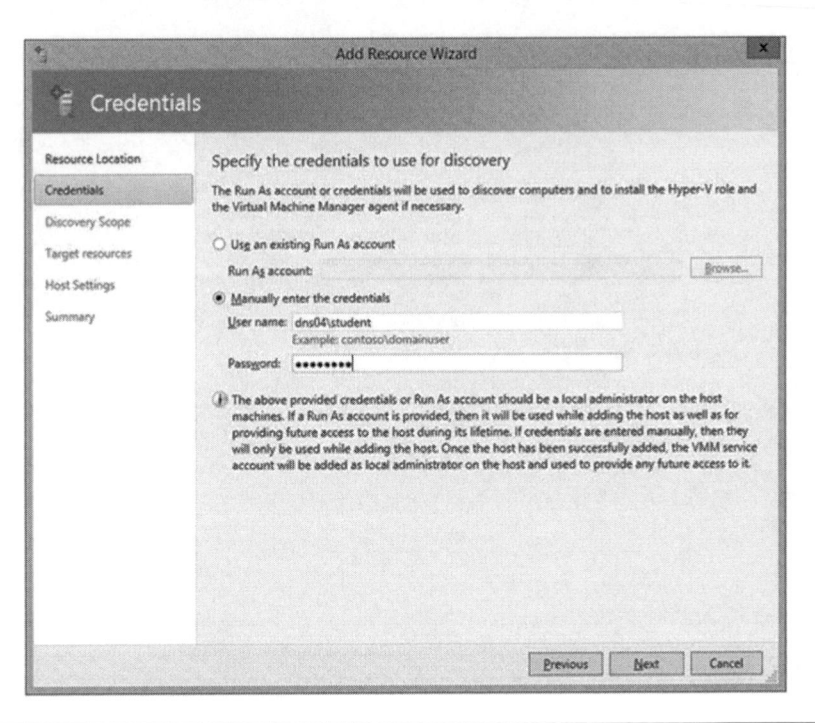

Figure 11.48   Specifying credentials.

6. On the **Credentials** page, enter the credentials for the domain account, *your_domain***student**, which was created earlier, enter the password, and then click **Next** (Figure 11.48).

7. On the Discovery scope page, check the option **Specify Windows Server computer by name**, enter your computer name, and then click **Next**.

8. On the Target resources page, select the check box next to your computer, and then click **Next**. When receiving the message "VMM will install the Hyper-V role and restart the server," click **OK** to continue.

9. On the Host Setting page, make sure that **lab** is the host group and click **Next**.

10. On the Summary page, confirm the settings, and then click **Finish**. You may see the warning "Multi path I/O is not enabled...." You can ignore it if you do not use a SAN storage device or run the following cmdlets in PowerShell.

```
Import-Module ServerManager
Add-WindowsFeature Multipath-IO
```

11. To verify that the host or host cluster has been successfully added, in the **Fabric** pane, expand the host group **lab**, and then in the **Hosts** pane, verify that the host status is **OK** as shown in Figure 11.49.

12. To configure network settings for a host, open the **Fabric** workspace.

13. In the **Fabric** pane, expand **Servers**, expand **All Hosts**, and expand the host group **lab**. Right click the host you just added to the host group and select **Properties**.

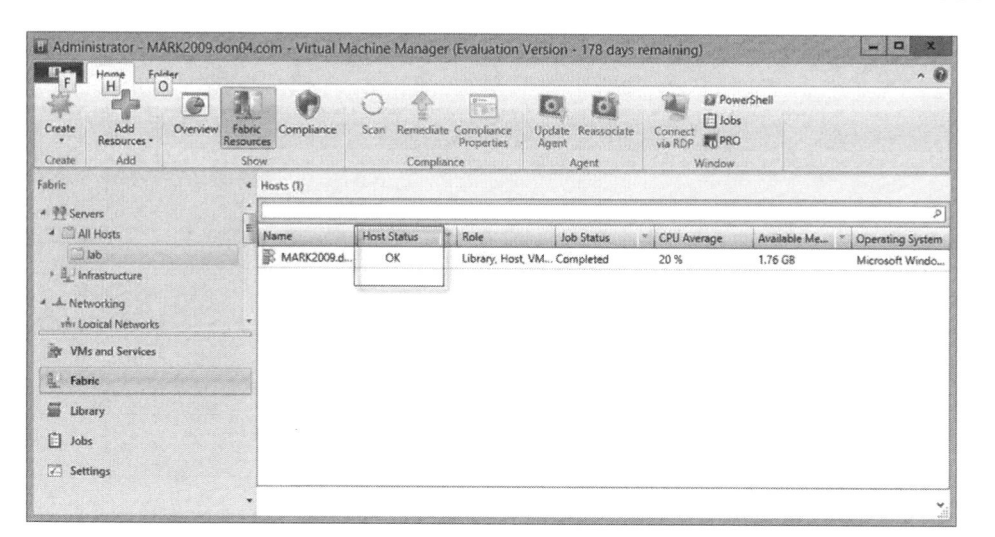

Figure 11.49 Host status.

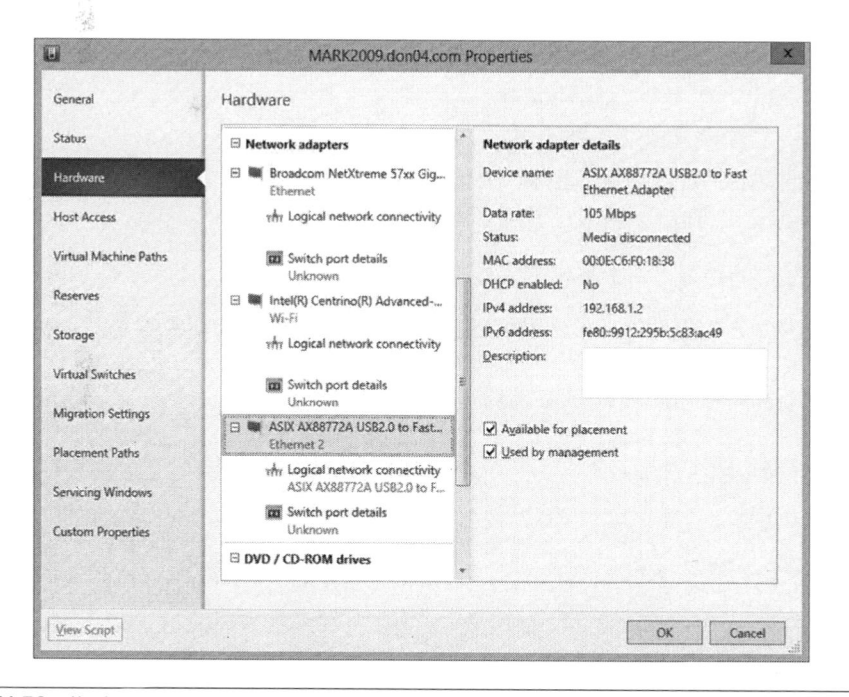

Figure 11.50 Hardware configuration.

14. Click the Hardware link on the left hand side of the screen as shown in Figure 11.50. Under **Network adapters,** click the physical network adapter **Ethernet 2** which is configured with the fixed IP address. Check the option **Available for placement** to use this network adapter for virtual machines. Check the option **Used by management** to use this network adapter for communication between the host and the VMM management server.

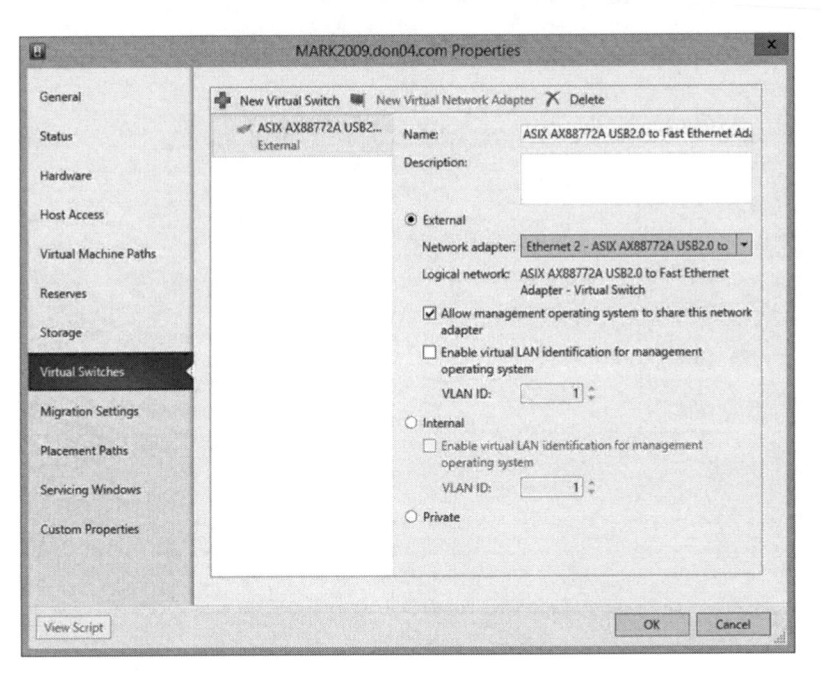

Figure 11.51 Virtual switch.

15. Click the **Virtual Switches** link on the left side of the screen.
16. In the Virtual Switches link, select the virtual switch created on **Ethernet 2** as shown in Figure 11.51. Then, click **OK**.

Part 3: Creating Private Cloud

1. To create a private cloud, click **VMs and Services** at the lower left side of the screen. Then, click on **Create Cloud** on the top as shown in Figure 11.52. This opens the Create Cloud Wizard.

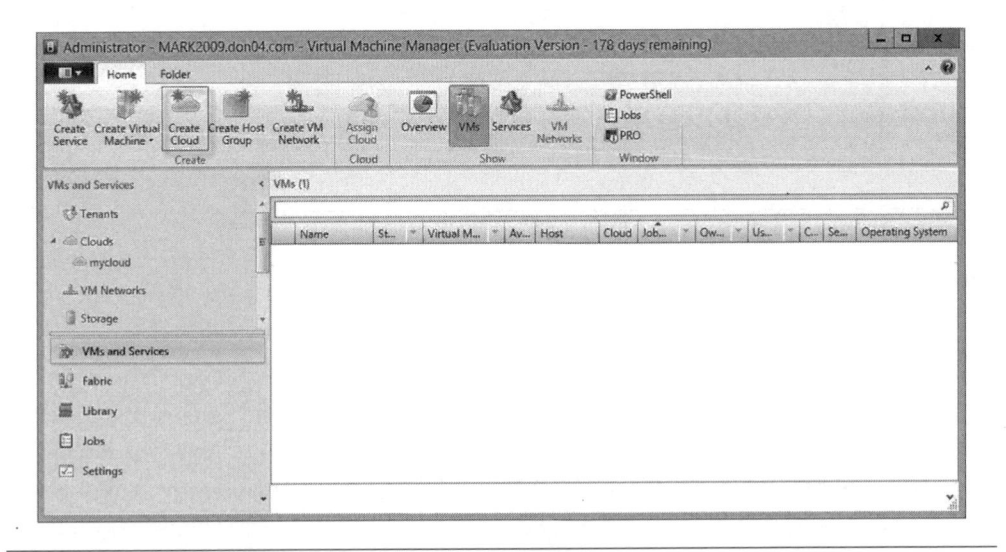

Figure 11.52 Creating cloud.

2. On the General page, specify the name and description for your cloud; for example, specify the name as **mycloud** and the description as **Lab experiment**. Then, click **Next**.
3. On the Resources page, select **All Hosts**. Then, click **Next**.
4. For Logical Networks, select the logical network created earlier and click **Next** as shown in Figure 11.53.
5. On the Load Balancers page, select **Microsoft Network Load Balancing (NLB)** and click **Next**.
6. On VIP Templates page, click **Next**.
7. On the Port Classifications page, click **Next**.
8. On the Storage page, select **Local Storage** and click **Next** as shown in Figure 11.54.
9. On the Library page, click **Browse** and select **MSSCVMMLibrary**, and click **OK**. Leave **Read-only library shares** blank (Figure 11.55). Then, click **Next**.
10. On the Capacity page, keep the default and click **Next**.
11. On the Capability Profiles page, check the option **Hyper-V** and click **Next**.
12. Review the summary and then click **Finish**.

Part 4: Creating VM Template Before you start adding VMs, you need to create a VM template that is compatible with the private cloud. The following steps explain how to create this template.

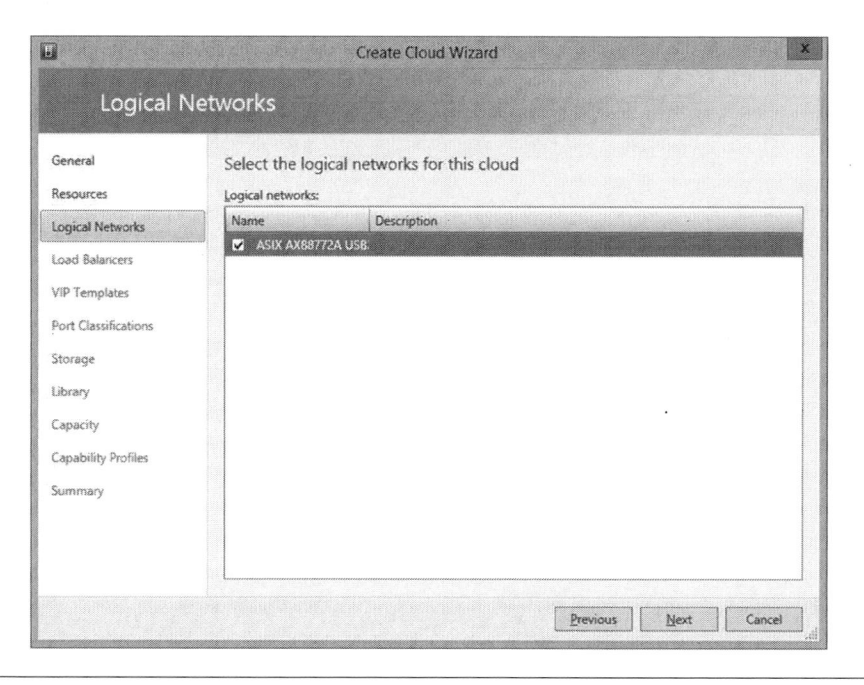

Figure 11.53 Logical network.

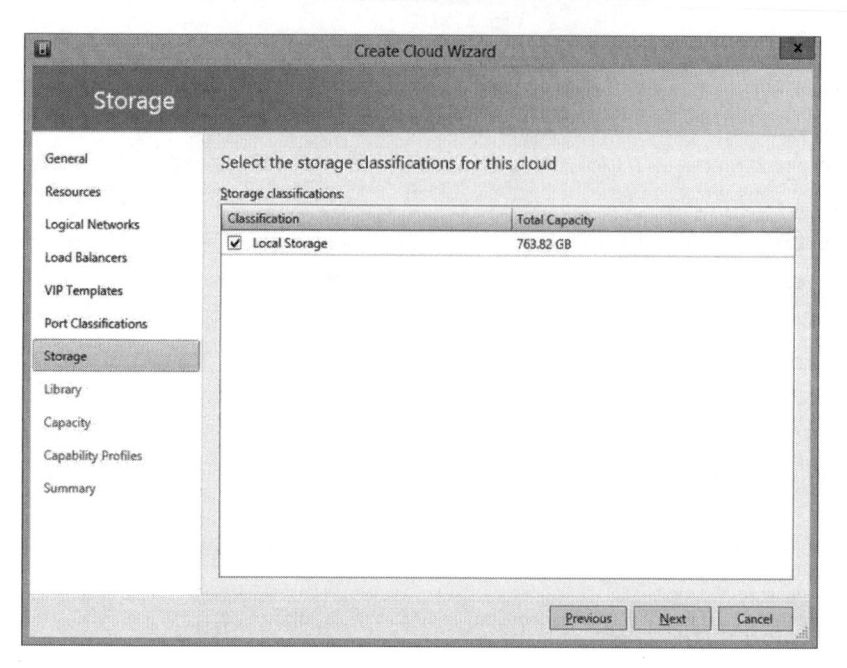

Figure 11.54 Local storage.

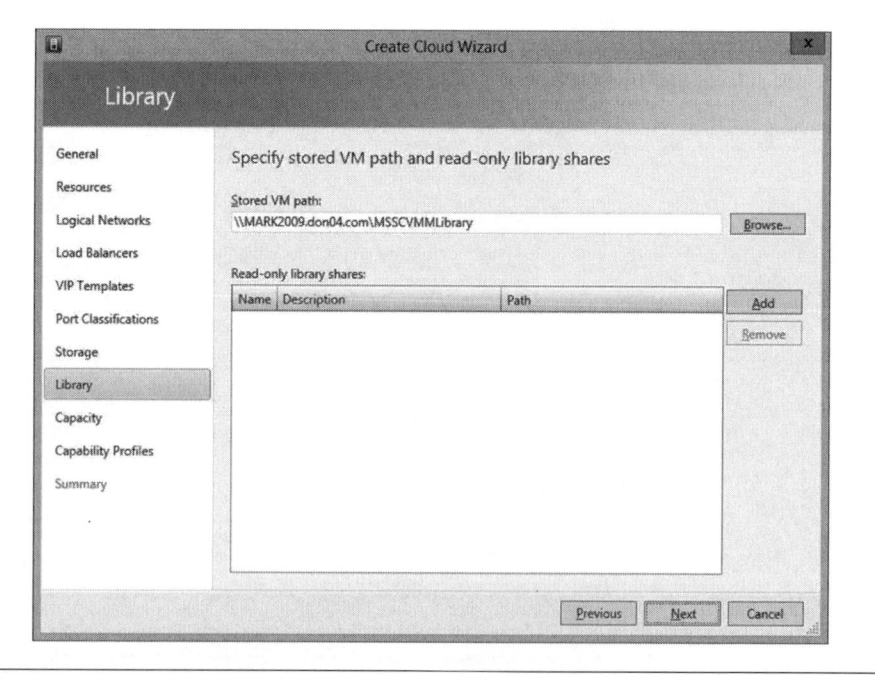

Figure 11.55 Library configuration.

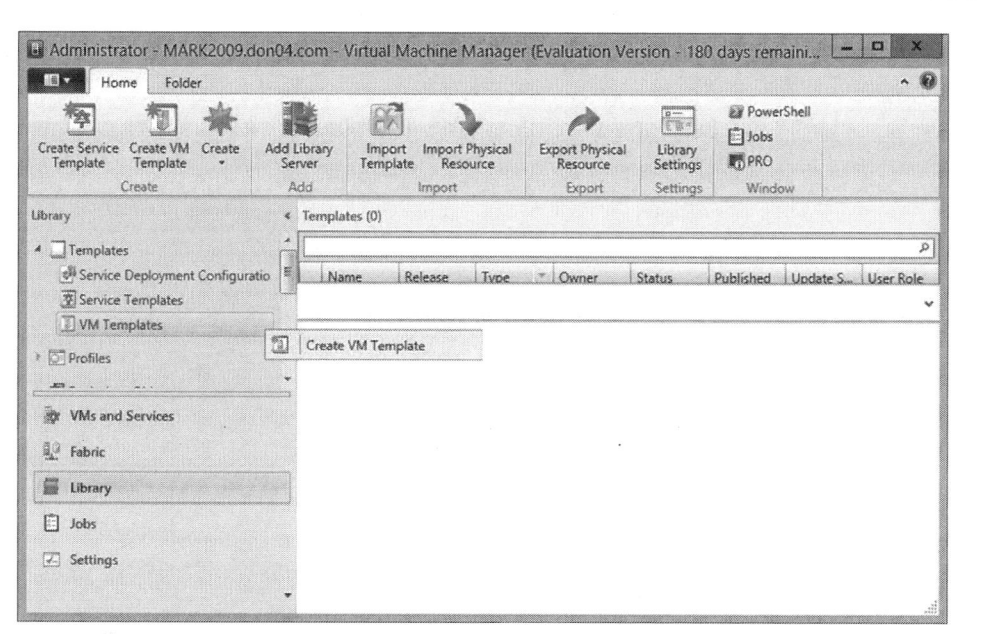

Figure 11.56   Creating VM template.

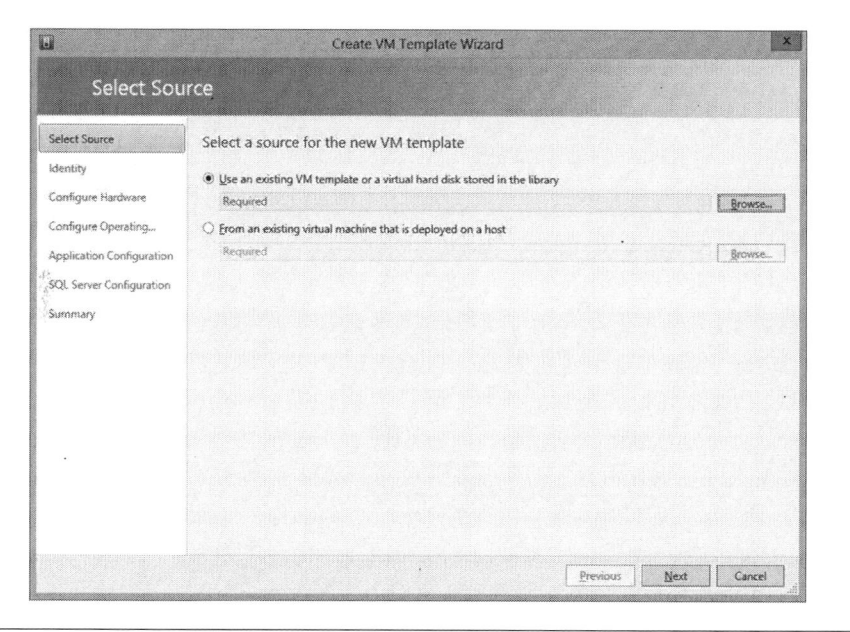

Figure 11.57   Using existing VM template.

1. In the Virtual Machine Manager console, click the **Library** link.
2. Expand the **Templates** node and right click **VM Templates** and select **Create VM Template** as shown in Figure 11.56.
3. The wizard will open and select the option **Use an existing VM...** as shown in Figure 11.57.

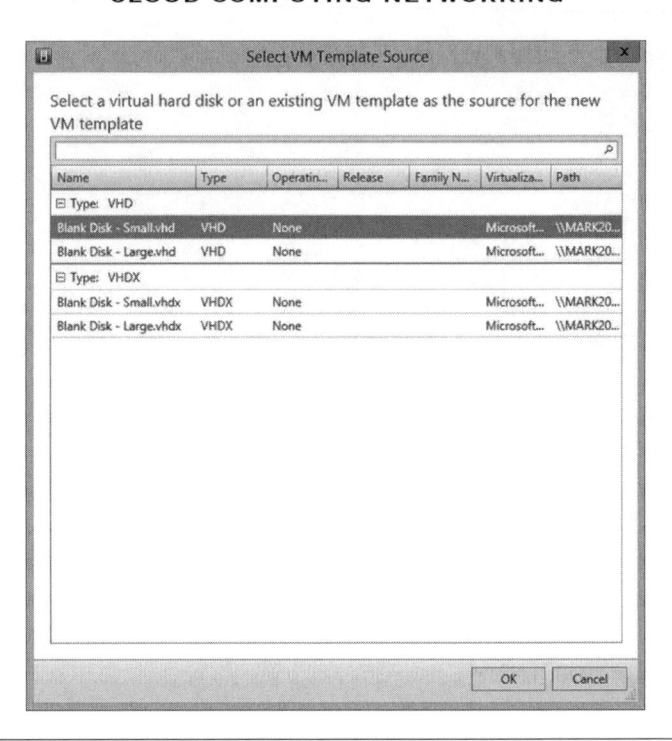

Figure 11.58   Using large VHD as template.

4. Click **Browse** and select **Blank Disk- Large.vhd** (Figure 11.58) and click **OK**. Then, click **Next**.

5. On the Identity page, name the template **mytemplate** and describe it as **Used for creating VMs in the lab**. Then, click **Next**.

6. On the Configure Hardware page, check the option **Hyper-V** (Figure 11.59). You may also set the memory as **512 MB** and set Network Adapter 1 to connect to the virtual network created earlier. (Note: If your computer has only 4 GB RAM, make sure to use 512 MB. If your computer has more than 4 GB RAM, you can set the memory as 1 GB or more.) Then, click **Next**.

7. On Configure Operating System page, select **None-customization not required** in the Guest OS profile drop-down menu as shown in Figure 11.60. Then, click **Next**.

8. Review the summary and click **Create**.

Part 5: Creating Virtual Machines   With the template created, you can now create your VM.

1. Click on **VMs and Services** and expand **Clouds**, right click your cloud and select **Create Virtual Machine** as shown in Figure 11.61.

2. Select **Use an existing...** and click **Browse**. Now select the VM template **mytemplate** as shown in Figure 11.62. Then, click **OK**.

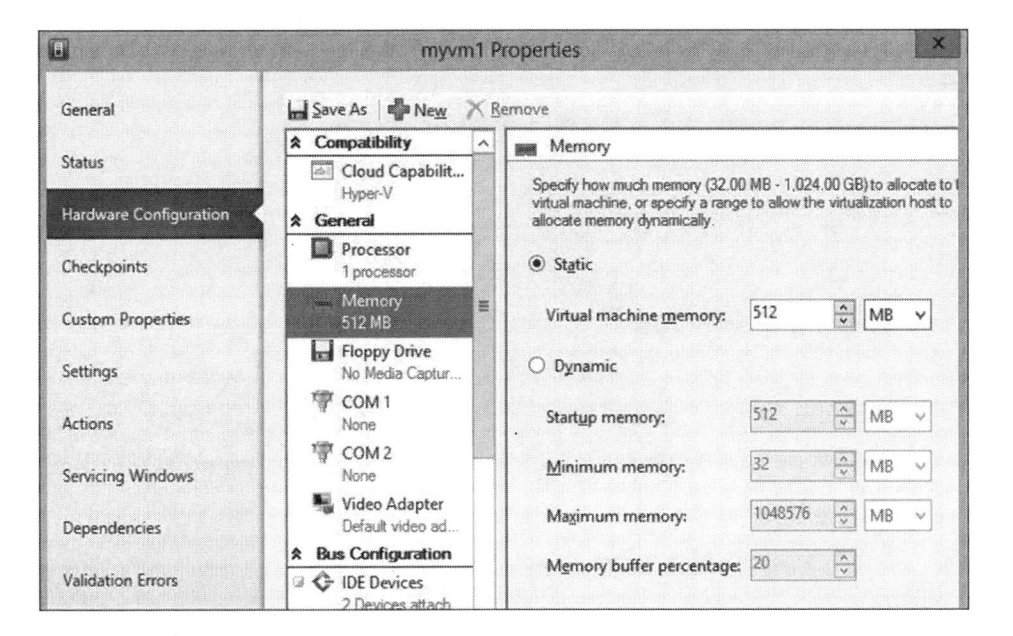

Figure 11.59   Hyper-V option.

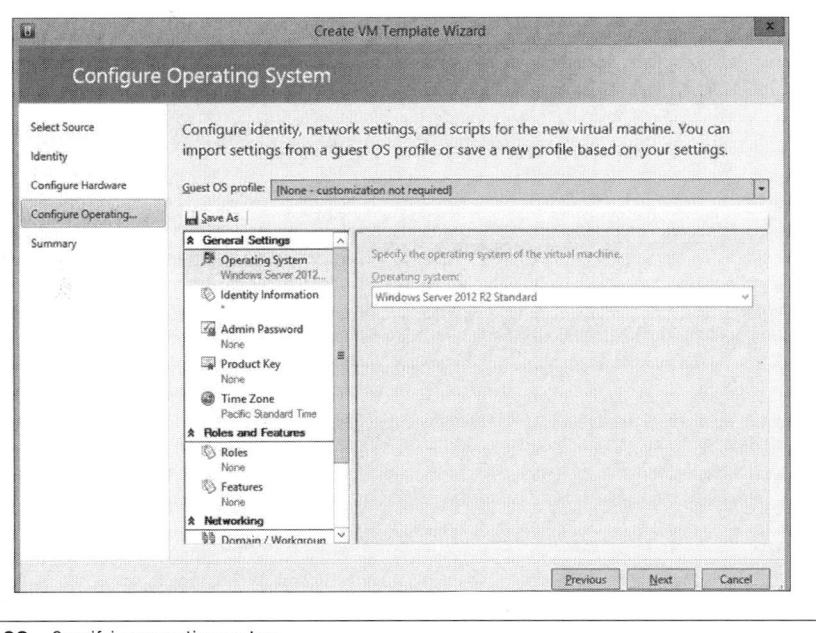

Figure 11.60   Specifying operating system.

3. Click **Next** to go to the Identity page. Name your VM as **myvm1** and describe it as **First virtual machine on cloud**. Then, click **Next**.

4. On the Configure Hardware page, click **Virtual DVD...** and check the option **Existing ISO image**. Click **Browse** and select the iso file added earlier as shown in Figure 11.63. Then, click **Next**.

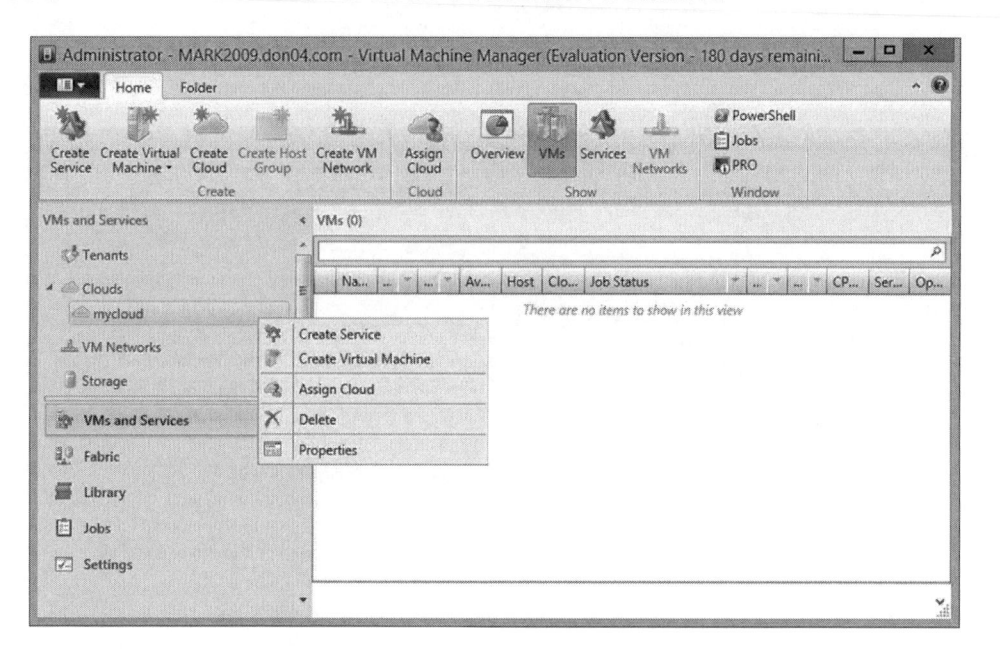

Figure 11.61   Creating virtual machine.

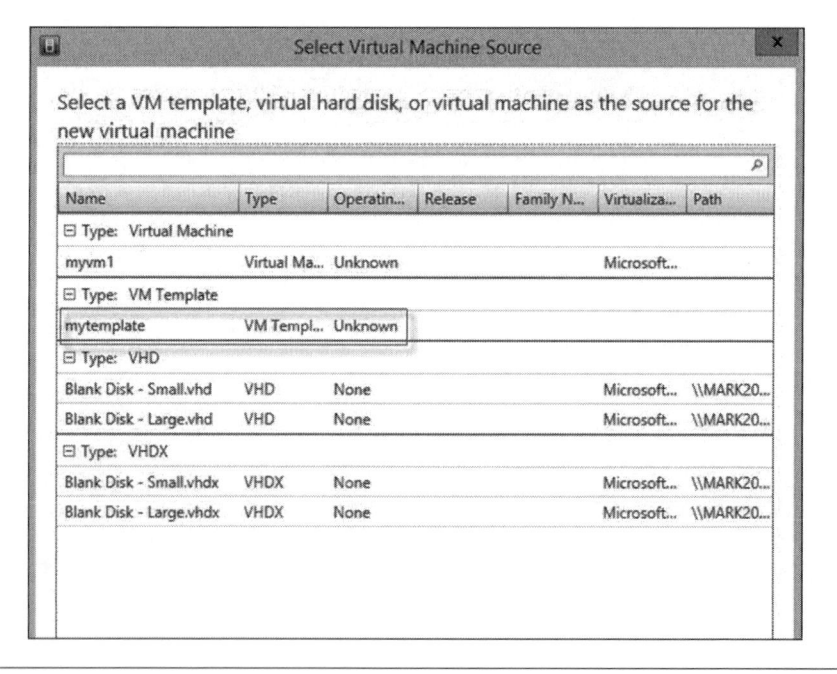

Figure 11.62   Selecting VM template.

5. On the Select Destination page, check the option **Deploy the VM to a private cloud**. Then, click **Next**.

6. On the Select Cloud page, make sure that your server is listed as the destination (Figure 11.64) and make sure that the Rating Explanation tab has no error. Then, click **Next**.

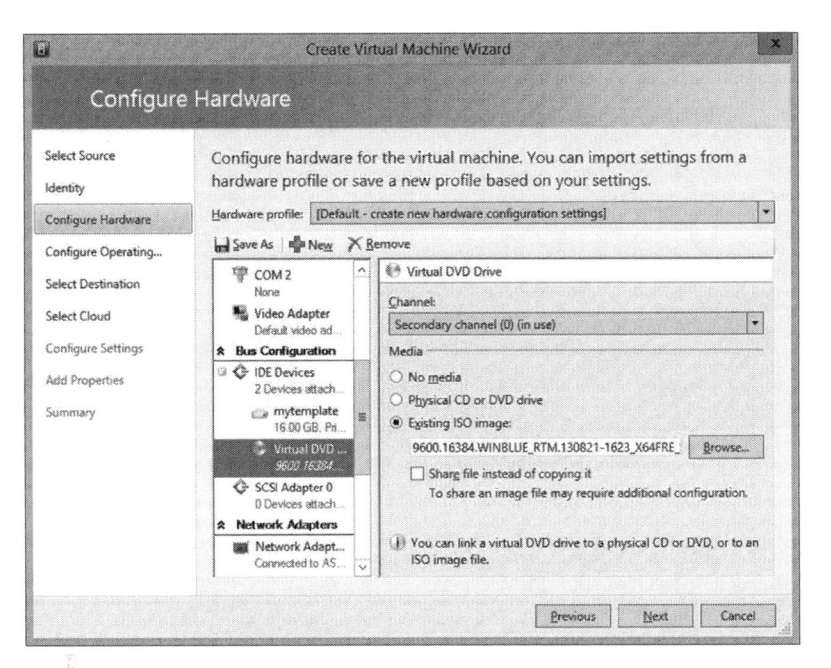

Figure 11.63 Adding iso file.

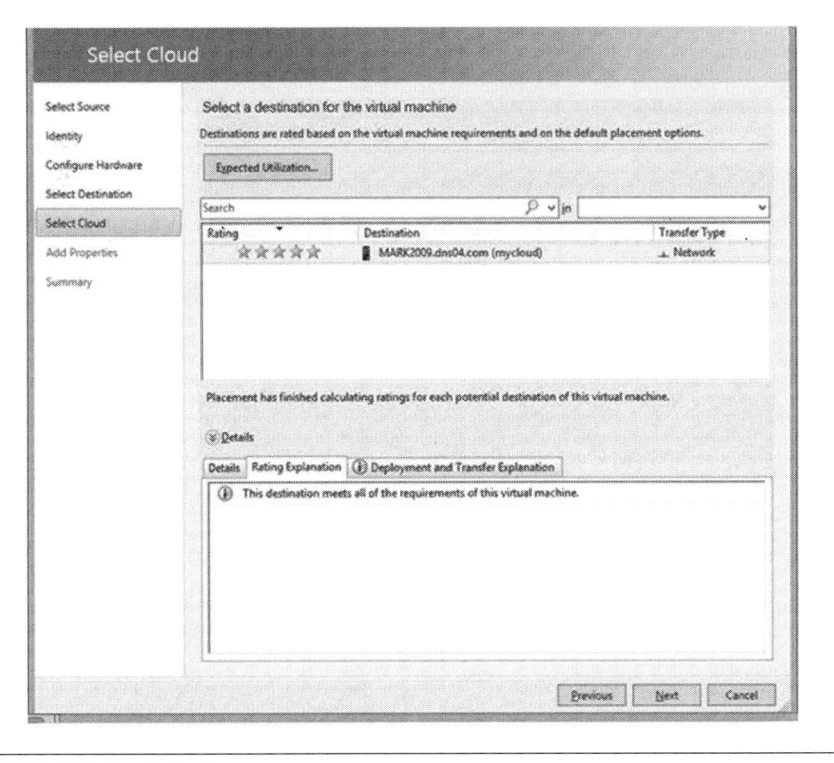

Figure 11.64 Selecting destination.

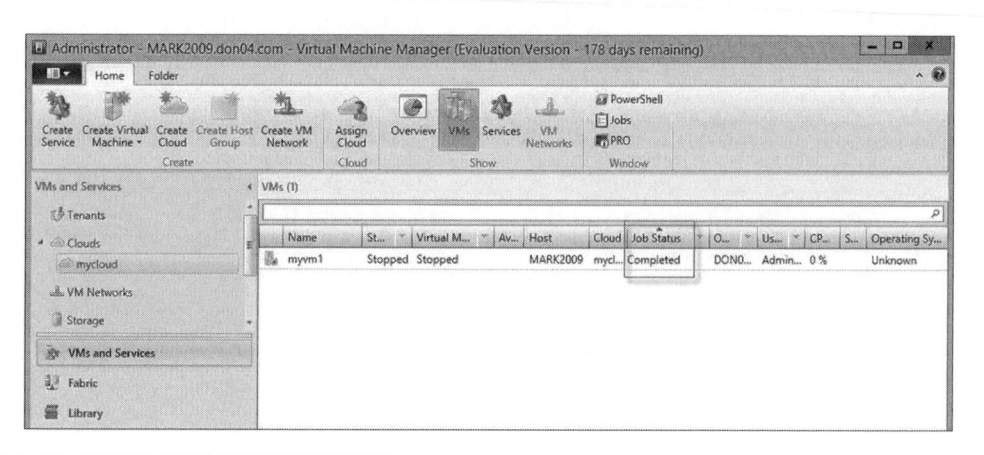

Figure 11.65 Virtual machine created on private cloud.

7. For Add Properties, keep the default and click **Next**.
8. Verify the summary and click **Create**.
9. You should now see in your cloud the created VM. The Job Status shows **Completed** (Figure 11.65).
10. Select the newly created virtual machine, click the **Power On** icon. Right click the running virtual machine and select **Connect or View** and then **Connect via Console**.
11. You will be prompted to install the OS to the VM. If you have only 4 GB RAM on your computer, choose **Windows Server 2012 R2 Standard Evaluation (Server Core Installation)** which has no GUI included (Figure 11.66). Then, click **Next**.

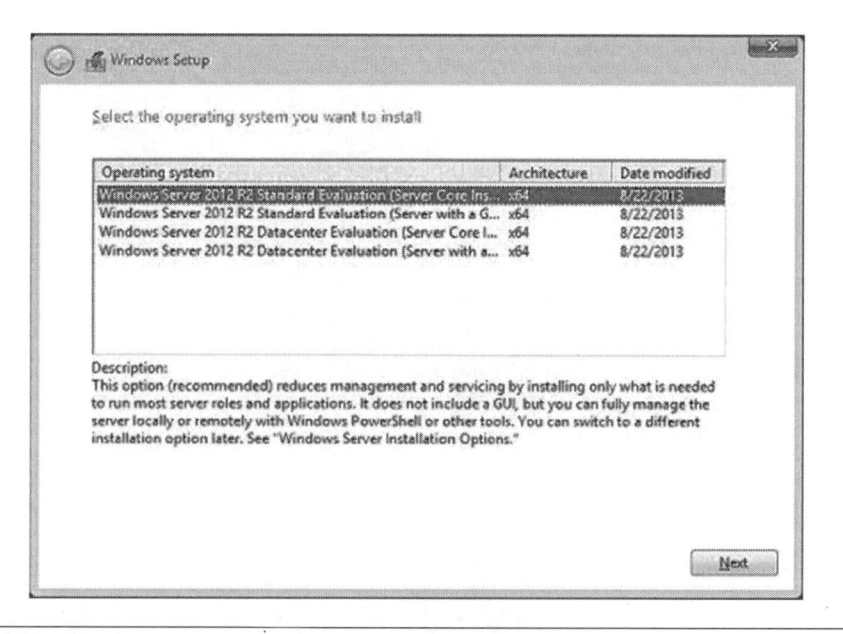

Figure 11.66 Selecting operating system for virtual machine.

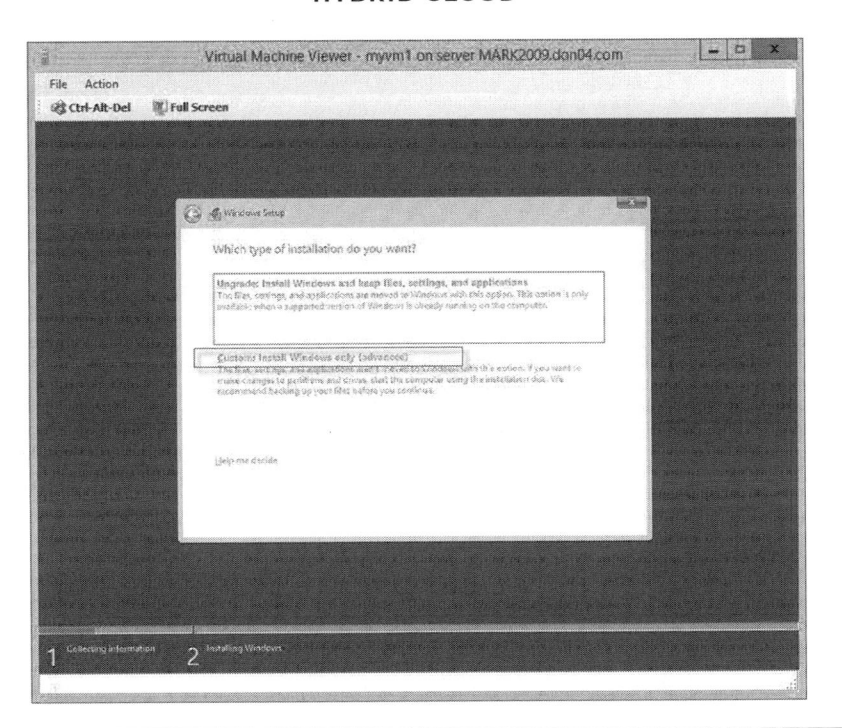

Figure 11.67   Selecting custom installation type.

12. Accept the license agreement and click **Next**.
13. When you are asked to select the installation type, choose **Custom** as shown in Figure 11.67.
14. Then, continue to install the operating system similar to the steps in Task 1. Once the installation is completed, right click the newly created virtual machine and select **Connect via Console**. You should be able to see the created virtual machine on your private cloud (Figure 11.68).

Part 6: App Controller Connection   App Controller allows the management of virtual machines through a browser. The following steps show how to connect App Controller to Virtual Machine Manager (VMM).

1. Open IE browser.
2. Go to the webpage for your private cloud. This will be https://192.168.1.2.
3. Sign in using the domain account with the **student** account created earlier (Figure 11.69).
4. To connect to your VMM, expand the **Settings** node and click **Connections**. Then, click the **Connect** drop-down list to select **SCVMM** as shown in Figure 11.70.
5. Specify the connection name and click **OK** as shown in Figure 11.71.

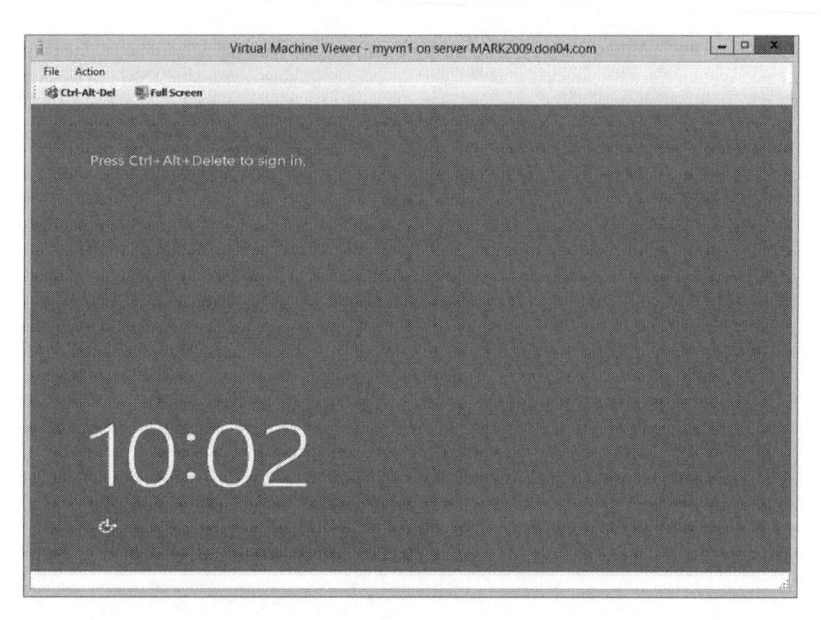

Figure 11.68   Installed virtual machine.

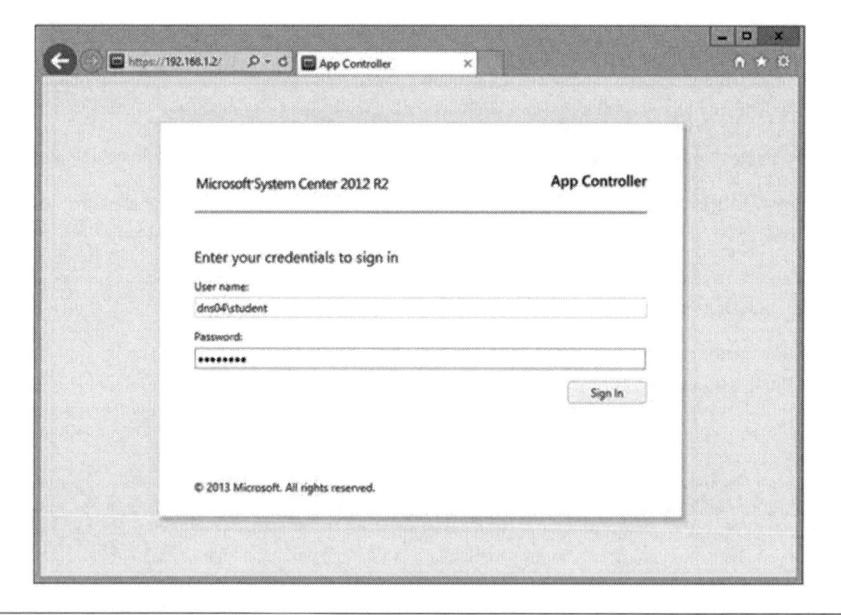

Figure 11.69   Signing in to app controller.

6. You should see that the 192.168.1.2 SCVMM is added to the list as shown in Figure 11.72.
7. Click the **Virtual Machines** link on the left-hand side; you should now see the VM shown in Figure 11.73.
8. Now, you are able to start and view it from the web browser. Right click the virtual machine myvm1, and select **Start**. After the virtual machine is opened,

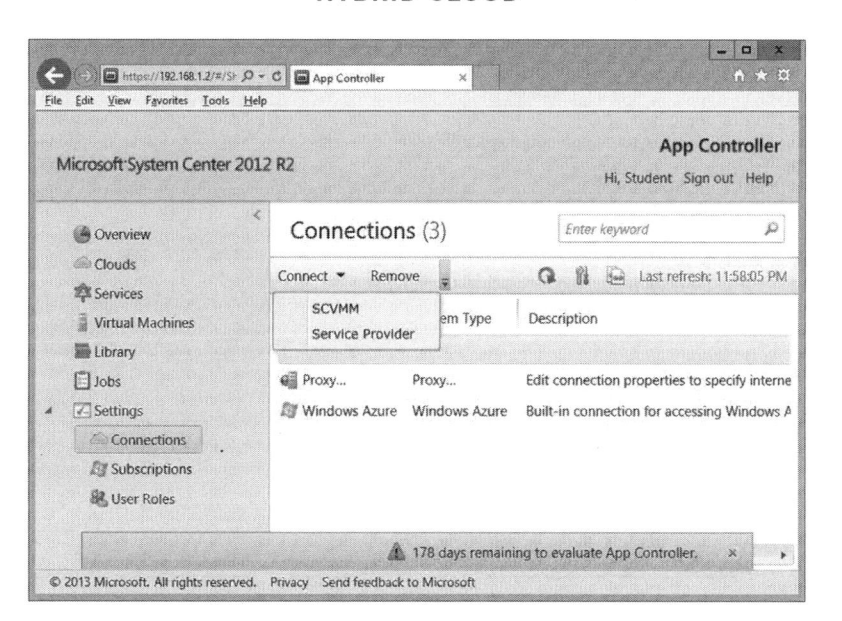

Figure 11.70 Connecting to SCVMM.

Figure 11.71 Specifying connection name.

right click the virtual machine myvm1 and select **Console**. You should be able to see the virtual machine as shown in Figure 11.74. (Note: You may need to install the certificate for your web browser. Also, if you are planning on connecting from multiple clients, you need to configure the DNS, certificate, and load balancing properly.)

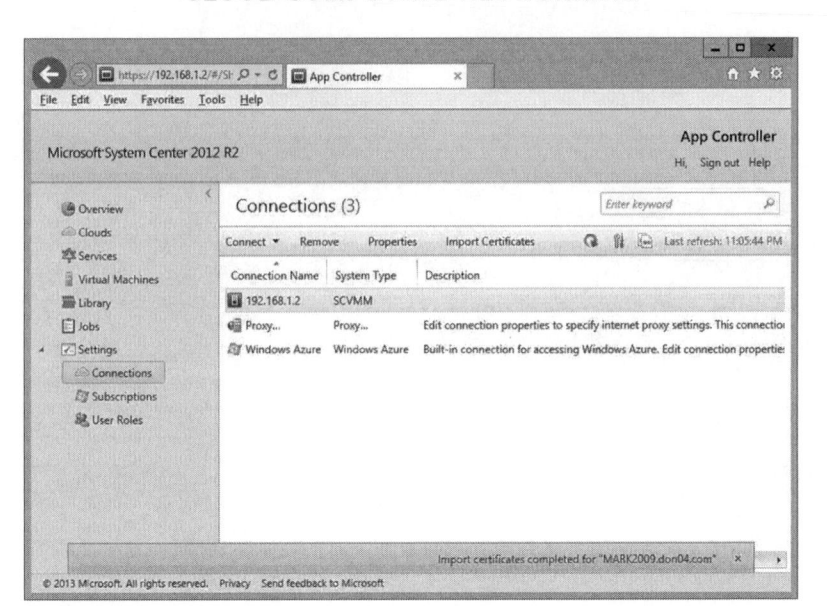

Figure 11.72 Listed SCVMM.

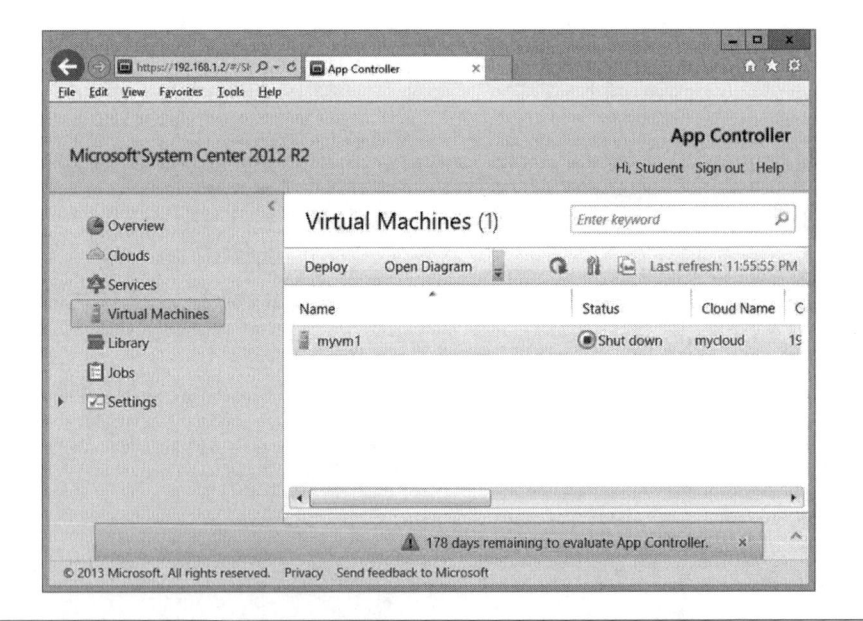

Figure 11.73 Virtual machine shown in app controller.

Task 5: Hybrid Cloud Development

In the preceding text, you have created a private cloud on the on-premises network. This task demonstrates how to connect the private cloud to Microsoft Azure which is the public cloud to form a hybrid cloud. The task can be accomplished with App Controller.

Figure 11.74   Viewing Virtual Machine from browser.

Part 1: Connecting Private Cloud to Public Cloud   To connect to Microsoft Azure, you first need to create a certificate. There are two types of certificates: The .cer type of certificate which will be uploaded to Microsoft Azure and the .pfx type of certificate which will be used to connect to App Controller. During the installation of SCAC, a self-signed certificate has been created. All you need to do is to export this existing self-signed certificate to create a .pfx certificate. Also, you can import this certificate to the personal certificate store and export it to create a .cer certificate. Let us start to export the .pfx certificate.

1. To create a certificate, in Server Manager, click **Tools** and select **Internet Information Services (IIS) Manager**. Then, double click **Server Certificates** as shown in Figure 11.75.
2. To export the self-signed certificate generated by App Controller to a .pfx file, select **System Center 2012 R2 App Controller Self-Signed Certificate** and click **Export** in the **Actions** pane. After the Export Certificate dialog is opened, enter a file name and destination for the file. Here, the file to be exported is named **myappcert**. Then, set a password and click **OK** as shown in Figure 11.76.

    This is the .pfx certificate you will use later to connect App Controller to your Microsoft Azure subscription.
3. Once the .pfx certificate is exported, you need to import the .pfx certificate into the personal certificate store and then export it as a .cer certificate from there. To do so, click the **Start** icon and type cmd to open the **Command Prompt** window.
4. In the Command Prompt window, type **certmgr.msc** and press **Enter**.
5. Once certmgr is opened, navigate to Personal and Certificates.

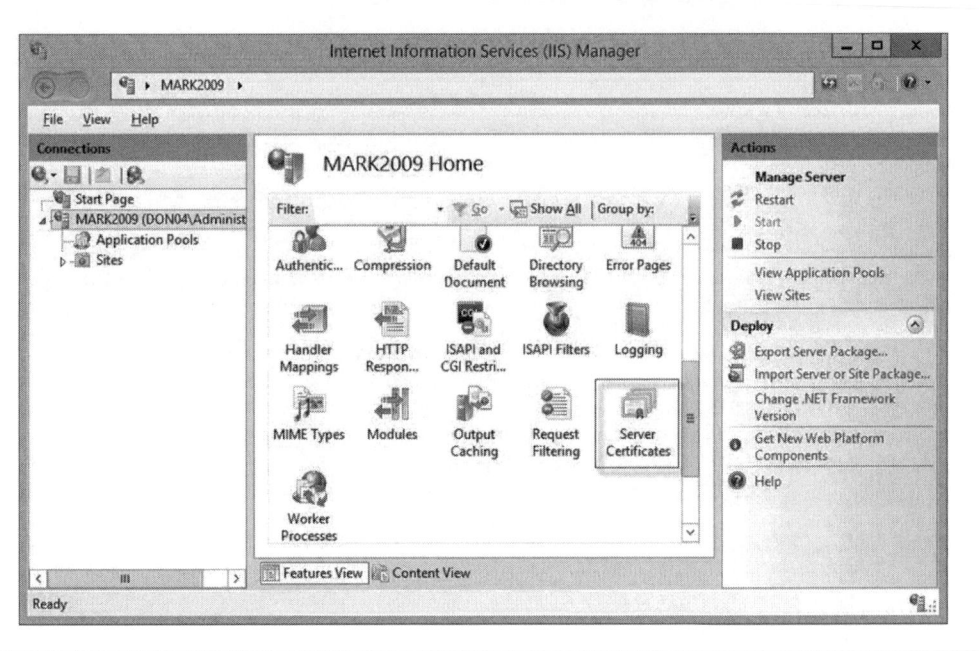

Figure 11.75 Opening server certificates.

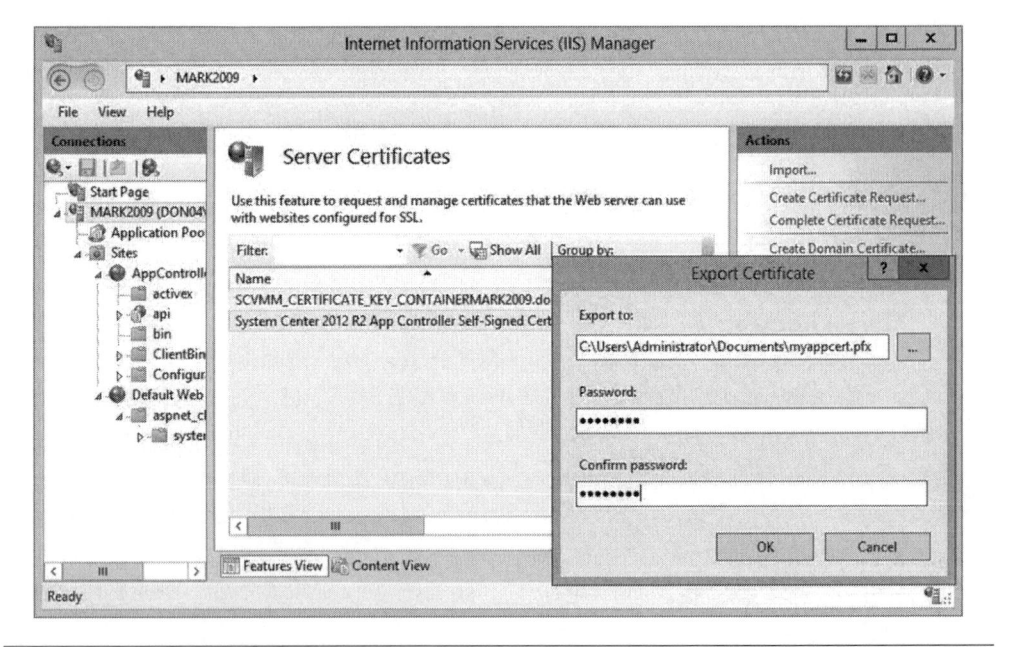

Figure 11.76 Exporting certificate.

6. Right click the **Certificates** node (Figure 11.77), and select **All Tasks** and **Import**.

7. In the Certificate Import Wizard, click **Next**, and then browse to and open the .pfx certificate exported in the previous step as shown in Figure 11.78. Then, click **Next**.

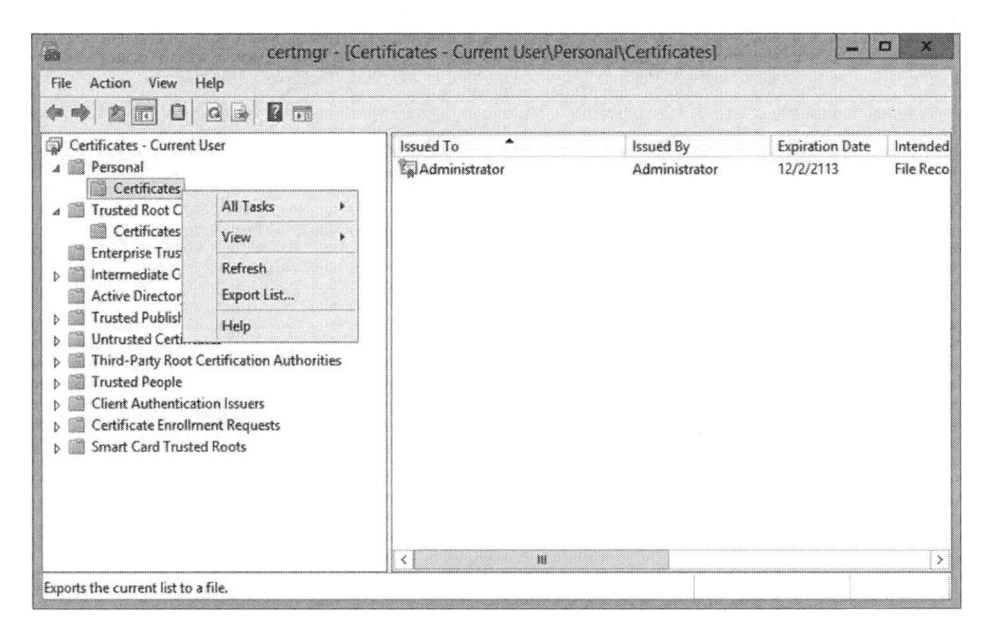

Figure 11.77 Importing certificate.

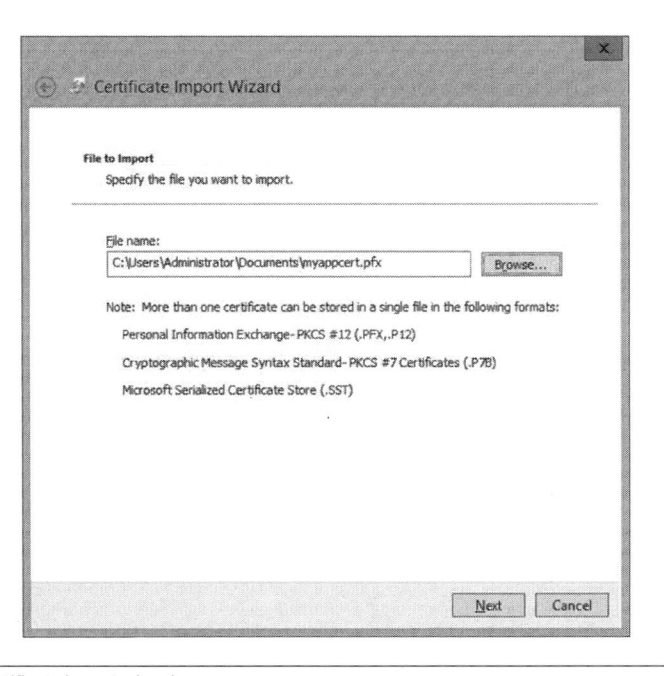

Figure 11.78 Certificate import wizard.

8. On the Private key protection page, enter the password used to protect your .pfx certificate and click **Next** as shown in Figure 11.79.

9. On the Certificate Store page, keep the certificate store as **Personal** (Figure 11.80). Click **Next**, and then click **Finish** to complete the import.

10. In the certificate manager, you will see the imported certificate as shown in Figure 11.81. Right click your certificate, and select **All Tasks** and **Export**.

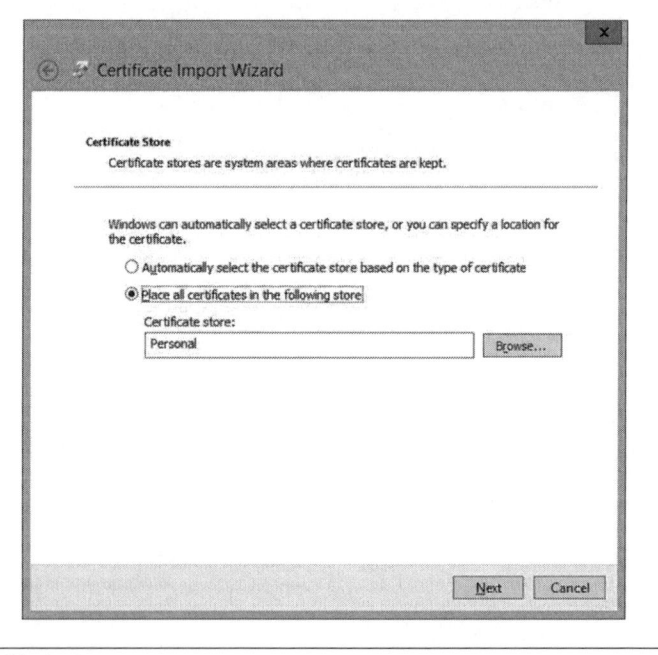

Figure 11.79 Private key protection.

Figure 11.80 Certificate store.

11. On the Export Private Key page, keep the default and click **Next**.
12. On the Export File Format page, keep the default and click **Next**.
13. On the File to Export page, browse to a location to export your .cer certificate and save the certificate by giving it a name as shown in Figure 11.82. Click **Next** and **Finish**.

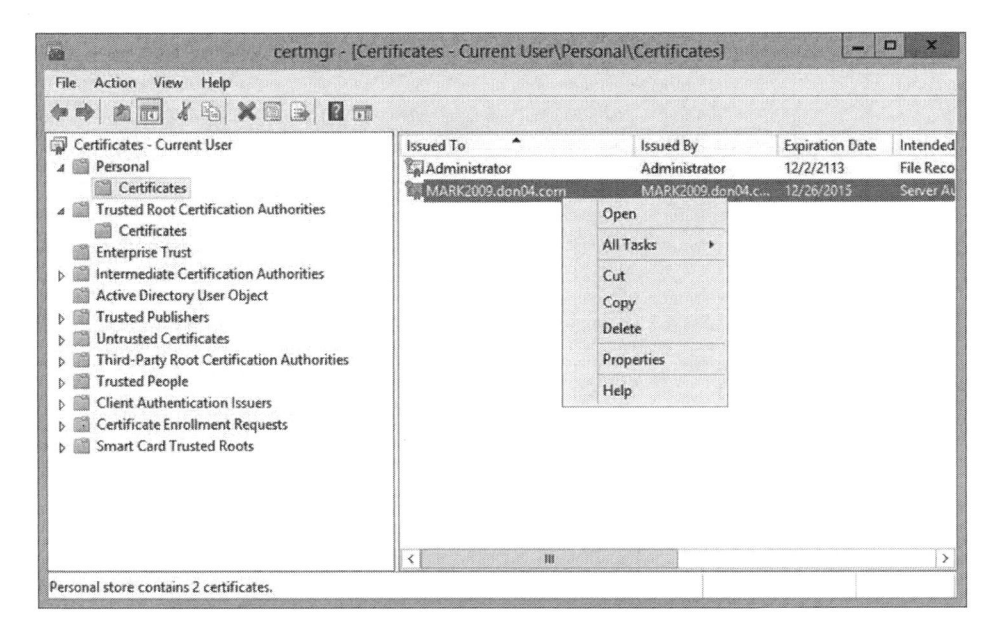

Figure 11.81 Imported certificate.

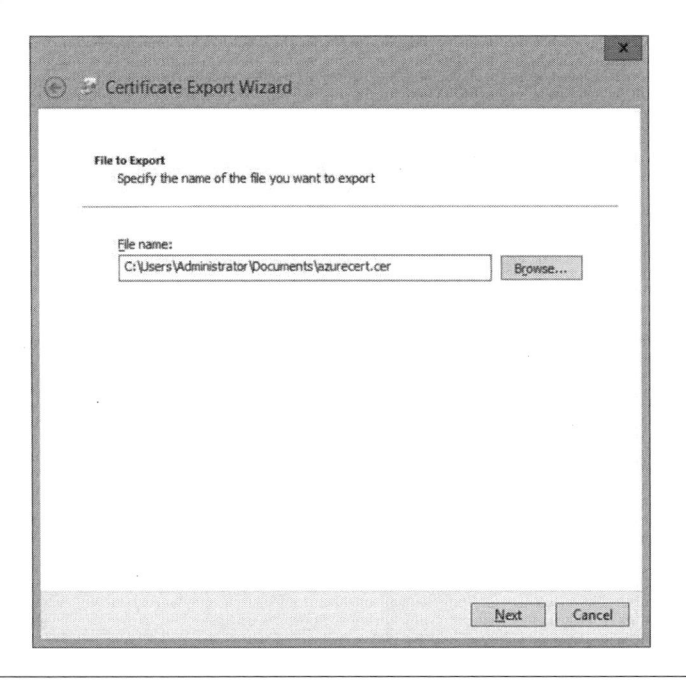

Figure 11.82 File to export.

14. To upload the .cer certificate to Microsoft Azure, log on to the **Microsoft Azure Management Portal**.

15. In the Microsoft Azure Management Portal, at the bottom left, select **SETTINGS**, **MANAGEMENT CERTIFICATE**, and then click **UPLOAD** as shown in Figure 11.83.

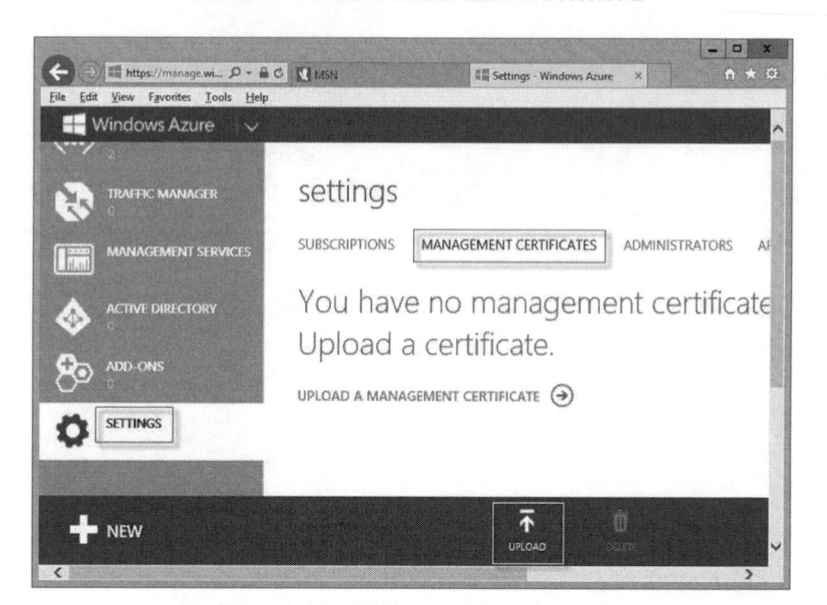

Figure 11.83   Uploading certificate.

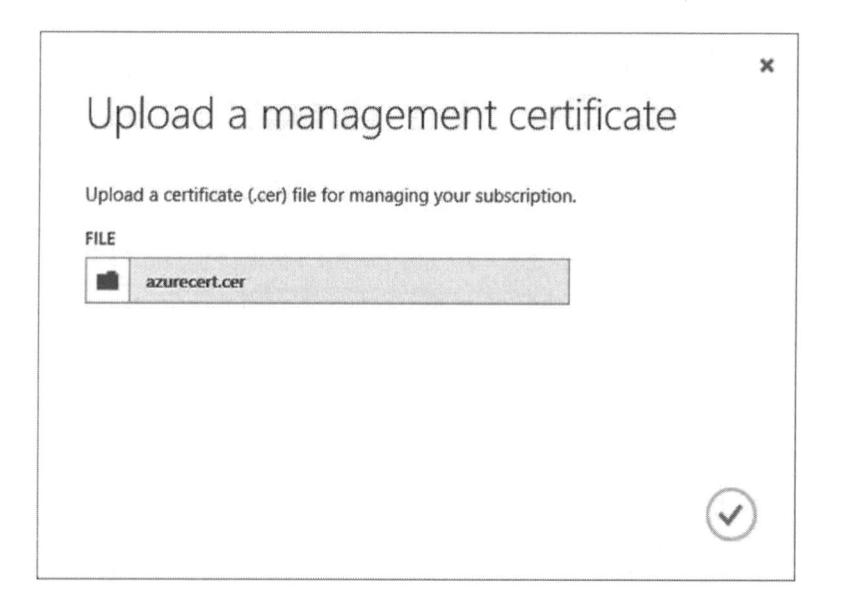

Figure 11.84   Selecting certificate to upload.

16. Browse to the folder where the exported .cer certificate is located to open the certificate. Then, click the **check mark** as shown in Figure 11.84.

17. Once the certificate is uploaded, in the Microsoft Azure Management Portal, click **SUBSCRIPTIONS** and copy the subscription ID to the clipboard as shown in Figure 11.85.

18. To connect to Microsoft Azure, open **App Controller**. In the Overview pane, under Public Clouds, click **Connect a Windows Azure subscription** (Figure 11.86).

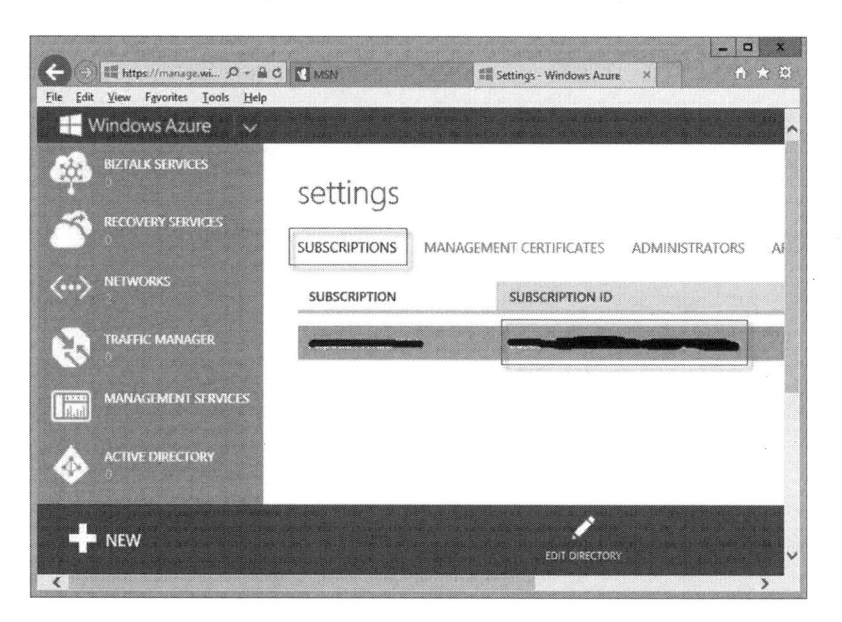

Figure 11.85 Copying subscription ID.

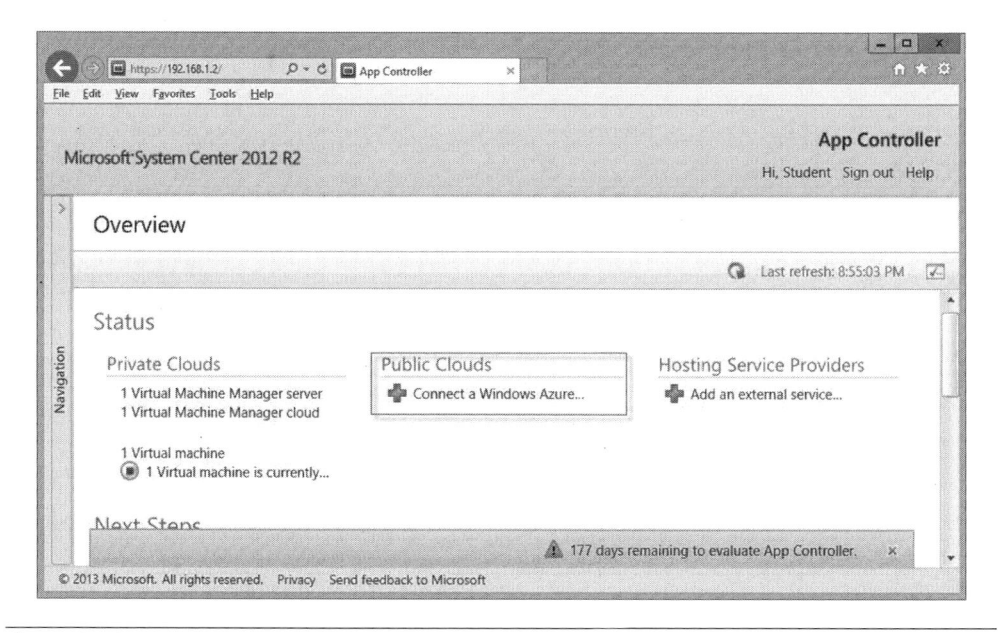

Figure 11.86 Connecting to microsoft azure.

19. After the Connect a Windows Azure Subscription dialog is opened, enter the subscription name, the subscription ID, the private certification file name, and the password for the private key as shown in Figure 11.87. Then, click **OK**.

20. If the connection is successful, you should be able to see that the public cloud has a Microsoft Azure subscription in App Controller as shown in Figure 11.88. Also, there are two virtual machines available on the public cloud. Now, your private cloud is linked to the public cloud to form a hybrid cloud.

Figure 11.87   Windows azure subscription configuration.

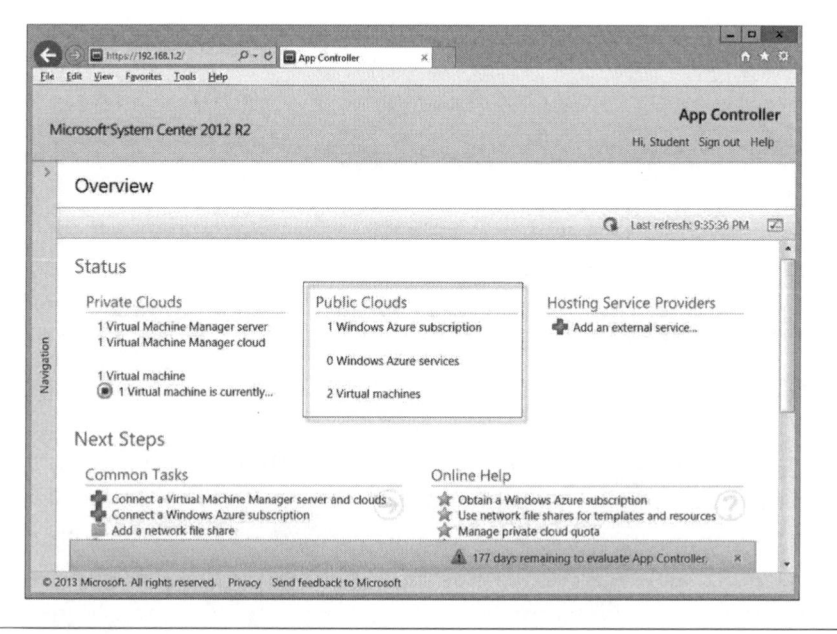

Figure 11.88   Connected to microsoft azure.

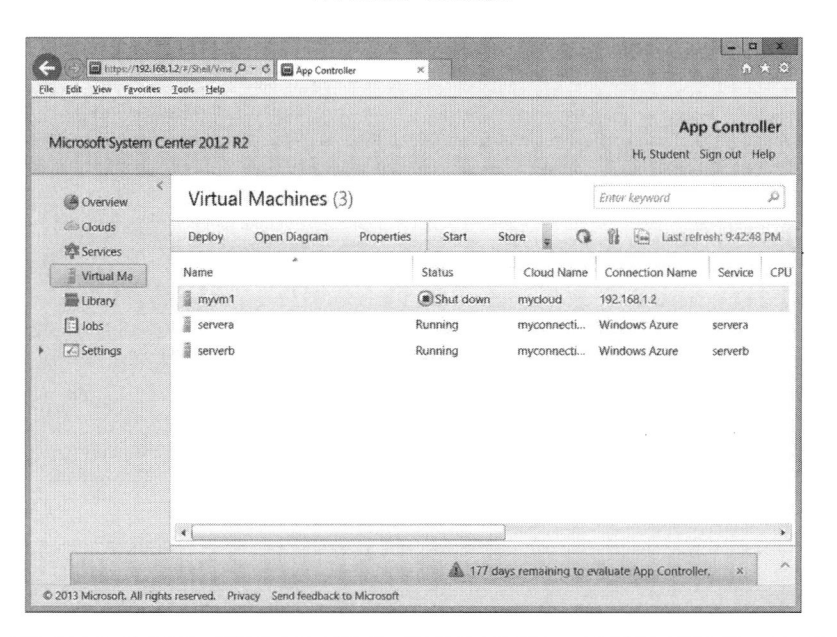

Figure 11.89 Virtual machines on hybrid cloud.

21. Click the **Virtual Machine** link on the left-hand side of the screen; you will see three virtual machines, one on the private cloud and two on the public cloud as shown in Figure 11.89.

Part 2: Creating Virtual Machine on Hybrid Cloud Due to the limitation of the academic account, you are not able to create additional virtual machines on Microsoft Azure. However, you can create more virtual machines on your private cloud. The following steps show how to achieve this goal.

1. Assume that App Controller is still open, click the **Virtual machines** link. Then, click **Deploy** to open the New Deployment window as shown in Figure 11.90.
2. In the New Deployment Window, click **Configure** to open the Select a cloud for this deployment page.
3. On the Select a cloud for this deployment page, click the private cloud link, **mycloud**, as shown in Figure 11.91. Then, click **OK**.
4. You will be prompted to select a template. Click the **Select a template...** link as shown in Figure 11.92. Select the template created before and click **OK**.
5. After the template is selected, click **Configure**. On the Properties of new virtual machine page, name your new virtual machine as **myvm2** as shown in Figure 11.93. Then, click **OK**.
6. Click **Deploy**. You now should be able to see the new virtual machine, myvm2, created on the hybrid cloud as shown in Figure 11.94.

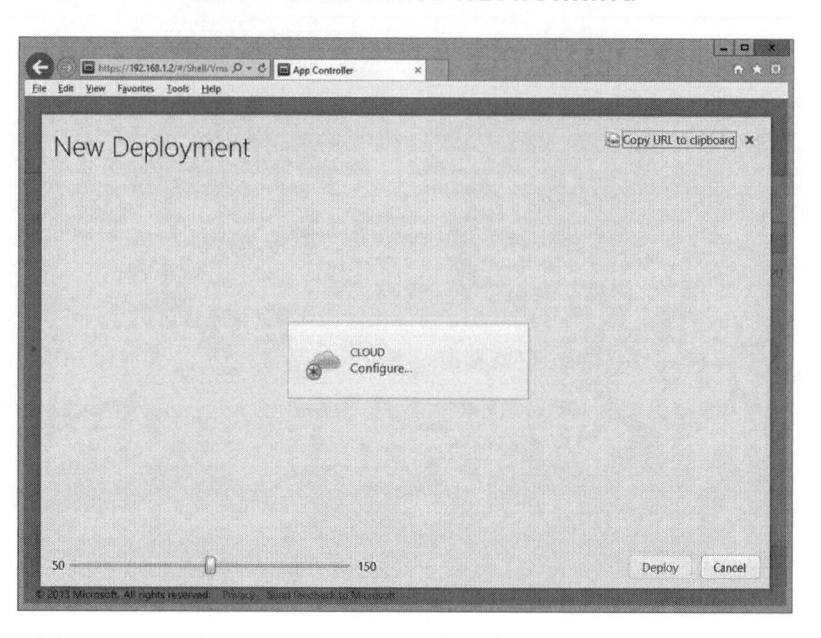

Figure 11.90   New deployment window.

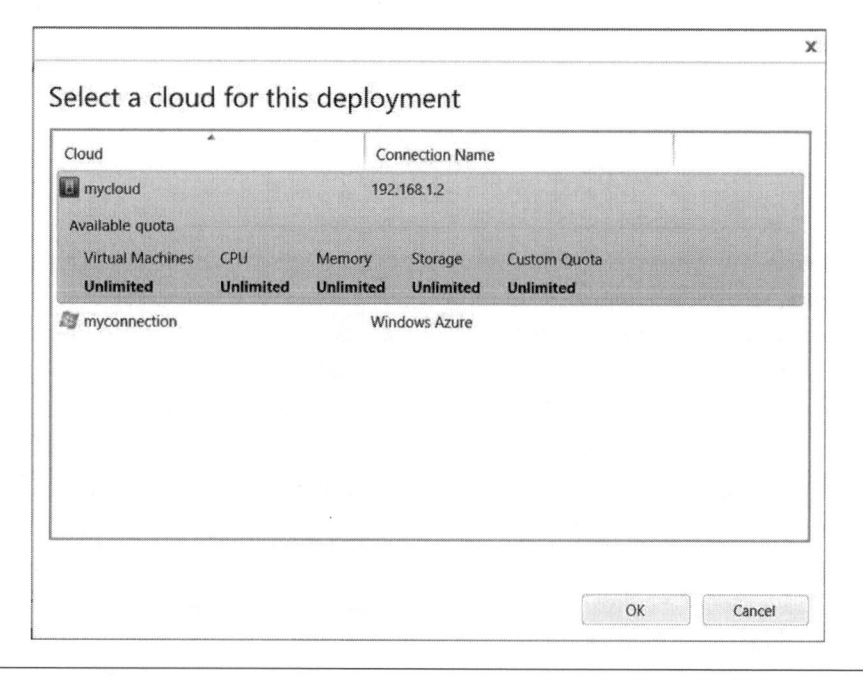

Figure 11.91   Selecting cloud for this deployment.

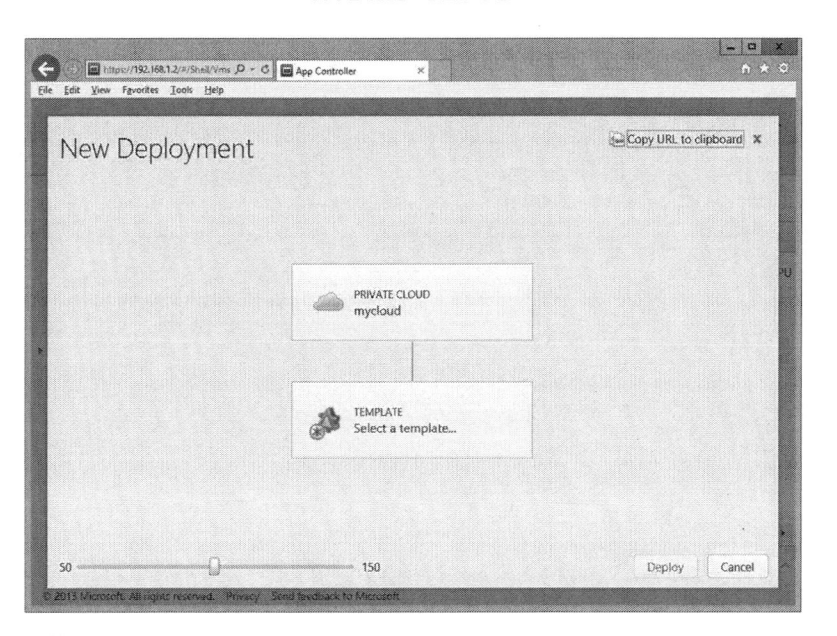

Figure 11.92   Selecting template.

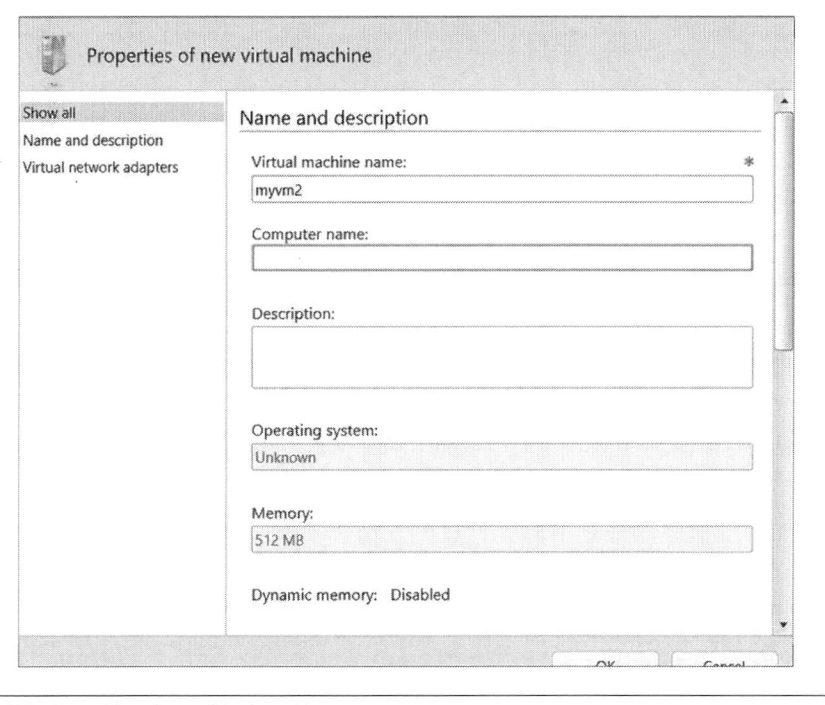

Figure 11.93   Properties of new virtual machine.

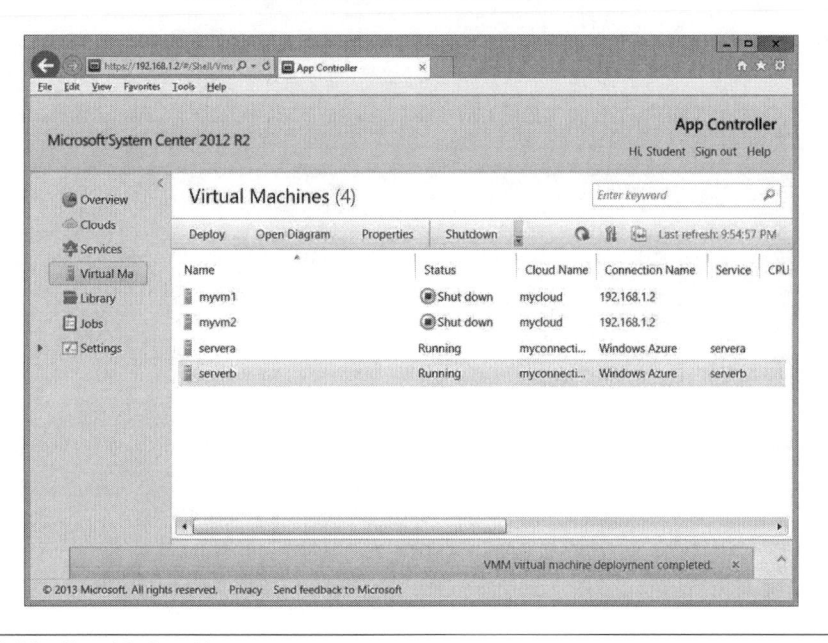

Figure 11.94   New virtual machine.

Now that the virtual machines have been created, these virtual machines can be configured to be on the same local network and be assigned dynamic IP addresses by the same DHCP server, to join the same domain and share the same DNS server.

11.5 Summary

This chapter presents scenarios where a hybrid cloud does a better job. By integrating a private cloud and a public cloud, the hybrid cloud can have the advantage offered by both types of clouds. The chapter explains why the hybrid cloud is a better solution for a project that requires high-level security as well as scalability. Like a public cloud, the hybrid cloud also has high flexibility. Like a private cloud, the mission-critical data are stored in the local storage devices so that an organization has full control of the data.

This chapter describes the technologies used in constructing the hybrid cloud. For the hybrid cloud, the chapter introduces the cloud management platform software. It provides information about the commonly used cloud management platform. For private cloud construction, this chapter introduces the virtualization technology. Three commonly used hypervisors, VMware vSphere, Microsoft Hyper-V, and Citrix XenServer have been discussed in this chapter.

The private cloud is a component of the hybrid cloud. SCVMM is the software that is used to create and manage private clouds. This chapter shows how to create a fabric which is the infrastructure where the private cloud will be constructed. After the fabric is created, this chapter illustrates how to create a private cloud with the Create Cloud Wizard. Then, it shows how to connect the private cloud to the public cloud, Microsoft Azure, to form a hybrid cloud. For the hands-on practice, this chapter demonstrates how to install, develop, and manage a private cloud. It also demonstrates how to connect the private cloud to Microsoft Azure with the tool App Controller.

Review Questions

1. Why is it not easy to deal with both the public cloud and private cloud?
2. How can a hybrid cloud benefit by taking advantage of a public cloud?
3. How can a hybrid cloud benefit by taking advantage of a private cloud?
4. How can a hybrid cloud be used in data protection?
5. How can a hybrid cloud be used in data center outsourcing?
6. How can a hybrid cloud be used in application hosting?
7. How can a hybrid cloud be used in web hosting?
8. What features should be included in a hybrid cloud?
9. What are the common cloud management tasks?
10. How do we address the responsibility of IT service in a cloud management policy?
11. What functionalities are provided by the cloud management platform software?
12. Describe the cloud management software vCloud Director.
13. Describe the cloud management software App Controller.
14. Describe the cloud management software OpenStack.
15. What do you do with the virtualization technology?
16. What do you do with a hypervisor?
17. Name three commonly used hypervisors.
18. Describe vSphere suite.
19. Describe Hyper-V.
20. Describe Xen.

Bibliography

Websites

The following websites are about the recent development of cloud computing related technologies.

Websites that provide comprehensive coverage of some major cloud providers

IBM, IBM Cloud Academy, May, 2015. http://www.ibm.com/solutions/education/cloudacademy/us/en/cloud_academy_3.html.

Amazon, Get Started with AWS for Free, May, 2015. http://aws.amazon.com/.

Apple, iCloud, May, 2015. http://www.apple.com/icloud/.

Microsoft Azure, The cloud for modern business, May, 2015. http://azure.microsoft.com/en-us/.

Google, Google Cloud Platform, May, 2015. https://cloud.google.com/.

Microsoft, OneDrive, May, 2015. https://onedrive.live.com/about/en-us/.

Websites that provide tutorials of Windows Azure:

Microsoft, How Windows Azure Works, May, 2015. http://dotnetslackers.com/articles/aspnet/How-Windows-Azure-Works.aspx.

Julie Lerman, Microsoft Azure Table Storage—Not Your Father's Database, May, 2015. http://msdn.microsoft.com/en-us/magazine/ff796231.aspx.

Microsoft, Microsoft Azure training, May, 2015. http://www.microsoft.com/learning/en/us/azure-training.aspx.

DELL, Cloud Computing, May, 2015. http://content.dell.com/us/en/enterprise/dell-cloud-computing-strategy.aspx.

Microsoft, Documentation Center, May, 2015. http://www.windowsazure.com/en-us/develop/overview/.

Microsoft, Managing Databases and Logins in Azure SQL Database, May, 2015. http://msdn.microsoft.com/en-us/library/ee336235.aspx.

CodePlex, SQL Database Migration Wizard v3.15.6, v4.15.6 and v5.15.6., May, 2015. http://sqlazuremw.codeplex.com/.

Brent Ozar, Playing Around with SQL Azure and SSMS, May, 2015. http://www.brentozar.com/archive/2009/11/playing-around-with-sql-azure-and-ssms/.

Tamram, How to use Queue storage from .NET, May, 2015. http://www.windowsazure.com/en-us/develop/net/how-to-guides/queue-service/.

Microsoft, SQL Azure: Cloud Database Security, May, 2015. http://technet.microsoft.com/en-us/hh352139.

Microsoft, How to: Extract a DAC From a Database, May, 2015. http://technet.microsoft.com/en-us/library/ee210526(v = sql.105).aspx.

Paul Yuknewicz and Boris Scholl, Developing and Deploying Microsoft Azure Cloud Services Using Visual Studio, May, 2015. http://msdn.microsoft.com/en-us/magazine//jj618299.aspx.

Cloud Resource Websites:

DELL, Take the Simpler Path to Cloud Computing, May, 2015. http://content.dell.com/us/en/enterprise/dell-cloud-computing.aspx.

Microsoft Azure, Free One-Month Trial, May, 2015. http://www.windowsazure.com/en-us/pricing/free-trial/.

Microsoft Azure, Documentation Center, May, 2015. http://azure.microsoft.com/en-us/documentation/.

Microsoft Azure, Sign in, May, 2015. http://blogs.msdn.com/b/sqlazure/.

Microsoft Azure, Virtual Machines, May, 2015. http://azure.microsoft.com/en-us/services/virtual-machines/.

VMware, Cloud Computing, May, 2015. http://www.vmware.com/solutions/cloud-computing.

Windows Azure, Windows Azure Virtual Machines & Networking, May, 2015. http://channel9.msdn.com/Series/Windows-Azure-Virtual-Machines-and-Networking-Tutorials.

Michael Washam, Introduction to Windows Azure Virtual Machine Networking, May, 2015. http://channel9.msdn.com/Series/Windows-Azure-Virtual-Machines-and-Networking-Tutorials/Introduction-to-Virtual-Machine-Networking.

Microsoft, Create VM Networks for Windows Azure Pack, May, 2015. http://technet.microsoft.com/en-us/library/dn502517.aspx.

Books

The following books provide in-depth coverage of cloud computing theories and related technologies.

Arora, P., A. Duchene. *To the Cloud: Cloud Powering an Enterprise.* New York: McGraw-Hill Osborne Media, 2012.

Crookes, D. *Cloud Computing in Easy Steps.* Warwickshire, U.K.: In Easy Steps Limited, 2012.

Finn, A., H. Vredevoort, P. Lownds, D. Flynn. *Microsoft Private Cloud Computing.* Indianapolis, IN: Sybex, 2012.

Jackson, K. *OpenStack Cloud Computing Cookbook.* Birmingham, U.K.: Packt Publishing, 2012.

Josyula, V., M. Orr. *Cloud Computing: Automating the Virtualized Data Center (Networking Technology).* Indianapolis, IN: Cisco Press, 2011.

Nielsen, L. *The Little Book of Cloud Computing,* 2011 Edition. Wickford, RI: New Street Communications, LLC, 2011.

Rhoton, J., R. Haukioja. *Cloud Computing Architected: Solution Design Handbook.* Richmond, TX: Recursive, Limited, 2011.

Rosenberg, J., A. Mateos. *The Cloud at Your Service.* Greenwich, CT: Manning Publications, 2010.

Savill, J. *Mastering Hyper-V 2012 R2 with System Center and Windows Azure.* Indianapolis, IN: Sybex, 2014.

Sosinsky, B. *Cloud Computing Bible.* Hoboken, NJ: Wiley, 2011.

Washam, M. *Automating Microsoft Azure Infrastructure Services: From the Data Center to the Cloud with PowerShell.* Sebastopol, CA: O'Reilly Media: Microsoft Press, 2014.

Wilder, B. *Cloud Architecture Patterns: Using Microsoft Azure.* Sebastopol, CA: O'Reilly Media, 2012.

Vic Winkler, J.R.. *Securing the Cloud: Cloud Computer Security Techniques and Tactics.* Waltham, MA: Syngress, 2011.

Index